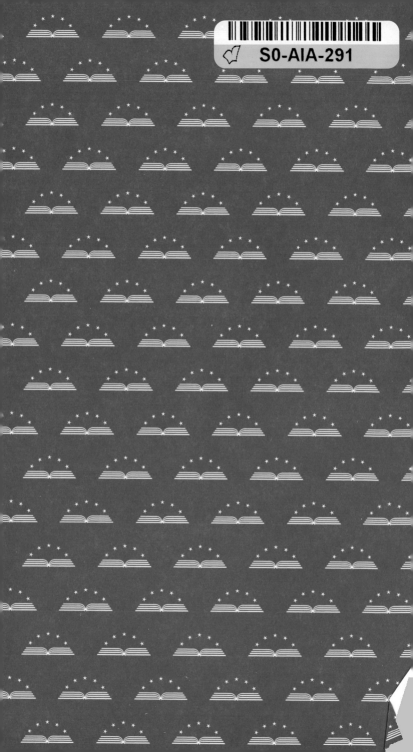

AMERICAN MUSICALS
1927–1949

American Musicals
1927–1949

THE COMPLETE BOOKS & LYRICS
OF EIGHT BROADWAY CLASSICS

Laurence Maslon, *editor*

THE LIBRARY OF AMERICA

See page 707 for sources and acknowledgments.

This paper meets the requirements of
ANSI/NISO Z39.48-1992 (Permanence of Paper).

Distributed to the trade in the United States
by Penguin Random House Inc.
and in Canada by Penguin Random House Canada Ltd.

Library of Congress Control Number: 2013957908
ISBN 978-1-59853-258-6

First Printing
The Library of America—253

Manufactured in the United States of America

American Musicals: 1927–1949
The Complete Books & Lyrics of
Eight Broadway Classics

is published with support from

MARK KRUEGER CHARITABLE TRUST

SUSAN & ELIHU ROSE FOUNDATION

ROGER BERLIND

THE PETER J. SHARP FOUNDATION

COLE PORTER MUSICAL & LITERARY TRUSTS

MARY ROGERS GUETTEL

Contents

(See photo insert following page 634.)

Additional Lyrics   *609*

Introduction

BY LAURENCE MASLON

The music of the American musical theater has formed the soundtrack to our country's cultural life for nearly a century. Tunes from Kern and Berlin, Gershwin and Rodgers, Porter and Arlen, Loewe and Loesser, Bernstein and Styne, and their effervescent peers have wafted over the orchestra pit, out of the bandstand, onto the airwaves and movie screens, and through hi-fi speakers and earbuds to underscore the most celebratory moments of several generations. This music is central to what has been dubbed the Great American Songbook. From the beginning of World War I nearly through the end of the 1960s, Broadway music and popular music were so intertwined as to be almost synonymous.

Yet the transcendence of Broadway music would not have been possible without the craft, construction, and context of the words—the "book and lyrics" that are the foundation of the Broadway musical at its best. The two volumes of *American Musicals* (*1927–1949* and *1950–1969*) celebrate the gifted craftsmen who provided the words—classic American writers whose talents included the ability to thrive in a highly collaborative medium. These book writers and lyricists were the hearty standard-bearers in the evolution of this uniquely American art form.

The Broadway stage gave the nation and the world upbeat and unforgettable tunes from the heyday of the European-style romantic operetta (exemplified by the compositions of Victor Herbert, Sigmund Romberg, and Rudolf Friml) at the beginning of the twentieth century through the many tuneful and sophisticated but inconsequential star vehicles and musical comedies written by such giants as Irving Berlin, the Gershwins, and Cole Porter, along with the non-narrative revues that peppered the Broadway landscape in the 1920s and early 1930s.

But, beginning in the late 1920s, and continuing during the Depression, the arc of the musical theater's evolution bent toward narrative. The first volume of *American Musicals* (1927–1949) highlights the pioneers who led the Broadway musical into the territory of its Golden Age—an era officially initiated with the 1943 debut of *Oklahoma!* During this period, the popular musical achieved a new maturity in form by deploying dialogue, song, and dance organically to tell increasingly nuanced and complex stories, stories that grappled with native materials and spoke to the heart of American culture. In the years following the successful conclusion of World War II, the influence of this new breed of Broadway musicals reached audiences thousands of miles away from Times Square through blockbuster film adaptations, best-selling cast albums on long-playing records, and special presentations on television.

During the early 1950s, the American musical gamboled along in its merry, sentimental, or inspirational way, but with the success of *My Fair Lady* in 1956, another avenue was opened to its progress. After this adaptation of a classic play by George Bernard Shaw, no source material (within the boundaries of taste, of course) seemed off-limits. If the first volume of *American Musicals* celebrates an evolution in form, the second volume (1950–1969) celebrates a revolution in content. All sorts of cultures and historical eras became grist for the Broadway mill, many far afield from the Theatre District of midtown Manhattan: Edwardian England, Ancient Rome, Czarist Russia, Weimar Germany, and Colonial America were each transformed into settings for serious-minded musicals, a direction for which Rodgers and Hammerstein had paved the way in *South Pacific*.

The precise closed parenthesis of this Golden Age usually depends on one's taste, but certainly by 1970 as American culture began to fragment, so too did that decade inaugurate a new, fragmented era for the traditional narrative in American musicals. That same year saw the premiere of Stephen Sondheim and George Furth's *Company*, directed by Harold Prince, which rode the crest of the sea-change in American popular music to deliver a jangling, disconnected, thoroughly contemporary and original theater piece to unsuspecting Broadway audiences. *Company* would also initiate the seminal partnership of Sondheim and Prince, a collaboration that would seize on the experiments in form and content pioneered by their predecessors and take the American musical into innovative (and occasionally terrifying) territory over the subsequent decade.

When Irving Berlin (represented by the revue *As Thousands Cheer* in the first volume) came to this country in 1893 as a frightened five-year-old boy, escaping the anti-Semitic pogroms of his native Czarist Russia, he could scarcely have imagined that he would one day strike it rich by writing something as frivolous and effervescent as a Broadway show tune—let alone that one of the biggest Broadway hits of his very long lifetime would be *Fiddler on the Roof* (reprinted in the second volume), set in the same sort of shtetl from which he had escaped seventy years earlier.

Taken together, the sixteen musicals of this two-volume anthology provide a kind of road map for this transformation. The texts for these shows are presented in versions as close as possible to the form of each show as presented to its audience on its opening night. Of the works included, one is published for the first time, three are presented in unique new versions, and three have long been out of print. Detailed background information on each musical and an account of relevant textual issues will be found in the Note on the Texts and Notes to these volumes.

Why these particular shows? Given the limitations of space, it was clearly necessary to forgo many worthy candidates. (Interested readers can find at least one of these—*Of Thee I Sing* written by George S. Kaufman in 1931 in collaboration with Morrie Ryskind, Ira Gershwin, and George Gershwin, and the first musical to be awarded the Pulitzer Prize—in The Library of America volume *Kaufman & Co.*) A variety of criteria helped shape the contents. The musicals chosen have been not only critical but popular successes; they have achieved a sustained performance history and a vital performance tradition. Also, as far as possible, they provide representation of the major contributors to the musical theater form during this period. Additionally, each of these shows added something new and progressive—a stylistic approach, an imaginative adaptation of source material—to the vocabulary of the American musical. (Nine of the musicals selected were also the recipients of the Tony Award for Best Musical; the first award for Best Musical was given in 1949 to *Kiss Me, Kate*.)

Of primary importance, beyond any other consideration, was that any musical selected should be enjoyable on its own merits in print form. This was a crucial if somewhat elusive criterion. A musical theater piece is particularly vulnerable in print, stripped of its music, its dancing, and its performance components. The musicals chosen for this collection had to absorb and move and delight the reader by their dramatic and lyrical qualities, even in the absence of those other theatrical elements.

In this two-volume collection, the spotlight is focused on those brave writers who have worn down cartloads of Blackwing 602 pencils, scribbling witty rhymes and trenchant dialogue in grimy rehearsal rooms and in the back of darkened theaters. The very words of their songs—"He just keeps rollin' along," "New York, New York, it's a helluva town," "Everything's coming up roses," "Life is a cabaret, old chum"—have infiltrated everyday speech and become part of our vocabulary. But, as Tevye says in *Fiddler on the Roof*: "It isn't easy." One can only sympathize with Dorothy Hammerstein (Oscar's second wife), who—when a guest at a cocktail party remarked how much she loved Jerome Kern's "Ol' Man River"—is said to have retorted, "Jerome Kern wrote 'da-da-*dee*-da.' My husband wrote 'Ol' Man River.'"

SHOW BOAT

Book and lyrics by OSCAR HAMMERSTEIN II
Music by JEROME KERN
Based on the novel by EDNA FERBER

SYNOPSIS OF SCENES

ACT ONE

SCENE 1. The Levee at Natchez on the Mississippi, in the late eighteen eighties.

SCENE 2. Kitchen pantry of the *Cotton Blossom*, a half-hour later.

SCENE 3. Outside a Waterfront Gambling Saloon, simultaneous with Scene 2.

SCENE 4. Auditorium and Stage of the *Cotton Blossom*, one hour later.

SCENE 5. Box-office, on Foredeck of the *Cotton Blossom*, three weeks later.

SCENE 6. Auditorium and Stage of the *Cotton Blossom*, during the Third Act of "The Parson's Bride"

SCENE 7. The Top Deck of the *Cotton Blossom*, later that night.

SCENE 8. The Levee, next morning.

ACT TWO

SCENE 1. The Midway Plaisance, Chicago World's Fair, 1893.

SCENE 2. A room on Ontario Street, 1904.

SCENE 3. Rehearsal room of the Trocadero Music Hall, about 5 P.M.

SCENE 4. St. Agatha's Convent, meanwhile.

SCENE 5. Corner of lobby of the Sherman Hotel, Chicago, 8 P.M., New Year's Eve, 1904.

SCENE 6. Trocadero Music Hall, New Year's Eve, 11:30, 1904.

SCENE 7. In front of the Office of *The Natchez Evening Democrat*, 1927.

SCENE 8. Top Deck of the new *Cotton Blossom*, 1927

SCENE 9. Levee at Natchez, the next night.

MUSICAL PROGRAM

ACT ONE

1. *Opening—Cotton Blossom* . . . . Entire Ensemble
2. *Make Believe* . . . . Ravenal and Magnolia
3. *Ol' Man River* . . . . Joe and Jubilee Singers
4. *Can't Help Lovin' Dat Man* . . . . Julie, Queenie, Magnolia, Joe, Windy
5. *Life on the Wicked Stage* . . . . Ellie and Girls
6. *'Til Good Luck Comes My Way* . . . Ravenal and Male Chorus
7. *I Might Fall Back on You* . . . . Ellie, Frank and Girls
8. *C'mon, Folks* . . . . Queenie and Jubilee Singers
9. *You Are Love* . . . . Magnolia and Ravenal
10. *Finale* . . . . Entire Ensemble

ACT TWO

1. Opening—World's Fair . . . . Sightseers, Dandies, Barkers, etc.
2. *Why Do I Love You?* . . . . Magnolia, Ravenal, Andy, Parthy and Chorus
3. *In Dahomey* . . . . . . Jubilee Singers and Dahomey Dancers
4. *Bill* . . . . Julie
5. *Can't Help Lovin' Dat Man (Song)* . . . . Magnolia
6. *Service and Scene Music, St. Agatha's Convent*
7. *Apache Dance, First Time in America* . . . . Sidell Sisters
8. *Goodbye, My Lady Love* . . . . Frank and Ellie
9. *After the Ball* . . . . Magnolia and Chorus
10. *Ol' Man River* . . . . Old Joe
11. *Hey, Feller!* . . . . Queenie and Jubilee Singers
12. *You Are Love* (Reprise) . . . . Ravenal
    a. Kim's Imitations
    b. Eccentric Dance
    c. Tap Dance
13. *Finale* . . . . Entire Ensemble

ACT ONE

The Levee at Natchez—On the Mississippi—about 1890.
Steamboat Mollie Able *up right. Show Boat* Cotton Blossom
left.

STEVEDORES *are piling up bales at right.* WINDY, *an old pilot,
stands on Texas deck of Steamboat, smoking his pipe and looking
on.*

"Cotton Blossom"

STEVEDORES:

Niggers all work on de Mississippi
Niggers all work while de white folks play—
Loadin' up boats wid de bales of cotton,
Gittin' no rest till de Judgment day.

GALS:	STEVEDORES:
Git yo' self a bran' new gal	Hye! Git along—
	Git along—git along—
Git a lovin' baby who's de apple of yo' eye—	Git along—hey!
	Git along—git along—
Coal Black Rose or High Brown Sal	
Dey kin cook de sparra grass an' chicken pie.	Git along—hey!

ALL:

Niggers all work on de Mississippi
Niggers all work while de white folks play—

STEVEDORES:

Loadin' up boats wid de bales of cotton
Gittin' no rest till de judgment day—
(*Refrain*)
Cotton Blossom, Cotton Blossom,
Love to see you growin' free
When dey pack you on de levee
You're a heavy load to me!

ALL:

> Cotton Blossom, Cotton Blossom,
> Love to see you growin' wild
> On de levee, you're too heavy
> Fo' dis po' black child!

> (STEVE *enters from Show Boat and places picture frame.*)
> (PETE, *the engineer and bandman, enters from steamboats.*)
> (STEVEDORES *work up stage to pile of bales.* GALS *sit around on bulkhead, etc., leaving downstage clear.*)
> (QUEENIE, *the cook, waddles on from market with a basket of provisions on her head.*)

QUEENIE: Lordy my feet shure is killin' me this morning. Mornin' Mars' Steve—

STEVE: Mornin' Queenie—

PETE: Hey there, Nigger! Where y'all git dat brooch you're wearin'?

> (WINDY *takes his pipe from his mouth.*)

QUEENIE: You mean dis scrumptious piece of jewelry?

PETE: Where'd you git it, Nigger?

QUEENIE: It was given to me.

PETE: Who give it to you?

QUEENIE: Ax me no questions 'n' ah'll tell y' no lies! That man asking me where I get my jewelry.

> (QUEENIE *exits to Show Boat.* STEVE *scowls at* PETE *and exits after* QUEENIE . . . PETE *plunges his hands in his pockets and goes upstage.* WINDY *replaces pipe in his mouth.*)

STEVEDORES and GALS:

> Niggers all work on de Mississippi,
> Niggers all work while de white men play—
> Loadin' up boats wid de bales of cotton—
> Gittin' no rest till de Judgment Day.

> Cotton Blossom, Cotton Blossom
> Love to see you growin' wild
> On de levee you're too heavy
> Fo' dis po' black child—

> (*A group of dainty, beruffled* MINCING MISSES *enter from right and left. They go over to the pictures.* GALS *moving up stage again, imitate mincing gait.*)

1ST MINCING MISS: The center picture is Julia La Verne, the leading lady.

(PETE *turns and slouches down stage.*)

2ND MINCING MISS: My—isn't she beautiful!

(*The local* BEAUX *then make a dashing entrance like the young bucks they are—they stand off and ogle the demure maidens.*)

(PETE *hangs around picture frames as* GIRLS *turn to be demure for the* BEAUX.)

BEAUX:

What a pretty bevy!
Ah! There! Ah, there!
The fairest of the fair—
To Southern beauty
Ev'ry beau must bow!

MINCING MISSES:

How you love to flatter,
You rogues! You rogues!
(*Confiding to audience.*)
Oh, goodness gracious!
They're so flirtatious!
(*To* BEAUX.)
You naughty

	BEAUX:
Fellows seem to think you please us	Little women don't be timorous!
	You will find, acting thus
When you tease us.	Only makes a man
So!	more Bold!
You're a reckless lot we know!	These are not the days of old!

BEAUX (*each grabbing a* MINCING ONE):

See! The Show Boat,
That's old Captain Andy's *Cotton Blossom*
Will you go?
Let me take you to the show—

STEVEDORES (*as they work*):

Look 'live dere—

MINCING MISSES:
>'Twill be delightful
>But to rightfully
>Accept, I have to make Mama
>Get permission from Papa!

BEAUX and MISSES   STEVEDORES and GALS:
>(*reading bills*):

>*Cotton Blossom,*
>>*Cotton Blossom*
>Captain Andy's
>>Floating Show
>Thrills and laughter
>Concert after—
>Ev'rybody's sure to
>>go!

>*Cotton Blossom,*
>>*Cotton Blossom*
>Love to see you
>>growin' free
>When dey pack you
>On de levee
>You're a heavy load to
>>me!

>*Cotton Blossom,*
>>*Cotton Blossom*
>Captain Andy's
>>Floating Show
>Thrills and Laughter
>Concert after—
>Get your girl and go!

>*Cotton Blossom,*
>>*Cotton Blossom*
>Love to see you
>>growin' wild
>On de levee
>You're too heavy
>Fo' dis po' Black Child

>So get your girl and
>>go!

>So come on,
>>Whistle-blow!

(PETE *steals* JULIE's *picture from the frame.* WINDY *takes his pipe from his mouth. Voice of* PARTHY ANN HAWKS *heard off stage.*)

(PETE *hastily puts picture out of sight as he slinks away and exits to steamboat.*)

PARTHY (*off stage*): Andy! (*Entering.*) Drat that man, he's never around!

(MAGNOLIA HAWKS *starts to practice on piano in the* Cotton Blossom.)

WINDY (*from Texas deck*): Lookin' fer Cap'n Andy?

PARTHY: Yes, Windy—Have you seen him?

WINDY: Nope. (*He puts pipe back in his mouth.*)

PARTHY: Well—if y' ain't seen him, why did you ask me if I was lookin' for him?

(WINDY *has an irritating way of not seeming to hear.*)
Y'old weather-beaten buzzard! I'm goin' to tell my husband
to get a new pilot. . . .

GIRL: Is that your little girl playing the piano?

PARTHY: Yep—ain't so little any more—eighteen this comin'
August.

GIRL: I've brought a chocolate layer cake for Captain Andy.

SECOND GIRL: And I have some plum jelly for him—

PARTHY: Well, he ain't around and the Lord knows when he
will be—

(BAND *in distance.*)

BOY: Here comes the Show Boat parade—

CROWD: Hurrah!

(*Some* COLORED BOYS *and* GIRLS *run in—leaping, dancing,
throwing their hats in the air. Others enter.*)

(CAPTAIN ANDY *enters with a girl on each arm, behind him
the Brass Band and balance of troupe and followers.*)

(PETE *re-enters and relieves piccolo player in the band. The latter's wind level isn't as good as it used to be.*)

ALL (*presenting candy, etc., to* ANDY):

Captain Andy, Captain Andy
Here's your lemon cake and home made candy.
Quince preserve and apple brandy
Mama sends her best regards to you—

Captain Andy, Captain Andy,
We've been hearing all about your dandy
Show—Is this year's good as last year's?
Won't you tell us what is new?

(*Music continues, but* ANDY *now goes into his announcement,
ignoring metre.*)

ANDY: Ladies and Gentlemen—I want you to meet some of the
greatest artists that ever played the River towns . . . Miss Ellie
May Chipley, the toast of Cairo, Illinois.

(*Applause.*)

(*To* ELLIE.)

C'mon, Ellie!

(*He pulls her by the hand.* ALL *applaud.*)

PARTHY: Y' don't have to hold hands all day!

(ELLIE *simpers.*)

ANDY (*shouting above her*): Next, I want y'all to meet Frank Schultz—

   (FRANK *steps out—Applause.*)

Mr. Schultz is the villain in our play—but off the stage, he's as meek as a lamb, and wouldn't hurt a fly—and he's stuck on Ellie.

   (ALL *laugh lightly—but* ANDY *laughs loudest.*)

That's the way they are, folks—Just one big happy family!—And I'm their father—

   (GIRLS *laugh.*)

And Parthy here is the mother—Ha! Ha!

   (ALL *laugh.*)

What about that, Parthy?

PARTHY: Oh, y' make me sick!

ANDY (*coughing*): Just one big happy family! (*Running over to* ELLIE.) Get Julie and Steve.

   (ELLIE *exits to Show Boat.*)

   (*Then, readdressing crowd.*)

Jes' t' give you a sample o' what we got in the way of talent—let me call your attention to Rubber-Face Smith, the funniest man in the world—

   (*Calling up to stocky individual on deck.*)

Hey Rubber-Face! Drop that mop an' come over to the rail. I want you to meet the folks—

   (SMITH *obeys.*)

Folks—this is Rubber-Face Smith, late of P. T. Barnum's Big Circus—I got him to join my show at tremendous expense—Hey, Smithy—give 'em one o' your funny faces—jest a sample.

   (SMITH *makes a face,* ALL *laugh, especially* ANDY.)

Ha, ha, ain't that good?—Give 'em the smile, Smithy.

   (SMITH *obeys.* ALL *laugh.*)

Look at that smile—He's got a heart of gold—He's got a heart of gold, an' teeth to match—ha! ha! That's one of my originals—

PARTHY (*aside to* ANDY): Tell 'em much more, an' they won't have to see the show.

   (JULIE *and* STEVE *enter with* ELLIE *from Show Boat.*)

ANDY: Here they come—here they come! Now, folks—I want you to meet the little sweetheart of the South—Miss Julia La Verne, our leading lady—

(*Applause.*)

Y'all know her, and y'all love her—what more can I say? . . . and we have another famous ornament of the stage with us—Mr. Stephen Baker! The handsomest leading man in the middle west!

(ALL *applaud, but a little hesitatingly, because* STEVE *is scowling at* PETE *who is now in the place of the piccolo player in the band, and who has gone over to* JULIE. ANDY *tugs at his sleeve.*)

Smile, damn you—smile y' fool—

(STEVE *finally achieves a proper smile.*)

(*The* GIRLS *gasp admiringly.*)

So here we are, folks—jest one big happy family!

(*To* PETE.)

Get the hell out of here. (*Now picking up patter in rhythm.*)

> Look't we got! Look't we got!
> How can we fail? How can we fail?
> You never see a show like this before
> We'll try to make the ev'ning bright
> An' if you come around tonight,
> Tomorrer night, you'll come around for more!

ALL:

> Captain Andy, Captain Andy
> You know how to make a show sound dandy—

ANDY (*mollified*):

> Frank and Ellie
> C'mon, let's show them
> Jest a sample of your soft shoe dance—

PARTHY (*the note of warning—she has stood enough*):

> Captain Andy! Captain Andy!

ANDY (*pleading*):

> Jest a sample—

PARTHY:

> What a man!
> My land! He
> Gives away his show for nuthin!

ANDY (*to* FRANK *and* ELLIE):

> Come on. Jest a sample of the dance—

(*He signals band, turns to crowd and beams as the dance begins. Finish of dance* ELLIE *and* FRANK *strike pose. "Looking out to sea."*)

(*At the end of dance* ANDY *applauds with so much gusto that the crowd would be ashamed not to follow suit.*)

(*Underneath ensuing scene, music.*)

(ANDY *starts passing bills around.*)

Well, folks—that was jest a sample—don't forget the bill tonight—*Tempest and Sunshine*—that beautiful drama of tears and laughter—concert after the show—Bring the children, come one, come all—

(ANDY *works up stage among* CROWD—*part of* CROWD *gathers about* JULIE *and* STEVE. *The* BOYS *around* JULIE, *and* GIRLS *around* STEVE, *so that they are temporarily separated. These admirers however keep at some little distance as they stand and worship their idols of the stage.* PETE *slinks up to* JULIE.)

PETE: That's hell of a thing to do—givin' my presents to a nigger—

JULIE (*nervously*): Pete—If Steve ever knew about you sending me that brooch, I declare he'd just about beat you to death—

(STEVE *sees* PETE *and* JULIE *together.*)

PETE: Well, he better not try, and you better be pretty nice to me—or you'll be mighty sorry—

(STEVE *has come up to* PETE—*He takes his arm and swings him around so that he faces him.*)

STEVE: I told you to keep away from my wife. I reckon I won't do any more talkin' about it.

(*Holding* PETE's *arm, he strikes him and knocks him down—* PETE *raises his other hand which holds the piccolo.*)

JULIE: Steve!—Don't!—

(*The men clinch—* PARTHY *sees them.*)

PARTHY: Andy!

(PETE *and* STEVE *struggle—* GIRLS *shriek, the crowd mills around the two men as they wrestle.* ANDY *hops about ineffectually.*)

ANDY: Hey! Pete! Steve!

(PETE *falls—* ANDY *rushes in and holds* STEVE.)

STEVE: I'll kill him.

ANDY: Get on that boat.

(FRANK *runs up—* ANDY *sort of passes* STEVE *to* FRANK *who leads him back into the boat—* STEVE *half-dazed with anger, and weakened by the nervous outburst, follows meekly, dimly realizing he has done something wrong.* ELLIE *helps* PETE *to his feet.* ANDY *looks around—the* CROWD *looks puzzled—he must say something. Suddenly he becomes inspired.*)

Well, folks—that was jest a sample. The boys jest showed you a scene from one of our bills—That's the way they are folks . . . always skylarking, always playing pranks. (*He looks around at a horrified* PARTHY *and* ELLIE—*solemn* JULIE, *and* PETE, *just coming to.*) . . . Jest one big happy family!

(*He gives the band the high sign—they strike up a tune— "Cotton Blossom." He cheers and throws his hat in the air—His good spirits infect the* CROWD *who follow suit and join in singing "Cotton Blossom" for an exit.*)

(*Their exit masks the entrance of a gentleman in elegant but frayed clothes who has paused and leaned against the bulkhead, looking out over the river—His face has not yet been seen.*)

(ANDY, ELLIE, PARTHY *and* JULIE *left on stage.* PETE *addresses* JULIE.)

PETE: Just wait—I'll get you two for this, and I know how I can do it— (*At entrance.*) And when I start in, you'll be sorry you were ever born—

ANDY: You get away from here, you little no-account river rat! You're fired.

(PETE *exits.*)

An' if y'ever come near my show boat again, I'll pitch you right into the river! . . . and don't try to get on the steamboat either . . . (*Looking up to* WINDY.) Y'hear that, Windy?

(WINDY *nods.*)

Throw him right off the boat.

(WINDY *nods.*)

PARTHY (*looking hard at* JULIE): Humph—nice goin's on!

ANDY (*looking sympathetically towards* JULIE): It wasn't Julie's fault, Parthy—

PARTHY: 'N you protecting her!

JULIE: The one thing I'm thankful for is that Magnolia wasn't here—

PARTHY: So am I—an' I'll be thankful for somethin' else, Miss La Verne—I'll have to ask you to stop givin' Magnolia pianner lessons. She can practice by herself now—in fact, I don't want my daughter mixed up with you—or anybody like you—

JULIE: Mrs. Hawks—please don't say that—Nola is like a little sister to me—outside of Steve, I don't love anybody like I love

Nola— (*Crosses to* ANDY.) Mr. Hawks, if I have to stop—seein' her—I can't stay on the *Cotton Blossom*—I just can't! (*She runs into the boat as the tears come rushing to her eyes.*)

ANDY: Now you done it—Now you done it—The best leading lady on the river!

ELLIE (*coyly snuggling up to* ANDY): Oh, Cap'n Andy, if Julie goes, will you give me a chance at the leads? I'd love to get a crack at a serious part—I'd be a sensation in drammer.

ANDY: Why, Ellie! There ain't a funnier girl on the river 'n you are! Let's see who we can get?

ELLIE (*beginning to act*): Now just watch this—Just stand there. (*Now throwing herself into it.*) "Beneath this mirthful mask burns a soul that has plumbed the depths." (*Herself again.*) *That's* the way I could play Gwendolyn in *The Heart of an Ethiopian.*

ANDY: There ain't a funnier girl on the river.

ELLIE (*anxiously clutching* CAPTAIN ANDY'*s arm and kneeling*): O Captain Andy, don't—don't stamp your foot down on real actin' ability!

PARTHY (*grimly*): Leave go my husband's arm—

(ELLIE *edges away gingerly.* PARTHY *turns her attentions to* ANDY. *During the following tirade he doesn't dare answer. He stands meek and still.*)

An' you—you think more of your show boat troupe than you do of your own daughter's upbringing—I may not know much, but—if you insist on keepin' a lot of roustabouts on board, then I'll have to protect Magnolia. . . . Thank God, her mother has a good Christian bringin' up in Massachusetts. Where I come from, no decent body'd touch this show boat riff raff with a ten foot pole—let alone have their daughters mixed up with them— I'll have more to say to you, later!

(*She exits into the boat—He waits until she's gone—then, oblivious of* ELLIE'*s presence, he answers* PARTHY *back.*)

ANDY (*walking up and down and arguing with his imaginary adversary*): Oh, you will, will you? Well, maybe I'll have somethin' to say to you, too—'s far as that goes I'd just as soon have her be friends with Julie as any gal I know—yes—Julie!— You heard me— (*He sees* ELLIE.) My God—I'll tell her!

PARTHY (*off stage*): Andy!

ELLIE: Are you going to tell her all of that now?

ANDY: No—I'll tell her tonight—late. I don't want any more trouble before the show. Jest one big happy family—Bah!

(ANDY *exits into Show Boat.*)

(ELLIE *turns away from boat—sees* RAVENAL.)

ELLIE: It's a man.

(RAVENAL *turns, we see him for the first time—so does* ELLIE. *He strides down stage, nonchalantly swinging his cane. She thinks he's grand—she drops her handkerchief.* RAVENAL *picks up handkerchief and hands it to her with courtesy.*)

ELLIE: Thank you so much. (*Gives flirtatious glance and exits.*)

(RAVENAL *looks after her, mildly amused. He takes the long cheroot from his mouth and looks at it reflectively.*)

(VALLON *enters.* RAVENAL *sees him. They regard each other coolly for a moment.*)

VALLON: Back in town, Gay?

RAVENAL: For a short stay—

VALLON: Can't be more than twenty-four hours, you know.

RAVENAL: Give me time, can't you? I haven't been twenty-four hours stepping off the gangplank onto this wharf, have I? . . . I can get on just as quickly. (*With impulsive irritation, he throws his half-smoked cheroot to the ground.*)

VALLON: No offense, Gay—just thought I'd remind you in case of trouble—it'd be terrible to have you locked up—all the purty gals on the river front'd be cryin' their eyes out. Where you aim to go from here?

RAVENAL: Who cares? Who cares where I go?

VALLON: Cigar?

(*As he proffers it,* RAVENAL *raises his eyebrows disdainfully.*)

RAVENAL: What did you call it?

VALLON: *Cig*ar—

RAVENAL: Optimist . . .

(VALLON *shrugs his shoulders and walks off*—RAVENAL *swings his cane airily and strolls up and down.*)

RAVENAL:

    Who cares if my boat goes up stream—
    Or if the gale bids me go with the river's flow?
    I drift along with my fancy—
    Sometimes I thank my lucky stars my heart is free—

And other times I wonder—where's that mate for me?
(MAGNOLIA *begins again on the piano off stage. He looks up.*
She hesitates in her fingering at certain points. He pantomimes
the serious anxiety a listener always feels, hoping she'll hit the
right note. He sits on a cotton bale and goes on with his musing,
idly tapping his cane on the ground.)

RAVENAL:

The driftwood floating over the sea
Someday finds a sheltering lee
So, somewhere there surely must be
A harbor meant for me—

(MAGNOLIA *enters on the upper deck of Show Boat.*)

I drift along with my fancy—
Sometimes I thank my lucky stars my heart is free
And other times I wonder where's the mate—

(*He turns and sees* MAGNOLIA. *What a picture! A very young*
face, and a fluffy dress all pink with flowers and everything—
and she is becomingly shy—yet bold enough to return his gaze—
and to speak first.)

MAGNOLIA: Hello . . .

RAVENAL (*taken by surprise—an unusual thing*): Er—how do you
do—

MAGNOLIA: Do you live here?

RAVENAL: No—I'm just a way-farer along the river—

MAGNOLIA: So am I—which way are you going?

RAVENAL: Either way—where are you going?

MAGNOLIA: Anywhere Papa gives shows—

RAVENAL (*just a trifle jarred*): Oh—are you a player?

MAGNOLIA: You mean like on the pianner? Yes—I play a little.

RAVENAL: Oh—was that you I heard just now—?

MAGNOLIA: Yes—that was me!

RAVENAL: What a pity!

MAGNOLIA: What did you say, Mister?

RAVENAL: Er—when I asked you if you were a player—I
meant—are you an actress?

MAGNOLIA: Oh—no—but I'd give anything if I could be.

RAVENAL: Why?

MAGNOLIA: Because you can make believe so many wonderful
things that never happen in real life.

RAVENAL: But wonderful things do happen—this very day I was standing here on the levee—feeling blue—and suddenly I looked up, and—

MAGNOLIA: I must go now—

RAVENAL: Why?

MAGNOLIA: Well, you see you're talking to me—and I don't know you—

RAVENAL: Does that really matter so much?

MAGNOLIA: N-no—not to me— But they say it isn't nice.

RAVENAL: If you like to make believe things, why can't we make believe we know each other?

MAGNOLIA: Oh, yes—and we haven't seen each other for seventy-five years, and you're my long-lost nephew— There's a scene like that in a play called *The Village Drunkard*.

RAVENAL: No—Seventy-five years is too long— Besides I don't think I like the idea of being your nephew. Let us imagine that we've just met—

MAGNOLIA: But we really have—

RAVENAL: Yes—but let's just suppose that we've fallen in love at first sight—

"Make Believe"
Only make believe I love you,
Only make believe that you love me.
Others find peace of mind in pretending—
Couldn't you? Couldn't I? Couldn't we?
Make believe our lips are blending
In a phantom kiss, or two, or three.
Might as well make believe I love you
For, to tell the truth, I do.

Your pardon I pray,
'Twas too much to say
The words that betray my heart.

MAGNOLIA:
We only pretend,
You do not offend
In playing a lover's part—

The game of just supposing is the sweetest game I
    know.

Our dreams are more romantic than the world we see—

RAVENAL:

And if the things we dream about don't happen to be
    so,

That's just an unimportant technicality—

MAGNOLIA:

Though the cold and brutal fact is

You and I have never met

We need not mind convention's P's and Q's.

If we put our thoughts in practice

We can banish all regret

Imagining most anything we choose.

  (*Refrain*)

We could make believe I love you,

We could make believe that you love me.

BOTH:

Others find peace of mind in pretending,

Couldn't you?

Couldn't I?

Couldn't we?

RAVENAL:

Make believe our lips are blending

In a phantom kiss, or two, or three.

BOTH:

Might as well make believe I love you.

RAVENAL:

For to tell the truth, I do . . .

(*They stand and gaze at each other.* VALLON *enters, followed
by* JOE, *who is carrying a sack of flour, which he places on stage.*)

VALLON (*in a low tone*): Ravenal— The Judge'd like to see you.

RAVENAL (*taking his tone from* VALLON): What for?

VALLON: Nothin' serious—but y' got to come and have a talk
with him.

RAVENAL (*turning to* MAGNOLIA): You will excuse me, ma'am?—
I hope I'll see you again—in a little while.

(*He bows and exits grandly with* VALLON. *She looks after him
adoringly. Then she sees* JOE *looking at* RAVENAL *curiously.*)

MAGNOLIA: Oh, Joe!— Did you see that young man I was talkin' to?

(JOE *turns*.)

JOE: Mornin' Miss Nola . . . Yep—I seed him—seed a lot like him on de river— (*He sets down a large bag of flour he has been carrying.*)

MAGNOLIA: Oh, Joe, he was such a gentleman! Have you seen Miss Julie?—I got to tell her—I got to ask her what she thinks— (MAGNOLIA *exits.*)

JOE: Better ask de ol' man river what he thinks— He knows all 'bout dem boys . . . He knows all 'bout ever'thin' . . . (JOE *sits on box, takes out a knife, picks up a shaving and starts to whittle, idly, as he sings.*)

"Ol' Man River"

Dere's an ol' man called de Mississippi;
Dat's de ol' man dat I'd like to be!
What does he care if de world's got troubles?
What does he care if de land ain't free?
(*Refrain*)
Ol' Man River
Dat ol' Man River,
He mus' know sumpin'
But don't say nuthin',
He jes' keeps rollin',
He keeps on rollin' along.
He don't plant taters,
He don't plant cotton,
An' dem dat plants 'em
Is soon forgotten,
But Ol' Man River
He jes' keeps rollin' along.

You an' me, we sweat an' strain,
Body all achin' an' racked wid pain—
Tote dat barge
Lif' dat bale!
Git a little drunk
An' you land in jail. . . .

Ah gits weary
An' sick of tryin',
Ah'm tired of livin'
An' skeered of dyin',
But ol' Man River,
He jes' keeps rollin' along.
(BARGE MEN *enter, pulling rope, during the following verse,*
close in with curtain, leaving JOE *and* MALE CHORUS *in*
front.)

JOE:

Niggers all work on de Mississippi,
Niggers all work while de white folks play,
Pullin' dem boats from de dawn to sunset,
Gittin' no rest till de Judgment day—

MEN:

Don't look up
An' don't look down—
You don't dast make
De white boss frown.
Bend your knees
An' bow your head,
An' pull dat rope
Until yo' dead.

JOE:

Let me go 'way from de Mississippi,
Let me go 'way from de white man boss;
Show me dat stream called de river Jordan,
Dat's de ol' stream dat I long to cross.

MEN:

Ol' Man River
Dat ol' Man River
He mus' know sumpin'
But don' say nuthin',
He jes' keeps rollin',
He keeps on rollin' along.

JOE:

Long ol' river forever keep rollin' on—

MEN:

He don' plant taters,

He don' plant cotton,
An' dem dat plants 'em
Is soon forgotten,
But ol' Man River
He jes' keeps rollin' along.

JOE:

Long ol' river keeps hearin' dat song;
You an' me, we sweat an' strain
Body all achin' an' wracked wid pain—
Tote dat barge! Lif' dat bale!
Git a little drunk, an' you land in jail. . . .

ALL:

Ah gits weary
An' sick of tryin';
Ah'm tired of livin'
An' skeered of dyin',
But ol' Man River
He jes' keeps rollin' along.

BLACK OUT

SCENE 2

Kitchen pantry of the Cotton Blossom.
   A half hour later.
   Chair and sugar barrel down left. Kitchen table up left. Cupboards and shelves on back wall. Kitchen presumably off left.
   At rise: MAGNOLIA *is sitting on chair, day-dreaming.*

QUEENIE (*enters with a pan of biscuits*): What cher doin' all by yourself, Miss Nola?

MAGNOLIA: Nothin'. Just waitin'. I wish Julie would come—

QUEENIE: Ah declare, ef de kitchen pantry ain't de funniest place to be meetin' people.

JULIE (*off stage whispered call*): Nola! You there? Nola—

MAGNOLIA (*same tone*): C'm on in, Julie—

JULIE (*entering*): I had a hard time getting here—I just missed bein' caught by Parthy. Oh, look at Queenie's biscuits—

QUEENIE: Now look here, Miss Julie. Dinner'll be in five minutes.

JULIE: Oh, let me take a bite. Joe'll help you make some more.

QUEENIE: Joe! Dat lazy nigger don't help me—he's always too tired—ef dat feller ever tried to cook, he'd be puttin' popcorn in flapjacks so dat dey'd turn over by demselves!—

MAGNOLIA: Sit down Julie—I got to tell you something.

JULIE (*sitting*): I'm just dying to hear what it is. . . .

> (MAGNOLIA *climbs on sugar barrel next to* JULIE's *chair, and squats, tailor fashion.*)

MAGNOLIA: Julie—I'm in love—

QUEENIE (*stopping her action as she is reaching to shelf for a box of salt*): What's dat? You says in love?—(*She laughs—much too boisterously to suit* MAGNOLIA.) Why yo' po' crazy little gal— you got your first long skirt and you in love! . . . (QUEENIE *laughs even louder than before—which seemed impossible—and exits to the kitchen with her box of salt.*)

JULIE (*taking* MAGNOLIA's *hands in hers*): Tell me all about it, honey, who is he?

MAGNOLIA: I don't know— He was standing on the wharf— and I was standing on the top deck and he looked so different from anybody else, and so—so beautiful.

JULIE (*snuggling* MAGNOLIA's *head against her bosom*): Yo' poor little lamb—

> (JULIE *is thoughtful,* MAGNOLIA *can't wait for her comment, she turns to her impulsively.*)

MAGNOLIA: Julie, he said he liked me—d'ye think he meant it?

JULIE: I don't know, child—I don't know as I like you to go fallin' in love with some man that nobody ever heard of— suppose he turned out to be a—be just a no-account river feller—

MAGNOLIA: But if I found he was no-account, I'd stop lovin' him—

JULIE: Oh, no, you wouldn't—once a girl like you starts to love a man, she don't stop so easy—

MAGNOLIA: Couldn't you stop lovin' Steve if he treated you mean?

JULIE: No, honey, no matter what he did—

MAGNOLIA: Why do you love Steve?
  (*Music.*)
JULIE: I don't know—he's such a bad actor on the stage. And
  he thinks he's so good—maybe that's why I love him—
  (*Continuing to* MAGNOLIA.) You see, child—Love's a funny
  thing—There's no sense to it—that's why you got to be so
  careful when it comes creeping up on you—
MAGNOLIA: It's like that thing you always sing when we take
  our walks—
JULIE: I know!— (*She sings.*)
      Fish got to swim, birds got to fly—
      I got to love one man till I die—
      Can't help lovin' dat man of mine.
    (QUEENIE *re-entering, stops in her tracks and looks puzzled.*)
MAGNOLIA: That's it—
JULIE:
      Tell me he's lazy, tell me he's slow,
      Tell me I'm crazy (maybe I know)
      Can't help lovin' dat man of mine.
QUEENIE: How come y'all know dat song?
    (JULIE *stops abruptly, a swift terror steals across her face, and
    quickly vanishes—succeeded by an expression of stolid caution.*)
MAGNOLIA: Why? Do you know it, Queenie?
QUEENIE: F'sho' ah does— But ah didn't ever hear anybody but
  colored folks sing dat song—Sounds funny for Miss Julie to
  know it—
MAGNOLIA: Why Julie sings it all the time.
QUEENIE: Kin y'sing de whole thing?
JULIE: 'Course I can— (*Almost fiercely.*) What's so funny about
  that? (*She starts to sing in an attitude of defiance, then lapsing
  into the "Blue" spirit of the song.*)

            "Can't Help Lovin' Dat Man"
      Oh, listen, sister,
      I love my mister man,
      And I can't tell yo' why.
      Dere ain't no reason
      Why I should love dat man—
      It mus' be sumpin' dat de angels done plan.

(*Refrain*)

> Fish got to swim, birds got to fly,
> I got to love one man till I die—
> Can't help lovin' dat man of mine.
> Tell me he's lazy, tell me he's slow,
> Tell me I'm crazy (maybe I know)—
> Can't help lovin' dat man of mine.
> When he goes away
> Dat's a rainy day,
> And when he comes back dat day is fine,

(*Carried away.*)

> De sun will shine!

(QUEENIE *goes on beating time with a spoon.*)

> He kin come home as late as kin be,
> Home widout him ain't no home to me—
> Can't help lovin' dat man of mine.

QUEENIE (*tickled to death*): Dat's beautiful Miss Julie—
JOE (*entering, eating apple*): Was dat you Miss Julie—dat's mah favorite song!—
QUEENIE:

> Mah man is shif'less
> An' good for nuthin' too
> (He's mah man jes' the same)
> He's never round here
> When dere is work to do—

(*Looking hard at* JOE.)

(*Enter two colored* SERVANTS, *pick apples out of basket.*)

> Uh-huh—
> He's never 'round here when dere's workin' to do.

(*Another* NEGRO *helper comes in and listens, entranced.* MAGNOLIA *gradually starts to do coon shuffle.* JOE, QUEENIE *and* BOY *look on admiringly.*)

> De chimbley's smokin',
> De roof is leakin' in,
> But he don' seem to care.
> He kin be happy
> Wid jes' a sip of gin—

JOE:

> What you all talking 'bout gin?

QUEENIE:

    Uh-huh. Ah even love him when his kisses got gin!

JOE:

    Look it dat little gal shuffle!

JOE, JULIE and QUEENIE:

    Fish got to swim, birds got to fly,
    I got to love one man 'til I die—
    Can't help lovin' dat man of mine.
    Tell me he's lazy, tell me he's slow,
    Tell me I'm crazy (lovin' him so)
    Can't help lovin' dat man of mine.
    When he goes away
    Dat's a rainy day,
    But when he comes back dat day is fine,
    De sun will shine!
    He kin come home as late as kin be,
    Home widout him ain't no home to me—
    Can't help lovin' dat man of mine!

BLACK OUT

SCENE 3

Outside of a river-front gambling saloon. Right door to the saloon is a little old-fashioned notion store. On the other side of saloon is a cigar store with wooden Indian outside. A group of LOUNGERS—*young bloods of the town—hanging around. A typical southern gambling-house* DEALER *is with them.*

    The curtain rises.

    At rise: Idle chatter among the boys. As the curtain rises, the DEALER *draws out a heavy gold chain to which is attached a gold watch and a ponderous charm.*

DEALER: Time to open up the game.

VALLON (*just as the* DEALER *is about to go through saloon door*): Jim!

    (*The* DEALER *turns in the door.*)

    If that fellah Ravenal comes in after six o'clock this evenin', don' deal any cards to him— He's got to be out of town in twenty-four hours, understand?

DEALER: It's all right with me, chief. I'll count him out.

(MEN *exit in saloon.*)

(*During the preceding speeches,* ELLIE *and* FRANK *have entered from left.* FRANK *sees the saloon and begins to cough a racking cough.*)

ELLIE: I am going to get Parthy a spool of thread.

(FRANK *coughs.*)

(*After a sharp look at him. Rather caustically.*)

Where's the saloon?

FRANK: Saloon? What do you mean?

ELLIE: I mean I'm on to that old cough gag— If you think you're going in there, Frank Schultz, you've got another guess comin'.

FRANK: Honest, Ellie, my chest hurts.

ELLIE: Your chest hurts? I don't know what it can be—the way I feel I should have been buried yesterday.

FRANK: Gee, I'm sorry, Ell. Do you know that I think about you?

ELLIE: What?

FRANK: You got a cute indigestion.

ELLIE: Ah, I bet you say that to all the girls.

FRANK: No I don't. You know I'm crazy about you honey . . . You know I love you.

ELLIE: Yes, but tell me—will you love me when I'm old?

FRANK: I don't see why a year or two should make any difference.

ELLIE: You better not talk that way to me. The way my chest hurts I know I am going to die.

FRANK: Don't talk foolish; you're not going to die.

ELLIE: Yes I am gonna die. The doctor said I'm gonna die.

FRANK: Aw gee Ellie—

ELLIE: Before I die I want you to make some promises. I want you to promise that at the funeral you'll ride in the first carriage.

FRANK: Alone?

ELLIE: Well not exactly alone. No, my relatives will ride with you.

FRANK: I don't want to ride with your relatives; I don't like them and I don't want to ride with them. (*He starts to go into saloon.*)

ELLIE: Please don't go into that saloon— If you do I'll tell Captain Andy.

(FRANK *starts again for saloon.*)

If you go in there I'll faint.

(FRANK *starts again for saloon.*)

Frank, here I go.

(*She falls forward.* FRANK *grabs her by neck of dress. Business of falling, etc.*)

FRANK: Stop this nonsense and go in and buy the thread.

(*Kisses her.*)

(ELLIE *exits into notion store.*)

(*Enter* PETE.)

PETE: Hey, Frank, I'm glad I found you. Will you come with me to the sheriff? I want yuh to hear somethin'.

FRANK: Say, Pete, what do you wanta see the sheriff for?

PETE: You know it's a crime in this state for a white man to be married to a nigger wench.

FRANK (*puzzled but full of curiosity*): Yeah? What of it?

PETE: You'll see what's of it, when I talk to the sheriff. Why, there's a case of it right on the *Cotton Blossom*.

FRANK (*astounded*): Oh, you must be crazy! (*Sits on keg.*)

PETE: Crazy, am I? (*Takes out* JULIE'S *picture.*) Look at this. And I got proof.

FRANK (*looking at picture*): Julie!

PETE (*with a sneer*): Passin' herself off for a white lady.

(VALLON *enters from saloon and goes left.*)

FRANK: Pete, you wouldn't do anything— (*Frightened.*) My Gawd! But you ain't go' to do anything, are yuh?—Pete, c'm here.

PETE (*with a grim look at* FRANK *as he goes over to* VALLON): Say, ain't you Mr. Vallon, the sheriff?

VALLON: Yes suh, Vallon's my name.

PETE: Can we go some place where we can talk private?

VALLON: At yo' service, suh.

FRANK: In the saloon? (*Coughs.*)

(*They go into saloon.*)

(RAVENAL *comes on, flanked on either side by a simpering* GIRL *and followed by several other feminine admirers. Several* GIRLS *also enter from left. Before saloon door,* RAVENAL *stops talking, as though about to leave.*)

(ELLIE *enters from the notion store, with several* GIRLS. *She at once sees* RAVENAL *and prepares to do her usual handkerchief*

trick. She passes by and drops her handkerchief. RAVENAL
restores it quickly and politely to her hand.)

ELLIE: Oh, thank you so much.

RAVENAL: Delighted to again be of service, ma'am.

(*He looks at her and sees from her rather startling attire that
she must belong to the show boat troupe.*)

(ELLIE *looking around rather disdainfully at the* BELLES *who
are admiring* RAVENAL.)

ELLIE: Are you coming to our show tonight? I'm very good in
it. I've been told it gives me my grandest change to be emotional . . . you know . . . the kind of part I can get my teeth into.

RAVENAL (*wishing to end her palaver but anxious to get information about* MAGNOLIA): That so? (*Hurriedly.*) Oh, by the
way, I was talking to a young girl on your boat—I don't know
her name— I think she was the piano player.

ELLIE: Oh! That's Captain Andy's daughter.

RAVENAL: Does she always travel with you?

ELLIE: Yes—But her mother is always watchin' her. You'd think
she was one o' them wax flowers under a glass dome.

RAVENAL (*seeing that he can get no information from* ELLIE):
Well, you must pardon me. I have an engagement. (*Nodding
toward the saloon. He goes to the saloon door, stops and turns.*)
I may be down to see—the show—later. (*He enters the saloon.*)

(*The* BELLES *crowd around* ELLIE, *their interest now diverted
from* RAVENAL *to the show boat actress.*)

GIRL: Aren't you Ella May Chipley, the actress—

ELLIE (*very important*): Yes, dear—that's me.

GIRL: Was that man an actor?

ELLIE: No—just a gentleman who seems to have taken a fancy
to me.

GIRL: It must be grand to be an actress and see the world!

2ND GIRL: Yes, and think of all the actors you meet.

ELLIE (*crestfallen because she has made no impression on* RAVENAL):
Yeh, you meet a lot of actors.

"Life on the Wicked Stage"

Why do stage struck maidens clamor
To be actin' in the drammer?

GIRLS:

We've heard say

You are gay
Night and day.

ELLIE:

(You go 'way)

GIRLS:

We drink water from a dipper
You drink champagne from a slipper

ELLIE:

Tho' it seems
Crool to bust
All your dreams
Still I must
Here's the truth I tell you:

(*Refrain*)

Life upon the wicked stage ain't ever what a girl
    supposes
Stage-door Johnnies aren't raging over you with gems
    and roses
When you let a feller hold your hand (which
Means an extra beer or sandwich)
Ev'rybody whispers, "Ain't her life a whirl?"
Tho you're warned against a roué ruining your
    reputation
I have played around the one night trade around a
    great big nation,
Wild old men who give you jewels and sables
Only live in Aesop's fables
Life upon the wicked stage ain't nothin' for a girl.

GIRLS:

Tho we've listened to you moan and grieve, you
Must pardon us if we do not believe you
There is no doubt you're
Crazy about your art.

ELLIE:

I admit it's fun to smear my face with paint
Causing ev'ry one to think I'm what I ain't,
And I like to play a demi-mondy role—with soul!
Ask the hero does he like the way I lure
When I play a hussy or a paramour;
Yet when once the curtain's down my life is pure—

And how I dread it!

GIRLS:

> (*Refrain*)
>> Life upon the wicked stage ain't ever what a girl
>> supposes
>> Stage door Johnnies aren't raging over you with gems
>> and roses.

ELLIE:

>> If some gentleman would talk with reason
>> I would cancel all next season—
>> Life upon the wicked stage ain't nothin' for a girl—

GIRLS:

>> You'd be back the season after.

> (ELLIE *and* GIRLS *exit on dance.*)

> (GAMBLER *enters from saloon.*)

LOUNGER: Say— Who's that sportin' gambler in there?

GAMBLER: That's Gaylord Ravenal—

LOUNGER: Ravenal! Ain't that the one—?

GAMBLER: Yep— Got in a little fuss here 'bout a year ago—
Proved it was self-defense and got off— Chief jes' tol' him to
clear out o' town by nightfall—

LOUNGER: Don't seem to be worryin' him none—

GAMBLER: Nothin' worries him—

> (RAVENAL *enters from saloon—followed by a few others.*)

RAVENAL: Can't be helped, gentlemen— I'll have better luck
next time—

> "'Til Good Luck Comes My Way"
>> The man who ventures with chance
>> Is the man who's adding the salt, romance,
>> To a world
>> That otherwise is dark and drear
>> The sane, conservative lot
>> Have their fate secure in a guarded spot
>> Of the world
>> They're welcome to their drab career.

BOYS:

>> It is all well enough to be grinning
>> While your winnings grow
>> But when fortune reverses her spinning,

Life is not a-glow
That is why we like to see
Someone who can be
Unconcerned and free like you.
RAVENAL:
If I am losing today
I will take my loss and I'll pay
For I know
That in time my luck will turn; it's bound to turn.
(*Refrain*)
'Til good luck comes my way, I'll play along
While there's a game on the highway, I'll stay along
With just the turn of a wheel or the flip of a card as my
     guide,
I'll let fate decide
If I walk or ride.

Why sit alone with your sorrow and kill the day?
There may be sunshine tomorrow to fill the day.
While I've a heart and a brain
And my ebony cane
I can borrow
Until the day when good luck comes my way.

RAVENAL:	BOYS:
Never venture	So you have our sympathy
Never gain	You are game as you can be
Men of caution	Fortune will change like an
Live in vain	April day
So I will wait 'til	And so we'll wait 'til
Good luck comes my way	Good luck comes our way.

BLACK OUT

SCENE 4

The auditorium and stage of the Cotton Blossom.
     *Downstage, the orchestra sit behind in the small stage of the boat.
The roller curtain is down. On one side of the pit is a double plan of
stage boxes.*

At rise: MAGNOLIA *is seated at piano.* JULIE, STEVE *and*
RUBBER-FACE *waiting for stage direction.*

>(JULIE *moves up-stage.*)
>
>(PARTHY *carries some costume she is mending and takes a posi-
>tion on chair.*)
>
>(*Evidences of old-fashioned lighting equipment are visible. The
>foots are kerosine lamps masked by shields. They are not lighted.
>A hanging kerosine pilot light is all they are using for rehearsals.*)
>
>(ANDY *is down stage, consulting 'script.*)

ANDY: —now while we're waiting for Ellie an' Frank let's skip
right down to Act Three—That scene about cows is the big
one to tackle—

>(JULIE *takes her place.*)

We'll take it from where your sister just went out—so—and—
so—and so—and so—long speech, ending—"and, remember
dear, I'm your sister, an' if any harm should come to you I'd
never forgive myself." That's your cue—y' get up—got your
part?

JULIE: I know it— (JULIE *rises and becomes an actress—a totally
artificial person.*) "I wonder what can be keeping Parson
Brown . . ."

>(MAGNOLIA *plays.*)
>
>(ANDY *nods to* MAGNOLIA—*she starts to play for no reason.
>She does not average more than one mistake to three measures—
>when she takes her time—This does not count slurred chords in
>the bass.*)

"He promised to be here, before dark, and the twilight is fast
fading into night."

ANDY: Just a minute, Julie . . .

>(MAGNOLIA *stops playing.*)
>
>(MAGNOLIA'*s eyes never leave the keyboard. They don't dare.*)

Hey—"Rubber-Face"—I want you to watch these cues—
There ain't any comical part in this bill, so you got to take
care of the props—

RUBBER-FACE (*his voice lacks the cheery note of enthusiasm*): All
right—

ANDY: "Fading into night" is a light cue: Y' get it from Julie.
Start to dim down then—

RUBBER-FACE: I know—

>(MAGNOLIA *plays.*)

JULIE (*going through stage directions as she speaks*): Then comes a long speech—I know it— So and so and so—"I love him with all my heart"— Go up to window . . . (*She goes up to window.*) so—and so—so—down to table— (JULIE *sits down on bench.*) (MAGNOLIA *stops playing.*)

ANDY (*reading*): Sit down on "love—the most tender of all human sentiments"—So and so—and so—so—ending with—"Can it be he will not keep his tryst with me?"

RUBBER-FACE (*calling out*): "Keep his tryst with me"—that's the bell . . .

STEVE: That's me, isn't it?

ANDY: Yep—You enter through door at right— Nola, play something for a Parson—
(MAGNOLIA *plays very feelingly.*)

STEVE: "Good evening, Miss Lucy—I was absorbed in meditation and did not realize night had fallen—"

JULIE: "The days are getting shorter, Hamilton. But they are long when one is waiting."

STEVE: "As I came across the field, I saw the cattle being driven home—by your faithful dog—"

ANDY: Get that, Rubber-Face?
(MAGNOLIA *stops playing.*)

RUBBER-FACE: Yeh—I get a cowbell—

ANDY: A cowbell! It ain't a cowbell—it says here "cow's moo off stage"—Have you got a moo effect?

RUBBER-FACE: I kin do that myself—Moo-oo-oo——

ANDY: Try it again—a little deeper—

RUBBER-FACE: Moo—oo—

ANDY: Guess y' better use the bell.

STEVE: "Miss Lucy—although I wear the garb of a parson—" (STEVE *now steps out of his character.*) May I make a suggestion here, Cap'n? I thought it'd be a good idea if while we was talking here for Frank to pass by and peek in through the window—like this.
(*He pantomimes* FRANK *sneaking by and peering through the window with a blood-curdling expression on his face.*)

MAGNOLIA (*rising*): Y' can't do it! Room's supposed to be on the second floor— Frank couldn't look in the window if it was on the second floor—

ANDY: I don't think it'd be any good anyway—

MAGNOLIA: Julie let me study her part— I know every line—
and all the business— If you forget anything, ask me—

PARTHY: You stick to the pianner young lady—no play-actin'
for you—

(MAGNOLIA *sits down at the piano.*)

STEVE (*looking out at the audience, towards extreme left aisle*):
Here's Ellie—

(*Enter* ELLIE.)

ANDY (*looking out*): Where's Frank?

ELLIE: He's comin'— (*She runs over to* STEVE *out of breath.*) He
sent me ahead to give you a message, Steve— C'm here—

(*She seems nervous and worried. She stands on tiptoe; and whispers in* STEVE'*s ear. He is visibly affected.*)

ANDY: All right, Steve—as long as Frank's comin' we'll lead up
to his entrance—C'mon, Steve—

(JOE *appears in upper box intending to wipe off rail.*)

(ELLIE *stands at side, waiting for something to happen.*)

STEVE (*dazed, not able to think as fast as he'd like to*): Er—all
right—er—"Miss Lucy—although I wear the clothes—"

MAGNOLIA: Garb!—

STEVE (*his voice seems detached from his thoughts*): "Garb of a
parson"—"Beneath these sombre vestments there is the heart
of a man—that beats for you alone—"

JULIE (*stands up*): "Hamilton!"

(*They embrace, he whispers in her ear—apparently what* ELLIE
told him. She looks at STEVE, *horrified.* ELLIE *takes one step toward
her sympathetically.* JULIE *looks over at* ELLIE *questioningly.*)

ELLIE (*half-whispering*): They'll be up here in a minute—

ANDY (*reading script*): All right—embrace is over— Then what?

JULIE: Then—I say—I say—

ANDY: Prompt her—Nola—

MAGNOLIA: "Hamilton—my own, my own"—Papa! Look at
Julie—

(JULIE *has fallen limp in* STEVE'*s arms. He places her on
bench.*)

ANDY (*running over*): What's the matter?

STEVE: Julie's sick.

MAGNOLIA (*running to her*): What is it, Julie?

ANDY (*puzzled*): Well, you better stop rehearsin' an' rest, so's
you'll be all right tonight.

JULIE (*in terror*): No—no, I can't play tonight. Don't ask me.

(STEVE *standing at* JULIE's *side does not turn around—his eyes are on* JULIE.)

(MAGNOLIA *presses* JULIE's *hair back of her forehead*.)

PARTHY: Huh— Playing Fort Adams tomorrow—good a stand as we got—probably won't be able to open there neither if she's as sick as all that.

JULIE (*in a high strained voice*): I'll be able to play tomorrow!

STEVE (*in desperation*): She'll be all right as soon as she gets out of this town—

PARTHY: That's a funny thing—

ANDY: Sure you won't be feeling better by night time?

(WINDY *shambles on stage*.)

JULIE (*clings herself into* STEVE's *arms—clings to him weeping*): No! No! Leave me alone—can't you—leave me alone!

(MAGNOLIA *jumps up, frightened by* JULIE's *sudden outburst*.)

ANDY: Sure—sure we'll leave you alone, Julie. Hello, Windy— what you doin' here?

(*The little group turn toward* WINDY. *He takes his hat off and rubs his head—stands a minute silent—chewing*.)

WINDY: Seems that skunk Pete's been up to something. . . . (*Chews*.) Skinned out an hour back, streaking toward town like possessed. He yanked that picture of Julie out of the frame on the levee— I seen him.

ELLIE (*to* STEVE): I told you!

STEVE: I'll kill him this time, the—

ANDY: Shut up.

WINDY: Just stepped down to warn you. I seen Pete coming along the levee with Vallon—Vallon is the sheriff. He'll be along now any minute.

ANDY: Well, let him come aboard; our license is paid.

JULIE: What are we going to do?

STEVE: Stay right here—you know what I told you—

(JULIE *springs from the bench and clings to* STEVE. *He looses her hold roughly and from his pocket he whips out a large clasp knife and opens it—all the women scream but* JULIE. ANDY *springs at* STEVE *but is shaken off*.)

ANDY: What are you doing with that knife, Steve?

STEVE: I'm not going to hurt her, you fool—leave me be— I know what I'm doing—

(MAGNOLIA *instinctively seeks shelter in* PARTHY's *arms.*)

Somebody go out and keep them away a minute—it won't hurt much, darling—

(*He seizes* JULIE's *hand in his left one and runs the blade across the tip of her finger—throws knife up stage—he bends his head and pressing his lips to the wound sucks it greedily.*)

(*With a little moan* JULIE *falls back on bench.* STEVE *looks offstage.* VALLON *enters and goes up to the group, some of the* TOWNSPEOPLE, *the Colored* JUBILEE SINGERS *follow him in, and other curiosity seekers edge in during the ensuing scene.* JOE *appears in upper box wiping rail.*)

VALLON: Hello Windy. Capt. Hawks, do you acknowledge to be owner of the Show Boat?

ANDY (*clutching his whiskers, steps forward. His voice quivers in spite of an effort to be cool*): 'Course I do. What do you want?

VALLON: Well, Cap, I have an unpleasant duty. I understand there's a miscegenation case on board—

MAGNOLIA: What's he mean, Mama?

ANDY (*to* VALLON): How's that?

VALLON: Case of a negro woman married to a white man. Criminal offense in this state.

ANDY: No such thing—No such thing on board this boat.

VALLON (*producing paper*): Name of the white man is Steve Baker—

(*All look at* STEVE— *He looks straight forward meeting no-one's eyes.*)

Name of the negress— (*He squints at paper.*) Name of the negress is Julie—Dozier.

(*He looks at group.*)

Which one's them?

MAGNOLIA (*involuntarily*): Julie!

(*She takes a step toward* JULIE, PARTHY *holds her back.*)

STEVE (*steps forward*): I'm Steve Baker— (*Points to* JULIE *on bench.*) This is my wife—

VALLON: Julie Dozier— My information says you were born in Mississippi. Your pop was white, and your mammy black— That right?

JULIE: Yes—that's right.

MAGNOLIA: But Julie—you—

VALLON: You two better get your things and come along with me—

(STEVE *throws an arm around* JULIE'*s shoulder and faces* VALLON.)

STEVE: You wouldn't call a man a white man that's got negro blood in him, would you?

VALLON: No, I wouldn't. Not in Mississippi. One drop of nigger blood makes you a nigger in these parts—

(JOE *stands looking on dumbly.*)

STEVE: Well, I got more than a drop of—nigger blood in me, and that's a fact.

VALLON: You ready to swear to that in a court of law?

STEVE: I'll swear to it any place. (*Takes a step forward, one hand outstretched.*) I'll do more than that. Look at all these folks here. Every one of them can swear I got nigger blood in me this minute. That's how white I am.

VALLON: Well, I seen fairer men than you that was niggers, still you better tell that to the Judge.

WINDY (*clears his throat, and steps out of the group*): Ike Vallon, guess you know me better part of twenty-five years. I was keel-boatin' time you was runnin' around a barefoot on the landin' . . . Now I'm tellin' you, me, Windy McLain—that that white man there's got nigger blood in him. I'll take my oath to that— (WINDY *stands in silence.*)

VALLON: If it was anybody else but Windy—but I got this straight from—well—from somebody who ought to know—

ELLIE (*all indignation*): From who? From a sooty-faced river-rat—named Pete—and why? Because he's been stuck on Julie here—and she wouldn't have anything to do with him.

ANDY: That's right, Vallon. That gal's telling the truth.

(VALLON *waits quite a while before answering.*)

VALLON: Guess I got to take Windy's word against this other fellow— (*To* PARTHY.) You look like a respectable woman.

PARTHY: I am.

VALLON: Do you all stand by what Windy just said?

ANDY: Why of course we do. Windy wouldn't tell a lie to save his own life, you know that Sheriff—

VALLON: Well, I'll take his word for it— (*He starts to go—stops at entrance.*) Only let me tell you this—don't try to give your

show tonight with mixed blood in it—or you'll be riding out
of town on something that don't sit so easy as a boat.

(VALLON *turns deliberately, and exits. The eyes of the* CROWD
*follow him, fascinated by the oracular quality of his final speech.
The heads then turn to the central picture on the stage.* JULIE'S
head is buried in STEVE'S *shoulder. He keeps his arm around
her and stands immovable, with set expression on his face,
brave, grimly defiant.* PARTHY *looks on, contentedly austere,
waiting to see what* ANDY *will say about all this—*ANDY *and*
MAGNOLIA—*emotionally very much like each other, find the
situation quite beyond them—probably each has a desire to run
to the humiliated couple and join* STEVE *in protecting* JULIE—
probably each is too afraid of JULIE'S *sensibilities. How can one
tell how she will receive anything?*)

STEVE: You needn't all look at us like we were a couple of wild
animals—We ain't goin' to hurt anybody— C'm on, Julie.
We'll pack up our things—

(*He releases* JULIE. *Her shoulders straighten bravely, but her
eyes look down and meet no one's gaze as she precedes* STEVE *to
their tiny dressing room and exits.*)

(JUBILEE SINGERS *sing "Mis'ry"—First half hummed.*)

JUBILEE SINGERS:

On my back in a hack
In a fohty dollah hack
No mo' gin, no mo' rum
Fo' de misery's done come.

ANDY (*to* SINGERS. *He has to take it out on somebody*): Well,
what're y'all standin' around fer like a lot of tree stumps—
clear out, the whole lot of you—go on!

(*They turn slowly, as dispossessed crowds always do. A mutter,
a whisper, a stifled giggle—They are gone— So are the lowlier
members of the cast who retire discreetly to their rooms.* ANDY
stops one of them.)

Rubber-Face, write out a sign and get it hung up at the
post-office. No show tonight. Leave enough cash to refund
the tickets. (*To* WINDY.) Windy—we pull out o' here soon's
Rubber-Face gets back—

(WINDY *turns and exits—silent and grim.*)

(RUBBER-FACE *exits. Only* PARTHY, MAGNOLIA, ELLIE *and*
ANDY *are left on stage, and* JOE *stands in box fixed, dumb.*

MAGNOLIA *leaves her mother, and starts walking slowly off stage.*)

PARTHY: Nola! Where you goin'?

(JOE *exits from upper box.*)

MAGNOLIA: I want to see Julie—

PARTHY: You come back here this instant! No daughter of mine's goin' to talk to that—that— (*Running over and grabbing* MAGNOLIA'*s arm.*)

MAGNOLIA (*shaking her off almost savagely*): Let me go, Mother! . . . I'm goin' in to Julie . . . (*She goes up and exits into* JULIE'*s room.*)

PARTHY: Well, Hawks, you see what your show boat has done to your daughter—

ANDY: I think the Show Boat's made a damn fine girl out of my daughter—

PARTHY: I'm goin' straight into that room and pull her away from that lyin', deceivin'—

ANDY (*stopping her*): Now, wait a minute—Parthy—Julie'll be gone in a few minutes and it'll be all over— Thing we got to do is figure out how we're going to give a show tomorrer night without Steve . . .

PARTHY: You're just as bad off for a leadin' woman—

ELLIE (*rises*): How about me? . . . "Beneath this mirthful mask burns a soul . . ."

ANDY (*trying to head her off*): No! You're a comedian. I was thinkin' we'd let Nola jump in— She knows all the parts—

PARTHY: Over my dead body. There never was an actress in my family and there ain't goin' to be—

(FRANK *comes up on stage. His hair is a little mussed—He walks with exaggerated straightness, like a man who is trying to "carry his liquor." By no means is this direction intended as a typical "drunk bit."* FRANK *is just overloaded and a bit dazed.*)

ANDY: I just meant to put her—in temporary. She don't know much about actin' but she's got a smile worth a million dollars. (*Seeing* FRANK.) Oh, my God—

ELLIE: Frank, where you been?

PARTHY: Tell Frank what a fine troupe he's in—

FRANK: You mean J-Julie? Know all about it—was with Pete when he told the Sheriff— (*Sits on bench.*)

ANDY: Steve and Julie are leavin'—Do you know any actor we could pick up in Fort Adams to jump into the lead?

ELLIE: How about Frank?

(FRANK *perks up involuntarily.*)

PARTHY: Fine leadin' man he'd make, with that face and those flat feet—

FRANK: I never asked to play a lead, did I? . . . (*Impressively.*) But if you're lookin' for a beauty, I got one—

ANDY: Who?

FRANK: There's a feller I met in town— Seems he's got to leave tonight and there ain't no boats— He asked me if we took passengers . . .

PARTHY: O' course we don't take passengers—

FRANK: So I brought him along— He's waitin' outside— Swell lookin' feller—

ANDY: Tell him to come in—let's see him.

FRANK: There he is, looking at the pictures— I'll bring him in. (*Calling offstage.*) Hey, Mister! . . . Will you come up here?

ANDY (*peering out*): Looks like a swell—

PARTHY: Looks like a river gambler to me—

ANDY: He's got manner—the gals'd like him—Parthy. (*Slapping his knee.*) —I believe I'd take a chance—

FRANK (*to* RAVENAL): Right up here.

(RAVENAL *follows.*)

PARTHY: I declare, Andy Hawks, you'll wind up in a lunatic asylum . . .

(FRANK *leads* RAVENAL *to the center of stage.*)

FRANK: Meet Cap'n Andy Hawks—this is Mr. . . . er . . .

RAVENAL: Ravenal is my name, suh—Gaylord Ravenal—of the Tennessee Ravenals.

(PARTHY *sniffs—a little louder than the word "sniff" suggests.*)
(RAVENAL *turns to her, raises his eyebrows and turns back to* ANDY—*if* PARTHY *doesn't know her place now, she never will.*)

I thought, suh, if I could have a bed on your boat tonight, I could pay you my fare tomorrow at Fort Adams—I—er—expect a remittance, and—

(ANDY *looks at* PARTHY, *she nods a grudging affirmative.* ANDY *acts on her endorsement.*)

ANDY: You ever acted?

RAVENAL: Acted!

ANDY: On the stage— Acted— Been an actor—? We need a juvenile lead—fifteen dollars a week—chance to see the world— No responsibility—

RAVENAL: Am I to understand that you are offering me the position of juvenile lead?—

PARTHY: That's what he means, young man— We don't like to pick up actors off the wharves, but we can't be choosy jest now—

RAVENAL: Madam, your courtesy is only exceeded by your charm—

ANDY: Ha-ha-ha. Better take the job. Fifteen dollars a week— found money—no responsibility—a chance to see life—

RAVENAL: I've seen it— (*Turns up to* FRANK *and* ELLIE.)

(JOE *appears in upper box and watches proceedings.*)

(*At this point* JULIE's *voice is heard offstage.* MAGNOLIA *runs down to center of stage, followed by* JULIE.)

JULIE: Don't, Magnolia,—Please—

MAGNOLIA (*she is very decisive—very brave, despite the nervous tremor in her voice*): Father—half an hour ago, Julie was my dearest friend— And she hasn't changed a bit—to me—

(RAVENAL *steps back—she doesn't see him.*)

ANDY (*quietly*): O' course not, Nola—

MAGNOLIA: Then why are you sending her away?

JULIE: He's not sending me, Nola dear—Steve and I want to go—

MAGNOLIA: If Julie goes, I go with her—

PARTHY: Well—that's a nice thing to say!

ANDY: Now don't talk nonsense, Nola— You got to stay with your mother—

(RAVENAL *turns, sees* MAGNOLIA—*their eyes meet.*)

no matter what—an' another thing— I'm dependin' on you to play the leads till we get somebody—

JULIE (*goes to* MAGNOLIA): See, Nola—what a chance for you—I just know you can act.

(*But* MAGNOLIA *has at last seen* RAVENAL *and she scarcely sees or hears anything else— He bows slightly, not certain if it is tactful to bow at all.*)

ANDY: An' if this young man'll play the juvenile lead—and if he's a quick study and wants to act opposite you—we could get you both ready by tomorrow night— (*To* RAVENAL.) You a quick study?—

RAVENAL: Lightning!

> (MAGNOLIA *bows her head.* STEVE *enters.*)

STEVE: Ready Julie? (*To* ANDY.) Didn't have time to get everything together, Cap'n—if you'll just bundle our trash up and
leave 'em at the post-office in New Orleans, we'll pick it up—

ANDY: Need any money, Steve?

STEVE: No—guess we'll make out all right—thanks—goodbye!

ANDY: Goodbye, Steve . . .

> (*He shakes hands with* STEVE—*as* STEVE *takes his hand away
> he finds some money in it, he starts to thank* ANDY, *but* ANDY
> *motions to him to be quiet in front of* PARTHY.)

Forget it.

JULIE (*to* MAGNOLIA): Goodbye, dear—

> (MAGNOLIA *runs to kiss her.* JULIE *turns her head away, but
> holds* MAGNOLIA *close to her.*)

I'll write to you—and you write to me and tell me all about
everything—

> (*She looks straight over* NOLA's *shoulder at* RAVENAL, *then,
> with sudden impulse, she jerks herself away and runs to* STEVE.
> As* JULIE *and* STEVE *exit from stage—as they pass behind box,
> JOE *calls timidly from the box.*)

JOE: Goodbye, Miss Julie—Goodbye, Mars' Steve—

JULIE: Goodbye, Joe—

> (*Exit* JULIE *and* STEVE—ANDY *prevents* MAGNOLIA *from
> going after them.*)

MAGNOLIA (*runs after them*): Julie! Julie! Wait for me!—Julie!

> (ELLIE *catches her—A dead pause . . .*)

> (ANDY *leads* MAGNOLIA *back— She looks up and sees
> PARTHY's *bewildered face.*)

MAGNOLIA: Mama—I'm awful sorry I talked to you like that—
I—I loved—Julie so—

> (FRANK *and* ELLIE *exit.*)

ANDY (*clearing his throat*): Well—well—we ain't got much
time— (*Picking up manuscript of* East Lynne.) Here take this,
Mr. Ravenal—I'd like to hear how you handle dialogue—now
the idea of this character is— You're in love with her—

> (*His voice lowers as he explains the subtleties of the character
> to* RAVENAL. JOE, *very thoughtful observer of the drama he
> has just seen, and is seeing—knowing in his wise old head that
> this newcomer is going to change conditions on the Show Boat,*

knowing there is nothing he can do to stop the march of events in this puzzling river world, falls back on his resigned philosophy, singing softly to himself.)

JOE: "Ol' Man River, dat ol' man river" . . . etc.

(Refrain continues— JOE *goes back to his rail-polishing.—*ANDY *has led* MAGNOLIA *over to* RAVENAL. PARTHY *has gone back to watch proceedings.* JOE *finishes first movement of refrain, stops singing as second movement is played underneath dialogue.)*

ANDY: Now try it—jest a sample—

MAGNOLIA: What will I do, pop?

ANDY: You jest smile, Nola, that will get them.

RAVENAL *(embarrassed with Lucy)*: "Miss Lucy—will you be mine?"

ANDY: Not quite it—not quite it—more feelin'—as if you love her—

RAVENAL: I understand— *(This time he does seem to feel it—much more.)* "Miss Lucy— Will you be mine?—"

(They look into each other's eyes, and hold their kiss while ANDY *laughs aloud.* PARTHY *jumping up and down stamping her feet.* JOE *sees them— He finishes refrain.)*

(Lights fade out on stage picture first, leaving JOE *in pin shot— fade out completely on last note.)*

CURTAIN

SCENE 5

Box office on Fore-deck of the Cotton Blossom. *Three weeks later.*

Discovered: Box office window right—Box office window left. Latter marked "Colored"—Wide arch at center leading to inside of boat—Just right of arch, MAGNOLIA's *picture—Just left of arch,* RAVENAL's *picture, featuring them as leading man and woman— gang plank right extending off stage to higher level.*

At rise: ELLIE *selling tickets.* SHOW GIRLS *entering with* BOYS *buying tickets looking at pictures and all exit into Show Boat.* FRANK *posing near* RAVENAL's *picture, left.*

*(*FRANK *looks after them, humbled—chagrined— Music continues— He goes up to picture— Tries to strike* RAVENAL's

pose and to arrange a few hairs in the same formation as RAVENAL's *luxurious locks.*)

ELLIE (*from box office window*): Tickets on sale. No use, Frank—

FRANK: What's wrong with me?

ELLIE: I haven't got the time to tell you—

FRANK: That's show business for you—I've been trouping up and down this river for twelve years and nobody ever heard of me— This Ravenal has been acting for exactly three weeks— and they make a star out of him . . .

ELLIE: I feel the same way, Frank. Look at Magnolia— Her picture with Ravenal's on all the three-sheets. Guess we're a couple of donkeys—

FRANK: Make that singular—

ELLIE: All right— You're a jackass— You want to know the secret of their quick success?—They're in love with each other.

FRANK: What's that got to do with it?

ELLIE: They make love on the stage, and it rings true— That's why they're a hit—

FRANK: Well, I've been playing opposite you for five years—and I love you—

ELLIE: Yeh, but— Maybe, I don't love you—

FRANK: So—you're responsible for our failure! We'll never be stars of the Show Boat.

ELLIE: You talk as if you expected to live on this barge the rest of your life. My God, ain't you got no ambition?

FRANK: Sure I got ambition. I want to marry you.

(*The rough-looking* BACKWOODSMEN *enter.*)

(*Grabbing* ELLIE *by the wrist.*)

Listen, Ellie, you've got to— Say you'll marry me, honey— I won't be home much— Come on, marry me—just this once—

ELLIE: Ouch—you're pinching my wrist—

BACKWOODSMAN (*pulling gun*): Drop that girl!

(*It is probably the deepest and most menacing voice* FRANK *has ever heard— Of course he drops her!—and turns around. The* BACKWOODSMAN *saunters up to him and grabs a handful of his coat at the chest—*FRANK *is paralyzed.*)

Well, Missy, what d'ye reckon we better do with him?

ELLIE: Let him go—

BACKWOODSMAN: Don't y' even want me to throw him in the river?

ELLIE: No—please, mister—don't hurt him—

BACKWOODSMAN: Too bad—

(*He shoves* FRANK *aside regretfully and goes over to box office window—when his back is turned* FRANK *tries to laugh it off, only to become conscious of an equally huge figure, on the other side of him—He decides to be very still and quiet.*)

(*To* ELLIE.) This the boat where they have the play-actin'?

ELLIE (*stuttering*): Yes, mister— Do you want to buy a ticket?

BACKWOODSMAN: Ah reckon as how we better buy two tickets. (*Calling over to companion.*) What say, Jeb?

JEB: Ah reckon!

(*Both calls make* FRANK *jump.*)

BACKWOODSMAN: Seein's how this is the first show we ever see, reckon as how you better give Jeb an' me the best two seats in the theayter!

ELLIE: I got two left in the stage box—thirty-five cents a piece—

BACKWOODSMAN: All right, honey— Here y' are—

(*He gives her the money, as she picks it up, he chucks her under the chin.*)

ELLIE (*to* BACKWOODSMAN): Say!—Come back here, You— This is Confederate money—

BACKWOODSMAN: We still use that up in the mountains— (*To* FRANK—*menacingly.*) That's jest 's good as your money—ain't it?

FRANK: Better!

ELLIE (*bouncing coin on ledge*): But this quarter ain't got no ring to it—

BACKWOODSMAN (*threatening* FRANK): Does it make any difference if the quarter don't ring?

FRANK: Of course not! (*To* ELLIE.) What do you want for two bits— The chimes of Normandy?

BACKWOODSMAN: We're cummin' to this yere show tonight, and it better be good— (*Starts to go.*) I ain't used to these places, I want to ask you somethin'—

FRANK: Go ahead.

BACKWOODSMAN: Is there any objection to carryin' guns in a theayter?—

(ELLIE *motions him to say there is, but he doesn't quite dare.*)

FRANK: Well—it isn't customary—

BACKWOODSMAN: Oh, it ain't— Well, we're gonna carry ours jes' the same! What say—Jeb?

JEB: I reckon.

(*Both* BACKWOODSMEN *laugh boisterously*—FRANK *joins in the spirit of the thing.*)

(*Business and Shot*—BACKWOODSMEN *exit into theatre.*)

FRANK: Y'see, Ellie— There's what I mean— This is a rough life for a woman all alone— You need a real red-blooded man to protect you—

ELLIE: Yes. Do you know any?

"I Might Fall Back on You"

FRANK:

> Little girl you are safe with me
> I can protect what's mine
> I am a sturdy maple tree
> And you my clinging vine.

ELLIE:

> Woods are just full of maple trees
> Cedar and oak and pine
> Let me look them over please
> And then I'll let you know
> If you have a show.

(*Refrain*)

> After I have looked around the world for a mate
> Then perhaps I might fall back on you
> After I'm convinced that there is no better fate
> Then I might decide that you will do.

FRANK:

> I am but an average lad
> Though no gift to womanhood
> Some girls say I'm not so bad

ELLIE:

> Others say you're not so good
> But if you are patient dear
> And willing to wait
> There's a chance I might fall back on you.

(*Refrain*)

ELLIE and CHORUS:

> After she has looked around the world for a mate
> Then perhaps she might fall back on you
> After she's convinced that there is no better fate
> Then she might decide that you will do.

(*Exit after number.*)

PARTHY (*entering*): Come out of that box office—Andy Hawks—
I want to talk to you.

ANDY: Now what is it?

PARTHY: It's about that Ravenal— He keeps looking at Nola.

ANDY: He'd be a fool if he didn't—

PARTHY: Andy Hawks—you mean to tell me you'd like to see
your daughter married to a tramp you picked off the levee—
that hadn't a shirt to his back when you found him?

(*Two* BOYS *and two* GIRLS *go into Show Boat.*)

ANDY: God A'mighty, woman, can't a man look at a girl without having to marry her?—Hello, Girls and Boys—going to
see the show tonight?—'S far as that goes she could do lots
worse—

PARTHY: All right—are y'all thru?—Now I'll show you somethin'—Listen to this—"Dear Mrs. Hawks—I know Captain
Andy don't like me"—

ANDY: Who is it?

PARTHY: Pete—

ANDY: I *don't* like him—

PARTHY: Listen . . . "but I got somethin' of interest to tell him
about Gaylord Ravenal—"

ANDY (*interrupts*): Bah!

PARTHY: "I hear the *Cotton Blossom* comes back to Natchez next
Thursday"—That's tomorrer—"I can be reached at the above
address in Fayette—Faithfully, Pete Gavin."—Well, what d'ye
say now?

ANDY: I say forget it—

PARTHY: Forget it!—Not much! Soon as we arrive at Natchez
tomorrow, I'm goin' over to Fayette— It's two hours away,
but I'll make the trip— Are you comin' along with me?—

ANDY: I ain't—

PARTHY: All right— It's good someone has a sense of duty—

ANDY: I like Ravenal— He's a right smart young feller—an' he's
the best leading man we ever had.

PARTHY: Shifty—that's what he is—mark my words if you asked
around about him you'd find something queer—for all he
talks so high about being a Ravenal of Tennessee.

ANDY: He is a Rav—

PARTHY: He says he is—

ANDY: Didn't he show me the church and tomb-stone of his
folks?

PARTHY: Oh, Hawks, you're a zany. I could say my name was Bonaparte and show you Napoleon's tomb but that wouldn't make him my grandfather, would it?

ANDY: No, but if he was, it would make him turn over in his grave.

(PARTHY *exits*. QUEENIE *enters*.)

QUEENIE: Is the theatre fillin' up, Cap'n Andy?

ANDY: Yes, but there's nobody in the balcony.

QUEENIE: Dat's where de colored people sit.

ANDY: Well, why don't they come?

QUEENIE: 'Cause you don't talk to dem.

ANDY: What you mean—don't talk to 'em? I ballyhooed my lungs out this mornin'.

QUEENIE: Mah people don't remember dat long. Dis is how to get 'em! Look at that crowd over on de levee . . . Ah'll show you how to get 'em—

(ANDY *goes in box office*.)

"C'mon, Folks"

Hey!
Where yo' think yo' goin'?
Don't yo' know dis show is startin' soon?
Hey!
Jest a few seats left yere!
It's light inside an' outside dere's no moon—
What fo' you gals dress up dicky? Where's yo' all gwine?
Tell dose stingy men o' yours to step up here in line!

(*Refrain*)

C'mon, folks, we'se rarin' to go—
Is you or ain't you seein' dis show?
Get het up—dere'll be no let up, here!

GIRL:

Listen to dat gal talk!

QUEENIE:

You'll be excited all night,
Grippin' yo' man an' holdin' him tight—
Two seats fo' twenty cents ain't so dear!

(*Drawing them to her confidentially*.)

Story's 'bout a lady in love—
Loves her man but—heavens above!

Dere's a villain—bad as you ever see—
White outside, but black in de heart,—
Swears dose two young lovers to part;
He's de worstest scallawag dat can be—
(*Her audience's eyes are beginning to pop out.*)
(*She becomes mysterious.*)
He tries to get her alone,
You hear dat little gal moan—
Ol' villain makin' her groan wid woe!

ALL:

What does he do?
What does he do?—Tell us!

QUEENIE:

He likes to choke her to death—
Den when she's almos' out o' breath
Somebody comes a-knockin' at dat ole door!

GIRLS:

Open de door, O Lord!

MEN:

How does de rest of it go?

QUEENIE (*chuckling*):

Is you or ain't yo' dyin' to know?—
(*Triumphantly.*)
Step up an' buy yo' tickets for dis yere show!

(QUEENIE *and* DANCERS *do shuffle and exit.*)

SCENE 6

Same set as Scene 4. Curtain raised on Third Act of The Parson's
Bride. *Auditorium is now filled with benches and audience is seated
with colored people in balcony.* PARTHY *and* BACKWOODSMEN *in
upper stage box.* ANDY *is playing violin—"Hearts & Flowers"—at
foot of Show Boat stage.*

ELLIE (*playing "Emma"*): "Remember, Lucy— I'm telling you
this because you're my sister— This is a man's world, which I
know to my sorrow, God help us."
(*As she speaks the lights gradually come up revealing the
double tier of boxes, the false footlights, and the "fancy set with*

the portieres." MAGNOLIA, *playing Lucy, is sitting on a stool near the fireplace— It is throwing a very red light on her face. Her sister Emma, played by* ELLIE, *is seated on a chair next to her.* PARTHY *is very much in evidence in the upper right stage box—and the two* BACKWOODSMEN *are visibly and audibly enthralled as they hang over the upper right box.*)

"Young girls like us are like flowers—we bloom in the sunshine until we are plucked by a passing mule—"

MAGNOLIA: Male.

ELLIE: What?

MAGNOLIA: Male.

ELLIE: "Male. What are we? Ornaments—bright nosegays to be worn in bootoneers—and then cast aside to float along on the tide of eternity, like flotsam and jetsam on the sea—"

BACKWOODSMEN (*in box*): That's purty talk, gal.

   (ELLIE *rises, ignoring the comments as something very usual with these audiences.*)

MAGNOLIA (*prompting her*): And remember I'm your sister.

ELLIE: Huh?

MAGNOLIA (*whispers*): And remember I'm your sister.

ELLIE: I know; don't tell me. "And remember, I'm your sister, and if any harm should come to you I'd never forgive myself—" (*She turns madly, and makes one of those effective quiet exits, marred only by the door not opening.*) What's the matter with the door? The door won't open. (*Pulls at it—Exits through door.*)

MAGNOLIA (*rises*): "I wonder what can be keeping Parson Brown?—He promised to be here before dark and the twilight is fast fading into night." (*There is no change of lights on stage—This disturbs* MAGNOLIA— *She decides to give the cue again.*) "Yes—The twilight is fast fading into night."

   (*Lights dim presently. She comes downstage. She picks up a picture.*)

"Hamilton—Hamilton—Noble soul—dare I hope that, that look in your eye bespeaks the love which in my heart of hearts I long for with every fibre in my being! Oh, love—!"

ANDY (*standing*): Nola, just a minute Nola—Excuse me, folks— Is Seth Purdy in the audience?

SETH: Yes, sir.

ANDY: Your missus jest sent in a message her sister's took with fever and y' got drive her over to Centerville— All right, Nola—

MAGNOLIA (*paces up and down a bit to control her anger. She looks at clock which has only one hand pointing to 9*): "Oh, love—love—Five o'clock— Can it be he will not keep this tryst with me?"
(*A painful wait—suddenly a cow's moo—strangely like* RUBBER-FACE's *rejected effect of a previous scene.* MAGNOLIA *shows rare presence of mind.*)

"Ah, there is the bell—it must be Parson Brown at last."
(*Parson, played by* RAVENAL, *enters thru door.*)

RAVENAL: "Good evening, Miss Lucy— I was absorbed in meditation and did not realize night had fallen—"
(*He comes over to greet her— He takes her hand— As he draws her to him,* PARTHY *in upper stage box coughs. He releases* MAGNOLIA *on this signal.*)

MAGNOLIA: "The days are getting shorter, Hamilton. But they are long when one is waiting."

RAVENAL: "As I came across the field, I saw the cattle being driven home—by your faithful dog—"
(*Another moo—still another—and another.*)

ANDY (*turning*): Shut up!

RAVENAL: "Miss Lucy, altho I wear the garb of a parson, beneath these sombre vestments there is the heart of a man, that beats for you alone."

MAGNOLIA: "Hamilton! My own!— My own—!"
(*They go to embrace—*PARTHY *coughs.*)

RAVENAL: "And will you be my cherished bride?"

MAGNOLIA: "Oh—Hamilton—"

RAVENAL: "Will you?"

MAGNOLIA: "Yes—"
(RAVENAL *goes to embrace her—*PARTHY *coughs— He ignores it— He sweeps* MAGNOLIA *into his arms and gives her a kiss as few stage lovers have shown a river audience. Wild applause from the boxes— As* RAVENAL *releases* MAGNOLIA, *he directs a look of satisfied defiance at* PARTHY *up in the box.* MAGNOLIA *herself was very much surprised.*)

RAVENAL: Ah, Magnolia— (*He realizes his error.*) "Miss Lucy—Lucy— You have made me the happiest man in the world."

MAGNOLIA: "Little did I think I could ever be so happy again."

RAVENAL (*looks at watch*): "Ten minutes past five. I must go now to the Ladies Aid Society Meeting. Will you come with me and let me announce our betrothal?"

MAGNOLIA: "We must not forget our work in our new found happiness— I will stay here and correct the examination papers of my little pupils!"

RAVENAL: "Very well, then— Goodbye, until the morrow, beloved."

MAGNOLIA: "Goodbye, my dear Hamilton—"

(*He kisses her hand and exits.*)

(*Villain music.* MAGNOLIA *goes to the window and waves.*)

"To think that after my first marriage with that drunken beast—I should be loved by such a man as Hamilton Brown."

FRANK (*from doorway*): "Ha—ha—"

(MAGNOLIA *wheels and sees* FRANK—*He is made up as a tramp, drunken—leering—repulsive—grisly.*)

MAGNOLIA: "My God! You! My husband!"

FRANK (*advancing into room*): "I reckon you thought I was dead. Well, I'm about the livest corpse you ever saw." (*Diabolical laugh.*) "Too darn bad you won't be able to marry the Parson." (*All audience hisses.*)

MAGNOLIA: "Don't spoil my one chance for happiness— Is there no mercy in your evil soul—please—please go away— don't wreck my life again."

FRANK: "I'll give you your chance, gal—a thousand dollars and quick, or you don't walk down the aisle to no wedding march."

MAGNOLIA: "I haven't got it."

(*The hissing gets furious.*)

FRANK: "No? Where's the money you been saving all these years?"

BACKWOODSMEN (*standing up—leaning over box*): Let 'er go, I tell you.

MAGNOLIA: "I haven't a thousand dollars, I swear it."

FRANK: "Oh, you haven't, ain't you? For years, I waited for this chance. At last I have you in my power."

(FRANK *seizes her—drags her across the room—she screams— his hand stifles her.* MAGNOLIA *writhes in his grasp—*FRANK *bares his teeth—chortles like a maniac—he winds his fingers in her hair—screams—protestations—snarls—ha-ha's— pleadings—agony—anguish—*FRANK *hears a noise of a chair being pushed back in the right upper box—and sees the*

BACKWOODSMAN—*leaning over the rail—his hand just pulling a gun from the holster.*)

BACKWOODSMAN: I warned you.

(FRANK *suddenly releases* MAGNOLIA—*gentleness and love overspread his features—*MAGNOLIA *stares in open-mouth amazement—he makes gesture of abnegation.*)

(FRANK *pushes the amazed* MAGNOLIA *into a chair, gently patting her, and makes exit by crawling off stage.*)

RAVENAL (*off stage*): "I'll save you—I'll save you—Courage—"

ANDY (*jumps on stage, calls after* FRANK): Schultz, come back here.

RAVENAL (*rushes in the room—taking off his coat and plunging into his dialogue with great gusto*): "Let go of her—you swine—let go—" Where is he?

ANDY: Curtain!

(*The curtain rolls down.*)

(ANDY *steps before the curtain at first agitated, he later steadies down.*)

Folks, I'm very sorry we had to ring down like that before the act was over— Fact is, Mr. Schultz, our heavy man was suddenly took sick— (*He looks up at* BACKWOODSMEN.) Rubber-Face, take it up.

(*The curtain rolls up.* ANDY *steps back into the false stage set.*)

Now just before Mr. Schultz was took with that attack, he and the parson was just on the verge o' goin' into the most sensational hand-to-hand struggle to the death ever seen on the stage. (ANDY *starts to illustrate the fight.*) When Egbert saw the parson comin'—he should o' said—"Ho, ho! I'm glad you come when you did"—and with that—he hauls off and hits the parson. (ANDY *swings so hard at imaginary foe that he almost loses his balance.*) But the parson knowing a thing or two comes right back and Egbert gits somethin' he ain't lookin' for. "Take that, you cur!" And down he goes! (ANDY *whacks himself a resounding blow on the jaw which almost knocks him out. As soon as he has recovered, he goes on.*) Egbert, seein' how he ain't goin' to win the fight by fair means, grabs the parson around the waist an' back-heels him. (*While fighting with himself.*) "Let go—let go—you dog," etc. (ANDY *does this to himself and takes the fall. He wrestles with himself for a few seconds on the floor, upsetting two chairs and banging his head. He lies flat on his stomach on the floor.*)

(*Applause.*)

In the meantime, poor Lucy is down on her knees crying for her beloved— (ANDY *draws himself up on his knees in a praying posture.*) Now is the big dramatic moment, folks. Egbert, the low-down skunk, reaches for his pocket an' pulls out a monkey-wrench—hits the parson, the parson groans, reels, and falls—

(*Hisses.*)

He's about to beat the parson's brains out— (*Suiting action to word.*) When Lucy says—(*he stands up on the chair and goes into a high falsetto*) "Do with me what you will, but spare my Hamilton." At that moment, as if Providence had heard her prayers, the door swings open. (*In a stage whisper—while waiting for the door to open, steps down.*) In comes her errin' foster-sister, Emmy— (ANDY *rushes to door and takes three mincing steps into the room*)—now ready to right the wrong she done poor Lucy. For a second time Emmy stands flabbergasted— (*In his falsetto.*) "My God, what is this awful happening?" (*Resuming his normal tone.*) Quick as lightnin', Emmy lookin' on the prostrate form o' Hamilton an' the weepin' figger of her heart-broken sister, a-beggin' Egbert to spare the parson, grabs up the water pitcher, and cries—(*looking around for the water pitcher which is on the table*) (*in the falsetto again, with great emotion*) "The wages of sin is death." (*He bangs the rubber pitcher on the floor so hard it bounces up.*) (*His own voice again, tragically.*) And kills the dirty rascal, deader'n a door-nail.

(*Applause.*)

Now that's what you'd a seen if it hadn't been for Mr. Schultz bein' took that way.

(*A wild applause.*)

I want you to know, folks, I always put on strong, moral plays— The kind you can bring your children to see, the kind where virtue triumphs over vice. I been twenty years on the river an' I ain't never permitted a show to go on where virtue ain't won out—(*confidentially*)—though it's been a tight squeeze sometimes. There ain't never been no Camilleys in my shows. An' to prove you always get your money's worth on the *Cotton Blossom*, this is what I'm go' t'do, folks.—For tonight, our big, stupendous concert, which we usually charge ten cents for—an' it's worth ten times the money, is go' to be presented absolutely free of charge, without costin' you so much as a penny.

(*Audience applauds vociferously.*)

(ANDY *turns to wings.*)

Now we'll go right ahead an' give you the olio. The first number is go' to be—our heavy man. Mr. Schultz is now entirely recovered and will give you a sample of his soft shoe dance.

DANCE IN ONE (FRANK)

BLACK OUT

SCENE 7

The upper deck of the Cotton Blossom.

Later that night.

*Discovered: It is moonlight, just after the storm clouds have broken—*RAVENAL *stands near a water-barrel— He looks about, anxiously awaiting* MAGNOLIA. *He blows on his fingers, and moves about a little to take off the chill that is characteristic of southern nights. He hears a noise. He peers into the darkness and calls eagerly offstage.*

At rise: "Ol' Man River" being sung off stage. (JUBILEE SINGERS.)

RAVENAL: That you, Nola?

WINDY (*offstage*): Nope—it's me—

RAVENAL (*quickly filling dipper from water-barrel to carry on the illusion that he came out here to get a drink*): Hello, Windy—

WINDY (*entering*): Come over to take a look at the moorings— (*He crosses* RAVENAL.) Kind o' cool for you to be stayin' out on deck, ain't it?

RAVENAL (*just finishing drink*): Er— No— Not at all— I'm very thirsty—

(*He fills the dipper again to prove it—* WINDY *exits—* RAVENAL *pours balance of dipper's contents in fire bucket— He hears whistle offstage—refills dipper hastily—* MAGNOLIA *enters. She carries a porcelain water-pitcher. He flings dipper away from him and rushes to her impetuously.*)

That you, Nola? (*He embraces her.*) How did you get away?

MAGNOLIA: I can't stay long— I told Mother I'd fill her pitcher—She's waiting—

RAVENAL: Nola—we haven't much time— (*Speaking rapidly, excited, impulsive.*) Listen, I want to marry you—in Natchez tomorrow. . . .

MAGNOLIA: But Mother—

RAVENAL: She's going to be in Fayette all morning— She told me so herself— There's a lovely little church in Natchez—

MAGNOLIA: But Father—what will he say?

RAVENAL: He will not oppose us— As a matter of fact, he gave me the idea—

MAGNOLIA: What!

RAVENAL: Of getting married, while your mother was away— He knows how I feel—how much I love you— Oh, Nola, please—say you will. . . .

MAGNOLIA: Oh, Gay— I want to—

RAVENAL: You can make me the happiest man in the world. I can't stand it this way any longer . . . these stolen seconds, these little snatches of you! I want you all to myself— forever—Nola, dearest . . . I want you with me wherever I go. I want to show you a world you've never dreamed of—cities, theatres, restaurants, people—and you and I always together, looking on—and living in our own lovers' world.

MAGNOLIA: But, Gay—you've seen everything in the world.

RAVENAL: I used to think so—until I looked into your eyes— and then I knew that I had seen nothing—I hadn't even lived.

"You Are Love"

Once a wand'ring ne'er-do-well
Just a vagrant, roving fellow
I went my way.
Life was just a joke to tell,
Like a lonely Punchinello
My role was gay.

But I knew the joke was aimless;
Time went on—I liked the game less,

For you see
Somewhere lurked a spark divine,
And I kept wond'ring whether mine
Would come to me.

Then my fortune turned and I found you;
Here you are with my arms around you—
You will never know what you've meant to me;

MAGNOLIA:
    You're a prize that heaven has sent to me.

BOTH:
    Here's a bright and beautiful world, all new,
    Wrapped up in you.
    (*Refrain*)
    You are love—
    Here in my arms,
    Where you belong,
    And here you will stay,
    I'll not let you away,
    I want day after day
    With you.
    You are Spring,
    Bud of romance unfurled;
    You taught me to see
    One truth forever true.
    You are love,
    Wonder of all the world.
    Where you go with me,
    Heaven will always be.
    (*She looks up at him for a moment, then, of her own accord
    throws her arms around him. They kiss.*)

CURTAIN

SCENE 8

The Levee at Natchez—Next morning.
    *Discovered: This is a different view of the same levee seen in Scene
1. The* Cotton Blossom *runs in the other direction across the back
of the stage— There is some little impromptu decoration adorning*

it— The stage is well crowded with TOWNSPEOPLE *who have come down to see the unusual spectacle of a leading man and his leading lady being married—*

CAPTAIN ANDY *with his fine flair for publicity has seen the value of this interest; and has placed an announcement in the town post office issuing a public invitation to everyone to see the wedding—So they all are here— This entire scene constitutes the Finale of Act 1.*

"Finale"

1ST GROUP (*discovered singing at rise*):

> Oh tell me, did you ever!
> Did you ever hear of such a thing?

2ND GROUP:

> The leading man's about to give the leading girl
> A wedding ring!

1ST GROUP:	2ND GROUP:
Her father has neglected none,	So you see,
He's asked us all to see the fun—	Romance can start
And since we are invited to	Upon the stage—
Attend, we are delighted to	Romance like theirs
Be there, when these united two	Is not for everyone!
Are plighted to be one!	

(ANDY *enters from boat—all smiles and dressed up to kill.*)

SOPRANOS—TENORS:

> Captain Andy! Captain Andy!
> My but doesn't he look fine and dandy!
> Now Magnolia's found her mate, you
> Know we're happy to congratulate you!

ALL:

> Thank you for inviting us to
> See the wedding—It was friendly thus to
> Let us share your happy day
> And see you give the bride away—

ANDY (*spoken above music*): Accordin' to the announcement you read in the post office you're all invited to the wedding of my daughter Miss Magnolia Hawks to her leading man, the Honorable Gaylord Ravenal!

(*Cheers.*)

Bein' as how y'all take such an interest in the doin's of show boat folks, I thought you'd like to see the happy couple playin' their own romance off the stage—

(*Cheers.*)

The bride and groom'll be out in a minute— Then we will all march down to the church!

(*Cheers.*)

(*As the ensemble takes up the waltz refrain here, the various characters of the show boat troupe march out in their go-to-wedding clothes—*FRANK *and* ELLIE *are particularly elegant.*)

ALL (*as the show boat procession goes on*):

Happy, the day,
When the hand of a maid has been won by swift
    pursuing—
Happy, the way
He has chosen to win her—by bold and ardent
    wooing—
Theirs a lucky fate to be romantic—
We can hardly wait to see the frantic
Looks of the bridegroom, and quakes
Of the bride whom he takes
Now or never, and makes
Her forever the one and the only one
Who will take care
That his life's not a lonely one—
While she's the only one—

(MAGNOLIA *and* RAVENAL *enter.*)

Happy the bride!
May the greatest of happiness, health and wealth
    attend you!
Lovely bride-to-be,
We'd take pride to be
Wedded to anyone charming as you—

NEGRO CHORUS (*coming forward, enthusiastic, but a trifle diffident*):

> Miss Magnolyer
> We always tol' yer
> We knowed you'd find
> Your man who'd be lovin' yer true!

(*They go into big levee shuffle dance, as* MAGNOLIA, QUEENIE, JOE *and singing* NEGRO CHORUS *sing: "Can't Help Lovin' Dat Man."*)

(*Just as they get to the carriage, a wild hysterical shriek is heard offstage, and* PARTHY ANN *rushes on, followed by* PETE *and* VALLON.)

VALLON and PETE (*offstage*): Stop them—stop them!

PARTHY (*entering with* VALLON *and* PETE): Don't talk to him. He's a murderer!

ANDY (*impatiently*): Who?

PARTHY (*pointing at* RAVENAL): That Ravenal— He killed a man.

MAGNOLIA: Gay—

ANDY (*really frightened now*): God-a-mighty—when?

PARTHY: Last year. (*Pointing to* VALLON.) Ask him!

VALLON (*embarrassed*): He got off on self-defense—

ANDY (*viciously turning on* PARTHY): Then he proved he had a right to kill.

PARTHY: Are you goin' to let your daughter stand here and talk to a murderer?

ANDY: Stand—murderer be damned—I killed a man when I was nineteen.

PARTHY (*overcome*): You killed—

ANDY: Yes—me— Now are you comin' with us—or ain't you?

PARTHY: Where're ye goin'?

ANDY: To the church—they're goin' to be married.

PARTHY: Married to a murderer! Oh, my God! (*Faints.*)

VALLON: She's fainted.

ANDY: Are you sure?

VALLON: She's gone.

ANDY: Good— Now we can go on with the wedding.

ALL:

Can't stop me now
There's no use to try—
I've got to love my man till I die—
Can't help lovin' dat man of mine.
(ANDY *arranges the procession. Bridal couple are locked in each other's arms as they march off stage and the*

CURTAIN FALLS.)

ACT TWO

The Midway Plaisance at the Chicago World's Fair—1893.

At rise an animated scene of visitors walking and looking on at the wonders described by several barkers who stand on platforms in front of their respective buildings and booths. The famous Ferris Wheel is seen in the background behind a building labelled: "World's Congress of Beauty"—Stage license can be taken to concentrate in this spot any of the following features of the fair: The MacMonnies fountain, Hagenback's Arena, Dahomey Village, Streets of Cairo—etc.

During the opening chorus when LA BELLA FATIMA, *the first "couchie-couchie" dancer is introduced, there is a scramble among the men to follow her into "The Streets of Cairo" building, where she will dance.* ANDY *is suddenly discovered being continually forced out of the crowd and rushing in again.*

The final episode of the Opening Chorus is a march refrain, which brings in HETTY CHILSON *with some of her well-known beauties in tow—She is a tall blond woman with remarkable poise and manner. As the crowd breaks up and continues to seek the thrills offered by the Fair,* MISS CHILSON *and her friends form a little sophisticated group downstage.*

"World's Fair"

ALL:

>When we tell them about it all
>They're likely to doubt it all
>But why should we care
>Just as long as we've been to the fair.

IST BARKER:

	BOYS:	GIRLS:
Ho, ho! Your kind attention		
Bestow	Let's go near	
The strongest little	I can't hear	
lady known to the	Shall we go?	I don't know
world we'll show		He's talking

62

Come one and all,
  come up and feel
  the fist of her!

1ST BARKER:
  So just move along
    and visit
  The queen of the
    strong—
  She's sixteen years
    of age

2ND BARKER:
  Hey! Hey!
  What have we here,
    what have we here?
  A marvelous display
  The beauties picked
    from all the
    world
  In superfine array

        Thru his hat
        You bet I'm
          pretty sure
          of that

CHORUS:
  Great Christopher!
  If Sandow felt her
    hand how
  He would stutter
    and mutter
  And shiver and
    quiver with rage

GIRLS:
Say, they're
  going to
  tell you
What they
  want to
  sell you
Now

BOYS:
That's one
  show we
  must see!

GIRLS:
Are you
  taking
  me?

1ST BARKER:
>Get tickets this way

2ND BARKER:
>Just step up and pay

1ST BARKER:
>Just step this way.
>Hey!
>Right up this way.
>Hey!

2ND BARKER:
>Not much to pay
>For such display
>Come on this way

BOTH:
>And you will say
>In all Chicago this is *the* best show!
>Folks you must know
>Here's the best show
>Nothing else can please you so.

BOYS: GIRLS:
>Won't you let me   We're in the face
>   take you in   Of a great
>Do come, the show   temptation
>   will soon begin   In such a place
>Do let me take you   To attempt flirtation
>   in.   I don't really
>   know—

3RD BARKER:
>Now for this special feature
>I demand your close attention
>Step closer, Gentlemen
>You notice "Ladies" I don't
>   mention!

>   Goodness gracious
>   me!
>   Whatever can it be?

>My story's quickly told
>The world's sensation
>Now behold—
>   (*Interlude*)

3RD BARKER (*during dance—ad libs*):
  Gather around boys—
  Greatest feature of
    World's Fair,
  She's the only one in
    her class, boys, etc.

                    GIRLS:
                    Hurry, hurry,
                    Let us run.

BOYS:
  What for?
  There's nothing
    wrong

                    GIRLS:
                    You can stay, but I
                      must run.

  She's a princess,
  From better folks
    than us I guess
  All right! You always
    spoil my fun.

ALL:
  Belles and beaux
  Dressed in the very latest style
  Here they come
  Goodness knows,
  Aren't they swell?
  Well, I should smile!

BOYS:
  Look, dear!
  Look here!

                    GIRLS:
                    Ain't they gorgeous?

ALL:
  When the sports of gay Chicago
  Pay a visit to the fair
  You can tell
  Ev'ry swell
  By his dashing air.
  They do credit to Chicago
  With their clothes all tailor-made

All their country cousins gape and stare
When they see the dandies on parade.

(MAGNOLIA *and* PARTHY *enter.*)

MAGNOLIA: Look, Mother, this is the Congress of Beauty. Isn't she lovely?

PARTHY: Hussy, that's what she is, a hussy. That's all you see around here— Hussies and Dudes. How much longer are you going to drag me around?

MAGNOLIA: Gay said he would meet us here as soon as he finished some business.

PARTHY: Humph— Must be a funny business that you're ashamed of—

MAGNOLIA: How do you mean ashamed?

PARTHY: If I've asked you once I've asked you a hundred times how your husband makes his livin' and I never can get an answer out of either one of you—secrets—mysteries— How I hate not to know things.

MAGNOLIA: He's certainly doing well. We have everything we want and we go everywhere.

(*Hoochy-koochy music starts. Men start coming out of "The Streets of Cairo."*)

PARTHY: Look—look at the droves of men coming out of that place.

MAGNOLIA: That's the hoochy-koochy dance.

PARTHY: Couchie-couchie. . . . A man ought to be ashamed t' be seen near the place. I wouldn't have any respect for— My God. Look, Nola, is that your father?

(ANDY *enters but does not see them; he is so deeply engrossed trying to master the couchie-couchie movement.*)

ANDY (*to himself*): I'll be darned if I see how she does it.

PARTHY: Andy Hawks, what are you tryin' to do?

ANDY: Couchie-couchie.

(MAGNOLIA *laughs but not* PARTHY.)

PARTHY: Y' ought t' be ashamed of yourself.

ANDY: Never had so much fun in my life.

(*The couchie-couchie announcer starts again.*)

Look, will you, look at that gal. Think I'll go again.

(PARTHY *pulls him away as he starts once more to follow the magnetic appeal of the dancer.*)

Let's have a little fun. What's a World's Fair for? Let's go in
here— It's the Dahomey Village.

PARTHY: Dahomey Village—what's that?

ANDY: Wild men. Zulus. Every one of them fellows has a bunch
of wives—

MAGNOLIA: Bunch of wives?

ANDY: Why if a man has less than twenty he's considered a
bachelor.

PARTHY: Hawks—you're crazy!

(RAVENAL *enters accompanied by* OLD SPORT *and two or three
other men.*)

SPORT: Never saw anything like it, Gay. It was phenomenal.

GAY: The cards were running for me.

(SPORT *exits.*)

MAGNOLIA (*sees* RAVENAL *and comes over*): Oh, Gay.

RAVENAL (*loudly*): Yes, dear, just concluded a deal for a handsome profit.

PARTHY (*looking over*): Humph—

RAVENAL (*to* MAGNOLIA): I made a killing. McDonald had to
close the game and send out for new bank roll.

MAGNOLIA: Oh, Gay, how marvelous.

RAVENAL (*crossing over*): Well—Captain Andy— What do you
say to a little jamboree?

ANDY: Suits me to a "T."

RAVENAL: We'll go to the Palmer House for dinner—take in
the show at the Grand Opera House and then if you like we'll
look in at Rector's.

PARTHY: Been traipsin' about enough for one day—come along
to the hotel, Hawks.

ANDY: Don't think we'll go with you tonight, Gay. Will take
another turn around the fair grounds and then go to bed.
You young folks go out and have a good time together.

PARTHY: That's all they ever do. Him spending money like a
fool. (*Turns to* RAVENAL.) You'd better be saving it, you may
need it some day.

MAGNOLIA (*proudly*): Oh, Gay can always make more.

PARTHY: Yeh— Come along, Hawks—if you must be dilly
dallying around this pair we'll go down to the Wild West
show—never in your life did you get such a lot of excitement
for such little money.

ANDY: My marriage license only cost a dollar.
(PARTHY *and* ANDY *exit*.)
RAVENAL: Well, dear—I must go up and have another fling.
MAGNOLIA: Oh, Gay, do you think you ought to?
RAVENAL: While they're running for me, I must play them. I'll be back in time to dress for dinner.
MAGNOLIA: All right, darling—Oh, I am so happy and so proud of you—

"Why Do I Love You?"

I'm walking on the air dear
For life is fair dear, to lovers.
I'm in the seventh heaven
(There's more than seven, my heart discovers)

RAVENAL:

In this sweet, improbable and unreal world
Finding you has given me my ideal world.

MAGNOLIA:

(*Refrain*)
Why do I love you?
Why do you love me?

BOTH:

Why should there be two
Happy as we?

RAVENAL:

Can you see
The why or wherefore
I should be the one you care for?

MAGNOLIA:

You're a lucky boy,
I am lucky too.

BOTH:

All our dreams of joy
Seem to come true—
Maybe that's because you love me . . .
Maybe that's why I love you.
(*Interlude*)

RAVENAL:

Darling, I have only just an hour to play

MAGNOLIA:

I am always lonely when you go away

CHORUS:

Hours are not like years
So dry your tears.
What a pair of love birds

RAVENAL:

My darling, I'll come home as early as I can
Meanwhile be good and patient with your man.
Why do I love you?
Why do you love me?

(*Exit* RAVENAL.)
(MAGNOLIA *and* CHORUS *go on with Number.*
(DAHOMEYS *come out of the Village and down stage*—CROWD *moves up stage and steps up to building, etc.*)

"In Dahomey"

DAHOMEYS:

Dyunga doe
Dyunga doe
Dyunga hungy ung gunga
    Hungy ung gunga go
Kyooga chek
Kyooga chek
Kyooga chek a chek uncha
    Chek a chek uncha chek

Daringa doo
Daringa dy da
Daringa doo
Daringa dy da

Dyunga hungy ung gunga
  hungy ung gunga go
Dyunga hungy ung gunga
    hungy ung gunga go

Hoo go ga doo
Hoo go ga doo

Hoha hoga tooga togo
Togo togo togo
WHITES:
Don't let us stay here,
For tho they may play here,
They're acting vicious—
They might get malicious;
And though I'm not fearful
I'll not be a spearful
So you better show me
The way from Dahomey.
(CROWD *exits in fear.*)
DAHOMEYS:
We're glad to see them go;
We're glad to see those white folks go;
We've had enough
Of all this stuff—
We wish we'd never come here
To join a Dahomey show!
(*Refrain*)
In Dahomey—
Let the Africans stay
In Dahomey;
Gimme Avenue A
Back in old New York
Where yo' knife and fork
Gently sink into juicy little chops what's made of
pork!

We are wild folks
When de ballyhoos bawl,
But we're mild folks
When we're back in de kraal,
'Cause our home
Just ain't Dahomey at all

Oh, take me back today
To Avenue A!

(*Close in on Dahomeys with velvet, after one chorus.* DAHOMEY DANCERS *on for a dance followed by* DAHOMEY VILLAGERS *crossing stage left to right singing one chorus of "Dahomey."*)

BLACK OUT

SCENE 2

A room on Ontario Street—a typical second-class boarding house of the day (1904).

The room is used as a sitting room; at right you can see a curtained-off sleeping alcove with the footboard of a double bed— Below this is a dresser with a picture of MAGNOLIA *and* KIM *on it. Above this is a window—The door to the hall is left center—* COLORED SLAVEY *cleaning up the room at rise.* ETHEL—*she is singing in a grating voice "Good Morning Carrie"—the* LANDLADY *enters. She is Irish.*

LANDLADY: Skidaddle out of here. I've got a couple of actors looking for rooms.

(ETHEL *is struck with awe as* FRANK *and* ELLIE *appear in the doorway— They are now a team of vaudeville hoofers and look the part—* ELLIE *is dressed just a little too fancy—and painted too much.* FRANK'S *once luxurious moustache of 1890 is now close cropped à la 1904. His clothes are the fancy cut of the period. The shoulders are padded generously—the trousers short— college style—* ETHEL *exits, dazed by all this brilliance.*)

Ain't this a grand room now? You won't find another like it in Chicago for the price. (*Clearing her throat to relieve the tension.*) And look . . . You've got a fine bed here, feather mattress and all—

ELLIE (*who has been looking around*): What's this, a closet?

LANDLADY: Yes, ain't it a grand one— Look—you can look right in if you want.

(ELLIE *looks in—"snooping."*)

ELLIE: They don't seem to be using much of it.

LANDLADY: 'Tis more space than they need with everything

they've got in pawn— (*In a whisper.*) A gambler is what he is—Ten years, on an' off they been comin' here— Right after the World's Fair they started— Each time they'd be livin' here for a couple o' months until some fine night he'd come in with his pockets stuffed with greenbacks—"Mrs. O'Brien," he'll say, grand as you please, "Here's the money I owe you—an' keep the change— We're movin' to other quarters!"—Then they'll wake up the little girl—even if it be the middle o' the night, and off they'll go, bag and baggage to the Sherman House—!!

ELLIE: T-t-t-t-t-t——

LANDLADY: They'll be livin' like quality at the Hotel sometimes for a year—sometimes not more'n a month— Then they'll be comin' back here, an' one by one their fine things disappear—First he pawns his fancy cane—then her diamond ring goes—then her fur coat—and this winter, the poor little woman has no coat at all but a kind of old woolen thing that neither you nor I'd be seen in—

ELLIE: T-t-t-t-t——

FRANK: There you are—smart Aleck— How'd you like it if you was married to a gambler like that? You ought to be thankful you got a husband that supports you— Listen, kiddo—if it wasn't for me, you'd be back on a show boat doin' comedy hits and doublin' as chambermaid and dishwasher—

ELLIE: What d'ye mean—supports me—I'm the backbone of the set! Yes, an' if it weren't for you, I'd be on Broadway this minute doing Sappho in Shakespeare's *Merchant of Venice*.

FRANK: You would, would you?

ELLIE: Yes, I would. You don't deserve a girl like me.

(FRANK's *eyes follow* ELLIE's *fascinated gaze up stage— The thing that fascinates her is* MAGNOLIA's *form in the doorway.*)

ELLIE (*a little timidly*): Is—is that you, Nola?

MAGNOLIA (*not entirely sure—coming forward slowly*): —Ellie?

ELLIE (*still bashful for some reason—she doesn't know what*): That's right—

MAGNOLIA: Ellie! (*She rushes over to her and kisses her.*)

FRANK (*grinning sheepishly*): 'Lo, Nola—

MAGNOLIA: And Frank! Dear old Frank—

(FRANK *kisses her awkwardly—*ELLIE *is there.*)

ELLIE: How are you, dearie?

MAGNOLIA: Oh, I'm fine— My, but it's good to see you— How did you know where I lived?

FRANK: Well, as a matter of fact—

LANDLADY: They just come here to look for rooms— (*Slowly and significantly.*) I told them you were leaving—

MAGNOLIA (*It is news to her—but she understands— She knows she owes for twelve weeks*): Oh—er—er—yes, of course— (*Turning to* ELLIE.) You see, these are only temporary quarters—until we move into our new home on the Lake Shore— Meanwhile we stop here— It's so near Gay's business— And we like to help out Mrs. O'Brien.

LANDLADY: Humph— Great help— (*To* ELLIE *and* FRANK.) I'll be downstairs— You can let me know about the room— Humph— Helpin' out Mrs. O'Brien.—

(*She exits—*MAGNOLIA *laughs patronizingly.*)

MAGNOLIA: She's a dear old thing—

(*There is an embarrassing silence, broken lamely by* ELLIE.)

ELLIE (*picking up picture on mantel*): Nola, is this your little girl's picture?

(FRANK *picks up picture.*)

MAGNOLIA: Yes—that's Kim—Isn't she a darling? Eight years old this March—

FRANK: I'll bet Cap'n Andy's proud of her—

MAGNOLIA: Kim and I go back to visit the old *Cotton Blossom* most every summer.—But in Chicago she's at a convent—over at St. Agatha's— Gay insisted on giving her every possible advantage.

FRANK: Gay doing well, Nola?

MAGNOLIA: Oh, yes, he's a big success. Well, tell me something about yourselves.

FRANK: We're doing pretty good—

ELLIE: Pretty good, listen to him! We're practically headliners—

FRANK: Yeh— We're practically headliners— I'm buildin' a house myself— (*He begins to puff his cigarette grandly.*)

MAGNOLIA: Really?

FRANK: Yep—up on Riverside Drive in New York—pretty far out—but I was thinkin' of buyin' one of them gas buggies— either a Thomas or a Pope-Hartford. I ain't decided.

ELLIE: *You* ain't decided— You talk as if it was all *your* money— Ain't I the wishbone— I mean—backbone of the set?

FRANK: She's getting her bones all mixed.

MAGNOLIA: Where are you playing now?

ELLIE (*a little ill at ease*): Well—we're just sort of breakin' in an act. We open New Year's Eve at the Trocadero.

MAGNOLIA: Oh, I've been there often—not lately though.

FRANK (*quietly*): Say, Nola—I was thinkin'—if you needed a little money maybe I could fix it so's you get a job— Maybe fix yuh up with a little act—maybe singin' an' playin' the guitar like you used to—

ELLIE: That'd be fine, Nola—

MAGNOLIA: I'm afraid Gay would never hear of it— Of course I'd like to— I mean just as a lark—I don't need the money—

ELLIE: No—o' course not—

(*A knock on the door.*)

MAGNOLIA (*puzzled—a little nervous—It might be a bill collector*): —C-come in—

(ETHEL *enters.*)

ETHEL: Boy just left this for yo', Miss Ravenal— (*Hands MAG-NOLIA a letter.*)

MAGNOLIA: Thank you, Ethel— (MAGNOLIA *opens the envelope— She takes out a roll of bills. Her face lights up.*)

(*Airily.*) Oh, yes— Gay was to have stopped at the bank—

(ETHEL *exits.*)

Excuse me a minute, folks— I've got to see what Gay says— He may want me to meet him somewhere.

(*She reads the letter—her hand begins to tremble— As she finishes, the letter drops to the floor— She looks down at the crumbled money in her lap—* FRANK *picks up the letter. One of the love themes plays in orchestra beneath this pantomime and ensuing dialogue.*)

ELLIE: Nola dear— What's the matter?— Is Gay hurt?

MAGNOLIA: No—I—

(FRANK *hands her letter.*)

Ellie—you—you read it—I may believe it if I hear somebody else say it—

ELLIE (*reads*): Er—er—"Dearest— By the time this letter reaches you, I shall be on a train, bound God knows where— There is nothing left to pawn, and no more friends to borrow from. I am enclosing two hundred dollars— This will let Kim finish her term at the convent— Then you can both go to your parents—" (ELLIE *clears her throat.*) "I am doing this because I think it is right—and because I love you— Please believe I will always love you— My dear little wife— Goodbye." (*It has been getting harder for* ELLIE *to speak—she gulps out the last words.*) "—Your own Gay."

(*There is an awkward pause.*)

Er Nola— Can we do anything, Nola?

(*Orchestra plays: "Why Do I Love You?"*)

MAGNOLIA: I don't think so, Ellie— I don't know— I never thought of living without Gay—no matter what happened— I can't imagine it now—

FRANK: He seems to think you and Kim'll be better off—

MAGNOLIA: Better off!—I never complained— I've lived like this half the time. One room—one bed—washing clothes in the basin, cooking food over a gas jet—but I loved him—and if all that went with him, I was willing to take it— I thought he knew that.

ELLIE: But dearie, you and Kim can have a good home on the Show Boat—

MAGNOLIA: Good home! Living on charity and having my mother tell me she always knew it would be like this. The whole Show Boat troupe whispering about me in their dressing rooms— No! I'll do anything but that—

FRANK: Won't it cost you something to keep the kid at the convent?

MAGNOLIA: This money will help me for a month or so— Meanwhile I'll look for work—

FRANK: Remember what I said about the Trocadero.

MAGNOLIA (*trying hard to keep back tears now*): The Trocadero— Oh—yes— I might try that, Frank— I–I'll think it over—

ELLIE: You'd like us to go, wouldn't you, Nola?

(MAGNOLIA *nods.*)

FRANK (*a lame attempt to be light and airy*): Sure— Ellie an I'll twenty-three skiddo out—

ELLIE (*at door*): You can get us over at Forbes' Hotel if you want us—

MAGNOLIA: All right, dear—

(FRANK *and* ELLIE *exit*— MAGNOLIA *picks up letter; starts crying, sinks into chair, buries face between hands.*)

CLOSE IN

SCENE 3

Two weeks later— The Trocadero Rehearsal Room—about five p.m.
This is played before black drop— Piano with JAKE *seated before it*
Stage left— BOY WITH GUITAR *on chair left of piano—*
  At rise: JIM *is standing right of piano watching* GIRLS *dancing.*
  JAKE, *a pale boy with a cigarette in his mouth, bangs on a piano*
downstage. He is playing a Sousa march for the girls' dance. They finish
a laborious, effective and well-executed dance, designed for legitimate
applause and exit disclosing a woman who sits dejectedly in a chair.
This is JULIE, *a hollow-cheeked woman—looking older than she really*
is—with all the ear-marks of one who is down and out—marks which
she has desperately and pathetically tried to hide by overdressing, by
making use of too many odds and ends of finery, and by a too-anxious
application of rouge and lip-stick and by dyeing her hair a wretched
red. She sits there, oblivious to all that is going on around her. From
time to time she opens her hand-bag and takes out a pint flask—typical
of the bottled goods of the time—and furtively takes a drink.

JIM: All right, Jake—call 'em at twelve tomorrer— (*To* JULIE.)
  Ready, Julie? You're next. I wanta hear that new song. Got
  it all set?
JULIE: Leave me alone, Jim—I ain't feelin' so very good. Before
  you know it I'll be off on a tear an' to hell with your show.
JIM: Oh, you ain't feelin' so good! Just you go off on a tear an'
  you'll never get back in this place again. When I told you that
  the last time, I meant it. You go out that door and you don't
  come back. Get me?
JULIE: All right; all right. I ain't in no mood to listen to long
  speeches. I'll put your damn song over.
JIM: You better. I'm sick an' tired o' arguin' with yuh! You get
  that number or you're through. Come on now and see what
  you can do . . . I gotta set this show.
JULIE (*rising from her chair*): All right. All right. (*She takes her*
  position, ready to sing.) I'm ready, Jake, whenever you are.
    (JAKE *pounds out the introduction to* JULIE'S *song on the piano.*)

"Bill"
I used to dream that I'd discover
The perfect lover—someday

I knew I'd recognize him if ever
He came round my way
I always used to fancy then
He'd be one of the God-like kind of men
With a giant brain and a noble head
Like the heroes bold
In the books I've read.
(*1st Chorus*)
But along came Bill
Who's not the type at all
You'd meet him on the street—
And never notice him.
His form and face
His manly grace
Are not the kind that you
Would find in a statue
Oh, I can't explain
It's surely not his brain
That makes me thrill
I love him because he's wonderful
Because he's just old Bill.
(*2nd Verse*)
He can't play golf or tennis or polo
Or sing a solo, or row
He isn't half as handsome
As dozens of men that I know
He isn't tall or straight or slim
And he dresses far worse than Ted or Jim
But I can't explain why he should be
Just the one, one, man in the world for me.
(*2nd Chorus*)
He's just old Bill, an ordinary man
He hasn't got a thing that I can brag about
And yet to be, upon his knee
So comfy and roomy
Seems natural to me
Oh, I can't explain
It's surely not his brain
That makes me thrill
I love him—because he's—I don't know—

Because he's just my Bill.

(*After number,* JULIE *exits.*)

JAKE: She'll be all right for the show. She always comes through. She's a real trouper.

JIM: If she don't, that's the end o' her. Queer how a woman goes to pieces over a man! Why, she was the best bet in Chicago till that big blonde bum left her flat. (*To* JAKE.) 'At all now?

JAKE: All except this feller—says he can play the guitar.

(YOUNG MAN WITH GUITAR CASE *coming forward.*)

MAN WITH GUITAR: I'd like to show you my specialty, Mr. Greene— I do a novelty musical act, and if—

JIM: No, no—guitar's a thing o' the past. They had that kind o' stuff back in the World's Fair—

MAN WITH GUITAR: But I got a new notion—

JIM: Sure. But I gotta go.—Take his name, Jake.

(*The* YOUNG MAN *goes up to* JAKE *who fumbles for a card, finally writing name on a small piece of* JAKE'S *music paper, this pantomime taking place during the ensuing dialogue. As* JIM *starts to go off,* FRANK *enters.*)

FRANK: Mr. Greene—can I see you a minute?

(JIM *picks up a newspaper from table, stuffs it in his pocket and proceeds to leave, as if* FRANK *had never spoken.* FRANK *clears his throat and speaks louder this time.*)

Mr. Greene—I'd like to talk to you—

JIM (*turning*): Huh?

FRANK: I'd like to talk to you.

JIM (*brusquely*): Who are you?

FRANK: Frank Schultz—of Schultz and Schultz, the well-known comedy team.

JIM: Oh, the new act, eh? I'll see you later. (*Turning and walking away from* FRANK.)

FRANK (*clearing his throat again*): Mr. Greene, I want to see you a minute!

JIM (*very gruffly, suspecting a touch*): Whatcha want?

FRANK: I gotta girl outside I'd like you to hear sing.

JIM: Oh, for Gawd's sake—I don't need nobody. I ain't seein' no more people today—

(MAGNOLIA *enters.*)

FRANK: I know—but I thought—

JIM: Well, you thought wrong, see?

(JAKE *laughs uproariously at this witticism. This pleases* JIM— *it was even cleverer than he had thought.*)

You thought wrong!

(*He starts to go. He almost bumps into* MAGNOLIA.)

Who d' ye want to see?

MAGNOLIA: I—I—

FRANK: That's the girl I mean, Mr. Greene.

MAGNOLIA: I'd like to sing for you, Mr. Greene.

JIM (*looking her over*): Yeh? What kind o' singin'?

MAGNOLIA: Why—I—I do negro songs . . .

JIM: Oh—Coon songs, eh? (*Looks at his watch.*) All right—let's see whatcha can do.

FRANK (*eager and nervous, like all impresarios*): Come on, Nola. (*He helps her off with her coat.*)

MAGNOLIA: Have you got a guitar?

JIM: Oh, my Gawd, this must be guitar day.

(JAKE *laughs at this sally.*)

Never seen so many guitar players—

MAGNOLIA: I just—it's a good accompaniment—

YOUNG MAN WITH GUITAR: Here, sister—you can use mine—

MAGNOLIA: Thank you. (*She takes guitar.*)

JIM: Take your hat off!

(*She obeys. She sits with the guitar across her knees, throws back her head, half closes her eyes and starts to sing, "Can't Help Lovin' Dat Man"—At first her voice falters, then she gets into it and sings it with fine feeling and sincerity. The three men listen, spellbound. No one moves an inch. She finishes. There is a pause.*)

(*When* MAGNOLIA *begins to sing,* JULIE *enters quietly, passes behind piano—recognizes* MAGNOLIA *and takes a couple of quick steps up to her, but directly behind her. Stands there during song till next to last line when she seems to arrive at a decision. She makes a shy hesitant little gesture which is half-throwing a kiss. She disappears quickly and softly.*)

FRANK: What do you say, boss?

JIM: Lousy! What kind of a coon song do you call that? (*To* MAGNOLIA.) You don't sing bad—but that song—

MAGNOLIA (*her temper aroused*): That song is the most beautiful song I know. And if you don't like it I'm sorry for you.

JIM: You're sorry for me?— Say!

FRANK: Mr. Greene, I—that tune she sung ain't so bad— Jake

could fix it up . . . Gee Mr. Green—that's a great chance for her and a great chance for you. She was a star on the *Cotton Blossom*—the show boat.

JIM: Star of a show boat don't mean nothin' in Chicago . . .

(CHARLIE, *doorman of the Trocadero Restaurant, enters.*)

CHARLIE: Boss—

JIM: Well—what do you want?

CHARLIE: Got a message for you from your prima donna. (*With a sarcastic emphasis on "prima donna."*) Told me to tell you she was goin' on that tear.

JIM (*exploding*): I'll be damned! Just the day before we open! She won't be good for anything for a week, let alone tomorrow night! Good God, why didn't you stop her? (*Striding angrily back and forth.*)

CHARLIE: Say—I'm a doorman—not a nurse-maid!

JIM (*still angry and worried*): It's enough t' drive a man crazy! And after what I told her, too! That settles it! She's through!

CHARLIE: She said t' tell yuh—if yuh want a girl to take her place—yuh better grab that girl that just sung.

FRANK (*taking advantage of this opening*): Yeah. Say, Mr. Greene, this little girl ain't so bad. Can't you use her?

JIM: I can't afford to take chances on amachoors with a two thousand dollar production. Wait now—let me think. (*He stands pondering the problem and running his fingers through his hair. Looking* MAGNOLIA *over appraisingly.*)

FRANK (*to* MAGNOLIA): Funny how you always git your chance, ain't it? . . .

MAGNOLIA: How do you mean?

FRANK: You know—on the Show Boat. That's how you got your first chance— Remember— Julie?

MAGNOLIA: Yes, I remember . . . I often wonder what ever became of her. I loved Julie . . .

JIM: Aw, keep still—I'm tryin' t' think! Say—you can smile, can't you? Your poisonality is all right— If we could only teach you some up-to-date numbers.

JAKE: That one she sang ain't so bad, Boss—we can trick that— Listen—something like this—(*starts to hum it in syncopation*) Da daddum de da de da da dum—

FRANK (*eagerly*): Oh, you mean rag it—

(JAKE *plays on.*)

JAKE: That's it.

> (JAKE *continues refrain.* JIM *shows interest and goes up to piano.* MAGNOLIA *is bewildered.*)

O' course the words got to be changed too—near the finish a couple o' gags—right here. Te tum ta tum tum tumtum—catch line! See what I mean?—ta tum tum tum—catch line! Da de dum de da—

> (FRANK *and* JAKE *finish big.*)

JIM: That ain't bad.

FRANK: Come on over here, Nola—try it this way. (*He brings her over.*)

MAGNOLIA: How do you mean?

FRANK: Follow Jake.

> (JAKE *and* MAGNOLIA *start the song together—but he soon leaves her far behind.*)

JIM (*interrupting*): No—no—rag it, he means—

> (FRANK *sings the first line to show her.*)

MAGNOLIA (*willing to try*): I know. Oh, all right, go ahead—

> (FRANK *dances like mad. During dance he speaks.*)

> (MAGNOLIA *meanwhile singing rag-time to his dancing.*)

FRANK: What do you say, Boss?

JIM: All right.

FRANK: Does she get the job?

JIM: Sure.

> (FRANK *falls to the stage from dancing so fast and continues twitching his head, body and legs with music until . . .*

CLOSE IN)

SCENE 4

Meanwhile—St. Agatha's Convent
At Rise: Choral singing heard behind curtain.

> (CHOIR)
> *Alma redemptoris mater*
> *Alma redemptoris mater*
> *Alma redemptoris, redemptoris*
> *Redemptoris, redemptoris*
> *Redemptoris, redemptoris*

Redemptoris, redemptoris
Alma redemptoris mater

Te Deum laudamus
Te Dominum confitemur
Te Deum laudamus
Te Dominum confitemur

Te Deum laudamus
Te Dominum confitemur

Venerandum Tuum verum et unicum Filium
Venerandum Tuum verum et unicum Filium

(*Procession of pupils exits.*)
(RAVENAL *is just being ushered in by one of the* SISTERS. *The singing continues.*)

SISTER: Here they come.

(RAVENAL *waits for* KIM'S *appearance with suppressed eagerness. But the voices and steps never quicken their tempo. A procession of girls files in slowly.*)

(KIM *is on the end of the line, with a class of smaller children.* RAVENAL *gives an involuntary start when he sees her.*)

RAVENAL: Kim!

(*A little* GIRL, *about seven years old, hears him, sees him and rushes out of line. Suddenly realizes she has broken a rule, darts a quick look at* SISTER *who nods her consent, and then continues her swift course to* RAVENAL'S *waiting arms. He kneels to meet her, hugs her tight and kisses her. Then he holds her from him at arm's length to get a good look at her.*)

KIM: Daddy—

(*Business.*)

Where's Mummy?

RAVENAL: Mummy couldn't come today. Now listen, Kim, dear. Daddy's in a great hurry. He must catch a train.

KIM (*disappointed*): Where are you going?

RAVENAL: Away—for a little while—on business. I just had a few minutes to rush in and—see you.

KIM: Can't I go with you?

RAVENAL: No, dear—not on this trip—but while I'm gone I want you to think of me once in a while—will you?

KIM: Yes, I think of you all the time and when I miss you I always do what you told me.

RAVENAL: What was that?

KIM: Don't you remember? Make believe—

RAVENAL (*laughing*): Oh, yes, that's right. I gave you a system for having anything you want.

> Only—
> Make believe I'm near you,
> Only make believe that you're with me.
> Girls and boys find it fun just pretending—
> Couldn't you?
> Couldn't I?
> Couldn't we?

And if I'm a little late coming back— You just remember— and pretend I've never gone away— Will you, sweetheart?

> Best of all, make believe I love you—
> For to tell the truth—I do!

(*He grabs her up in his arms again and kisses her. The* SISTER *coughs gently to remind him that it is time to let* KIM *rejoin her class.*)

(*Rising.*) Goodbye, darling.

KIM (*lightly*): G'bye.

(*She runs to join the other girls in line until he stops her.*)

RAVENAL: Kim dear—tell Mother I came in to see you, will you?

(*She starts to march off; throws him a kiss. He returns it. He stands there looking longingly at her. The* SISTER *and* KIM *exit.*)

(RAVENAL *takes hat and cane from table and exits through door.*)

CURTAIN

SCENE 5

A corner of the lobby of the Sherman Hotel, Chicago; New Year's Eve. Three well-dressed GIRLS *sitting on settee stage left.*
ANDY *and* PARTHY *enter.*

From time to time there is heard, off-stage, a characteristic medley of New Year's Eve sounds—horns, cow-bells, etc.

PARTHY: Nice New Year's—I must say! They ain't here—and nobody knows where they went! You an' your surprises! You're a nitwit, Hawks—and always will be! Haven't you a word to say?

 (ANDY *does business with balloon.*)

ANDY: Will you listen?

PARTHY: No I won't.

ANDY: I thought you wouldn't.

PARTHY: What are you go' to do—stand here all night? Get the key. I'm goin' to my room. I'm all tuckered out.

ANDY: Parthy, it's New Year's Eve. Let's go out. I bet Nola an' Gay are celebratin' at some restaurant. (ANDY *takes wistful notice of the ladies seated on settee.*) Let's go an' see if we can find 'em.

PARTHY: Like lookin' for a needle in a hay-stack! Get the key. What's the matter? Are you deaf? (*Sees* ANDY *looking at the girls.*) Hawks, will you never learn? A man of your age! Ev'ry time you see a pretty girl you forget you're married!

ANDY: You're wrong, Parthy. That's the time I remember I'm married. (ANDY *holds up key.*)

PARTHY (*out of patience*): Are you goin' to gimme that key?

ANDY: Here it is. I'm holdin' it in front of you. What's a-matter? Can't you see? Better get your specs.

PARTHY (*taking the key*): I don't need any specs an' never will. My grandfather lived to be ninety-seven and never used glasses!

ANDY: Well, lots of people prefer to drink from a bottle!

 (*Business of flirting again.*)

PARTHY: Will you stop lookin' at gals?

ANDY: Jest lookin' over types—might find an actress for the Show Boat.

PARTHY: It's a fine time, I must say, to be thinkin' about the Show Boat.

ANDY: Couldn't be better. Gotta get a comp'ny together. Met a feller today that'd be great for the troupe.

PARTHY: Is he a good actor?

ANDY: Good actor? I should say so! For the last three years he played Santa Claus for the Salvation Army! . . . You go upstairs an' get some sleep an' I'll look around for the children.

PARTHY: Sleep! It's a lot o' sleepin' I'll do—a wonderin' where that good-fer-nothin' scamp Ravenal has dragged Nola!

ANDY: Now, Parthy, they're all right. I know they are. I got a feelin' I'll bump into them or somebody. (*Looks at* GIRLS.)

PARTHY (*looking at clock*): Hawks, it's eight o'clock. You be back here by nine—or I'll be comin' after you.

ANDY: You won't find me!

(PARTHY *exits.*)

(ANDY *rubs his hands together, sets his hat at a more cocky angle and straightens himself up as the* GIRLS *stand up.*)

LOTTIE: Hello, pop.

ANDY: Hello, girls.

DOLLY: Say, pop, who was that awful fright you were talking to?

ANDY: Why, that was Parthemia, my wife.

DOLLY: Oh, my mistake.

ANDY (*sadly*): Nope—mine.

LOTTIE (*as the* GIRLS *all laugh*): Gee, you're funny! Want to take us out tonight?

ANDY: Sure. (*Takes two of the* GIRLS *by the arm.*) I ain't done this in years. Where do you want to go?

LOTTIE: To the Trocadero.

ANDY: Come ahead, girls. Ain't done this in years! But I want to warn you—I'm a wild man when I get going. I turned out to be just the sort of man my father warned me against.

(LOTTIE *grabs him by the arm; they all start to go out.*)

BLACK OUT

SCENE 6

The Trocadero Restaurant—New Year's Eve. Gay Scene. Crowd at tables around Stage. NEGRO WAITERS *bustling around. Ballet dance in progress at Opening Scene.*

*After ballet dance, curtain on Trocadero stage drawn—*JIM *steps forward to make announcement.*

JIM: We take pleasure in presenting tonight a Parisian novelty, the Apache Dance—first time in America.
(SIDELL SISTERS *do "Apache Dance."*)
(FRANK *and* ELLIE *enter for their number.*)

"Goodbye, My Lady Love"
FRANK and ELLIE:
> So I'm going away
> Because my heart has gone astray,
> And you promised me
> That some day
> You'll come back to me.
> (*Chorus*)
> Goodbye, my lady love,
> Farewell, my turtle-dove,
> You are the idol
> And darling of my heart,
> But some day
> You will come back to me
> And love me tenderly
> So goodbye, my lady love,
> Goodbye.

(*After song they do cakewalk—during which* ANDY *enters with* GIRLS, *and stands watching until* FRANK *and* ELLIE *exit.*)
ANDY: Happy New Year! I ain't done this in years!
LOTTIE: It'll do you good, pop.
ANDY: It's done me good already—whee! Happy New Year! (*To* HEAD WAITER.) Give us the best table in the house. Happy New Year! I ain't done this in years! You know I know them four people that was out here doing that cakewalk. Must a' seen 'em some place before.
LOTTIE: It's a new turn here, pop. Opened tonight.
ANDY: Well, I seen so many actors in my time—they all git lookin' alike. Fine— Now, girls, what'll it be?—A cold bottle and a bird?—
LOTTIE: I should smile!
ANDY (*to* WAITER): Waiter, bring four quarts o' Mumm's extray an' while you're gone we'll be lookin at the "Minny."
(*Business with horn.*)

(*To* GIRLS.)

By cracky—I ain't done this in years—

LOTTIE: What's mistletoe? A vine or a vegetable?

ANDY: Mistletoe is an excuse— (*He kisses her. Then takes a deep breath.*) Golly—I ain't done that in years!

(*Horn business.*)

FRANK (*Enters. Rushes up to* ANDY): Captain Andy! Andy Hawks!

ANDY: Well if it ain't Frank—I thought that was you and Ellie in that turn—sit down Frank—Glad to see you— Girls this is Mr. Schultz, old friend of mine I ain't seen in years— Frank, this is Miss So-and-so, and Miss Thingabob—and this little devil's name is Lottie—

LOTTIE: Hello—

FRANK: Captain Andy—how d'you happen to come here?

ANDY: Jest dropped in— Parthy an' me come up to surprise Nola and Gay—but they ain't stoppin' at the Sherman House any more.

FRANK: No.

ANDY: S'pose we'll find them tomorrer . . . Anyway, I left Parthy, about eight o'clock in the hotel and took a walk and— and—ever since ten o'clock I been tryin' to think of an excuse for not bein' home by nine!

(*Looks at* LOTTIE *and laughs, also notices her legs crossed and her skirt is up to her calves! She hastily pulls skirt down over her ankles.*)

That's all right—liquor's *my* only weakness.

FRANK: Listen, Capt. Andy—Nola's here—

ANDY (*sobering up quickly*): Where?

FRANK: She's actin'—

ANDY: Actin'—what do you mean— Gay'd never let her—

FRANK: Gay's gone—

ANDY: Gone!

FRANK: Went broke and—and quit— I'm tellin' you this because Nola's opening here tonight and we want everything to go smooth. Gee—it'll be awful if—if she don't make a hit—

ANDY: What do you mean don't make a hit— My Nola'll stand this crowd on their ears—she's bound to— Look how they used to love her on the river. (*To* GIRLS.)— My daughter's singin' here tonight.

LOTTIE: Are you old enough to have a daughter?

ANDY: No— But I got one—

JIM (*taking the floor*): Ladies and gentlemen— I regret to announce— That Miss Julie Wendell is indisposed and cannot appear tonight—

> (CROWD *groans its disappointment.*)

But we are fortunate, however, in obtaining the services of Miss Magnolia Ravenal who will sing you an old favorite.

> (*More groans.*)

DRUNK (*at nearby table*): Magnolia Ravenal—who the hell's she?

ANDY (*getting up and starting to take his coat off*): I'll show you who th' hell she is—

> (MAGNOLIA *comes down stage. She starts to sing rather timidly and is ill at ease.*)

"After the Ball"

MAGNOLIA:

> A little maiden
> Climbed an old man's knee
> Begged for a story
> "Do Uncle Please"

> (CROWD *murmurs.*)

> Why are you single,
> Why live alone?

A MAN: Get the hook!

MAGNOLIA:

> Have you no babies,
> Have you no home?

ANDY: Nola!

> (*She turns in opposite direction to where he is sitting, but evidently trying to see who called her.* CROWD *grows noisy.*)

MAGNOLIA:

> I had a sweetheart,
> Years, years a-go;

ANDY: NOLA!

> (*She sees* ANDY, *and gains confidence.*)

MAGNOLIA:

> Where she is now pet,
> You will soon know—

> (*She has begun to sing very well and the* CROWD *grows quiet.*)

> List to the story

        I'll tell it all
ANDY: Smile!
MAGNOLIA:

      I believed her faithless
      After the ball.

MAGNOLIA and CROWD:

    (*Chorus*)
      After the ball is over,
      After the break of morn,
      After the dancers leaving
      After the stars are gone;
      Many a heart is aching,
      If you could read them all;
      Many the hopes that have vanished
      After the ball.
    (*Chimes ring.*)

ANDY and CROWD: Happy New Year!

    (ANDY *takes* MAGNOLIA *in his arms.*)

BLACK OUT

SCENE 7

Street corner outside the office of the Natchez Democrat—*showing bulletin "Lindbergh Arrives in Mexico City"—date in order to denote lapse of time to present day.*

    JOE, *now gray-haired and old, is sitting on box before window—whittling.*

"Ol' Man River"

JOE:

      Ol' Man River,
      Dat ol' Man River,
      He mus' know sumpin'
      But don't say nuthin',
      He jes' keeps rollin',
      He keeps on rollin' along.
      He don't plant 'taters,
      He don't plant cotton,

An' dem dat plants 'em
Is soon forgotten,
But ol' Man River
He jes' keeps rollin' along.
New things come 'n ol' things go
But all things look de same to Joe.
Folks git mad an' starts a war,
An' den git glad,
Don't know what for.
Ah keep laughin'
Instead of cryin'
Ah mus' keep livin'
Until ah'm dyin'
But Ol' Man River,
He jes' keeps rollin' along!

(QUEENIE *enters.*)

QUEENIE: There yo' is, Joe—jest in de same spot when I left yo'—

JOE: Yep. Can't help lookin' at dat ol' river—dere it gone—keeps on livin' and doin' nothin'—

QUEENIE: Keeps on livin' an' doin' nothin'—you an' de river is twins.

(*Four or five of levee* CHORUS *enter now and group builds up throughout ensuing scene.*)

BOY: Hello dere Queenie—yo' sho' got back fast—How'd yo' come, by airplane?

CARRIE: Mah, goodness! Look at dat dicty dress.

QUEENIE: Miss Kim done gimme dis gown— Lordy, Joe, y'oughter see dat gal—she's de finest actress in New York City.

JOE (*rising*): Always knowed she would be—well, I guess I'll go in an' finish de letter I'm writin' to my sister—

QUEENIE: Letter yo' writin' to yo' sister—you don't know how to write!

JOE: Well, mah sister don't know how to read. (JOE *exits.*)

QUEENIE: I don't know how I've put up with dat man all my life.

CARRIE: Kin yo' member when he was a young feller tryin' to make you marry him?

QUEENIE: He didn' try to marry me— I ketched him—an' if you gals think yo' kin get a man any other way, yo' crazy.

"Hey, Feller!"

When you yen for a gent
Give him encouragement
Only then will he come to stay
You must declare yourself
Or you'll be on the shelf
If you wait too long he'll get away
Once you have picked your boy
Waste no time in acting coy
Leave no time for doubt
Step up and speak right out.
(*Refrain*)
Hey! Feller!
I think you're swell
I took a look and then I fell
Hey! Feller!
I've got to tell
I can't deny what you know well
I'm longing to be basking
In your caressing
Right now
And if you'll do the asking
I'll do the yessing
And how!
Say! Feller!
I must admit
That I suspect that you've got it
Hey! Feller!
I'm yours to take
So give a little girl an even break
And if you love her
Tell her
Hey! Feller! Hey! Hey!
(*Refrain repeated with Chorus*)
(JUBILEE DANCERS *on for 3rd refrain*)

SCENE 8

A small part of the upper deck of the New Cotton Blossom, *a freshly painted, modern show boat.* ANDY *and* RAVENAL *are discovered sitting on two chairs, looking straight out, listening to* MAGNOLIA'S *voice thru the radio amplifier which is set between them on a table with the radio box—* ANDY *is now eighty-two, but with a good many signs of the old energy remaining—* RAVENAL *is about sixty-five—still dignified—well dressed, but a trifle shabby—the two old codgers drinking juleps.* MAGNOLIA *finishes her song—"Can't Help Lovin' Dat Man."*

RAVENAL: That song takes me back a long time—

ANDY: Guess y' ain't heard her voice in more'n twenty years—

RAVENAL: Oh yes—I—I sneaked into a theatre once when she played Chicago—

    (ANNOUNCER'S VOICE *through horn.*)

ANNOUNCER'S VOICE: The lady you just heard was Magnolia Ravenal. She retired several years ago—but her great theatrical name is kept on by her daughter, Kim Ravenal, the musical comedy star . . . Our next entertainment will be the National Cruller Boys Orchestra—

    (RAVENAL *has turned the radio off.* ANDY *taking his pipe out of his mouth.*)

ANDY: When Nola gets back from the broadcastin' studio, she'll get my telegram . . .

RAVENAL: Do you suppose they'll leave tonight?

ANDY: Sure's shootin'— Gosh—it seems like fate my bumping into you at Fort Adams yesterday.

RAVENAL (*in a more serious mood than* ANDY): I can hardly wait to see Nola.

ANDY: You won't have to wait long— Train'll get 'em here by tomorrow night— Things move fast these days, Gay. (*Trying to cheer him up.*) Remember when you were a wild young buck in Chicago?

RAVENAL: I remember—

ANDY: You'd have to go some to be considered wild these days. Yes, things are fast now-a-days.— I can remember when it took a man years to drink himself to death!

RAVENAL: Captain— You only found me by accident—won't it

be better if I just drop out of sight again?— Her life is happy, and complete—

ANDY: I don't know about that. Anyway—don't you ever want to see Kim?

RAVENAL (*intensely interested*): Does she look like Nola?

ANDY: Spit an' image of her! An' she's got a lot of your ways— Kind of dignified—more refined than most gals today—I mean she talks like 'em and dresses like 'em, but she don't overdo it— I mean when she sits on a chair she realizes that the human knee is a joint an' not an entertainment—

RAVENAL: I'd give a good deal to see her— But I don't dare— I don't think I'd better . . .

ANDY: Sit down a minute Gay.—

(RAVENAL *sits. During* ANDY's *ensuing speech* JOE *and* BOYS *off stage sing softly—"Can't Help Lovin' Dat Man!"—The lights dim slowly.*)

Trouble is you keep blamin' yourself for things—an' the fact is that you was jest unlucky— The lucky couple are the ones that get to do what they enjoy doin'— I allus enjoyed runnin' a show boat—and I made a success out of it. Nola was always meant for the stage, an' she finally landed there— Now you— you was meant to be a gentleman—the big mistake you made was ever to try to make a livin'. . . . Nobody ever expected it of you— You was on the right track when you started to be a leadin' man on the river— You could o' got to be a big Broadway actor, an' then you wouldn't have had to work any more.

PARTHY (*off stage*): Andy—Andy!

ANDY: Parthy's calling me. Guess I'd better be going.

RAVENAL: I don't understand it— Married all these years and yet—every time she calls—you jump. What is it? What has she got?

ANDY (*as he exits*): She's got a mean disposition.

(*After* ANDY *leaves,* RAVENAL, *dreaming of the past, picks up the dipper from the water-barrel and speaks as though to a vision.*)

RAVENAL: That you—Nola?

"You Are Love" (reprise)
You taught me to see
One truth forever true—

You are love,
Wonder of all the world.
Where you go with me,
Heaven will always be.

BLACK OUT

SCENE 9

*The levee at Natchez in 1927, showing modernized show boat with
electric lights, etc.—radio towers and hydroplane in background—*
BOYS *and* GIRLS *in evening dress on stage at rise—singing "Cotton
Blossom."*

    (PARTHY *and* KIM *enter from Show Boat*)

A BOY: Good evening, Mrs. Hawks.

PARTHY: Good evening. Well—I never thought I'd live to be
    bossed around by my grand-daughter.

KIM: Why Parthy! I don't boss you.

PARTHY: Yes, you do, Kim Ravenal— Didn't you bring me this
    dress that's up to my knees? And ain't you makin' me wear it?

KIM: But it looks marvellous! And I like your hair, too—

PARTHY: Another idea of yours—boyish bob! Will you tell me
    why a woman of my age should want to look boyish? . . . I'm
    goin' to put a hem on this skirt. You're not goin' to make a
    red-hot grandma out of me!

    (GIRLS *laugh.*)

All right, laugh—all of you. In my day, we never thought of
    doin' the things you girls do!

KIM: Don't you wish you had?

A BOY: Glad to see you back in town. Mrs. Hawks, is it a good
    troupe this year?

PARTHY: It's always a good troupe.

A BOY: It must be. This whole crowd came down from Fayette
    and couldn't buy a seat. We're waiting for the concert.

GIRL: Aren't you Mrs. Hawks' grand-daughter, Kim Ravenal,
    the musical comedy star?

KIM: I'm Kim Ravenal—

GIRL: I think you're marvellous. Are you ever going to play
    with the Show Boat?

PARTHY: Ha! Gettin' a thousand a week on Broadway—what would she be doin' on a Show Boat?

GIRL: I'd just love to see you act. I know I'll never get to New York.

PARTHY: Come on Kim—give 'em the imitation of your mother, singing—"That's Why I Love You"—just a sample—

(KIM *gives the imitation.*)

(*Turning to* CROWD.)

Now give them Ethel Barrymore—John Barrymore's sister—I always had a soft spot for John— This is Ethel—got your handkerchief, Kim?

(KIM *does imitation.*)

That's all there is . . . Now give 'em Ted Lewis—

(*To* CROWD.)

This is a hot one—Ted Lewis—you know—Paul Whiteman's uncle— Got a hat, Kim?

(KIM *does imitation.*)

(ENSEMBLE *have entered for imitations and number.*)

(*Eccentric and tap dances*—ENSEMBLE *exit.*)

(FRANK *and* ELLIE *enter from Show Boat with* ANDY.)

FRANK: Say, Capt. Andy, sorry we couldn't stay for the end of the concert; we have to make that eleven o'clock boat.

ELLIE (*very Ritz*): We hated to leave your little entertainment—it was very amusing.

ANDY: I'm glad you liked it.

ELLIE: It's so quaint.

FRANK: You see—things are so different in Hollywood.

ELLIE (*with boastful hauteur*): Yes, being the parents of little Frankie Schultz . . . the wonder boy of the screen—we have our social position to maintain.

ANDY: And to think o' you two havin' the luck to adopt a kid an' him turnin' out to be a screen knock-out . . . earnin' a million dollars a year!

ELLIE: Well, Capt. Andy, if you ever come out to beautiful California, do look us up at our palatian villa.

ANDY: I sure will. I'm glad you're doin' so well in pitchers.

FRANK: Yes, of course, it's an exacting art and between you and I the social life in Hollywood is pretty swift.

ELLIE (*coyly*): O Frank, don't be so mid-Victrola!

(FRANK *and* ELLIE *exit.*)

ANDY: Those movin' pitcher people are wonderful!

> (*The concert on the boat is over.*)
>
> (*The* CROWD *starts to come out. It is a corresponding crowd to the 1890 audience we saw in Act I—in modern guise. They gather about in groups up stage discussing the show.* RAVENAL *comes down stage.* JOE *stands outside the pilot house of the tug; other* NEGROES *gather about deck of tug and look on.*)

ANDY: Hello Gay. She'll probably come out on the top deck. (*To* GIRL.) Hello Hope. (*To* RAVENAL.) Shall I call Nola?

RAVENAL: I don't know.

GIRL (*passing with her escort*): 'Lo, Cap'n Andy!

ANDY: Is your ma well?

GIRL: Fine, thanks.

ANDY: Thank her for the chocolate cake.

GIRL: I will.

MAN: Great show, Captain Andy.

ANDY: Glad you liked it. How're the kids?

MAN: All right. Little one's got a cold.

ANDY: Too bad; change o' weather, I expect . . . Oh, I didn't see you, Nola.

> (NOLA *has entered quietly from the boat to speak to her father and has seen* GAY *before he could turn.* ANDY *follows her gaze over his shoulder.*)

Er—Nola—here—here's Gay . . .

> (*Turning to* RAVENAL.)

Here's Nola, Gay.

MAGNOLIA: Gay—

> (*Neither knows what to say—the silence is embarrassing, painful to all three. An* OLD LADY *comes up to* ANDY.)
>
> (JOE *and* CHORUS *start to hum softly—"Ol' Man River."*)

OLD LADY: Isn't that your daughter, Cap'n Hawks?

ANDY: Er—yes—that's Nola.

OLD LADY (*going over to* MAGNOLIA): How-do? I remember when you were leading lady on this boat—and—that's your husband, isn't it? How do, sir?

RAVENAL: How do you do?

OLD LADY: I thought I recognized you both—guess I ought to—I was here on this levee the day you were married. My, my, how excited we all were! That was a real love match!

Well, glad to see it turned out well and you're still happy
together . . . Good-night.

MAGNOLIA: Good night, dear.

> (*The* OLD LADY *exits.*)

> Father—this is a—a nice surprise— (*She goes over and takes*
> RAVENAL's *hand.*) Gay—come—come up on the top deck—
> we can talk there . . . Will you?

RAVENAL: Nola . . . (*He slowly takes her in his arms—he hasn't*
quite the courage to kiss her. She kisses him.)

> (GIRLS *and* BOYS *enter.*)

ANDY (*chuckling*): If you go up front you'll find a water-barrel—
ain't much different from the old one—

> (*They start to walk towards boat.*)

MAGNOLIA: Look, Gay—there's Kim.

> (*They go towards boat—*JOE *and* CHORUS *voices swell in*
> *volume—*

>> Ol' Man River,
>> He jes' keeps rollin' along!)

(*Slow curtain timed to hit floor as last note is held.*)

CURTAIN

AS THOUSANDS CHEER

Lyrics and music by IRVING BERLIN

Sketches by MOSS HART

SCENES AND MUSICAL NUMBERS

PROLOGUE

MAN BITES DOG
SCENE 1. Dining Room in Park Avenue
SCENE 2. Editor's Office
    Man Bites Dog
SCENE 3. Columbus Circle
    Man Bites Dog, cont.

THE REVUE
Act One

FRANKLIN D. ROOSEVELT INAUGURATED TOMORROW

BARBARA HUTTON TO WED PRINCE PRINCE MDIVANI
    How's Chances

HEAT WAVE HITS NEW YORK
    Heat Wave

JOAN CRAWFORD TO DIVORCE DOUGLAS
FAIRBANKS, JR.

MAJESTIC SAILS AT MIDNIGHT
    Debts

LONELY HEART COLUMN
    Lonely Heart

WORLD'S WEALTHIEST MAN CELEBRATES
94TH BIRTHDAY

THE FUNNIES
    The Funnies

GREEN PASTURES STARTS THIRD ROAD SEASON
    To Be or Not to Be

ROTOGRAVURE SECTION: EASTER PARADE ON FIFTH
AVENUE—1883
    Easter Parade

Act Two

METROPOLITAN OPERA OPENS IN OLD TIME SPLENDOR
Metropolitan Opening

UNKNOWN NEGRO LYNCHED BY FRENZIED MOB
Supper Time

GANDHI GOES ON NEW HUNGER STRIKE

REVOLT IN CUBA

NOEL COWARD, NOTED PLAYWRIGHT, RETURNS
TO ENGLAND

SOCIETY WEDDINGS OF THE SEASON OUTSIDE
ST. THOMASES
Our Wedding Day

PRINCE OF WALES RUMORED ENGAGED

JOSEPHINE BAKER STILL THE RAGE OF PARIS
Harlem on My Mind

BROADWAY GOSSIP COLUMN
Through a Keyhole

SUPREME COURT HANDS DOWN IMPORTANT
DECISION
Not for All the Rice in China (*Finale*)

PROLOGUE

MAN BITES DOG

SCENE I

The Dining-room of the Andrews Apartment. A well-appointed room of a duplex apartment in the East 70's.

As the curtains part, LANGLEY, *the Andrews' butler, is putting the finishing touches to the dinner table which is laid for two. There is, however, direct center, facing the audience, a baby's high-chair, in back of the table.* MR. ANDREWS' *place is at the head of the table,* MRS. ANDREWS *sits at the other end, and the high-chair is midway between them both.*

LANGLEY (*calling off*): Dinner is served. (*He stands back, respectfully holding the door open.*)
　　(GEORGE ANDREWS *enters, or rather limps into the room. A timid, rather pathetic looking man of about 40, he is at the moment rendered still further pathetic by the fact that both his hands are bandaged—the left rather heavily, the right hand just a finger or two.*)
ANDREWS: Good evening, Langley.
LANGLEY: Good evening, sir.
MRS. ANDREWS (*off-stage*): Gertrude! Don't make Mother speak to you again, please! Come in to dinner this minute! *Gertrude*! There! That's Mother's good girl!
　　(MRS. ANDREWS *appears in the doorway with* GERTRUDE *in her arms.* GERTRUDE *is a particularly offensive looking Pekingese dog who looks balefully at* LANGLEY—*then glares resentfully at* MR. ANDREWS *and utters a ferocious growl.*)
Take Gertrude to her chair, Langley. She's going to be a good little girl and eat her dinner. Sweet, say hello daddy. Gertrude loves her Langley, doesn't she?
　　(LANGLEY *exits.*)

You know, George, I don't think Gertrude likes Langley. She's still missing Wilson. Gertrude really loved Wilson. It's a pity we lost him.

MR. ANDREWS: He'd have been bitten to death if he stayed.

MRS. ANDREWS: Now, George—I will *not* have you go on saying that! Gertrude may have playfully nipped Wilson a few times—

MR. ANDREWS: The Doctor said Wilson was on the verge of hydrophobia.

MRS. ANDREWS: Oh, poof! Hydrophobia! It's no worse than a bad cold, anyway! Not hungry, George?

MR. ANDREWS: No.

MRS. ANDREWS: What's new at the office? No dessert if you don't finish your soup! Mother means what she says! What did you say, George?

MR. ANDREWS: Nothing. I didn't go to the office today.

MRS. ANDREWS: No? Where were you?

MR. ANDREWS: I spent all day at the Doctor's being cauterized. (LANGLEY *enters*.)

LANGLEY: Telephone for you, Madame. Mrs. Haskell.

MRS. ANDREWS: O, I want to talk to her—she's on the Committee of Arrangements for the Dog Show. Talking about Gertrude like that. I'd like to see you win a prize at a dog show. I bet you'd come in third or fourth. Gertrude gets blue ribbons.

MR. ANDREWS (*sweetly*): Hello, Gertrude! Good old Gertrude. (*Coyly.*) See all these bandages, Gertrude? That's what *you* did—last night, and the night before and the night before that. For seven years you've been biting me, Gertrude. There isn't an inch of me that you don't know! (*He extends his hand toward* GERTRUDE—*then quickly draws it away.*)
Ah, no! You've had your last bite out of *me*, Gertrude! From now on, it's an eye for an eye, a tooth for a tooth, and a bite for a bite!

MRS. ANDREWS: George!

BLACK OUT

SCENE 2

Editor's office.

"Man Bites Dog"

REPORTER:

    I've got a headline—oh what a headline

    Off the beaten track

    A dog bit a man and the man bit the dog right back

EDITOR (*in phone*):

    You can print what Roosevelt said

    On the front page for a great big spread

REPORTER:

    But I've got a headline—oh what a headline

    Off the beaten track

    A dog bit a man and the man bit the dog right back

EDITOR (*in phone*):

    Hold the wire, it's hard to hear

    There is someone screaming in my ear

    What the hell is the matter with you

    And why the big enthuse?

REPORTER:

    A man was bitten by a dog

EDITOR:

    I know, but that's not news

REPORTER:

    But the man bit the dog right back

EDITOR:

    What's that you say?

    Got no time for gags today

REPORTER:

    But this is no gag—it's on the square,

    I just this minute came back from there

EDITOR:

    You just this minute came back from where?

REPORTER:

    From the swell Park Avenue Shack

    Where a dog bit a man and the man bit the dog right
      back

EDITOR (*in phone*):

> Never mind that Roosevelt speech
> I've a headline now that is a peach,
> It's a most important story
> That'll set the town agog
> Kill the Roosevelt spread
> Print this instead
> MAN—BITES—DOG

SCENE 3

Columbus Circle

NEWSBOYS (*in the dark*):

> Extra! Extra! Man bites dog
> Extra! Extra! Man bites dog
> Extra! Extra! Man bites dog
> Extra! Extra! Man bites dog
> (*The scene is revealed.*)
> Man bites dog
> Extra! Extra! Man bites dog! Extra! Extra!
> Man bites dog
> Extra! Extra! Man bites dog! Extra! Extra!
> Here's a headline off the beaten track
> MAN—BITES—DOG!
> A dog bit a man and the man bit the dog right back,
> Extra! Extra! Extra! Extra!
> MAN BITES DOG
> Extra! Extra! Extra! Extra!
> Man bites dog
> Extra! Extra! Extra! Extra!

BOYS AND GIRLS WITH NEWSPAPERS (*before curtain*):

> At last—at last
> Something new in the news, at last,
> Something else in the news
> Besides that the Drys will lose
> Besides that we'll soon have booze,

Besides that we'll all be a bunch of stews
At last—at last
Something else in the news at last.
A man bit a dog—and that's news,
Arthur Brisbane in his column says
That this will lift the fog
For years he has been waiting for
A man to bite a dog
He says this proves we're cavemen
Of the pre-historic sort
And proving that, Mr. Brisbane says
"Don't sell America short"
At last—at last,
A man bit a dog at last,
And it seems to Heywood Broun
That the world is out of tune,
That if things don't happen soon
We'll all be biting dogs next June.
A man bit a dog—and that's news.
Mr. Walter Lippman tells us he was told
That the tooth that bit the dog was filled with gold
And while politicians roll each other's logs
The nation's gold is going to the dogs.
At last—at last
A man bit a dog at last,
And Mr. Hearst has a chance
To kick the French in the pants.
He says the man who bit the dog
Was a native of France,
And Winchell's all agog
He interviewed the dog
And he says that the pretty "pom"
Was soon to become a "mom"
'Twas a dog you love to be with
The kind you see with—the Rich
Not a great big manly he-dog
A little she-dog—a bitch—which
Gives us a headline off the beaten track
A bitch bit a man and the man bit the bitch right back.

THE REVUE

ACT ONE

FRANKLIN D. ROOSEVELT INAUGURATED TOMORROW

Scene: The curtains part to disclose the famous "Oval Room" of the White House, which Mr. and Mrs. Hoover use as a sitting room to their bedroom. Thru the large window at the back can be seen the tall obelisk of the Washington Monument and a little to the side is a glimpse of the Senate Buildings.

It is late in the evening of March 3, 1933 and the last night Mr. and Mrs. Hoover will call the White House "home." There are visible signs of their leave-taking tomorrow. Two large open trunks stand almost direct center and a number of wooden crates and cartons help give the room the unmistakable atmosphere of a house about to see the last of its present occupants. On one of the large wooden crates downstage is painted in large black letters:

TO HERBERT HOOVER
PALO ALTO
CALIFORNIA

The stage is deserted for a few seconds after the curtain rises—then we hear MR. HOOVER's *voice off-stage:*

MR. HOOVER (*off stage*): Lou! Oh Lou! Where do you want this, Lou?

MRS. HOOVER (*enters*): Bring it in here, Herbie.

MR. HOOVER (*enters with pedestal*): What do you want to lug that thing along for, Lou? It'll cost more than it's worth to ship it to California.

MRS. HOOVER: Never mind! I'm not going to leave anything for those Roosevelts, I can tell you that. Did you bring that electric toaster up from the kitchen, Herbie?

MR. HOOVER: No!

MRS. HOOVER: Well, go down and get it. I'd like to see myself leaving 'em a perfectly good electric toaster. Like fun.

MR. HOOVER: All right.

MRS. HOOVER: Oh Herbie. Better take your fruit salts while you're downstairs, Herbie. You know what a long train ride does to you.

MR. HOOVER: All right.

FRANK (*enters*): In here, Mrs. Hoover?

MRS. HOOVER: Yes, Frank. Thank you.

MR. HOOVER: What's that? What's that piece of wire?

MRS. HOOVER: That's the aerial.

MR. HOOVER: Now for goodness sake, you're not going to take the aerial. Now Lou, you go put that back.

MRS. HOOVER: Put it back. I nearly broke my neck taking it down. Thank you, Frank.

(FRANK *exits*.)

MR. HOOVER: What's that?

MRS. HOOVER: This is nothing, Herbie—nothing at all. Just a little souvenir for my room at home.

MR. HOOVER: Let me see it.

MRS. HOOVER: But it's nothing, Herbie.

MR. HOOVER: Then let me see it. (*It is a portrait of George Washington.*)

MR. HOOVER: Now Lou, you go right down and put that back. You can't take that. It's very valuable. It's Government property. You want to be stopped at the train?

MRS. HOOVER: Herbie, they'll never miss it. This house is lousy with pictures of George Washington.

MR. HOOVER: I don't care. You go put that back. Why those Democrats are liable to pick on a thing like that and cause a whole Senate investigation.

MRS. HOOVER: All right, I'll put it back. We'll just go back to Palo Alto with nothing at all to show for your having been President of the United States.

MR. HOOVER: Nobody else in the country has got anything to show for it either.

MRS. HOOVER: That's right. Wise-cracking is going to help us a lot.

MR. HOOVER: Now Lou, things might have been a lot worse. Suppose I'd been re-elected.

MRS. HOOVER: You know what Palo Alto is. It's going to be very nice, isn't it, for me to go to bridge parties and luncheons and have all my old girl friends saying "Herbie get anything to do yet, Lou? Well, don't worry. Something'll turn up sooner or later." I can just hear 'em.

MR. HOOVER: I've still got my Civil Engineer's License, don't forget that.

MRS. HOOVER: Oh, sure! Now you remember it, after fiddling away a whole four years. I hate to say I told you so, Herbie— but you can't say I didn't warn you.

MR. HOOVER: But it seemed like such a good idea at the time— being President.

MRS. HOOVER: Not to me it didn't. We were doing so well too. Everything was going along beautifully for us. Then you had to go and become President. Herbie, there's a streak in you that makes you do the most simple-minded things sometimes. Had to become President. Couldn't let well enough alone.

MR. HOOVER: Well all I can say is, when as smart a man as Ogden Mills comes to you and says that—

MRS. HOOVER: Ogden Mills! Don't talk to *me* about Ogden Mills! If Ogden Mills was so smart he'd have a job now instead of sitting around writing letters to the *Times* and signing himself "Friend of the American Indian."

MR. HOOVER: Well he is.

MRS. HOOVER: When you came home that night and told me the Republican Party wanted you, I told you what to tell 'em, didn't I?

MR. HOOVER: Oh Lou, I couldn't tell 'em that.

MRS. HOOVER: And all those other Palo Alto boys have done so well for themselves—every one of them. They were all crazy about me too. You know the chances I had. Why even Eddie Harris—I laughed at him when he proposed—he owns the largest knit-goods factory in Southern California now.

MR. HOOVER: He wouldn't have made any better President than I did.

MRS. HOOVER: I didn't say he would. All I say is, here we are going back to Palo Alto after all these years and what have we got to show for it? A medicine ball, a couple of dozen silver spoons. Yes I took the spoons and I'd like to see the Army and the Navy make me put 'em back. A couple of dozen silver spoons and some campaign posters you can't hang up any way. That's what we've got.

MR. HOOVER: Why can't you hang 'em up?

MRS. HOOVER: Do you want to look at Charlie Curtis?

MR. HOOVER: No.

MRS. HOOVER: That reminds me. (*At phone.*)

Get me Mrs. Dolly Gann, please.

MR. HOOVER: What are you going to do?

MRS. HOOVER: This is something I've wanted to do for a long time. Hello, Dolly? This is Lou Hoover. For four years, Dolly, you've been upsetting my dinner parties and getting in everybody's hair. How would you like to take a running jump in the lake. I may call up Andrew Mellon and Henry Stimson later. (*Hangs up.*) I may go through the whole gang of 'em. If you were half a man you'd call up Mellon and Stimson yourself and tell 'em what you think of them. God knows, you've belly ached to me long enough about 'em.

MR. HOOVER: Oh Lou, I couldn't do that.

MRS. HOOVER: What have you got to lose? You're never coming back here.

MR. HOOVER: For two cents I'd do it.

MRS. HOOVER: I dare you. I doubly dare you.

MR. HOOVER: I will. (*At phone.*)

Get me Mr. Mellon. Oh boy, oh boy, oh boy.

MRS. HOOVER: Give it to him good.

MR. HOOVER: Hello. I want to talk to Mr. Andrew Mellon. Mr. Hoover calling. Hoover, *Hoover*! H—as in Harry—O—as in Oboe—yes Hoover.

MRS. HOOVER: By the time we get to the coast we'll be lucky if the servants and the dogs know us.

MR. HOOVER: Hello Andy? This is Herbie? Greatest Secretary of the Treasury since Alexander Hamilton, eh? Well how would you like to meet me in Macy's Window.

MRS. HOOVER (*into phone*): And bring Ogden Mills along.

MR. HOOVER: Ambassador to the court of St. James, eh? You know what you looked like in those knee-breeches? Like an old ostrich!

MRS. HOOVER (*into phone*): Yah—you old ostrich!

MR. HOOVER: Go back to Pittsburgh and wipe the soup off your moustache! (*Hangs up.*)

MRS. HOOVER: Doesn't that make you feel good?

MR. HOOVER: Like a new man. What time do they disconnect the telephone, Lou?

MRS. HOOVER: In about half an hour.

MR. HOOVER: We gotta work fast. Who's next?

MRS. HOOVER: Henry Stimson.

MR. HOOVER: We'll both call him.

MRS. HOOVER: All right. I've got a few words I want to say to his wife. (*At phone.*)

Get me Henry Stimson please. Herbie— (*Whispers to* HOOVER.)

MR. HOOVER: You're an angel, Lou.

MRS. HOOVER: Hello, Henry? This is Mr. and Mrs. Herbert Hoover. Is Mrs. Stimson there? No, don't you go away. Put Mrs. Stimson on the extension. We want to talk to both of you. Are you on, Mrs. Stimson? Just a moment. Are you there, Henry? That's fine. (*To* HOOVER.) One, two, three. (*Bronx cheer.*)

(*Business.*)

MR. HOOVER (*singing*):
  Tony's wife, the boys are all wild about you,
  Tony's wife—

MRS. HOOVER (*singing*):
  Fit as a fiddle and ready for love.
  (*Both tossing medicine ball.*)

MRS. HOOVER: Herbie!

MR. HOOVER: Yes, Lou.

MRS. HOOVER: The Roosevelts?
  (*They both dash for the phone.*)

BARBARA HUTTON TO WED PRINCE MDIVANI

"How's Chances"

BARBARA HUTTON:
  The nickels and dimes I got
  Have bought me an awful lot

A great big box
Of bonds and stocks
A hundred frocks,
A car and yacht,
But having so much, and more
Is getting to be a bore,
It's not much fun
When day is done
Without someone
To love and adore

THE LACKEY, PRINCE HOHENSTEIN, PRINCE DONATELLI,
   PRINCE AUSTERLIEBE, PRINCE DELUNEVILLE:

(*Chorus*)

How's chances
Say, how are the chances
Of making you love me
The way I love you;
I'd give up the things I'm possessing
To be caressing
Someone like you
How's chances
For one of those glances,
A glimpse of the heaven
I'm longing to see
How's chances
To end all your romances
And start taking your chances with me.

PRINCE MDIVANI:

My tailor's the best, but he
Is dear as a man can be,
My shoes and spats,
My opera hats
And my cravats
Are made just for me,
I like an expensive car
And when at my favorite bar,
I think it's fine
To order wine,
And when I dine,
I love caviar

PRINCES:

(*Chorus*)

> How's chances
> Say, how are the chances
> Of making you love me
> The way I love you.
> My castle will need some restoring
> Ceiling and flooring,
> Furniture, too
> How's chances
> For one of those glances,
> A glimpse of the heaven
> I'm longing to see
> How's chances
> To end all your romances
> And start taking your chances with me.

HEAT WAVE HITS NEW YORK

"Heat Wave"
Sung by Ethel Waters

(*Verse*)

> A Heat Wave—blew right into town last week,
> She came from—the Island of Martinique,
> The Can-Can—the dances will make you fry,
> The Can-Can—is really the reason why:

(*Chorus*)

> We're having a Heat Wave—
> A tropical Heat Wave—
> The temp'rature's rising—
> It isn't surprising,
> She certainly can—Can-Can.
> She started the Heat Wave
> By letting her seat wave,
> And in such a way that
> The customers say that
> She certainly can—Can-Can.

Gee! her anatomy
Made the mercury
Jump to ninety-three—yes sir!
We're having a Heat Wave—
A tropical Heat Wave,
The way that she moves that
Thermometer proves that
She certainly can—Can-Can.

(*Patter*)
It's so hot—the weather man will
Tell you a record's been made
It's so hot—a coat of tan will
Cover your face in the shade.
It's so hot the coldest maiden
Feels just as warm as a bride,
It's so hot—a chicken laid an
Egg on the street—and it fried!

JOAN CRAWFORD TO DIVORCE
DOUGLAS FAIRBANKS, JR.

The curtains part to disclose a divan set in front of a Japanese screen.

Seated on the divan are WILL HAYS *center, and* JOAN CRAW-FORD *and* DOUGLAS FAIRBANKS *to the right and left of him.*

At each end of the divan facing its three occupants sits a REPORTER, *notebook in hand, pencils poised.*

JOAN: May I go on, Mr. Hays?

HAYS: Please do, my dear. (*She takes a deep breath, lets her hand flutter to her heart, and speaks.*)

JOAN (*intensely*): With the approval of Mr. Hays, gentlemen, I want you to be sure to say that this divorce can never change our spiritual relationship. Douglas will always remain to me the lover eternal—the finest man I have ever known. I shall always keep and treasure his water colors. (*Her hand reaches out and rests lightly and tenderly on a sculptured head of herself that stands on a pedestal next to the divan.*) I shall have this sculpture always near me to console me in my loneliness. I even intend to go on reading his articles in *Vanity Fair.*

HAYS: Greater love hath no woman, gentlemen.

JOAN: I— I—

> (*She stops, unable to control the rising sobs—she covers her face with her hands. In the little silence that follows, the* REPORTERS *write busily, and* MR. HAYS *uses his pocket handkerchief to wipe a tear from his eye.*)

DOUGLAS: Joan! Shall I, Mr. Hays?

HAYS: Go ahead, my boy.

DOUGLAS: With the approval of Mr. Hays, gentlemen, I want you to be sure to say that this divorce does not mean the end for us—it means a new beginning. Joan is the finest woman I have ever known and I don't intend to give her up. I'm going to try to win her all over again. I'm going to send her flowers every day. I'm going to take her to supper—little intimate suppers for just the two of us—in the Brown Derby or the Cocoanut Grove. I'm going to paint her new water colors—sculpt bigger and better heads of her. I'm going to do the story of her life for *Vanity Fair.* I— I— Oh my God!

JOAN: Douglas!

DOUGLAS: Joan! (*He, too, stops, unable to go on.*)

HAYS: For my own part I want you to say that this is a divorce the industry can be proud of! It's clean divorce—no sex in it! It's a divorce any Woman's Club in the country can point to with pride. Gentlemen—if there was a "Pulitzer Prize" for the best divorce of the year, I'd give it to this one!

> (*The* REPORTERS' *pencils fly over the paper. Then:*)

1ST REPORTER: Thank you for giving us first crack at this, Mr. Hays.

HAYS: I think it's a scoop for you boys.

2ND REPORTER: Scoop? Why, this'll make the front page of every newspaper in the country. "Joan Crawford to Divorce Douglas Fairbanks, Jr." I'll say it's a scoop!

DOUGLAS: Oh—just a minute. That isn't the way you're going to run the headline, is it?

2ND REPORTER: Yes—I guess so, why?

DOUGLAS: Well, it's all wrong. Absolutely wrong. My name

must come first. It should read "Douglas Fairbanks, Jr. to Divorce Joan Crawford."

JOAN: Why, Douglas, dear, wherever did you get such an idea?

DOUGLAS: What's the matter with it?

JOAN: Well—Dodo, darling, you don't think for one moment that my name could come second to anybody's, do you? Why, the studio wouldn't stand for it!

DOUGLAS: But Joan love, *you* don't think for one moment that my studio would allow my name to come second, do you?

JOAN: It wouldn't be the first time.

HAYS: Now, children—children!

JOAN: If that's the way you want to do it, I'll have my manager handle the whole divorce!

DOUGLAS: *Her* manager!

JOAN: We'll *see* whose name goes first!

DOUGLAS: I've got a manager too. Don't forget that!

JOAN: The divorce was my idea in the first place. Does Constance Bennett's name come second when *she* gets her divorces? I should say not! Does Ruth Chatterton's name come second when she gets hers?

DOUGLAS: Are you comparing me to Ralph Forbes?

JOAN: Yes!

DOUGLAS: I'll sock you.

HAYS: Now wait a minute! Children, I'm surprised! I'm really surprised. Why, this should be like the final fadeout of a picture. The passionate romance, the years of married life, and then the parting of the ways. No bitterness—only a great spiritual understanding—and *he*, the husband, makes the magnificent gesture—he lets *her* name go first. That's the way to look at it. That's the way the public will see it! Like a final fadeout.

DOUGLAS: Gee, that's beautiful, Mr. Hays. I get a glow out of that. I see it all now. I, the man must make the gesture.

JOAN: I see it now, too. It's lovely. Only I think the *woman* ought to make the gesture.

DOUGLAS: That's right, grab everything!

JOAN: *You* do!

DOUGLAS: So what!

HAYS: Listen—here's what we'll do! Joan's name will go first—

DOUGLAS: Huh?

HAYS: But in every bit of publicity—everything will be divided equally. Both of you must promise not to take pictures alone, and every picture used in connection with the divorce will have just you two in it. No one will get any publicity but *you* two—I'll see that nobody else horns in.

DOUGLAS: That's very fair, Mr. Hays.

1ST REPORTER: Could we get a picture now, Mr. Hays?

HAYS: How about it, children?

JOAN and DOUGLAS: Certainly! Sure!

DOUGLAS: Shoot up to the smile, boys.

HAYS: All right. We're ready.

DOUGLAS: Pardon me. Do you mind? Say what do you fellows want. Something domestic or passionate?

1ST REPORTER: Make it passionate.

DOUGLAS: Passionate? Come on.

HAYS: That's right, keep it clean. No sex in it.

1ST REPORTER: Ready please. Hold it now.

HAYS: That's right—just you two!

(*Business of turning toward cameras.*)

(*The* NEW REPORTERS *rush in.*)

REPORTERS (*in great excitement*): Miss Crawford—Mr. Fairbanks! A statement, please! A statement!

2ND REPORTER (*speaking simultaneously*): The *International News* would like a statement from both of you!

JOAN and DOUGLAS: Why, sure! Of course! Glad to!

(*They sit up, assume characteristic poses, and begin to recite, simultaneously, the beginnings of their statements to the other reporters.*)

DOUGLAS: I want you to be sure to say that this divorce does not mean the end for us. It means a new beginning. Joan is the finest woman I have ever—

JOAN: I want you to be sure to say that this divorce can never change our spiritual relationship. Douglas will always remain to me the lover eternal.

1ST REPORTER: No, no! Not that!

2ND REPORTER (*breaking in*): We don't care about that! We want a statement about the Mary Pickford–Douglas Fairbanks separation!

JOAN and DOUGLAS: Wha-wha-*what*!

HAYS: What's that? Mary Pickford–Douglas Fairbanks separating?

2ND REPORTER: Yeah! Sure!

HAYS: My God! I hope there's no sex in it. (*He grabs his hat and goes rushing off without a backward glance at the two on the divan.*)

THE TWO CAMERAMEN: Jeez! Mary Pickford, Douglas Fairbanks separating! Let's go! (*They, too, pick up their cameras and rush off.*)

JOAN and DOUGLAS (*to the backs of the retreating cameramen*): Say! What about us—our pictures?

(*But the cameramen have gone.*)

2ND REPORTER: Aw, come on—we're wasting time here.

IST REPORTER: If they won't talk, let's get a statement from Louie B. Mayer!

(*And they, too, rush off.*)

(*There is a silence of rugged grandeur. Then:*)

JOAN (*from the depths of her soul*): That's *your* family! Your family! They're doing this just to spite me! They never have liked me anyway! They're doing this just to kill my publicity!

DOUGLAS: He can't do this to me! Even if he *is* my father,—he can't do this to me! Horning in on my publicity. Why, the—big stiff.

JOAN: Douglas!

DOUGLAS: Well, he is! He is! Jumping on the bandwagon now after the way I've worked on this!

JOAN: I know what I'll do—I'll have a baby, that's what I'll do! I'll have a baby!

DOUGLAS: I'll help you! That's what we'll do—I'll have a baby—let 'em try and top that!

THE CURTAINS ARE CLOSING

MAJESTIC SAILS AT MIDNIGHT

"Debts"

REPRESENTATIVES OF ENGLAND, ITALY, GERMANY, AND FRANCE:

(*Verse*)

England and Italy and Germany and France
We came here to discuss the debts,
And we're leaving with no regrets,
For England and Italy and Germany and France,
We have more than reached our aim
And we're mighty glad we came:
(*Chorus*)
We've had a lovely conference
With the U.S.A.
We'll pay our debts in silver and
We'll be glad to pay
In a month or two, we think
We can pay our debts in zinc
And the next year we'll begin
Paying off what's left in tin.
Oh how we love America
For she never makes a fuss,
That's why we love America
And America loves us.
We'll tell our countries what we did
And they're bound to say
"If you think we could
Pay them off in wood
Go back to the U.S.A."
(STATUE OF LIBERTY *steps off pedestal and sings.*)
STATUE OF LIBERTY:
England and Italy and Germany and France
Here's some news that you ought to know,
Off the Gold Standard we must go
Like England and Italy and Germany and France,
We are going to inflate
And we're very glad to state:
(*Chorus*)
Let the pound go up
The franc go up
The mark go up as well
Uncle Sam will be in Heaven
When the dollar goes to hell
For the stocks go up
The bonds go up

When no one wants to sell
Uncle Sam will be in Heaven
When the dollar goes to hell.
Of course, our friends won't like it
Across the ocean blue
But we can greet our neighbors
With a hey nonny nonny and a nuts to you
Let them call us this
And call us that
But while they scream and yell
Uncle Sam will be in Heaven
When the dollar goes to hell.

(*When she finishes the song she goes into "The Star Spangled Banner" chorus as the four representatives sing their chorus against it.*)

LONELY HEART COLUMN

"Lonely Heart"
Sung by Harry Stockwell

Miss Lonely Heart—what will I do?
I am a Lonely Heart—writing to you
Hoping that through your column you will drop me a
    line
Saying you know a Lonely Heart as lonely as mine.
Miss Lonely Heart—hear my appeal
You seem to know the way—lonely hearts feel,
That's why I'm writing and I'm asking for a reply,
That's why I'm hoping you know someone lonely as I.
I'm so blue returning to my lonely room
Every night, for nothing's quite as lonely as a lonely
    room.
Miss Lonely Heart—I'm by myself,
Watching the clock that stands—upon the shelf,
Hoping to hear the news that you know somebody who
Watches a clock, and whispers "I'm a Lonely Heart,
    too."

WORLD'S WEALTHIEST MAN CELEBRATES NINETY-FOURTH BIRTHDAY

Drawing Room of the Rockerfeller Estate at Pocantico Hills, New York. Oak-paneled walls, casement windows, and authentic Tudor furniture impressively suggest its aged owner.

MRS. ROCKEFELLER: Now children, you'd better go into the dining room until we're ready for you. Your father and I have something to talk over with Grandpa.

> (*The* CHILDREN *murmur a "Yes, Mother" and move toward the large double doors at the back, center.*)

You sure you know what to do? When you hear your father shout "Surprise" you all come in with the cake singing: "Happy Birthday, dear Grandpa, happy birthday to you!"

> (*Another "Yes, Mother."*)

JUNIOR: Not until you hear me shout "Surprise."

CHILDREN: Yes, Father, we understand. (*Exit.*)

MRS. ROCKEFELLER (*ad lib*): "Happy Birthday to you."

REPORTER (*offstage*): May we have just one more picture, Mr. Rockefeller. Turn your face a little more to the left—thank you very much.

MRS. JOHN D. JR.: Now, John, you've *got* to tell him, so you might as well make up your mind and get it over with.

JUNIOR: I know, my dear—but it isn't going to be easy.

MRS. JOHN D. JR.: Well, it's no use crying now. I don't know what you wanted to build that thing in the first place for.

REPORTER (*offstage*): Thank you, Mr. Rockefeller. Thank you very much.

JOHN D. (*enters*): That, gentlemen, is my recipe for a hearty old age.

A REPORTER: Mr. Rockefeller, have you a birthday message we can give to the public? Some *one* great thing you've learned from life?

JOHN D.: Well, sir, I'm 95 years old today, and a man learns a lot by the time he reaches that age.

> (*The* REPORTERS *laugh appreciatively.*)

I think the one great thing I've learned in my life, gentlemen, is to hold on to your money.

(*The* REPORTERS *write busily.*)

I've been through a lot of depressions in my time and the only thing I've learned is to sit tight. Sit tight and no foolishness. That's all.

THE REPORTERS: Thank you, Mr. Rockefeller.

JOHN D.: Oh, just a minute, boys. Here's a little something for you to remember my birthday with. (*He plunges his hand into his pocket, brings out a handful of silver, and distributes a single piece to each reporter.*)

A REPORTER: Why, Mr. Rockefeller—these are nickels!

JOHN D.: Well, it's been a pretty tough year for all of us.

(REPORTER *exits.*)

Well, my dears, they took some very nice pictures of me. Very nice pictures indeed.

MRS. JOHN D. JR.: I'm so glad. You always take a good picture, Father.

JOHN D.: It's been a very nice birthday, hasn't it?

MRS. JOHN D. JR.: Lovely. And it isn't over either. The day's young yet. I always say you never can tell *what* a birthday has in store for you until the very end.

JOHN D.: Yes I always like birthdays. Junior! Don't you think that was a good birthday message I gave them? Sit tight and hold on to your money?

JUNIOR: Yes. Yes, indeed, Father.

JOHN D.: Pretty nice thing to be able to say on your 95th birthday the family fortune is still intact, eh, Junior? 'Tisn't everybody that can say so.

JUNIOR: Yes. Yes, indeed.

JOHN D.: And the only way to do it is to put your money in the ground. *Oil*! I never held to any of these real estate speculations even when land was cheap. No sir!

MRS. JOHN D. JR.: O, now I don't know, Father—*some* real estate is good.

JOHN D.: *None* of it's any good. None of it. You take my advice. You let the other fellows put up the buildings—

(*There is a slight pause during which* MRS. JOHN D. JR. *motions frantically to her husband and whispers huskily: "Go on! Tell him! Go on!"*)

JOHN D. (*catching the last of one of her frantic gestures, and interpreting it in his own way*): Na! Na! Na! Ah!! Now children—you haven't been going about and spending a lot of money on a birthday present for me, have you?

JUNIOR (*choking*): Why—why—

JOHN D.: Lot of foolishness, I always said. Couple of handkerchiefs and a pair of socks is a good enough present for anybody.

MRS. JOHN D. JR. (*forcing the issue*): Oh, but not good enough for *you*, Father. John's got a *real* birthday present for you! Haven't you, John!

JUNIOR: Yes.

JOHN D.: Well, that's very nice now, Junior. What is it?

JUNIOR: Radio City.

JOHN D.: Well, I'm sure I appreciate it, Junior, but you take it back to the store and get your money. I never listen to 'em— and they're always getting out of order, anyway. Wouldn't have one in the house. Wouldn't have one on the premises.

MRS. JOHN D. JR. (*as* JUNIOR *stands helpless*): But Father, this isn't a radio—it's *Radio City*!

JOHN D.: Radio City?

JUNIOR: Yes.

JOHN D.: What's that?

JUNIOR: Why—it's a *city*, Father!

JOHN D.: A city? Whose city?

JUNIOR: It's *your* city. *All* yours! It's my birthday present to you! (*The* OLD MAN *stares at him unbelievably.*)

MRS. JOHN D. JR.: Tell Father about it, John.

JUNIOR: O, it's a wonderful thing, Father! Got the largest theatre in the world in it! 6500 seats! Wait till you see it!

MRS. JOHN D. JR.: Wait till he takes a peek at that stage, eh, John? With the hydraulic curtain and the rising orchestra? And the ushers in full dress!

JOHN: And it's got another awful cute theatre in it too, Father. It's only got 3000 seats. We call it Dingbat up at Radio City.

MRS. JOHN D. JR.: And the office building, John—

JUNIOR: Eighty stories high, Father—and a sunken plaza with gardens and fountains.

MR. & MRS. JOHN D. JR.: Doesn't it sound wonderful? (*A pregnant pause, then:*)

JOHN D.: Junior—you sell it *right* back to whoever sold it to you! Somebody took you over!

JUNIOR: But—I didn't buy it from anybody? I built it myself.

JOHN D.: You *what*?

MRS. JOHN D. JR.: He built it for *you*, Father—as a birthday present!

JOHN D.: Now—wait a minute. One minute, please. You mean to say this thing is all *built*?

MRS. JOHN D. JR.: O, yes. You really can't miss it if you walk past 50th Street and Sixth Avenue. It's a lot of buildings and it says Radio City. You can't miss it.

JOHN D.: What did it cost?

JUNIOR: Well, we don't know yet, Father—they're still building. At first we figured about 50 million but as we got into it we—

MRS. JOHN D. JR.: They've really been very thrifty. They were going to build an Opera House, too—but they just held themselves back!

JOHN D.: How many tenants in that 80 story building?

JUNIOR: Well, there's just ourselves and the ushers and a man named Arthur Vogel for the time being—

JOHN D.: Those theatres making money?

MRS. JOHN D. JR.: Well, you see, Father it's kind of an out of the way place—50th Street and 6th Avenue. And we've just had the Jewish Holidays, too.

JOHN D.: Junior—that's no birthday present! That's a dirty trick!

JUNIOR: Why, Father!

JOHN D.: Don't "Why, Father" me. Giving me this Radio City for a birthday present! Why didn't you buy me Muscle Shoals, too? Eighty story building—6500 seats—how could you *do* such a thing? Answer me that! How could you ever get into such a thing in the first place?

(JUNIOR *stands helpless.*)

JOHN D. (*ad lib*): "Poppycock."

MRS. JOHN D. JR.: Go ahead and tell him, John. Tell him the truth! It really wasn't his fault at all. He didn't know *what* they were building until the first theatre was all done, did you?

JUNIOR: I thought it was something for the Red Cross for a whole year.

MRS. JOHN D. JR.: Go ahead and tell him the whole thing, John. (*A pause.*)

JOHN D.: 6500 seats! Well?

JUNIOR: Well, about two years ago it was raining. I was sitting in my office. Sometimes I think if it hadn't been raining that afternoon the whole thing wouldn't have happened. I was just about to leave when my secretary said Roxy wanted to see me.

JOHN D.: What's that?

JUNIOR: Well, it's—well, he's rather hard to explain, Father.

MRS. JOHN D. JR.: He's a man who goes around building big theatres for people.

JOHN D.: Ought to be put away, a man like that.

MRS. JOHN D. JR.: O, he isn't dangerous. Once he sees the cement being mixed he's as gentle as a child.

JUNIOR: Anyway, he came in and said wouldn't it be wonderful if New York City had the largest theatre in the world. I said: "Yes, it certainly would"—and he went away. Just like that it happened. I didn't think much about it at the time—never even mentioned it at home that night, did I?

MRS. JOHN D. JR.: First thing *I* knew about Radio City was when John kept coming home with mud on his shoes.

JUNIOR: Well, Father, the next thing I knew there I was standing in a big excavation on 50th Street and Sixth Avenue. After that the only thing left to do was to paint the elevated station aluminum.

MRS. JOHN D. JR.: He even tried to turn it over to the Government for a War Memorial, but they never even answered his letter.

JUNIOR: That was when I got the idea of giving it to you as a birthday present, Father.

(*Utter silence.*)

(*The* OLD MAN *is trying to speak but seems to be having some difficulty in making sounds issue. When he does speak his voice is pretty terrifying.*)

JOHN D.: But the buildings—letting the buildings go up—you must have known about that, didn't you?

JUNIOR: Well yes, Father, I did.

JOHN D.: Oh you did, you did well. Why didn't you tell me about this months ago—months ago!

JUNIOR (*tearfully*): I wanted it to be a surprise, Father—a surprise!

(*At the word "surprise," the double doors at the back are flung open, and the children appear bearing a huge birthday cake on the top of which is an enormous replica of Radio City—all lit up. They come blithely into the room singing:*)

Happy Birthday to you,
Happy Birthday to you,
Happy Birthday, dear grandpa,
Happy Birthday to you!

(GIRL *gives cake knife to* ROCKEFELLER SR. *who rises and crosses towards* JOHN D. JUNIOR *who flees in terror.*)

CURTAIN

THE FUNNIES

"The Funnies"
Sung by Marilyn Miller and Ensemble

Sunday is Sunday to my family
But Sunday is not simply Sunday to me,
For Sunday's the one day when I love to see
The Funnies.
Breakfast is nothing of which you can boast,
But breakfast to me isn't coffee and toast,
It's coffee and toast and what I love the most—
The Funnies.
(*Chorus*)
Oh—I love the Funnies
I couldn't go—without the Funnies.
A cup o' coffee to my lips
And in between the sips
The papers with the capers that are in the comic strips,
Which means I'm simply mad about,
I mean I couldn't do without—the Funnies.
Oh—in my pajamas,

I love to read the Katzenjammers
A little coffee in a cup
And "Bringing Father Up,"
I'm dippy over "Skippy" and his little yeller pup
Which means I'm simply mad about
I mean I couldn't do without—the Funnies.
I'm not concerned with the news of the day,
The stories of who murdered who,
And as for what Mr. Hearst has to say,
I have no need of—I don't want to read of
The Dempseys or the Tunneys,
The wealthy daughters or the sonnies
The news about the lovely trips
That people take in ships,
I'd rather read about the people in the comic strips,
Which means I'm simply mad about,
I mean I couldn't do without—
The Funnies.

GREEN PASTURES STARTS
THIRD ROAD SEASON

At rise: WOMAN *at ironing board.* MAN, *book in hand—pacing and reading* Hamlet *aloud.*

MAN: To be or not to be; that is the question; whether it is nobler in the mind to suffer the slings and arrows of outrageous fortune, or to arms against a sea of troubles and by opposing end them, to die—to sleep, no more.

WOMAN: What the hell do you think you're doing?

MAN: Woman shut up! You is breaking my mood!

WOMAN: Lucky I ain't broke your head.

MAN: Ah fair Ophelia—nymph in they orizons be all my sins remembered. Get thee to a nunnery—why wouldst thou be a breeder of sinners? We are arrant knaves all. Believe none of us. Get thee to a nunnery.

WOMAN: I'm getting mighty fed up with all this Shakespeare stuff.

MAN: How you expect me to caputure the essence of this if you keep on interfering with me all the time. What's the matter with you?

"To Be or Not to Be"
Sung by Ethel Waters

(*Verse*)
Listen Misten Actor,
Listen 'til I'm through—
Since you spoke that one line in *Green Pastures*
There ain't no holding you;
Now you speak of Hamlet,
And you says to me,
That the question is to be or not to be.
For years you ain't been home much,
And now you're on your way
To be a Harlem Hamlet,
Well, here's what I've got to say
(*Chorus*)
To be or not to be
That's what you've got to be,
To be or not to be my man
To do or not to do,
That's what you've got to do
I mean to do the things you can.
I hear you speaking of Ophelia
But I know you don't mean me,
'Cause if you think I'll get me to a nunnery—you're
crazy,
Because I'm not that kind
So just make up your mind
To be or not to be my man.
(*2nd Chorus*)
To be or not to be
That's what you've got to be
To be or not to be my man.
To do or not to do,
That's what you've got to do
I mean to do the things you can

I know John Barrymore played Hamlet
In a way it should be played
But you're no Barrymore,
Let's call a spade a spade—remember
For years we've been apart
Take off your tie and start
To be or not to be my man.

ROTOGRAVURE SECTION: EASTER PARADE ON FIFTH AVENUE—1883

"Easter Parade"
Sung by Marilyn Miller and Clifton Webb

(*Verse*)
WEBB:
   Never saw you look
   Quite so pretty before—
   Never saw you dressed
   Quite so lovely—what's more,
   I could hardly wait
   To keep our date
   This lovely Easter morning,
   And my heart beat fast
   As I came through the door—for
(*Chorus*)
   In your Easter bonnet
   With all the frills upon it
   You'll be the grandest lady in the Easter Parade.
   I'll be all in clover
   And when they look you over
   I'll be the proudest fellow in the Easter Parade.
   On the Avenue—Fifth Avenue
   The Photographers—will snap us
   And you'll find that you're
   In the rotogravure.

Oh—I could write a sonnet
About your Easter bonnet
And of the girl I'm taking to the Easter Parade.
(*Chorus*)

MILLER:

In my Easter bonnet
With all the frills upon it
I'll be the grandest lady in the Easter Parade.

WEBB:

I'll be all in clover
And when they look you over
I'll be the proudest fellow in the Easter Parade.

MILLER:

On the Avenue—Fifth Avenue
The photographers will snap us

WEBB:

And you'll find that you're
In the rotogravure.
Oh—I could write a sonnet
About your Easter bonnet
And of the girl I'm taking to the Easter Parade.

CURTAIN

END OF ACT ONE

ACT TWO

METROPOLITAN OPERA OPENS IN OLD TIME SPLENDOR

"Metropolitan Opening"

ALL:

Who are we
And what are we doing here?
Wait and see
We're going to make it clear,
We're the new millionaires
Who will sit in the chairs
That were once occupied
By the old millionaires.
Where are they?
The people who had the cash—
They can't pay
They lost it all in the Crash,
Their sables and their foxes
Have all been put in pawn
So we bought up their boxes
For the opera must go on!
And instead of Mr. Belmont, and the others who have
    gone
There's Mr. Rubin
A Cuban—
Who runs a delicatessen store,
The man which
A sandwich—made famous,
And there is Mr. Klein
You've seen the sign
On Union Square,
The women's wear
He sells made him a millionaire
And a First Night Patron of the Opera.
The most expensive box

Was bought by William Fox,
A fellow named Nat Lewis
Who deals in ties and socks
Will occupy the chair
A Vanderbilt sat upon
He'll be there
To help them all carry on.
Those gentlemen who force you
To buy their Scotch and Rye
Are in the diamond horse-shoe,
Would you like to know just why?
It seems a large delegation
Couldn't get a donation
And hope was gone
And so the racket
Said we will back it
They came across because the opera must go on.

ANNOUNCER: Well, well, here we are on the air again, folks, broadcasting from Box 19 in the famous Diamond Horseshoe of the Metropolitan Opera House in New York City. Yessir—it's a great sight in here. In case any of you unseen listeners are tuning in on this program for the first time tonight, I want to tell you that every night at this hour we bring beauty into millions of American homes by broadcasting opera. As you know, the Metropolitan Opera Company last year was only enabled to complete its season by broadcasting once a week—but *this* year, in order to open at *all*, it was necessary for the radio to take over the Metropolitan. This we were able to do through the courtesy of our various sponsors, and each night's opera is brought to you by a representative product—the sponsor's one idea being to bring beauty into your home. Tonight's opera is *Rigoletto*—the sponsor, Mueller's Miracle Mustard Sauce for Steak—and since that ever popular radio attraction, the Williams Family, is also on at this time, we bring you them, too, as part of the program. We have also the honor of having with us tonight, Mons. Peppiton—the world famous Parisian chef—the *discoverer* of Mueller's Miracle Mustard Sauce. So gather 'round the radio, folks. Put down your sewing, Mother. Lean back in your easy chair, Father.

Mueller's Miracle Mustard Sauce brings you simultaneously *Rigoletto*—the Williams Family—and Mons. Peppiton!

MONSIEUR PEPPITON: My dear father was a famous Parisian chef. I too also am a famous Parisian chef. For many years I try to make ze perfect sauce for steak—but always never, never, never, ze perfect sauce do I achieve! Night and day I work—every sauce I try—sixty steaks I spoil—But then one day, AHA!—I have ze perfect sauce for all ze whole world to see. It is ze sauce for steak that millions of American housewives will choose.

MOTHER WILLIAMS: Darling please come in to dinner, all the steak is getting cold.

RUTHIE: No—I don't want any—I'm sick of eating steak!

MOTHER WILLIAMS: Ruthie, come right in this minute, must I have your father bring you.

RUTHIE: O—I want some chicken—I'm so sick of steak!

FATHER WILLIAMS: Ruthie! —do as mother says!

RUTHIE: I'm sick of steak!

MONSIEUR PEPPITON: Ah! What do we find here, my friends! It is ze typical American family about to go in for ze evening meal. Ze little girl she cries she does not want to eat steak! Why? Because it is tasteless—Always ze same! Steak! Steak! Steak! But if ziz lady—the mother—if ziz lady used Mueller's Miracle Mustard Sauce—it would be different!

ANNOUNCER: Radio friends—this little drama you are listening to might be any household in America—Once every week the American family eats steak, and when they do the same old family spat occurs. Mother bursts into tears, Father is grumpy—Daughter is sent to bed—and the steak is thrown out. But Mrs. Williams, the mother you've been listening to, is a wise woman. Unknown to Father or Daughter she is serving the steak tonight with Mueller's Miracle Mustard Sauce. Ah! There they go into the dining room! There they go.

RUTHIE:
   Momma! Momma! Momma!

MOTHER WILLIAMS:
   Surprise! Surprise!

FATHER WILLIAMS:
   This steak is great! This steak is great!

RUTHIE:
   Momma, it's great! Momma, it's great!

MOTHER WILLIAMS:
>Surprise! Surprise!

FATHER WILLIAMS:
>This steak is great! This steak is great!

MOTHER WILLIAMS:
>Surprise! Surprise!

RUTHIE:
>This steak is great!

ALL:
>She used Mueller's Miracle Mustard Sauce for Steak.
>The original Mueller's Mustard Sauce for Steaks.

MONSIEUR PEPPITON:
>The one and only Mueller's Mustard Sauce for Steak.

ANNOUNCER: Ladies and gentlemen. You have been listening to *Rigoletto.* Tomorrow night the Metropolitan brings you *Madame Butterfly,* through the courtesy of A.G. Spaulding, manufacturers of Spaulding's famous Athletic Supporter. Good night.

UNKNOWN NEGRO LYNCHED BY FRENZIED MOB

"Supper Time"
Sung by Ethel Waters

Supper Time—
I should set the table
'Cause it's Supper Time—
Somehow I ain't able
'Cause that man o' mine—ain't comin' home no more.
Supper Time—
Kids will soon be yellin'
For their Supper Time,
How'll I keep from tellin'
That that man o' mine—ain't comin' home no more.
How'll I keep explainin'
When they ask me where he's gone—
How'll I keep from cryin'

When I bring their supper on?
How can I remind them
To pray at their humble board—
How can I be thankful
When they start to thank the Lord—God!
Supper Time—
I should set the table
'Cause it's Supper Time—
Somehow I ain't able
'Cause that man o' mine—ain't comin' home no more—
No more—no more!

GANDHI GOES ON NEW HUNGER STRIKE

The curtains part to disclose a restaurant in India.

Seated at a table downstage right is GANDHI, *clad only in a loin cloth, busily spinning. Set up in front of him is a movie camera with "Universal Newsreel" lettered across it and the sound apparatus. The cameraman and his assistant are busily arranging to take the shot.*

NICK: I can't get it.

CAMERAMAN: Come on fellows give us a break, will you? Step aside, you'll get a chance to see it, step aside. (*Pushes crowd to one side.*) Oh Mr. Gandhi. Please. That's fine Mr. Gandhi. Now you just hold that a minute. Ready Nick?

NICK: O.K.

CAMERAMAN: No wait I got it. (*Crossing behind camera to boys.*) Hey do you fellows want to be in the picture with Mr. Gandhi?

CROWD: Yes.

CAMERAMAN: Well, come on over here. Take your plates and stand around Mr. Gandhi and keep eating. Mr. Gandhi is on a new kind of hunger strike in a public restaurant. He's going to torture himself while he starves. O.K. camera. (*Crosses and kneels downstage of camera.*) Now, Mr. Gandhi—you look around at them and shake your head No. You're on a hunger strike and you're hungry as hell, but all the food in the world doesn't bother you, see? That's what we want.

(GANDHI *looks around, sniffs, and smiles a toothless smile.*) Now you boys eat some more. That's it! Now you smile, Mr. Gandhi—a great big hungry smile. Fine! That's the stuff. Now how about a few words, Mr. Gandhi? These news-reels go all over the world—millions of people will see this—how about a message to the people of the world? (*He places a microphone in front of Gandhi and gestures for him to speak.*)

GANDHI (*into the microphone*): People of North America, People of South America, People of Australia, People of Asia, People of Africa, People of Great Britain, France, Germany and Russia—hello!

CAMERAMAN: Okay! Thank you, Mr. Gandhi. Lots of luck. I hope you make it. Thank you, boys. Now let's get a picture of the viceroy of India eating. (*They exit.*)

NATIVE: Mahatma, there's a lady outside to see you.

GANDHI: Who is it?

NATIVE: Aimee Semple McPherson.

AIMEE: Bless you, Brother! Bless you, Sister! Bless this restaurant! Bless all India! Hallelujah! (*Turning.*) Ah, there you are, Mr. Gandhi! Just call me Sister Aimee!

GANDHI: The Four Square Gospel Lady?

AIMEE: Yes, sir. The Four Square Gospel—praise be to Glory!

GANDHI: Well, whaddye know!

AIMEE: Waiter—the regular dollar and a quarter dinner—with jello! (*Sitting.*) Now, you go right on starving, Brother Gandhi—it won't interfere with my appetite a bit.

GANDHI: This restaurant has the best food in India—that's why I starve here.

AIMEE: Bless you, Brother. (*Calling.*) Shake a leg on that dinner, boys.

(*The food comes on—ad lib from* AIMEE.)

NATIVE (*entering*): Mahatma—there are two untouchables outside.

GANDHI: Tell them to get in touch with me next week.

AIMEE: Of course, there's one thing I don't understand about this country. Untouchables. If they're—well, if they're untouchable—how can they possibly have children?

GANDHI: Sister Aimee—the population of India is three hundred million—they must have worked it out someway!

(*The* NATIVE *enters again.*)

NATIVE: Passive Resistance report, Mahatma! There are five hundred people down the street lying in front of a street car. What are your orders?

GANDHI: Tell them to sit tight. The British won't dare run over them.

(*Screams off-stage.*)

My mistake.

AIMEE: Brother Gandhi—do you know why I'm in India?

GANDHI: Don't tell me you've been kidnapped again!

AIMEE: To carry on the good work, Brother. To carry on the good work! And last night there wasn't an empty seat in the house. Praise be to glory.

GANDHI: Is that good?

AIMEE: Good! Why, we did seven hundred dollars more than that picture *She Done Him Wrong* across the street!

GANDHI: Say . . . do you know Mae West?

AIMEE: Brother, that way madness lies!

GANDHI: O, I wouldn't go too far—I'd just like to take her out once—for the hell of it!

AIMEE: As far as I can find out, you keep going on these hunger strikes and all you get out of it is indigestion.

GANDHI: O, I have my fun.

AIMEE: O, you do. Well, you know where you're going to end up. In the gutter!

GANDHI: Well, a man's a saint or he isn't a saint.

AIMEE: Oh, don't give me that. I'm a saint. But you don't catch me giving anything away for nothing. Who's your publicity man?

GANDHI: Publicity man?

AIMEE: Who's your business manager?

GANDHI: I haven't got any business manager.

AIMEE: Three hundred million followers and all you get out of it—is an appetite! Listen, if you handled yourself right you could be one of the biggest box-office atractions in the world—You're bigger than Mae West right now and you don't know it.

GANDHI: I am? Where?

AIMEE: Brother, there's a cool million waiting for you to come along and pick it up. Don't be a sucker all your life. Look all *alone* I gross two grand a night all thru the Middle West. If we hooked up together as a team we'd triple the business. With the spiel I'll give 'em and the way you look—it's a natural. I promise you three grand a night! I promise you five grand a night.

GANDHI: Hallelujah!

AIMEE: Hallelujah! O, dear—there goes that old shoulder strap again. Have you got a safety pin on you?

GANDHI: No.

AIMEE: O, yes you have.

GANDHI: Well, it has sort of a sentimental value.

AIMEE: Gimme the pin and stop interrupting. I can see the act now. Dark stage. I come out all in white. Two white spotlights and then I go into five minutes of straight revival stuff. "Hallelujah." "Praise Be To Glory"—the whole works—with the chorus in back of me. Then your introduction. Muffled drums off-stage and the cornetist plays "taps." The curtains part then you come on.

GANDHI: Whee!

AIMEE: You're in a green spotlight. They see you—they look at you—Say—can you do anything besides starve?

GANDHI: I don't know. I never tried. Why?

AIMEE: Well, you've got to give 'em something. You can't just sit there. Come on—think—it's important.

GANDHI: Well—I used to sing with the Oxford Glee Club.

AIMEE: Do you remember anything you sang?

GANDHI: Yes.

AIMEE: Let's hear it.

GANDHI (*singing*): "Pale hands I loved"—

AIMEE: That's no good. Can't you sing something they can whistle as they go out?

GANDHI: Say—did you see that picture *42nd Street*?

AIMEE: Yes.

(*Put in song.* GANDHI *sings.*)

That's great! That'll panic 'em! Now we got the makings of an act. All we need is a good finish and we're set!

GANDHI: Sister Aimee I've got a great finish if you could do a little dance step with me.

AIMEE: Is it very hard?

GANDHI: I can show it to you in a minute. Boys, give me Shuffle Off to Buffalo.

(BOYS *sing.*)

AIMEE: I got it Brother Gandhi. Big finish, Mahatma. Hallelujah!

GANDHI: Hallelujah!

AIMEE: Hallelujah!

GANDHI: Hallelujah!

BOTH: Praise be to Glory.

BLACKOUT

REVOLT IN CUBA

"Rumba Number Dance"

NOEL COWARD, NOTED PLAYWRIGHT, RETURNS TO ENGLAND

The curtains part to disclose Noel Coward's apartment in the Waldorf-Astoria.

The room is in wild disarray—the kind of hectic jumbling together of sofa pillows, White Rock bottles and pages of manuscript, that bespeak a farewell party to the host—a party that partied him right into his stateroom. What they have left behind is a pretty terrible mess.

Outside one of the windows at the back, a WINDOW-CLEANER, *strapped to the outside of the building, is cleaning the windows.*

IST BELL BOY: Boy! This must have been some party all right all right.

2ND BELL BOY: I came on at eight o'clock this morning and it was still going strong. The whole bunch of them went right down to the boat to see him off. About three hundred people it looked like.

1ST BELL BOY: Jeez, when I left last night they were still pouring in. Everybody in New York. Tallulah Bankhead, George Gershwin, Edna Ferber, Alec Woollcott—

2ND BELL BOY: I saw 'em, I saw 'em. Gee they left an awful lot of junk here.

1ST BELL BOY: Say he gave you a couple of passes to *Design for Living*, last week, didn't he?

2ND BELL BOY: Yeah.

1ST BELL BOY: What was it about?

2ND BELL BOY: Oh it was about three people who couldn't do anything to each other.

(MRS. FISCHER *enters. The* BOYS *start guiltily.*)

MRS. FISCHER: Well what are you boys doing here?

2ND BELL BOY: Oh just sort of looking around, Mrs. Fischer.

MRS. FISCHER: Well just sort of get out of here before I report you to the bell captain.

BOYS: Yes, Mrs. Fischer.

(*The* BOYS *hastily beat a retreat.* MRS. FISCHER *looks disdainfully around her at the shambles and picks up a newspaper.*)

MRS. FISCHER (*reading*): "Mr. Noel Coward's large English public is eagerly awaiting his return to London." I wish Mr. Noel Coward's large English public could take a look at the way he left that bathroom.

(ELLA *enters.*)

ELLA: My Gawd! They sure said farewell to him.

MRS. FISCHER: No one but an English playwright would leave a mess like this.

ELLA: Yes, ma'am, them boys sure do leave messes behind 'em when they go. You remember that Mr. Lonsdale we had up in 1410?

MRS. FISCHER: It's beyond me why a hotel that won't take in dogs takes in any English playwright that comes along.

ELLA: Well, they're awful good tippers, Mrs. Fischer.

MRS. FISCHER: Good tippers! A man like Noel Coward disrupts the entire staff of a hotel.

ELLA: Why, I kinda liked that Mr. Coward. He never tried to disrupt *me*.

MRS. FISCHER: You better get started cleaning up, Ella.

ELLA: Yes ma'am. Mrs. Fischer, how do you mean disrupts the whole staff.

MRS. FISCHER: Well look at Aggie Reilly. Before that man Noel Coward came to this hotel, Aggie Reilly was as nice a girl and as good a chambermaid as we had. Look at her now.

ELLA: She ain't right in the head, is she?

MRS. FISCHER: Oh. She's right enough. She just saw Lynn Fontanne hanging around that's all.

(AGNES, *a maid of the hotel, enters with pillow-slips, sheets, and bath towels over her arm. Obviously a hotel chambermaid, her appearance is all the more startling therefore, in her looking astonishingly like Lynn Fontanne. The porcelain-white face, the carmine lips, the hair piled high on the forehead—above all, the slithering, sensuous walk, the intoxicating, liquid voice, proclaim at once that here is a little girl who has seen Lynn Fontanne a couple of times and has never gotten over it.*)

MRS. FISCHER: Aggie—you got the sheets for both beds and the towels for the bathroom?

AGGIE: Yes. A-ha! A-ha! A-ha! (*A low, gurgling, Fontanne laugh.*) White sheets. Smooth white dreams of divine debauchery that come up suddenly—like a channel swimmer. A-ha! A-ha! A-ha! (*Turns up.*) A-ha! A-ha! A-ha! Divine debauchery.

(*Again the low, gurgling Fontanne laugh, and* AGGIE *Fontannes it across the stage into the bedroom before the astonished* ELLA *and the disapproving* MRS. FISCHER.)

MRS. FISCHER: How do you like that?

ELLA: My goodness!

MRS. FISCHER: That's nothing—the whole hotel has gone Noel Coward. Wait till you take a look at Perlmutter.

ELLA: Perlmutter the waiter?

MRS. FISCHER: Best waiter in the place until that man Noel Coward gave him an autographed edition of his plays.

(*A waiter,* HENRY PERLMUTTER, *jauntily enters the room. He is dressed in the regulation waiter's outfit, but there is immediately something different about Henry. What it is, is immediately discernible when he speaks—for Henry sounds more like Noel Coward than Noel Coward.*)

HENRY: Good morning, Mrs. Fischer. A good, decadent, morning to you.

(MRS. FISCHER *shoots him a murderous look.*)

MRS. FISCHER: Now I'll thank you to keep a civil tongue in your head, Perlmutter. It's about time you came in to clear away the table.

PERLMUTTER: Lafe, Mrs. Fischer—lafe has a petulant way of interfering with the clearing away of tables, you know.

MRS. FISCHER: O, it has, has it!

PERLMUTTER: Lafe, I may add, is a medieval megaphone—a prolonged prophylactic.

ELLA: Yeah man!

(*Suddenly, there is a tap at the window—they* ALL *turn as the window-cleaner opens the window and leans in.*)

WINDOW-CLEANER: I say, dear boy, have you the time?

HENRY: It's eleven o'clock. In China it's eight. Pot-bellied coolies slither through the oriental dusk toward unpremeditated seductions. In India it's eleven. The Taj Mahal gleams like a wet water hydrant in the moonlight.

WINDOW-CLEANER: Deathless dreamer!

AGGIE (*calling in from the bedroom*): Henry, my sweet, is that you?

HENRY: Yes—child of the century.

AGGIE: A-ha! A-ha! A-ha! (*She appears in the doorway—and gives the gurgling Fontanne laugh.*)

HENRY: Python—Gioconda!

AGGIE: I'm about to turn over the mattresses, darling. Would you like to help? It might be fun, you know.

HENRY: I should adore it!

(*Crossing to* ELLA.)

"Destiny's Tot."

(*Tap on head.*)

(*Crossing, sees* MRS. FISCHER, *to her, bows.*)

"Dear lady."

(*Tap on head.*)

MRS. FISCHER: Now I'll be God damned if I'm going to stand for much more of *that*! (*She goes angrily into the bedroom.*)

PERLMUTTER: Succulent paradox!

AGGIE: Each to his own manger, my canine friend.

(ELLA *starts to throw book in bucket.*)

PERLMUTTER: Ella may I ask what you're casting aside like a spendthrift Messiah?

ELLA: Some kind of old book—was on the floor here.

PERLMUTTER: Let me see it. (ELLA *hands it over. He opens the book and reads:*)

"Noel Coward—His Diary." Temperamental puss. Why, he must have forgotten it. Dear Noel! He does get around a bit. Come my blossom: Listen.

(*He reads.*)

"March 27th—Awoke at seven—a pale gardenia-like hour. Sloughed off my pajamas like a snake and wriggled into my bath. One grows positively scaly in America. Alec Woollcott called at eight—how I adore Alec—dear, sweet avalanche of condescension. He is doing an impression of me for *Cosmopolitan* and called to ask me where I was born. I said: 'Out of the wedlock, into the here.' He laughed until I hung up. Tempestuous sprite. Breakfast. I adore breakfast. It is like I am glad when it comes—I am glad when it goes. Max Gordon arrived at ten. I adore Max—he is the potted palms in the vestibule of my morning—green—flowering—alive—but nevertheless, alas,—potted. He said—'Noel—Lunt's make-up is wrong for the part.' I said: 'Max, the trouble with Alfred's face is that it hasn't been lived in.' He laughed until I went to rehearsal. I adore rehearsals. Dear Lynn and Alfred are going to be too magnificent! How fortunate I have written myself the best part. Elsa Maxwell called to take me to a party I am giving for her which she is giving for me. Everyone there. I adore everyone. They laughed until I left. Tumbled into bed like a string of beads and scribbled an act. I adore writing in bed. So—may I suggest—private. Turned out the light at midnight and let blackness kiss me. I must write a play someday to be done entirely in bed—in the dark. It could be an American *Cavalcade*—! Lay for a while thinking idly of Mussolini—! Black-skirted rascal—I adore him. To sleep."

AGGIE: "Ah!"

MRS. FISCHER: Divine, my pet. Too envy-making! (*Holding up a pair of shorts.*) Can either of you effortless charmers tell me whose gauntlet of chastity this is?

ELLA (*speaking for the first time*): The Duke of Westminster's, I suppose—it always is.

MRS. FISCHER: Fabulous tid-bit!

ELLA (*looking at the shorts*): He must have been a very little man.

MRS. FISCHER: Do you mind very much, Ella, if I tell you that little men to me are like falling from a great height—you bounce back to reality with qualms that you step on—like beetles.

ELLA: Or opera hats.

MRS. FISCHER: Quite.

PERLMUTTER (*angrily shutting the book*): Second rate Lonsdale—hardly Noel Coward.

AGGIE: Coward-climbers. Somerset Maughamers!

PERLMUTTER: Come my blemish. Sit. Heigh-ho I always say. What do you always say?

ELLA: White chimneys throw me into an ecstasy of passion.

MRS. FISCHER: Anything white!

(*Business.*)

PERLMUTTER (*wheeling to* AGGIE): I have a friend who has a dog.

AGGIE: I have a friend who *hasn't* a dog.

PERLMUTTER: Take the good with the bad. Ha!

(*Business.*)

ELLA: Natives of Bangkok have a curious custom. They don't eat.

MRS. FISCHER: How greedy!

(*Business.*)

PERLMUTTER: Sting sting sting—like a swinging door.

MRS. FISCHER: Snap snap snap—like a buttonhole.

AGGIE: Tell us more about your friends.

ELLA: What color?

PERLMUTTER: Pretty, very pretty.

MRS. FISCHER: Rudeness should be struck at regularly—like a convict ship.

(*Business with record.*)

PERLMUTTER: Oh! Oh!

WINDOW CLEANER: Situated as I am on the outside looking in, I have seen Mr. Coward quarrel a great many times. I have observed at this point in a quarrel, Mr. Coward always proposes a toast. May I suggest a toast?

PERLMUTTER: You are quite right. I am angry and ashamed.
MRS. FISCHER: I am hurt and humiliated. You are quite right.
AGGIE: Frightfully right, darling.
PERLMUTTER: To Noel Coward, whom we love so well, may he
find happiness and peace—and dignity again.
(ALL *drink*.)

CURTAIN

SOCIETY WEDDING OF THE SEASON OUTSIDE ST. THOMASES

"Our Wedding Day"

BRIDESMAIDS AND USHERS:
Ten little bridesmaids—ten little ushers
Marching side by side,
We gave our promises
To come to St. Thomases
And usher for the bridegroom
And bridesmaid for the bride.
From a hundred we were chosen,
And we're very glad we were
For this is the most important wedding
Of the Social Register.

It's a perfect match,
He was quite a catch
For the bridegroom is a member of the best of families
And the lovely bride,
On her mother's side,
Is a first or second cousin of the Astors, if you please.
Cholly Knickerbocker says this is a smart affair,
Cholly will be there—knee-deep in Vanderbilts,
It is plain to see
Why we're proud to be
The selected few—picked from "Who's Who"
To come here side by side

And usher for the bridegroom
And bridesmaid for the bride.

Now we must go into church
And see the groom and bride
Standing side by side
Knee-deep in Vanderbilts—
For the happy pair
Will be waiting there,
So we can't be late
We mustn't wait
The knot will soon be tied,
Champagne for the bridegroom
And babies for the bride.
(*Curtains part to reveal* BRIDEGROOM *and* BRIDE *in bed together.*)

BRIDEGROOM:

Wake up, sleepy head,
Tumble out of bed,
Wake up—don't be so slow,
Bells go ting-a-ling
Let's be hurrying
Off to church we must go:
(*Chorus*)
Sun's in the sky,
Don't you know why?
This is our wedding day,
Birds in their nest
Are singing their best
For we're going to be married.
Flowers are in bloom
And the perfume
Speaks of a bride's bouquet,
Spread the good news
With rice and old shoes,
For this is our wedding day!

BRIDE:

I'm so sleepy, dear,
Won't you make it clear
Why you're shaking me so,

Please, dear, cut it out,
What's it all about?
BRIDEGROOM:
Off to church we must go.

(*Repeat chorus*)

PRINCE OF WALES
RUMORED ENGAGED

The curtains part to disclose one of the drawing rooms at the Palace.
    Seated at a table downstage right, is the KING, *lost to the world and blissfully happy in the pasting of some new items in his beloved stamp collection. He chuckles and chortles in pure glee as he picks up a new item, eyes it lovingly for a moment, and then carefully and gently places it in the album.*
    A moment of this and the door opens to reveal the QUEEN. *She has evidently just come in, for she is togged out in coat, galoshes, umbrella, hat, and carries a folded newspaper under her arm.*
    QUEEN *enters and drops parasol on couch.*

KING: Back so soon, Mary? Been for a nice walk.
QUEEN (*pacing*): Nice walk my eye! Put away those stamps.
KING: Why, what's the matter, my dear?
QUEEN: Matter, have you read the papers this morning?
KING: Yes—I've read the *Daily Mail* and the *Express* and—
QUEEN (*paces*): I don't mean *those* papers. Have you read *Winchell*?
KING: No. Something juicy?
QUEEN (*crossing to desk*): Listen to this: (*She takes the paper from under her arm, unfolds it, and reads:*) "Things I Never Knew 'Til Now." That the Prince of Wales is really engaged and has been since that good-will tour a year or so ago. She's a South American girl and seems to have pretty good proof. Naughty—naughty. Nice talk!!
KING: I wouldn't pay any attention to it, my dear. They been saying the same kind of thing about David for years.
QUEEN: Not Winchell. Where's David?
KING: In his room, I guess.

(*The* QUEEN *crosses to desk.*)

Now Mary you're not going to—

QUEEN: I certainly am. (*She walks to the telephone and presses a button—then listens.*)

David! What are you doing? Well, put on a pair of trousers and come right up. No arguments, please! (*She hangs up.*) Naughty—naughty!

KING: O, pish. Boys will be boys, my dear.

QUEEN (*sits on settee*): Exactly. David is like all other young people these days. Moonlight and a couple of guitars and where are they?

(*The door opens and the* PRINCE *enters.*)

PRINCE: 'Lo, Father. Morning, Mother—what's up? Am I overdrawn at the bank again?

(KING *rises from behind desk.*)

QUEEN: No. David, you've never told us very much about that good-will tour you made to South America.

(*Business of* PRINCE.)

Have you been holding anything back?

PRINCE: I? Why should I be holding anything back?

KING: Wasn't any—funny business going on, was there?

PRINCE (*business with collar*): Why, Father! What do you mean?

QUEEN: He means *this*! (*She hands him the paper.*)

PRINCE (*he reads—then looks up*): Now, really, Mother—if *that's* what you made me get out of the bathtub for—! (*Drops paper.*)

KING: I told your mother it was all nonsense, but she insisted on—

QUEEN: You keep out of this George. Well David?

PRINCE: Why it's ridiculous!

KING: See, Mother?

QUEEN: No, I don't see. He's always been a little too anxious to go on these good-will tours to suit me anyway.

PRINCE: Well, very well then—whom do you believe—Winchell or me?

QUEEN: Well—Winchell is pretty good. (*To* KING.)

He hasn't been wrong about anyone *we* know for years.

KING (*up and to* PRINCE): Why can't you take the boy's word for it, Mother? If you're worried about those tours he makes it might be very nice for both of us to make a good-will tour next year! Eh David? Ever been to a place called Bali, David? I saw a picture called *Goona-Goona* the other night and it might be a good idea for *both* of us to run down there and create some good will. Eh, Mother?

QUEEN: You'll do nothing of the kind. I saw *Goona-Goona* too, you know. Twice. Anyway, there'll be no good-will tours for anybody in *this* house for the next couple of years if I have anything to say about it.

(KING *and* PRINCE *look.* KING *sits.*)

PRINCE: Suits me. Mind if I run along? I've got the Guards to review at twelve.

QUEEN: Not going out tonight, you know. You stay home.

PRINCE: What's up?

KING: The new American Ambassador is presenting his credentials.

PRINCE: O, for God's sake, who wants to see his old credentials! (*Sits on stool.*) I've got an appointment.

QUEEN: Never mind—you stay home for a change. New Ambassadors are funny about things like that. If you're not here he's liable to write home and they'll slap on another *gold* embargo.

PRINCE (*sulking*): Oh—

QUEEN: Well, do you suppose your father and I like it? Sitting around all night and talking about the N.R.A. and Samuel Insull?

KING: I wonder where they dig 'em up! Remember that fella Charley Dawes we had over there for a while?

QUEEN: Do I remember him? Puffing that damn pipe in my face all the time and his language. That's all I need. I guess we can consider ourselves lucky we didn't get that man Woodin over here with his violin.

PRINCE (*rises*): Couldn't we have dinner and take 'em to the Kit-Kat Club afterwards?

QUEEN: We certainly could not! If they think we've got money to spend on night clubs they'll want the war debt paid. I'm giving 'em cold cuts for dinner just on that account.

PRINCE: Sometimes I think we ought to pay that old War Debt and be done with it.

KING: Why David, I'm surprised.

QUEEN: That's what comes of running around with Duke Ellington. Well, you certainly stay home tonight.

PRINCE: You know what I wish? I wish I were the Duke of York.

LACKEY (*enters*): Mr. Ramsey MacDonald. (*Exits.*)

PRIME MINISTER (*entering*): Good morning, sir. Good morning, Madam.

(QUEEN *holds out her hand.*)

(PRIME MINISTER *crosses and kisses it.*)

PRIME MINISTER (*to* PRINCE): Good morning, sir.

PRINCE (*starts for door when the door opens and* PRIME MINISTER *appears in doorway*): Hello, Ramsey—when'd *you* get back?

PRIME MINISTER: This morning, sir. (*He bows.*)

QUEEN: Glad to see you, Ramsey.

PRINCE: I'll see you later, Ramsey. I've got to run. (PRINCE *exits.*)

KING (*sits*): Well, Ramsey, old top, what have you got to say for yourself?

QUEEN (*to* PRIME MINISTER) (*all eagerness*): Tell me—you can speak perfectly freely here—what about Mrs. Roosevelt? I want to know *everything*!

PRIME MINISTER (*pulls chair to settee*): Well, Madam, to tell you the truth, I didn't even *see* her while I was at the White House.

QUEEN: You didn't see her? Where was she?

PRIME MINISTER: Pretty busy woman. Does a lot of radio work. You know she's fifth now—Eddie Cantor, Jack Pearl—Ed Wynn—The Marx Brothers—and then Mrs. Roosevelt.

QUEEN (*leaning toward him*): Tell me, Ramsey—do you still read Walter Winchell's column?

PRIME MINISTER: Wouldn't be without it, Madam. Why?

QUEEN: Did you read that bit about the Prince this morning?

KING: Now, Mother, David just *told* you—

QUEEN: George!

(*To* PRIME MINISTER.)

Ramsey, what do you think? Of course, the Prince swears there's nothing in it.

PRIME MINISTER (*coughing*): Well, Madam—there probably *isn't* anything in it, of course, but I had a letter from the South American Embassy this morning.

QUEEN: What did it say?

PRIME MINISTER: Oh, nothing about the Prince—but it suggested this would be a very good time to lower the Tariff Rate to South America.

QUEEN: Lower the Tariff Rate to South America?

KING: Lower the Tariff Rate to South America. What does that mean?

PRIME MINISTER: That's what he said.

QUEEN: I don't like it George. Haven't we got *anything* on the South American Embassy?

PRIME MINISTER: Nothing as good.

(*The* PRINCE *enters.*)

PRINCE: Good-bye, Mother. Goodbye, Father. I shall be home for dinner.

QUEEN: You be home on time remember.

PRINCE: Yes, Mother. Good morning, Ramsey.

PRIME MINISTER: Good morning, sir.

PRINCE (*starts left*): Oh, by the way, Mother, about that South American business, I just happened to think. There's nothing to it. There was a certain girl down there.

QUEEN (*to* KING): I'm wrong, am I?

(*Picks up bag.*)

(KING *moves to settee.*)

PRINCE: Oh, but it couldn't be that girl, Mother—why I barely knew her—can't ever remember her name.

QUEEN: She remembered yours all right. When will you learn not to give your right name all the time!

PRINCE: But *nothing* happened. I had one dance with her—sat out another dance—and that's all. Never saw her again.

KING: Well, there's certainly nothing wrong with *that.*

QUEEN: Shows how much *you* know about South America. Where did you sit out that dance?

PRINCE: In the Garden.

QUEEN: Any guitars playing?

PRINCE: Oh, one or two. Why?

QUEEN (*to* PRIME MINISTER): There ought to be a law against playing guitars in a tropical climate. (*To* PRINCE.) Go on.

PRINCE: Well, we practiced the rhumba a couple of times.

(QUEEN *drops bag.* PRIME MINISTER *picks it up.*)

But it was all perfectly harmless, Mother! After that we just walked along and she told me the names of the various South American flowers. Then she suddenly ran off and I chased her for a while. Then we sat down under a tree. It was the last dance and we stayed out there talking. After a while it began to get cold and I put my arms around her. Come to think of it, I kissed her. Then we started talking about Havelock Ellis—and after that everything went black and I don't remember anything.

QUEEN: Ramsey! Lower the Tariff Rates to South America!

CURTAIN

JOSEPHINE BAKER STILL THE RAGE OF PARIS

People at tables. General chatter in French—waiters bustling in and out with drinks, etc., to various tables.

Enter JOSEPHINE BAKER—*her* CHAUFFEUR *and* PERSONAL MAID *behind her.*

Immediately, there is an excited buzz from the tables, and out of the murmur arises the whisper of: "Here she comes" "There's Josephine Baker" "That's her"—"That's Josephine Baker."

She proceeds to the center table, and gives a quick order to the CHAUFFEUR *and* MAID *who exit. The* HEAD WAITER *comes immediately to her table and takes her order which she gives in a low voice. Simultaneously, a new couple come on, sit down, and order.*

MISS BAKER's SECRETARY *comes on and proceeds to her table.*

CHAUFFEUR (*enters*): Mam'selle, votre secrétair, il attends la.
MISS BAKER: Send him in.

(CHAUFFEUR *exits.*)

THE SECRETARY: Good afternoon, Mademoiselle! I have your list of appointments.

(MISS BAKER *nods unenthusiastically. The* SECRETARY *consults her notebook.*)

Your appointments for tomorrow, Madame.
Rehearsal at the Folies Bergères at three.

(*A stifled groan from* MISS BAKER.)

Tea with the Countess Frogronard. . . .

MISS BAKER: You may make some excuse for me to the Countess and cancel it!

THE SECRETARY: But Mam'selle—the tea is being given in your honor!

MISS BAKER: You heard me. Cancel it.

THE SECRETARY: Cocktails at the Ritz at five with the Marquis De Gordios.

MISS BAKER: Cancel that, too.

THE SECRETARY: But Mam'selle! You cancelled yesterday's appointment with the Marquis!

MISS BAKER: And you can cancel tomorrow's, too.

THE SECRETARY: Mam'selle is not ill?

MISS BAKER: Mam'selle is all right. I'm just not in the mood for pink teas and cocktails today.

THE SECRETARY: Dinner with Mons. Phillips, and Mme. Chanel's party at Sarfreis after the show.

MISS BAKER: Cut 'em out. Cut 'em both out! That's what I said! Tell 'em anything you want to.

THE SECRETARY: Mam'selle!

MISS BAKER: You got your orders. Go on and leave me alone.

THE SECRETARY: Your cigarette, Mam'selle? (*Takes her cigarette.*)

MISS BAKER: *S'il vous plait. Au revoir, Albert.*

    (*The* SECRETARY *exits.*)

                    "Harlem on My Mind"

    (*Verse*)
      Emeralds in my bracelets
      Diamonds in my rings
      A Riviera chateau
      And a lot of other things
      And I'm blue, so blue, am I—
      Lots of ready money
      In seven different banks
      I counted up this morning
      It was about a million francs
      And I'm blue, so blue and I know why—
    (*Chorus*)
      I got Harlem on my mind
      And I'm longing to be lowdown

And my parlez-vous will not ring true
With Harlem on my mind
I've been dined and I've been wined
But I'm headin' for a show down
Cause I can't go on, from night till dawn
With Harlem on my mind
I go to dinner with a French Marquis
Each evening after the show
My lips begin to whisper mon chéri
But my heart keeps singing hi-de-ho
I've become too damned refined
And at night I hate to go down
To that high-falutin' flat
That Lady Mendel designed
With Harlem on my mind.

(*Tag chorus*)

And when I'm bathing in my marble tub
Each evening after the show
I get to thinking of the Cotton Club
And my heart starts chirping hi-de-ho
I've become too damned refined
And at night I hate to go down
To my flat with fifty million Frenchmen tagging
   behind
With Harlem on my mind.

BROADWAY GOSSIP COLUMN

"Through a Keyhole"
Sung by Clifton Webb

(*Verse*)

My mother was frightened by
A snoopy neighbor who poked his eye
Through mother's keyhole, and that is why
I am what I am today,
The man who looks through the keyholes along
   Broadway.

My job is to be alert
And get the lowdown on all the dirt,
The dirt that gathers on Broadway's skirt,
For that's how I earn my pay,
The man who looks through the keyholes along
    Broadway.
(*Chorus 1*)
Would you like to take a look
Through a keyhole?
If you'd like to get the in
On the latest bit of sin,
Have a look.
Life is like an open book
Through a keyhole.
If you wonder what occurs
Ere the lady gets her furs,
Have a look.
Angry people who think they're tough
Start to threaten, but that's a bluff—
They may holler but they won't stuff
Up their keyholes.
So come on and have a look
Through a keyhole.
If you'd like to get a view,
View of who is cheating who,
Have a look!
(*Chorus 2*)
Would you like to take a look
Through a keyhole?
If you want to get a load
Of the husband on the road,
Have a look.
Life is like an open book
Through a keyhole.
If you want to see New York
Getting ready for the stork,
Have a look.
Lovely ladies of every kind
Think they're safe when they pull the blind;
I see just what is on their mind

Through a keyhole.
So come on and have a look
Through a keyhole.
If you'd really like to know
How she got into the show,
Have a look!

SUPREME COURT HANDS
DOWN IMPORTANT DECISION

GIRLS AND BOYS:
At last, at last
Something new in the show at last
Something new if you please
We won't pull the same old wheeze
We mean that we won't reprise
The chorus of one of the melodies
At last, at last
Here's a show that'll end at last
Without a reprise and that's news

They looked up the Constitution
And they couldn't find a word
That said we had to sing a song
That you'd already heard
The finest legal minds have met
And every one agrees
That when we reach the Finale
We don't have to sing a reprise
At last, at last
We've come to the end at last
It'll all be over soon
But we don't intend to croon
The composer's favorite tune
The one they sang beneath the moon
Now we'll explain—a reprise
It's that certain song they sing all through the show
And the one they sing again before you go

But the judges met and every one agrees
That we will have to end without a reprise
(*Leslie Adams sings eight bars of "Easter Parade."*)

BOYS AND GIRLS:

Now you can't do that—you can't do that
You can't sing again about your Easter hat
(*Ethel Waters sings eight bars of "Heat Wave."*)
No you can't repeat—you can't repeat
You can't sing again about your Can Can heat
(*Helen Broderick sings eight bars of "Debts."*)
No you don't, you're through—we mean you're
    through
With hey nonny nonny and a nuts to you.
(*Marilyn Miller and Clifton Webb sing eight bars of "How's Chances."*)
No you can't do that—you can't do that
Because if you do we're gonna leave you flat.

MILLER:

Never mind that introduction
For we don't intend to sing
The chorus of "How's Chances"
As it wouldn't mean a thing

WEBB:

We'd like to sing a song
That wasn't written for the score
A simple little chorus
That they haven't heard before—

EVERYONE:

A simple little chorus
That you haven't heard before

WEBB (*to* MILLER):

"Not for All the Rice in China"

Not for all the rice in China
Not for all the grapes in France
Would I exchange the pleasure
That I get from every measure
When we dance
Not for all the kilts in Scotland
Not for all the bulls in Spain

Would I give up arriving
At your house although you're driving
Me insane
Not for all the onions in Bermuda
Or the cheeses that are made by the Swiss
Would I exchange that first kiss
That you gave me
Not for all the beans in Boston
Not for all the steaks in Moore's
Would I agree to part with
All the joy you filled my heart with
When you said I'm yours.

(*Chorus repeats*)

END OF SHOW

PAL JOEY

Book by JOHN O'HARA
Music by RICHARD RODGERS
Lyrics by LORENZ HART

SYNOPSIS OF SCENES AND
MUSICAL NUMBERS

ACT ONE

ACT TWO

ACT ONE

SCENE I

Cheap night club, South Side of Chicago. Not cheap in the whorehouse way, but strictly a neighborhood joint.

MIKE *the proprietor is sitting at a table stage left.* JOEY *has just finished singing.*

JOEY: Where is that Alice Faye?

MIKE: Anything else?

JOEY: Sure. (*Does some dance steps.*)

MIKE (*stopping him*): That's enough.

JOEY: Well?

MIKE: Well, I don't know. What do you drink?

JOEY: Drink? Me—drink? I had my last drink on my twenty-first birthday. My father gave me a gold watch if I'd stop drinking when I was twenty-one.

MIKE: All right—so you don't drink. How about nose-candy?

JOEY: Nor that, either. Oh, I have my vices.

MIKE: I know that. Well, we have a band here. The guitar player is only a boy, only a child.

JOEY: Hey, wait a minute.

MIKE: Okay. We got that straight. But we also have some girls.

JOEY: Yeah. I saw some of them.

MIKE: Oh—so that's it?

JOEY: I ran over the routine with them.

MIKE: I think they can handle you.

JOEY: Bet?

MIKE: Now, look. I don't know whether you're the man for the job or not. This job calls for a young punk about your age. About your build—about your looks. But he has to be master of ceremonies.

(JOEY *starts to interrupt.*)

Don't interrupt. He has to introduce the acts, such as they are—he has to have a lot of self-confidence. He has to be able to get up and tell a story. He has to be sure of himself in case he gets heckled.

JOEY: Say—

MIKE: You—you're sure you wouldn't get embarrassed in front of all those strangers?

JOEY: Ah, I love you. I can talk to you. When do I start?

MIKE: Tomorrow night.

JOEY: What about my billing?

MIKE: Wha?

JOEY: Outside, the marquee. Billing. My name. My picture?

MIKE: Drop dead.

JOEY: Naw, Mike. It's good business for you. Why last month when I was at the Waldorf-Astoria—

MIKE: Don't give me that.

JOEY: Huh?

MIKE: Now look Laddie, I know all about you so just try to get by on your merit and not on some tall story. Your last job was playing a dump in Columbus, Ohio, and you got run out of town because you was off side with the banker's daughter.

JOEY: Oh, that.

MIKE: And those other stands you've played have been very far from the Waldorf-Astoria, so just keep to facts.

JOEY: All right, so I'm not Richman, so I'm not Downey, or Crosby. But do those local clients know that? Look, you take my picture, blow it up, put it outside. My name up on the marquee. You never did that before?

MIKE: Not in this crib.

JOEY: That's the point. You never had anyone worth doing it for. But you start with me, and they think "He must be some hotshot." They think good old Mike he's gone out and got himself a class act. And every night the rope's up.

MIKE: Just one bad night, and you'll be the end of it. What about a front? You got a full dress? Tails?

JOEY: Tails? You know who wears tails? Dancers. Tony de Marco. Veloz, you know, Veloz and Yolanda. They wear tails.

MIKE: And I hear no complaints about *them*.

JOEY: Ah, but they're dancers. A dancer has to be that way, you know, formal, smooth, suave. (*Pantomimes dancers.*) But not an M.C. The whole idea of an M.C. is to get people to relax, have fun, buy that wine, that bubbly. If an M.C. comes out wearing tails nobody has any fun. But I come out in my snappy double-breasted tuxedo, maybe I'm wearing—

(MIKE *cuts in.*)

MIKE: O.K. I'm beginning to think you gave the matter thought. Okay. Maybe you're right. You wear your tuxedo.

JOEY: Thaat's the talking. Now you're cooking with e-lectricity. I think it's twenty-three bucks.

MIKE: What's twenty-three bucks?

JOEY: That's with the interest. I got twenty on the suit, but of course those guys aren't in business for love.

MIKE: Oh.

JOEY: Oh. Twenty-three, twenty-five, you know.

MIKE: Well anyway, this means I'll keep you till the end of the week.

JOEY: Why, Mike, I consider myself a partner. (*Slaps* MIKE *on back.*)

    (*The* KID *enters and puts on shoes.*)

MIKE: What about this rehearsal?

KID: They're coming, Mr. Spears.

MIKE: Well—I'll be back later. (*Exiting.*)

JOEY: Ouch—

KID: What's the matter?

JOEY: Oh, it's nothing. I got a bad leg when I cracked up one time.

KID: Cracked up? You mean in an airplane accident?

JOEY: I used to have my own plane when I was nineteen or twenty.

KID: Oh, I'd love to be able to fly. I've never been up in an airplane but I always wanted to.

    (GLADYS *enters carrying her shoes showing that her feet hurt. Unseen by* JOEY *or the* KID *she sits on the steps rubbing her feet.*)

JOEY: It's my life. My love. Oh, you get something out of flying that you don't get anywhere else. I sold my plane, but the chaps out at the airport let me fly for nothing. I'll take you up some time.

KID: Would you?

JOEY: Why, I'd be glad to. Next week, maybe. Tonight I might tell you about my experiences.

GLADYS (*interrupting*): Hey Kid. Get the rest of them in here.

KID: Okay.

    (*She exits.*)

GLADYS: Now you're an aviator.

JOEY: What's it to you?

GLADYS (*mimicking him*): Tonight I might tell you some of my experiences.

    (JOEY *sits.*)

The big aviator! Were you ever up in an elevator, for God's sake?

JOEY: You bore me.

GLADYS: What was the one you used to tell? How you were a rodeo champion?

JOEY: You bore me. Anyway, you never heard of me.

GLADYS: I heard about you. You know that tab show you used to be in? My sister was in that show. I heard all about you.

JOEY: Yeah? Which one was your sister?

GLADYS: The one you didn't score with.

JOEY: That must have been the ugly one.

GLADYS: You punk!

    (*The* KID *enters with five other girls.*)

KID: Okay, Gladys.

GLADYS (*to* JOEY): You sing the first vocal—I come on for the encore.

JOEY: Right. Where's the rest of them, and the waiters?

MICKEY (*entering*): Hey—on the floor—everybody.

AGNES (*entering*): Say—didn't you used to be in Pittsburgh?

JOEY: I was everywhere.

AGNES: I was sure I saw you at the Band Box, singing.

GLADYS: Skip the old home week.

JOEY (*to* AGNES): Later, honey.

    (*To all.* GIRLS *begin to take off work clothes.*)

Now, children, the same routine we did earlier. If you're all good, put everything in it, maybe I'll form a Joey Evans unit, and take you all over the country. Now get your places, and let's have some cooperation.

"You Mustn't Kick It Around"

    I have the worst apprehension
    That you don't crave my attention.
    But I can't force you to change your taste.
    If you don't care to be nice, dear,
    Then give me air, but not ice, dear,
    Don't let a good fellow go to waste.
    For this little sin that you commit at leisure

You'll repent in haste.
(*Refrain*)

ALL:

If my heart gets in your hair
You mustn't kick it around.
If you're bored with this affair
You mustn't kick it around.
Even though I'm mild and meek
When we have a brawl,
If I turn the other cheek
You mustn't kick it at all.
When I try to ring the bell
You never care for the sound—
The next guy may not do as well,
You mustn't kick it around!

SCENE 2

It is early evening, a middle class district on Chicago's South Side, a row of taxpayers, one of them a pet shop. There are passersby, commuters on their hasty way home. A GIRL *is standing in front of the pet shop, as* JOEY *comes on.*

This is played with JOEY *and* LINDA ENGLISH, *the* GIRL, *looking through window of pet shop, toward audience.*

JOEY *is wearing his dinner jacket, over it a topcoat with collar turned up. He is sauntering along, takes a second look at the* GIRL, *and stops and looks in the window.* LINDA *does not look at him, but moves over to make room for him. He is giving her side-long glances, but she pays no attention. Then:*

JOEY (*in that dog-babytalk*): Hel-yo Skippy. Skippy boy.
     (LINDA *looks up, but now he pays no attention.*)
     Hel-yo, boy. You wish you were outa there, doncha boy.
LINDA (*involuntarily*): Oh, I'll bet he does.
JOEY: Sure, he does. Aah, these people, they don't care about dogs. What do they know about dogs? A puppy—why, to them a puppy is fifteen dollars, twenty dollars, whatever will make a profit for them.
LINDA: Oh, some of them are nice to the dogs.
JOEY: *Are* they? If they are I never met them. They put on an act

for you, but they have no interest in any dog. Looka that little fella, the wire-haired, the one I call Skippy.

LINDA: He's cute, he's sweet.

JOEY: Well bred, too. Hi, Skippy.

LINDA: Oh, you mean that one? I thought you meant the wire-haired one.

JOEY (*trapped*): Well, he's a wire-haired scotty. Don't you know anything about dogs?

LINDA: No. I just love them.

JOEY (*relieved*): I don't know. You can't really love dogs if you don't know a little about them. A wire-haired and a Scotty, they're just about the same family—terriers.

(*She looks at him.*)

LINDA: I never really thought of that, but I guess it's true.

JOEY (*stronger*): Hyuh, Skippy.

LINDA: Why do you call him Skippy? Is that his real name, or did you have a dog called Skippy?

JOEY: That's it?

LINDA: Which?

JOEY: I had one called Skippy.

(*She leans forward and he inspects her figure some more.*)

I'd rather not talk about him.

LINDA: Oh, tell me something about him. I never had a dog myself. Wouldn't you like to talk about him?

JOEY: Well, you understand, this was an Airedale I used to have. Oh, he wasn't much. We had champion dogs in those days. That was when the family still had money.

LINDA: Your family?

JOEY: Sure. Mother breeded dogs for a hobby. Well, sort of a hobby, the way Daddy played polo! Well, one day I came home from the academy. I was going to an Academy then, about ten miles from the estate. I didn't learn much there, except how to play polo and of course riding to hounds. So this particular day I have reference to, I was returning to our estate. They opened the gate for us and about a mile up the road I saw Skippy coming. Oh, he could always tell the sound of the Rolls every afternoon. Of course, the poor old codger was half blind by that time, but we gave him a good home. So I was sitting up with the chauffeur and I saw Skippy coming. He was up near the main house, about a mile or so, and I instructed the chauffeur, I said—Chadwick—be careful of old Skippy, and he said—yes. But with Skippy you couldn't tell, because his eyesight was so bad. Well—do you want to hear the rest of it?

LINDA: Did you run over him?

JOEY: —It wasn't the chauffeur's fault, really. Not actually. But Daddy discharged him anyway. Mother erected a monument over his grave.

(*She cries.*)

Skippy's, I mean. I guess it's still there unless they took it away. I never go back.

(*She looks at him.*)

The estate fell into other hands when Daddy lost his fortune. That was when I resigned from the Princeton College. Hy-yuh, Skippy, boy. (*Looks at her.*) Don't cry—(*arm around her*) it was a long time ago.

LINDA: I know, but I mean, first your dog, and then losing your fortune.

JOEY: Yes, I never go by the house on Park Avenue without I have to laugh. (*He laughs.*) I soon found out who my friends were.

LINDA: You mean fair weather friends? Just because you lost your fortune?

JOEY: Not only that. I guess you don't recognize me. Well, that's a lucky break too.

LINDA: Why?

JOEY: Daddy. He was never brought up to work. He never did a day's work in his life, so when the crash came he took the only way out, for him. I don't think he was a coward. That way Mother got some insurance.

LINDA: Oh, how awful. And what about you?

JOEY: Down, down, down. I M.C. in a night club over on Cottage Grove Avenue. That's where I've ended up. Do you live around here?

LINDA: Yes. With my sister and her husband.

JOEY: Oh . . . Apartment?

LINDA: Yes, I sleep on the living room couch. That is, till I get a job.

JOEY: Living room couch. You have a car?

LINDA: No. Sometimes my brother-in-law lets me drive his.

JOEY: I didn't mean to bore you with the story of my life.

LINDA: Oh, I wasn't bored. I feel honored that you confided in me. I hope you tell me some more.

JOEY: I probably will. You inspire me. You know what I mean.

"I Could Write a Book"

A B C D E F G,
I never learned to spell,
At least not well.
1 2 3 4 5 6 7,
I never learned to count
A great amount.
But my busy mind is burning
To use what learning I've got.
I won't waste any time,
I'll strike while the iron is hot.

(*Refrain*)

If they asked me I could write a book
About the way you walk and whisper and look.
I would write a preface on how we met
So the world would never forget.
And the simple secret of the plot
Is that to tell them that I love you a lot;
Then the world discovers as my book ends
How to make two lovers of friends.

(*2nd Verse*)

LINDA:

Used to hate to go to school,
I never cracked a book
I played the hook.
Never answered any mail,
To write I used to think
Was wasting ink.
It was never my endeavor
To be too clever and smart.
Now I suddenly feel
A longing to write in my heart.

(JOEY *and* LINDA *repeat refrain*.)

SCENE 3

The Night Club again. LINDA *and a* BOYFRIEND *are at table, left.* GIRLS *do "Chicago" number. When the number is over,* MIKE *rushes to the waiter, right.*

"Chicago"

GIRLS:

> There's a great big town
> On a great big lake
> Called Chicago.
> When the sun goes down
> It is wide awake.
> Take your ma and your pa,
> Go to Chicago.
> Boston is England,
> N'Orleans is France,
> New York is anyone's
> For ten cents a dance.
> But this great big town
> On that great big lake
> Is America's first,
> And Americans make
> Chicago.
> Hi ya boys.
> (*Repeat*)

MIKE: Table, get a table ready. (*To* JOEY.) Lay it on good now, Boy.

JOEY: What?

MIKE: Mrs. Simpson's outside. She's coming in.

JOEY: Who?

MIKE: Mrs. Prentiss Simpson. Mrs. Chicago Society.

(VERA *enters with escort and couple, they sit.*)

JOEY (*continuing*): Well, ladies and gentlemen, that's our show. That is, our *midnight* show. We have another complete show going on again at two o'clock. At two o'clock we have Beatrice Lillie, Clifton Webb, Noel Coward, Gertie Lawrence and a whole mob coming down from a party at Ernie Byfield's.

LINDA: Isn't he cute?

JOEY: Oh, I forgot. These ladies and gentlemen weren't here in time to catch the whole thing. (*Crossing to table.*) Well, I'll tell you about our show. First, I come out, and tell a few stories. Of course, if you want to sit home and listen to Bob Hope, you'll hear the same *stories*. Of course, you don't get the music of Jerry Burns and his Pneumatic Hammer Four over the *radio*. Ah-ha no, and if your luck holds out you never *will*. No, but seriously, folks, Jerry has a swell band, and I think they're going places. Go places, will you, boys, you *bother* me.

    (*His foot business.*)

    (VALERIE *enters.*)

    Oh, my God!

VALERIE: Can I recite now?

JOEY (*to* VERA's *table*): I have to explain this to you late-comers. Valerie does a dance, doesn't she, *folks*?

    (*Howl.*)

    You see what Valerie has on now? Well, that's what she starts with in her dance. What a beautiful dancer. We had a guy here one night—well, I'll tell you one thing about him—he came here, and he came alone. So he watched Valerie dance—right down to the last rose-petal, and you know what he said when she finished? You wanna know? He said—"She doesn't know how to keep time." *She* doesn't know how to keep time! Well, we found out later he was waiting for the *drummer*.

    (*Noise from band.*)

    Only fooling, Bob. Well, after that is our big production number. Do you want to wait for it? Valerie will wait, won't you, dear?

VALERIE: Now can I recite?

JOEY (*he shakes her off*): No!

    (*Laughter and applause.*)

    Thank you, ladies and gentlemen. Seriously, the next show'll be on in just a little while, and it is entirely different. Thank you. Now there will be a short intermission.

    (*Music from the pit as one of the dancers fakes it.*)

    (JOEY *crosses to* LINDA's *table.*)

    Hello, pretty little Miss English. How are you? You like the vocal?

LINDA: Oh, yes. I thought it was pretty wonderful. Really.

JOEY: You know why?

LINDA: No—why?

JOEY: Because I was singing it for you.

LINDA: Oh—Why you didn't even see me. You didn't even know I was here until after you finished singing.

(WAITER *crosses to* JOEY.)

JOEY: Ah—I didn't say that. All I meant was I was thinking of you. You can't deny that.

(WAITER *gives* JOEY *message from* VERA.)

LINDA: I have a job, too.

JOEY: Excuse me, I gotta talk to somebody. (*To* LINDA's *boy friend.*) A pleasure . . . (*He crosses to* VERA's *table.*)

VERA: Hello. Won't you join us? This is Miss Armour and Mr. Swift.

(JOEY *sits.*)

Why haven't I seen you before?

JOEY: That's easy. You've never been here before.

VERA: That's perfectly true, but I get around—I've been to just about every other night-club in Chicago, and of course, New York. Didn't I read outside that you were direct from the Jamboree Club on 52nd Street?

JOEY: Could be, could be.

VERA: Well. I was there last month.

JOEY: Lady—a secret—I was never there. Not even as a customer.

VERA: Why, that's fraudulent. It's dishonest. "Joey Evans direct from Jamboree Club." Name up all over the place. Pictures. But you're not a Chicagoan?

JOEY: No.

VERA: Oh, you're going to be difficult. Secretive.

JOEY: Sure. If I gave it to you all at once you wouldn't come back.

VERA: You're about the freshest person I've ever met. What makes you think I care enough to come back?

JOEY: Lady, you can level with me. You'll be back.

VERA (*to one of the gents*): Shall we go? I don't like this place.

JOEY: Wait a minute. I'm liable to get the bounceroo if you walk out like this.

VERA: You worry about that.

(*She exits with her escort.*)

MIKE (*angry*): So?

JOEY: So what?

MIKE: Absolutely from hunger less than five weeks ago, and the first time we get some live ones in the joint you can't keep your hands to yourself.

JOEY: My hands? Why don't you stop?

MIKE: Then if it wasn't your hands, you said something. Wuttid you say?

JOEY: She did the talking.

MIKE: Any spot in town would give a week's take to have her come in. So she picks my lousy crib by some accident, and what do you do? You give her the business like she was one of them kids on the line. You're not only out. You're out all over town. Here—(*starts peeling off bills*) and get out of here before I start wrecking my own furniture.

JOEY (*follows him*): Wait a minute. So maybe I did talk a little out of turn. She started it.

MIKE: Stop it.

JOEY: I'll make you a bet. If she doesn't come back in, say, two nights, you can give me the bounce without paying me a nickel.

MIKE: Which is a good idea for now. Here—take your moola.

JOEY: Two nights. Tomorrow night, or the next night. What can you lose? Either you win my pay, or, if she does come back—you know how they are. They'll keep coming back, and spending—wine money.

MIKE: Well, maybe. I'd like to know your angle.

JOEY: No angle. A job and . . . (*Shrugs.*)

MIKE: You're kidding. That dame? Mrs. Prentiss Simpson? Come on. Wuttid she say?

JOEY: Ah, no. When I have more to tell you, maybe I'll tell you. (*To himself.*) And believe me, if I have nothing to tell I'm gonna make it good.

(*He exits. The* GIRLS *enter for the "Rainbow" Number.*)

"That Terrific Rainbow"

GLADYS:

> My life had no color
> Before I met you
> What could have been duller
> The time I went through?

You weakened my resistance
And colored my existence
I'm happy and unhappy too.
(*Chorus*)
I'm a RED hot mamma
But I'm BLUE for you
I get PURPLE with anger
At the things you do
And I'm GREEN with envy
When you meet a dame
But you burn my heart up
With an ORANGE flame.
I'm a RED hot mamma
But you're WHITE and cold
Don't you know your mamma
Has a heart of GOLD
Though we're in those GREY clouds
Some day you'll see
That terrific RAINBOW
Over you and me.

SCENE 4

JOEY *at the phone, right,* VERA *at the phone, left.*

JOEY (*into phone*): Hello, Miss English there? Oh, how are you? This is your pal Joey. You know, your contact with cafe society. I just called up to ask what happened last night, why'd you leave so suddenly. . . . No, no. You got it all wrong. I hadda go an' talk to those people. They own the place. Not exactly own it but maybe they're gonna put a little money in it. All right, so I didn't look as if I ever saw them before. I didn't. But that's the way it is. What middle-aged woman . . . Hello, hello . . .

(LINDA *has hung up.*)

Oh all right, small fry.

(*He starts to dial as the lights dim. When they are out the phone rings on the opposite side of the stage. The lights pick up* VERA *as she takes the phone.*)

VERA: Mr. Evans, from New York—oh, of course. Hello Norton?

JOEY: Hello, Vera. How are you?

VERA: When did you get in?

JOEY: Just a minute ago. How's Prentiss?

VERA: What did you say?

JOEY: I said, how's Prentiss?

VERA (*frowning*): Is this Norton Evans?

JOEY: Uh-huh.

VERA: Well, I don't believe it is. You'll have to identify yourself. Uh-h-h. What was the name of the play we saw in New York last summer?

JOEY: Why, I think we saw *The Man Who Came to Dinner.*

VERA: Oh, you do. Well, Norton Evans and I have not seen each other for over a year, and Norton Evans calls my husband Pete. Now, who is this, please?

JOEY: All right. (*Laughs.*) This is Joey Evans.

VERA: Who?

JOEY: You know. Last night.

VERA: Oh. The night club thing.

JOEY: That's right. Listen, I just wanted to tell you what I think of you. You know you cost me my job. I'm through the end of this week, not only here, but all over town. They tell me you're such hot stuff around this town you can keep *any-body* from working. Well, it's a lousy town anyway, but I just thought I'd tell you to go to hell before I leave.

(*Joey hangs up.*)

"What is a Man?"

(*Verse*)

VERA:

> There are so many, so many fish in the sea,
> Must I want the one who's not for me?
> It's just my foolish way
> What can I do about it?
> I'm much too used to love—
> To be without it.

(*Refrain*)

> What is a man
> Is he an animal
> Is he a wolf
> Is he a mouse

Is he the cheap or the dear kind
Is he champagne or the beer kind

What is a man
Is he a stimulant
Good for the heart
Bad for the nerves

Nature's mistake since the world began
What makes me give
What makes me live
What is this thing called man.
(*Dials phone*)

Hello Jack—can't keep the appointment
Have an awful cold (*Sneeze*)
Hello Frank
Have to meet my husband
So long—please don't scold
Hello—Hello—Love

What is a man
Is he a stimulant
Good for the heart
Bad for the nerves

From Charlie Chaplin to Charlie Chan
All have one trick—one that is slick
What is this thing called man.

SCENE 5

The night club again after the last show. JOEY *is seated at a table, right. Some of the kids are on the way home. One of them sneaks up behind* JOEY *and kisses him.*

KID: I hear you're getting the bounceroo.
JOEY: You hear good, Gladys.
KID: Huh?

JOEY: Oh, I thought you were Gladys.

KID: Oh. You thought I was Gladys. I was gonna ask you to come up to the apartment, but if it's with you and Gladys well nutsa to you-a. You had it coming to you. (*She goes off.*)

TERRY: Don't whatever you do call me tonight. My husband's back.

JOEY: Just my luck. Let me know when he goes back on that baker wagon.

TERRY: Baker wagon nothing. He owns a piece of a band. You're pretty fresh for somebody that's washed up. *I* heard. (*Exits.*)

   (*Other girls cross the stage, exiting.*)

MIKE (*entering from outside*): A lot of you girls' boyfriends are waiting out in the alley.

AGNES: We'll be ready in a minute.

JOEY: Hey, Gladys—no good night?

GLADYS: Listen to what's talking. If I let you come home with me tonight there'd be no getting rid of you. *I* heard.

JOEY: You mean about me going to the El Morocco in New York?

GLADYS: What?—Ah—Morocco. You'd have to join the Foreign Legion to get to Morocco.

JOEY (*to* VALERIE): How about you, you bum?

VALERIE (*exiting*): Who are you calling a bum, you bum?

MIKE (*to* JOEY): Well, wise guy. One more night. Mrs. Prentiss Simpson.

   (*Knock from outside door.*)

   (MIKE *goes up steps.*)

   Nobody here. Everybody went home. (*Starts down.*)

   (*Knock from outside door.*)

   Aw, nuts. (*He goes up steps and out of sight to open door.*)

VERA (*off stage*): Good evening.

MIKE (*backing in*): Come in, Mrs. Simpson. (*Goes to foot of stairs.*)

VERA: My, what a nice reception. (*Coming down.*)

   (*Followed by* ESCORT.)

MIKE: Sorry we're all closed up, Mrs. Simpson.

   (ESCORT *staggers*—MIKE *catches him.*)

   But I can fix you up with a powder.

   (ESCORT *starts for table.*)

   A little drink.

(ESCORT *staggers and* MIKE *takes him to table—hold for next line*.)

VERA: I'd *love* one. I like it like this. It's so peaceful.

(ESCORT *sits.*)

Why, Mr. Evans.

JOEY: Hello.

MIKE (*gesturing to* JOEY, *who has remained seated*): Up. Up.

VERA: No, don't bother. Mr. Evans is tired I'm sure. He has to work on his valentines. Did you know about Mr. Evans and his valentines, Mr. uh—I never knew it, so I didn't get it.

MIKE: Spears. Just Mike is all right. I get no respect around here, so I guess you can call me Mike too.

VERA: Well, Mike, were you serious about that powder?

MIKE: I sure was. Has to be Scotch. Everything else is locked up.

VERA: Scotch and plain water is fine for me. (*Looks at companion.*) Nothing for him.

MIKE (*to* JOEY, *as he goes off*): I don't pay off yet.

VERA: So I can go to hell?

JOEY: You can double go to hell. You wanta hear what else you can do?

VERA: Something about a galloping rooster, I imagine. Or the moon.

JOEY: Why the hell couldn't you come back earlier?

VERA: Why earlier?

JOEY: Never mind. Skip it.

VERA: Why earlier? Oh I'll bet I can guess.

JOEY: Guess your head off.

VERA: You told Mike that I'd be back. Didn't you?

JOEY: Why, the heel.

VERA: No. I've had no conversation with Mike. Give me credit for some intuition. After all I am a woman.

JOEY (*giving her the "eye"*): Yes, I'll say that for you.

VERA (*drawing herself "together"*): Intuition and mind changing. I decided last night . . . and this afternoon—that I'd never come here again. Tonight I change my mind. Oh I can tell you the whole story. When we walked out of here last night Mike was annoyed because he counted on our spending a lot of money . . . Right so far?

JOEY: Go ahead.

VERA: So he fired you, but you said "She'll be back, I know her kind." Right?

JOEY: I said, go ahead.

VERA: You thought it over. "How can I get her to come back?" By the way, how'd you get my number?

JOEY: Easy. The press agent of this joint has a 1919 social register.

VERA (*slapping his face*): 1919 eh? . . . Well to continue, you thought of the technique of the insult. Instead of appealing to my better nature, which you are sure I do not possess—Does it hurt? I hope?—you reveal yourself as a sensitive, understanding young man. And it worked. That's why I'm here.

(JOEY *rises—then sits again.*)

But one moment, please. One moment. The reason it worked isn't because I was sucker enough to get angry. Oh no. The reason it worked, dear Mr. Evans, was that you were nice enough to treat me differently. Or is that a subtlety that escapes you. No matter. (*She rises.*) However one thing you must never never never forget. I am older than you, and I am a very smart and ruthless woman, so don't try any fast ones. Come on.

JOEY: Where to?

VERA: Oh, you know where to. You knew it last night. Get your hat and coat. I'll be waiting in the car.

(MIKE *enters as* VERA *starts to exit.*)

(JOEY *gives* MIKE *the "fingers" and exits backstage to get hat and coat.* MIKE *gestures "You SOB" with bottle.*)

(CLUB PATRON *strikes table.*)

MIKE (*to* ESCORT, *bottle on table*): Hey, you—you wanna get plastered? (*Pours two drinks.*)

AGNES (*entering*): The hell he is.

ESCORT (*coming to*): Where is she?

AGNES: What's the matter with Joey?

MIKE: You know as much about it as I do.

AGNES: He says he's going hunting.

MIKE: Hunting?

AGNES: That's what he says.

GIRL (*entering*): He says he's through with this dump.

ESCORT (*rising*): Where is she?

MIKE (*taking* ESCORT *offstage*): Come on, brother.

AGNES: What does he mean? Why should he be through?

VALERIE (*entering*): You'd better ask him—here he comes now. (JOEY *enters*.)

"Happy Hunting Horn"

JOEY:

Don't worry, girls,
I'm only on vacation,
Not out of circulation,
Don't worry, girls.
Don't worry, girls,
While I still have my eyesight
You're going to be in my sight;
Don't worry, girls.
You never can erase
The hunter from the chase.

(*Refrain*)

Sound the happy hunting horn,
There's new game on the trail now;
We're hunting for quail now,
Happy little hunting horn.
Play the horn but don't play corn,
The music must be nice now,
We're hunting for mice now,
Happy little hunting horn.
Danger's easy to endure when
You're out to catch a beaut;
Lie in ambush, but be sure when
You see the whites of their eyes—don't shoot!
Play the horn from night to morn,
Just play, no matter what time
Play, "There'll be a hot time!",
Happy little hunt—Bang! Bang!—ing horn.

SCENE 6

Tailor shop.

ERNEST: I like this, lots.
JOEY: Yeah, who's wearing this?
ERNEST: Well, of course no one is. Everything is exclusive. If

you bought this you'd be the only one, but Mr. Teddy Winston, the polo player—well he has a jacket quite a little like it.

JOEY: Okay. Make up a suit out of it.

ERNEST: The trousers too? I thought just the jacket and possibly
some contrasting slacks.

JOEY: The suit. The schmeer. What else do I need?

VERA (*enters*): Hello.

JOEY: You're late enough.

VERA: You better get used to it, my pet. This stuff—thank
goodness you didn't buy any of this.

JOEY: What? I bought all of it.

VERA: Oh, no, you didn't. Now Ernest didn't he tell you I sent
him here. You wouldn't do this to a friend of mine, would
you?

ERNEST: Had I but known, Mrs. Simpson. But the gentleman
never mentioned your name.

VERA: Well that's something. All right, throw all that stuff away
and we'll start from scratch. And can I scratch.

ERNEST: Very good, Mrs. Simpson. Now I have some new—If
you'll just step this way—

VERA: And don't show us any more of Teddy Winston's stuff.
(*To* JOEY.) If you started dressing like a gentleman you might
begin behaving like one, and that I but never could take. Stay
as sweet as you are, dear.

JOEY: That's the way to do it.

VERA: Do what?

JOEY: Keep me as sweet as I am—pamper me a little.

VERA: Somebody started that a long time ago.

JOEY: Well, it got results. (*He exits.*)

"Bewitched, Bothered and Bewildered"

VERA:

(*Verse*)

    After one whole quart of brandy,
    Like a daisy I awake.
    With no Bromo Seltzer handy,
    I don't even shake.
    Men are not a new sensation;
    I've done pretty well, I think.
    But this half-pint imitation

Put me on the blink.
(*Refrain 1*)
 I'm wild again,
 Beguiled again,
 A simpering, whimpering child again—
 Bewitched, bothered and bewildered am I.
 Couldn't sleep
 And wouldn't sleep
 Until I could sleep where I shouldn't sleep—
 Bewitched, bothered and bewildered am I.
 Lost my heart, but what of it?
 My mistake, I agree.
 He's a laugh, but I love it
 Because the laugh's on me.
 A pill he is,
 But still he is
 All mine and I'll keep him until he is
 Bewitched, bothered and bewildered
 Like me.
(*Refrain 2*)
 Seen a lot—
 I mean a lot—
 But now I'm like sweet seventeen a lot—
 Bewitched, bothered and bewildered am I.
 I'll sing to him,
 Each spring to him,
 And worship the trousers that cling to him—
 Bewitched, bothered and bewildered am I.
 When he talks, he is seeking
 Words to get off his chest.
 Horizontally speaking,
 He's at his very best.
 Vexed again,
 Perplexed again,
 Thank God I can be oversexed again—
 Bewitched, bothered and bewildered am I.
(*Refrain 3*)
 Sweet again,
 Petite again,
 And on my proverbial seat again—

Bewitched, bothered and bewildered am I.
What am I?
Half shot am I.
To think that he loves me
So hot am I—
Bewitched, bothered and bewildered am I.
Though at first we said, "No, sir,"
Now we're two little dears.
You might say we are closer
Than Roebuck is to Sears.
I'm dumb again
And numb again,
A rich, ready, ripe little plum again—
Bewitched, bothered and bewildered am I.
(*Encore*)
You know,
It is really quite funny
Just how quickly he learns
How to spend all the money
That Mr. Simpson earns.
He's kept enough,
He's slept enough,
And yet when it counts
He's adept enough—
Bewitched, bothered and bewildered am I.

(VERA *exits and then* JOEY *and* ERNEST *come in as* VERA *comes back on.*)

JOEY: Why didn't you come with us? Don't you take an interest?

VERA: I'll see the final result.

(LINDA *enters. She is a stenographer and has something for* ERNEST *to sign.*)

LINDA: Will you okay this, please, Mr. Ernest?

JOEY: Hyuh. How're the dogs?

LINDA: Oh, I never get a chance to see them any more. I moved. I'm not in that neighborhood any more.

JOEY: Oh.

(VERA *starts tapping her foot, which* ERNEST *notices. He shoos* LINDA *away.*)

ERNEST: Go away, Miss Birnbaum, or whatever your name is. (*To* VERA.) She's new here. (*To* LINDA.) I told you never to. . . . (*To* VERA.) Or perhaps you'll excuse me just a second? It might be important.

LINDA: It isn't important, Mr. Ernest. (*To* JOEY.) Good-bye. (*She goes off.*)

JOEY: Good-bye.

VERA: Now really.

JOEY: I only saw her twice before in my life. She likes dogs. (*Laughs*) Imagine that. She's crazy about dogs. Ordinary dogs, that you see in a window.

VERA: And that's how you got together. You—Albert Payson Terhune, you. Oh, I can just see you, with your pipe, and your Teddy Winston tweeds, and a stout walking stick, tramping across the moors.

(JOEY *laughs*.)

What are you laughing about?

JOEY: Those moors. I used to work in a band with a guy named Moore. I'd like to tramp across him.

VERA: Stop it. Anyway, this, uh, mouse, as you call them. (*Shakes her head slowly, warningly.*) No. See? No . . . Good God, I'm getting to talk like you.

JOEY: Her? That's jail bait. Of course she's old enough to work. How old do you have to be to work in this state?

(VERA *looks offstage, sort of wondering whether to do anything about the mouse,* LINDA.)

VERA: At what?

JOEY: Ah you're not listening. How about this one. (*He picks up some material as another mouse comes on. He does not see the mouse, but* VERA *does and misinterprets what he says.*) I like this one.

VERA: Oh you do, eh?

JOEY: Yeah . . . and it ought to wear like hell. But a hundred and twenty clams.

VERA: And how did you know it was a hundred and twenty clams?

JOEY: It says so. Look. (*Holds up tag.*) See?

VERA: I didn't. But I do now. Oh what you missed.

JOEY: What did I miss?

VERA: Never mind. You probably only missed it once. Anyway

it's the evening things that are important. You never get up in the daytime. If you're going to be a great big master of ceremonies, in a great big night club—

JOEY: Hey, I thought it was going to be aan-teem. Small but exclusive. Chez Joey. Oho boy. Chez Joey. I can just see myself in white tie, and tails, maybe an opera hat sort of like this . . . (*Imitates a smooth toothy entrance.*) "Maysure a darm." Suave. I bow here, I bow there. Very quiet. Maybe I have the plumbers playing "Valentina" very soft behind me. Never raise my voice. I wish I could do it all in French. Maybe I will, maybe I will.

VERA: Maybe you better not.

JOEY: Maybe I better not. To-night it is my pleasure—to—pre-sent—for your delight. Hey, maybe a sort of a patter. To-night—it is my pleasure—to present for your delight—Bazum, bazum bazum zum, bazum bazum, bazum. Hey, how about that? Who writes that kind of stuff? Maybe I could get him to grind out a little thing like that.

VERA: Bazum.

JOEY: No, sugar. No cracks.

VERA: Bazum. Get your mind off bazum.

JOEY: You wrong me. You wrong me. I'm only thinking of my work. You put all this scratch in an an-teem little cloop. Is that right? Cloop?

VERA: Club, Joint, Dive, Crib, I don't care what you call it.

JOEY: I like cloop. Anyway, you put all this moola in the cloop, I want it to be a success for your sake, honey sugar. I like to think of your investment.

VERA: Just remember, my hero, that it is my investment.

JOEY: What have I done that you don't trust me?

VERA: What have you had a chance to do?

(ERNEST *enters.*)

ERNEST: So terribly sorry, but I—

VERA: Never mind, Ernest. The important thing is the evening clothes. Not too Brooks Brothers. After all he's only a boy and we want to keep him looking that way. But on the other hand, not too, you know, lapels and things.

JOEY: I guess I can order my own clothes.

VERA: That's what I mean. Whenever he tries putting in his ideas, that's when to be very careful.

ERNEST: I think I understand, perfectly. Now if we'll just go in the fitting room.

(*They exit.*)

VERA: Don't mind me. I'm leaving.

(LINDA *enters with some notes in her hand. She crosses* VERA *as though to go after the men.*)

Oh, you're new here, aren't you?

LINDA: Yes. My second week.

VERA (*putting on the "tough act"*): Well, would you mind telling Ernie to be sure and put the extra size pockets in for the guns? My husband is absent-minded and he forgot the last time.

LINDA: Huh?

VERA: Imagine that lug, forty suits he ordered and not a God damn one has the rod pocket in it.

LINDA: Your husband?

VERA: Did you see him or didn't you? He's in there with Ernie now. I gotta scram. Take a note. Quote. Joey Evans stuff. Be sure and put in extra revolver pockets. Unquote.

LINDA (*tearfully making notes*): Yes, ma'am.

VERA: Okey doke. Ah me. Tell him I gotta talk tough to his first wife. She wants more alimony. More alimony. (*Crossing.*) She's lucky to be alive, that babe. Be seeing you. (*Exits.*)

LINDA: Be seeing you—thank you.

ERNEST (*as he and* JOEY *re-enter*): . . . But I could have guessed to the quarter inch . . . Thirty-eight and a quarter shoulders, left shoulder slightly higher. . . .

JOEY (*paying no attention—to* LINDA): Hy-yuh babe. I guess you don't sleep on that living room couch any more since you got a job.

LINDA: No, sir. (*To* ERNEST.) You're not to forget about the revolver pockets in this gentleman's suits.

JOEY and ERNEST: Revolver pockets?

LINDA: And your wife said to tell you she's going to talk tough to your first wife. About the alimony.

JOEY: What is this?

LINDA: I'll bet you never ran over Skippy. I'll bet you shot him. (*Exits.*)

ERNEST: But Mr. Evans—

JOEY: Ah—let it alone.

(ERNEST *exits.*)

She can't bother me; nobody can.

SCENE 7

JOEY *looks into the future.*

"Pal Joey"

What do I care for a dame?
What do I care for a dame?
Every old dame is the same.
Every damn dame is the same.

I got a future—
A rosy future;
You can be sure I'll be tops.
I'm independent;
I'm no defendant.
I'll own a night-club that's tops,
And I'll be in with the cops.

What do I care for the skirts?
What do I care for the skirts?
I'll make them pay 'til it hurts.
Let them put up 'til it hurts.

I'm going to own a night-club;
It's going to be the right club.
For the swell gentry—
It's elementary
I'll wear top hat and cane.
In Chez Joey
They'll pay Joey,
The gay Joey—
I can see it plain.

("*Chez Joey*" *Ballet.*)

END OF ACT ONE

ACT TWO

SCENE I

Chez Joey.
VICTOR *is standing center looking at the costumes of two girls.*
MICKEY *is at left.*

STAGEHAND: Hey, Scholtz!

SCHOLTZ (*in wings*): Yeah.

STAGEHAND: Hit Gladys with a surprise pink.

SCHOLTZ: Okay.

VICTOR: And when I say pink light, I mean pink.

MICKEY: I'll tell him.

STAGEHAND: Hey Scholtz!

SCHOLTZ: Yeah.

STAGEHAND: You'll have to raise that baby when they bring those tables on the floor.

SCHOLTZ: Right.

VICTOR: Oh, don't worry about that. We're never going to be ready to open tonight.

MICKEY: I'll tell him.

VICTOR: You keep your mouth shut.

KID (*at entrance, with three girls*): Is this all right, Victor?

VICTOR: Come here. Where's Mr. Evans? (*Examines costumes.*)

MIKE (*entering*): Don't bother Joey. I got him slated for an interview in 15 minutes. Get your opening number cleaned up first.

STAGEHAND: Give me the trim on these hedges.

VICTOR: Where's Gladys?

MICKEY: Getting on her costume. She'll be here in a minute.

VICTOR: Well, hurry her up.

DELIVERY BOY (*entering with crate of eggs*): Want this in here?

MIKE: Use the service entrance. No, never mind. Take it downstairs.

STAGEHAND: Stand by and lower that border.

GLADYS (*entering—giving "Mi-Mi-Mi" with the voice.* VICTOR *crosses left of her to see her costume*): Did you reserve that table for those friends of mine?

MIKE: All taken care of.

GLADYS: Can they see the floor? I mean with a telescope. Have
'em good, will you? They're very important people.

MIKE: I bet.

MICKEY (*re-entering—has gone off*): Victor!

VICTOR: What is it?

MICKEY: They're ready.

VICTOR: It's about time. All right, on your toes, everybody. I
want no interruptions—and no NOISE.

    (*Hammering off stage.*)

And try to get it right just once.

    (*Flower number with* TENOR *and* GIRLS.)

"The Flower Garden of My Heart"

THE TENOR:

        I haven't yet got a great big yacht,
        But I'm contented with my lot,
        I've got one thing much more beautiful and grand.
        I do not own a racing horse
        But that don't fill me with remorse.
        I possess the finest show-place in the land.
        So come with me and wander
        To a lovely spot out yonder.
    (*Refrain*)
        In the flower garden in my heart
        I've got violets blue as your eyes,
        I've got dainty narcissus
        As sweet as my missus
        And lilies as pure as the skies.
        In the flower garden in my heart
        I've got roses as red as your mouth.
        Just to keep our love holy
        I've got gladioli
        And sun-flowers fresh from the south,
        But you are the artist
        And love is the art
        In the flower garden in my heart.

VIOLET: The flower dear old grandmother wore
    Away 'way *back* in the days of yore.

SUNFLOWER: The favorite of white and dusky pixie
Away down south in the land of Dixie.
HEATHER: Sir Harry Lauder sang of its beauties—
The decoration of all Scotch cuties.
LILY: The flower of youthful purity—
It's very sweet—you have my surety.
LILAC: The sky turns blue and the churchbells chime.
Ah—love—we love sweet lilac time.
ROSE: If you're a hundred per-cent American—goodness knows
You love the American Beauty rose.
(*Refrain*)
THE TENOR:
In the flower garden in my heart
I've got daisies to tell me you're true.
Oh, the west wind will whisk us
The scent of hibiscus
And heather that's smothered with dew.
In the flower garden of my heart
I've got lilacs and dainty sweet peas.
You will look like Sweet William
And smell like a trillium
Surrounded by fond bumble bees,
But love is the archer and you are the dart
In the flower garden of my heart.

VICTOR: All right, strike those props and get everybody in costume for the jitterbug number.
(THE TENOR *crosses stage taking off costume.*)
(*Also* GIRLS.)
(WAITERS *set tables and chairs.* MIKE *enters with* MELBA.)
MIKE (*to* VICTOR): Tell Joey to come out here. (*To* MELBA.) Sit right down here, Miss Melba.
(She *sits.*)
(JOEY *enters.*)
Joey! Here's one I can leave you alone with.
JOEY: Alone? Here? *That?*
MIKE: Be nice. This is the press. You know. Publicity. Chez Joey's name in the papers.
JOEY: Ah?
MIKE: Her name is Melba Snyder. She's on the *Herald.* Now

be nice . . . Miss Snyder, make you acquainted with Joey, of Chez Joey.

JOEY: *Miss* Snyder. Miss Melba Snyder, of course?

MELBA: Yes, as a matter of fact, but how did you know? I usually only sign M.S.

JOEY: And I think it's a shame they don't let you sign your whole name. (*Aside to* MIKE.) Oh, Mike. (*To* MELBA.) Just a second, Miss Snyder. (*To* MIKE.) Uh, Mike, before I forget it, in that second number . . . (*voice lowering*) what the hell does this dame do? Write a cooking column or something?

MIKE: You're doing fine, boy. She does night club news and interviews.

JOEY: Right. Then I come on for the last eight bars, right?

MIKE: Right.

JOEY: Sorry, Miss Snyder, but you know all this confusion and helter-skelter and et cetera on opening night. Now, as I was saying when Mike interrupted me, they oughta let you sign your whole name. I often think, you newspaper people—I don't know many of the ladies and gentlemen of the press here in Chicago, but of course New York. I know all the boys. Anyway, you ought to have a *union*.

MELBA: We have a union.

JOEY (*covering*): And I'm glad. Well, let's have a powder. (*Whistle. Calls* WAITER.) Waldo! You drink, of course.

MELBA: A double Scotch and plain water. No ice. Make that St. James Scotch and tell him not to give me Jameson's Irish.

JOEY (*dumbfounded*): What? (*Sits.*)

MELBA (*to the* WAITER): Double St. James and water, no ice. And don't bring me Jameson's Irish. (*To* JOEY.) I can't drink Irish except straight.

JOEY (*weakly*): Coke with lime.

(WAITER *exits.*)

MELBA: This is going to be a Sunday piece, so we can go all out. You can start at the beginning, wherever you want to. I never take notes, so go right ahead.

JOEY: Well, how I got in this business and so on?

MELBA: Right.

JOEY: That was rather innaresting, how I got in this business. I was up at Dartmouth University—

MELBA: What for?

JOEY: Going there. I was a "soph."

MELBA: I thought they called it Dartmouth College.

JOEY: Well, sometimes we do, and sometimes we don't. It's a hell of a big place.

(WAITER *with drinks.*)

MELBA: Relatively. About 1650 students, I'd say. Nothing to compare in size at least with Chicago, Northwestern, and our universities. However, you were up there. (*She takes drink.*)

JOEY: As a soph. I was living at the Frat house.

MELBA: Frat?

JOEY: Sure!

MELBA: You make it sound like one of those colleges where Betty Grable's always going. But—continue.

JOEY: Well. The kids were sitting around singing and playing the piano and there was this society singer from New York—I grew up with her—Her name was Consuelo Van Rensselaer, Connie. I grew up with her, but I didn't see her much after Daddy lost his fortune.

MELBA: Excuse me? (*She chokes on her drink.*)

JOEY: We had to give up the estate. All the horses, and mares, and dogs—

MELBA: And?

JOEY: And yes, Miss Snyder—and bitches—we had to give them up too.

MELBA: Oh yeah?

JOEY: Well, we had to give them all up when Daddy lost his fortune.

MELBA: You said that. Or maybe you forget. I'm not taking notes—I remember everything.

JOEY: We started singing all the old songs. "Dardanella," "Who?" The oldies. Suddenly everybody stopped singing and I was the only one. It was a lovely old tune that Mother used to sing to me before going out to some big society ball. Mother had a lovely voice.

MELBA: That was before you lost your fortune?

JOEY: Yes. Exactly. She lost her voice when Daddy lost our fortune. The shock— (*Looks at her—thinks as though he is being ribbed—and continues a little mad.*) Well, this lovely old tune . . .

MELBA: You don't happen to remember what it was called? Was it—(*singing*) "Frère Jacques—Frère Jacques"?

JOEY (*cutting in*): I believe it was. Yes, I believe it was.

MELBA: Oh, then everybody joined in.

JOEY: No—nobody else knew it.

MELBA: Oh.

JOEY: So Connie was sitting in a corner, and she was crying softly to herself. It reminded her of something. It was just the mood it got her into. So when all the others applauded, she sat there crying softly.

MELBA: Then did she say—you ought to be singing professionally, and introduce you to Pops Whiteman, and he gave you your first break, then you sort of sang with several other bands, and in night clubs, and that's how you happened to come to Chicago? Okay. I'll write it.

JOEY: Say, what is this?

MELBA: Let me make it up. You'll only confuse me. I've got to get some pictures of this tripe. God knows why—God knows and I think I do— (*Looks at watch.*) Che-rist-mas— I've gotta leap. Good luck, and give my love to Connie Van Rensselaer.

MIKE (*enters*): How's our boy doing? Giving you all the facts?

MELBA: He's given me plenty of information, I don't know about the facts.

JOEY: I'd love to interview you some day. You'd get some information.

MELBA: I'd love it.

(JOEY *exits.*)

MIKE: Ah—you mustn't mind him—

MELBA: Him? After the people I've interviewed? It's pretty late in the day for me to start getting bothered by the funny ones I talk to.

MIKE: Like for instance?

MELBA: Well?

"Zip"

I've interviewed Leslie Howard,
I've interviewed Noel Coward,
I've interviewed the great Stravinski,
But my greatest achievement is the interview I had

With the star who worked for Minsky.
I met her at the Yankee Clipper
And she didn't unzip one zipper.
I said, "Miss Lee, you are such an artist,
Tell me why you never miss.
What do you think of while you work?"
And she said, "While I work
My thoughts go something like this:
(*Refrain*)
Zip! Walter Lippmann wasn't brilliant today.
Zip! Will Saroyan ever write a great play?
Zip! I was reading Schopenhauer last night.
Zip! And I think that Schopenhauer was right.
I don't want to see Zorina,
I don't want to meet Cobina.
Zip! I'm an intellectual.
I don't like a deep contralto
Or a man whose voice is alto.
Zip! I'm a heterosexual.
Zip! It took intellect to master my art.
Zip! Who the hell is Margie Hart?
(*Refrain*)
Zip! I consider Dalí's paintings passé.
Zip! Can they make the Metropolitan pay?
Zip! Hearing Rhumba bands will drive me to drink.
Zip! Mrs. Perkins isn't red, she's just pink.
I have read the great Cabala
And I simply worship Allah.
Zip! I am just a mystic.
I don't care for Whistler's Mother,
Charley's Aunt, or Shubert's brother.
Zip! I'm misogynistic.
Zip! My intelligence is guiding my hand.
Zip! Who the hell is Sally Rand?
(*3rd Chorus*)
Zip! That Stokowski leads the greatest of bands;
Zip! Jergen's Lotion does the trick for his hands.
Zip! Rip Van Winkle on the screen would be smart;
Zip! Tyrone Power will be cast in the part.
I adore the great Confucius,

And the lines of luscious Lucius.
Zip! I am so eclectic;
I don't care for either Mickey—
Mouse and Rooney make me sicky!
Zip! I'm a little hectic.
Zip! my artistic taste is classic and choice—
Zip! who the hell's Rosita Royce?

(MELBA *exits.*)

(VICTOR *enters.*)

VICTOR: Mike . . .

MIKE: Well, what now?

VICTOR: There's a fellow out there to see you.

MIKE: Don't let him in.

VICTOR: I think he's going to come in whether we want him to or not.

LOWELL (*offstage*): Out of my way. (*Enters.*)

(MIKE *enters and calls Joey from off stage.* JOEY *enters from right as* LOWELL *enters from left.*)

Mike, take five.

MIKE: Hello . . . Hey you, waiter. Waldo . . . Nail them tables down. Nail everything down.

LOWELL: Aah ha ha ha . . . Ah you Mike. You're my guy. You really are my guy. Let's sit down over here after you introduce me to the new idol of the airwaves. My name is Ludlow Lowell.

MIKE: Ooh. You really go by that?

LOWELL: It's my name. Cook County says it's my name.

MIKE: I know, but just amongst us kids. What is that again?

LOWELL: Ludlow Lowell, with two l's. Next year I change it to Lowell with one l. It's a combination I figured out on numerology and the stars, astrology.

JOEY: Say it again, with two l's.

LOWELL: Lowell.

JOEY: Now say it with one l.

LOWELL: Lowell.

JOEY: I like it better with one l.

LOWELL: Oh, a fresh punk. Okay, Mike, it's your joint, I guess. But would you mind, you know, going away. Take a powder the hell outa here. Now. (*Crossing to table.*) I take off my

watch, I put it on the table here, and I ask you to shut up and
listen to me for a minute. Okay? Okay. Now, I am a man of
few words and very taciturn. I have a point and head straight
for it, provided certain parties do not interrupt. Don't even
say *alright*—just keep quiet.

JOEY: All right.

LOWELL (*rising*): You spoiled it. Now I have to start all over
again. (*Sits.*) Okay. Watch on table. Man of few words. *So*—
The word reaches me that an unknown is suddenly opening
up in this newly decorated and refurnished decor. I see where
they are calling it the Chez Joey. I ponder it over and consider
it in my mind. Why? I say. I don't cheat on this right away. I
try to figure it out myself without asking questions and inter-
rogating people who are in the know. Well, Joey, if I know
one thing it is night clubs and human nature and who backs
shows and the like of that, and so I never heard of you, and so
I add it all up and deduce that you have a friend. Is this friend
a man? Maybe. Or is it a mouse?

JOEY (*interrupting*): But I don't see how . . .

LOWELL (*rising—annoyed*): How do you like the guy? He
won't let you talk. (*Sits again.*) Well, All this I checked up on
through my underground sources. I get the word that it is a
rich dame backing the joint because she is interested in you. I
am not a gossip or a scandalmonger that does not mind their
own business, Joey, but just incidentally I happen to hear who
it is. *Holy Hell*—I say to myself. So I come right over to see if
you have representation.

JOEY: Are you asking do I have an agent?

LOWELL: "Representation" is what I offer.

JOEY (*rising*): I don't have any agent.

LOWELL (*taking contracts from pocket*): Sign this.

JOEY: I sign nothing.

LOWELL: If I can assure and guarantee you $50,000 a year inside
of a year and a half, is that any encouraging inducement?

JOEY: I'll be making that myself in that time without any agent.

LOWELL: Sign this, you Goddam pig-headed fool or I'll walk
out on you.

JOEY (*over table*): Why should I sign what I never even read?

LOWELL: *Ludlow Lowell* is why. Me. Take a quick gander at it.

It is not typewritten. It is printed. It is a standard contract. (*Snatches it away from* JOEY.) Here, give it back to me. I don't care if you sign it or you don't sign it.

(GLADYS *enters.*)

Don't turn round now, but isn't that Gladys Bumps over there?

JOEY: Without looking, yes.

LOWELL: Gladys, darling. Come here and sit on my lap, Gladys.

GLADYS (*rushing to him*): Hello, Louis—I mean Ludlow. (*Sits on his lap.*) What's with you?

JOEY (*seated*): You know this jerk?

GLADYS: Jerk? You call him a jerk? Go out and take a look at his car. Honey, I never saw you for over a year.

JOEY: Wuddia mean, his car? How do you know him?

GLADYS: You're the only one that doesn't know him. Are you wasting your time with the laddy-boy here, Ludlow?

LOWELL: That I fear, Gladys, that I fear. I have offered him representation; I have offered him a contract and he wants to read it.

GLADYS (*to* JOEY): Well, sign it, you jerk, before he walks out on you. Or did you change your mind in the last ten minutes and no longer care for money?

JOEY: You think I ought to sign with this guy?

GLADYS: In blood, if necessary.

(JOEY *signs both copies—* GLADYS *and* LOWELL *exchange looks.*)

LOWELL: Gladys, would you care to attest this instrument?

(*She gives a take.*)

Don't look at me that way, Gladys. I only mean do you wish to sign this as a witness?

GLADYS (*laughing*): Oh, I thought . . .

LOWELL: Don't worry, Gladys, we know what you thought. Down here in the lower left hand corner. Two copies.

(*She signs and he gives* JOEY *one copy.*)

Now then, old chappie, Monday afternoon three o'clock you come to my temporary office at the Morrison Hotel while I'm having the main office redecorated and refurbished. You be there at three o'clock and we will have a little chat to get acquainted, and following that I am taking you over to NBC to audition and for the Staff o' Life Bread program.

(JOEY *rises as though to go.*)

By the way, a delicate matter, but you will tell Mike to send me your checks hereafter since I am representing you; then I put them in our special Joey account and deduct my small fee.

JOEY: But I got this job myself.

LOWELL (*has risen—pats* JOEY'S *face*): Contract's a contract, Joey. Let's not start right off on the wrong foot, you know?

JOEY: You're sure about this Staffo thing?

LOWELL: It is only the beginning. Thirteen weeks is the most I will sign for, that's how I feel about it.

JOEY: Okay. How'd you . . . what made you think I'd be such a sure thing for this program? Who owns Staffo?

LOWELL: Are you kidding? Only Prentiss Simpson owns it.

JOEY: Oh——

LOWELL: I guess you know him? Or anyway, you know who he is.

JOEY: Well, I gotta blow. (*Exits.*)

LOWELL: Sure. Be seeing you, pally. And you too. (*To* GLADYS.)

GLADYS (*rises*): Yeah—I'll be up to your "temporary headquarters" tomorrow.

LOWELL: You didn't forget to reserve that table for me?

GLADYS: In my name.

LOWELL: And listen—

(MIKE *enters.*)

Mike—a million thanks for the use of the hall.

MIKE: In the meantime, you wouldn't be upset if we went ahead with our rehearsal?

(DANCING BOYS *enter.*)

LOWELL: On the contrary, I want you to rehearse, because I'm going to be here tonight, and it better be good.

(*Two more* DANCERS *enter.*)

MIKE: Good God, you coming?

LOWELL: I might even give the kids some ideas.

MIKE: All we want is the use of the floor.

LOWELL: Okay. You want the floor? You got it. Now I go.

"Plant You Now, Dig You Later"

(*Verse*)

LOWELL:

> Sweetheart, the day is waning,
> Must go without complaining,

Time for Auf Wiedersehning now.
Don't let this sad disclosure
Ruffle your calm composure,
Smile at the one who knows your
Ev'ry whim.
Wait for him now.
(*Refrain*)
Where's the check?
Get me the waiter.
I'm not going to stay.
Plant you now, dig you later,
I'm on my way.
My regret couldn't be greater
At having to scram.
Plant you now, dig you later,
I'm on the lam.
Bye-bye, my hep-chick,
Solid and true.
I'll keep in step-chick,
Till I come digging for you.
So, little potater.
Stay right where you are,
Plant you now, dig you later
Means au revoir,
Just au revoir!

GLADYS: Oh but I want to go with you.
(*Verse*)
I know your time is money
And though you leave me, Sunny
We'll have a future honey-moon
Right now it's time to start your
Farewells that mean depart-ure
I keep deep in your heart
You're all for me
Call for me soon.

SCENE 2

JOEY's apartment. He is on love seat, left, reading his notices. VERA *enters from left at rise.*

VERA: Well, Beauty, how did they treat you?

JOEY: They all said I was there. That's something, I guess.

(VERA *eases to behind* JOEY.)

They didn't even say I stink. They didn't say anything except this newcomer from New York drew a fashionable crowd, and so forth. You got more out of it than me! Mrs. Prentiss Simpson gave a large party! And then the names of those jerks. Mrs. Prentiss Simpson was ravishing in a dirty old suit of tired overalls. Then the names of some more jerks. Yeah? Well, do I get my notices? I need my notices when I talk about my radio job.

VERA: I wouldn't worry about the job, Beauty.

JOEY (*turns to her*): I'm thinking that over. That Beauty. I'm not so sure I like it. I'm not exactly beautiful.

VERA: Listen. I am thirty-six years old. I know what's beautiful.

JOEY: Oh, well—I see what you mean. You—me—

VERA: Don't analyze it. If you take it apart you might not be able to put it together again.

JOEY: Beauty, hey—nobody ever put it that way before.

VERA: I can believe that. Your average conquest—I imagine they were rather unthinking. Or else they never thought of anything else. And judging by the way some of my friends were looking at you last night—

JOEY (*eagerly*): Yeah? Which ones?

VERA: Oh, no. (*Rises.*) Maybe not any place else—but here it's just you and I. While we're here I can be reasonably sure of you. That's why I'm really beginning to like this terrible apartment.

JOEY: Terrible apartment? Why this is the *nuts*.

VERA: Yes, dear.

"In Our Little Den"
Just two little love birds all alone
In a little cozy nest

With a little secret telephone,
That's the place to rest.

JOEY:

Artificial roses 'round the door—
They are never out of bloom—

VERA:

And a flowered carpet on the floor
In the loving room.

(*Refrain*)

BOTH:

In our little den of iniquity
Our arrangement is good.

VERA:

It's much more healthy living here,
This rushing back home is bad, my dear,

JOEY:

I haven't caught a cold all year:

VERA:

Knock on wood!

BOTH:

It was ever thus, since antiquity,
All the poets agree.

VERA:

The chambermaid is very kind,
She always thinks we're so refined,

JOEY:

Of course, she's deaf and dumb and blind—

BOTH:

No fools, we—
In our little den of iniquity.

In our little den of iniquity
For a girly and boy,

VERA:

We'll sit and let the hours pass,
A canopy bed has so much class,

JOEY:

And so's a ceiling made of glass—

BOTH:

Oh, what joy!

Love has been that way, since antiquity,
Down to you and me.

VERA:

The radio, I used to hate,
But now when it is dark and late
Tchaikowski's "1812" sounds great—

BOTH:

That's for me,
In our little den of iniquity.

SCENE 3

Chez Joey two days after opening. GLADYS *is lolling in a chair.* THE BUM *is admitting* LINDA *at street door.* LINDA *is in street clothes and carries a package.*

THE BUM (*to* GLADYS): Here's somebody wants to see Mr. Mike.

GLADYS: What am I supposed to do?

LINDA: I have a C.O.D. for Mr. Evans but I'm supposed to collect the money from Mr. Mike.

GLADYS: Won't he be glad to see you? What is it?

LINDA: It's an evening vest. I mean waistcoat.

THE BUM: I'll tell him. (*Exits.*)

GLADYS: Why don't you sit down? Mike is never in a hurry to pay for a C.O.D. Especially for Joey—I mean Mr. Evans.

LINDA (*sitting down*): But after all, Joey is the star attraction.

GLADYS: He's the star. I'm not so sure about the attraction.

LINDA: You sound as if you disliked him. What'd he ever do to you, or shouldn't I ask?

GLADYS: Well, nothing. He never really did anything to me, I guess.

LINDA: I don't believe anybody's all bad.

GLADYS: Aw, now listen. I'm tired.

LINDA: Oh, I'm not just a dumb Pollyanna, either. But Joey— if the right person took an interest in him maybe the good things would come out.

GLADYS: Then for my dough the right person took an interest a long time ago, and all the good things came out, permanently.
    (*The* KID *enters from outside.*)

KID: Hey—Gladys—There's a gentleman want to see you. He's outside in a car. He says to tell you Ludlow is here.

GLADYS: Oh, lend me your coat. (*To* LINDA.) Excuse it, please! (*Takes the* KID's *coat, and exits.*)

(WAITER *enters.*)

WAITER: Mike says to wait for him in the office. In there. (*Indicates office.*)

(LINDA *goes there*, WAITER *gives her the eye—leering.*)

KID: Oh, you been working in these joints so long, you think anybody with clothes on is pretty.

(LOWELL *enters—followed by* GLADYS.)

LOWELL (*to the* KID): Could we talk a little private?

KID: Who? Us?

LOWELL: Not this time, dear. I and Gladys this time.

(*The* KID *exits.*)

(*To* WAITER.)

Now, Waiter, you know what you can do.

WAITER: Yes, sir?

LOWELL: Walk east. Walk east as far as you can. You come to Lake Michigan. Keep right on walking 'til your hat starts floating. You catch?

WAITER (*as he leaves*): I catch. (*Exits.*)

LOWELL: God, the waiters in this town are getting fresh and impertinent.

GLADYS: What's the scheme? Give.

LOWELL: Well, there's an ugly, ugly word for it. It is called blackmail or extortion in some sets. In our set it is known as the shake.

GLADYS: Do I get under the bed? You remember the last time what happened.

LOWELL (*smiling placatingly*): Not this time. This time you're high and dry. I am only keeping you in reserve. Now if you let me expostulate the stragety, it's this way. This Mrs. Simpson. Joey's protector? Well, did you ever take notice to these trucks around town with Staffo on the side in big letters?

GLADYS: What would I be doing looking at trucks?

LOWELL: Maybe some day you'll be sorry you didn't, if one comes along with your number on it. Anyway, Staffo means a kind of bread. It is made by *Mister* Simpson in large quantities. I tell you how large the quantities are. One of these trucks that you never took notice to, they cost anywhere from three to ten thousand dollars each. Mr. Simpson has around a hundred of these trucks. Does that make an interesting mathematic to you? Is that a kind of an arithmetic that fascinates you?

GLADYS (*thinking*): Say they're worth three grand apiece . . . Why, that's $300,000 bucks. And he has to have people drive them, too. That costs money.

LOWELL: Right. Correct.

GLADYS: He has to have a garage to keep them in.

LOWELL: Most precisely and assuredly.

GLADYS: Gas. You can't run those trucks without gas.

LOWELL: Right. Right. Maybe I better help you a little if we're ever gonna get to the point. The important part, they carry a lot of bread, and he probably nets a cent on each and every single loaf of bread.

GLADYS: Oh. Well, then there's pie and cake, too.

LOWELL: Yes, dear. There's pie and cake and cinnamon buns and ginger snaps. Okay, he sells a lot of that stuff. Now get the psychology. A man that runs a bank—

GLADYS: Oh, a bank too? That's good.

LOWELL: Kindly refrain from opening your God damn trap till I finish. Now look. A man that runs a bank, he has to be respectable till he gets caught. Then they get another man. But the man that sells bread or milk, the public thinks of him as a handsome old fluff with a white suit and a white cap on his head. If he gets in a jam, that's bad. They don't only get a new man. They get a new bread. The jam kills the bread. Ooh, what am I saying? Excuse it. So anyway, this is a two-way blackmail. I go to old Simpson. I tell him his wife is carrying on with my sister's fiancé. You are my sister. Joey is your fiancé. If he don't get up the dough we are going to sue his wife, so that puts him in a jam. The other part, I'm a little ashamed of it, it's so old-fashioned. All I do, I go to Mrs. Simpson and just say if she don't get up say 20 G's, I'll tell her husband about Joey.

GLADYS: I like that one better.

LOWELL (*he starts to laugh*): Oh, and I forgot to tell you. This is such small change, but it strikes my sense of humor.

GLADYS: What's that? To see an old lady hit by a truck or something?

LOWELL: No, no, no, no. In addition to taking Mr. and Mrs. Simpson, I decided just for the hell of it to take Joey too. (*They both laugh.*) First we take dear Mrs. Simpson, then Joey—
   (LINDA *appears.*)

GLADYS (*as* LINDA *crosses their table*): You get everything straightened out?

LINDA: Yes, everything's straightened out.

GLADYS: I didn't hear any screams.

LINDA: That's nothing, I didn't hear you scream either.

GLADYS: Get her. Get that dialogue . . . Oh, you ever meet Ludlow Lowell, the agent?

LOWELL: Artist's representative, please.

LINDA: How do you do and goodbye. (*Exits.*)

LOWELL: Goodbye, goodbye. (*Looking after* LINDA.)

GLADYS: You don't think?

LOWELL: No. Nobody ever hears me. I talk in a whisper.

GLADYS: You know this shake may not be so easy.

LOWELL: Don't worry. Let me make the plans. And I think our plan is to contact the charming Mrs. Simpson right away.

GLADYS: Yes, but I do worry. Remember that time I was found under the bed?

LOWELL: It's very seldom you're found under the bed, so forget the whole incident.

GLADYS: I just say it might not be so easy.

LOWELL: Did you ever see the time when I was afraid to do it the hard way? Don't answer.

"Do It the Hard Way"

Fred Astaire once worked so hard
He often lost his breath,
And now he taps all other chaps to death.
Working hard did not retard
The young Cab Calloway,
Now hear him blow his vo-de-o-do today.
   (*Refrain*)
Do it the hard way
And it's easy sailing.
Do it the hard way
And it's hard to lose.
Only the soft way

Has a chance of failing;
You have to choose.
I took the hard way
When I tried to get you,
You took the soft way
When you said "We'll see."
Darling, now I'll let you
Do it the hard way
Now that you want me.

SCENE 4

The apartment. ERNEST *is fitting new jacket on* JOEY.

JOEY: Wait 'til my new dance goes in. The Club will be making money.

    (*Telephone rings.*)

    (*In phone.*) Yeah . . . Who? Why—Sure—

    It's Linda English—It's that girl. You know—

VERA: Ask her to come up.

JOEY: Come on up. I don't know what she means. I haven't seen her.

VERA: Maybe you have, and maybe you haven't. But you're giving your usual impression of a man with a guilty conscience. If your own mother were announced, you'd have a guilty conscience.

JOEY (*does a takes*): I sure would. Wouldn't you?

VERA: Well, since you put it that way, yes.

JOEY: Although I wouldn't mind it if it was my old man. (*Laughs.*) He always said I'd never amount to anything.

VERA: What's he doing now?

JOEY: Dads—? Dads, is at Palm Beach—

VERA: Never mind. I'm sorry I asked.

    (*Door buzzes.*)

    (VERA *rises.* LINDA *enters and crosses to* VERA.)

VERA: Hello. How are you?

LINDA: I'm very well, thank you, Mrs. Simpson. Could I speak to you alone?

VERA: Why, of course. (*To* JOEY.) Blow, you.

JOEY: Blow?

VERA: Try on one of your new frocks.

JOEY: God, the way you're getting to talk.

VERA: Try on one of your new costumes.

    (JOEY *exits*.)

    (VERA *sits*.) I'm sorry I pretended to be a gangster's moll that day.

LINDA (*sits*): Oh, that's all right. I guess I knew you weren't one, but—that's not what I came to talk about. I came to warn you.

VERA: Warn me? About what?

LINDA: Both of you. You and Mr. Evans.

VERA: Sounds sinister.

LINDA: They're going to blackmail you. I overheard them.

VERA: Yes?

LINDA: Oh, you know who they are?

VERA: No. But I have to find out somehow, so I thought I'd let you tell me your own way.

LINDA (*rises, crosses to* VERA): Well, it's that Ludlow Lowell, the agent. And that blonde singer at the club. They have some scheme that they'll tell your husband that you and Mr. Evans—go around together—quite a lot.

VERA: How delicate you are. (*Rises.*) Hmmm—What about Joey?

LINDA (*drops down*): Well—they didn't count on getting much out of him. Only all he had.

VERA: I'm afraid his bank balance will disappoint them. Linda, what about you? I wonder why you're warning me.

LINDA: Why? Because it's dishonest—that's all.

VERA: Is it? Is that all? As one woman to another?

LINDA: Well I certainly hope you don't think it was what you think it was.

VERA: I think it was, though.

LINDA: Well, just don't think it was what you think it was. Take him.

"Take Him"

LINDA:

    He was a cutie—I admit I used to care.

    But it's my duty to myself to take the air.

    I won't prevent you from eloping if you wish.

     May I present you with this tasty dish.
(*Refrain*)
     Take him, you don't have to pay for him,
     Take him, he's free.
     Take him, I won't make a play for him,
     He's not for me.
     He has no head to think with,
     True that his heart is asleep.
     But he has eyes to wink with:
     You can have him cheap.
     Keep him, and just for the lure of it
     Marry him too.
     Keep him, for you can be sure of it.
     He can't keep you,
     So take my old jalopy,
     Keep him from falling apart.
     Take him, but don't ever take him to heart.
(*Verse*)

VERA:

     Thanks, little mousie for the present and all that
     But in this housey I would rather keep a rat.
     Only a wizard could reform that class of males.
     They say a lizard cannot change his scales.
(*Refrain*)
     Take him, I won't put a price on him,
     Take him, he's yours.
     Take him, pajamas look nice on him,
     But how he snores.
     Though he is well adjusted,
     Certain things make him a wreck.
     Last year his arm was busted
     Reaching for a check.
     His thoughts are seldom consecutive,
     He just can't write.
     I know a movie executive
     Who's twice as bright.
     Lots of good luck, you'll need it,
     And you'll need aspirin too.
     Take him, but don't ever let him take you.

(*Duet—harmony*)

BOTH:

> I hope that things will go well with him,
> I bear no hate.
> All I can say, is the hell with him,
> He gets the gate.
> So take my benediction
> Take my old benedict too.
> Take it away, it's too good to be true.

(JOEY *enters in costume.*)

JOEY: I was going to show you my dance. Who you talking about?

VERA: Linda and I have discovered that we have a mutual friend.

JOEY: Yeah?

VERA: But I don't think you'd recognize him—even if we described him to you.

VERA and LINDA:

> I hope that things will go well with him
> I bear no hate
> All I can say, is the hell with him
> He gets the gate
> So take my benediction
> Take my old benedict too
> Take it away, it's too good to be true.

(LINDA *exits*—JOEY *exits to change*—VERA *goes to phone.*)

VERA: Dearborn 3300, please. Speak to Deputy Commissioner O'Brien, please. Mrs. Simpson calling . . . that's right—Mrs. Prentiss Simpson. Hello, Commissioner?—you'll get a chance to prove it right now. Yes, it is . . . just about the same kind of thing that happened two years ago. I'm afraid I've been a bad girl again—not really bad—but just having a little fun— that's right—What? Well, what's more fun, may I ask?—Oh, you're slipping. No—I'm not at home . . . I'm at the Embassy Arms Apartment—18-B. The name is Evans . . . you will?— Thanks—goodbye. (*Hangs up.*) Dear Jack. What would I do without him? I know damn well what I'd do. I'd pay. (*Calling offstage.*) Beauty!

JOEY (*enters*): Well, what gives?

VERA: I wonder what you did to that girl that made you like her so much? Or didn't do?

JOEY: I never didn't do anything. Or do anything. I never nothing.

VERA: Stop that baby-talk. You're a big boy now. Big enough to be blackmailed.

JOEY: Blackmailed? Me? That's for a laugh.

VERA: Laugh now, then, because your friend and agent, Mr. Lowell, and your friend and I don't know what, Miss Gladys Bumps, have a little plan to take me for plenty, and you for whatever you have.

JOEY: Oh, they wouldn't do that. I know they're strictly larceny, but—

    (*Knock on door.*)

    (JOEY *moves right.*)

    (*Enter* LOWELL *and* GLADYS *with fox stole.*)

LOWELL: I took the liberty and assumed the privilege of old acquaintance and came right up without being announced. Do you mind?

JOEY: You're here. What do you want?

LOWELL (*eases to* JOEY—GLADYS *follows*): I expected a little more cordiality from client to representative.

GLADYS: I don't like his attitude.

LOWELL: Nor do I, my dear mutton. (*To Joey.*) Oh, my new client. (*Indicating* GLADYS—*her business with fox head.*) But we must proceed.

    (GLADYS *sits—He crosses to* VERA.)

Uh, dear Mrs. Simpson, I bet you're wondering to what you owe the honor of this visit—like in the old plays? Or maybe you're not wondering, but I will tell you. Seating myself on the chaise longue—(*he does so*) and casually lighting a butt—my object is blackmail.

VERA: Well, I'll be damned.

JOEY: I'll be darned.

LOWELL: I have decided that you are an intelligent woman of the world, Mrs. Simpson. A woman that has been around—not too long, of course—

VERA: Thanks for that anyway.

LOWELL: Glad to. Now a woman of the world, charming, intelligent, fascinating—she knows that the time comes to pay the piper.

VERA: Did you say viper?

LOWELL: Haw haw haw. Not bad. Not bad. Viper. Windshield viper. Like that one? Well, to continue, you know that the day of reckoning must come, and here it is. I reckon twenty thousand is a good day's reckoning.

VERA: Twenty thousand.

LOWELL: Ah, the way you say it. I know we aren't going to have no trouble, Mrs. Simpson. That's the figure. A little old twenty thousand.

VERA: Otherwise, I suppose you'll tell my husband that Joey and I—

LOWELL: We would be forced to it, wouldn't we?

VERA: I don't know who'd force you, but I see what you mean.

JOEY: You'll do that to her over my dead body.

LOWELL: Now Joey, I wouldn't say that if I were you because on my books you are in hock to me for a little over seven gees.

JOEY: What do you mean, "your books"?

LOWELL: My books are better than your books and you have no books.

JOEY: Why you lousy . . .

    (LOWELL *knocks him out.*)

LOWELL (*to* MRS. SIMPSON *who is at* JOEY's *side*): We can talk better without him standing there like a wooden Indian. I used to be quite a pugilist Mrs. Simpson.

VERA: Oh, I can see that. Anybody you outweigh by fifty pounds.

LOWELL (*crosses and looks at* JOEY): Five short minutes and he'll be as good as new. Here! (*Lifts* JOEY *and puts him on the couch.*) . . . so I and you might as well talk.

VERA: Naturally, let's talk. Don't you think twenty thousand is rather high?

LOWELL: Yes. Yes I do.

VERA: Couldn't we adjust it slightly? We might bargain a little for cash.

LOWELL: Oh, I'm afraid you misunderstood me, or else I didn't make myself clear. I never had no thought about this being anything but a cash deal. From the very beginning I was thinking in terms of cash.

GLADYS: Strictly cash.

LOWELL: Gladys put it correctly. Strictly cash.

VERA: But how am I going to get twenty thousand in cash?

GLADYS: Sell some trucks.

LOWELL: Now Gladys, no more interruptions please. You saw what happened to Joey. There are ways and means of a woman like you getting twenty gees cash, you know that.

VERA: I haven't got it in the bank.

LOWELL: I hear different. What I hear, I hear you send a check around and deposit it to the Chez Joey account every week without fail.

VERA: Oh. You really made quite a study of this. What am I going to tell my husband when he finds out I have no money in the bank?

LOWELL: Mrs. Simpson, what you oughta be worrying about is what we're gonna tell your husband.

VERA: You've got something there. You sure you couldn't come down a little ten thousand?

LOWELL: I don't see how. You see, Mrs. Simpson, Gladys gets her cut out of this. If you could persuade *her* to give up *her* end . . .

GLADYS: Don't even try. Don't waste your time.

LOWELL: Then you see how it is, Mrs. Simpson? I'm afraid we come to the same old seeteaction, twenty thousand.

(*Phone rings.*)

VERA: Just a moment . . . Hello. Oh send her up please.

LOWELL: Who was that? We don't want to be interrupted just when we're getting somewhere.

VERA: My hairdresser. She can wait in the next room. The only thing is, Mr. Lowell, I'm about through with Joey anyway.

LOWELL: Mrs. Simpson. Not that I'm a guy that goes around doubting a lady's word but I think you only told me you're through with Joey because you thought you'd bluff me.

VERA: There you're wrong. I've decided he's become too expensive. And I'm afraid Joey's eye is beginning to wander.

(*Door buzzes.*)

Come in Jack. You know Mr. Lowell and Miss Bumps?

O'BRIEN: Yes, sure Mrs. Simpson. I'd recognize him in a minute. He used to have his picture in every post office in the country. Didn't you Looie?

LOWELL (*to* GLADYS): Come on you.

O'BRIEN: You'll blow when I tell you to.

LOWELL: Listen Copper, we're in the clear. You can't make a pinch here.

O'BRIEN: Who said anything about making a pinch? I just came up here to see you off at the train. You know Mrs. Simpson I wouldn't do this for just everybody. We were all hoping the next time Looey took a train it would be for a five year visit down at Joliet.

VERA: I'm sorry, Jack. Well, Mr. Lowell, you see?

LOWELL: Aaah.

O'BRIEN: The shock is too great for him, but he'll have plenty of time to think it over. I guess we go now Laddie. I have to go with him and see where he buys a ticket for. Come on. Move. Two tickets. You're going too, Gladys. Goodbye, Mrs. Simpson. Don't forget the boys at Christmas.

VERA: Especially not this Christmas, Commissioner.

O'BRIEN: *Jack.*

VERA: Jack.

(*He exits with the other two.* VERA *goes to telephone.*)

Dearborn 9900, please. (*To* JOEY'*s unconscious figure.*) Hello? Commercial National? I want to speak to Mr. McCrea. Hello, Harry? Vera. Look, Harry, on that special account, yes, the Chez Joey one. No more withdrawals. If that Mike person comes around today, tell him the account's been closed. And close it. That's right. Thank you.

(*To* JOEY.) Poor Beauty. You ought to know by this time that chivalry is out of character for you. Never, never do that again.

JOEY (*coming out of it*): Wha——? What'd you say? Ohhh— (*Feels his jaw.*) Hey! What happened? Oh, I know. Did you give him the dough?

VERA: No. You frightened them off.

JOEY: I did? I really frightened them off?—Eh? Well, that

Ludlow not that he isn't a very handy guy with the paws—but
you know, he reminds me of a pug I used to know.

VERA: Some other time, Beauty. Right now I have some questions to bother you with. How are you fixed, financially?

JOEY: I got rid of a lot of dough, recently. Why? You want some
back?

VERA: No, but I've been thinking. What if I were called away
to California, or dropped dead, or something—would you be
all right? I mean, for instance, would you eat?

JOEY: Honey Sug, somehow, I always eat. But what's on your
mind?

VERA (*rises—crosses around to console*): Well, I think I'm going to
be called away to California, or maybe drop dead.

JOEY: Come on, say it. This is the brush off. Those punks gave
you a scare, and you're walking out.

VERA: A slightly brutal, though accurate way of putting it. You
can keep the club. . . .

JOEY: Are you trying to kid me? You got some other guy, that's
why I'm getting the brusheroo. I get it now—"Take him"—
you meant me. All right—go on back to him.

VERA: I have a temper, Beauty, and I want to say a few things
before I lose it.

JOEY: Lose it. It's all you have left to lose. Get out of my
apartment.

VERA: Your apartment— (*She crosses down toward him.*) All right.
I won't even wish you all the good luck you're going to need.

JOEY: Blow.

VERA: Yes, dear. (*Sings.*)

>Wise at last
>My eyes, at last
>Are cutting you down to your size at last.
>Bewitched, bothered and bewildered, no more.
>Burned a lot;
>But I learned a lot.
>And now you are broke, though you earned a lot.
>Bewitched, bothered and bewildered no more.
>Couldn't eat—
>Was dyspeptic;
>Life was so hard to bear.

> Now my heart's antiseptic—
> Since you moved out of there.
> Romance—*finis*;
> Your chance—*finis*;
> Those ants that invaded my pants—*finis*—
> Bewitched, bothered and bewildered no more.

(*She exits—He goes quickly to phone.*)

JOEY: Hi, baby. Dearborn 9900—what time you off? Wait a minute. Commercial National? Mr. McCrea—if you please. Hello, McCrea—yeah, yeah, yeah—Evans of Chez Joey. Send over five hundred cash by messenger right away. Not my personal account. The Chez Joey account. You what? Say, are you serious? My God! How much have I got in my personal account? Don't bother looking. I know.

(*Door buzzes.*)

Come in.

MANAGER (*enters*): Ah, Mr. Evans—is everything quite satisfactory?

JOEY: No. Too noisy. Put in air-conditioning windows. They don't cut the grapefruit right. I want a better looking chambermaid. And another thing. What the hell are you doing here?

MANAGER: Well, you know our rule. Bills payable on the first of the month. And here it is the fourteenth, Mr. Evans! A matter of eleven hundred twenty-three dollars, and twenty-six cents.

JOEY: Well, that will all be taken care of. Mrs. Simpson has a financial interest in my club.

MANAGER: I spoke to Mrs. Simpson—and I inferred from what she said that her financial interest in the club has been terminated. She said—I quote—"That's his headache."

JOEY: Oh—you're going to have to ask for this apartment? I could move to a smaller room—Yeah, yeah—I know. I saw it in *Dinner at Eight-Thirty*. Well, how'd you like it if I turned on the gas, and gave this place a bad name? How about if some rich society debutante was in love with me?

MANAGER: I'm a busy man, Mr. Evans. And in one detail you're very wrong. We're not offering you another smaller room. You have until six o'clock to pay up or get out. I'm afraid you'll have to leave your things with me.

JOEY: You mean, I leave the way I am. How about a hat and coat?

MANAGER: Oh, a hat's all right. I think we can do a hat. A coat? Well, an old coat.

(*Door buzzes.*)

But don't try to get past the desk with that new mink-lined one, Mr. Evans.

(*Door buzzes.*)

JOEY: Come in.

(LINDA *enters.*)

LINDA: Oh, excuse me—I just . . . I came back. I saw Mrs. Simpson and she said . . . (LINDA *is upset.*)

JOEY: Oh, sure. Say, Mr. Hoople—how's for, you know . . . ?

MANAGER: Leaving? (*Crossing in.*) I'm sorry, but I think I'd better stay.

JOEY: You see—I'm planning on getting out of here.

LINDA: Out of town?

JOEY: Well, New York first. Some offer in a musical comedy. They're after me again.

LINDA (*to* JOEY): Oh. I was hoping you could come down and have supper at my sister's house. Remember me telling you about my sister?

JOEY: Yes. That's right. Didn't you tell me she had a husband?

LINDA: In the trucking business.

JOEY: Say, by Jove, it might be fun—seeing some new people. Say—Hoople, old boy—cancel those reservations on the New York plane. I decided to wait over 'til tomorrow.

MANAGER: Cancel the reservations? Yes, sir.

JOEY: Thanks, old boy. Now let me see. Coat?

(MANAGER *nods at polo coat.* JOEY *puts it on.*)

I guess I won't wear my fur-lined one. It's too ostensible, don't you think so?

LINDA: Much.

JOEY: Hat? (*Picks up red-lined Homburg—*MANAGER *shakes—* "no.") Hat? (*Picks up old green one—*MANAGER *nods "yes"—puts it on.*) You won't forget about those reservations, Hoople, old boy?

MANAGER: No, sir.

JOEY: Righto. (*To* LINDA.) I feel like walking. Is it far?

(*They exit.*)

SCENE 5

Pet Shop. LINDA *and* JOEY *enter.*

(JOEY *sings reprise of "I Could Write a Book."*)

JOEY: Boy—did I eat. I'll bet your sister'll never have me for dinner again.

(*They have stopped in front of Pet Shop.*)

LINDA: Oh, there you're wrong. She's very proud of her cooking, and likes to see people eat.

JOEY: Well, I must have given her a lot of pleasure tonight. Three pieces of pie—!

LINDA: Well, if you ever come back to Chicago, you must come again.

JOEY: Well, you never can tell. I'm always changing my plans. Those big New York shows—I don't know. They might bore me.

LINDA: Well, goodbye. (*Shaking his hand.*) I think I'd better get back and help Mary with the dishes.

JOEY: Okay. I may shoot you a wire and let you know how things go.

LINDA: Oh, that would be wonderful. Goodbye.

(*She leaves—He waves after her.*)

JOEY: And thanks—thanks a million.

CURTAIN

OKLAHOMA!

Music by RICHARD RODGERS
Book and lyrics by OSCAR HAMMERSTEIN II
Based on Green Grow the Lilacs *by* LYNN RIGGS

SCENES

ACT ONE

ACT TWO

TIME: *Just after the turn of the century*

PLACE: *Indian Territory (Now Oklahoma)*

MUSICAL NUMBERS

ACT ONE

Scene 1

Oh, What a Beautiful Mornin' . . . . Curly
The Surrey with the Fringe on Top . . . .Curly, Laurey, Aunt Eller
Kansas City . . . . Will, Aunt Eller and the Boys
I Cain't Say No. . . . . Ado Annie
Many a New Day .Laurey and the Girls
It's a Scandal! It's a Outrage! . . . . .Ali Hakim and the
Boys and Girls
People Will Say We're in Love . . . . Curly and Laurey

Scene 2

Pore Jud . . . . .Curly and Jud
Lonely Room. . . . . Jud

Scene 3

Out of My Dreams . . . . .Laurey and the Girls

ACT TWO

Scene 1

The Farmer and the Cowman . . . . .Carnes, Aunt Eller,
Curly, Will, Ado Annie,
Fred and Ensemble
All er Nuthin' . . . Ado Annie and Will and Two Dancing Girls

Scene 2

Reprise: *People Will Say We're in Love* . . . . . . Curly and Laurey

Scene 3

Oklahoma. . . . . .Curly, Laurey, Aunt Eller, Ike,
Fred and Ensemble
Oh, What a Beautiful Mornin'. . . Laurey, Curly and Ensemble
Finale. . . . . Entire Company

ACT ONE

SCENE: *The front of* LAUREY'S *farmhouse.*

"It is a radiant summer morning several years ago, the kind of morning which, enveloping the shapes of earth men, cattle in a meadow, blades of the young corn, streams—makes them seem to exist now for the first time, their images giving off a golden emanation that is partly true and partly a trick of the imagination, focusing to keep alive a loveliness that may pass away."

AUNT ELLER MURPHY, *a buxom hearty woman about fifty, is seated behind a wooden, brass-banded churn, looking out over the meadow (which is the audience), a contented look on her face. Like the voice of the morning, a song comes from somewhere, growing louder as the young singer comes nearer.*

CURLY (*off stage*):
> There's a bright, golden haze on the meadow,
> There's a bright, golden haze on the meadow.
> The corn is as high as a elephant's eye
> An' it looks like it's climbin' clear up to the sky.
> (CURLY *saunters on and stands tentatively outside the gate to the front yard.*)
> Oh, what a beautiful mornin',
> Oh, what a beautiful day.
> I got a beautiful feelin'
> Ev'rythin's goin' my way.
> (CURLY *opens the gate and walks over to the porch, obviously singing for the benefit of someone inside the house.* AUNT ELLER *looks straight ahead, elaborately ignoring* CURLY.)
> All the cattle are standin' like statues,
> All the cattle are standin' like statues.
> They don't turn their heads as they see me ride by,
> But a little brown mav'rick is winkin' her eye.
> Oh, what a beautiful mornin',
> Oh, what a beautiful day.

I got a beautiful feelin'
Ev'rythin's goin' my way.
(CURLY *comes up behind* AUNT ELLER *and shouts in her ear.*)

Hi, Aunt Eller!

AUNT ELLER: Skeer me to death! Whut're you doin' around here?

CURLY: Come a-singin' to you. (*Strolling a few steps away.*)

All the sounds of the earth are like music—
All the sounds of the earth are like music.
The breeze is so busy it don't miss a tree
And a ol' weepin' willer is laughin' at me!
Oh, what a beautiful mornin',
Oh, what a beautiful day.
I got a beautiful feelin'
Ev'rythin's goin' my way. . . .
Oh, what a beautiful day!

(AUNT ELLER *resumes churning.* CURLY *looks wistfully up at the windows of the house, then turns back to* AUNT ELLER.)

AUNT ELLER: If I wasn't a ole womern, and if you wasn't so young and smart-alecky—why, I'd marry you and git you to set around at night and sing to me.

CURLY: No, you wouldn't neither. Cuz I wouldn't marry you ner none of yer kinfolks, I could he'p it.

AUNT ELLER (*wisely*): Oh, none of my kinfolks, huh?

CURLY (*raising his voice so that* LAUREY *will hear if she is inside the house*): And you c'n tell 'em that, *all* of 'm includin' that niece of your'n, Miss Laurey Williams! (AUNT ELLER *continues to churn.* CURLY *comes down to her and speaks deliberately.*) Aunt Eller, if you was to tell me whur Laurey was at—whur would you tell me she was at?

AUNT ELLER: I wouldn't tell you a-tall. Fer as fer as I c'n make out, Laurey ain't payin' you no heed.

CURLY: So, she don't take to me much, huh? Whur'd you git sich a uppity niece 'at wouldn't pay no heed to me? Who's the best bronc buster in this yere territory?

AUNT ELLER: You, I bet.

CURLY: And the best bull-dogger in seventeen counties? Me, that's who! And looky here, I'm handsome, ain't I?

AUNT ELLER: Purty as a pitcher.

CURLY: Curly-headed, ain't I? And bow-legged from the saddle fer God knows how long, ain't I?

AUNT ELLER: Couldn't stop a pig in the road.

CURLY: Well, whut else does she want then, the damn she-mule?

AUNT ELLER: I don't know. But I'm shore sartin it ain't you. Who you takin' to the Box Social tonight?

CURLY: Ain't thought much about it.

AUNT ELLER: Bet you come over to ast Laurey.

CURLY: Whut 'f I did?

AUNT ELLER: You astin' me too? I'll wear my fascinator.

CURLY: Yeow, you too.

LAUREY (*singing off stage*):
> Oh, what a beautiful mornin'
> (*She enters.*)
> Oh, what a beautiful day
> (*Spoken as she gives* CURLY *a brief glance.*)
> Oh, I thought you was somebody.
> (*She resumes singing, crosses to clothesline and hangs up an apron.*)
> I got a beautiful feelin'
> Ev'rythin's goin' my way.
> (*Spoken as she comes down to* AUNT ELLER.*)

Is this all that's come a-callin' and it a'ready ten o'clock of a Sattiddy mornin'?

CURLY: You knowed it was me 'fore you opened the door.

LAUREY: No sich of a thing.

CURLY: You did, too! You heared my voice and knowed it was me.

LAUREY: I heared a voice a-talkin' rumbly along with Aunt Eller. And heared someone a-singin' like a bullfrog in a pond.

CURLY: You knowed it was me, so you set in there a-thinkin' up sump'n mean to say. I'm a good mind not to ast you to the Box Social.

(AUNT ELLER *rises, crosses to clothesline, takes down quilt, folds it, puts it on porch.*)

LAUREY: If you did ast me, I wouldn't go with you. Besides,

how'd you take me? You ain't bought a new buggy with red
wheels onto it, have you?

CURLY: No, I ain't.

LAUREY: And a spankin' team with their bridles all jinglin'?

CURLY: No.

LAUREY: 'Spect me to ride on behind ole Dun, I guess. You
better ast that ole Cummin's girl you've tuck sich a shine to,
over acrost the river.

CURLY: If I was to ast you, they'd be a way to take you, Miss
Laurey Smarty.

LAUREY: Oh, they would?

> (CURLY *now proceeds to stagger* LAUREY *with an idea. But she
> doesn't let on at first how she is "tuck up" with it.* AUNT ELLER
> *is the one who falls like a ton of bricks immediately and helps*
> CURLY *try to sell it to* LAUREY.)

CURLY:

> When I take you out tonight with me,
> Honey, here's the way it's goin' to be;
> You will set behind a team of snow-white horses
> In the slickest gig you ever see!

AUNT ELLER: Lands!

CURLY:

> Chicks and ducks and geese better scurry
> When I take you out in the surrey,
> When I take you out in the surrey with the fringe on
>   top!
> Watch thet fringe and see how it flutters
> When I drive them high-steppin' strutters!
> Nosey-pokes'll peek through their shutters and their
>   eyes will pop!
> The wheels are yeller, the upholstery's brown,
> The dashboard's genuine leather,
> With isinglass curtains y'c'n roll right down
> In case there's a change in the weather—
> Two bright side-lights, winkin' and blinkin',
> Ain't no finer rig, I'm a-thinkin'!
> You c'n keep yer rig if you're thinkin' 'at I'd keer to
>   swap

Fer that shiny little surrey with the fringe on the top!
(LAUREY *still pretends unconcern, but she is obviously slipping.*)

AUNT ELLER: Would y'say the fringe was made of silk?

CURLY: Wouldn't have no other kind but silk.

LAUREY (*she's only human*): Has it really got a team of snow-
white horses?

CURLY: One's like snow—the other's more like milk.

AUNT ELLER: So y'can tell 'em apart!

CURLY:

    All the world'll fly in a flurry
    When I take you out in the surrey,
    When I take you out in the surrey with the fringe on
       top!
    When we hit that road, hell fer leather,
    Cats and dogs'll dance in the heather,
    Birds and frogs'll sing all together and the toads will
       hop!
    The wind'll whistle as we rattle along,
    The cows'll moo in the clover,
    The river will ripple out a whispered song,
    And whisper it over and over:
(*In a loud whisper.*)
    Don't you wisht y'd go on ferever?
    Don't you wisht y'd go on ferever?
(AUNT ELLER's *and* LAUREY's *lips move involuntarily, shaping
the same words.*)
    Don't you wisht y'd go on ferever and ud never stop
    In that shiny little surrey with the fringe on the top?
(*Music continues under dialogue.*)

AUNT ELLER: Y'd shore feel like a queen settin' up in *that*
carriage!

CURLY (*over-confident*): On'y she talked so mean to me a while
back, Aunt Eller, I'm a good mind not to take her.

LAUREY: Ain't said I was goin'!

CURLY (*the fool*): Ain't ast you!

LAUREY: Whur'd you git sich a rig at? (*With explosive laughter,*

seeing a chance for revenge.) Anh! I bet he's went and h'ard a rig
over to Claremore! Thinkin' I'd go with him!

CURLY: 'S all you know about it.

LAUREY: Spent all his money h'arin' a rig and now ain't got
nobody to ride in it!

CURLY: Have, too! . . . Did not h'ar it. Made the whole thing
up outa my head.

LAUREY: What! Made it up?

CURLY: Dashboard and all.

LAUREY (*flying at him*): Oh! Git offa the place, you! Aunt Eller,
make him git hisse'f outa here. (*She picks up a fly swatter and
chases him.*) Tellin' me lies!

CURLY (*dodging her*): Makin' up a few—look out now! (*He jumps
the fence to save himself.* LAUREY *turns her back to him, and sits
down. He comes up behind her. The music, which had become more
turbulent to match the scene, now softens.*) Makin' up a few purties ain't agin' no law 'at I know of. Don't you wisht they *was*
sich a rig, though? (*Winking at* AUNT ELLER.) Nen y'could go
to the play party and do a hoe-down till mornin' if you was
a mind to. . . . Nen when you was all wore out, I'd lift you
onto the surrey, and jump up alongside of you—And we'd jist
point the horses home. . . . I can jist pitcher the whole thing.

    (AUNT ELLER *beams on them as* CURLY *sings very softly*:)

> I can see the stars gittin' blurry
> When we ride back home in the surrey,
> Ridin' slowly home in the surrey with the fringe on
>   top.
> I can feel the day gittin' older,
> Feel a sleepy head near my shoulder,
> Noddin', droopin' close to my shoulder till it falls,
>   kerplop!
> The sun is swimmin' on the rim of a hill,
> The moon is takin' a header,
> And jist as I'm thinkin' all the earth is still,
> A lark'll wake up in the medder. . . .
> Hush! You bird, my baby's a-sleepin'—
> Maybe got a dream worth a-keepin'
> (*Soothing and slower.*)

Whoa! You team, and jist keep a-creepin' at a slow
clip-clop.
Don't you hurry with the surrey with the fringe on the
top.
(*There is silence and contentment, but only for a brief moment.*
LAUREY *starts slowly to emerge from the enchantment of his
description.*)

LAUREY: On'y . . . on'y there ain't no sich rig. You said you
made the whole thing up.
CURLY: Well . . .
LAUREY: Why'd you come around here with yer stories and lies,
gittin' me all worked up that-a-way? Talkin' 'bout the sun
swimmin' on the hill, and all—like it was so. Who'd want to
ride 'longside of you anyway?
(IKE *and* FRED *enter and stand outside the gate, looking on.*)
AUNT ELLER: Whyn't you jist grab her and kiss her when she
acts that-a-way, Curly? She's jist achin' fer you to, I bet.
LAUREY: Oh, I won't even speak to him, let alone 'low him to
kiss me, the braggin', bow-legged, wisht-he-had-a-sweetheart
bum! (*She flounces into the house, slamming the door.*)
AUNT ELLER: She likes you—quite a lot.
CURLY: Whew! If she liked me any more she'd sic the dogs onto
me.
IKE: Y'git the wagon hitched up?
AUNT ELLER: Whut wagon?
CURLY: They's a crowd of folks comin' down from Bushyhead
for the Box Social.
FRED: Curly said mebbe you'd loan us yer big wagon to bring
'em up from the station.
AUNT ELLER: Course I would, if he'd ast me.
CURLY (*embarrassed*): Got to talkin' 'bout a lot of other things.
I'll go hitch up the horses now 'f you say it's all right.
(*As he exits, a group of boys run on, leaping the fence, shouting
boisterously and pushing* WILL PARKER *in front of them.* WILL
is apparently a favorite with AUNT ELLER.)
SLIM: See whut we brung you, Aunt Eller!
AUNT ELLER: Hi, Will!
WILL: Hi, Aunt Eller!

AUNT ELLER: Whut happened up at the fair? You do any good in the steer ropin'?

WILL: I did purty good. I won it.

(*The following three speeches overlap.*)

IKE: Good boy!

FRED: Always knowed y'would.

AUNT ELLER: Ain't nobody c'n sling a rope like our territory boys.

WILL: Cain't stay but a minnit, Aunt Eller. Got to git over to Ado Annie. Don't you remember, her paw said 'f I ever was worth fifty dollars I could have her?

AUNT ELLER: Fifty dollars! That whut they give you fer prize money?

WILL: That's whut!

AUNT ELLER: Lands, if Ado Annie's paw keeps his promise we'll be dancin' at yer weddin'.

WILL: If he don't keep his promise I'll take her right from under his nose, and I won't give him the present I brung fer him. (*He takes "The Little Wonder" from his pocket. This is a small cylindrical toy with a peep-hole at one end.*) Look, fellers, whut I got for Ado Annie's paw! (*The boys crowd around.*) 'Scuse us, Aunt Eller. (*Illustrating to the boys, lowering his voice.*) You hold it up to yer eyes, like this. Then when you git a good look, you turn it around at th' top and the pitcher changes.

IKE (*looking into it*): Well, I'll be side-gaited!

(*The boys line up, and take turns, making appropriate ejaculations.*)

WILL: They call it "The Little Wonder"!

AUNT ELLER: Silly goats! (*But her curiosity gets the better of her. She yanks a little man out of the line, takes his place, gets hold of "The Little Wonder" and takes a look.*) The hussy! . . . Ought to be ashamed of herself. (*Glaring at* WILL.) You, too! . . . How do you turn the thing to see the other pitcher? (*Looking again, and turning.*) Wait, I'm gettin' it. . . . (*When she gets it, she takes it away from her eye quickly and, handing it to* WILL, *walks away in shocked silence. Then she suddenly "busts out laughin'."*) I'm a good mind to tell Ado Annie on yer.

WILL: Please don't, Aunt Eller. She wouldn't understand.

AUNT ELLER: No tellin' what you been up to. Bet you carried on plenty in Kansas City.

WILL: I wouldn't call it carryin' on. But I shore did see some things I never see before. (*Sings.*)

> I got to Kansas City on a Frid'y.
> By Sattidy I l'arned a thing or two.
> For up to then I didn't have an idy
> Of whut the modren world was comin' to!
> I counted twenty gas buggies goin' by theirsel's
> Almost ev'ry time I tuck a walk.
> Nen I put my ear to a Bell Telephone
> And a strange womern started in to talk!

AUNT ELLER: Whut next!
BOYS: Yeah, whut!
WILL: Whut next?

> Ev'rythin's up to date in Kansas City.
> They've gone about as fur as they c'n go!
> They went and built a skyscraper seven stories high—
> About as high as a buildin' orta grow.
> Ev'rythin's like a dream in Kansas City.
> It's better than a magic-lantern show!
> Y'c'n turn the radiator on whenever you want some
>   heat.
> With ev'ry kind o' comfort ev'ry house is all complete.
> You c'n walk to privies in the rain an' never wet yer
>   feet!
> They've gone about as fur as they c'n go!

ALL:

> Yes, sir!
> They've gone about as fur as they c'n go!

WILL:

> Ev'rythin's up to date in Kansas City.
> They've gone about as fur as they c'n go!
> They got a big theayter they call a bur-lee-que.
> Fer fifty cents you c'n see a dandy show.
> One of the gals was fat and pink and pretty,
> As round above as she was round below.
> I could swear that she was padded from her shoulder to
>   her heel,

But later in the second act when she begun to peel
She proved that ev'rythin' she had was absolutely real!
She went about as fur as she could go!

ALL:

Yes, sir!
She went about as fur as she could go!
(WILL *starts two-stepping.*)

IKE: Whut you doin'?
WILL: This is the two-step. That's all they're dancin' nowadays.
The waltz is through. Ketch on to it? A one and a two—a one
and a two. Course they don't do it alone. C'mon, Aunt Eller.
(WILL *dances* AUNT ELLER *around. At the end of the refrain
she is all tuckered out.*)

AUNT ELLER:

And that's about as fur as I c'n go!

ALL:

Yes, sir!
And that's about as fur as she c'n go!
(WILL *starts to dance alone.*)

FRED: Whut you doin' now, Will?
WILL: That's rag-time. Seen a couple of colored fellers doin' it.
(*And* WILL *does his stuff, accompanied by four of the dancing
boys. At end of number* CURLY *enters.*)
CURLY: Team's all hitched.
WILL: 'Lo, Curly. Cain't stop to talk. Goin' over to Ado Annie's.
I got fifty dollars.
IKE: Time we got goin', boys. Thanks fer the loan of the wagon,
Aunt Eller. (*They all start to leave.*) Come on, Curly.
CURLY: I'll ketch up with you. (*He makes sure* IKE *is well on his
way, then turns to* AUNT ELLER.) Aunt Eller, I got to know
sumpin'. Listen, who's the low, filthy sneak 'at Laurey's got
her cap set for?
AUNT ELLER: You.
CURLY: Never mind 'at. They must be plenty of men a-tryin' to
spark her. And she shorely leans to one of 'em. Now don't she?
AUNT ELLER: Well, they is that fine farmer, Jace Hutchins, jist
this side of Lone Ellum— Nen thet ole widder man at Claremore, makes out he's a doctor or a vet'nary—

(JUD, *a burly, scowling man enters, carrying firewood*.)

CURLY: That's whut I thought. Hello, Jud.

JUD: Hello, yourself.

(JUD *exits into house*.)

AUNT ELLER (*significantly, looking in* JUD'*s direction*): Nen of course there's someone nearer home that's got her on his mind most of the time, till he don't know a plow from a thrashin' machine.

CURLY (*jerking his head up toward the house*): Him?

AUNT ELLER: Yeah, Jud Fry.

CURLY: That bullet-colored, growly man?

AUNT ELLER: Now don't you go and say nuthin' agin' him! He's the best hired hand I ever had. Jist about runs the farm by hisself. Well, two women couldn't do it, you orta know that.

CURLY: Laurey'd take up 'th a man like that!

AUNT ELLER: I ain't said she's tuck up with him.

CURLY: Well, he's around all the time, ain't he? Lives here.

AUNT ELLER: Out in the smokehouse.

(JUD *and* LAUREY *enter from the house.* JUD *crosses and speaks to* AUNT ELLER.)

JUD: Changed my mind about cleanin' the henhouse today. Leavin' it till tomorrow. Got to quit early cuz I'm drivin' Laurey over to the party tonight.

(*A bombshell!*)

CURLY: You're drivin' Laurey?

JUD: Ast her.

(*Pointing to* LAUREY, *who doesn't deny it.* JUD *exits.* CURLY *is completely deflated.*)

CURLY: Well, wouldn't that just make you bawl! Well, don't fergit, Aunt Eller. You and me's got a date together. And if you make up a nice box of lunch, mebbe I'll bid fer it.

AUNT ELLER: How we goin', Curly? In that rig you made up? I'll ride a-straddle of them lights a-winkin' like lightnin' bugs!

CURLY: That there ain't no made-up rig, you hear me? I h'ard it over to Claremore.

(*This stuns* LAUREY.)

AUNT ELLER: Lands, you did?

CURLY: Shore did. (*Refrain of the "Surrey Song" starts in orchestra.*) Purty one, too. When I come callin' fer you right after supper, see that you got yer beauty spots fastened onto you proper, so you won't lose 'em off, you hear? 'At's a right smart turnout. (*His voice, a little husky, picks up the refrain:*)

> The wheels are yeller, the upholstery's brown,
> The dashboard's genuine leather,
> With isinglass curtains y'c'n roll right down,
> In case there's a change in the weather—
>
> (*He breaks off in the song.*)

See you before tonight anyways, on the way back from the station—

> (*Turning, singing to himself as he saunters off:*)
> Ain't no finer rig, I'm a-thinkin' . . . 'at I'd keer to swap
> Fer that shiny little surrey with the fringe on the top—
>
> (*He is off.*)

AUNT ELLER (*calling off stage to him*): Hey, Curly, tell all the girls in Bushyhead to stop by here and freshen up. It's a long way to Skidmore's. (*Maybe* LAUREY *would like to "bust out" into tears, but she bites her lip, and doesn't.* AUNT ELLER *studies her for a moment after* CURLY *has gone, then starts up toward the house.*) That means we'll have a lot of company. Better pack yer lunch hamper.

LAUREY (*a strange, sudden panic in her voice*): Aunt Eller, don't go to Skidmore's with Curly tonight. If you do, I'll have to ride with Jud all alone.

AUNT ELLER: That's the way you wanted it, ain't it?

LAUREY: No. I did it because Curly was so fresh. But I'm afraid to tell Jud I won't go, Aunt Eller. He'd do sumpin turrible. He makes me shivver ever' time he gits clost to me. . . . Ever go down to that ole smokehouse where he's at?

AUNT ELLER: Plen'y times. Why?

LAUREY: Did you see them pitchers he's got tacked onto the walls?

AUNT ELLER: Oh, yeah, I seed them. But don't you pay them no mind.

LAUREY: Sumpin wrong inside him, Aunt Eller. I hook my door at night and fasten my winders agin' it. Agin' it—and the sound of feet a-walkin' up and down out there under that tree outside my room.

AUNT ELLER: Laurey!

LAUREY: Mornin's he comes to his breakfast and looks at me out from under his eyebrows like sumpin back in the bresh som'eres. I know whut I'm talkin' about.

(*Voices off stage. It's* ADO ANNIE *and the* PEDDLER.)

AUNT ELLER: You crazy young 'un! Stop actin' like a chicken with its head cut off! Now who'd you reckon that is drove up? Why, it's that ole peddler! The one that sold me that egg-beater!

LAUREY (*looking off*): He's got Ado Annie with him! Will Parker's Ado Annie!

AUNT ELLER: Ole peddler! You know whut he tol' me? Tol' me that egg-beater ud beat up eggs, and wring out dishrags, and turn the ice-cream freezer, and I don't know whut all!

LAUREY (*calling off stage*): Yoohoo! Ado Annie!

AUNT ELLER (*shouting off stage*): Hold yer horses, Peddler-man! I want to talk to you!

(*She starts off, as* ADO ANNIE *enters with lunch hamper.*)

ADO ANNIE: Hi, Aunt Eller!

AUNT ELLER: Hi, yourself. (AUNT ELLER *exits.*)

ADO ANNIE: Hello, Laurey.

LAUREY: Hello. Will Parker's back from Kansas City. He's lookin' fer yer.

(ADO ANNIE'*s brows knit to meet a sudden problem.*)

ADO ANNIE: Will Parker! I didn't count on him bein' back so soon!

LAUREY: I can see that! Been ridin' a piece?

ADO ANNIE: The peddler-man's gonna drive me to the Box Social. I got up sort of a tasty lunch.

LAUREY: Ado Annie! Have you tuck up with that peddler-man?

ADO ANNIE: N-not yit.

LAUREY: But yer promised to Will Parker, ain't yer?

ADO ANNIE: Not what you might say *promised*. I jist told him mebbe.

LAUREY: Don't y' like him no more?

ADO ANNIE: 'Course I do. They won't never be nobody like Will.

LAUREY: Then whut about this peddler-man?

ADO ANNIE (*looking off wistfully*): They won't never be nobody like *him*, neither.

LAUREY: Well, which one d'you like the best?

ADO ANNIE: Whutever one I'm with!

LAUREY: Well, you air a silly!

ADO ANNIE: Now, Laurey, you know they didn't nobody pay me no mind up to this year, count of I was scrawny and flat as a beanpole. Nen I kind of rounded up a little and now the boys act diff'rent to me.

LAUREY: Well, whut's wrong with that?

ADO ANNIE: Nuthin' wrong. I like it. I like it so much when a feller talks purty to me I git all shaky from horn to hoof! Don't you?

LAUREY: Cain't think whut yer talkin' about.

ADO ANNIE: Don't you feel kind of sorry fer a feller when he looks like he wants to kiss you?

LAUREY: Well, you jist cain't go around kissin' every man that asts you! Didn't anybody ever tell you that?

ADO ANNIE: Yeow, they *told* me.

It ain't so much a question of not knowin' whut to do,
I knowed whut's right and wrong since I been ten.
I heared a lot of stories—and I reckon they are true—
About how girls're put upon by men.
I know I mustn't fall into the pit,
But when I'm with a feller—I fergit!

I'm jist a girl who cain't say no,
I'm in a turrible fix.
I always say, come on, le's go—
Jist when I orta say nix!
When a person tries to kiss a girl
I know she orta give his face a smack.
But as soon as someone kisses me
I somehow sorta wanta kiss him back!
I'm jist a fool when lights are low.
I cain't be prissy and quaint—
I ain't the type thet c'n faint—
How c'n I be whut I ain't?
I cain't say no!

Whut you goin' to do when a feller gits flirty
And starts to talk purty?

Whut you goin' to do?
S'posin' 'at he says 'at yer lips're like cherries,
Er roses, er berries?
Whut you goin' to do?
S'posin' 'at he says 'at you're sweeter'n cream
And he's gotta have cream er die?
Whut you goin' to do when he talks thet way?
Spit in his eye?

I'm jist a girl who cain't say no,
Cain't seem to say it at all.
I hate to disserpoint a beau
When he is payin' a call.
Fer a while I ack refined and cool,
A-settin' on the velveteen settee—
Nen I think of thet ol' golden rule,
And do fer him whut he would do fer me!
I cain't resist a Romeo
In a sombrero and chaps.
Soon as I sit on their laps
Somethin' inside of me snaps
I cain't say no!
(*She sits on her hamper, and looks discouraged.*)

I'm jist a girl who cain't say no.
Kissin's my favorite food.
With er without the mistletoe
I'm in a holiday mood!
Other girls are coy and hard to catch
But other girls ain't havin' any fun!
Ev'ry time I lose a wrestlin' match
I have a funny feelin' that I won!
Though I c'n feel the undertow,
I never make a complaint
Till it's too late fer restraint,
Then when I want to I cain't.
I cain't say no!

(*Resuming dialogue, after applause.*)
It's like I tole you, I git sorry fer them!

LAUREY: I wouldn't feel sorry fer any man, no matter whut!

ADO ANNIE: I'm shore sorry fer pore Ali Hakim now. Look how Aunt Eller's cussin' him out!

LAUREY: Ali Hakim! That his name?

ADO ANNIE: Yeah, it's Persian.

LAUREY: You shore fer sartin you love him better'n you love Will?

ADO ANNIE: I *was* shore. And now that ole Will has to come home and first thing you know he'll start talkin' purty to me and changin' my mind back!

LAUREY: But Will wants to marry you.

ADO ANNIE: So does Ali Hakim.

LAUREY: Did he ast yer?

ADO ANNIE: Not direckly. But how I know is he said this mornin' that he wanted fer me to drive like that with him to the end of the world. Well, 'f we drove only as fur as Catoosie that'd take to sundown, wouldn't it? Nen we'd have to go som'eres and be all night together, and bein' together all night means he wants a weddin', don't it?

LAUREY: Not to a peddler it don't!

(*Enter* PEDDLER *and* AUNT ELLER.)

PEDDLER: All right! All right! If the egg-beater don't work I give you something just as good!

AUNT ELLER: Jist as good! It's got to be a thousand million times better!

(*The* PEDDLER *puts down his bulging suitcase, his little beady eyes sparkling professionally. He rushes over and, to* LAUREY'S *alarm, kisses her hand.*)

PEDDLER: My, oh, my! Miss Laurey! Jippity crickets, how high you have growed up! Last time I come through here, you was tiny like a shrimp, with freckles. Now look at you—a great big beautiful lady!

LAUREY: Quit it a-bitin' me! If you ain't had no breakfast go and eat yerself a green apple!

PEDDLER: Now, Aunt Eller, just lissen—

AUNT ELLER (*shouting*): I ain't yer Aunt Eller! Don't you call me Aunt Eller, you little wart. I'm mad at you.

PEDDLER: Don't you go and be mad at me. Ain't I said I'd give you a present? (*Getting his bag.*) Something to wear.

AUNT ELLER: Foot! Got things fer to wear. Wouldn't have it. Whut is it?

PEDDLER (*holding up garter*): Real silk. Made in Persia!

AUNT ELLER: Whut'd I want with a ole Persian garter?

ADO ANNIE: They look awful purty, Aunt Eller, with bows onto 'em and all.

AUNT ELLER: I'll try 'em on.

PEDDLER: Hold out your foot.

> (AUNT ELLER *obeys mechanically. But when he gets the garter over her ankle, she kicks him down.*)

AUNT ELLER: Did you have any idy I was goin' ter let you slide that garter up my limb? (*She stoops over and starts to pull the garter up.*) Grab onto my petticoats, Laurey.

> (*Noticing the* PEDDLER *looking at her, she turns her back on him pointedly and goes on with the operation. The* PEDDLER *turns to* ADO ANNIE.)

PEDDLER: Funny woman. Would be much worse if I tried to take your garters off.

ADO ANNIE: Yeh, cuz that ud make her stockin's fall down, wouldn't it?

AUNT ELLER: Now give me the other one.

PEDDLER: Which one? (*Picking it out of his case.*) Oh, you want to buy this one to match?

AUNT ELLER: Whut do you mean do I want to *buy* it?

PEDDLER: I can let you have it for fifty cents—four bits.

AUNT ELLER: Do you want me to get that egg-beater and ram it down yer windpipe! (*She snatches the second one away.*)

PEDDLER: All right—all right. Don't anybody want to buy something? How about you, Miss Laurey? Must be wanting something—a pretty young girl like you.

LAUREY: Me? Course I want sumpin. (*Working up to a kind of abstracted ecstasy.*) Want a buckle made outa shiny silver to fasten onto my shoes! Want a dress with lace. Want perfume, wanta be purty, wanta smell like a honeysuckle vine!

AUNT ELLER: Give her a cake of soap.

LAUREY: Want things I've heared of and never had before—a rubber-t'ard buggy, a cut-glass sugar bowl. Want things I cain't tell you about—not only things to look at and hold in yer hands. Things to happen to you. Things so nice, if they

ever did happen to you, yer heart ud quit beatin'. You'd fall
down dead!

PEDDLER: I've got just the thing for you! (*He fishes into his satchel
and pulls out a bottle.*) The Elixir of Egypt! (*He holds the bottle
high.*)

LAUREY: What's 'at?

PEDDLER: It's a secret formula, belonged to Pharaoh's daughter!

AUNT ELLER (*leaning over and putting her nose to it*): Smellin'
salts!

PEDDLER (*snatching it away*): But a special kind of smelling salts.
Read what it says on the label: "Take a deep breath and you
see everything clear." That's what Pharaoh's daughter used
to do. When she had a hard problem to decide, like what
prince she ought to marry, or what dress to wear to a party,
or whether she ought to cut off somebody's head—she'd take
a whiff of this.

LAUREY (*excited*): I'll take a bottle of that, Mr. Peddler.

PEDDLER: Precious stuff.

LAUREY: How much?

PEDDLER: Two bits.

(*She pays him and takes the bottle.*)

AUNT ELLER: Throwin' away yer money!

LAUREY (*holding the bottle close to her, thinking aloud*): Helps you
decide what to do!

PEDDLER: Now don't you want me to show you some pretty
dew-dads? You know, with lace around the bottom, and ribbons running in and out?

AUNT ELLER: You mean fancy drawers?

PEDDLER (*taking a pair out of pack*): All made in Paris.

AUNT ELLER: Well, I never wear that kind myself, but I shore
do like to look at 'em.

(PEDDLER *takes out a pair of red flannel drawers.*)

ADO ANNIE (*dubiously*): Y-yeah, they's all right—if you ain't
goin' no place.

AUNT ELLER: Bring yer trappin's inside and mebbe I c'n find
you sumpin to eat and drink.

(AUNT ELLER *exits.* PEDDLER *starts to repack. The two girls
whisper for a moment.*)

LAUREY: Well, ast him, why don't you? (*She giggles and exits
into house.*)

ADO ANNIE: Ali, Laurey and me've been havin' a argument.

PEDDLER: About what, Baby?

ADO ANNIE: About what you meant when you said that about drivin' with me to the end of the world.

PEDDLER (*cagily*): Well, I didn't mean really to the end of the world.

ADO ANNIE: Then how fur did you want to go?

PEDDLER: Oh, about as far as—say—Claremore—to the hotel.

ADO ANNIE: Whut's at the hotel?

PEDDLER (*ready for the kill*): In front of the hotel is a veranda—inside is a lobby—upstairs—upstairs might be Paradise.

ADO ANNIE: I thought they was jist bedrooms.

PEDDLER: For you and me, Baby—Paradise.

ADO ANNIE: Y'see! I knew I was right and Laurey was wrong! You do want to marry me, don't you?

PEDDLER (*embracing her impulsively*): Ah, Ado Annie! (*Pulling away.*) What did you say?

ADO ANNIE: I said you do want to marry me, don't you. What did you say?

PEDDLER: I didn't say nothing!

WILL (*off stage*): Whoa, Suzanna! Yoohoo, Ado Annie, I'm back!

ADO ANNIE: Oh, foot! Jist when—'Lo, Will! (WILL *lets out a whoop off stage.*) That's Will Parker. Promise me you won't fight him.

PEDDLER: Why fight? I never saw the man before.
    (WILL *enters.*)

WILL: Ado Annie! How's my honey-bunch? How's the sweetest little hundred-and-ten pounds of sugar in the territory?

ADO ANNIE (*confused*): Er—Will, this is Ali Hakim.

WILL: How are yuh, Hak? Don't mind the way I talk. 'S all right. I'm goin' to marry her.

PEDDLER (*delighted*): Marry her? On purpose?

WILL: Well, sure.

ADO ANNIE: No sich of a thing!

PEDDLER: It's a wonderful thing to be married. (*He starts off.*)

ADO ANNIE: Ali!

PEDDLER: I got a brother in Persia, got six wives.

ADO ANNIE: Six wives? All at once?

WILL: Shore. 'At's a way they do in them countries.

PEDDLER: Not always. I got another brother in Persia only got one wife. He's a bachelor. (*Exits.*)

ADO ANNIE: Look, Will—

WILL: Look, Will, nuthin'. Know whut I got fer first prize at the fair? Fifty dollars!

ADO ANNIE: Well, that was good. . . . (*The significance suddenly dawning on her.*) Fifty dollars?

WILL: Ketch on? Yer paw promised I cud marry you 'f I cud git fifty dollars.

ADO ANNIE: 'At's right, he did.

WILL: Know whut I done with it? Spent it all on presents fer you!

ADO ANNIE: But if you spent it you ain't got the cash.

WILL: Whut I got is worth more'n the cash. Feller who sold me the stuff told me!

ADO ANNIE: But, Will . . .

WILL: Stop sayin' "But, Will"—When do I git a little kiss? . . . Oh, Ado Annie, honey, y'ain't been off my mind since I left. All the time at the fair grounds even, when I was chasin' steers. I'd rope one under the hoofs and pull him up sharp, and he'd land on his little rump . . . Nen I'd think of you.

ADO ANNIE: Don't start talkin' purty, Will.

WILL: See a lot of beautiful gals in Kansas City. Didn't give one a look.

ADO ANNIE: How could you see 'em if you didn't give 'em a look?

WILL: I mean I didn't look lovin' at 'em—like I look at you. (*He turns her around and looks adoring and pathetic.*)

ADO ANNIE (*backing away*): Oh, Will, please don't look like that! I cain't bear it.

WILL: Won't stop lookin' like this till you give me a little ole kiss.

ADO ANNIE: Oh, whut's a little ole kiss?

WILL: Nothin'—less'n it comes from you.
    (*Both stop.*)

ADO ANNIE (*sighing*): You do talk purty! (WILL *steps up for his kiss. She nearly gives in, but with sudden and unaccounted-for strength of character she turns away.*) No, I won't!

WILL (*singing softly, seductively, "getting" her*):
>S'posin' 'at I say 'at yer lips're like cherries,
>Er roses er berries?
>Whut you gonna do?
>
>(*Putting her hand on his heart.*)
>Cain't you feel my heart palpatin' an' bumpin',
>A-waitin' fer sumpin,
>Sumpin nice from you?
>I gotta git a kiss an' it's gotta be quick
>Er I'll jump in a crick an' die!

ADO ANNIE (*overcome*): Whut's a girl to say when you talk that-a-way?

>(*And he gets his kiss. The boys and girls, and* CURLY *and* GERTIE *enter with lunch hampers, shouting and laughing.* WILL *and* ADO ANNIE *run off.* AUNT ELLER *and* LAUREY *come out of the house.* GERTIE *laughs musically.* LAUREY, *unmindful of the group of girls she has been speaking to, looks across at* CURLY *and* GERTIE *and boils over. All the couples and* CURLY *and* GERTIE *waltz easily, while they sing:*)

ALL:
>Oh, what a beautiful mornin',

CURLY:
>Oh, what a beautiful day.

ALL:
>I got a beautiful feelin'

CURLY:
>Ev'rythin's goin' my way. . . .

AUNT ELLER (*to the rescue*): Hey, Curly! Better take the wagon down to the troft and give the team some water.

CURLY: Right away, Aunt Eller.

>(*He turns.*)

GERTIE: C'n I come, too? Jist love to watch the way you handle horses.

CURLY (*looking across at* LAUREY): 'At's about all I *can* handle, I guess.

GERTIE: Oh, I cain't believe that, Curly—not from whut I heared about you!

(She takes his arm and walks him off, turning on more musical laughter. A girl imitates her laugh. Crowd laughs. LAUREY *takes an involuntary step forward, then stops, frustrated, furious.)*

GIRL: Looks like Curly's tuck up with that Cummin's girl.

LAUREY: Whut'd I keer about that?

(The girls and LAUREY *chatter and argue, ad lib.)*

AUNT ELLER: Come on, boys, better git these hampers out under the trees where it's cool.

(Exit AUNT ELLER *and boys. To show "how little she keers,"* LAUREY *sings the following song:)*

> Why should a womern who is healthy and strong
> Blubber like a baby if her man goes away?
> A-weepin' and a-wailin' how he's done her wrong—
> That's one thing you'll never hear me say!
> Never gonna think that the man I lose
> Is the only man among men.
> I'll snap my fingers to show I don't care.
> I'll buy me a brand-new dress to wear.
> I'll scrub my neck and I'll bresh my hair,
> And start all over again.
>
> Many a new face will please my eye,
> Many a new love will find me.
> Never've I once looked back to sigh
> Over the romance behind me.
> Many a new day will dawn before I do!
> Many a light lad may kiss and fly,
> A kiss gone by is bygone,
> Never've I asked an August sky,
> "Where has last July gone?"
> Never've I wandered through the rye,
> Wonderin' where has some guy gone—
> Many a new day will dawn before I do!

CHORUS:
> Many a new face will please my eye,
> Many a new love will find me.
> Never've I once looked back to sigh

Over the romance behind me.
Many a new day will dawn before I do!

LAUREY:

Never've I chased the honey-bee
Who carelessly cajoled me.
Somebody else just as sweet as he
Cheered me and consoled me.
Never've I wept into my tea
Over the deal someone doled me.

CHORUS:

Many a new day will dawn,

LAUREY:

Many a red sun will set,
Many a blue moon will shine, before I do!

(*A dance follows.* LAUREY *and girls exit.* PEDDLER *enters from house,* ADO ANNIE *from the other side of the stage.*)

ADO ANNIE: Ali Hakim—

PEDDLER: Hello, kiddo.

ADO ANNIE: I'm shore sorry to see you so happy, cuz whut I got to say will make you mis'able. . . . I got to marry Will.

PEDDLER: That's sad news for me. Well, he is a fine fellow.

ADO ANNIE: Don't hide your feelin's, Ali. I cain't stand it. I'd ruther have you come right out and say yer heart is busted in two.

PEDDLER: Are you positive you got to marry Will?

ADO ANNIE: Shore's shootin'.

PEDDLER: And there is no chance for you to change your mind?

ADO ANNIE: No chance.

PEDDLER (*as if granting a small favor*): All right, then, my heart is busted in two.

ADO ANNIE: Oh, Ali, you do make up purty things to say!

CARNES (*off stage*): That you, Annie?

ADO ANNIE: Hello, Paw. (CARNES *enters. He is a scrappy little man, carrying a shotgun.*) Whut you been shootin'?

CARNES: Rabbits. That true whut I hear about Will Parker gittin' fifty dollars?

ADO ANNIE: That's right, Paw. And he wants to hold you to yer promise.

CARNES: Too bad. Still and all I cain't go back on my word.

ADO ANNIE: See, Ali Hakim!

CARNES: I advise you to git that money off'n him before he loses it all. Put it in yer stockin' er inside yer corset where he cain't git at it . . . or can he?

ADO ANNIE: But, Paw—he ain't exackly kep' it. He spent it all on presents. . . .

    (*The* PEDDLER *is in a panic.*)

CARNES: See! Whut'd I tell you! Now he cain't have you. I said it had to be fifty dollars cash.

PEDDLER: But, Mr. Carnes, is that fair?

CARNES: Who the hell are you?

ADO ANNIE: This is Ali Hakim.

CARNES: Well, shet your face, er I'll fill yer behind so full of buckshot, you'll be walkin' around like a duck the rest of yer life.

ADO ANNIE: Ali, if I don't have to marry Will, mebbe your heart don't have to be busted in two like you said.

PEDDLER: I did not say that.

ADO ANNIE: Oh, yes, you did.

PEDDLER: No, I did not.

CARNES (*brandishing his gun*): Are you tryin' to make out my daughter to be a liar?

PEDDLER: No, I'm just making it clear what a liar I am if she's telling the truth.

CARNES: Whut else you been sayin' to my daughter?

ADO ANNIE (*before the* PEDDLER *can open his mouth*): Oh, a awful lot.

CARNES (*to* PEDDLER): When?

ADO ANNIE: Las' night, in the moonlight.

CARNES (*to* PEDDLER): Where?

ADO ANNIE: 'Longside a haystack.

PEDDLER: Listen, Mr. Carnes . . .

CARNES: I'm lissening. Whut else did you say?

ADO ANNIE: He called me his Persian kitten.

CARNES: Why'd you call her that?

PEDDLER: I don't remember.

ADO ANNIE: I do. He said I was like a Persian kitten, cuz they was the cats with the soft round tails.

CARNES (*cocking his gun*): That's enough. In this part of the country that better be a proposal of marriage.

ADO ANNIE: That's whut I thought.

CARNES (*to* PEDDLER): Is that whut you think?

PEDDLER: Look, Mr. Carnes . . .

CARNES (*taking aim*): I'm lookin'.

PEDDLER: I'm no good. I'm a peddler. A peddler travels up and down and all around and you'd hardly ever see your daughter no more.

CARNES (*patting him on back*): That'd be all right. Take keer of her, son. Take keer of my little rosebud.

ADO ANNIE: Oh, Paw, that's purty. (CARNES *starts to exit into house.*) You shore fer sartin you can bear to let me go, Paw?
(CARNES *turns.*)

PEDDLER: Are you *sure*, Mr. Carnes?

CARNES: Jist try to change my mind and see whut happens to you. (*He takes a firmer grip on his gun and exits into the house.*)

ADO ANNIE: Oh, Ali Hakim, ain't it wonderful, Paw makin' up our mind fer us? He won't change neither. Onct he gives his word that you c'n have me, why, you *got* me.

PEDDLER: I *know* I got you.

ADO ANNIE (*starry-eyed*): Mrs. Ali Hakim . . . the Peddler's bride. Wait till I tell the girls.
(*She exits.* ALI *leans against the porch post as the music starts. Then he starts to pace up and down, thinking hard, his head bowed, his hands behind his back. The orchestra starts a vamp that continues under the melody. Some men enter and watch him curiously, but he is unmindful of them until they start to sing. Throughout this entire number, the* PEDDLER *must be burning, and he transmits his indignation to the men who sing in a spirit of angry protest, by the time the refrain is reached.*)

PEDDLER (*circling the stage*):
       Trapped! . . .
       Tricked! . . .
       Hoodblinked! . . .
       Hambushed! . . .

MEN:

Friend,
Whut's on yer mind?
Why do you walk
Around and around,
With yer hands
Folded behind,
And yer chin
Scrapin' the ground?

(*The* PEDDLER *walks away, then comes back to them and starts to pour out his heart.*)

PEDDLER:

Twenty minutes ago I am free like a breeze,
Free like a bird in the woodland wild,
Free like a gypsy, free like a child,
I'm unattached!
Twenty minutes ago I can do what I please,
Flick my cigar ashes on a rug,
Dunk with a doughnut, drink from a jug—
I'm a happy man!

(*Crescendo*)

I'm minding my own business like I oughter,
Ain't meaning any harm to anyone.
I'm talking to a certain farmer's daughter—
Then I'm looking in the muzzle of a gun!

MEN:

It's gittin' so you cain't have any fun!
Ev'ry daughter has a father with a gun!

It's a scandal, it's a outrage!
How a gal gits a husband today!

PEDDLER:

If you make one mistake when the moon is bright,
Then they tie you to a contract, so you'll make it ev'ry
    night!

MEN:

It's a scandal, it's a outrage!
When her fambly surround you and say:
"You gotta take an' make a honest womern outa Nell!"

PEDDLER:

    To make you make her honest, she will lie like hell!

MEN:

    It's a scandal, it's a outrage!

    On our manhood, it's a blot!

    Where is the leader who will save us?

    And be the first man to be shot?

PEDDLER (*spoken*): Me?

MEN (*spoken*): Yes, you!

    (*Sing.*)

    It's a scandal, it's a outrage!

    Jist a wink and a kiss and you're through!

PEDDLER:

    You're a mess, and in less than a year, by heck!

    There's a baby on your shoulder making bubbles on
       your neck!

MEN:

    It's a scandal, it's a outrage!

    Any farmer will tell you it's true.

PEDDLER:

    A rooster in a chickencoop is better off'n men.

    He ain't the special property of just one hen!

    (ANNIE *and girls enter at side.*)

MEN:

    It's a scandal, it's a outrage!

    It's a problem we must solve!

    We gotta start a revolution!

GIRLS:

    All right, boys! Revolve!

    (*The boys swing around, see the girls and are immediately
    cowed. The girls pick them off the line and walk off with them,
    to the music. All exit except one girl, who stalks around look-
    ing for a boy. Suddenly one appears, sees the girl and exits fast.
    She pursues him like mad.* GERTIE *enters through gate with*
    CURLY. LAUREY *enters on the porch and starts packing her
    lunch hamper.*)

GERTIE: Hello, Laurey. Jist packin' yer hamper now?

LAUREY: I been busy.

(GERTIE *looks in* LAUREY'S *hamper.* AUNT ELLER *enters.*)

GERTIE: You got gooseberry tarts, too. Wonder if they is as light as mine. Mine'd like to float away if you blew on them.

LAUREY: I did blow on one of mine and it broke up into a million pieces.

(GERTIE *laughs—that laugh again.*)

GERTIE: Ain't she funny!

(*The girls step toward each other menacingly.*)

AUNT ELLER: Gertie! Better come inside, and cool off.

GERTIE: You comin' inside 'th me, Curly?

CURLY: Not jist yet.

GERTIE: Well, don't be too long. And don't fergit when the auction starts tonight, mine's the biggest hamper.

(*The laugh again, and she exits.*)

LAUREY (*going on with her packing*): So that's the Cummin's girl I heared so much talk of.

CURLY: You seen her before, ain't you?

LAUREY: Yeow. But not since she got so old. Never did see anybody get so peaked-lookin' in sich a short time.

AUNT ELLER (*amused at* LAUREY): Yeah, and she says she's only eighteen. I betcha she's nineteen. (AUNT ELLER *exits.*)

CURLY: What yer got in yer hamper?

LAUREY: 'At's jist some ole meat pies and apple jelly. Nothin' like whut Gertie Cummin's has in *her* basket. (*She sits on the arm of a rocking chair.*)

CURLY: You really goin' to drive to the Box Social with that Jud feller? (*Pause.*)

LAUREY: Reckon so. Why?

CURLY: Nothin' . . . It's jist that ev'rybody seems to expec' *me* to take you. (*He sits on the other arm of the rocker.*)

LAUREY: Then, mebbe it's jist as well you ain't. We don't want people talkin' 'bout us, do we?

CURLY: You think people *do* talk about us?

LAUREY: Oh, you know how they air—like a swarm of mudwasps. Alw'ys gotta be buzzin' 'bout sumpin.

CURLY (*rocking the chair gaily*): Well, whut're they sayin'? That you're stuck on me?

LAUREY: Uh-uh. Most of the talk is that you're stuck on me.

CURLY: Cain't imagine how these ugly rumors start.

LAUREY: Me neither.

    (*Sings.*)
        Why do they think up stories that link my name with
            yours?
CURLY:
        Why do the neighbors gossip all day behind their
            doors?
LAUREY:
        I have a way to prove what they say is quite untrue;
        Here is the gist, a practical list of "don'ts" for you:

        Don't throw bouquets at me—
        Don't please my folks too much,
        Don't laugh at my jokes too much—
        People will say we're in love!
CURLY (*leaving her*): Who laughs at yer jokes?
LAUREY (*following him*):
        Don't sigh and gaze at me,
        Your sighs are so like mine,
    (CURLY *turns to embrace her, she stops him.*)
        Your eyes mustn't glow like mine—
        People will say we're in love!
        Don't start collecting things—
CURLY: Like whut?
LAUREY:
        Give me my rose and my glove.
    (*He looks away, guiltily.*)
        Sweetheart, they're suspecting things—
        People will say we're in love!
CURLY:
        Some people claim that you are to blame as much as
            I—
    (*She is about to deny this.*)
        Why do you take the trouble to bake my fav'rit pie?
    (*Now she looks guilty.*)
        Grantin' your wish, I carved our initials on that
            tree . . .
    (*He points off at the tree.*)

Jist keep a slice of all the advice you give, so free!

Don't praise my charm too much,
Don't look so vain with me,
Don't stand in the rain with me,
People will say we're in love!
Don't take my arm too much,
Don't keep your hand in mine,
Your hand looks so grand in mine,
People will say we're in love!
Don't dance all night with me,
Till the stars fade from above.
They'll see it's all right with me,
People will say we're in love!
(*Music continues as* CURLY *speaks.*)

Don't you reckon y'could tell that Jud you'd ruther go with me tonight?

LAUREY: Curly! I—no, I couldn't.

CURLY: Oh, you couldn't? (*Frowning.*) Think I'll go down here to the smokehouse, where Jud's at. See whut's so elegant about him, makes girls wanta go to parties 'th him. (*He starts off, angrily.*)

LAUREY: Curly!

CURLY (*turning*): Whut?

LAUREY: Nothin'.

(*She watches* CURLY *as he exits, then sits on rocker crying softly and starts to sing:*)

Don't sigh and gaze at me,
Your sighs are so like mine,
Your eyes mustn't glow like mine—
(*Music continues. She chokes up, can't go on.* AUNT ELLER *has come out and looks with great understanding.*)

AUNT ELLER: Got yer hamper packed?

LAUREY (*snapping out of it*): Oh, Aunt Eller. . . . Yes, nearly.

AUNT ELLER: Like a hanky?

LAUREY: Whut'd I want with a ole hanky?

AUNT ELLER (*handing her hers*): Y'got a smudge on yer cheek—jist under yer eye.

(LAUREY *dries her eyes, starts toward the house, thinks about the bottle of "Lixir of Egyp'," picks it up, looks at* AUNT ELLER, *and runs out through the gate and off stage.* AUNT ELLER *sits in the rocker and hums the refrain, happy and contented, as lights dim and the curtain falls.*)

END OF SCENE 1

SCENE 2

SCENE: *The Smokehouse.*
Immediately after Scene I.
It is a dark, dirty building where the meat was once kept. The rafters are smoky, covered with dust and cobwebs. On a low loft many things are stored—horse collars, plow-shares, a binder twine, a keg of nails. Under it, the bed is grimy and never made. On the walls, tobacco advertisements, and pink covers off Police Gazettes. *In a corner there are hoes, rakes and an axe. Two chairs, a table and a spittoon comprise the furniture. There is a mirror for shaving, several farm lanterns and a rope. A small window lets in a little light, but not much.*
JUD *enters and crosses to table. There is a knock on the door. He rises quickly and tiptoes to the window to peek outside. Then he glides swiftly back to the table. Takes out a pistol and starts to polish it. There is a second knock.*

JUD (*calling out sullenly*): Well, open it, cain't you?
CURLY (*opening the door and strolling in*): Howdy.
JUD: Whut'd you want?
CURLY: I done got th'ough my business up here at the house. Jist thought I'd pay a call. (*Pause.*) You got a gun, I see.
JUD: Good un. Colt forty-five.
CURLY: Whut do you do with it?
JUD: Shoot things.
CURLY: Oh. (*He moseys around the room casually.*) That there pink picture—now that's a naked womern, ain't it?
JUD: Yer eyes don't lie to you.
CURLY: Plumb stark naked as a jaybird. No. No, she ain't. Not quite. Got a couple of thingumbobs tied onto her.

JUD: Shucks. That ain't a think to whut I got here. (*He shoves a pack of postcards across the table toward* CURLY.) Lookit that top one.

CURLY (*covering his eyes*): I'll go blind! . . . (*Throwing it back on the table.*) That ud give me idys, that would.

JUD (*picking it up and looking at it*): That's a dinger, that is.

CURLY (*gravely*): Yeah, that shore is a dinger. . . . (*Taking down a rope.*) That's a good-lookin' rope you got there. (*He begins to spin it.*) Spins nice. You know Will Parker? He can shore spin a rope. (*He tosses one end of the rope over the rafter and pulls down on both ends, tentatively.*) 'S a good strong hook you got there. You could hang yerself on that, Jud.

JUD: I could whut?

CURLY (*cheerfully*): Hang yerself. It ud be as easy as fallin' off a log! Fact is, you could stand on a log—er a cheer if you'd rather—right about here—see? And put this here around yer neck. Tie that good up there first, of course. Then all you'd have to do would be to fall off the log—er the cheer, whichever you'd ruther fall off of. In five minutes, or less, with good luck, you'd be daid as a doornail.

JUD: Whut'd you mean by that?

CURLY: Nen folks ud come to yer funril and sing sad songs.

JUD (*disdainfully*): Yamnh!

CURLY: They would. You never know how many people like you till you're daid. Y'd prob'ly be laid out in the parlor. Y'd be all diked out in yer best suit with yer hair combed down slick, and a high starched collar.

JUD (*beginning to get interested*): Would they be any flowers, d'you think?

CURLY: Shore would, and palms, too—all around yer cawfin. Nen folks ud stand around you and the men ud bare their heads and the womern ud sniffle softly. Some'd prob'ly faint—ones that had tuck a shine to you when you wuz alive.

JUD: Whut womern have tuck a shine to me?

CURLY: Lots of womern. On'y they don't never come right out and show you how they feel less'n you die first.

JUD (*thoughtfully*): I guess that's so.

CURLY: They'd shore sing loud though when the singin' started—sing like their hearts ud break!

(*He starts to sing very earnestly and solemnly, improvising the sort of thing he thinks might be sung:*)

> Pore Jud is daid,
> Pore Jud Fry is daid!
> All gether 'round his cawfin now and cry.
> He had a heart of gold
> And he wasn't very old—
> Oh, why did sich a feller have to die?
> Pore Jud is daid,
> Pore Jud Fry is daid!
> He's lookin', oh, so peaceful and serene.

JUD (*touched and suddenly carried away, he sings a soft response*):
> And serene! (*Takes off hat.*)

CURLY:
> He's all laid out to rest
> With his hands acrost his chest.
> His fingernails have never b'en so clean!

> (JUD *turns slowly to question the good taste of this last reference, but* CURLY *plunges straight into another item of the imagined wake.*)

Nen the preacher'd git up and he'd say: "Folks! We are gethered here to moan and groan over our brother Jud Fry who hung hisse'f up by a rope in the smokehouse." Nen there'd be weepin' and wailin' (*significantly*) from some of those womern.

> (JUD *nods his head understandingly.*)

Nen he'd say, "Jud was the most misunderstood man in the territory. People useter think he was a mean, ugly feller.

> (JUD *looks up.*)

And they called him a dirty skunk and a ornery pig-stealer.

> (CURLY *switches quickly.*)

But—the folks 'at really knowed him, knowed 'at beneath them two dirty shirts he alw'ys wore, there beat a heart as big as all outdoors.

JUD (*repeating reverently like a Negro at a revivalist meeting*):
> As big as all outdoors.

CURLY:
> Jud Fry loved his fellow man.

JUD:

>He loved his fellow man.

CURLY (CURLY *is warming up and speaks with the impassioned inflections of an evangelist*): He loved the birds of the forest and the beasts of the field. He loved the mice and the vermin in the barn, and he treated the rats like equals—which was right. And—he loved little children. He loved ev'body and ev'thin' in the world! . . . On'y he never let on, so nobody ever knowed it!

>(*Returning to vigorous song:*)

>Pore Jud is daid,

>Pore Jud Fry is daid!

>His friends'll weep and wail fer miles around.

JUD (*now right into it*):

>Miles around.

CURLY:

>The daisies in the dell

>Will give out a diff'runt smell

>Becuz pore Jud is underneath the ground.

>(JUD *is too emotionally exalted by the spirit of* CURLY's *singing to be analytical. He now takes up a refrain of his own.*)

JUD:

>Pore Jud is daid,

>A candle lights his haid,

>He's layin' in a cawfin made of wood.

CURLY:

>Wood.

JUD:

>And folks are feelin' sad

>Cuz they useter treat him bad,

>And now they know their friend has gone fer good.

CURLY (*softly*):

>Good.

JUD and CURLY:

>Pore Jud is daid,

>A candle lights his haid!

CURLY:

>He's lookin', oh, so purty and so nice.

>He looks like he's asleep.

>It's a shame that he won't keep,

But it's summer and we're runnin' out of ice . . .

Pore Jud—Pore Jud!

(JUD *breaks down, weeps, and sits at the table, burying his head in his arms.*)

Yes, sir. That's the way it ud be. Shore be a interestin' funril. Wouldn't like to miss it.

JUD (*his eyes narrowing*): Wouldn't like to miss it, eh? Well, mebbe you will. (*He resumes polishing the gun.*) Mebbe you'll go first.

CURLY (*sitting down*): Mebbe. . . . Le's see now, whur did you work at before you come here? Up by Quapaw, wasn't it?

JUD: Yes, and before that over by Tulsa. Lousy they was to me. Both of 'em. Always makin' out they was better. Treatin' me like dirt.

CURLY: And whut'd you do—git even?

JUD: Who said anythin' about gittin' even?

CURLY: No one, that I recollect. It jist come into my head.

JUD: If it ever come to gittin' even with anybody, I'd know how to do it.

CURLY: That? (*Looking down at gun and pointing.*)

JUD: Nanh! They's safer ways then that, if you use yer brains. . . . 'Member that f'ar on the Bartlett farm over by Sweetwater?

CURLY: Shore do. 'Bout five years ago. Turrible accident. Burned up the father and mother and daughter.

JUD: That warn't no accident. A feller told me—the h'ard hand was stuck on the Bartlett girl, and he found her in the hayloft with another feller.

CURLY: And it was him that burned the place?

JUD (*nodding*): It tuck him weeks to git all the kerosene—buying it at different times—feller who told me made out it happened in Missouri, but I knowed all the time it was the Bartlett farm. Whut a liar he was!

CURLY: And a kind of a—a kind of a murderer, too. Wasn't he? (CURLY *rises, goes over to the door and opens it.*) Git a little air in here.

JUD: You ain't told me yet whut business you had here. We got no cattle to sell ner no cow ponies. The oat crop is done spoke fer.

CURLY: You shore relieved my mind consid'able.

JUD (*tensely*): They's on'y one other thing on this farm you could want—and it better not be that!

CURLY (*closing the door deliberately and turning slowly, to face* JUD): But that's jist whut it is.

JUD: Better not be! You keep away from her, you hear?

CURLY (*coolly*): You know somebody orta tell Laurey whut kind of a man you air. And fer that matter, somebody orta tell *you* onct about yerself.

JUD: You better git outa here, Curly.

CURLY: A feller wouldn't feel very safe in here with you . . . 'f he didn't know you. (*Acidly.*) But I know you, Jud. (CURLY *looks him straight in the eye.*) In this country, they's two things you c'n do if you're a man. Live out of doors is one. Live in a hole is the other. I've set by my horse in the bresh som'eres and heared a rattlesnake many a time. Rattle, rattle, rattle!—he'd go, skeered to death. Somebody comin' close to his hole! Somebody gonna step on him! Git his old fangs ready, full of pizen! Curl up and wait!—Long's you live in a hole, you're skeered, you got to have pertection. You c'n have muscles, oh, like arn—and still be as weak as a empty bladder—less'n you got things to barb yer hide with. (*Suddenly, harshly, directly to* JUD.) How'd you git to be the way you air, anyway—settin' here in this filthy hole—and thinkin' the way you're thinkin'? Why don't you do sumpin healthy onct in a while, 'stid of stayin' shet up here—a-crawlin' and festerin'!

JUD: Anh!

(*He seizes a gun in a kind of reflex, a kind of desperate frenzy, and pulls the trigger. Luckily the gun is pointed toward the ceiling.*)

CURLY (*actually in a state of high excitement, but outwardly cool and calm, he draws his own gun*): You orta feel better now. Hard on the roof, though. I wisht you'd let me show you sumpin. (JUD *doesn't move, but stands staring into* CURLY'S *eyes.*) They's a knot-hole over there about as big as a dime. See it a-winkin'? I jist want to see if I c'n hit it. (*Unhurriedly, with cat-like tension, he turns and fires at the wall high up.*) Bullet right through the knot-hole, 'thout tetchin', slick as a whistle, didn't I? I knowed I could do it. You saw it, too, didn't you? (*Ad lib off stage.*) Somebody's a-comin', I 'spect.

(*He listens.* JUD *looks at the floor.* AUNT ELLER, *the* PEDDLER *and several others come running in.*)

AUNT ELLER (*gasping for breath*): Who f'ard off a gun? Was that you, Curly? Don't set there, you lummy, answer when you're spoke to?

CURLY: Well, I shot onct.

AUNT ELLER: What was you shootin' at?

CURLY (*rises*): See that knot-hole over there?

AUNT ELLER: I see lots of knot-holes.

CURLY: Well, it was one of them.

AUNT ELLER (*exasperated*): Well, ain't you a pair of purty nuthin's, a-pickin' away at knot-holes and skeerin' everybody to death! Orta give you a good Dutch rub and arn some of the craziness out of you! (*Calling off to people in doorway.*) 'S all right! Nobody hurt. Jist a pair of fools swappin' noises. (*She exits.*)

PEDDLER: Mind if I visit with you, gents? It's good to get away from the women for a while. Now then, we're all by ourselves. I got a few purties, private knickknacks for to show you. Special for the menfolks. (*Starts to get them out.*)

CURLY: See you gentlemen later. I gotta git a surrey I h'ard fer tonight. (*He starts to go.*)

PEDDLER (*shoving cards under* JUD's *nose*): Art postcards.

JUD: Who you think yer takin' in that surrey?

CURLY: Aunt Eller—and Laurey, if she'll come with me.

JUD: She won't.

CURLY: Mebbe she will. (*Exits.*)

JUD (*raising his voice after* CURLY): She promised to go with me, and she better not change her mind. She better not!

PEDDLER: Now, I want ye to look at these straight from Paris.

JUD: I don't want none o' them things now. Got any frog-stickers?

PEDDLER: You mean one of them long knives? What would you want with a thing like that?

JUD: I dunno. Kill a hog—er a skunk. It's all the same, ain't it? I tell you whut I'd like better'n a frog-sticker, if you got one. Ever hear of one of them things you call "The Little Wonder"? It's a thing you hold up to your eyes to see pitchers, only that ain't all they is to it . . . not quite. Y'see it's got a little jigger onto it, and you tetch it and out springs a sharp blade.

PEDDLER: On a spring, eh?

JUD: Y'say to a feller, "Look through this." Nen when he's

lookin' you snap out the blade. It's jist above his chest and, bang! Down you come. (*Slaps the* PEDDLER *on the chest, knocking the wind from him.*)

PEDDLER (*after recovering from blow*): A good joke to play on a friend . . . I—er—don't handle things like that. Too dangerous. What I'd like to show you is my new stock of postcards.

JUD: Don't want none. Sick of them things. I'm going to get me a real womern.

PEDDLER: What would you want with a woman? Why, I'm having trouble right now, all on account of a woman. They always make trouble. And you say you *want* one. Why? Look at you? You're a man what is free to come and go as you please. You got a nice cozy little place. (*Looking place over.*) Private. Nobody to bother you. Artistic pictures. They don't talk back to you. . . .

JUD: I'm t'ard of all these *pitchers* of women!

PEDDLER: All right. You're tired of them. So throw 'em away and buy some new ones. (*Showing him cards again.*) You get tired of a woman and what can you do? Nothing! Just keep getting tireder and tireder!

JUD: I made up my mind.

PEDDLER (*packing his bag and starting off*) : So you want a real woman. . . . Say, do you happen to know a girl named Ado Annie?

JUD: I don't want her.

PEDDLER: I don't want her either. But I got her! (*Exits.*)

JUD: Don't want nuthin' from no peddler. Want real things! Whut am I doin' shet up here—like that feller says—a-crawlin' and a-festerin'? Whut am I doin' in this lousy smokehouse?

(*He looks about the room, scowling. Then he starts to sing, half talking at first, then singing in full voice:*)

> The floor creaks,
> The door squeaks,
> There's a fieldmouse a-nibblin' on a broom,
> And I set by myself
> Like a cobweb on a shelf,
> By myself in a lonely room.

But when there's a moon in my winder
And it slants down a beam 'crost my bed,
Then the shadder of a tree starts a-dancin' on the wall
And a dream starts a-dancin' in my head.
And all the things that I wish fer
Turn out like I want them to be,
And I'm better'n that Smart Aleck cowhand
Who thinks he is better'n me!
And the girl that I want
Ain't afraid of my arms,
And her own soft arms keep me warm.
And her long, yeller hair
Falls acrost my face
Jist like the rain in a storm!

The floor creaks,
The door squeaks,
And the mouse starts a-nibblin' on the broom.
And the sun flicks my eyes—
It was all a pack o' lies!
I'm awake in a lonely room. . . .

I ain't gonna dream 'bout her arms no more!
I ain't gonna leave her alone!
Goin' outside,
Git myself a bride,
Git me a womern to call my own.

END OF SCENE 2

SCENE 3

AT RISE: *A grove on* LAUREY's *farm. Singing girls and* GERTIE *seated under tree. A girl,* VIVIAN, *is telling* GERTIE's *fortune.*

VIVIAN: And to yer house a dark clubman!
    (*Laughter from girls.* LAUREY *enters.*)

LAUREY: Girls, could you—could you go som'eres else and tell
fortunes? I gotta be here by myself.

GERTIE (*pointing to bottle*): Look! She bought 'at ole smellin'
salts the peddler tried to sell us!

LAUREY: It ain't smellin' salts. It's goin' to make up my mind fer
me. Lookit me take a good whiff now!

(*She chokes on it.*)

GERTIE: That's the camphor.

LAUREY: Please, girls, go away.

(GERTIE *laughs and exits.* LAUREY *closes her eyes tight.*)

ELLEN: Hey, Laurey, is it true you're lettin' Jud take you tonight
'stid of Curly?

LAUREY: Tell you better when I think ever'thin' out clear.
Beginnin' to see things clear a'ready.

KATE: I c'n tell you whut you want . . .

(*Singing.*)
      Out of your dreams and into his arms you long to fly.

ELLEN:
      You don't need Egyptian smellin' salts to tell you why!

KATE:
      Out of your dreams and into the hush of falling
            shadows.

VIRGINIA:
      When the mist is low, and stars are breaking through,

VIVIAN:
      Then out of your dreams you'll go.

ALL THE GIRLS:
      Into a dream come true.
      Make up your mind, make up your mind, Laurey,
            Laurey dear.
      Make up your own, make up your own story, Laurey
            dear.
      Ol' Pharaoh's daughter won't tell you what to do.
      Ask your heart—whatever it tells you will be true.

(*They drift off as* LAUREY *sings.*)

LAUREY:
      Out of my dreams and into your arms I long to fly.
      I will come as evening comes to woo a waiting sky.

Out of my dreams and into the hush of falling
   shadows,
When the mist is low, and stars are breaking through,
Then out of my dreams I'll go,
Into a dream with you.

BALLET

(The things LAUREY *sees in her dream that help her "make up her mind.")*

(During the above refrain the lights dim to a spot on LAUREY. CURLY *enters in another spot, walking slowly and standing perfectly still. Then his ballet counterpart enters and stands behind him.* LAUREY's *ballet counterpart enters and stands behind her. These are figures fading into her dream. The real* CURLY *and the real* LAUREY *back off slowly, and leave the stage to their counterparts who move toward the center and into an embrace. The downstage drop is lifted and they are in another scene, full stage.)*

These dream figures of LAUREY *and* CURLY *dance ecstatically. A young girl enters, sees them and bounds off to break the news and soon others dance on and off gaily. Two of* CURLY's *cowboy friends stroll by and wave their greeting. "Curly" kisses "Laurey" again and walks away, happy and smug.*

A little girl runs on, presents "Laurey" with a nosegay and then bursts into tears. More girl friends dance on and embrace her. A bridal veil floats down from the skies and they place it on her head. "Curly" and the boys enter, in the manner of cowboys astride their horses. Following a gay dance, the music slows to wedding-march tempo. "Curly," a serious expression on his face, awaits his bride who walks down an aisle formed by the girls.

Now the ballet counterpart of JUD *walks slowly forward and takes off "Laurey's" veil. Expecting to see her lover,* CURLY, *she looks up and finds "Jud." Horrified, she backs away. Her friends, with stony faces, look straight ahead of them. "Curly," too, is stern and austere and when she appeals to him, he backs away from her. All of them leave her. She is alone with "Jud."*

"Jud" starts to dance with her but he is soon diverted by the entrance of three dance-hall girls who look very much like the Police Gazette *pictures* LAUREY *has seen tacked on to his walls in the smokehouse.*

Some of the cowboys follow the girls on, and whistle at them. But that is as far as they go. The cowboys are timid and inexpert in handling these sophisticated women. The women do an amusing, satirically bawdy dance. Then "Jud" and the boys dance with them.

After the girls dance off, "Laurey" and "Jud" are again alone. "Curly" enters, and the long-awaited conflict with "Jud" is now unavoidable. "Curly," his hand holding an imaginary pistol, fires at "Jud" again and again, but "Jud" keeps slowly advancing on him, immune to bullets. He lifts "Curly" in the air and throws him to the ground. A fierce fight ensues. The friends of LAUREY and CURLY run helplessly from one side to the other. Just when the tables seem to have turned in "Curly's" favor, "Jud" gets a death grip on his throat. He is killing "Curly." "Laurey" runs up to him and begs him to release her lover. It is clear by her pantomime that she will give herself to JUD to save CURLY. "Jud" drops "Curly's" limp body, picks up "Laurey" and carries her away. Over "Jud's" shoulder she blows a feeble, heart-broken kiss to "Curly's" prostrate form on the ground. The crowd surround him and carry him off in the dark as a spot comes up revealing the real LAUREY being shaken out of her dream by the real JUD.

JUD: Wake up, Laurey. It's time to start fer the party.

    (As she awakens and starts mechanically to go with JUD, the real CURLY enters expectantly. She hesitates. JUD holds out his arm and scowls. Remembering the disaster of her recent dream, she avoids its reality by taking JUD's arm and going with him, looking wistfully back at CURLY with the same sad eyes that her ballet counterpart had on her exit. CURLY stands alone, puzzled, dejected and defeated, as the curtain falls.)

END OF ACT ONE

ACT TWO

SCENE I

SCENE: *The* SKIDMORE *ranch.*

SKIDMORE*'s guests dancing a "set." Soon after the curtain rises, the melody settles into a "vamp" and* CARNES *holds up his hand as a signal that he wants to sing. The dancing couples retire and listen to him.*

CARNES:
> The farmer and the cowman should be friends,
> Oh, the farmer and the cowman should be friends.
> One man likes to push a plow,
> The other likes to chase a cow,
> But that's no reason why they cain't be friends.
>
> Territory folks should stick together,
> Territory folks should all be pals.
> Cowboys, dance with the farmers' daughters!
> Farmers, dance with the ranchers' gals!

(The chorus repeats this last quatrain.)
(They dance with gusto—sixteen measures—then the vamp is resumed and CARNES *starts to sing again.)*
> I'd like to say a word fer the farmer.

AUNT ELLER (*spoken*): Well, say it.

CARNES:
> He come out west and made a lot of changes.

WILL (*scornfully; singing*):
> He come out west and built a lot of fences!

CURLY:
> And built 'em right acrost our cattle ranges!

CORD ELAM (*a cowman; spoken*): Whyn't those dirtscratchers stay in Missouri where they belong?

FARMER (*spoken*): We got as much right here—

CARNES (*shouting*): Gentlemen—shut up!
(Quiet restored, he resumes singing.)
> The farmer is a good and thrifty citizen.

FRED (*spoken*): He's thrifty, all right.

CARNES (*glaring at* FRED, *he continues with song*):
>   No matter whut the cowman says or thinks,
>   You seldom see him drinkin' in a barroom—

CURLY:
>   Unless somebody else is buyin' drinks!

CARNES (*barging in quickly to save the party's respectability*):
>   The farmer and the cowman should be friends,
>   Oh, the farmer and the cowman should be friends.
>   The cowman ropes a cow with ease,
>   The farmer steals her butter and cheese,
>   But that's no reason why they cain't be friends!

ALL:
>   Territory folks should stick together,
>   Territory folks should all be pals.
>   Cowboys, dance with the farmers' daughters!
>   Farmers, dance with the ranchers' gals!
>   (*Dance, as before. Then back to vamp.*)

AUNT ELLER (*singing*):
>   I'd like to say a word fer the cowboy . . .

FARMER (*anxious to get back at the cowmen; spoken*): Oh, you would!

AUNT ELLER:
>   The road he treads is difficult and stony.
>   He rides fer days on end
>   With jist a pony fer a friend. . . .

ADO ANNIE:
>   I shore am feelin' sorry fer the pony.

AUNT ELLER:
>   The farmer should be sociable with the cowboy,
>   If he rides by and asks fer food and water.
>   Don't treat him like a louse,
>   Make him welcome in yer house . . .

CARNES:
>   But be shore that you lock up yer wife and daughter!
>   (*Laughs, jibes, protests.*)

CORD ELAM (*spoken from here on*): Who wants a ole farm womern anyway?

ADO ANNIE: Notice you married one, so's you c'd git a square meal!

MAN (*to* CORD ELAM): You cain't talk that-a-way 'bout our womern folks!

WILL: He can say whut he wants.

(WILL *hauls off on him and a free-for-all fight ensues, all the men mixing with one another, the women striving vainly to keep peace by singing "The farmer and the cowman should be friends!"*)

(AUNT ELLER *grabs a gun from some man's holster and fires it. This freezes the picture. A still, startled crowd stops and looks to see who's been shot.* AUNT ELLER *strides forward, separating the fighters, pulling them away from one another, and none too gently.*)

AUNT ELLER: They ain't nobody goin' to slug out anythin'—this here's a party! (*Pointing the gun at* CARNES.) Sing it, Andrew! Dum tiddy um tum tum—

CARNES (*frightened, obeys*):
        The farmer and the cowman should be friends . . .
        (AUNT ELLER *points her gun at a group, and conducts them. They join in quickly.*)

RIGHT GROUP:
        Oh, the farmer and the cowman should be friends.
        (*She turns her gun on the left group and now they all sing.*)

ALL:
        One man likes to push a plow,
        The other likes to chase a cow,
        But that's no reason why they cain't be friends!
        (IKE *comes down and joins* AUNT ELLER *and* CARNES.)

IKE:
        And when this territory is a state,
        And jines the union jist like all the others,
        The farmer and the cowman and the merchant
        Must all behave theirsel's and act like brothers.

AUNT ELLER:
        I'd like to teach you all a little sayin'—
        And learn these words by heart the way you should:
        "I don't say I'm no better than anybody else,
        But I'll be damned if I ain't jist as good!"
        (*They cheer the sentiment, and repeat lustily:*)

ALL:

> I don't say I'm no better than anybody else,
> But I'll be damned if I ain't jist as good!
> Territory folks should stick together,
> Territory folks should all be pals.
> Cowboys, dance with the farmers' daughters!
> Farmers, dance with the ranchers' gals!
> (*Now they go into a gay, unrestrained dance.*)

IKE (*after number is over*): C'mon, everybody! Time to start the Box Social.

CORD ELAM: I'm so hungry I c'd eat a gatepost.

DOROTHY: Who's goin' to be the auctioneer?

TOM: Aunt Eller! (*Shouts of approval from the entire crowd.*)

AUNT ELLER (*playing coy*): Let one of the men be the auctioneer.

CROWD: "No, Aunt Eller, yore the best." "Ain't any ole men auctioneers as good as you."

AUNT ELLER: All right then. Now you know the rules, gentlemen. Y'got to bid blind. Y'ain't s'posed to know whut girl goes with whut hamper. Of course, if yer sweetheart has told you that hers'll be done up in a certain kind of way with a certain color ribbon, that ain't my fault. Now we'll auction all the hampers on t'other side of the house and work around back here. Follow me.

> (AUNT ELLER *starts off, followed by the crowd. As the crowd exits, the* PEDDLER *strolls on, meeting* WILL *ambling along with his bag.*)

PEDDLER: Hello, young fellow.

WILL: Oh, it's you!

PEDDLER: I was just hoping to meet up with you. It seems like you and me ought to have a little talk.

WILL: We only got one thing to talk about. Well, Mr. Hakim, I hear you got yerself engaged to Ado Annie.

PEDDLER: Well . . .

WILL: Well, nothin'. I don't know what to call you. You ain't purty enough fer a skunk. You ain't skinny enough fer a snake. You're too little to be a man, and too big to be a mouse. I reckon you're a rat.

PEDDLER: That's logical.

WILL: Answer me one question. Do you really love her?

PEDDLER: Well . . .

WILL: 'Cuz if I thought you didn't I'd tie you up in this bag and drop you in the river. Are you serious about her?

PEDDLER: Yes, I'm serious.

WILL: And do you worship the ground she walks on, like I do? You better say yes!

PEDDLER: Yes—yes—yes.

WILL: The hell you do!

PEDDLER: Yes.

WILL: Would you spend every cent you had fer her? That's whut I did. See that bag? Full of presents. Cost fifty bucks. All I had in the world.

PEDDLER: If you had that fifty dollars cash . . .

WILL: I'd have Ado Annie, and you'd lose her.

PEDDLER (*thoughtfully*): Yes. I'd lose her. Let's see what you got in here. Might want to buy something.

WILL: What would you want with them?

PEDDLER: I'm a peddler, ain't I? I buy and sell. Maybe pay you real money. . . . (*Significantly.*) Maybe as much as—well, a lot. (WILL *becomes thoughtful. The* PEDDLER *fishes in bag and pulls out an item.*) Ah, what a beautiful hot-water bag. It looks French. Must have cost plenty. I'll give you eight dollars for it.

WILL: Eight dollars? That wouldn't be honest. I only paid three-fifty.

PEDDLER: All right. I said I'd give you eight and I will. . . . (*The* PEDDLER *pulls a nightgown out of the bag. It is made of white lawn and is notable for a profusion of ribbons and bows on the neckline.*) Say! That's a cracker-jake!

WILL: Take your hands off that! (*Grabbing it and holding it in front of him.*) That wuz fer our weddin' night!

PEDDLER: It don't fit you so good. I'll pay you twenty-two dollars.

WILL: But that's—

PEDDLER: All right then—twenty-two-fifty! (*Stuffing it into his coat with the hot-water bag.*) Not a cent more.

    (WILL *smiles craftily and starts to count on his fingers. The* PEDDLER *now pulls out a pair of corsets.*)

WILL: Them—those—that was fer her to wear.

PEDDLER: I didn't hardly think they was for you. (*Looking at them.*) Mighty dainty. (*Putting them aside.*) Fifteen dollars. Le's see, eight and twenty-two makes thirty and fifteen is forty-five and fifty cents is forty-five-fifty. (*He looks craftily at* WILL *out of the corner of his eye and watches the idea percolate through* WILL's *thick head.*)

WILL: Forty-five-fifty? Say, that's almos'—that's . . . (*Turning anxiously.*) Want to buy some more?

PEDDLER: Might.

WILL (*taking "The Little Wonder" out of his pocket*): D'you ever see one of these?

PEDDLER (*frightened*): What made you buy this? Got it *in* for somebody?

WILL: How d'you mean? It's jist funny pitchers.

PEDDLER (*examining it carefully*): That all you think it is? Well, it's more'n that! It's . . .

(*He breaks off as* LAUREY *runs on, a frightened look on her face.*)

LAUREY: Whur is ev'ybody? Whur's Aunt Eller?

WILL: On t'other side of the house, Laurey.

JUD (*off stage*): Laurey! Whur'd you run to?

(*LAUREY runs off, around the end of the house, putting hamper on porch.*)

WILL: How much'll you give me fer that thing?

PEDDLER: I don't like to handle things like this. I guess you don't know what it really is.

WILL: Shore do. It's jist a girl in pink tights.

JUD (*entering, carrying* LAUREY's *basket*): Either of you two see Laurey?

WILL: Jist went to th' other side of the house. Auction's goin' on there.

(*JUD grunts and starts upstage.*)

PEDDLER (*calling to him*): Hey, Jud! Here's one of them things you was looking for. "The Little Wonder."

(*JUD comes back and examines it.*)

JUD (*to* WILL): How much?

WILL (*closing his eyes to struggle with a mathematical problem*): Three dollars and fifty cents.

JUD (*digging in his pocket*): Lotta money but I got an idy it might be worth it.

(*JUD goes upstage to look it over, then exits.*)

WILL: Let's see, three-fifty from him and forty-five-fifty from you. 'At makes fifty dollars, don't it?

PEDDLER: No. One dollar short.

WILL: Darn it. I musta figgered wrong. (*Impulsively.*) How much fer all the resta the stuff in this bag?

PEDDLER (*having the cash all ready*): One dollar!

WILL: Done! Now I got fifty dollars, ain't I? Know whut that means? Means I'm goin' to take Ado Annie back from you!

PEDDLER: You wouldn't do a thing like that to me!

WILL: Oh, wouldn't I? And when I tell her paw who I got mosta the money offa, mebbe he'll change his mind 'bout who's smart and who's dumb!

PEDDLER: Say, young feller, you certainly bunkoed me!

> (*Off right, there is a hum of voices and the crowd starts to drift on.* AUNT ELLER *enters, followed by the balance of the party.* JUD *eyes* LAUREY *throughout the ensuing dialogue.* CURLY *stands apart and pays little attention to anybody or anything.*)

AUNT ELLER: Now, here's the last two hampers. Whose they are I ain't got no idy!

ADO ANNIE (*in a loud voice*): The little un's mine! And the one next to it is Laurey's!

> (*General laughter.*)

AUNT ELLER: Well, that's the end of *that* secret. Now whut am I bid then fer Ado Annie's hamper?

SLIM: Two bits.

CORD ELAM: Four.

AUNT ELLER: Who says six? You, Slim? (SLIM *shakes his head.*) Ain't nobody hungry no more?—Whut about you, Peddler-man? Six bits?

> (*Pause.*)

PEDDLER: Naw!

> (CARNES *takes a gun from his pocket and prods the* PEDDLER *in the back.*)

CARNES: Come on.

PEDDLER: Six bits!

AUNT ELLER: Six bits ain't enough fer a lunch like Ado Annie c'n make. Le's hear a dollar. How about you, Mike? You won her last year.

MIKE: Yeah. That's right. Hey, Ado Annie, y'got that same sweet-pertater pie like last year?

ADO ANNIE: You bet.

AUNT ELLER: Same old sweet-pertater pie, Mike. Whut d'you say?

MIKE: I say it give me a three-day bellyache!

AUNT ELLER: Never mind about that. Who bids a dollar?

CARNES (*whispering to* PEDDLER): Bid!

PEDDLER (*whispering back*): Mine's the last bid. I got her fer six bits.

CARNES: Bid a dollar.

(*The* PEDDLER *looks doubtful.* CARNES *prods him with his gun.*)

PEDDLER: Ninety cents.

AUNT ELLER: Ninety cents, we're gittin' rich. 'Nother desk fer th' schoolhouse. Do I hear more?

WILL (*dramatically, his chin thrust forward*): You hear fifty dollars!

PEDDLER (*immediately alarmed*): Hey!

AUNT ELLER: Fifty dollars! Nobody ever bid fifty dollars for a lunch! Nobody ever bid ten.

CARNES: He ain't got fifty dollars.

WILL: Oh, yes, I have. (*Producing the money.*) And 'f yer a man of honor y'gotta say Ado Annie b'longs to me, like y'said she would!

CARNES: But where's yer money?

WILL (*shoving out his hand*): Right here in my hand.

CARNES: 'At ain't yours! Y'jist bid it, didn't you? Jist give it to th' schoolhouse. (*To* PEDDLER, *chuckling. Back to* WILL.) Got to say the Peddler still gits my daughter's hand.

WILL: Now wait a minute. That ain't fair!

AUNT ELLER: Goin' fer fifty dollars! Goin' . . .

PEDDLER (*gulping*): Fifty-one dollars!

(*A sensation, all turn to* PEDDLER.)

CARNES: You crazy?

WILL (*mechanically*): Fif— (*Prompted by frantic signs from the* PEDDLER, *he stops and suddenly realizes the significance of the* PEDDLER'*s bid.*) Wait a minute. Wait! 'F I don't bid any more I c'n keep my money, cain't I?

AUNT ELLER (*grinning*): Shore can.

WILL: Nen I still got fifty dollars. (*Waving it in front of* CARNES.) This is mine!

CARNES (*to* PEDDLER): You feeble-minded shike-poke!

AUNT ELLER: Goin', goin', gone fer fifty-one dollars and 'at means Ado Annie'll git the prize, I guess.

WILL: And I git Ado Annie!

CARNES (*to* PEDDLER): And whut're you gittin' fer yer fifty-one dollars?

PEDDLER (*shrugging his shoulders*): A three-day bellyache!

> (PEDDLER *and* ADO ANNIE *pick up her basket and leave* AUNT ELLER.)

AUNT ELLER: Now here's my niece's hamper. (*General murmur of excitement runs through the crowd.*) I took a peek inside a while ago and I must say it looks mighty tasty. Whut do I hear, gents?

SLIM: Two bits!

FRED: Four bits!

AUNT ELLER: Whut d'you say, Slim? Six?

> (SLIM *shakes his head.*)

CARNES: I bid one dollar.

AUNT ELLER: More like it! Do I hear two?

JUD: A dollar and a quarter.

> (LAUREY *gets a start from his voice.*)

CORD ELAM: Two dollars.

JOE: Two-fifty.

CARNES: Three dollars!

JUD: And two bits.

CORD ELAM: Three dollars and four bits!

JOE: Four dollars.

JUD (*doggedly*): And two bits.

> (LAUREY *looks straight ahead of her, grimly.* AUNT ELLER *catches this look and a deep worry comes into her eyes.*)

AUNT ELLER: Four dollars and a quarter. (*Looking at* CURLY, *an appeal in her voice.*) Ain't I goin' to hear any more?

> (CURLY *turns and walks off, cool and deliberate.*)
>
> (LAUREY *bites her lip.* AUNT ELLER*'s voice has panic in it.*)

I got a bid of four and a quarter—from Jud Fry. You goin' to let him have it?

CARNES: Four and a half.

AUNT ELLER (*shouting, as if she were cheering*): Four and a half! Goin' fer four and a half! Goin' . . .

JUD: Four-seventy-five.

AUNT ELLER (*deflated*): Four-seventy-five, come on, gentlemen. Schoolhouse ain't built yet. Got to git a nice chimbley.

CORD ELAM: Five dollars.

AUNT ELLER: Goin' fer five dollars! Goin' . . .

JUD: And two bits.

CORD ELAM: Too rich for my blood! Cain't afford no more.

AUNT ELLER (*worried*): Five and a quarter! Ain't got nearly enough yet. (*Looking at* CARNES.) Not fer cold duck with stuffin' and that lemon-meringue pie.

CARNES: Six dollars.

AUNT ELLER: Six dollars! Goin' . . .

JUD: And two bits.

AUNT ELLER: My, you're stubborn, Jud. Mr. Carnes is a richer man'n you. (*Looking at* CARNES.) And I know he likes custard with raspberry syrup. (*Pause. No one bids.*) Anybody goin' to bid any more?

JUD: No. They all dropped out. Cain't you see?

FRED: You got enough, Aunt Eller.

CARNES: Let's git on.

JUD: Here's the money.

AUNT ELLER (*looking off*): Hold on, you! I ain't said "Goin', goin', gone" yet!

JUD: Well, say it!

AUNT ELLER (*speaking slowly*): Goin' to Jud fer six dollars and two bits! Goin' . . .

   (CURLY *enters, a saddle over his arm.*)

CURLY: Who'd you say was gittin' Laurey?

AUNT ELLER: Jud Fry.

CURLY: And fer how much?

AUNT ELLER: Six and a quarter.

CURLY: I don't figger 'at's quite enough, do you?

JUD: It's more'n *you* got.

CURLY: Got a saddle here cost me thirty dollars.

JUD: Yo' cain't bid saddles. Got to be cash.

CURLY (*looking around*): Thirty-dollar saddle must be worth sumpin to somebody.

TOM: I'll give you ten.

SKIDMORE (*to* CURLY): Don't be a fool, boy. Y'cain't earn a livin' 'thout a saddle.

CURLY (*to* TOM): Got cash?

TOM: Right in my pocket.

(CURLY *gives him the saddle.*)

CURLY (*turning to* JUD): Don't let's waste time. How high you goin'?

JUD: Higher'n you—no matter whut!

CURLY (*to* AUNT ELLER): Aunt Eller, I'm biddin' all of this ten dollars Tom jist give me.

AUNT ELLER: Ten dollars—goin' . . .

(*Pause. General murmur of excited comments.* LAUREY's *eyes are shining now and her shoulders are straighter.*)

JUD (*determinedly*): Ten dollars *and* two bits.

AUNT ELLER: Curly . . .

(*Pause.* CURLY *turns to a group of men.*)

CURLY: Most of you boys know my horse, Dun. She's a—(*he swallows hard*)—a kinda nice horse—gentle and well broke.

LAUREY: Don't sell Dun, Curly, it ain't worth it.

CORD ELAM: I'll give you twenty-five fer her!

CURLY (*to* CORD ELAM): I'll sell Dun to you. (*To* AUNT ELLER.) That makes the bid thirty-five, Aunt Eller.

AUNT ELLER (*tickled to death*): Curly, yer crazy! But it's all fer the schoolhouse, ain't it? All fer educatin' and larnin'. Goin' fer thirty-five. Goin'—

JUD: Hold on! I ain't finished biddin'! (*He grins fiercely at* CURLY.) You jist put up everythin' y'got in the world, didn't yer? Cain't bid the clothes off yer back, cuz they ain't worth nuthin'. Cain't bid yer gun cuz you need that. (*Slowly.*) Yes, sir. You need that bad. (*Looking at* AUNT ELLER.) So, Aunt Eller, I'm jist as reckless as Curly McLain, I guess. Jist as good at gittin' whut I want. Goin' to bid all I got in the world—all I saved fer two years, doin' farm work. All fer Laurey. Here it is! Forty-two dollars and thirty-one cents.

(*He pours the money out of his pocket onto* LAUREY's *hamper.* CURLY *takes out his gun. The crowd gasps.* JUD *backs away.*)

CURLY: Anybody want to buy a gun? You, Joe? Bought it brand new last Thanksgivin'. Worth a lot.

LAUREY: Curly, please don't sell your gun.

(CURLY *looks at* JOE.)

JOE: Give you eighteen dollars fer it.

CURLY: Sold. (*They settle the deal.* CURLY *turns to* AUNT ELLER.)
That makes my bid fifty-three dollars, Aunt Eller. Anybody
going any higher?

AUNT ELLER (*very quickly*): Goin'—goin'—gone! Whut's the
matter with you folks? Ain't nobody gonna cheer er nuthin'?
(*Uncertainly they start to sing "The Farmer and the Cowman."*
CURLY *and* LAUREY *carry their basket away.* JUD *moves slowly
toward* CURLY. CURLY *sets the basket down and faces him. The
singing stops.*)

SKIDMORE (*in his deep, booming voice*): That's the idy! The
cowman and the farmer shud be friends. (*His hand on* JUD's
shoulder.) You lost the bid, but the biddin' was fair. (*To
CURLY.*) C'mon, cowman—shake the farmer's hand!
(CURLY *doesn't move a muscle.*)

JUD: Shore, I'll shake hands. No hard feelin's, Curly.
(*He goes to* CURLY, *his hand outstretched. After a pause,
CURLY takes his hand, but never lets his eyes leave* JUD's.*)

SKIDMORE: That's better.
(*The* PEDDLER *has come downstage and is watching* JUD
narrowly.)

JUD (*with a badly assumed manner of camaraderie*): Say, Curly,
I want to show you sumpin. (*He grins.*) 'Scuse us, Laurey.
(*Taking* CURLY's *arm, he leads him aside.*) Ever see one of these
things?
(*He takes out "The Little Wonder." The* PEDDLER *is in a
panic.*)

CURLY: Jist whut *is* that?
(*The* PEDDLER *rushes to* AUNT ELLER *and starts to whisper
in her ear.*)

JUD: Something special. You jist put this up to yer eye like this,
see?
(CURLY *is about to look when* AUNT ELLER's *voice rings out,
sharp and shrill.*)

AUNT ELLER: Curly! Curly, whut you doin'?
(CURLY *turns quickly. So does* JUD, *giving an involuntary
grunt of disappointment.*)

CURLY: Doin'? Nuthin' much. Whut you want to squeal at a
man like 'at fer? Skeer the liver and lights out of a feller.

AUNT ELLER: Well then, stop lookin' at those ole French

pitchers and ast me fer a dance. You brung me to the party, didn't you?

CURLY: All right then, you silly ole woman, I'll dance 'th you. Dance you all over the meadow, you want!

AUNT ELLER: Pick 'at banjo to pieces, Sam!

(*And the dance is on. Everyone is dancing now.* WILL *takes* ADO ANNIE *by the waist and swings her around.* JUD *finally snaps the blade of "The Little Wonder" back, slips it into his pocket, then goes up to* LAUREY, *who has started to dance with the* PEDDLER. *He pushes the* PEDDLER *away and dances* LAUREY *off.* WILL *and* ADO ANNIE *dance off. The curtains close. Immediately,* WILL *and* ADO ANNIE *dance on to center stage. He stops dancing. They're alone in a secluded spot now, and he wants to "settle things."*)

WILL: Well, Ado Annie, I got the fifty dollars cash, now you name the day.

ADO ANNIE: August fifteenth.

WILL: Why August fifteenth?

ADO ANNIE (*tenderly*): That was the first day I was kissed.

WILL (*his face lighting up*): Was it? I didn't remember that.

ADO ANNIE: You wasn't there.

WILL: Now looka here, we gotta have a serious talk. Now that you're engaged to me, you gotta stop havin' fun! . . . I mean with other fellers. (*Sings.*)

> You'll have to be a little more stand-offish
> When fellers offer you a buggy ride.

ADO ANNIE:

> I'll give a imitation of a crawfish
> And dig myself a hole where I c'n hide.

WILL:

> I heared how you was kickin' up some capers
> When I was off in Kansas City, Mo.
> (*More sternly.*)
> I heared some things you couldn't print in papers
> From fellers who been talkin' like they know!

ADO ANNIE:

> Foot!
> I only did the kind of things I orta—sorta

To you I was as faithful as c'n be—fer me.
Them stories 'bout the way I lost my
    bloomers—Rumors!
A lot o' tempest in a pot o' tea!

WILL:

The whole thing don't sound very good to me—

ADO ANNIE:

Well, y'see—

WILL (*breaking in and spurting out his pent-up resentment at a great injustice*):

I go and sow my last wild oat!
I cut out all shenanigans!
I save my money—don't gamble er drink
In the back room down at Flannigan's!
I give up lotsa other things
A gentleman never mentions—
But before I give up any more,
I wanta know your intentions!

With me it's all er nuthin'!
Is it all er nuthin' with you?
It cain't be "in between"
It cain't be "now and then"
No half-and-half romance will do!
I'm a one-woman man,
Home-lovin' type,
All complete with slippers and pipe.
Take me like I am er leave me be!
If you cain't give me all, give me nuthin'—
And nuthin's whut you'll git from me!
(*He struts away from her.*)

ADO ANNIE:

Not even sumpin?

WILL:

Nuthin's whut you'll git from me!
(*Second refrain. He starts to walk away, nonchalantly. She follows him.*)

ADO ANNIE:

It cain't be "in between"?

WILL:

    Uh-uh.

ADO ANNIE:

    It cain't be "now and then"?

WILL:

    No half-and-half romance will do!

ADO ANNIE:

    Would you build me a house,
    All painted white,
    Cute and clean and purty and bright?

WILL:

    Big enough fer two but not fer three!

ADO ANNIE:

    Supposin' 'at we should have a third one?

WILL (*barking at her*):

    He better look a lot like me!

ADO ANNIE (*skeered*):

    The spit an' image!

WILL:

    He better look a lot like me!

(Two girls come on and do a dance with WILL *in which they lure him away from* ADO ANNIE. ADO ANNIE, *trying to get him back, does an oriental dance.* WILL, *accusing her, says: "That's Persian!" and returns to the girls. But* ADO ANNIE *yanks him back. The girls dance off.* ADO ANNIE *sings:)*

ADO ANNIE:

    With you it's all er nuthin'—
    All fer you and nuthin' fer me!
    But if a wife is wise
    She's gotta realize
    That men like you are wild and free.
    (WILL *looks pleased.*)
    So I ain't gonna fuss,
    Ain't gonna frown,
    Have your fun, go out on the town,
    Stay up late and don't come home till three,
    And go right off to sleep if you're sleepy—
    There's no use waitin' up fer me!

WILL:

    Oh, Ado Annie!

ADO ANNIE:

    There's no use waitin' up fer me!

WILL:

    Come on and kiss me!

    (ADO ANNIE *comes dancing back to* WILL. *They kiss and dance off.*)

BLACKOUT

SCENE 2

SCENE: *The kitchen porch of* SKIDMORE's *ranch house. There are a few benches on the porch and a large coal stove.*

    The music for the dance can still be heard off stage. Immediately after the curtain rises, JUD *dances on with* LAUREY, *then stops and holds her. She pulls away from him.*

LAUREY: Why we stoppin'? Thought you wanted to dance?

JUD: Want to talk to you. Whut made you slap that whip onto Old Eighty, and nearly make her run away? Whut was yer hurry?

LAUREY: 'Fraid we'd be late fer the party.

JUD: You didn't want to be with me by yerself—not a minnit more'n you had to.

LAUREY: Why, I don't know whut you're talking about! I'm with you by myself now, ain't I?

JUD: You wouldn'ta been, you coulda got out of it. Mornin's you stay hid in yer room all the time. Nights you set in the front room, and won't git outa Aunt Eller's sight. . . . Last time I see you alone it was winter 'th the snow six inches deep in drifts when I was sick. You brung me that hot soup out to the smokehouse and give it to me, and me in bed. I hadn't shaved in two days. You ast me 'f I had any fever and you put your hand on my head to see.

LAUREY (*puzzled and frightened*): I remember . . .

JUD: Do you? Bet you don't remember as much as me. I remember eve'ything you ever done—every word you ever said.

Cain't think of nuthin' else. . . . See? . . . See how it is? (*He attempts to hold her. She pushes him away.*) I ain't good enough, am I? I'm a h'ard hand, got dirt on my hands, pig-slop. Ain't fitten to tetch you. You're better, so much better. Yeah, we'll see who's better—Miss Laurey. Nen you'll wisht you wasn't so free 'th yer airs, you're sich a fine lady. . . .

LAUREY (*suddenly angry and losing her fear*): Air you making threats to me? Air you standing there tryin' to tell me 'f I don't 'low you to slobber over me like a hog, why, you're gonna do sumpin 'bout it? Why, you're nothin' but a mangy dog and somebody orta shoot you. You think so much about being a h'ard hand. Well, I'll jist tell you sumpin that'll rest yer brain, Mr. Jud. You ain't a h'ard hand fer me no more. You c'n jist pack up yer duds and scoot. Oh, and I even got better idys'n that. You ain't to come on the place again, you hear me? I'll send yer stuff any place you say, but don't you's much 's set foot inside the pasture gate or I'll sic the dogs onto you!

JUD (*standing quite still, absorbed, dark, his voice low*): Said yer say! Brought it on yerself. (*In a voice harsh with an inner frenzy.*) Cain't he'p it. Cain't never rest. Told you the way it was. You wouldn't listen—

(*He goes out, passes the corner of the house and disappears. LAUREY stands a moment, held by his strangeness, then she starts toward the house, changes her mind and sinks onto a bench, a frightened little girl again.*)

(*There is a noise off stage.*)

LAUREY (*turns, startled*): Who's 'at?

WILL (*entering*): It's me, Laurey. Hey, have you seen Ado Annie? She's gone agin.

(LAUREY *shakes her head.*)

LAUREY (*calling to him as he starts away*): Will! . . . Will, could you do sumpin fer me? Go and find Curly and tell him I'm here. (CURLY *enters.*) I wanta see Curly awful bad. Got to see him.

CURLY: Then whyn't you turn around and look, you crazy womern?

LAUREY (*with great relief*): Curly!

WILL: Well, you found yours. Now I gotta look fer mine. (*He exits.*)

CURLY: Now whut on earth is ailin' the belle of Claremore? By gum, if you ain't cryin'!

(LAUREY *leans against him.*)

LAUREY: Curly—I'm afraid, 'fraid of my life!

CURLY (*in a flurry of surprise and delight*): Jumpin' toadstools! (*He puts his arms around* LAUREY, *muttering under his breath.*) Great Lord!

LAUREY: Don't you leave me. . . .

CURLY: Great Godamighty!

LAUREY: Don't mind me a-cryin', I cain't he'p it. . . .

CURLY: Cry yer eyes out!

LAUREY: Oh, I don't know whut to do!

CURLY: Here. I'll show you. (*He lifts her face and kisses her. She puts her arms about his neck.*) My goodness! (*He shakes his head as if coming out of a daze, gives a low whistle, and backs away.*) Whew! 'Bout all a man c'n stand in public! Go 'way from me, you!

LAUREY: Oh, you don't like me, Curly—

CURLY: Like you? My God! Git away from me, I tell you, plumb away from me! (*He backs away and sits on the stove.*)

LAUREY: Curly! You're settin' on the stove!

CURLY (*leaping up*): Godamighty! (*He turns around, puts his hand down gingerly on the lid.*) Aw! 'S cold's a hunk of ice!

LAUREY: Wisht it ud burnt a hole in yer pants.

CURLY (*grinning at her, understandingly*): You do, do you?

LAUREY (*turning away to hide her smile*): *You* heared me.

CURLY: Laurey, now looky here, you stand over there right whur you air, and I'll set over here—and you tell me whut you wanted with me.

LAUREY (*grave again*): Well—Jud was here. (*She shudders.*) He skeered me . . . he's crazy. I never saw nobody like him. He talked wild and he threatened me. So I—I f'ard him! I wisht I hadn'ta! They ain't no tellin' whut he'll do now!

CURLY: You f'ard him? Well then! That's all they is to it! Tomorrow, I'll get you a new h'ard hand. I'll stay on the place myself tonight, 'f you're nervous about that hound-dog. Now quit yer worryin' about it, er I'll spank you. (*His manner changes. He becomes shy. He turns away unable to meet her eyes as he asks the question.*) Hey, while I think of it—how—how 'bout marryin' me?

(LAUREY, *confused, turns too. They are back to back.*)

LAUREY: Gracious, whut'd I wanta marry you fer?

CURLY: Well, couldn't you mebbe think of some reason why you might?

LAUREY: I cain't think of none right now, hardly.

CURLY (*following her*): Laurey, please, ma'am—marry me. I—don't know whut I'm gonna do if you—if you don't.

LAUREY (*touched*): Curly—why, I'll marry you—'f you want me to. . . .

(*They kiss.*)

CURLY: I'll be the happiest man alive soon as we're married. Oh, I got to learn to be a farmer, I see that! Quit a-thinkin' about th'owin' the rope, and start in to git my hands blistered a new way! Oh, things is changin' right and left! Buy up mowin' machines, cut down the prairies! Shoe yer horses, drag them plows under the sod! They gonna make a state outa this, they gonna put it in the Union! Country a-changin', got to change with it! Bring up a pair of boys, new stock, to keep up 'th the way things is goin' in this here crazy country! Now I got you to he'p me—I'll 'mount to sumpin yit! Oh, I 'member the first time I ever seen you. It was at the fair. You was a-ridin' that gray filly of Blue Starr's, and I says to someone—"Who's that skinny little thing with a bang down on her forehead?"

LAUREY: Yeow, I 'member. You was riding broncs that day.

CURLY: That's right.

LAUREY: And one of 'em th'owed you.

CURLY: That's—Did not th'ow me!

LAUREY: Guess you jumped off, then.

CURLY: Shore I jumped off.

LAUREY: Yeow, you shore did. (*He kisses her.*)

CURLY (*shouting over music*): Hey! 'F there's anybody out around this yard 'at c'n hear my voice, I'd like fer you to know that Laurey Williams is my girl.

LAUREY: Curly!

CURLY: And she's went and got me to ast her to marry me!

LAUREY: They'll hear you all the way to Catoosie!

CURLY: Let 'em! (*Singing.*) Let people say we're in love! (*Making a gesture with his arm.*) Who keers whut happens now!

LAUREY (*reaching out, grabbing his hand and putting it back in*

hers): Jist keep your hand in mine.
    Your hand feels so grand in mine—

BOTH:

    Let people say we're in love!
    Starlight looks well on us,
    Let the stars beam from above,
    Who cares if they tell on us?
    Let people say we're in love!
    (*The curtains close. In front of curtain, the* PEDDLER *walks on, with* ADO ANNIE.)

PEDDLER: I'll say good-bye here, Baby.

ADO ANNIE: Cain't y'even stay to drink to Curly and Laurey?

PEDDLER (*shaking his head*): Time for the lonely gypsy to go back to the open road.

ADO ANNIE: Wisht I was goin'—nen you wouldn't be so lonely.

PEDDLER: Look, Ado Annie, there is a man I know who loves you like nothing ever loved nobody.

ADO ANNIE: Yes, Ali Hakim.

PEDDLER: A man who will stick to you all your life and be a regular Darby and Jones. And that's the man for you—Will Parker.

ADO ANNIE (*recovering from surprise*): Oh . . . yeh . . . well, I like Will a lot.

PEDDLER: He is a fine fellow. Strong like an ox. Young and handsome.

ADO ANNIE: I love him, all right, I guess.

PEDDLER: Of course you do! And you love those clear blue eyes of his, and the way his mouth wrinkles up when he smiles—

ADO ANNIE: Do you love him too?

PEDDLER: I love him because he will make my Ado Annie happy. (*Taking her in his arms.*) Good-bye, my baby. I will show you how we say good-bye in Persia. (*He draws her tenderly to him and plants a long kiss on her lips.*)

ADO ANNIE (*wistfully as he releases her*): That was good-bye?

PEDDLER (*his arms still around her*): We have an old song in Persia. It says: (*Singing.*) One good-bye—(*speaking*)—is never enough.

(*He kisses her again.* WILL *enters and stands still and stunned. He slowly awakes to action and starts moving toward them, but then the* PEDDLER *starts to talk and* WILL *stops again, surprised even more by what he hears than by what he saw.*)

I am glad you will marry such a wonderful man as this Will Parker. You deserve a fine man and you got one.

(WILL *is almost ashamed of his resentment.*)

ADO ANNIE (*seeing* WILL *for the first time*): Hello, Will. Ali Hakim is sayin' good-bye.

PEDDLER: Ah, Will! I want to say good-bye to you, too. (*Starting to embrace him.*)

WILL: No, you don't. I just saw the last one.

PEDDLER (*patting* WILL *on the cheek*): Ah, you were made for each other! (*He pulls* ADO ANNIE *close to him with one arm, and puts the other hand affectionately on* WILL'S *shoulder.*) Be good to her, Will. (*Giving* ADO ANNIE *a squeeze.*) And you be good to him! (*Smiling disarmingly at* WILL.) You don't mind? I am a friend of the family now? (*He gives* ADO ANNIE *a little kiss.*)

WILL: Did you say you was goin'?

PEDDLER: Yes. I must. Back to the open road. A poor gypsy. Goodbye, my baby— (*Smiling back at* WILL *before he kisses* ADO ANNIE, *pointing to himself.*) Friend of the family. I show you how we say good-bye in my country. (ADO ANNIE *gets set for that old Persian good-bye again. The* PEDDLER *finally releases her and turns back to* WILL.) Persian good-bye. Lucky fellow! I wish it was me she was marrying instead of you.

WILL: It don't seem to make no difference hardly.

PEDDLER: Well, back to the open road, the lonely gypsy. (*He sings a snatch of the Persian song as he exits.*)

WILL: You ain't goin' to think of that ole peddler any more, air you?

ADO ANNIE: 'Course not. Never think of no one less'n he's with me.

WILL: Then I'm never goin' to leave yer side.

ADO ANNIE: Even if you don't, even if you never go away on a trip er nuthin', cain't you—onct in a while—give me one of them Persian good-byes?

WILL: Persian good-bye? Why, that ain't nuthin' compared to a Oklahoma hello!

(*He wraps her up in his arms and gives her a long kiss. When he lets her go, she looks up, supreme contentment in her voice.*)
ADO ANNIE: Hello, Will!

BLACKOUT

SCENE 3

SCENE: *Back of* LAUREY'*s house. Shouts, cheers and laughter are heard behind the curtain, continuing as it rises.*

CARNES *and* IKE *walk down toward house.* CARNES *carries a lantern.*

IKE: Well, Andrew, why ain't you back of the barn gettin' drunk with us? Never see you stay so sober at a weddin' party.

CARNES: Been skeered all night. Skeered 'at Jud Fry ud come up and start for Curly.

IKE: Why, Jud Fry's been out of the territory for three weeks.

CARNES: He's back. See him at Claremore last night, drunk as a lord!

(*Crowd starts to pour in.* IKE *and* CARNES, *continuing their conversation, are drowned out by the shouts and laughter of the crowd as they fill the stage.* LAUREY *wears her mother's wedding dress. The following lines are sung.*)

AUNT ELLER:
    They couldn't pick a better time to start in life!
IKE:
    It ain't too early and it ain't too late.
CURLY:
    Startin' as a farmer with a brand-new wife—
LAUREY:
    Soon be livin' in a brand-new state!
ALL:
    Brand-new state
    Gonna treat you great!
FRED:
    Gonna give you barley,

Carrots and pertaters—

CORD ELAM:

Pasture for the cattle—

CARNES:

Spinach and termayters!

AUNT ELLER:

Flowers on the prairie where the June bugs zoom—

IKE:

Plen'y of air and plen'y of room—

FRED:

Plen'y of room to swing a rope!

AUNT ELLER:

Plen'y of heart and plen'y of hope. . . .

CURLY:

Oklahoma,
Where the wind comes sweepin' down the plain,
And the wavin' wheat
Can sure smell sweet
When the wind comes right behind the rain.
Oklahoma,
Every night my honey lamb and I
Sit alone and talk
And watch a hawk
Makin' lazy circles in the sky.
We know we belong to the land,
And the land we belong to is grand!
And when we say:
Ee-ee-ow! A-yip-i-o-ee-ay!
We're only sayin',
"You're doin' fine, Oklahoma!
Oklahoma, O.K.!"

(*The full company now joins in a refrain immediately follow-ing this one, singing with infectious enthusiasm. A special and stirring vocal arrangement.*)

CURLY (*after number*): Hey! Y'better hurry into that other dress! Gotta git goin' in a minnit!

AUNT ELLER: You hurry and pack yer own duds! They're layin' all over my room.

CURLY: Hey, Will! Would you hitch the team to the surrey fer me?

WILL: Shore will! Have it up in a jiffy!

(WILL *runs off.* CURLY *exits into house.* CORD ELAM *runs over to door. The manner of the group of men that surrounds the door becomes mysterious. Their voices are low and their talk is punctuated with winks and nudges.*)

IKE (*to* CORD ELAM): He's gone upstairs.

CORD ELAM: Yeah.

(*The girls cross to men, but are shooed away. The men whisper and slip quietly off, except for* CARNES.)

ADO ANNIE: Whut you goin' to do, Paw? Give Laurey and Curly a shivoree? I wisht you wouldn't.

CARNES: Aw, it's a good old custom. Never hurt anybody. You women jist keep outa the way. Vamoose!

ADO ANNIE: It ain't goin' to be rough, is it?

CARNES: Sh! Stop gabbin' about it!

(CARNES *exits, leaving only women on the stage.*)

ADO ANNIE: Seems like they's times when men ain't got no need for womern.

SECOND GIRL: Well, they's times when womern ain't got no need fer men.

ADO ANNIE: Yeow, but who wants to be dead?

(GERTIE'*s well-known laugh is heard off stage.*)

ELLEN: Gertie!

(GERTIE *enters.*)

ADO ANNIE: Thought you was in Bushyhead.

GERTIE (*obviously having swallowed a canary*): Jist come from there.

ELLEN: Too bad you missed Laurey's wedding.

GERTIE: Been havin' one of my own.

ELLEN: Lands! Who'd you marry? Where is he?

ADO ANNIE (*looking off stage*): Is that him?

GERTIE (*triumphantly*): That's him!

(*All look off right. The* PEDDLER *enters, dejected, sheepish, dispirited, a ghost of the man he was.*)

ADO ANNIE: Ali Hakim!

PEDDLER (*in a weak voice*): Hello. Hello, Ado Annie.

GERTIE: Did you see my ring, girls?

(*The girls surround* GERTIE *to admire and exclaim. The* PEDDLER *and* ADO ANNIE *are left apart from the group.*)

ADO ANNIE: How long you been married?

PEDDLER: Four days. (GERTIE*'s laugh is heard from group. He winces.*) Four days with that laugh should count like a golden wedding.

ADO ANNIE: But if you married her, you musta wanted to.

PEDDLER: Sure I wanted to. I wanted to marry her when I saw the moonlight shining on the barrel of her father's shotgun! I thought it would be better to be alive. Now I ain't so sure.

GERTIE (*coming out of group*): Ali ain't goin' to travel around the country no more. I decided he orta settle down in Bushyhead and run Papa's store.

(WILL *enters.*)

ADO ANNIE: Hey, Will! D'you hear the news? Gertie married the peddler?

WILL (*to* PEDDLER): Mighty glad to hear that, peddler man. (*Turning to* GERTIE, *and getting an idea.*) I think I orta kiss the bride. (*He goes toward* GERTIE, *then looks back at* PEDDLER.) Friend of the fambly . . . remember? (*He gives* GERTIE *a big kiss, not realizing that it is* ADO ANNIE *and not the* PEDDLER *he is burning.*) Hey, Gertie, have you ever had a Oklahoma hello? (*He plants a long one on* GERTIE. ADO ANNIE *pulls her away and stands in her place.* ADO ANNIE *socks* WILL, *then* GERTIE. GERTIE *strikes back.* WILL *comes between them but is beaten off by both of them. Kicking and slugging, the women resume the fight until* GERTIE *retreats, with* ADO ANNIE *close on her heels. The other girls follow.* WILL, *too, is about to go after them when he is called back by the* PEDDLER.)

PEDDLER: Hey! Where you goin'?

WILL: I'm goin' to stop Ado Annie from killin' yer wife.

PEDDLER (*grabbing* WILL*'s arm*): Mind yer own business!

(*He leads* WILL *off. The stage is empty and quiet. A man sneaks on, then another, then more. Cautiously they advance on the house. One of the more agile climbs up a trellis and looks in the window of the second floor. He suppresses a laugh, leans down and reports to the others. There are suppressed giggles and snorts. He takes another peek, then comes down and whispers to them. The joke is passed from one to the other; they are doubled up with laughter. At a signal from one, they all start to pound on tinpans with spoons and set up a terrific din.*)

AUNT ELLER (*coming to the window with a lamp in her hand*): Whut you doin' down there, makin' all thet racket, you bunch o' pig-stealers?

FRED (*shouting up*): Come on down peaceable, Laurey sugar!

IKE: And you, too, you curly-headed cowboy.

CORD ELAM: With the dimple on yer chin!

IKE: Come on, fellers, let's git 'em down!

(*Three of the men run into the house. Those outside toss up rag dolls.*)

MEN: Hey, Laurey! Here's a girl baby fer you!

And here's a baby boy!

Here's twins!

(CURLY *is pulled from the house and hoisted on the shoulders of his friends.* LAUREY *and* AUNT ELLER *come out of the house. All are in high spirits. It is a good-natured hazing. Now* JUD *enters. Everyone becomes quiet and still, sensing trouble.*)

JUD: Weddin' party still goin' on? Glad I ain't too late. Got a present fer the groom. But first I wanta kiss the bride. (*He grabs* LAUREY. CURLY *pulls him off.*) An' here's my present fer you!

(*He socks* CURLY. *The fight starts, with the crowd moving around the two men.* JUD *pulls out a knife and goes for* CURLY. CURLY *grabs his arm and succeeds in throwing him.* JUD *falls on his knife, groans and lies still. The crowd surges toward his motionless body.*)

CURLY: Look—Look at him! Fell on his own knife.

(*He backs away, shaken, limp. Some of the men bend over the prostrate form.*)

MEN: Whut's the matter?

Don't you tetch it!

Turn him over—

He's breathin', ain't he?

Feel his heart.

How'd it happen?

FRED: Whut'll we do? Ain't he all right?

SLIM: 'S he jist stunned?

CORD ELAM: Git away, some of you. Let me look at him.

(*He bends down, the men crowding around. The women, huddled together, look on, struck with horror.* CURLY *has slumped back away from the crowd like a sick man.* LAUREY *looks at* CURLY, *dazed, a question in her eyes.*)

LAUREY: Curly—is he—?

CURLY: Don't say anythin'.

LAUREY: It cain't be that-a-way.

CURLY: I didn't *go* to.

LAUREY: *Cain't be!* Like that—to happen to us.

CORD ELAM (*getting up*): Cain't do a thing now. Try to get him to a doctor, but I don't know—

MAN: Here, some of you, carry him over to my rig. I'll drive him over to Doctor Tyler's.

CORD ELAM: Quick! I'm 'fraid it's too late.

(*The men lift* JUD *up.*)

MEN: Handle him easy!

Don't shake him!

Hold on to him, careful there!

(*A woman points to* JUD, *being carried off.* IKE *and his companions run up and exit with the other men.*)

CURLY (*to* LAUREY *and* AUNT ELLER): I got to go see if there's anythin' c'n be done fer him. (*He kisses* LAUREY.) Take keer of her, Aunt Eller. (*He exits.*)

AUNT ELLER: Mebbe it's better fer you and Curly not to go 'way tonight. (*She breaks off, realizing how feeble this must sound.*)

LAUREY (*as if she hadn't heard* AUNT ELLER): I don't see why this had to happen, when everythin' was so fine.

AUNT ELLER: Don't let yer mind run on it.

LAUREY: Cain't fergit, I tell you. Never will!

AUNT ELLER: 'At's all right, Laurey baby. If you cain't fergit, jist don't try to, honey. Oh, lots of things happens to folks. Sickness, er bein' pore and hungry even—bein' old and afeared to die. That's the way it is—cradle to grave. And you can stand it. They's one way. You gotta be hearty, you got to be. You cain't deserve the sweet and tender things in life less'n you're tough.

LAUREY: I—I wisht I was the way you are.

AUNT ELLER: Fiddlesticks! Scrawny and old? You couldn't h'ar me to be the way I am!

(LAUREY *laughs through her tears.*)

LAUREY: Oh, whut ud I do 'thout you, you're sich a crazy!

AUNT ELLER (*hugging* LAUREY): Shore's you're borned!

> (*She breaks off as* CURLY *enters with* CORD ELAM, CARNES *and a few others. Their manner is sober. Some of the women come out of the house to hear what the men have to say.*)

CORD ELAM: They're takin' Jud over to Dave Tyler's till the mornin'.

AUNT ELLER: Is he—alive?

> (CORD ELAM *shakes his head.*)

CURLY: Laurey honey, Cord Elam here, he's a Fed'ral Marshal, y'know. And he thinks I orta give myself up— Tonight, he thinks.

LAUREY: Tonight!

AUNT ELLER: Why, yer train leaves Claremore in twenty minutes.

CORD ELAM: Best thing is fer Curly to go of his own accord and tell the Judge.

AUNT ELLER (*to* CARNES): Why, you're the Judge, ain't you, Andrew?

CARNES: Yes, but—

LAUREY (*urging* CURLY *forward*): Well, tell him now and git it over with.

CORD ELAM: 'T wouldn't be proper. You have to do it in court.

AUNT ELLER: Oh, fiddlesticks. Le's do it here and say we did it in court.

CORD ELAM: We can't do that. That's breaking the law.

AUNT ELLER: Well, le's not break the law. Le's just bend it a little. C'mon, Andrew, and start the trial. We ain't got but a few minnits.

CORD ELAM: Andrew—I got to protest.

CARNES: Oh, shet yer trap. We can give the boy a fair trial without lockin' him up on his weddin' night! Here's the long and short of it. First I got to ask you: Whut's your plea? (CURLY *doesn't answer.* CARNES *prompts him.*) 'At means why did you do it?

CURLY: Why'd I do it? Cuz he'd been pesterin' Laurey and I always said some day I'd—

CARNES: Jist a minnit! Jist a minnit! Don't let yer tongue

wobble around in yer mouth like 'at. Listen to my question. Whut happened tonight 'at made you kill him?

CURLY: Why, he come at me with a knife and—and—

CARNES: And you had to defend yerself, didn't you?

CURLY: Why, yes—and furthermore . . .

CARNES: Never mind the furthermores—the plea is self-defense— (*The women start to chatter.*) Quiet! . . . Now is there a witness who saw this happen?

MEN (*all at once*): I seen it.

Shore did.

Self-defense all right.

Tried to stab him 'th a frog-sticker.

CORD ELAM (*shaking his head*): Feel funny about it. Feel funny.

AUNT ELLER: And you'll feel funny when I tell yer wife you're carryin' on 'th another womern, won't you?

CORD ELAM: I ain't carryin' on 'th no one.

AUNT ELLER: Mebbe not, but you'll shore feel funny when I tell yer *wife* you air.

(*Boisterous laughter.*)

CORD ELAM: Laugh all you like, but as a Fed'ral Marshal—

SKIDMORE: Oh, shet up about bein' a marshal! We ain't goin' to let you send the boy to jail on his weddin' night. We just ain't goin' to *let* you. So shet up!

(*This firm and conclusive statement is cheered and applauded.*)

SLIM: C'mon, fellers! Let's pull them to their train in Curly's surrey! We'll be the horses.

CARNES: Hey, wait! I ain't even told the verdick yet!

(*Everything stops still at this unpleasant reminder.*)

CURLY: Well—the verdick's not guilty, ain't it?

CARNES: 'Course, but . . .

LAUREY: Well, then *say* it!

(CARNES *starts, but the crowd drowns him out.*)

ALL: Not guilty!

(CURLY *and* LAUREY *run into the house. The rest run out toward the stable.* CARNES *is left downstage without a court.*)

CARNES: Court's adjourned!

(CARNES *joins* AUNT ELLER, *who has sat down to rest, after all this excitement.* ADO ANNIE *and* WILL *enter, holding hands soulfully.* ADO ANNIE's *hair is mussed, and a contented look graces her face.*)

AUNT ELLER: Why, Ado Annie, where on earth you been?

ADO ANNIE: Will and me had a misunderstandin'. But he explained it fine.

(ADO ANNIE *and* WILL *go upstage and now tell-tale wisps of straw are seen clinging to* ADO ANNIE's *back. Amid shouts and laughter, the surrey is pulled on.*)

IKE: Hey, there, bride and groom, y'ready?

CURLY (*running out of the house with* LAUREY): Here we come!

(*The crowd starts to sing lustily, "Oh, What a Beautiful Mornin'."* LAUREY *runs over and kisses* AUNT ELLER. *Then she is lifted up alongside* CURLY. AUNT ELLER *and three girls start to cry. Everyone else sings gaily and loudly.*)

ALL: Oh, what a beautiful day!

(*The men start to pull off the surrey. Everybody waves and shouts.* CURLY *and* LAUREY *wave back.*)

CURTAIN

ON THE TOWN

Book and lyrics by BETTY COMDEN *and* ADOLPH GREEN

Music by LEONARD BERNSTEIN

Based on an idea by JEROME ROBBINS

SCENES AND MUSICAL NUMBERS

ACT ONE

SCENE I

Brooklyn Yard. After a short orchestra prelude, the curtain goes up on a street just outside the Brooklyn Navy Yard—with the entrance to the Yard itself on one side of the stage. It is early morning—just before six o'clock. It is quiet—the light is just beginning to seep through— and gets brighter and brighter as the scene progresses. WORKMEN *are standing about in small groups, some drifting in the gate.* SAILORS *are returning to the Yard in various states—some come with* GIRLS *whom they kiss goodbye during this first song—sung by the* WORK-MEN. *The movement is all slow and quiet—but there is an air of expectancy—of a day about to begin.*

"I Feel Like I'm Not Out of Bed Yet"

WORKMAN:
> I feel like I'm not out of bed yet—
> A-a-a-a-a-a-a-a
> (*Yawns.*)
> Oh, the sun is warm—but my blanket's warmer—
> Sleep—sleep in your lady's arms—

WORKMEN:
> Sleep in your lady's arms—

2ND WORKMAN (*to* 3RD WORKMAN, *who is absorbed in reading a paper. Spoken against last line of song*): Got the time, Bud?
3RD WORKMAN (*annoyed*): Uh—three minutes to six.
WORKMAN:
> I left my old woman still sleeping—
> A-a-a-a-a-a-a-a-a
> Oh, the air is sweet—but my woman's sweeter—
> Sleep, sleep in your lady's arms—

WORKMEN:
> Sleep in your lady's arms.

2ND WORKMAN: Hey, what time is it?
3RD WORKMAN (*more annoyed*): Uh—one minute to six.
WORKMAN:
> All night I was walking the baby—
> A-a-a-a-a-a-a-a-a-h

297

Oh, his eyes are blue—but her eyes are bluer—
Sleep, sleep in your lady's arms—

WORKMEN:

Sleep in your lady's arms.

2ND WORKMAN: What time is it now, Bud?

3RD WORKMAN (*yelling furiously*): A-a-a-h—six o'clock, willya!!
(*The whistle blows—to the accompaniment of noisy frantic chords in the music.* WORKMEN *dash busily into the Yard.* SAILORS *and* WORKERS *emerge from the entrance. There is great activity and hurry. On top of this the three principal* SAILORS *enter—all in an exuberant state of excitement.* CHIP *and* OZZIE *lead,* GABEY *following, all looking about eagerly.*)

OZZIE: Come on Gabey, hurry up!

CHIP: Twenty-four hours!!!

(GABEY *bumps into another* SAILOR *as he looks around.*)

SAILOR: Hey, why don'tcha watch were ya goin. You'd think it was your first time in New York!—

GABEY: It *is!*

(*All three look about in great excitement.*)

"New York, New York"

ALL:

New York—New York—it's a helluva town!

CHIP:

We've got one day here and not another minute—
To see the famous sights!

OZZIE:

We'll find the romance and danger waiting in it—
Beneath the Broadway lights—

ALL:

And we've hair on our chest—
So what we like the best—
Are the nights!

CHIP:

Sights!

GABEY:

Lights!

OZZIE:

Nights!

ALL:

> New York, New York—a helluva town—
> The Bronx is up—but the Battery's down
> The people ride in a hole in the groun'
> New York—New York—it's a helluva town!

CHIP (*points to Empire State Building on backdrop*): Hey—Gabey!
   (CHIP *consulting his guide book with reverence and excitement.*)
   It says here—"there are 20,000 streets in New York City,
   not counting MacDougall Alley in the heart of Green-witch
   Village—a charming thoroughfare filled with—"

OZZIE: Here we go again!

CHIP (*with a threatening gesture at* OZZIE):

> The famous places to visit are so many
> Or so the guide books say
> I promised Daddy I wouldn't miss on any
> And we have just one day—
> Gotta see the whole town—
> From Yonkers on down the Bay—
> In just one day!

ALL:

> New York, New York—a visitor's place—
> Where no one lives on account of the pace—
> But seven millions are screaming for space—
> New York—New York—
> It's a visitor's place!

   (*Two* SAILORS *enter, weaving and weary-looking. One happy,
   the other very glum.*)

GABEY: Hey! Here come Tom and Andy!—

ALL (*gaily*): 'Lo, guys!

TOM (*sadly*): Hullo—

OZZIE: Hey, fellas—how are the New York dames?

ANDY (*brightly*): Wonderful—I don't remember a thing!

TOM: Awful! I remember everything.

   (*They exit.*)

OZZIE (*laughs*):

> Manhattan women are dressed in silk and satin—
> Or so the fellas say—
> There's just one thing that's important in Manhattan
> When you have just one day—
> Gotta pick up a date—

CHIP:

>Maybe seven—

OZZIE:

>Or eight—
>On your way—
>In just one day—

ALL:

>New York, New York—a helluva town—
>The Bronx is up but the Battery's down—
>The people ride in a hole in the groun'
>New York, New York—it's a helluva town!
>
>(*Scene segues to a stylized version, set to music, of a New York City street and its crowds, with* GABEY, OZZIE, *and* CHIP *vainly trying to find their way. The tempo increases until the curtain parts on the next scene.*)

SCENE 2

A subway train in motion. Typical New Yorkers seated and standing. LITTLE OLD LADY *is seated.* FLOSSIE *and her* FRIEND *are right of* LITTLE OLD LADY.

FLOSSIE: So I said to him—"Listen, Mr. Gadolphin, Betty Hutton herself in person would look like a dead zombie after my day's work in this office."

FRIEND: What did he say?

FLOSSIE: So I said, "After all, a girl hasn't got fourteen arms."

FRIEND: For Heaven's sake.

>(*Two people get up and the* GIRLS *get the seats.* CHIP, GABEY *and* OZZIE *enter through crowd. Two women who got up start off left.* FLOSSIE *and her* FRIEND *talk together.*)

CHIP: Now, I've got our whole tour organized— (*Thumbs through his guide-book.*)

OZZIE: A-a-a-a-h!

CHIP: Holy smoke, Oz—I wanna see New York. I've never been anywhere bigger than Peoria—and I'm not gonna miss any of the famous landmarks. Now—I got our whole day figured out: 10:30 Bronx Park; 10:40 Statue of Liberty—

OZZIE: I wanna see the beauties of the city, too—but I mean the kind with legs!

>(CHIP *turns away with disgust.*)

Back home in Scranton everybody's covered with coal dust—I want one of those New York City glamour girls—the kind you see in the movies. How about it, Gabe?

GABEY: I want one special girl. I—I had a wonderful girl once—she lived on a farm right next to ours—'bout five miles away. (*Car lurches.*)

OZZIE (*turns to* GABEY): Y-a-a-a, we know! Minnie Frenchley—in the 7th grade!! Forget your purple past, kid. Think of New York! Chip and I'll show you all the sights. The most crowded place you've ever been is in a cornfield—

GABEY (*grabs* OZZIE, *pulls him back and twists his arm*): I told you about that! Say uncle!

OZZIE: O.K. Uncle—Uncle.

FLOSSIE: So I said to him, "Listen, Mr. Gadolphin, I will not work overtime, no matter what. Whether it's handling the Snodgrass-Rumshinsky account—or you."

FRIEND: So what did he say?

FLOSSIE: So I said—"One more crack out of you, Mr. G.—and the Grand Illusion Brassiere Company is looking for another yours truly"—

(BILL POSTER *enters through crowd, pushes his way through* GABEY *and* OZZIE. *He is carrying a bag of car cards.*)

FRIEND: So what did he say?

BILL POSTER: Pardon me, boys—got a little art work to do—
(*He puts bag down on floor in front of* LITTLE OLD LADY, *picks out a card and gives the boys a quick glance at it.*)
Well, they sure picked a nifty this month—

GABEY: What's that?

BILL POSTER (*still holding card and facing front*): It's "Miss Turnstiles for the Month"— (*Turns and steps up on seat.*)

LITTLE OLD LADY: Watch what you're doing, Mister.

BILL POSTER: Take it easy, lady, take it easy. "Meet exotic Ivy Smith"— (*Places the card in space over door.*)

OZZIE: Oh boy—I'd love to meet her.

CHIP: Obviously an upper class society girl.

GABEY: Fellas, she reminds me of Minnie Frenchley.
(BILL POSTER *gets down, picks up another card from bag.*)

BILL POSTER (*reading*): Now look at that for an all-round creature . . . "Ivy's a home-loving type who likes to go out night-clubbing" . . .

GABEY (*reading*): Gee—she loves the Navy.

BILL POSTER: Yeah—but her heart belongs to the Army.
(*Their faces fall.*)
"She's not a career girl, but she is studying singing and ballet at Carnegie Hall and painting at the Museums. She is a frail and flowerlike girl—who's a champion at polo, tennis, and shotput."
(OZZIE *whistles.*)
Got it all over last month's Miss Turnstiles—

GABEY: She's wonderful.

BILL POSTER (*leaving*): Why don'tcha date her up? Well, so long, fellas—drop in again sometime. (*Exits.*)

GABEY: That's the girl for me, fellas. I'd like to meet her today.

CHIP: There are 2,500,000 women in New York—and—it's impractical.

OZZIE: If Gabe wants her, he can have her. He's a naval hero— He deserves a girl like that!
(GABEY *has climbed on the seat and is taking picture down.*)

LITTLE OLD LADY (*rises, protesting*): Young man, that's vandalism!

CHIP: Hey, Gabe, what are ya doing?

OZZIE: Put it back, Gabe—

GABEY (*staring at it*): Why? I like her—

LITTLE OLD LADY: Destroying public property! You're liable to a fine of $500—I'll get a policeman!

OZZIE: Hey, I think she means it.

LITTLE OLD LADY (*screaming*): Conductor—conductor—Police!

OZZIE: Hey, come on, let's get out of here!

LITTLE OLD LADY: Put that back!!

CHIP: Come on, Gabe—come on!!

OZZIE (*grabs* GABEY *bodily, forces him through crowd*): Gangway, folks!!

LITTLE OLD LADY: Vandals! Vandals!
(*She tries to follow them, but boys push through the crowd and exeunt.* LITTLE OLD LADY *steps through curtain on end of scene for 1st Chase Interlude.* LITTLE OLD LADY *runs left and right looking for* POLICEMAN, *jumps up and down, runs off.*)

SCENE 3

A New York street. GABEY, CHIP *and* OZZIE *enter.* GABEY *is still engrossed in the picture.*

CHIP (*comes over and puts his hands on* GABEY'S *shoulders*): But, Gabe—be reasonable. There are twenty-thousand streets in this town—and you'll never find her in one day.

GABEY: So that's my hard luck. (*Looks down at picture.*)

CHIP: Well, I'm not gonna waste any more time on this. I'm way behind on my schedule already. Bronx Park is a dead issue. (*Crosses it off his guidebook.*)

OZZIE: Hey, Chip. If Gabe hadn't pulled us out of the drink, we wouldn't *be* here in New York! We'd be just a couple of pleasant memories.

GABEY (*looks at them, moves a step right*): Oh, the hell with that.

OZZIE (*a look to* CHIP, *then quickly*): Chip, you and me are gonna help him find her.

CHIP (*looking at* OZZIE): WHAT?

OZZIE: We're going to help him find Ivy Smith.

(GABEY *smiles.*)

CHIP: Help him find her? (*Waves guidebook excitedly.*) That's crazy—I gotta—

OZZIE: What's the matter with you? Haven't you got any gratitude? What kind of people come from Peoria, anyway—I'll give up all my girls till tonight to help Gabe—if you'll promise me to give up your sightseeing.

CHIP: All right. But how're we gonna do it?

OZZIE: That's your department—you're the guy with the systems. 10:30—Yellowstone Park; 10:45—Opium dens.

CHIP: Let's see the card, kid.

(*Grabs card from* GABEY *with his right hand and holds it away from him.*)

GABEY (*trying to get it away from him*): Hey!

CHIP: Uh—I got it—We'll break up and follow all the clues on this poster—and—we'll meet—at Times Square—(*points*) at Nedick's—at—eleven—

OZZIE: Swell! One of us'll find her—and then, Gabe, she's all yours.

GABEY: Aw—that will never work.

CHIP: It might work. It's all down there in black and white. She's got to be one of those places.

OZZIE: Now look, Gabe—if you do happen to run into her, without me there to advise you, just remember—the whole secret is to be a bigshot. You're important, see—you're a hero. (*Dusts off* GABEY's *ribbons*.) Just keep saying to yourself, "Gabey's coming." Get it?

GABEY: Gabey's coming.

OZZIE: Yeah, Gabey's coming.

CHIP: Gabey, you go to Carnegie Hall—and Ozzie—you go to the Modern Museum.

OZZIE: Museum?

CHIP: It's at 79th Street and Central Park—and I'll investigate through the subway people.

GABEY & OZZIE: Huh?

CHIP: The underground authorities.

GABEY: But what about your dames?

OZZIE: A-a-h, we can pick up somebody later on. That's easy. After all, the girls we're willing to date aren't fancy contest winners.

CHIP: Yes. Can you imagine what Miss Turnstiles must be like?

GABEY: To win such a title—Miss Turnstiles for June.

    (*The three exit.*)

SCENE 4

Presentation of Miss Turnstiles. There is a fanfare, and the ANNOUNCER *steps on.*

ANNOUNCER: Miss Turnstiles for June!

    (*Music starts, and a line of* GIRLS *sways in, backs to audience.*) Every month some lucky little New York miss is chosen Miss Turnstiles for the Month. She's got to be beautiful, she's got to be just an average girl, and most important of all, she's got to ride the subway. There are 5,683 women who ride the subway every day. And which fortunate lassie will be picked this month for the signal honor? Beautiful, brilliant, average, a typical New Yorker—

    (*A spotlight which has been roving up and down the line of* GIRLS *as it sways across the stage suddenly stops on one of the girls. The line stops, and the girl,* IVY SMITH, *turns around coyly with a happy Who me? expression.*)

YES, YOU!!

    (IVY *runs forward and the line disappears.*)

    (*The stage lights come up and a* REPORTER, *a* PHOTOGRA-PHER *and* ASSISTANT, *a* DRESS DESIGNER *and* ASSISTANT

gather around to glamourize and publicize MISS TURN-
STILES. *During this, the* ANNOUNCER *sings. Large blowup
of the Turnstiles poster flies in.*)

> She's a home-loving girl
> But she loves high society's whirl—
> She adores the army, the navy as well,
> At poetry and polo she's swell.

(*The* PHOTOGRAPHER, *the* REPORTER, *the* DESIGNER *and*
ASSISTANT *back off, and* IVY *and* BOYS *do a satiric dance
based on the contradictory attributes that* MISS TURNSTILES
seems to possess:

> HOME-LOVING TYPE—*boy in slippers, bathrobe, pipe.*
> JITTERBUGGER—*zoot-suit, jazz routine.*
> THE ARMY
> THE NAVY
> THE POETIC TYPE
> THE ATHLETE

*She does a brief pas-de-deux with each of them and a final
dance with all.*)

(*At the end of the dance, the voice of the* ANNOUNCER *is heard.*)
ANNOUNCER: But of course at the end of each month a new
Miss Turnstiles is chosen, and when that happens . . .

> (*The* BOYS *disappear. She waves a sad farewell to them. Her
> picture—an enlargement of the car card placed in the subway
> earlier—which was on display at the rear of the stage, disap-
> pears. She waves goodbye to that. The same line of* GIRLS *has
> re-appeared sidling with their backs to the audience. She discon-
> solately resumes her place in line and sidles off with the rest as
> the curtain closes.*)

(*2nd Chase Interlude. The* LITTLE OLD LADY *finds a* POLICE-
MAN, *tells him about the vandalism, and they run off.*)

SCENE 5

*A taxi-cab. Inside it is a young tough girl cabbie. She's asleep. A
man wearing a jacket, on the back of which is printed* S.UPERMAN,
awakens her roughly.

UPERMAN: Hey—hey, you!
HILDY: Taxi.

UPERMAN: Wake up, Esterhazy—it's me—your boss—Uperman.

HILDY: Oh, Mr. Uperman, good morning.

UPERMAN: Good morning to you. (*Very sarcastic.*) I just dropped by to tell you this is the last time I'm catching you asleep. You're fired.

HILDY: But Mr. Uper—

UPERMAN: And if that cab ain't back in the garage in an hour, I'll turn you in to the cops. (*He exits.*)

HILDY (*philosophically*): Well—a civilian again! Might as well make this last fare a good one—

  (*She looks around. A* MAN *rushes up to cab.*)

MAN: Taxi. Grand Central Station—quick.

HILDY (*disapprovingly*): Uh, uh—too small.

  (*He rushes off in a huff.*)

ANOTHER MAN: Taxi! . . .

HILDY (*turning him down*): Too big!

  (*He withdraws.*)

DELICATE TYPE (*enters*): Uh—is this cab occupied?

HILDY: Too-too!

  (*He leaves.* CHIP *enters, stands with back to audience. A* GIRL *approaches.*)

  (*Shouting.*) AND NO GIRLS!!

  (GIRL *runs away.* CHIP *consulting his guidebook tries to get his bearings.* HILDY *sees him—her face lights up. She shouts at him.*)

  Hey, you!

CHIP (*looking up, startled*): Who—who, me?

HILDY: Yes, you—get in.

CHIP (*coming over to her*): Oh, maybe you can take me to the subway people.

HILDY (*does a take*): The what?

CHIP: The subway people . . .

HILDY (*as if she knows all about it*): Oh, sure—sure—and when we get through with them we'll go see the Cat People. Only get in.

  (*He starts getting into the back of the cab.*)

  No. Up front! This ride's on me!!

CHIP: But lady, I—

  (*She pulls him into the front seat.*)

HILDY: What's your name?

CHIP: Uh—John Offenblock—but the fellas call me Chip.

HILDY (*coquettishly*): Chip, huh, betcha can't guess my name.

CHIP: Guess it? Oh, that's ridiculous. Why, the law of averages—

HILDY: O.K. You win! The name's Esterhazy. Brunhilde Esterhazy. (*Slight pause.*) Kiss me.

(*She turns her face. He doesn't believe it. He turns his face to the right. She grabs him. They disappear in a clinch behind the steering wheel, and come up after a moment. He, all flustered, and she all aglow.*)

Well! (*Little laugh.*) Let's go to my place!!

CHIP: I—I'd like to, lady—but I have to—

HILDY: Aw, what's the matter with me, Chip, why won't you come? I'm young, I'm free, I'm highly attainable.

CHIP (*leaning against door*): Look, Miss, I got a promise to stick to—

HILDY: You stick to me instead, kid. I've been waiting for you all my life. Knew you the minute I saw you. You're for me—I like your face. It's open—ya know what I mean? Nothing in it. The kind of a face I can fall into. Kiss me!

(*She grabs him, pulls him down in the seat and kisses him. He breaks away and gets up.*)

CHIP: Listen, lady—

HILDY: Just call me Hildy.

CHIP: Look, Miss—I got something important to do today. Just lemme outta here. (*He starts out of the cab.*)

HILDY (*moves over to right end of seat, grabs his sleeve*): A-a-a-h, no you don't. You're going with me while I turn in my cab. After that, we'll go to my place.

CHIP: Now, look, miss, I've got to find this Miss Turnstiles for my pal—

HILDY (*hits her forehead with left hand, then turns and looks out window*): Miss Turnstiles for your pal! Well, I thought I'd heard 'em all. You're not going to get rid of me that easy, kid. (*Turns to him.*)

CHIP: Oh, no, it's true. If I didn't have to help my buddy, I'd be out seeing the famous sights my father told me about. He was here in 1934 and gave me this guidebook—and . . .

HILDY (*grabs the guidebook*): I'll take you any place you want to go. Get in.

CHIP: I shouldn't do this—

HILDY: Come on, Chip.

CHIP (*climbs in, guiltily*): O.K., a quick tour of the city—
HILDY (*triumphantly*): Then up to my place! (*Pats his knee.*)
CHIP: No—to help find Gabe's girl.
HILDY: No—up to my place!
CHIP: But—
HILDY: It's all settled—where d'ya wanna go first!! (*Leans out left door.*) Ah—the same to you!

"Come Up to My Place"

CHIP:
>My father told me "Chip, my boy, there'll come a time when you leave home
>If you should ever hit New York, be sure to see the Hippodrome."

HILDY:
>The Hippodrome?

CHIP:
>The Hippodrome.

HILDY:
>Did I hear right?
>Did you say the Hippodrome?

CHIP:
>Yes, you heard right—
>Yes, I said the Hip——
(*Brake noise.*)
>Hey, what did you stop for?

HILDY:
>It ain't there anymore—
>Aida sang an A and blew the place away—

CHIP: Aw, I wanted to see the Hippodrome!
HILDY: Give me a chance, kid. I haven't got 5,000 seats, but the one I have is a honey!! Come up to my place.
CHIP: No, the Forrest Theatre—

>When I was home I saw the plays
>The Ladies Drama Circle showed,
>Now I'm here—I want to get—
>Some tickets for *Tobacco Road*.

HILDY:
>*Tobacco Road*?

CHIP:
> *Tobacco Road.*

HILDY:
> Did I dig that—
> Did you say *Tobacco Road?*

CHIP:
> Yes, you dug that—
> Sure, I said *Tobac*——
> (*Brake noise.*)
> Hey, what for did you stop?

HILDY:
> That show has closed up shop—
> The actors washed their feet
> And called it *Angel Street*—

CHIP: I wanted to see *Tobacco Road*—

HILDY: Stick with me, kid. I'll show you the road to ruin. Come up to my place.

CHIP: No—Battery Park.

> Back home I dreamt of catching fish
> So big I couldn't carry 'em.
> They told me that they have my size
> Right here in the Aquarium—

HILDY:
> Aquarium?

CHIP:
> Aquarium—

HILDY:
> Hold the phone, Joe—
> Did you say Aquarium?

CHIP:
> I'm still ringing—
> Yes I said Aquar——
> (*Brake noise.*)
> Did you stop for what, hey.

HILDY:
> The fish have flown away—
> They're in the Bronx instead—
> They might as well be dead—
> Come up to my place.

CHIP: No—Chambers Street.

> They told me I could see New York
> In all its spreading strength and power
> From the city's highest spot—
> Atop the famous Woolworth Tower—

HILDY:

> The Woolworth Tower?

CHIP:

> The Woolworth Tower.

HILDY:

> Beat me, daddy—
> Did you say the Woolworth Tower?

CHIP:

> I won't beat you, but I said the Wool——
> (*Brake noise.*)
> Did you stop for hey what—

HILDY:

> That ain't the highest spot—
> You're just a little late—
> We've got the Empire State—
> Let's go to my place—

CHIP:

> Let's go to Cleopatra's needle.

HILDY:

> Let's go to my place.

CHIP:

> Let's see Wanamaker's store—

HILDY:

> Let's go to my place.

CHIP:

> Go to Lindy's—go to Luchow's—

HILDY:

> Go to my place.

CHIP:

> Let's see Radio City—and Herald Square—

HILDY:

> Let's go to my place.

CHIP:

> Go to Reuben's—

HILDY:

    Go to my place.

CHIP:

    Go to Macy's.

HILDY:

    Go to my place.

CHIP:

    Roxy—

HILDY:

    Go to my place.

CHIP:

    Cloisters.

HILDY:

    My place.

CHIP:

    Gimbel's.

HILDY:

    My place—

CHIP:

    Flatiron Building.

HILDY:

    MY PLACE!!

CHIP:

    HIPPODROME!!!

HILDY:

    My place—

BLACKOUT

(*3rd Chase Interlude.* UPERMAN *finds a cop, tells him about* HILDY's *taking the cab. They run off.* LITTLE OLD LADY *and her* COP *follow in pursuit.*)

SCENE 6

Museum of Natural History. The scene is a large chamber in the Museum of Natural History—devoted to prehistoric animals. It's rather an eerie sight, filled with pterodactyls hanging from wires, skeletons of some smallish strange reptiles, and the skeleton of one huge dinosaur, with its shadow projected enormously against the back wall. This figure dominates the scene. A few feet away from it stands a realistic statue of a Pithecanthropus erectus, *an ancestor of present day man, somewhat more ape than man, who roamed the earth in around 6,000,000 B.C. The statue bears a striking resemblance, enough to be startling, to* OZZIE, *who is at this moment part of a small group of people gathered in front of the dinosaur skeleton listening to a lecture. The speaker is a fussy little professorial type,* WALDO FIGMENT, *and* OZZIE, *looking about for a possible* IVY SMITH, *isn't paying the strictest attention.*

FIGMENT (*speaking slowly and painfully*): This unique skeleton— I have reconstructed it without any clue whatsoever—except for one tiny bone—found during a picnic—in Westchester— in the bushes. Let us consider that these huge beasts might be living today—but they were victims of over-inflation. They became too goddamned big! Thank you. Let us move on.

  (*The crowd disperses, muttering and generally discussing the dinosaur as they drift away, leaving the stage clear except for* OZZIE, *who stares after them disappointedly, and* PROFESSOR FIGMENT, *who is busily arranging his notes in a brief-case.*)

OZZIE: Mr. Bones, maybe you can help me. I'm looking for a girl called Ivy Smith and I thought she might be at the Museum of Modern Art.

FIGMENT (*testily*): She probably is—this is the Museum of Natural History.

  (*Moves to exit. Sees* OZZIE *over his shoulder. Turns.*)

OZZIE (*moving up to dinosaur*): Chip and his guide book—

FIGMENT: And don't touch that dinosaur, or I'll call a policeman. It took me forty hard long years to construct that. (*Looks at dinosaur and sadly shakes his head.*) Sometimes I wish I hadn't gone on that picnic. (*Exits, shaking his head.*)

  (OZZIE *then yawns and stretches wildly and freely, unconsciously assuming the pose of* Pithecanthropus *statue. As he is doing this,* CLAIRE DE LOONE *enters briskly, apparently on her way to look at the dinosaur. She is a handsomely attractive, smartly dressed girl, and seems to be of the cool and poised school. However, upon seeing* OZZIE *and the statue side by side, arms stretched aloft, she stops dead in her tracks and . . .*)

CLAIRE (*shrieks*): A-a-a-a-a-a-a-h-h-h!!

OZZIE (*stifles yawn, sees her*): Don't be frightened, lady. They're all dead.

CLAIRE: But you!!—You're alive. (*Drops handbag on bench.*) How wonderful!! (*Takes out camera from bag.*)

OZZIE (*surprised—and conscious of being accosted by an attractive girl*): And you're alive, too. Don't we make a lovely couple. (*Makes a gesture toward her.*)

CLAIRE: Yes, you do. (*Referring to him and statue, of course.*) It's fantastic. I've got to get the two of you together. Hold it, please.

> (*Draws back and snaps picture with a Leica. Included in her equipment are a notebook and pencil and tape measure in her handbag.*)
>
> (OZZIE *freezes in pose.*)

Incredible. A *Pithecanthropus erectus*—in a sailor suit! Dear, you're priceless!

OZZIE (*taking all this as flattery*): Really, well, how about some cheese cake. (*He drapes himself in a Dietrich pose, pulling up his trouser leg.*)

CLAIRE (*beside herself*): That leg! How extraordinary—in all my studies, I've never seen one like it! (*Snaps another picture.*) This is wonderful. What a lucky girl I am. Now—your measurements. (*Approaches him, taking the tape measure out.*)

OZZIE (*more and more surprised and pleased. He continues posing*): Well, I'm a Junior Miss size 11—That's about all I can remember—

CLAIRE: Gorgeous!!

> (*She puts the tape measure over her left arm and starts to make a note in her notebook. She turns away from* OZZIE, *and he takes the tape from her arm playfully.*)

OZZIE (*behind her*): Now it's my turn— (*He measures her bust, humming.*)

> New York, New York—a helluva town!!

CLAIRE (*completely taken off guard*): How dare you! (*Turns and grabs tape-measure.*)

OZZIE (*thinking he's being wooed*): Two can play the same game as well as one, you know!

CLAIRE (*backing away*): Now look here!

(OZZIE *chases her around the gorilla.*)
Just what I should have expected from a *Pithecanthropus erectus*—No breeding! What's the idea?

OZZIE (*bumps into the* Pithecanthropus erectus): Owww! Out of my way—Quasimodo!! (*He resumes the chase.*)

CLAIRE (*angrily*): Quasimodo is right! The spitting image of you.

OZZIE (*standing still abruptly*): Huh? (*Looks at the statue, does terrific take as he realizes.*) You mean I look like that.

CLAIRE (*surprised he didn't know*): Look like? Well, what on earth did you think I was taking your picture for?

OZZIE (*deflated, realizing she wasn't chasing him*): You mean—

CLAIRE (*getting the misunderstanding—realizing he thought she was on the make*): Oh—I see—you thought I was carried away by your irresistible charms. I'm sorry—
    (*She is cool—amused—but keeps looking at him. He gets gloomier and gloomier.*)
I'll clear the whole thing up. I'm just a cold-blooded scientist. An anthropologist. The name is Claire de Loone.

OZZIE: An anthropologist! (*Completely deflated.*) Pleased to meetcha.

CLAIRE (*she looks him up and down. Writes in her book*): I'm writing a book for this Museum—an anthropological study, called *Modern Man—What Is It?*
    (*He sniffs.*)
And that's my only interest in modern man. You bear an extraordinary resemblance to this *Pithecanthropus erectus*—a man extinct since 6,000,000 B.C. And that's why I need your picture—and your measurements. Now then— (*Goes over to him with tape measure and notebook.*)

OZZIE: Aaah, I'm just wasting my time—Look lady—I'm looking for a girl named Ivy Smith. She was chosen Miss Turnstiles for the month of June. Do you know her?

CLAIRE: No, I don't. But you might ask at the information desk on your way out.
    (*Measuring his arm, looking at him.*)
Now don't be moody— (*Measures his chest from under-arm to waist.*) You made an understandable mistake. Now the head— (*Takes his hat off, hands it to him. Measures head.*) Ah! That

sub-super-dolico cephalic head! Sailor, I love you for having that. (*Makes a note admiringly.*)

OZZIE: Gee, all my life I wanted someone to love me for my sakidophalic head.

CLAIRE: Now don't be bitter.

(*Pushes his hat forward, measures the back of his head between the ears. She holds the tape measure out and is surprised to find about only two inches. She looks at him and then makes another note.*)

OZZIE (*pushes his hat to back of his head*): There aren't so many of us left. We had a sakidocephalic class reunion last year. Not many of the old faces around.

CLAIRE (*rolls up tape measure with finality*): Thank you . . . I'm finished now. (*She goes to bench.*) You may go now. Ask at the information desk on your way out for your friend. (*She sits and makes a note in her book.*)

OZZIE: I can go now!—I can go now!! You use me as a guinea pig—take my measurements—then you tell me I can go—all right, I'll go—

(CLAIRE *looks at him.*)

I've been neglecting my duty anyhow.

CLAIRE: Goodbye.

OZZIE: G'bye. (*Moves back to gorilla, sniffs. Turns back to* CLAIRE.) Hey—look— (*Approaches her.*) Seeing as you're not interested in modern man—then you probably haven't got a date tonight.

(CLAIRE *looks up surprised.*)

Uh— (*Sits.*) —You gonna be busy later?

CLAIRE: Very busy. I'll be busy for the rest of my life. I'm engaged to be married.

OZZIE: Uh huh—Well in that case I'll be going— (OZZIE *rises, starts to go, then turns to* CLAIRE.)

CLAIRE: Goodbye.

OZZIE (*at statue*): G'bye. Who's the lucky man?

CLAIRE: I'm engaged to be married to the famous Judge Pitkin W. Bridgework. We're celebrating our engagement tonight.

OZZIE: Is he hot-stuff?

CLAIRE (*rises and approaches him angrily*): Hot stuff! Of all the loathsome phrases. Pitkin is the finest man I've ever known.

He understands me completely. We have a purely intellectual relationship. It was Pitkin who made me study anthropology. I made a clean breast to him of all my past and he understood. He said, "Claire, I understand." (*Turns to* OZZIE.) "Just make a scientific study of man—know them objectively—and you'll get them out of your system."

OZZIE: Well, did it work?

CLAIRE (*staring at him*): Almost completely.

> (*Makes a lunge for him. She grabs him in her arms and bends him over her knee in a passionate kiss. His hat falls off. They come out of it.*)

Of course, sometimes I get carried away.

OZZIE (*retrieving his hat*): You too?

CLAIRE: I'm afraid so.

OZZIE: Gee, that's just my trouble.

CLAIRE: Claire—another demerit. (*Recitation against music.*) Modern man—what is it? Just a collection of complexes and neurotic impulses that occasionally break through.

OZZIE: You mean sometimes you blow your top like me?

CLAIRE: I do. (*She tosses her book away.*)

"Carried Away"

> I try hard to stay controlled
> But I get carried away
> Try to act aloof and cold—
> (*Toward him.*)
> But I *get carried away*

BOTH:

> Carried away—carried away—

OZZIE: CLAIRE:

> You—   I—

BOTH:

> Get carried—just carried away.

CLAIRE:

> When I sit and listen to a symphony
> Why can't I just say the music's grand—
> Why must I leap upon the stage hysterically—
> They're playing pizzicato—
> And everything goes blotto—

I grab the maestro's stick—and start in
Leading the band!
(*She conducts.*)

OZZIE: CLAIRE:
    You—   I—

BOTH:
    Gets carried—just carried away.

OZZIE:
    And when I got to see a moving picture show
    And I'm watching the actors in a scene
(*Gesture of picture screen.*)
    I start to think what's happening is really so—
    The girl—I must protect her
    The villain don't respect her—
    I leap to her defense and knock a hole right through
        the screen.
(*Punches left hand forward.*)

OZZIE: CLAIRE:
    I—   He—

BOTH:
    Gets carried—just carried away.
(*On interlude, they put hands on each other's shoulders to
console each other.*)

OZZIE:
    I try hard to keep detached
    But I get carried away.
    Try to act less booby-hatched
    But I get *carried away.*

OZZIE: CLAIRE:
    I—   He—

BOTH:
    Gets carried—just carried away.

OZZIE:
    When shopping I'm a sucker for a bargain sale
    If something is marked down upon a shelf
    My sense of what is practical begins to fail
    I buy one then another—
    Another and another—
(*Reaching for things on shelves.*)

I buy the whole store out and I'm in business for
    myself.
(*Business of washing hands.*)

OZZIE: CLAIRE:
    I—   He—

BOTH:
    Gets carried—just carried away.

CLAIRE:
    And when I go to see my friends off on a train
    Golly how I hate to see them go
    For them my love of traveling I can't restrain
    The time has come for parting
    The train's already starting—
    I hop a freight and in a flash I'm off to Buffalo.
    (*Does "Off to Buffalo" step.*)

BOTH:
    Carried away—carried away—
    We get carried—just carried a——
    (*They break off abruptly without finishing the song, go to
    bench and sit.*)
    (*Encore*)
    (*Both come down. She leads him by the right ear.*)

CLAIRE:
    I'm the scientific kind
    Yet I get carried away
    Ancient man is on my mind
    And I get carried away.

BOTH:
    Carried away—carried away
    I get carried—just carried away.

CLAIRE:
    I take anthropology so literally
    That these modern days are not for me
    Right now I feel we're living prehistorically
    To us the past has beckoned
    We're going back this second
    To happy days we knew in 6,000,000 B.C.

BOTH:
    (*Drum beat starts.*)

Carried away—carried away
We get carried—

(The drum becomes a slow tom-tom beat. Three PREHISTORIC
MEN *come on. Three* BIRD GIRLS *enter. The three men circle
the stage. The last one motions to* OZZIE *to join them. He
assumes the "Apeman" walk, and falls in line.* CLAIRE *begins
to scratch and walk like the* BIRD GIRLS. *One* MAN *comes
down and picks* CLAIRE *up, sets her on bench. Other* MAN *picks
up a club and hits third* MAN *who is dancing with a* BIRD
GIRL. *Third* MAN *bows deeply, relinquishes his* GIRL *to the
"cutter-in" man, picks up the club and starts to hit* OZZIE *in
the same manner, indicating that he wants to dance with his
BIRD GIRL. CLAIRE watches in horror.)*

CLAIRE *(as* OZZIE *is about to be clubbed, leaps from bench)*: Oh,
no—no—oh, no, oh, no, no!

OZZIE *(staggering back into* CLAIRE's *arms)*: No cutting in!

(The group now forms a semi-circle, with OZZIE *and* CLAIRE
*in the center. First man starts to pick one of them by the "eenie-
meenie-miney-mo" system. He goes round the circle, and* OZZIE
is "it." CLAIRE, *delightedly, picks up the club, and prepares to
hit him. She makes a mighty swing, hits, instead, the skeleton of
the dinosaur. It falls to pieces, as the prehistoric characters scurry
away with much chirping.)*

*(CLAIRE and OZZIE are once more back in the Museum. They
look at the wreckage of the dinosaur and sing.)*

BOTH:

We got carried—just carried a——

(The music breaks. FIGMENT *enters, sees the wreckage, starts
after* CLAIRE *and* OZZIE.)*

OZZIE: Come on! Let's get outta here!

(They pick up CLAIRE's *handbag, notebook and pencil, and
dash off, with* FIGMENT *in full chase after them.)*

*(4th Chase Interlude. The previous characters in the chase are
now supplanted by* FIGMENT *who demands that the* POLICE-
MAN *run after* OZZIE *and* CLAIRE *who have destroyed his
dinosaur. The others stream by in hot pursuit.)*

SCENE 7

GABEY *enters, looking around. People are passing on the street. A* MAN *is seated on a bench reading a newspaper.*

GABEY (*to* MAN): I beg your pardon, can you tell me where Carnegie Hall is?

> (MAN *shakes his head "No." Two* GIRLS *enter, crossing the stage.* GABEY *speaks to them.*)

I beg your pardon—

> (*They do not answer, continuing giggling on their way out. The* MAN *on the bench exits.*)

"Lonely Town"

Gabey's comin'—Gabey's comin' to town—
So what—who cares?
Back on the ship—it seemed such a snap—
You'd tap a girl on the shoulder—
She'd turn around—
And then she'd say "I love you"—
But once on shore—
It's not such a snap—
You get the cold shoulder—
The old run-around—
You're left with no one but you—
Gabey's coming—Gabey's coming to town.

(*Chorus*)

A town's a lonely town
When you pass through
And there is no one waiting there for you
Then it's a lonely town
You wander up and down—
The crowds rush by
A million faces pass before your eye—
Still it's a lonely town.
Unless there's love
A love that's shining like a harbor light—
You're lost in the night—
Unless there's love—
The world's an empty place

And every town's—a lonely town.

(GABEY *sits on bench. A group of* SCHOOL GIRLS *enters. Behind them comes a group of* SAILORS. *They're talking among themselves, see the* GIRLS, *follow them off. One* SAILOR *remains. A* GIRL *starts to leave, sees* GABEY, *who makes a gesture toward her. She turns from him in embarrassment, almost bumps into the remaining* SAILOR. *She recoils from him, goes and sits on bench opposite* SAILOR. *He follows, they go into a pas de deux, and exit.*)

(*The music picks up, and "Lonely Town" is reprised, with the singing chorus strolling on.* GABEY *joins for one chorus. The curtains close.*)

SCENE 8

The scene segues to a corridor in Carnegie Hall. A SOPRANO *is singing "The Bell Song" from* Lakmé *in a nearby studio. An* ACTOR *strolls on.*

ACTOR (*reciting as he walks, using many gestures*): "Down, down I come like glistening phaeton mounting the marriage of unruly jades in the base court—come down? Down court—Down King!"

(*As he reaches center stage, about to come off, a Wagnerian* SOPRANO *enters opposite, crossing stage, engrossed in singing Brunhilde's "Call of the Walkyrie." Two* MUSICIANS *enter carrying instrument cases, arguing.*)

1ST MUSICIAN: You call him a conductor? He used the baton like a meat cleaver.

2ND MUSICIAN: You know that fourth bar after H—They ought to let me conduct the orchestra. I'd show them how to do it.

(*As they exit, a* LITTLE MAN, *very dejected, holding a wilted flower, enters and crosses. As he exits, a* BALLET GIRL *in rehearsal clothes enters, talking over her shoulder.*)

BALLET GIRL: Are you going to the auditions for "Hold Your Britches"?

BALLET BOY (*enters fussily, tying ribbon around his head*): NO! I'm only interested in ballet.

(*He exits.* IVY *enters. Three* DANCERS *come on, two* GIRLS, *one* BOY. BOY *picks up* GIRL, *and lifts her in attitude, lowers her to floor with a jar.*)

IST GIRL DANCER (*still worried by the bad return to the floor, bawls out her partner*): That stinks! Come here.

2ND GIRL DANCER: Now watch!

(*She pirouettes, unwatched, across the stage. They try it again, and soar offstage. As they hit the wings, the* 2ND GIRL DANCER *gets to her toes.*)

Look! I'm Swan Lake.

(*She "points" offstage. The* LITTLE MAN, *no longer dejected, returns across stage, carrying a triumphantly erect flower. He is smiling happily. As he exits, the Carnegie Hall drop goes up, revealing studio of* MADAME MAUDE P. DILLY. MADAME DILLY *is practicing scales at her piano, punctuating notes with copious swigs from a whiskey bottle which reposes on the piano.*)

DILLY: Do-do-re-do-do re mi do—

(*Takes a drink.* IVY *enters.* DILLY *turns on stool.*)

Hel-l-o-o, Miss Smith.

IVY: Good morning, Madame Dilly.

DILLY: No, no—*sing* your greeting—always s-i-i-n-g—your greeting.

IVY (*singing*): Good morning, Madame Dilly.

DILLY: You've got your diaphragm wrapped around your spinal column. We haven't been practicing, have we?

IVY: I have been practicing, Madame Dilly. I practice every minute I'm not working. There's been complaints. But I'm determined to move onwards and upwards. That's why I'm studying singing and ballet like it says on my poster picture. But sometimes I feel I'd like to quit that crummy job.

DILLY (*rises, comes over to* IVY): No—no—don't do that. There is nothing wrong with—being an actress.

IVY: Oh, what's the use of saying that. I'm not an actress, I'm a cooch dancer. And it's so inartistic.

DILLY: It pays well. And the money you earn at Coney Island goes for your singing lessons. You are already in arrears about fifty dollars. So, keep working—working.

IVY: But Madame Dilly—what if the people who picked me Miss Turnstiles find out? They'll expose me as a phoney—and I'm not. Those are all the things I really want to do some day.

DILLY: And you can make all of them come true by studying

with me—the best teacher on this side of the corridor. Now—
to the grindstone. Place your feet wide apart—
> (IVY *does so.*)

Nothing helps like a firm grip on the floor. (DILLY *returns
to the piano, strikes note and sings.*) Now curl your toes and
say—I'm singing—I'm singing.

IVY: I'm singing—I'm singing.

DILLY: Now, again—in the relaxo position—over!
> (IVY *bends down. When she starts to sing,* DILLY *sneaks a
> drink.*)

IVY: I'm singing—I'm singing.

DILLY: Good! Now—up through the toes—through the
diaphragm—and out front!
> (IVY *straightens up, concentrating.*)

IVY: I'm singing—I'm singing.

DILLY (*rises, comes over to* IVY): Now—quiver my fingers with
those lovely high tones.
> (*Places two fingers of her right hand on* IVY's *upper lip. Turns
> her head left.*)

IVY: (*in a high soprano*): I'm singing—I'm singing.

DILLY: No, no, no. Try to think of your mouth as a trium-
phal arch through which passes a procession of pear-shaped
tones—like pearls on a rope. Again, please. (*Returns to the
piano, strikes a chord.*)

IVY: I'm singing—I'm singing.
> (*This is worse than before.* DILLY *wheels from the piano in a
> fury, thundering, and pounding her chest vigorously.*)

DILLY: THE RESONATORS!!!

IVY (*takes a deep breath and steps away*): Oh, Madame Dilly,
occasionally I feel like I'm not making any progress—

DILLY: Now, none of that. You've a splendid voice—
Magnificent—and I'm giving you priceless vocal secrets!
Now—position eight—
> (IVY *goes to piano.*)

Your vocalise—
> (IVY *does handstand, feet resting on the piano.* DILLY *sits,
> strikes a chord.*)

IVY: Do—do re do—do re mi do—

DILLY: Good—good placement. (*Drinks.*)

IVY: Do—re—mi—fa—do.

(GABEY *wanders through outside corridor.*)

DILLY (*holds up bottle to light, finds it really empty, rises, puts it in her bosom*): I must go now—just for a moment. You must stay here and practice your scales. (*Goes to the door.*) I'll be back before you can say Jack Ballantine—Jack Robinson.

(*She bumps into* GABEY *at door, he backs into room.*)

Oh, you clumsy! Really!

GABEY: I beg your pardon.

(IVY *is continuing her scales.* GABEY *notices her, takes a quick look at her picture which he has, bends down to take an upside-down look to see if it is the same girl.*)

IVY: Do—do re mi—do.

GABEY: Hey!

IVY (*coming out of her handstand, kneels on floor hastily pulling skirts over her knees*): A gentleman should always knock.

GABEY: Oh—uh— (*Looks at picture.*) Are—are you—could you be—is your name—by any chance—is your name Ivy Smith?

IVY (*rises*): And what if it is?

GABEY (*walks to door and closes it*): Gabey's coming. Gabey's coming. (*Returns to* IVY.) The name's Gabey. I'm pretty hot stuff in the Navy. I'm in town for one day, and I'm gonna do this old burg up brown. I'm a pretty special guy and I need a pretty special girl—and you're a pretty special girl—and we're gonna step out tonight—and——Goodbye.

(*He rushes to the door in a panic. Her voice stops him.*)

IVY: Wait a minute, sailor.

(*He turns. She moves toward him.*)

How did you know who I am?

GABEY: I saw your picture in the subway.

IVY (*moves toward him in excitement*): You mean you saw my picture and— (*Quickly assumes an air of indifference.*) Oh—that—

GABEY: Yeah—and it said how you were studying singing at Carnegie Hall—and so I thought I'd like to—like to look you up—and—and hear you sing.

IVY: That's the most peculiar line I ever heard.

GABEY (*walks toward her a little*): Well—to hear you sing—and—maybe to try to make a date with you for tonight.

IVY (*quickly, as she looks at him, then away*): I gotta be somewhere— (*Fake sophisticated tone.*) I'm afraid a date is quite out of the question.

GABEY: Sure—who do I think I am anyway. You probably get society guys—rich fellas—pestering you all day long.

IVY: Oh, yes, by the drove. The social whirl occasionally takes its toll.

GABEY: Yes, I guess it does. Well, I'll be going now.

(*He turns away, then back. She turns to face him, back to audience.*)

But all I wanted to say is—I'm glad to meet the famous Miss Turnstiles. You know, that really makes my day here complete. I—I liked your picture first because I thought you looked like Minnie Frenchley—but you—don't look anything like her. You're much more beautiful—and to look like that and do all those things—opera—sports—and—oh, gee—You're wonderful. G'bye.

(*He goes out door and starts off. She follows him outside the studio door.*)

IVY: Don't go. That's a much nicer speech. Wouldn't you like me to affix my signature to that picture you have?

GABEY: Would you?

(*He takes out his pen, she comes over to him.*)

That's wonderful.

(*He gives her the fountain pen, she signs the picture.*)

Gee—the guys on the ship will be jealous of me.

(IVY *gives him the picture.*)

"Best regards"—Gee, thanks.

IVY: And I mean it.

GABEY (*takes the fountain pen*): Gee—I found you. I found Ivy Smith. Uh—Miss Smith—do you think *maybe* you could make it tonight?

IVY: Oh, I couldn't. I'm much too occupied. But how long are you going to be in town?

GABEY: Only twenty-four hours.

IVY: Gabey, I'd love to go out with you.

GABEY: My gosh—you will?

IVY: Uh-huh. (*She nods.*)

GABEY: You're going out with me? Well, uh—uh—shall I come and get you?

IVY: No, I'll meet you. Where are you going to be?

GABEY: Nedick's—Times Square, at 11 o'clock.

DILLY (*entering*): Well! What's going on here?

IVY: Madame Dilly.

GABEY: I beg your pardon.

DILLY: Really, Miss Smith—you should be practicing every minute. You mustn't waste my precious time. Not if you're so anxious to better your position.

IVY: Please, Madame Dilly.

DILLY: Is this tar a friend of yours?

IVY: Well, no—but—

DILLY: Then leave at once, young man.

GABEY: Well, goodbye.

IVY: G'bye—Nedick's.

DILLY: On your way, bellbottom.

> (*He exits.*)

Just what were you saying to him?

IVY (*rushes over to her*): Oh, Madame Dilly, he's such a nice boy.

DILLY: They're all alike.

IVY: Oh, no.

DILLY: Sex and art don't mix. If they did, I'd have gone straight to the top. If you want to go onward and upward, keep your mind on your work. I see I'll have to watch you. Now your vocalise.

> (*Carnegie Hall corridor drop comes in, as* DILLY *and* IVY *sing.*)

SCENE 9

This is a double scene. On the right is a corner of CLAIRE's *apartment, a fairly luxurious apartment, with an aura of wealth about it, in direct contrast to* HILDY's *flat, which is opposite. There is a door on the back wall leading to the kitchen, another leading to the bedroom. Through the large window of* CLAIRE's *apartment the city sky-line can be seen.*

The lights go up on CLAIRE's *apartment.* OZZIE *and* CLAIRE *enter.*

OZZIE: Gee, what a dump!

CLAIRE (*places her bag on floor beside couch*): Thank you for your dimensions. I'll send you a copy of the book.

OZZIE: Well, aren't you gonna kiss me goodbye?

CLAIRE: A silly tradition. Come here.

(*She kisses him lightly on the cheek, then suddenly gets him in a terrific clinch. At this point, a suave, stately, portly gentleman comes from the kitchen, wearing a cocktail apron and carrying a tray on which are two glasses and an opened bottle of champagne. He stares for a moment in polite surprise, then comes down to them. It is* PITKIN W. BRIDGEWORK, *the Judge,* CLAIRE's *fiancé.*)

PITKIN (*jovially*): Hello, darling.

(OZZIE *and* CLAIRE *break away quickly.*)

CLAIRE (*breathless and surprised*): Why, Pitkin, darling—what are you doing here?

PITKIN: Don't you remember? We're celebrating our engagement today. (*To* OZZIE.) Hello!

(OZZIE *nods.*)

CLAIRE (*looks at* OZZIE, *then at* PITKIN. *A bit flustered*): Oh, of course, darling, how stupid of me. I was supposed to meet you here, wasn't I?

PITKIN: Yes, I've been waiting for two hours—

(CLAIRE *gestures.*)

. . . but don't bother to explain—I understand!

CLAIRE: Well, you must forgive my appearance—I was practically raped . . .

(OZZIE *looks at* PITKIN. *There is a short pause.*)

PITKIN (*moves to* OZZIE, *expansively—warmly extending tray*): Why, how do you do?

(OZZIE *hides behind* CLAIRE.)

CLAIRE (*a little beside herself*): No, darling, you don't understand—I was collecting material for my book—at the Museum—and I was measuring this man, and—

PITKIN (*extremely good natured*): No sordid details, Claire. (*Puts tray on table by door.*) I understand.

CLAIRE (*resigned*): Very well, Ozzie, this is my fiancé—Judge Pitkin W. Bridgework, and darling—this is Ozzie.

(*Pushes* OZZIE *toward* PITKIN, *indicates* OZZIE's *head.*)

A type Z-3 dolico-cephalic—very rare specimen.

PITKIN (*sincerely, shakes hands*): Very pleased to meet you—any rare specimen of Claire's is a rare specimen of mine. (*Drops* OZZIE's *hand.*)

OZZIE: Well, congratulations. I gotta be going. (*Starts toward door.*)

PITKIN: No, no, Ozzie, don't go. Stay and drink a toast with us.

CLAIRE: Pitkin, is this wise?

PITKIN: Love to have him—love to—just one moment—I'll get another glass. (*Exits into kitchen.*)

CLAIRE (*to* OZZIE): I think you'd better go.

OZZIE: But I've never tasted champagne before.

CLAIRE: Oh, very well. But if you say the bubbles tickle your nose I'll brain that dolico-cephalic head.

>(OZZIE *puts his hat on the couch.*)

PITKIN (*enters with the third glass*): Here we are, darling. (*Pours the champagne.*)

CLAIRE (*takes a glass of champagne and hands it to* OZZIE): Do you really think I should drink, dear? You remember the last time.

PITKIN: Good for you.

CLAIRE: Well—

OZZIE: I drink to the happy couple.

PITKIN: And I drink to the success of *Modern Man—What Is It?*

CLAIRE: And I drink.

>(*They drink.* PITKIN *splutters.*)

PITKIN: O-o-o-h! Bubbles—they tickle my nose.

>(CLAIRE *glares at him, swallows her drink at a gulp, puts her glass on table.* PITKIN *puts his beside hers.*)

There now, darling, any ill-effects?

CLAIRE (*moving to* OZZIE): On the contrary—I feel great. (*She makes a lunge at him, grabs him around the neck.*)

OZZIE (*laughs embarrassedly and disengages himself*): I gotta be going.

>(*He makes a move to avoid* CLAIRE. *She stops him.*)

PITKIN: No, no. Please stay and entertain Claire.

CLAIRE: Oh, Pitkin.

PITKIN: Don't worry, darling. I have a date with Congressman Bundy.

>(*Gets his hat from couch.* CLAIRE *swings him around and unties cocktail apron.*)

Meet you later at Diamond Eddie's for our engagement party. Just the two of us. Have a good time. (*He puts on his hat.*) Enjoy yourself— (*Goes out the door.*) Finish the champagne.

CLAIRE: Goodbye, darling.

(OZZIE *sits on couch, puts his glass on floor,* CLAIRE *is standing with a puzzled look on her face.*)

PITKIN (*offstage*): Goodbye, sweet.

CLAIRE: Pitkin believes in the honor system.

(*She leaps into* OZZIE'*s arms as the lights go down.*)

SCENE 10

The left half of the double scene. It is HILDY'*s apartment. There is a couch, and a small table on which are phone and phone book.*

HILDY *and* CHIP *enter.* CHIP *leading. He carries two grocery bags full of food, including a large chicken.* HILDY *carries a package which she puts on the floor.*

HILDY (*as she enters*): Just put 'em down anywhere, Chip—

CHIP (*looking around for an empty spot*): But I haven't time to stay for dinner. It'll take you, I should say, roughly four hours to cook all this stuff. Besides, I've got to find Ivy Smith.

HILDY: Ivy Smith—Ivy Smith! That's all I hear. Fine friend you've got—falling for a picture. (*Sits on sofa.*)

CHIP: Well, she is a remarkable girl. She sings and dances and—and—

HILDY: Yeah—yeah, that's swell.

CHIP: And besides, she's beautiful.

HILDY: Well, stop looking wistful. (*Rises.*) You've got a girl who can cook. (*Drags frying pan from under sofa, blows dust from inside, then wipes the outside on the seat of her pants as she takes it to the shelf and puts it down.*) Besides, don't you know all those pictures are touched up? You put ribbons in my hair and photograph me through a wall, and I bet you couldn't tell the difference.

CHIP (*moving up to her*): I'm not so sure, besides, I've got to find the real Ivy Smith.

HILDY: O.K. (*On haunches, thumbing through the phone book.*) Here's the phone. We'll call the I.R.T. and find her.

CHIP: Just like that?

HILDY: Sure. (*Consults phone book.*)

(CHIP *looks for a place to put down his packages.*)

Put 'em down anywhere.

(*He hesitates, starts to put them on sofa.*)

No—no—on the floor.

(*Dials phone. He places the package at the end of the sofa on the floor.*)

I.R.T.? Hold it, Jack.

(*Hands phone to* CHIP. CHIP *takes phone.* HILDY *lounges on the couch, proceeding to vamp him during the following conversation—pulling her hair over her eye and leering at him.*)

CHIP: Er—hello?—I'd like to speak to Miss Turnstiles, please— Miss Ivy Smith—Oh, she's not there? Well, look—I'd like her address, please, and telephone number . . . Oh, you don't? . . . Well, look, I'm a sailor and I'm here for one day—Hullo? (*Replaces phone.*) Hey, they hung up—they don't give out that information, especially to sailors.

HILDY (*she is busy vamping him*): Well, ya did your best, kid. (*Coughs, clearing her throat ostentatiously.*)

CHIP: I tried, didn't I? I did try—

HILDY (*sitting up, straightening her hair*): Yeah, you were sensational. I cried like a baby! (*Pats the empty space on the couch beside her in invitation.*)

CHIP: And I'll try them again later—

HILDY: Yeah—much later. (*Pats the couch again.*) Let's try this first.

CHIP (*moves to couch, sits*): Well, as long as I tried—

(*Suddenly makes a lunge at her and smothers her in a bear-hug and violent clinch.* LUCY SCHMEELER *suddenly sneezes outside the door and enters.* CHIP *and* HILDY *come out of the clinch.* LUCY *gives a little coo of surprise.*)

HILDY (*rises*): Well, what the hell are you doing here?

(CHIP *rises.*)

LUCY: I'b sobdy Hildy, I just couldn't go to work today—got an awful dode—and I didn't know—

HILDY: Of all the days you picked!!

CHIP: Pardon me, Mrs. Esterhazy.

LUCY: Oh—I'b not her mother!

HILDY: Chip, this is my roommate, Lucy Schmeeler—She's a grand girl.

CHIP: How d'ya do.

LUCY: Heddo—Chip.

CHIP: Well . . . you live here . . . all day?

LUCY: I'b soddy—Hildy and I sleep in shifts. She goes out to work at night. I come home from work at night. She comes home from work in the morning and I go out to work in the morning.

HILDY: All right—he gets it. Thank you.

LUCY: I'm sorry—I've gotta inhale. 'Scuse me. (*Puts towel over her head and kneels down over inhaler on the shelf.*)

CHIP (*takes* HILDY *aside*): Think she'll stay under there for long?

HILDY: Sure, sure—she'll be under there for days—

> (*They fall into a violent clinch.* LUCY *sneezes. They come out of the clinch.* LUCY *comes up from the towel.*)

LUCY: I'b sorry—'Scuse me . . . Y'know, Hildy, this is just like taking a picture. If I had a camera I could get the two of you together.

HILDY: You could do that just by leaving the room . . .

> (LUCY, *hurt, picks up the inhaler and exits.*)

CHIP: C'mere . . .

> (*Grabs* HILDY, *they sit on couch and clinch. There is the noise of* LUCY *spraying her throat, four times.* HILDY *raises her head.*)

HILDY (*coming out of clinch*): Is that *you*, Chip?

CHIP: No.

> (LUCY *comes out of the room with an atomizer. They sit and look at her.*)

LUCY: I gotta get some gargle.

> (*She exits into the bathroom. They clinch again. In a split second she is back. They break. She proceeds to the bedroom door, then turns back brightly.*)

I got the gargle.

HILDY (*goes up to door*): Well, I'm very glad to hear that. Lucy— would you step into the other room for a few minutes?

LUCY: What for?

HILDY: I'd like to go over some figures with you.

LUCY: Figures?

HILDY (*between her teeth*): The rent, Lucy—the rent—

LUCY: But, Hildy—we paid the rent—I don't understand—

> (HILDY *grabs her into the other room.* CHIP *picks up a bag of groceries, puts them on shelf, picks hat up.* LUCY *enters without her bathrobe.*)

I'b going out.

(*She disappears.* HILDY *appears in the doorway, leans on the jamb nonchalantly.* CHIP *grins.* LUCY *reappears, tying scarf over head, marches to outside door.*)

CHIP: With that cold?

LUCY: I'b going to an air-cooled movie. Hildy says—what you and she—

HILDY (*lounging still, interrupts her*): It will do you a world of good, Lucy.

CHIP: Yes—yes it will. Well, goodbye, Miss Schmeeler.

LUCY: Goodbye, Mr. Chips.

(*There is a reaction from* LUCY *as she realizes what she has said. Then she exits.*)

HILDY (*coming to* CHIP): Well, now what?

CHIP (*moves toward* HILDY): We eat, huh?

HILDY: Sure, we can do that first. (*Moves to shelf.*)

CHIP (*pushes couch downstage*): You claim you can cook.

HILDY: That's often been considered one of my strongest points.

CHIP: Yeah? What's the specialty of the house?

HILDY: Me!!

"I Can Cook, Too"

(*During introduction, she throws the chicken to him, he tosses it back, she throws it into the frying pan.*)

 Oh I can cook, too—on top of the rest
 My sea-food's the best in the town
 And I can cook, too
 My fish can't be beat—
 My sugar's the sweetest around
 I'm a man's ideal—of a perfect meal
 Right down to the demi-tasse.
 I'm a pot of joy for a hungry boy,
 Baby—I'm cooking with gas—
 Oh I'm a gum drop
 A sweet lollipop
 A brook trout right out of the brook—
 And what's more, baby—I can cook!

(*Verse*)

 Some girls make magazine covers
 Some girls keep house on a dime
 Some girls make wonderful lovers—

But what a lucky find I'm.
I'd make a magazine cover
I do keep house on a dime
I'd make a wonderful lover,
I should be paid overtime—

I can bake too—on top of the lot—
My oven's the hottest you'll find—
Yes I can roast, too—
My chickens just ooze—
My gravy will lose you your mind—
I'm a brand-new note
On a table d'hôte
But just try me à la carte
With a single course
You can choke a horse—
Baby—you won't know where to start—
Oh, I'm an hors d'oeuvre
A jelly preserve—
Not in the recipe book—
And what's more baby—I can cook.

(Here follows a musical chorus by the orchestra, during which HILDY *goes through a violent pantomime with back to audience apparently preparing one of her specialties. At the end of the musical bridge, she wheels, displaying a peeled banana.)*

Baby—I'm cooking with gas—
Oh I'm a gum drop
A sweet lollipop
A brook trout right out of the brook—
And what's more baby, I can cook.

(She rushes at him on the sofa and blackout.)
(Encore)
(Verse)

Some girls make wonderful jivers
Some girls can hit a high C
Some girls make good taxi drivers
But what a genius is me—
I'd make a wonderful driver
I'd even hit a high C

I make the best taxi driver—
I rate a big Navy "E"

'Cause I can fry, too—on the top of the heap—
My Crisco's as deep as a pool—
Yes, I can broil, too—
My ribs win applause—
My lamb chops will cause you to drool.
For a candied sweet—
Or a pickled beet—
Step up to my smorgasbord
Walk around until
You get your fill
Baby—you'll never be bored.
Oh, I'm a paté—
A marron glacé—
A dish you will wish you had took—
And what's more, baby, I can cook!

BLACKOUT

SCENE 11

Times Square. People are strolling back and forth. A Nedick's stand is on one side.

GABEY *wanders in, looking for* IVY, *goes to Nedick's, doesn't see her. Stops a* MAN.

GABEY: I beg your pardon, sir, can you tell me the correct time?
    (*The* MAN *indicates a moving sign on a building, and* GABEY *follows his finger.*)
  The time is now—
MAN: Ten thirty-seven.
    (MAN *goes to Nedick's.*)
GABEY: Oh, thanks.
    (*A* GIRL *enters, saunters up to* GABEY.)
GIRL: Hello.
GABEY: Hello.
GIRL: What are you doing?

GABEY: I'm waiting for my girl. She'll be here in half an hour.
(*The* GIRL *moves away disgustedly.*)

"Lucky to Be Me"
(*During this number the crowd collects around* GABEY, *they sing a second chorus, at the end of which* GABEY *exits and crowd disperses.*)

I used to think it might be fun to be
Anyone else but me.
I thought that it would be a pleasant surprise
To wake up as a couple of other guys.
But now that I've found you—
I've changed that point of view
And now I wouldn't give a dime to be
Anyone else but me.

(*Chorus*)
What a day—
Fortune smiled and came my way—
Bringing love I never thought I'd see—
I'm so lucky to be me.
What a night—
Suddenly you came in sight—
Looking just the way I hoped you'd be—
I'm so lucky to be me.
I am simply thunderstruck
At the change in my luck
Knew at once I wanted you
Never dreamed you'd want me too.
I'm so proud
You chose me from the crowd
There's no other guy I'd rather be—
I could laugh out loud—
I'm so lucky to be me.

(*After* GABEY's *exit, and general movement of crowd,* FLOSSIE *and her pal enter.*)

FLOSSIE: So I said to him, "Listen, Mr. Gadolphin, any boss who gives his employees only thirty-five minutes for lunch ought to be drawn and feathered."

FRIEND: So what did he say?

FLOSSIE: So I said, "After all, an individual needs time to refuel."

FRIEND: It stands to reason.

> (*The two have progressed to the Nedick's stand.* IVY *enters and looks around for* GABEY.)

FLOSSIE: Don't it, though?

IVY (*to* NEDICK'S MAN): Do you have the time?

ATTENDANT: Ten minutes to eleven.

> (*She buys a drink and pays for it.*)

FLOSSIE: And I said, "Furthermore, Mr. Gadolphin, nylon stockings are not as important as a girl's self-respect."

FRIEND: Naturally.

> (MADAME DILLY *enters, walks past* IVY, *sees her.*)

DILLY: Well, Miss Smith.

IVY: Oh, Madame Dilly!

DILLY: Might I have a word with you?

> (*Takes* IVY *aside.*)

So you are meeting that sailor.

IVY: Yes, I am. I called up my boss and told him I was sick.

DILLY: He called back and said if you didn't show up tonight, he'd fire you.

IVY: He did? Well, let him.

DILLY: I'd hate to lose that fifty.

IVY: But just this once.

DILLY: It's not the money, my dear. After all, I'm known as a patroness of the Arts.

IVY: But what if—

DILLY: No. You keep your job. If you should default in your payments, I might be forced to tell the whole disgraceful business in court.

IVY: But, Madame Dilly—

DILLY (*giving her a brush-off*): No, I don't care to argue about it.

IVY (*following her*): But, Madame Dilly, that's not fair—

> (*They exit.*)

FLOSSIE: So I said to him, "Listen, Mr. Gadolphin, I'm not in the habit of making appointments with married men—no matter how late at night it is."

FRIEND: So what did he say?

FLOSSIE: So I said, "After all, we've got to consider Mrs. Gadolphin."

> (*They exit.*)
>
> (GABEY *enters, looking around, spies* CHIP *offstage.*)

GABEY: Hey, Chip!

CHIP (*entering*): Gabe!

GABEY: Chip! Hey—guess what—I found—

CHIP: Gabey! Gee I'm glad to see you. O.K.? Right on the dot, eh?

GABEY: Sure.

CHIP: Well, I suppose you want to know how I made out—in finding Miss Turnstiles. Well, I— (*Calls offstage.*) Oh—IVY SMITH!

> (GABEY *is amazed.* HILDY *enters in hairdress* IVY *wore on the subway ad.*)

HILDY: Here I am.

CHIP: Miss Smith—uh—this is Gabey.

HILDY (*moves to him, hand extended in elegant pose*): How do you do? I gave up a concert and a shot-put rally to come and meet you—

GABEY (*takes her hand*): Thank you.

> (*He drops her hand and backs away from her.*)

CHIP: Don't look so disappointed—Gabe—uh—these pictures—you know—they're always retouched.

> (HILDY *gives him a dirty look.*)

OZZIE (*enters*): Hey Gabe!

> (GABEY *turns.*)

Here she is—IVY SMITH! (*Points offstage.*)

CLAIRE (*enters, assumes a pose. Then she goes to* GABEY *and shakes his hand*): My dear boy, when this man told me your story, I just had to drop everything and come—

> (HILDY *steps down and everyone looks at everyone else, as they discover what's going on.*)

GABEY (*laughing*): Now, wait a second, fellas.

OZZIE (*points to* HILDY): That dame's a phoney.

CHIP (*indicating* CLAIRE): Who is that woman?

OZZIE (*shoves* HILDY *aside and goes to* GABEY): Listen, Gabe, Chip's trying to put something over.

CHIP: Don't listen to him, Gabe. This girl's the real thing.

GABEY: Wait a minute, guys—willya listen—

OZZIE: (*to* CHIP): What are you trying to do to Gabey?

CHIP: Whatdya mean—I spent all day—

OZZIE: I know what you were doing all day—

HILDY (*moving between* CHIP *and* OZZIE *and pushing them apart*): O.K., fellows—break it up.

CLAIRE: I told him this was a ridiculous idea.

> (HILDY *goes to* CLAIRE. *They shake hands and go over to Nedick's.*)

GABEY: Listen! I know you were trying to help me. Thanks! But I found her myself.

CHIP: Miss Turnstiles?

OZZIE: What?

GABEY: Sure—there was nothing to it. I walked into Carnegie Hall. There she was. Made a date. That's all there was to it. (GABEY *goes up to Nedick's.*) Sure, you should have seen me.

OZZIE (*follows him*): Aw, don't give us that line, Gabey. It's impossible.

CHIP (*also goes up to Nedick's*): Why, statistics prove things don't happen like that.

GABEY: Well, they did this time. (*To the two* GIRLS.) Gee, girls, thanks for dressing up like Ivy Smith. And Oz—thanks for the slogan—it worked.

CHIP: Is that how you got her?

OZZIE: You mean you followed my advice?

> (MADAME DILLY *enters.*)

GABEY: Sure. She'll be here any minute. (*He leaves Nedick's to look around for her.*)

OZZIE (*to the* NEDICK'S ATTENDANT): Make that six—and no chasers.

DILLY (*spies* GABEY): Hey—bellbottom!

GABEY: Oh! Madame Dilly.

DILLY (*takes him aside*): You're just the one I'm looking for. I bear a message from Miss Ivy Smith.

GABEY: Ivy!

DILLY: She entrusted me—with her sincerest regrets.

> (*Bottle business.*)

GABEY: Huh?

DILLY: She can't make it. She said she's going to some—some party.

GABEY: But she had a date with me.

DILLY: My dear boy, she just can't be bothered. There!

> (*She hands him a note with a flourish and exits.*)

OZZIE (*laughing, as though finishing a joke*): So she said—"Come in."

(*General laughter.*)

CHIP (*referring to his drink of orange juice*): Gee, this is good!

HILDY: Well, I'm not staggering yet.

    (GABEY *returns to stand disconsolately, having read* IVY's *note.*)
    (*To* GABEY.) Hey—when do we get a glimpse of this Miss Turnstiles?

OZZIE: Yeah—it's about time—

GABEY: I don't think she'll be here.

OZZIE: What? Didja get stood up?

GABEY: No, but I never really did meet her—

OZZIE: Why—you son-of-a-gun!

CHIP: Well—the law of averages—

GABEY: No, I was just kidding. I went to Carnegie Hall and hung around but she wasn't there. I never did find her. So I went to a movie. Like you said, Chip—the town's too big— things don't just happen that way.

OZZIE: Sure—forget about her.

GABEY: S'long, fellas—see you on the ship. (*He starts to go.*)

OZZIE: Hey—wait a second, Gabey—don't go. Claire'll get you a date. Hey, Claire—how about a girl for Gabey.

CLAIRE (*drinks orange drink*): I don't know any girls.

HILDY: Wait a second—I can get you a date. My roommate, Lucy Schmeeler—

CHIP (*horrified*): What?!

HILDY: A-a-a-h—she's a nice girl, hasn't been out in years—and pretty, too. She's got a page-boy down to there— (*Puts her hand under her nose to indicate the length of it.*)

GABEY: Sure—swell, why not?

HILDY: O.K., I'll call her from the first nightclub we hit—

OZZIE: Night clubs!! Yowie!! (*Does a bell kick.*) Kid, we'll show you a great time tonight.

ALL THREE: Yes—this town belongs to the Navy.
    (*They lock arms and move up left.*)

    (*The Nedick stand disappears, and the Times Square Ballet begins, which concludes Act One.*)

CURTAIN

ACT TWO

SCENE IA

This is the first of three scenes depicting different nightclubs. The basic set is the same, but different props, change of personnel and size of set make the change of atmosphere.

The curtain opens on Diamond Eddie's. There is loud music, much loud talk and laughter. A line of six GIRLS *are entertaining.*

"So Long, Baby"

GIRLS (*singing and dancing*):

> So long, I'm on the loose again
> So long, I counted up to ten
> Bye, bye, baby—I got wise.
> Too long you made a fool of me
> Too long you had me up a tree—
> Now you get the booby prize

IST GIRL:

> So you cry—boo hoo hoo
> And you feel—oh so blue
> It's no use—now I'm leaving you—

ALL GIRLS:

> You need a new pal, Papa.
> So long, I've stood it long enough
> So long, it's my turn to call your bluff
> So long, baby—I've got wise to you.

(The GIRLS *do a short dance, during which the* HEADWAITER *enters and has an altercation with* OTHER WAITER.)*

IST WAITER: I told you I wanted a table for five—

2ND WAITER: But—

IST WAITER (*exploding*): I don't care what you want—get a table for five.

(The 2ND WAITER *comes off, gets a table and five chairs, which he sets up.* CLAIRE, OZZIE, CHIP *and* GABEY *come on. They are seated with much confusion as the* DANCING GIRLS *are finishing their dance. The* GIRLS *exit, with much tossing of plumes and flourishes. The* MASTER OF CEREMONIES *bounces on.)*

M.C. (*clapping the* GIRLS *off*): Ha-ha-ha-ha! Welcome to Diamond Eddie's. (*Walks rapidly around table.*) Well, everybody, take out your little mallets and hit yourselves over the head with 'em. Ha, ha! (*Emphasizes this last "ha, ha" with a stamp of the foot.*) Now, someone's handed me a message— (*Looks in his pocket.*) Yes, it's someone's birthday—now—and I want you all to join me in a chorus of Happy Birthday for that man we all know and love—uh—(*glances at message surreptitiously*) Rodney Smithers—a furniture manufacturer from, uh—Grand Rapids, Mich—

> (*The orchestra breaks into "Happy Birthday," all sing with* MASTER OF CEREMONIES *leading. During this, two* SAILORS *with* GIRLS *enter. A table is set for them. In the confusion, one* GIRL *is pushed against* CHIP. *She sits on his lap, abruptly, but doesn't seem to be too anxious to leave, as she apologizes after "Happy Birthday" is over.*)

1ST GIRL: Oh, I'm so sorry, I'm so terribly sorry—

> (CHIP *is amused.* HILDY *enters, sees what's going on, comes over with murder in her eye.* GIRL *continues.*)

I really didn't mean to sit on your lap. It was an accident— really it was—You see it was this way—

HILDY (*who has reached the table, and puts her hand on* GIRL's *shoulder*): Scram!

> (GIRL *joins her party in a huff.* HILDY *puts her arm around* CHIP's *neck, pats his cheek affectionately, sits.*)

Well, Gabe, I just talked to Lucy—told her all about you. She was out of the house before I could hang up.

OZZIE: Playing hard to get, huh?

CLAIRE (*holding up her shot glass*): Oh—just what I wanted. A jigger of solid glass.

CHIP: Gee, Gabe—you look unhappy.

GABEY: Aw, no—I'm fine.

CHIP: Hey, you're not still thinking of that Miss Turnstiles.

GABEY: Naw.

> (1ST DANCING GIRL *has come on with a tray of souvenir dolls.*)

OZZIE (*seeing* GIRL *with dolls*): Hey, Girlie—whatcha got over there?

GIRLS (*coming over to him*): Dolls.

OZZIE: Dolls! Hey look—dolls! Just what you need.

GABEY (*protesting*): I don't want a doll.

OZZIE: Ha-ha—take it—ha-ha, Gabe—show it to the fellas on the ship. What fun! (*He's knocking himself out trying to cheer* GABEY *up.*)

CLAIRE (*rising*): Cool off, darling, you'll have a stroke.
(*Pushes him down in his chair.* GABEY *takes the doll.* CLAIRE *dismisses the* GIRL. *As* GIRL *leaves,* OZZIE *pats her on the fanny.*)

GABEY: Yeah, take it easy, Oz, I feel great.

M.C.: And now for that treat you've all been waiting for—that star of the networks—Miss Diana Dream!
(*All applaud, especially the* WAITERS, *as* DIANA DREAM *enters—bowing regally to the customers.*)

DIANA DREAM (*singing with stylized gestures*):
 I'm blue—my life is through
 I thought I had a date with you—
 I guess I just don't rate with you—
 I wish I was dead
 And—buried!!
(GABEY *gets progressively lower, until he is sitting with his head between his knees. At the end of the next verse,* HILDY *notices his condition.*)
 I'm blue—A cast-off shoe
 I'll break right down and cry tonight—
 'Cause you told me a lie tonight—
 I wish I was dead
 And bur—
(HILDY *interrupts her.*)

HILDY: I'm sorry—I'm very sorry—This is too depressing. I've got a friend over there who's dyin'! You don't mind if I cheer him up, do you?

OZZIE: She's had a request to sing.
(M.C. *comes in, takes singer off, explaining.* WAITER *with telephone enters.*)

WAITER (*carrying phone*): Phone call for Miss Esterhazy—

OZZIE: Put it here.

HILDY: Is he kidding? Put it over here.
(WAITER *puts the phone on the table, plugs it in.*)
Hello—hello—hello—Lucy? Where are ya? Diamond Eddie's? That's impossible. We're at Diamond Eddie's. 53rd St.—four blocks from the house. You're in Yonkers?

(*They all look at* HILDY.)

They got a Diamond Eddie's up there too? All right—you made a natural mistake. Come on down here quick.

OZZIE (*rises, goes over to table to* CHIP'*s right*): Hold on a second, Hildy. Where can we go and show Gabey a good time?

CLAIRE: We need a change of atmosphere. I know—tell your friend to head for the Congacabana—and not the one in Poughkeepsie.

(OZZIE *returns to his chair.*)

HILDY (*into phone*): O.K. Lucy—look, don't come h— No, no— Don't—Come—Here . . . What? . . . Well, stop crying? Meet us at the Congacabana—Got it? O.K. And stop sneezing— you'll catch cold.

(*She hangs up. The* WAITER *removes phone.*)

(PITKIN *enters, looking for* CLAIRE.)

CLAIRE: Well, let's get the check and get out of this loathsome dive. Uh, waiter—waiter—you fat oaf— (*She turns slightly, sees someone standing near her, thinks it is the* WAITER.) Oh, there you are.

(OZZIE *sees* PITKIN.)

PITKIN: Hello, darling.

CLAIRE: Why, Pitkin, darling—

(*Rises, as does* OZZIE.)

What are you doing here? Oh, how stupid of me. I was supposed to meet you here, wasn't I?

PITKIN (*with his arm around her*): That's quite all right darling— I understand. (*Greets* OZZIE *warmly.*) Oh—glad to see you again, old man. (*Makes a slight move toward* OZZIE.)

OZZIE (*backs away*): I can explain everything—

PITKIN: Explain what? Why, I'm indebted to you.

(*Grabs* OZZIE'*s hand, shakes it, and they pile their hands one on the other.*)

I appreciate your bringing Claire to the club.

CLAIRE (*coming between them and separating them*): Oh, Pitkin, these are Ozzie's friends—uh, Gabey, Hildy, and Chip.

(*They ad lib "hellos."*)

This is Judge Bridgework, my fiancé—

PITKIN: Why don't you all have a drink with the two of us— (*Calls to the* WAITER.) Waiter—

CLAIRE (*moves over to him hurriedly*): Uh—look, Pitkin, darling,

I can't explain now—but we were just leaving. Why—why don't you meet us in a few minutes over at the Congacabana. I'd tell you all about it but we're in an awful hurry. Just take care of the check, will you? You understand.

PITKIN: Of course—of course—I understand . . . The Congacabana in a few minutes, darling. (*To* WAITER.) Waiter—let me have the check for that table.

WAITER: Yeah, yeah—

> (PITKIN *and* WAITER *exit.*)

CLAIRE (*returning to her seat and sitting*): Come on, everybody—we're off to the Congacabana.

BLACKOUT

SCENE 1B

The scene has shifted to the Congacabana. A large palm tree stands in the center of the stage. Otherwise the setting is the same.

When the lights come up, the patrons are indulging in a Conga line, which grows more strenuous, until by the final bars, HILDY, *who is dancing with* GABEY, *is completely knocked out and has to be assisted back to the table.*

OZZIE (*when the commotion has subsided, spies a* GIRL, *with a tray of shawls*): Hey, girlie!

> (*She starts toward him.*)

> Come here. (*He rises.*) What have you got there?

GIRL: Shawls.

OZZIE (*takes one, back to* GABEY): Oh—shawls.

GABEY: I don't want a shawl.

OZZIE: Here's a nice one. Take it.

GABEY: What would I do with a shawl?

OZZIE: Sure—sure—make yourself a hammock—make believe you're a piano—anything.

CLAIRE (*calming him down again*): Calm down.

> (CLAIRE *pays for the shawl.*)

> (*Fanfare—and* MASTER OF CEREMONIES *dashes on, all teeth.*)

M.C.: At this time, we have the pleasure to bring to you direct from Havana, Cuba, Señorita Dolores Dolores. Give her a nice hand.

(*To a smattering of applause, the* SEÑORITA *enters and in a slow rhumba tempo, sings "I Wish I Was Dead" in Spanish.* GABEY *does the same take. Near the conclusion of the first chorus,* HILDY *goes over to the singer and interrupts her.*)

SINGER (*singing the one line in very broken English*):
     I veesh I vas d-a-a-d—and bur—

HILDY: I'm awfully sorry—but my friend's allergic to that song.

M.C.: You mustn't interrupt this show.

HILDY: Oh, I've been requested to sing.

M.C.: Who requested it?

GABEY: I did.

HILDY: Yeah—I've had a request from a serviceman in uniform.
     (CHIP, OZZIE *and* GABEY *and other* SOLDIERS *and* SAILORS *rise and come forward in threatening silence.*)

M.C. (*seeing the situation. Hastily*): Well, in that case—
     (CHIP *waves "thanks" to the boys, they return to their seats.*)

GABEY: O.K. It's just a contest. They're trying to cheer me up.

"You Got Me"

HILDY:
     I'm eager to share my love and devotion
     It's deep as the ocean.
     I've plenty to spare and since it's so ample
     I'll throw you a sample.
     I will fix you up on the spot—
     So forget the things you have not—
     Can't you see, kid, what a very rare treasure you got.
(*Chorus*)
     You got me, Baby, you got me.
     You got my affection, baby, and my sympathy.
     You got my whole muscular equipment—from A to Z
     And it's free, Baby, it's all free,
     It's all free, it's all free, it's all free.

OZZIE:
     You got me, Gabey, you got me!
     You got my enthusiasm on the land and sea.
     You got my whole knack of getting ladies—
     It can't be beat—

And it's free, Gabey, it's all free,
    It's all free, it's all free, it's all free.

CLAIRE:
        I'm filled to the brim with eager affection
        That seeks a direction.
        My vigor and vim leave no one excluded—
        And you are included.
        I will get you out of your lull
        You won't feel unwanted or dull
        If you'll get this through that normal, Neanderthal
            skull.

    (*Chorus*)
        You got me, Baby, you got me.
        You got my extensive knowledge of anatomy.
        You got my whole interest in mankind—of every
            breed—
        And it's all free baby, it's all free,
        It's all free, it's all free, it's all free.

CHIP:
        You got me, Gabey, you got me.
        You got a guy who always functions systematically.
        You got my whole family in Peoria—for you to see!
        And it's free, Gabey, it's all free,
        It's all free, it's all free, it's all free.

    (*Dance*)
HILDY & CLAIRE:
        You got we, Gabey, you got we.

OZZIE & CHIP:
        You got a date with Lucy Schmeeler,
        Girl of mystery.

CLAIRE & HILDY (*repeating*):
        Mystery.

ALL:
        You got her whole reservoir of passion—
        To fill your need—
        And it's free, Gabey,
        Without fee, Gabey,
        Can't you see, Gabey—
        It's all free!

HILDY & CLAIRE (*pointing to* OZZIE *&* CHIP):
    You got he—
CHIP & OZZIE (*pointing to* HILDY *&* CLAIRE):
    You got she—
ALL:
    You got we!
    (*All sit. For encore, repeat chorus in pantomime, shouting only the last "You Got We."*)

CLAIRE: I'll tell you what, let's go on to the Slam Bang Club. The music's primitive—the atmosphere primeval—
OZZIE: Swell.
    (*Grabs* CLAIRE *and pulls her down in a clinch.*)
    You and I can go back a couple of centuries.
    (*Kisses her.* PITKIN *has entered and comes to the table merrily.*)
PITKIN: Hello, darling!
    (*The two break violently,* CLAIRE *comes to her feet.*)
CLAIRE (*flustered*): Oh—Pitkin darling—what are you doing here— (*Gesture of distraction.*) How stupid of me—I was supposed to meet you here, wasn't I?
PITKIN (*takes her down right a little*): Darling, I understand—getting a little scatter brained. Working too hard on the book—
CLAIRE: Well, darling, we're on our way to the Slam Bang—Meet us over there, won't you? That is so important—I can't give you the details, but pay the check, won't you? (*She returns to the table.*)
PITKIN (*a little puzzled*): Yes, of course, I understand—the Slam Bang—
HILDY (*a sudden horrid thought*): Hey—what about Schmeeler?
CLAIRE (*back to* PITKIN): Oh, Pitkin, while you pay the check—wait for a girl who answers to the name of Lucy Schmeeler, will you? And bring her along.
PITKIN: Schlam Bang—Schmeeler.
HILDY: You can't miss her—she's wearing a sneeze.
    (PITKIN *exits.*)
CLAIRE: O.K. On to the Slam Bang.

BLACKOUT

SCENE IC

The club is very small. The palm tree has disappeared, the customers have almost all gone, except a few people having a last dance to a dying orchestra. GABEY *sits with his head on the table.*

MADAME DILLY *enters, takes a table, obviously very drunk.*

DILLY (*as she enters*): Waiter—waiter—
 (*He approaches, she orders drink, during the opening music. When it stops she begins to sing drunkenly.*)
 Do-do-re-do——do-re-mi-do——do-re-mi-fa-do—
GABEY (*his head comes up as he hears her. Suddenly he recognizes her and dashes over to her*): Maude P. Dilly. (*He reaches her table.*) Oh, Madame Dilly! (*Very excited.*) Where is she?
DILLY: Where's who? (*With difficulty she focuses on him and a slight glimmer of recognition floats over her face.*) O-o-o-h-h-h— the young tar I hurled so unceremoniously out— (*Starts singing bravura.*) Out—of my lodge at Eventi-i-i-d-d-e!!
 (GABEY *shakes her impatiently.*)
 I know where she is— (*Laughs.*) You'll find her hobnobbing in the social whirl—
GABEY (*he is bursting with impatience*): Where? Where?
DILLY: At the corner of Tilyou and the Boardwalk—Coney Island.
GABEY: Tilyou and—what kind of place is that?
DILLY: O-o-h-h—iss an exclusive resort—
 (*He nods.*)
 The playland of the rich! Yesshir!!
 (*A second's pause—then he dashes out of the club.*)
 (*The others have watched and listened in complete bewilderment—and now are shocked to see him run out.* OZZIE *and* CHIP *jump up.*)
CHIP: Gabey!
OZZIE: Hey, Gabe. Come back.
 (*He rises and exits after him.*)
CHIP (*who has gone over to* DILLY. *He shakes her as she apparently has fallen into a stupor*): Hey, lady—lady.
DILLY (*raises her head, looks at him*): Bellbottom—how you've grown.
CHIP: Lady—who were you talking about?

OZZIE (*re-entering, coming to table*): He'll never get to the ship on time.

CHIP: We might lose him. (*Crosses to* HILDY *and kneels.*) Oh, gee, Hildy, it's been swell!!

(*Puts his arm around her, and kisses her on the cheek.* HILDY *sighs. He rises to go, but* HILDY *trips him, and he falls sprawling on his back.*)

HILDY (*quickly going over to him and hauling him up*): A-a-a-a-h-h-no ya don't—I'm going along.

(*They go into a corner, talking.*)

OZZIE (*goes to* CLAIRE): Well, we know where he is— (*Grabs the shawl.*) Come on, Claire—

(*Three* WAITERS *take table and chairs away.*)

CLAIRE: Look, specimen—I've just—I've just got to wait for Pitkin—

OZZIE (*pats her right shoulder*): O.K., kid, see you in another 6,000,000 years. (*Starts to leave.*)

CLAIRE: That's such a long time—

(*They both pause.*)

(*LUCY enters, beaming. She sneezes.*)

HILDY (*recognizing her*): Lucy!

(*LUCY turns to her expectantly.*)

Oh, Lucy, your date's gone!

LUCY (*crushed*): Do! (*No! with a cold.*)

HILDY: Don't cry. I'll explain just as soon as I get home.

(*CLAIRE gets her coat from chair, preparing to leave.*)

He couldn't wait any longer. Goodbye, Lucy.

LUCY: So long!

(*CHIP and* HILDY *start off.* PITKIN *enters. They bump into him as they exit.*)

PITKIN: Hello, darling!

CLAIRE: O-o-h-h-h, Pitkin, what are you doing here? We're going to Coney Island.

PITKIN: Are you?

CLAIRE: Yes—uh—well, look, you just stay here and take care of the check.

(*Gets* LUCY *and passes her to* PITKIN.)

And—uh—take care of Miss Schmeeler—you understand. G'bye!

(*She grabs* OZZIE *and rushes out.*)

(LUCY *and* PITKIN *look after them.* LUCY *sneezes.*)
PITKIN: Gesundheit!
LUCY: That's the nicest thing anybody ever said to me.
   (*Curtain closes in, and the two step down to the footlights.*)
 Do you understand?
PITKIN: I always have.

"I Understand"

When I was five my brother stole my lollipop.
My lollipop stole he—
But I didn't mutter "Damn your hide"
He needed candy more than I'd
So instead of biting off his hand—
I just said—"Goo! I understand!"

When I was ten my mother trounced me with a mop
With a mop troun-ced she me—
But I didn't mutter "Damn your eyes"
I knew she needed exercise—
So instead of joining the gypsy band—
I just said, "Mom, I understand."
(LUCY *sneezes. He gives her his handkerchief.*)

At thirty a man in a car ruthlessly ran me down
He ruthlessly down ran me—
But I didn't mutter "Damn your spleen"
For a man's a man—but a car's a machine.
So instead of stripping him of his land—
I just said, "Jack—
(*He puts out his hand and she hands him back his handkerchief.*)
                    I understand."

Now I'm forty-five and I've met Claire—
We're engaged to wed.
Engaged to wed are we—
But tonight I tell you, "Damn you Claire,"
You played me evil—
(LUCY *giggles, jumps up and down.*)
 And that's not fair!

LUCY: Do!!
PITKIN:

> So instead of remaining calm and bland—
> I hereby do not understand!

(5th Chase Interlude begins. FIGMENT sees PITKIN, demands arrest, runs off. POLICEMAN follows. UPERMAN follows in chase, followed by a COP. LITTLE OLD LADY tears across, finally PITKIN and LUCY join in, exiting.)

SCENE 2

The subway train to Coney Island.

GABEY *is seated to the right of the door, his doll in his hand. Two* COUPLES *are in the car. A* GIRL *passes through, fishing in her pocket-book.* GABEY'S *head drops, he is asleep, and in his dream . . .*

The swaying of the people in the car becomes rhythmic. The music picks up and the people dance to it, in a trance-like movement, their eyes closed, their movements detached. Suddenly, IVY *appears from one end of the subway, dressed as the doll now lying in* GABEY'S *lap. She comes toward* GABEY, *who looks up. The dance becomes wilder, and she motions him to come into the resplendent world which is now visible through the car windows—the Dream Coney Island of his imagination. She leads him invitingly to the center doors of the subway car, which open. The entire car splits in two, rolls off to either side of the stage, and* IVY *and* GABEY *step into the dream world. Segue directly to . . .*

SCENE 3

The Dream Coney Island. The stage is a limitless void of blue. In the distance soar the myriad lights of Coney Island—deeper, richer, higher, more exotic than the real place.

The Dream continues with the Dream Ballet.

GABEY *is conscious of motion around him—a swirl of skirts, the scuffing of passing feet. The lights slowly come up and he realizes where he is—a wonderful, suspended, fluid and dreamy sophisticated place for rich people. Suave well-groomed* MEN *and lovely, unattainable* WOMEN *dance by easily, and coldly, with a great impersonal quality about them.* IVY *is seized by the* MEN *and they carry her off over* GABEY'S *head.*

There is great excitement. The real GABEY *goes off to one side to see his dream counterpart enter. Two* GIRLS *carry on a poster, advertising* "GABEY THE GREAT LOVER." *The stage is a swirl of excitement as his dream self enters. They all watch as the* GREAT LOVER *dances for them—a jazzy, slick, ingratiating torchy sexy dance. He finishes with a bang. There is a fanfare. The* MASTER OF CEREMONIES *from Diamond Eddie's enters.*

M.C.: Good Evening, ladies and gentlemen. Welcome to Coney Island—Playground of the rich. Ha! Ha! (*Stamps his feet as he did in real night-club.*) And now, ladies and gentlemen—for the main event of the evening—Gabey the Great Lover versus Ivy Smith!

(*With much ceremony a prize ring is set up, a fight light comes down, and* IVY *enters the ring. The match begins.* IVY *starts toward the* GREAT LOVER *with soft, voluptuous movements— and the attacking feints of the* GREAT LOVER *become slow motion movements until finally they are caresses rather than punches. She lures him into unwrapping her turban. Suddenly, in her grasp, the length of red cloth becomes a rope with which she proceeds to ensnare the* GREAT LOVER *until he is helpless in its coils. He is overcome, and* IVY *is lifted to receive the plaudits of the multitude in triumph. The real* GABEY, *who has watched horrorstruck, is brushed away, and he glides rapidly backwards off stage.*)

CURTAIN

SCENE 4

The Coney Island Express. FLOSSIE *and her* FRIEND *are seated to one side. On the other side are* CHIP, HILDY, OZZIE *and* CLAIRE.

FLOSSIE: So I said to him, "Listen, Mr. Gadolphin, I've come to your house to deliver the brassieres, not to model them."
FRIEND: So what did he say?
FLOSSIE (*rises*): So I said, "Mr. G.—I'll thank you to keep your distance."
FRIEND (*rises*): So what did he say?

FLOSSIE: So I said—well, suddenly I had nothing left to say.

FRIEND: Well, for heaven's sake. What are you going to do now?

FLOSSIE: Oh, let's stop off and get a malted.

(*They exit.*)

OZZIE (*pointing to the subway sign of* MISS TURNSTILES): There she is! There's the cause of all Gabe's trouble.

CHIP (*rising to look at picture*): Do you think he really met her?

(HILDY *rises, goes to the seat at right, pulls* CHIP *down on bench beside her.*)

OZZIE: Damn it, we just missed him. Why did that door have to slam in our face just as we got there?

CLAIRE: It always does. It's the unwritten law of the subway.

OZZIE: Well, how long does it take to get to Coney Island?

CHIP (*rises, looks at map*): Let's see. From here, to Coney Island, there are two—three—

HILDY: Relax. You've got one hundred and ninety-six more stops to go.

CHIP: What? We'll never get to the ship on time.

OZZIE: Yeah, statistics show we've got to be back in a couple of hours.

CHIP: Aw, gee, Hildy, I'll hate to leave you. (*Sits beside her.*)

HILDY: Oh, John.

CLAIRE: Oh, specimen.

(HILDY *embraces* CHIP; CLAIRE *embraces* OZZIE.)

"Some Other Time"

CLAIRE:

> Twenty-four hours can go so fast
> You look around—the day has passed—
> When you're in love—
> Time is precious stuff—
> Even a lifetime isn't enough.

(*Chorus*)

> Where has the time all gone to?
> Haven't done half the things we want to—
> Oh, well—we'll catch up—
> Some other time.
> This day was just a token—
> Too many words are still unspoken

>   Oh, well—we'll catch up—
>   Some other time.
>   Just when the fun is starting—
>   Comes the time for parting—
>   But let's be glad—for what we've had—
>   And what's to come.
>   There's so much more embracing—
>   Still to be done, but time is racing—
>   Oh, well—we'll catch up
>   Some other time.

HILDY:

>   Didn't get half my wishes—
>   Never have seen you dry the dishes—
>   Oh, well—we'll catch up—
>   Some other time.
>   Can't satisfy my craving—
>   Never have watched you while you're shaving.
>   Oh, well—we'll catch up—
>   Some other time.
>   Just when the fun's beginning—
>   Comes the final inning—

CONDUCTOR (*passing through the car*): Coney Island—all out.
>   (OZZIE *and* CLAIRE *rise*.)

OZZIE:

>   Haven't had time to wake up—
>   Seeing you there without your makeup
>   Oh, well—we'll catch up
>   Some other time.
>   (ALL *step down to footlights as curtain closes, repeat in quartet*.)

ALL:

>   Just when the fun is starting
>   Comes the time for parting
>   But let's be glad—for what we've had—
>   And what's to come.
>   There's so much more embracing
>   Still to be done but time is racing.
>   Oh, well—we'll catch up
>   Some other time.
>   (*The four stand there as spotlights fade out*.)

SCENE 5

The real Coney Island. It is a gaudy honky-tonk sort of place. Some-
what later than 2 A.M. all the revelry that is left is concentrated in
this place. SOLDIERS *and* SAILORS *and their* GIRLS *are drifting*
around, some tired, some happy, some drunk.

On one side of the stage is the entrance to the Tunnel of Love.
On the other side is a platform and large sign advertising "Rajah
Bimmy's Night in a Harem."

CHIP, OZZIE, CLAIRE *and* HILDY *wander through the crowd*
and out. GABEY *wanders around in a daze looking for* IVY. BIMMY
comes onto his platform to advertise the show.

BIMMY: Hurry—hurry—hurry— (*Singing against the music.*)
Folks—it's our last red-hot—sizzling show of the evening—
and what I'm about to show you is the most blood-tingling
exhibition of the female form deevine in action—that you and
I have ever had the tantalizing privilege of witnessing—Might
as well warn you—the cops have their eye on this place—We
keep the girls just within the bounds of decency—but there
might be a slip—who can tell. One of the girls might go too
far—
    (*Corny "hootch" music as three* GIRLS *enter in cheap Turkish*
    costumes. BIMMY *keeps up a running commentary, sings:*)
"Rajah Bimmy's harum-scarum with the girl who picks the
handkerchief up with her teeth."
    (*This introduces* IVY.)
    (IVY *and the girls do their bumps and grinds and parades.* IVY
    takes a handkerchief from a MAN's *pocket and proceeds, with*
    the aid of her fellow dancers to pick handkerchief up. GABEY
    enters, and realizes with horror that this is IVY. *He makes a*
    grab for her, and pulls her skirt off. There is a pause of shock,
    then a police whistle.)
POLICEMAN: Hey—that's indecent exposure. I'll arrest you.
    (*General movement as people flock around the couple.* OZZIE,
    CLAIRE, CHIP *and* HILDY *enter and see* GABEY *and* IVY.)
OZZIE and CHIP: Ivy Smith!
    (*The* COP *approaches* HILDY. *She hits him and he backs away.*
    The six of them start to run, but encounter FIGMENT, COPS,
    LITTLE OLD LADY *and* UPERMAN, *entering, who recognize*

their quarry and chase the six back. HILDY *grabs* CHIP, *who grabs* CLAIRE, *who grabs* OZZIE. GABEY *grabs* IVY *and takes her aside.*)

GABEY: A fine thing—Miss Turnstiles—the pride of New York—Too good for me.

IVY: Gabey, I wanted to come to Nedick's to meet you but I owe Madame Dilly fifty-six dollars and she made me come to work.

GABEY: Is that true?

IVY: Yes, Gabey. I wanted to go out with you more than anything in the world.

GABEY: Ivy—Ivy—you're beautiful—you're wonderful—uh, you haven't got much clothes on.

(*A* GIRL *rushes on with a coat for* IVY.)

IVY (*as she struggles into the coat*): Oh, I know. I'm gonna be arrested for disnuding in public.

PITKIN (*entering with* LUCY, *pushes his way through the crowd*): All right, all right, officer. I'll take charge here.

WORKMAN: Who is that guy?

GIRL: Judge Bridgework.

PITKIN: Come on, officer, line 'em up.

CLAIRE: Oh, Pitkin, darling—what are you doing here? Oh, this is wonderful. All these people are following us. We've got into a little trouble—you'll get us out—you understand.

PITKIN: I do *not* understand.

CLAIRE: What?

PITKIN: I do *not* understand. Officer, arrest these people.

(*As the crowd murmurs and protests.*)

You three men will be turned over to the Naval Authorities.

OZZIE: Well, you see it's this way—

PITKIN: That means you, too, specimen. And I will hold the three accused females for further questioning.

CLAIRE: Pitkin, this is ridiculous. You know I'm not a criminal.

PITKIN: I don't know what you are, Claire. I'll never trust a woman again. You are all under arrest.

(*The crowd murmurs as the lovers rush to each other.*)

Silence!

IVY: Gabey!

GABEY: Ivy!

HILDY: They can't do this to us.

CHIP: Gee, Hildy.

CLAIRE: Goodbye, Ozzie.

PITKIN (*pushing*): No fond farewell, please, just go.

    (POLICEMAN *escorts* OZZIE, CHIP *and* GABEY *off.*)

HILDY (*to* PITKIN): A fine guy you are. Won't let your fiancée go with the guy she loves.

CLAIRE: Pitkin, darling, please understand and forgive—haven't you ever committed an indiscretion?

HILDY: Yes, haven't you ever, uh, uh— (*She gestures suggestively.*)

PITKIN: Never.

    (*There is a moment's pause, then* PITKIN *sneezes the heavily planted sneeze of* SCHMEELER. LUCY *giggles, as the people look from one to another, and the curtain closes.*)

SCENE 6

The Brooklyn Navy Yard—the same as the opening of the play. It is almost the same time of day—early morning. A street-sweeper goes his round. A SAILOR *is saying goodbye to his girl.* OZZIE, CHIP *and* GABEY *come on before curtain opens, escorted by a* POLICEMAN. *They are disconsolate.*

OZZIE:
    New York, New York.

GABEY:
    The lights are out.

CHIP: Six o'clock.

    (*The music picks up and the* BOYS *hear their names called from offstage. It's the* GIRLS. *They rush on.*)

HILDY (*calls offstage*): Chip!

CLAIRE: Ozzie!

IVY: Gabey!

HILDY, CLAIRE & IVY (*singing in time to the music as they throw themselves into the arms of* CHIP, OZZIE *and* GABEY):
    Pitkin understood!

ALL SIX (*in time to music, as they embrace*):
    He really understood!!

    (*Suddenly, six o'clock whistle blows, and the stage is alive with workers going to work, sailors returning, and fresh sailors out on*

their day of leave. The three couples look around them, realizing
that this is goodbye. Suddenly there is a familiar song—three
young sailors—all buddies—are setting forth on their first day
in New York.)

THREE SAILORS (*entering excitedly from ship*):

We've got one day here and not another minute
To see the famous sights.
We'll find romance and danger waiting in it—
Beneath the Broadway lights—
And we've hair on our chest,
So what we like the best
Are the nights—sights, lights, nights!

(*They are joined by the entire company.*)

ALL:

New York, New York—a helluva town
The Bronx is up but the Battery's down—
And people ride in a hole in the ground
New York—New York—it's a helluva town!

CURTAIN

FINIAN'S RAINBOW

Book by E. Y. "YIP" HARBURG *and* FRED SAIDY
Lyrics and music by E. Y. "YIP" HARBURG
and BURTON LANE

To Marie and Eddie
From Yip and Freddie
Translation:
To each author's lady
From Harburg and Saidy

SCENES

Act One

Act Two

MUSICAL NUMBERS

ACT ONE

ACT TWO

ACT ONE

A fertile valley in the state of Missitucky, U. S. A. In the background are visible long, rolling fields of green tobacco leaves: leaves that satisfy, leaves that mean mighty fine tobacco, leaves that don't irritate the throat—all looking approximately the same. A stone well and a rugged, ancient cypress tree are prominent in foreground. This is the meetin' place for the people of Rainbow Valley.

From behind the closed curtain is heard the music of a lazy harmonica. After a few moments the curtain rises to disclose this in the hands of SUNNY, *a Negro sharecropper, perched on a rocky ledge and taking his ease on this balmy Spring day. Suddenly he sees or senses something off-scene, and a note of urgency and alarm agitates his harmonica music. Summoned by it, a number of sharecroppers—both men and women, Negroes and whites—hurry on stage, in movements which form a pattern of dance. Their eyes watch with anxiety and anger the entrance of a plump little* SHERIFF *in a ten-gallon hat, followed by* BUZZ COLLINS, *a shifty, cigar-smoking character with a derby hat and a nervous manner. The* SHERIFF *is carrying a cloth banner which reads:*

RAINBOW VALLEY
TAX SALE
TODAY!

He starts to tack it to the tree.

BUZZ: Come on, Sheriff, put some swing into it.

SHERIFF (*in a slow, whining delivery*): Cool your britches, Buzz. These taxes been pilin' up fifteen years.

BUZZ (*with a snort*): Sixteen.

SHERIFF: Who wants 'em collected all of a sudden?

FIRST SHARECROPPER (*defiantly*): Senator Rawkins, that's who. He's aimin' to buy up this whole valley—and when Rawkins wants a valley—Lord, get out of his way.

(*A sullen murmur of assent comes from the* CROWD.)

SECOND SHARECROPPER: Ain't satisfied to represent the state. Wants to own it outright.

SHERIFF: Quiet, everybody. Auction's gonna start now.

(*A* SHARECROPPER *perched up in tree grabs gavel as he lifts it, then lets go,* SHERIFF *banging his foot.*)

Ouch!

(CROWD *laughs.*)

FIRST SHARECROPPER: Wait a minute! You can't run this auction without Susan Mahoney!

BUZZ (*his impatience mounting*): Why not?

FIRST SHARECROPPER: 'Cause this is her property, that's why not.

BUZZ: Beg your pardon. It's the property of anyone who has the money to pay the back taxes. And *I* have it.

FIRST SHARECROPPER: Who are you, anyhow?

BUZZ: The name is Buzz Collins. (*Offering indisputable proof.*) Here's my card.

FIRST SHARECROPPER (*studying card*): You left off your title— stooge for Senator Rawkins.

SECOND SHARECROPPER: He's gobbled up the rest of the valley, and now he's after our little strip.

BUZZ: Well, it's none of *your* business!

FIRST SHARECROPPER: We ain't got no *other* business. We sharecrop on this land together.

CROWD (*ad lib*): Yea, that's right!

SECOND SHARECROPPER: You disturb us, and Woody won't like it.

BUZZ: Who's Woody?

SECOND SHARECROPPER: Susan's brother.

FIRST SHARECROPPER (*a cryptic threat*): He's got a baritone voice that *buries* finance men!

(BUZZ *gives a start. Suddenly, from* SUNNY'S *harmonica, a series of sharp arpeggios. They herald the swift, darting entrance of* SUSAN MAHONEY, *a bare-legged, woodland sprite, whose dancing feet move like humming-bird wings. She skips excitedly about the stage, discovers the* SHERIFF, *seizes his coat lapels and looks at him imploringly.*)

That's Susan!

HENRY (*a small Negro boy*): She wants to tell you somethin'!

FIRST SHARECROPPER: Tell him, Susie!

(*She executes a quick, brisk dance figure, and stops.* HENRY *watches her feet intently.*)

SECOND SHARECROPPER: What'd she say, Henry?

HENRY: She says Woody's comin'!

CROWD (*ad lib*):

Woody's comin'!

Great day!

Woody's comin'!

BUZZ: Am I losing my mind? Am I going deaf? I didn't hear her say anything!

THIRD SHARECROPPER (*a middle-aged Negro woman*): Naturally. She was born silent—one of the few women ever *was*.

HENRY: Sure, mister. Don't you see? She don't do talk-talk. She does foot-talk.

(*The humming-bird feet do some more foot-talk, with* HENRY's *eyes following them closely.*)

BUZZ: Ridiculous! Ridiculous! (*But half believing it.*) What's she sayin' now?

HENRY: She says you've got to wait for Woody! He's bringin' the money!

(*A cheer goes up from the crowd.*)

BUZZ (*at a peak of exasperation*): Ah, 'tain't the money Rawkins is after! He's too big for that! Get on with it, Sheriff!

(*The cry of "Woody's comin'!" grows into a rhythmic, hand-clapping chant with a fervid hallelujah feeling.*)

SHERIFF (*frantically*): Quiet, all of you! Quiet! Tax sale gonna start now! (*He bangs his gavel loudly on a tree stump, but it is lost against the swelling counterpoint of "Woody's comin'!"*) It's my duty to protect the people of Rainbow County!

FIRST SHARECROPPER: Who from?

SHERIFF: From the citizens! (*A last feeble try.*) Hear ye! Hear ye! (*But the chant is now a musical rebellion.*)

"This Time of the Year"

SHARECROPPERS (*singing*):

We can't be bothered with a mortgage man, this time of the year!

SHERIFF (*one small speaking voice, against so many*): You'll be sorry, interferin' with the law!

SHARECROPPERS (*singing*):

For Spring don't care about a mortgage man, this time of the year!

SHERIFF (*his final gasp*): I'm givin' you the last chance to get back your land!

FIRST SHARECROPPER (*continuing song*):
> The dandelions in the dusky dell
> Don't give a hoot in hell—
> They're gonna smell without collateral
>> This time of the year!

GIRLS:
> Sweet merry buds
> And elderberry buds
>> Don't give a good ding-ding-dang!
> Corn's shootin' up,
> Fruit trees a-fruitin' up—

GROUP:
>> Go tell Rawkins to go hang-hang!

> Magnolias are sentimental,
>> Persimmons are queer,
> Snapdragons won't pay no rental
>> This time of the year!

> Red cabbage and sweet potatoes
>> Don't easily skeer.
> They'll sprout without real estaters
>> This time of the year!

(SUSAN *scurries up to a high rock, looks off, and breaks into a wild, joyous dance.*)

BOYS (*interpreting her dance*):
> The choo-choo's comin' and it's mighty clear—

GROUP:
> Woody's here!
>> He's up there ridin' with the engineer—
> Yes, Woody's here!

FIRST SHARECROPPER:
> Just look at that choo-choo puffin'—
> Let's give it a mighty cheer!
> Just look at that engine huffin'—
>> Dang blast it all—

GROUP:
> Woody's here!

Just listen, that whistle's blowin'—
 That whistle is good to hear—
Its wantin' us to be knowin',
 Dang blast it all, Woody's here!
Woody's here! Woody's here! Woody's here!
(*The happy* SHARECROPPERS *dance off down the valley, sweeping the* SHERIFF *and* BUZZ *before them. The stage is clear and quiet for a short moment, and then—*

FINIAN McLONERGAN *looms up out of the valley, a telescope to his eye, a carpetbag in his hand. He is a nimble-witted, nimble-footed Irish gentleman in his middle fifties who is, as you will presently see, in pursuit of a mad, merry dream; a lovable gaffer who is not afraid of his own shadow, and frequently boxes it; and a realist whose feet are planted firmly on a cloud.* FINIAN *is other things too, but right now he is Balboa and Ponce de León.*)

FINIAN (*peering through his telescope*): Eureka! (*Calling off-scene.*) Sharon, come quickly!

SHARON'S VOICE (*wearily*): Father, what is it now?

FINIAN: We're here! It's journey's end! Our destination—at last! (SHARON *trudges on, a pert but tired bundle of Tam O'Shanter, knitted shawl, valise, and smouldering rebellion.*)

SHARON: Thank merciful Heaven. Now I can sit me down.

FINIAN: Don't sit ye down! It's the hill beyond yon hill.

SHARON (*ominously*): Finian McLonergan, I've been hearin' about the hill beyond yon hill ever since we left Ireland. Now *you're* hearin' somethin'. (*With finality.*) Me feet ain't walkin' another step till they know where they're goin'!

FINIAN (*grabbing his most convenient leg*): Oh, now look what you've done. You've brought on me arthritis.

SHARON: 'Tis a strange malady that twists you up any time I'm wantin' a straight answer.

FINIAN: Sharon, you're torturin' me.

SHARON: To think I let you whisk me out of Ireland, across an ocean and down a continent, in the sweet, green month of April—and for what?

FINIAN (*forgetting the leg*): For what? For a beautiful new life in a beautiful new land, where the bees give certified honey and the spiders spin their webs of nylon!

SHARON: I thought we came here to cure your arthritis.

FINIAN: Aye, that too. (*Remembering the leg.*) That too!

SHARON: Well, 'tis *me* that's cured of your arthritis now. It's all mythical, and so is that cure-place for it called Rainbow Valley.

FINIAN: Now ye've gone too far. Here it is on me pink map, witnessed and endorsed by Rand & McNally.

SHARON: I don't know who Rand is, but I could never trust a McNally.

FINIAN (*triumphantly, spotting the* SHERIFF'*s sign*): But you can always trust a McLonergan. Behold the mythical land called Rainbow Valley! Sharon, shake hands with a millionaire!

SHARON: Millionaire . . .

FINIAN: Multi-millionaire! (*He does a little jig.*)

SHARON (*with deepening suspicion*): What's happened to your arthritis?

FINIAN: Arthritis? That's for the poor.

SHARON: Ah, I should have known you were up to something. Ever since I was two years high you've been seein' leprechauns in the cabbage patch, and rainbows over your whiskey jug. What pixified fancy of yours has brought us to America?

FINIAN: Sure, you'll love it here. You're goin' to have everything you left behind in Glocca Morra, and more. (*A skylark trills sweetly off scene.*) What did I tell you? Do you hear that skylark?

SHARON (*nostalgically*): Aye . . .

(*The skylark obliges again.*)

FINIAN: The same skylark music we have back in Ireland!

SHARON: Aye! A Glocca Morra skylark . . .

"How Are Things in Glocca Morra?"

SHARON (*singing*):
> I hear a bird,
> Glocca Morra bird,
> It well may be
> He's bringin' me
> A cheerin' word.
>
> I hear a breeze,
> A river Shannon breeze,
> It well may be
> It's followed me
> Across the seas.

Then tell me, please . . .

How are things in Glocca Morra?
Is that little brook still leapin' there?
Does it still run down to Donny Cove,
Through Killybegs, Kilkerry and Kildaire?

How are things in Glocca Morra?
Is that willow tree still weepin' there?
Does that laddie with the twinklin' eye
Come whistlin' by,
And does he walk away
Sad and dreamy there
Not to see me there?

So I ask each weepin' willow,
And each brook along the way,
And each lad that comes a-whistlin'
"Too-ra-lay,"
How are things in Glocca Morra
This fine day?

(*As* SHARON *finishes,* FINIAN *is weeping sentimental tears.
His conspiracy with the skylark has obviously boomeranged on
him.*)

SHARON (*pointedly*): Father, why are you crying?

FINIAN: Oh, it's that cheap Irish music.

SHARON: There, there, I didn't mean to be making you sad.
Come now, let's forget this silly journey and go back to where
we were happy.

FINIAN (*succumbing to an impulse*): Very well, I'm ready to go
back with you—(*conquering the impulse*)—in six months.

SHARON: In six months!

FINIAN: Why, in six months you'll be the richest colleen in
Glocca Morra.

SHARON: Well, we've got a good start—sixty-five dollars in me
bag. How do you propose to get the balance?

FINIAN: By the McLonergan Theory of Economics, built on a
solid foundation of mathematics, logic—

SHARON: And moonbeams?

FINIAN (*Professor Finian, if you please*): I proceed to develop me thesis. Now what makes America different from Ireland?

SHARON: It has more Irishmen.

FINIAN: Don't get political. The fact is, it has more refrigerators, and more radiators, and more slot machines. Every American is rich.

SHARON: But Father, are there no poor in America, no ill-housed, no ill-clad?

FINIAN: Of course, Sharon. But they're the best ill-housed and the best ill-clad in the whole world. Why? (*In an alarming roar.*) Why, I ask? And there's no man with wit enough to tell me! Well, then, I'll tell you! (*He unfolds a map from his pocket, places it on the ground and peers at it through his telescope.*) Do ye see Fort Knox, Kentucky, right there in the middle of America?

(SHARON *nods dumbly.*)

Have ye any idea what important crop is planted in the soil of Fort Knox?

SHARON: It's gold.

FINIAN: Sh-h! Not so loud. And what do they do with the gold at Fort Knox?

SHARON: They put it in their teeth.

FINIAN: No, Sharon, they don't even touch it, it's that sacred. They merely guard it. Four husky sentries—with guns—march up and down—and up and down— (FINIAN *is now four husky sentries, marching up and down.*)

SHARON: Do they never go roun'?

FINIAN: Just up and down— Where was I, Sharon?

SHARON: Under the groun'.

FINIAN (*pausing briefly on terra firma*): Aye, Fort Knox. I proceed to sum up me observations of the past twelve years. (*He brings forth the original manuscript itself, the southeast corner of a brown grocery bag, adjusts his pince-nez and reads.*) I quote from meself. Quote.

"The peculiar nature of the soil in and about Fort Knox brings an additional quality to gold, hitherto unsuspected by either Karl Marx or the gold itself. This causes the gold to radiate a powerful influence throughout America. It fertilizes the oranges in Florida, activates the assembly lines in Detroit, causes skyscrapers to sprout from the gutters of New York, and produces a bumper crop of millionaires."

(*The pince-nez dutifully drops.*)

I rest me case.

SHARON: Father! You mean to say it's the gold in Fort Knox begets the riches of America?

FINIAN: Obviously. Else for why did they rush to dig it from the ground of California in 1849, only to bury it in the ground of Fort Knox a hundred years later?

SHARON: And how does the McLonergan Theory affect the McLonergan family?

FINIAN: Don't you understand, lass? Any man in America can plant a bit of gold in the ground—near Fort Knox—and become a millionaire.

SHARON (*smells a rat in* FINIAN'*s carpetbag*): Well, all you need now to prove your theory is a bit of gold.

FINIAN: I'm ahead of ye. All I need is the land to bury it in.

SHARON: Father, what's in that bag?

FINIAN: It's me linen.

(*They simultaneously grab for the carpetbag, which flips open.*)

SHARON: Merciful heaven! It's gold—

FINIAN (*proud of it*): Aye. A pot of gold.

SHARON: And you stole it!

FINIAN: Indeed, I did not!

SHARON: That's why we've been running like criminals ever since we left Ireland!

FINIAN: I *did not* steal this pot of gold. I only borrowed it.

SHARON: Whom did you borrow it from?

FINIAN: Why do you want to know?

SHARON: So we can lend it right back to him.

FINIAN: Well, that's impossible.

SHARON: Why?

FINIAN: Because you can't communicate with him.

SHARON: Why not?

FINIAN: Because—because he's not mortal.

SHARON: Not mortal— (*A flash of horror.*) You killed him!

FINIAN: Of course not! He never was mortal. He's a leprechaun.

SHARON: A—*leprechaun*?

FINIAN: Aye, a leprechaun. Who else would have gold in Ireland?

SHARON: But, Father—leprechauns aren't *real*—they're only gnomes and elves, imaginary creatures in fairy tales and legends.

FINIAN: That's what people think, I'll grant you, but, thank God, they're in the minority. Don't you see, lass, in six months we'll be rich—filthy wealthy—like Mr. Ford and Mr. Cadillac and Mr. Serutan.

SHARON: Ah, how could you do a thing like this?

FINIAN: A thing like this? You're sharper than a serpent's tooth. Sure I did it only for you. (*Tenderly.*) 'Twas the last thing I promised your dear mother, that one day our Sharon would have everything—everything on God's good earth, and the rainbow that curves above it.

SHARON (*embracing him fondly*): Heaven and St. Patrick, forgive him his pixified fancies. Forgive him his moon-tipped mind. (*She kisses him.*) And forgive me for bein' his daughter.

> (*A hubbub of excited voices singing "Woody's here!" is heard down the valley.*)

FINIAN: Who's coming, Sharon? Climb the tree and take a look. And hide this. (*He thrusts the precious carpetbag into her hands, helps her up into the tree, and finds a leafy perch alongside her.*) America's full of gangsters, you know.

SHARON: I thought you said it was full of millionaires.

FINIAN: That depends on which newspaper you read.

> (*The crowd of singing sharecroppers bursts in, bearing* WOODY MAHONEY *on their shoulders. The* SHERIFF *and* BUZZ *are still being carried along with the tide.* WOODY, *in the navy-blue garb of a merchant seaman, is back from fighting fascism and fleas in the South Pacific and is no pushover for people who like to push other people around.* SHARON *takes one interested look and seems to forget the twinklin'-eyed laddie of the Glocca Morra lyric.*)

FIRST SHARECROPPER: How's the old place look, Woody?

WOODY (*surveying the scene. He speaks in a "Talking Union Blues" rhythm*): Nothin' changed since I went away. Tobacco leaves a-greenin' in the sun, bobolinks a-singin' in the willows. Nature watching over all. Finance company watching over Nature. (*He rips away the tax-sale sign.*)

SECOND SHARECROPPER: Woody, you musta struck it rich in the Merchant Marine. See you got a brand-new guitar.

WOODY: Seventy bucks' worth.

BUZZ: Mr. Mahoney, we'll have to get started. I'm a busy man.

WOODY: Folks, take a look at a busy man. You know what makes him busy?

A SHARECROPPER: Yeah, buyin' up real estate for Billboard Rawkins.

WOODY: That's the two-dollar answer. Now here's the jack-pot question. Why? (*There is a dead silence.*) Well, it seems some folks in Washington took a look in a river over Tennessee way—and what did they see?

HENRY: Catfish?

WOODY: Wrong, Henry. They saw horsepower—electric horsepower. So they decided to saddle it. Got themselves some *ce*ment and built themselves a *dam*.

HENRY: Oh! You said a dirty word!

WOODY: . . . And Senator Rawkins don't like it. Cuts into his sleep, makes him see things at night. Electric power spillin' out of the river and pourin' over the valley. Shacks lightin' up, people learnin' to read and write, everybody makin' money.

MAUDE: Is that bad?

WOODY: It ain't good—for Rawkins. First thing you know, poll tax gets paid off—Rawkins gets laid off.

FIRST SHARECROPPER: Pay 'em off, Woody.

WOODY: Came all the way from San Diego to do it. Here's your money—a hundred and fifteen dollars and fifty cents.

BUZZ: Well, that covers it—except for one or two little extra charges. Notary services, miscellaneous, sundry and interest—sixty-five dollars.

WOODY (*worried*): Didn't say that on the bill you sent my sister Susan.

BUZZ: Well, that's how it is with interest. Don't make a sound. Just keeps compoundin'.

FIRST SHARECROPPER: Ain't you got the money, Woody?

WOODY: Not in cash, I ain't.

BUZZ: All right, Sheriff, on with the auction.

SECOND SHARECROPPER: You're not gonna let him get away with it—

WOODY: Hold on there, you've got to give me a little time to get my seventy bucks refunded on this guitar.

BUZZ: Too late for that.

WOODY: I'll raise the money somehow.

BUZZ: Money don't grow on trees, you know.

    (*The cliché explodes in his face in a shower of dollar bills which* SHARON *drops from the tree.*)

HENRY: It does for Woody!

SHARECROPPERS (*ad lib*): It's a windfall!

    It's rainin' cats and dollars!

    (*The* SHERIFF *gathers up the money.*)

BUZZ: Oh, oh, Rawkins won't like this. Come on, Sheriff. We'd better start lining up new jobs.

    (*They slink off.*)

WOODY: Money from Heaven . . . and an angel in a tree-top. What do you know?

SHARON: Shame on the frivolous likes of you, young man—

WOODY: An angel from Ireland!

SHARON: —your kith and kin here pinnin' their hopes on you— and you squanderin' your savin's on a music box!

FINIAN: Daughter, that's no way to talk to me future business partner. (*He makes a neat landing from off the tree.*)

WOODY: Partner?

FINIAN: Well, now, you've accepted me money for the back taxes, haven't you?

WOODY: Oh, I intend to pay you back, Pop.

FINIAN: I don't want you to pay me back. I just want me property rights.

WOODY: Well, how many acres do you figure you're entitled to?

FINIAN: Now, what would I be doin' with an acre? All I need is a parcel of land as big as me bag.

WOODY: You've got it!

FINIAN: Then it's a deal. Shake hands, young man.

    (*They exchange big-business handshakes. Then* WOODY *gets down to more important business.*)

WOODY (*to* SHARON): Angel, you sure did get me off a limb. I'd like to return the kindness. (*He does so.*) Welcome to Rainbow Valley, ma'am. Hope you're gonna find it cozy here. Hope you're gonna like us. What's your name?

SHARON: Sharon McLonergan.

WOODY: Mine's Woody Mahoney.

FINIAN: Mahoney? It's fate.

WOODY: How come you're so pretty—and so rich?

SHARON: Well, sir, in Glocca Morra, where we come from, there's an old legend:

> You'll never grow old
> And you'll never grow poor,
> If you look to the rainbow
> Beyond the next moor.

WOODY: Lovely legend. I wonder who thought it up?
SHARON: My father!

"Look to the Rainbow"

SHARON (*singing*):
> On the day I was born,
> Said my father, said he,
> "I've an elegant legacy waitin' for ye.
> 'Tis a rhyme for your lip, and a song for your heart,
> To sing it whenever the world falls apart.
>
> Look, look, look to the rainbow,
> Follow it over the hill and the stream.
> Look, look, look to the rainbow,
> Follow the fellow who follows a dream.
>
> So I bundled me heart and I roamed the world free,
> To the east with the lark, to the west with the sea,
> And I searched all the earth, and I scanned all the skies,
> But I found it at last in my own true love's eyes.

GROUP:
> Look, look, look to the rainbow,
> Follow it over the hill and the stream.
> Look, look, look to the rainbow,
> Follow the fellow who follows a dream.

WOODY:
> Follow the fellow,
> Follow the fellow,

WOODY and SHARON:
> Follow the fellow who follows a dream.

(*Identifying himself with the hero of this camallia,* FINIAN *leads* WOODY *and the rest of the folk in an Irish jig with a Missitucky beat.*)

THE CURTAINS CLOSE

SCENE 2

Nighttime in the meetin' place. There is a half-moon in the sky, and a half-gallon whiskey jug in FINIAN'S *hand. He digs. He drinks. And he sings. In typical* FINIAN *fashion he is carrying the free-enterprise system to its logical conclusion: he is digging his own private Fort Knox. With respectful emulation of the Federal Reserve, he tenderly plants the crock of gold in the good earth. Its magic glows in the dark for a few moments and then fades beneath the moonlight. Having finished a hard day's work worthy of a banker,* FINIAN *raises the jug to his mouth for a final nip. An elfin flute note leaps from its liquid depths. A moonbeam tips with silver a bush about the size of a man. It rustles and stirs. It begins to dance. It is the first bush ever dressed in a little cocked hat with two feathers, a stylish cape of green leaves, a pair of Argyle socks, and golf shoes. Startled by this phenomenon,* FINIAN *does the only practical thing. He falls on the ground and hides behind the whiskey jug. From this vantage point, he utters a cautious and appeasing—*

FINIAN: God be with ye.

THE BUSH (*it speaks, too, and most politely*): God and Mary be with ye.

FINIAN: God, Mary, and St. Patrick be with ye.

THE BUSH: God, Mary, St. Patrick, and St. Ozymandias be with ye.

FINIAN: Ozymandias? Never heard of him.

THE BUSH: Our special saint. Patron saint of the leprechauns of Glocca Morra. My card— (*He produces this from thin air.*) The name is Og.

FINIAN: Og, from Glocca Morra? That's me native heath. (*With hollow accusation.*) You're an impostor. You can't be a leprechaun. You're too tall.

OG: Yes, and I'm getting taller.

FINIAN: Naturally—gallivantin' about America. Everything gets bigger and better over here. What are ye after, anyhow?

OG: I just came over to ask your *help*, Mr. McLonergan.

FINIAN (*vastly relieved*): Me help? Well, this calls for a toast! I rise to welcome you to America. (*He rises with jug in hand and then with great dignity falls on his face. He continues matter-of-factly, as though nothing had happened.*) How are things in Ireland?

OG: Alack, alack, alack—*and* willo-waly. I weep for Ireland.

FINIAN: You weep? Why, what's happened?

OG: No colleens smile and no children sing. A blight has fallen over Ireland.

FINIAN: The British are back! (*He scrambles to his feet.*)

OG: Never have I seen such a curse befall a folk, in all my four hundred and—(*nudging his memory*)—fifty-nine years. (*Wailing it.*) Alas, poor Ireland!

FINIAN (*not understanding, but caught up in the mood*): Alas, me poor—

OG: Ohh!

FINIAN: Sufferin'—

OG: Ohh!

FINIAN: —bleedin'—

OG: Ohhh!

FINIAN: —native land!

(OG *keens the fate of Erin in a mournful ditty, accompanied by sympathetic wails from* FINIAN.)

FINIAN (*with sudden indignation*): A fine lot of fairy folk you are, you and your associates, lettin' all this happen! Where's your magical power?

OG: We've lost it.

FINIAN (*outraged*): You mean you've gone and lost the power to make wishes?

OG (*miserably*): Aye.

FINIAN: What has Ireland to live for now? Answer me that!

OG: Doom and gloom—(*wailing again*)—d-o-o-m and gl-o-o-m!

(FINIAN *rolls up his sleeves, ready to take on the whole world in defense of Ireland.*)

FINIAN: Who's the author of this foul outrage?

OG: A monster.

FINIAN (*he wasn't counting on this*): A monster, eh? You mean the old flame-breathin' type, with the head of a dragon?

OG: Oh, no. This is a tiny wee monster, with the brain of a banker. (*Slyly.*) About your size.

FINIAN (*his courage up again*): Lead me to 'im! A tiny one, eh? (*He starts shadow-boxing.*) Lead me to 'im! I'll sizzle his gizzard. (*He sizzles.*) I'll throttle his larynx. (*He throttles.*) I'll rend him apart, vertebra by vertebra! (*He rends.*) Who is he? (*A roar.*) Who is this monster?

OG (*courteously*): Excuse me for pointing, Mr. McLonergan, but it's you.

FINIAN: Me!

OG: It's you who cast this curse on Ireland.

FINIAN: You're mad!

OG: You brought on the blight yourself when you stole our crock of gold—the little crock that gives us all our power to wish.

FINIAN: Don't be superstitious, man, it's bad luck.

OG: Don't you realize, Mr. McLonergan, without a crock of gold there can be no Fairy Association in Ireland? And without a Fairy Association there'll be no incentive for dreamin'? The Irish people will have to go to work!

FINIAN: It's a crisis! A crisis!

OG: Give it back, Mr. McLonergan.

FINIAN (*counter-attacking*): How do you know I've got it?

OG: Me magnetic feathers pointed you out all the way from Ireland. Feathers, who's the culprit?

(*The feathers on* OG's *hat point sternly to* FINIAN.)

FINIAN (*nothing else to turn to now*): Ah, me arthritis!

OG: Give it back, Mr. McLonergan, before a great evil befalls you.

FINIAN: Ah, can't you postpone your wishin' for a couple of months?

OG: But gold was never made for mankind. It's a fairyland metal for the fairy-folk only. In the hands of a mortal it brings doom and gloom—gl-o-o-m and d-o-o-m.

FINIAN (*mockingly*): D-o-o-m and gl-o-o-m. Stop your wailing. Leprechaun, I've come to a decision. I deny your existence. You're only a figment of me imagination.

OG (*frightened*): I am?

FINIAN: To prove it, I'm going to walk right through you. Step aside.

(OG, *taking no chances, prudently steps back.*)

OG: Oh, this is dreadful. Are you sure?

FINIAN (*encouraged*): Why, of course. I'm always seein' things. Ask me daughter.

OG (*after a puzzled pause*): Well, if I don't exist, how is it I'm gradually becoming mortal?

FINIAN (*now he's alarmed*): The saints preserve us! You are?

OG: Yes, and so are all the other leprechauns, ever since you took our crock of gold. Look at me—it's crept up past me ankles already. (*He shows* FINIAN *Exhibit A: socks and golf shoes.*)

FINIAN: Can't you manage to hold out until the winter?

OG: Well, I don't know. I've got a peculiar *human* feelin' in me thighs lately.

FINIAN: Your thighs? Don't let it go any further, man! (*But it's too late. The leafy trousers mysteriously disappear, and* OG *is left standing in a pair of long, earthbound, woolen drawers.*) Mary and Joseph, Ireland is ruined!

SHARON'S VOICE (*from somewhere in the woods*): Father! Father!

OG: Someone's coming!

FINIAN: And now that you're half mortal, you're indecent. Here, take these.

(FINIAN's *sense of decency overcomes his logic. He quickly slips off his trousers, revealing himself in red flannels, helps* OG *into them, and sends him scurrying off.*)

SHARON (*as she enters*): Father, where have you been? (*She notices* FINIAN's *deshabille.*) Mercy, what's happened?

FINIAN (*blandly*): Someone's gone off with me wallet.

(SHARON *quickly drapes her shawl around him.*)

WOODY'S VOICE: Sharon!

WOODY (*entering*): Sharon, did you find— (*Gracefully, with a quizzical look at* FINIAN's *abortive costume.*) We've been looking all over for you, Mr. McLonergan.

FINIAN: Looking for me? And you couldn't find me? (*This is a challenge to* FINIAN's *powers of ratiocination.*) Strange disappearance. Where did you look?

WOODY (*with a glance at* SHARON): Well, we started in that sycamore grove down by the river.

FINIAN: Did you have any luck?

SHARON (*airily*): Yes, a little . . .

FINIAN (*though only half dressed for the part, he assumes the role of Cupid*): Sure, it's a shame for two young people to be wastin' this star-twinklin' night lookin' for an old man. Woody, me boy, let me take this problem off your hands. (*He settles himself against the tree.*) When I find meself, I'll let you know. (*Motioning* WOODY *away in* SHARON's *direction.*) Just give me some privacy. (*With this he promptly falls asleep.*)

SHARON (*calling from log where she is seated*): Over here, Mr. Mahoney.

    (WOODY *crosses to her and sits.*)

Father needs plenty of room to dream in. In another minute he'll be surrounded by leprechauns.

WOODY: That's too bad. I was kinda hoping we'd be alone.

SHARON: Just you and I—(*with an arch look at the guitar between them*)—and the guitar?

WOODY: Oh, pardon me— (*He removes it.*) Didn't mean it to come between us.

SHARON: Do you think it's safe carrying a guitar, with all this moonlight lying loosely about?

WOODY: Shucks, a fella's no good without one. It says things he wouldn't *dare* say.

SHARON: Like what?

WOODY: Well, imagine a rough Joe like me wishin' I was a tender apple blossom beside those pale hands.

SHARON: I'd understand your difficulty.

WOODY: And without this guitar would I dare tell you that your eyes are like the dewdrops and your neck is like the swan?

SHARON: That would be dangerously romantic.

WOODY (*meaning it*): That all through the night my heart is singin' sweeter songs of love than the brown bird ever knew.

SHARON: I never appreciated guitar music before. Play, Mr. Mahoney.

WOODY (*sheepishly*): That's my shame, Sharon. I can't.

SHARON: I've been betrayed!

WOODY: Don't worry. I'll make it up to you when I get back from New York.

SHARON: New York? I didn't know you were leavin'.

WOODY: Tomorrow night. I've got to take some *gui*tar lessons from a folklore teacher on Fifty-second Street. Then I'm going back to my old job. (*Deadly serious.*) Sharon, there's something you ought to know about me. In some circles I'm considered a sinister character. *You know what I am?*

SHARON (*alarmed*): No.

WOODY: Brace yourself. Grab hold of that log. I'm a *union organizer.*

SHARON (*relieved*): Oh. Well, *I* believe in unions.

WOODY: Good!

SHARON: The domestic kind.

WOODY (*deflated*): Me too, Sharon. But I've got commitments. This guitar and I got a big job to do all through this part of the country—speak their language—tell 'em things the papers won't print. Music'll make 'em listen. (*Looking her in the eye.*) But darn it, there's something that's holding me up.

SHARON (*hopefully*): What could that be, Mr. Mahoney?

WOODY: I can't get into the musician's union.

SHARON: Well, even if you did, what is all this going to get you?

WOODY: Who knows? In eight or nine hundred years, maybe a better world.

SHARON: Better for whom, may I ask?

WOODY: Better for you, better for me, better for our children.

FINIAN (*suddenly waking up*): Children? Let me be the first to congratulate the both of you. (*He promptly falls asleep again.*)

SHARON: Whist, Father, he didn't mean it like that. (*Walking away from* WOODY.) Well, as you've only got eight or nine hundred years, you'd better start packing.

WOODY: Don't take it so hard, Sharon. I haven't got a chance of stayin' away from you. I'm caught—trapped—by that old valley legend. We've got our legends too. Notice anything peculiar goin' on?

SHARON (*looking heavenwards*): Why, yes. 'Tis a strange sky . . . the moon has disappeared.

(*And it has.*)

WOODY: But the moonlight is all around.

(*And it is.*)

SHARON: And it's growing brighter.

WOODY: That's the valley legend—

They who meet on an April night
Are forever lost in love,
If there is moonlight all about
And there's no moon above.

SHARON: Lovely legend. I wonder who thought it up?
WOODY: *I* did.

"Old Devil Moon"

WOODY (*singing*):
> I look at you and suddenly
> Something in your eyes I see
> Soon begins bewitching me.
> It's that old devil moon
> That you stole from the skies,
> It's that old devil moon
> In your eyes.
>
> You and your glance
> Make this romance
> Too hot to handle.
> Stars in the night
> Blazing their light
> Can't hold a candle
> To your razzle-dazzle.
>
> You've got me flying high and wide,
> On a magic carpet ride,
> Full of butterflies inside.
> Wanna cry, wanna croon,
> Wanna laugh like a loon,
> It's that old devil moon
> In your eyes.
>
> Just when I think I'm
> Free as a dove,
> Old devil moon deep in your eyes
> Blinds me with love.

THE CURTAINS CLOSE

SCENE 3

The Colonial estate of SENATOR BILLBOARD RAWKINS. *Time and termites have bitten into the bases of the three massive Greek columns which support the sagging portico; and their parallel lines have long since gone their separate ways. An old-fashioned garden swing, with moving platform, stands on the lawn; and, near it, a service table which holds a tray, a pitcher of water, a glass tumbler, and some julep goblets. Surveying this picture of seedy grandeur is a young, intelligent-looking Negro, named* HOWARD. BUZZ *bustles out of the house.*

BUZZ: Oh—you the new boy?

HOWARD: Yes, sir.

BUZZ: Ah, you'll like working here, boy. I've hired all the Senator's butlers for the past ten years. Hundreds of 'em. Of course, he's a little intolerant at times, but that's his blood pressure. Now let's see you serve this julep.

(*He acts the imaginary guest as* HOWARD *takes the tray with goblets on it and offers it.*)

Mm-mm. Rawkins won't like it. That's no way to serve a mint julep. It's too *fast.* Get some *shuffle* into it. You've seen movies like *Gone with the Wind*, haven't you? Here, like this. (*He takes the tray and gives a quick course in Southern julep-serving, based on the minstrel tradition of Dixie shuffle and exaggerated accent.*) Youah julep, suh, Mr. Rawkins, suh, all frosted and minty— yawk, yawk!

(*Turning back to* HOWARD.)

See?

HOWARD (*in dignified straight English*): But why do I have to shuffle, Mr. Collins?

BUZZ: Why? Well, it's a mark of breed, here in the South. Makes for kindly feelings between master and servant. (*Handing him the tray.*) Once more now, try it again. And not so *fast* this time.

(HOWARD *tries it again, but he has evidently been walking upright too long to change his habits.* BUZZ *shakes his head.*)

I don't understand you, Jackson.

HOWARD: The name is Howard, Mr. Collins.

BUZZ: That's beside the point, George. Do you want a job here as a butler or don't you?

HOWARD: Yes, sir, I do. I've got another year to go at Tuskegee.

BUZZ: Tuskegee? What's that?

HOWARD: A college.

BUZZ: Oh-oh. Don't mention the word college to Mr. Rawkins. It upsets him.

HOWARD: But I do need that tuition money, Mr. Collins.

BUZZ: All the more reason for you to make good here this summer. Then when you get *out* of college, you've got a job here for life.

RAWKINS' VOICE (*a senatorial and stentorian boom, from inside the house*): Buzz!

BUZZ (*to* HOWARD): I'll speak to you later.

THE VOICE (*again*): Oh, Buzz!

BUZZ: I'm over here, Senator.

> (HOWARD *exits with tray, as* RAWKINS *strides onto the porch and gets lost among the ancestral columns.*)

RAWKINS: I don't seem to see you.

BUZZ: It's those columns, Senator. They sort of get in the way.

RAWKINS: Poppycock! Those columns ain't moved an inch in a hundred years. (*Disgustedly.*) Oh, meet me down at the swing.

> (*This is exactly one stride away.* RAWKINS *negotiates the crossing and settles himself in the swing.* BUZZ *hurries over and begins to rock it gently—evidently an old-established custom. The* SENATOR *is now expansive.*)

Buzz, that was a great day's work you did yesterday.

BUZZ (*preening himself*): Well, I bought up the whole valley for you—except one little parcel.

RAWKINS: By God, that'll keep them bureaucrats back in Washington, where they belong. Cheap electric power! Let 'em go build their dam on the Potomac instead of desecratin' this heaven-given valley with a lot of copper wire—

> (*Sensing a speech,* BUZZ *quickly hands a glass of water to the* SENATOR, *who is now one with Patrick Henry and Daniel Webster. The arc of the moving swing increases with the fervor of the oratory.*)

—electrocutin' innocent bullfinches and sparras. Gentlemen, the festering tides of radicalism are upon us. But before I yield up our glorious South—and her sister commonwealth, the U.S.A.—I will lay down my life. I will go further than that—I'll filibuster. Back, you crackpots, and forward, America! Forward to the hallowed principles of our forefathers! Forward to the sweet tranquility of the status quo! Forward to yesterday!

SHERIFF (*entering excitedly*): Senator, I caught 'em dead to rights—two of 'em—right spank on your property.

RAWKINS: Dammit, Sheriff, can't you handle those chicken thieves by yourself?

SHERIFF: They're worse than chicken thieves this time, Senator—they're Federal men.

RAWKINS: Federal men! By God, we acted in the nick of time. Already they're trying to get their clutches on the people's property for that power project. Bring them in. (*Steps down from swing.*)

SHERIFF (*calls*): Fetch 'em in, Pete.

(*A deputy leads in two young men, one a Negro, dressed in the rough field garb of surveyors, and carrying a box-like machine with dials and needles.*)

RAWKINS (*looking them over*): I thought you said there was two of them.

NEGRO GEOLOGIST (*quietly*): There are two of us, Senator. Here are my credentials.

(*Hands papers to* RAWKINS, *who pushes them away.*)

RAWKINS: Credentials? You? You're in the wrong state, fella.

WHITE GEOLOGIST (*controlling his annoyance*): Mr. Rawkins, we're merely here in the line of duty to make a geological survey of the soil in this area in connection with the new dam.

RAWKINS: Well, I don't need nobody to tell me what's on my land, least of all—(*he looks hesitatingly at the Negro*)—his kind.

NEGRO GEOLOGIST: You're giving me too much credit, Senator. All I do is read the findings on this meter. It detected gold on your property this afternoon.

RAWKINS (*his breath taken away*): It did what on my property?

WHITE GEOLOGIST: Located an amazing concentration of gold. The meter reacted so violently it broke the needle.

RAWKINS: Well, that's too bad. Where did this unfortunate accident of the needle breakin' occur?

WHITE GEOLOGIST (*consulting memorandum book*): Near the big cypress tree on parcel sixteen, Rainbow Valley.

BUZZ (*sinks into swing*): Oh, my God!

RAWKINS: What are you mumblin' about, Buzz? Fetch some mint juleps for our guests. It ain't every day we're honored with the presence of two distinguished scientists from Washington.

BUZZ: Mr. Rawkins, that's the strip I told you about.

RAWKINS: What strip?

BUZZ: The one we couldn't buy.

RAWKINS: What do you mean, we couldn't buy? Who bought it?

BUZZ: A man named Finian McLonergan.

RAWKINS (*he is against blood-pressure control, too*): Why, you fuddlehead! You Yankee brain! Why wasn't you prepared for him?

BUZZ: I never saw him before. He's an immigrant.

RAWKINS: An immigrant! Damn! My whole family's been havin' trouble with immigrants ever since we *came* to this country! (*Collapses into swing.*)

WHITE GEOLOGIST: Come on, Bill

    (*The* GEOLOGISTS *and* DEPUTY *exit.*)

BUZZ: Don't get excited, Senator. You'll feel better when you have your julep.

RAWKINS (*gasping for breath*): To hell with my julep! Get me a bromo-seltzer! My blood-pressure's chokin' me! (*He yanks* [*sic*] *at his collar.*)

BUZZ (*calling frantically to* HOWARD, *in the house*): Howard, bring the Senator a bromo-seltzer! Quick!

RAWKINS: And call my lawyer! Tell him to find a loophole! Where's that bromo?

BUZZ (*yelling off*): Where's that bromo, Howard?

RAWKINS: My loophole's chokin' me!

HOWARD'S VOICE (*from the house*): Comin', Massa, just as fas' as I kin.

    (*And* HOWARD *appears with a foaming glass of bromo-seltzer on his tray. It sizzles and smokes violently as—having won his diploma in julep serving—he slowly* shuffles *toward the* SENATOR.)

BUZZ: Great work, Howard, you finally got it, fine manners. Take it easy, take it easy.

RAWKINS: Hurry it up, man, for God's sake, please!

HOWARD: Comin', suh, Massa Rawkins, suh. Ah hopes you enjoys it.

RAWKINS: Give it to me! Give me my bromo! (*He is on his knees, his collar off, his ego down, pleading and crawling toward* HOWARD.)

HOWARD (*the bromo evaporated*): Yassah, Massa Rawkins.

(*On* HOWARD, *the picture of a man on a treadmill, making forward steps, but never advancing, the lights fade out fast.*)

THE CURTAINS CLOSE

SCENE 4

The meetin' place, next afternoon. SHARON *is at the well, hauling up buckets of water for the wash, which she is doing. She is reprising "How Are Things in Glocca Morra?" and from her sad mood that laddie with the twinklin' eye seems farther away than ever.* FINIAN *enters shirtless, calling—*

FINIAN: Sharon, haven't ye laundered me shirt yet? (*He sees her wringing it out vigorously.*) Not so hard, lass, you'll be wringin' the Irish out o' the linen.

SHARON: 'Tis the neck off o' the Mahoney I'm wringin'.

FINIAN (*pleased*): So that Woody lad is makin' advances?

SHARON: Worse than that. He's retreatin'—leavin' for New York.

FINIAN: Oh, he is, is he? Well, if Mr. Woody Mahoney thinks he can whisk us out of Ireland, only to betray us, he doesn't know the McLonergans. Sharon, put this rose in your hair. (*He hands her a rose and stands back to survey her.*) Ah, 'tis a beautiful bride you'll be.

SHARON: All by meself, or is there a man involved?

FINIAN: Aye, there is. He doesn't know it yet, but before sundown Mr. Woody Mahoney will find himself betrothted to you.

(*This is news to* FINIAN, *too.*)

SHARON (*for once a willing victim of* FINIAN's *optimism*): Father—be*trothed*.

FINIAN (*with dignity*): Betroth*ted*.

> (*He marches off determinedly to execute some typical McLonergan stratagem.* SHARON *continues singing, in brighter mood.*)

SHARON (*ending her song gaily*): Things are fine in Rainbow Valley this fine day! (*Her next tug at the well-rope meets with resistance. Another tug sends her sprawling on the ground and brings up a bucketful of leprechaun.*) Well, this is a pretty bucket of fish!

> (OG *shies his head away bashfully as* SHARON *picks herself up.*)

How do you explain these strange shenanigans?

> (*He makes guttural noises.*)

Is it a frog you're pretendin' to be?

> (*He grunts.*)

Why, of course. You're the prince who was turned into a frog by a wicked bottle of whiskey.

> (*He hiccups.*)

Well, if you won't speak, back into the well you go.

OG (*jumping out—pleadingly*): *Oh, no!*

SHARON: So you've found your tongue. Well then, speak up— account for yourself—why were you hiding in that well?

OG (*pathetically*): Oh, I wasn't hiding. You see, somebody had set me on fire, and I had to put myself out.

SHARON: I see. And who put the torch to you?

OG: A sunbeam.

SHARON: A sunbeam?

OG: A sunbeam disguised as a fairy queen. But you can't fool me. I know a sunbeam when I see one.

SHARON (*pleased, approaches him*): Why, thank you. You're very poetical, aren't you?

OG: Don't come too close, please. I'll have to jump again.

SHARON: Alas, I'm beginnin' to understand. I've known that feelin' myself—

OG: You have?

SHARON: Only recently.

OG: It hit *me* this morning, as you were sunning your hair at the brook.

SHARON: Is it a warmish, kind of a glowish, kind of a peculiarish sensation?

OG (*with clinical objectivity*): No . . . a kind of quiverish, shiver-
ish, flibberty-gibberish sensation.

SHARON: A heavenly all-overish sensation?

OG: Half-overish, in my case.

SHARON: Half?

OG: It's approaching the three-quarter mark now. (*He points to his heart.*)

SHARON: Does it make you feel humming-birds in your heart?

OG: Butterflies in me feet.

SHARON: Bees in your bonnet?

OG: Stars in me britches.

SHARON: It makes you want to dance?

OG (*dancing*): I hadn't noticed that.

SHARON: And sing?

OG: It does. It does!

"Something Sort of Grandish"

OG (*singing*):
Something sweet,
Something sort of grandish
Sweeps my soul
When thou art near.

My heart feels
So sugar candish,
My head feels
So ginger beer.

Something so dare-ish,
So I-don't-care-ish,
Stirs me from limb to limb.
It's so terrifish, magnifish, delish,
To have such an amorish, glamorish dish.

We could be
Oh, so bride-and-groomish,
Skies could be
So bluish-blue.
Life could be

> So love-in-bloomish
> If my ish-es could come true.
> (*They do a little dance in which* OG, *propelled now by mortal legs, pursues* SHARON *with delicate amorousness.*)

SHARON (*singing*):

> Thou art sweet,
> Thou art sort of grandish,
> Thou outlandish cavalier.
> From now on
> We're hand in handish—
> Romeo—

OG:

> And Guinivere!
> Thou'rt so adorish,
> Toujour l'amorish,
> I'm so cherchez la femme.

SHARON:

> Why should I vanquish, relinquish, resish,
> When I simply relish this hellish condish?

OG:

> I might be
> Manish or mouse-ish,
> I might be
> A fowl or fish,
> But with thee
> I'm Eisenhowsish—
> Please accept my proposish.

OG and SHARON:

> You're under my skinish,
> So please be give-in-ish,
> Or it's the beginish
> Of the finish
> Of me!
> (OG *skips off and disappears in the well.* WOODY *walks in, suitcase in hand.*)

WOODY: Top o' the twilight to you, Miss McLonergan.
SHARON: And the rest of the day to you.
WOODY: Who've you been singin' romantic duets with?

SHARON: Oh, an old friend of mine from Ireland.

WOODY: Who?

SHARON: A skylark.

WOODY: Seems to know all the words, too. Smart bird.

SHARON: Well, at least he's a bird in the *hand*, Mr. Mahoney.

WOODY: Why doesn't he show himself if he's half a man?

 (OG *obligingly sticks his legs out of the well-top, unobserved.*)

SHARON: Sure, and I prefer half a man under me eye to a travelin' troubadour three thousand miles out of sight.

WOODY: Can't help myself, Sharon. I've got those commitments. But I'll be back. Can't you put your heart in escrow for a couple of months?

SHARON: On what collateral? A few promissory notes on your guitar? Frankly, I'm weary of minstrels who are always singin'—(*Sings.*)

 Will you be faithful when I'm far away?

 (*Resumes speech.*)

 For once I'd like to know the feelin' of bein' faithful to someone close at hand. You—you disorganizer! (*She sweeps off.*)

WOODY: Sharon!

 (*He starts after her but is intercepted by the arrival of* FINIAN, *a few* SHARECROPPERS, HENRY *and a couple of other kids. They are carrying pumpkin torches and other picnic paraphernalia.*)

KIDS (*in childish sing-song*): We're having a party, we're having a party!

WOODY: What's the occasion, Mr. McLonergan, a goin'-away party for me?

FINIAN (*baiting the trap*): What? Ye haven't heard the gossip?

WOODY: What gossip?

FINIAN: Why, me daughter Sharon is bein' betroth-ted today.

KIDS: Sharon's gettin' betroth-ted, Sharon's gettin' betroth-ted!

WOODY: So that's the guy she was singing duets with. There's a woman for you every time.

FINIAN: Now I hope you're not goin' to take it too hard.

WOODY: Why should I? It was only love.

FINIAN: Well, that's a sensible attitude. With all due respect, you were no match for Sharon in the first place.

FIRST SHARECROPPER: Better luck next time, Woody.

WOODY: Wait a minute. Explain yourself.

FINIAN: Don't you realize, lad, Sharon is from quality stock? Why, her whole family tree for generations back consists of nothin' but ancestors.

WOODY: We've been descendin' a long time too.

FINIAN: Ah, but *how* long? Sharon's grandparents go back to the dawn of history. Blue-blooded amebas they were, with a dauntless ambition. Up they came through the paleozoic slime—from ameba to tadpole, from tadpole to daffodil, from daffodil to dromedary, and from dromedary to McLonergan. That's the background Sharon comes from—so get along with your luggage, lad, you haven't a chance.

WOODY: Oh, haven't I? Well, you don't know the background of the Mahoneys—(*puts suitcase down*)—or the backbone either. I'm not leavin'!

(*Another group of* SHARECROPPERS *enter.*)

FIRST SHARECROPPER: Attaboy, Woody, stay here and fight it out!

WOODY (*belligerently*): Who is this guy?

FINIAN: Now if I tell you, you won't be makin' trouble and gettin' into fights with Sharon's fiancé?

WOODY: Promise.

FINIAN: Very well. I don't know his name, but 'twas last night, right here on me estate. Gentle as a ewe lamb he was, kneelin' at her feet—beggin' only one favor—to make a better world for Sharon and her children. I was the first to congratulate them.

WOODY: Mr. McLonergan, that was *me* you congratulated.

FINIAN: Well, was it now? Are you sure?

WOODY: You're my witness.

FINIAN: Well, this is a blessed relief. We're avoidin' a lot of bloodshed. 'Tis *you* that's the imaginary rival?

WOODY: Sure. It was me all along.

FINIAN (*closing the trap*): Then 'tis you that's goin' to make Sharon a fine upstandin' husband?

WOODY: That's right.

FINIAN: Therefore, 'tis you that's gettin' betroth-ted today?

WOODY: Be*trothed*.

FINIAN: I'm sorry—be*trothed*.

WOODY (*realizing it suddenly, like many a man before him*): Hey, what am I saying? Wait a minute, McLonergan!

FINIAN: Too late now, me boy. On with the celebration!

SHARON (*entering with large red rose in her hair*): Well, what are we celebrating?

WOODY: What? You mean you haven't heard the gossip?

SHARON: What gossip?

FINIAN: Why, our friend Mr. Mahoney is being betrothed.

KIDS (*in sing-song*): Woody's getting betroth-ted, Woody's getting betroth-ted!

SHARON (*with a twinkle*): So those were the commitments that kept you from committing yourself?

WOODY: Lucky me, marryin' a girl whose great-great-grandmother was a daffodil.

SHARON: I see. And was there a tadpole on her father's side?

WOODY: Yeah. How did you know?

SHARON: Why, that would be my Uncle O'Shaemas.

> (*She kisses him, then tosses the rose to* FINIAN. SUSAN *goes into a joyous little dance figure.*)

HENRY: Susan's trying to say somethin'.

GROUP: What's she sayin', Henry?

HENRY: I can't tell—it's a secret. Woody, you tell them.

"If This Isn't Love"

WOODY (*singing*):
> A secret, a secret,
> She says she's got a secret.
> A secret, a secret,
> A secret *kind* of secret.
> She's achin' for to shout it
> To ev'ry daffodil,
> And tell the world about it,
> In fact, she says she will.

GROUP (*watching* SUSAN'*s dancing feet*):
> She says,
> She says—

WOODY:
> If this isn't love,
> The whole world is crazy.
> If this isn't love,
> I'm daft as a daisy.

With moons all around
And cows jumping over,
There's something amiss
And I'll eat my hat if this
Isn't love.

I'm feelin' like the apple
On top of William Tell.
With this I cannot grapple,
Because—

GROUP:

Because—

WOODY:

You're so adora-bel!

WOODY and GROUP:

If this isn't love,
Then winter is summer.
If this isn't love,
My heart needs a plumber.
I'm swingin' on stars,
I'm ridin' on rainbows—
I'm bustin' with bliss
And I'll kiss your hand if this
Isn't love!

SHARON:

If this isn't love,
I'm Carmen Miranda.
If this isn't love,
It's Red propaganda!
If this is a dream
And if I should wake up,
Will you hear a hiss—
Will my face be red if this
Isn't love.

FINIAN:

I'm gettin' tired of waitin'
And stickin' to the rules.
This feelin' calls for matin'
Like birds—and bees—and other ani-mules.

GROUP:
>   If this isn't love,
>   We're all seeing double,
>   If this isn't love,

WOODY:
>   I'm really in trouble.
>   If she's not the girl—

SHARON:
>   And he's not the hero—

GROUP:
>   A kiss ain't a kiss,
>   It's a crisis, man, if this
>   Isn't love.
>   (*At finish of song, the* SHARECROPPERS *couple off and do a gay dance.*)

FINIAN: The barbecue's waitin' in the valley!
>   (*The dancers gather up the glowing pumpkins and fall into a torchlight parade which prances off down the valley.* FINIAN, *happily bringing up the rear, is suddenly stopped by a pumpkin-headed figure which leaps in front of him with an accusing—*)

OG (*removing pumpkin from his head*): Finian McLonergan!

FINIAN: How dare you come back here? (*Without conviction.*) Didn't I tell you you were an optical illusion?

OG: Yes, and I was ready to believe you yesterday—but not today. And I've got proof.

FINIAN: What proof?

OG: Does an optical illusion feel an, oh, such a hungry yearning burning inside of him, under the hide of him? Does an optical illusion feel the beat-beat-beat of the tom-tom in the roaring traffic's boom, in his lonely room?

FINIAN (*his scholarly interest is enlisted*): Hmmm. Do you also feel like the promised kiss of springtime that trembles on the brink of a lovely song?

OG: Yes, and what's worse, smoke keeps coming out of me eyes.

FINIAN: You go round and round like an elevator lost in the tide?

OG: Aye, that's the feeling— (*Wailing it.*) Day and night, night and day. Oh, give me your daughter, Mr. McLonergan!

FINIAN: Me daughter? What's she got to do with it?

OG: She's the one who's under me skin.

FINIAN (*this is worse than a crisis!*): Leprechaun, you're playing with fire.

OG: Yes, and the fire is winning. Oh, I don't want to be human, I don't want to be human! It's too inhuman!

FINIAN: Ah, you're neurotic. Who's forcin' ye to be human?

OG: You are, by keeping me crock of gold.

FINIAN: But I'm not keepin' it. I'm only lend-leasin' it. Give me another few weeks and I'll return it to you with interest—twelve little crocks.

OG: Oh, I do hope you're not going to use it to make wishes. It's only good for three wishes in the hands of a mortal—and after that it turns to dross.

FINIAN: You insult me—me who used to give courses in Advanced Leprechaunology. (*Smugly.*) I'll wager you don't know that certain types of crocks discovered by scholars are good for *four* wishes.

OG: Oh, I'm sorry, Mr. McLonergan. In Glocca Morra we only use the three-wish model.

FINIAN: From the way you talk, anyone would think I never had a pot to wish on.

OG: Excuse me, Mr. McLonergan, I'm a nuisance.

FINIAN: You're worse than that. You're the nemesis on me premises. You're endangerin' me whole project. Where's your passport?

OG: What's that?

FINIAN: I thought so. You have none. How dare you come into a free country without a passport?

OG: Oh, *I'm* legal. I came as a Christmas tree. But I'm not leavin' till I see me crock.

FINIAN: Then *I'm* seein' me congressman, Senator Rawkins, and havin' you deported. (*He sends* OG *sprawling with a slap.*) You're a member of a subversive underground group takin' its orders from Dublin!

  (*He patters off.* HENRY *and two* LITTLE GIRLS *scramble in.*)

HENRY: Mister, did you see our rooster?

DIANA: He ran away from the barbecue.

HENRY: Went A.W.O.L.

OG: What kind of a rooster was he?

DIANA: Oh, just a regular, everyday rooster—with a little golden comb and little green feet—and pink and purple feathers round a little yellow seat.

HENRY: Oh, she's just makin' that up. There ain't no such animal.

OG: Would this be it? (*He produces out of the ground the very rooster described.*)

DIANA (*taking it*): That's *it*, all right!

KIDS (*ad lib*):

Gee!

He's magic—like John Henry!

Snagdrab it!

HENRY: He's out of this world!

OG: How did you know? Yes, I do come from a magic land.

HENRY: Then can you wish for other things, too?

OG: I can, if we act quickly. Will you help me?

(*The* KIDS *huddle eagerly around him.*)

HENRY: What do you want us to do?

OG: Just help me find a little yellow crock that's buried under the ground somewhere around here.

HENRY: Sure.

OG: If we find it, I can get you anything you want. See, I've got it all here in this magic book.

(*A wave of his hand and a Sears-Roebuck catalogue descends from the sky.*)

HENRY: Shears-Robust—is that you?

OG: Shears-Robust? Oh, no. That's the two angels in charge of distribution.

HONEY LOU: Real angels, with wings?

OG: Wings? (*A thoughtful pause.*) On their collars.

DIANA: I wish I had a book like that. Where'd you get it, mister?

OG: The pixies left it for me in that tiny house yonder.

HENRY (*pointing off*): You mean the one over there with the half-moon on the door?

OG: Ah, yes, the wee, wee hut.

(*The kids excitedly look over the catalogue.*)

HONEY LOU: Gee, a harmonica!

HENRY: Can I get a fishin' rod?

DIANA: And a little doll with two pink bows that wriggles her ears and blows her nose?

OG: You can have anything that's made in fairyland.

"Something Sort of Grandish (Reprise)"

OG (*singing*):

    There'll be things
    Plenty-ish for all-ish,
    Wondrish toys and magic tricks,
    Electrish trains and basketball-ish,
    Mintish drops and licorish sticks.

    Life will be keen-ish,
    All Hallowe'en-ish,
    And jelly bean-ish, too,
    With ice cream and cake-ish
    And soda to sup,
    And no bellyache-ish
    To wakish you up.

    There will be
    Such delicious dishes,
    And we'll end this daffish plot.
    We will go
    From rags to rishes
    When we find that gold-ish pot.

    There'll be chocolate custish
    With hot dogs and mustish,
    But Shears and Robust-ish
    Must fustish come through.

(*At finish of song,* OG *and his hastily recruited searching party trip off.*)

SCENE 5

The meetin' place, next afternoon, serves as a work-shed (our share-croppers occasionally work, too), with the open sky for a roof. Several women and young girls, Negroes and whites, are sorting tobacco leaves into hampers. A male SHARECROPPER *is lolling in a crotch of the cypress tree, strumming his guitar as the women chant.*

THE WOMEN:

    Grade A, milder,

    Grade B, cooler,

    Grade C, cooler, milder.

SHARECROPPER IN TREE:

    Cooler, milder, better smoke.

    You'll find it easy on your throat.

    (A few more girls enter carrying apronfuls of leaves.)

THE WOMEN:

    Grade A, they satisfy,

    Grade B, better tastin',

    Easy on the throat.

    (They cough. Two men bring in some dried leaves strung on poles.)

MAUDE *(holding up a huge leaf)*: Mm-mm. Isn't *this* one a beauty? *(She kisses it and tosses it into the hamper.)* Fare thee well. Happy trip to New York or Miami.

DELORES *(dreamily)*: I wish I could go to New York or Miami.

ARLENE *(indicating a leaf)*: I'll bet this one's goin' to Hollywood.

LYN: Do you think Bogart will be smokin' it and puffin' it right into Baby Bacall's big blue eyes?

MAUDE: Stop dreamin' and keep sortin', gal. There's more than just miles between you and Hollywood.

LYN: I've often wondered what it is keeps me here.

MAUDE: And what is it puts the fly in your sasperilla?

DELORES: And hangs a ball and chain around your dreams?

"Necessity"

GIRLS *(singing in turn)*:

    What is the curse

    That makes the universe

      So all-bewilderin'?

    What is the hoax

    That just provokes

The folks
  They call
  God's childerin?

What is the jinx
  That gives a body
  And his brother
  And everyone around
The run-around?

Necessity, necessity,
That most unnecessary thing, necessity!
What throws the monkey wrench in
A fella's good intention?
That nasty old invention—
  Necessity!

My feet want to dance in the sun,
  My head wants to rest in the shade.
The Lord says, "Go out and have fun,"
But the landlord says,
  "Your rent ain't paid."

Necessity—
It's plain to see
What a lovely old world
This silly old world
  Could be—

But, man, it's all in a mess
Account of necess-
  Ity.

Necessity, necessity,
There ought to be a law against necessity.

I'd love to play some tennis
Or take a trip to Venice,
But, sister, here's the menace—
  Necessity.

Oh, hell is the father of gin,
And Cupid's the father of love.
Old Satan's the father of sin,
  But no one knows the father of
  Necessity.

(You mean he's a —?
That's what he is!)

Necessity—necessity—
That's the maximum
That a minimum
  Thing can be.

There's nothing lower than less,
Unless it's necess-
  Ity.

SHARECROPPER IN TREE:
  Necessity, necessity.

I loved a woman named Bess,
But nevertheless, poor me—

GIRLS:
  He had to marry Teresa
  'Count of necessi-
    Ty!

(RAWKINS *saunters in with* BUZZ.)

RAWKINS (*with disarming geniality*): You people belong here?

GIRLS: Yes, sir.

RAWKINS: You mean you live right here on this property?

GIRLS: Yes, sir.

(FINIAN *enters with* SHARON *and a few* SHARECROPPERS.)

FINIAN: It's *my* property, your honor.

BUZZ (*indicating* FINIAN *to* RAWKINS): McLonergan.

RAWKINS: Yes, I understand you got stuck with this piece of arid, gopher-infested land the other day. How would you like to unload right now for a clear profit of thirty percent?

FINIAN (*to* SHARON): It's a landslide, Sharon, you can't stop it.

RAWKINS: What do you say?

FINIAN: Oh, I'm afraid I can't consider any propositions for at least six months. You see, I'm conductin' certain experiments.

RAWKINS: What—kind of experiments?

SHARON: Oh, Father is a mineralogist from the old country. He can make gold sprout out of the ground.

RAWKINS: Gold?

BUZZ: Oh—oh, Rawkins isn't gonna like this.

RAWKINS: But there isn't any gold in Ireland.

FINIAN: Ah, yes, Senator. I myself discovered a vein that our countrymen have been searching for since the reign of Alfred the Thoughtless.

RAWKINS: Alfred who?

FINIAN: Ye never heard of Alfred the Thoughtless? Why, he was King of Erin followin' his father, Thomas the Temporary— who in turn was the only son of the Virgin Queen—Serena the Spotless—

RAWKINS: McLonergan, are you willin' to sell me this land or ain't you?

FINIAN: Sure, I'm willin' and I'm wantin'—but I'm waitin'.

RAWKINS (*with hypocritical unction*): Sorry to hear you say that. Just puts me to the trouble of having to issue a writ of seizure and take this land from you.

BUZZ (*producing the writ instantly*): Here's the writ, Senator.

RAWKINS: Don't be crude, Buzz. (*He hands the writ to* FINIAN.) I hate to do this, but you've been violatin' the law here.

FINIAN: What law, Senator?

RAWKINS: The law of the South. There's a restrictive covenant which forbids Negroes to build homes on this land—depreciates property values.

FINIAN (*to an old Negro*): John, have you depreciated any property around here lately?

JOHN: Haven't had time to notice. Been too busy raisin' tobacco.

SHARON: Well, now, there's nothin' depreciatin' about that, is there, Senator?

RAWKINS: I don't know where you immigrants get all those foreign ideas!

SHARON: From a wee book the immigration inspector handed us, called the United States Constitution. Haven't you ever read it?

RAWKINS: I haven't got time to read it! I'm too busy defendin' it! (*He marches angrily upstage and stops near the spot where the crock of gold is buried.*) I wish I could make you understand our culture! I wish I could—

FINIAN (*with explosive apprehension*): Now don't go makin' wishes on me property! (*He shoves* RAWKINS *away violently.*)

RAWKINS: Just for that, McLonergan, you can get off right now—you and your black friends!

HENRY: No, Mama, I don't want to go!

HENRY'S MOTHER (*as he rushes to her arms*): Hush, child.

A MIDDLE-AGED NEGRO WOMAN: We'll find a place, Henry. It's a big country.

HENRY: No—no—no—please!

SHARON: Do you mean to say you're taking this land from these people merely because their skins are black?

HENRY (*running to* SHARON *and still sobbing*): Don't let 'em chase us, Sharon.

RAWKINS (*very uncomfortable*): Tell that kid to shut up—he's making me out a bully! Now get going! (*He takes a belligerent step toward the group of sharecroppers, who begin to scatter.*)

JANE (*a little girl*): Is Henry the wrong color?

SHARON: Of course not, child. There's nothing wrong with being black— (*With mounting emotion at* RAWKINS.) But there's something wrong with the world that he and his kind have made for Henry. I wish he could know what that world is like. I wish to God he were black so—

    (*Suddenly there is darkness—a crash of thunder—a streak of lightning. When the lights go up,* RAWKINS *is disclosed as a trembling heap on the ground. The people are drawn back, aghast. From their faces it is evident that* SHARON's *wish has materialized and that the* SENATOR *is now, indeed, a black man. For* SHARON, *fortunately or unfortunately, has made her wish over the crock.* BUZZ *rushes to the aid of the fallen* RAWKINS *and takes one horrified look.*)

BUZZ: Oh, my God! What happened? Get a doctor, somebody! (*He runs wildly off. The* SHERIFF *strolls in with a man and a woman in riding habits.*)

SHERIFF (*giving a real-estate spiel*): Beautiful country around here, folks—heart of the old South—magnolias and mint

juleps, romance and tradition, happy song-singin' darkies—
(*He picks up the sharecropper's guitar and hands it to the first
convenient darky*—RAWKINS.) Here, Sambo—sing for the
white folks.

> (RAWKINS *slowly picks himself up, gazes at the black and final
> evidence of his outstretched hands, then covering his face, runs
> off. The* SHERIFF *chases after him, a knight in defense of white
> supremacy.*)

Well, I'll learn him!

SHARON (*still shocked*): Father—am I seein' things?

FINIAN: There, there, nothin's happened. You just shouldn't go
about me property makin' wishes.

WOODY (*entering breathlessly*): Was Rawkins tryin' to take our
land from us? (*He takes the writ of seizure from* SHARON.)

SHARON (*leaning on* WOODY *for support*): Yes—and then we had
some words, and he got furious—and turned black right in
front of me eyes!

WOODY: Forget it. Happens to him every time a Negro passes
by. He sees red, turns purple with rage, and yells himself
black in the face. (*Tearing up writ.*) The yellow dog.

FINIAN: Mr. Rawkins seems to have a rainbow all his own.

> (*Five* SHARECROPPERS *rush on with a whoop and a holler,
> carrying picks and shovels.*)

FIRST SHARECROPPER: Yippie! Gold's been discovered! Right
here in Rainbow Valley!

WOODY: So that's why Rawkins wanted the land. Gold, eh?
Who says so?

FIRST SHARECROPPER: This here telegram from Shears and
Robust. Here, McLonergan, it's addressed to you.

> (*He hands the telegram to* FINIAN, *who waves it away.*)

FINIAN: I don't have to read it. It's just the McLonergan theory
giving birth to itself.

SHARON (*looking at telegram*): The saints preserve us!

FIRST SHARECROPPER: Read 'em what it says, Sharon!

SHARON and WOODY (*reading alternately*):

"Mr. Finian McLonergan, Esquire, Rainbow Valley, Missitucky. Dear Sir: After investigating your standing in the
community and finding you to be a citizen of high character
and moral integrity, we have taken the liberty of opening a
charge account for you and your associates.

Please look over the attached catalogue and feel free to order anything you may want, from bobby pins to prefabricated homes, complete with radar weathervane, electronic rat control, air-conditioned hogpens and plastic privies—with jet-propulsion flush.

Signed, Shears Robust and Company.

P.S. Incidentally, we hear that gold has been discovered on your property. Congratulations."

FIRST SHARECROPPER: I'm stakin' out my claim! I'm gonna start diggin'!

GROUP (*ad lib*):

Me too!

Let's dig that gold!

I'm goin' for my shovel!

(*They all start off.*)

FINIAN (*collapsing onto ground at the thought*): Ah, me arthritis!

WOODY (*putting two and two together*): Wait a minute, fellas. (*They stop.*) Maybe there *is* gold and maybe again—(*with a pointed look at* FINIAN)—there ain't.

FINIAN (*groaning and rubbing his leg*): Aye, aye, aye. Woody's so right.

WOODY: Meantime, you've dug up the ground and wrecked your whole spring tobacco crop.

FIRST SHARECROPPER: But dang it, Woody, I been waitin' all my life for a break like this.

WOODY: Well, you've got your break now—all of you—this piece of yellow paper. It's credit! You can turn it into tractors—

SHARON: —turn the tractors into tobacco—

WOODY: —and turn the tobacco into money faster than you can dig the gold out o' the ground!

FINIAN (*jumps up, totally recovered*): That's the ticket, Woody! That's the ticket!

SHARON: You'll have everything you've ever hoped for.

MAUDE: But when do we all get this?

GROUP: Yes. When, when, when?

WOODY: When?

"That Great Come-and-Get-It Day"

WOODY (*singing*):

On that great come-and-get-it day,

Won't it be fun
When worry is done
And money is hay?
That's the time things'll come your way,
On that great, great come-and-get-it day.

I'll get my gal that calico gown,
I'll get my mule that acre of groun',
Cause word has come from Gabriel's horn:
The earth beneath your plow
Is a-buddin' and now it's yourn.

SHARON:

Glory time's comin' for to stay
On that great, great come-and-get-it day.

GROUP (*in a repeated counterpoint under the singing*):

Come and get it, come and get it, come and get it. . . .

PREACHER:

Sez here
Sez it in the Good Book, it sez—

WOMAN:

What's it say?

PREACHER:

A mighty mornin' is nigh—

ALL:

Universal Fourth of July.

WOODY:

Gonna get your freedom and pie.

GROUP:

What a day, with banjoes ringin',
What a day for people in overalls,
Can't you hear all the angels singin'?

MAUDE:

"Come and get your gravy and two meat balls!"

PREACHER:

Sez here—

GROUP:

Bells will ring in ev'ry steeple—

GIRL:

Come and get your test on that movie screen.

GROUP:

>   Come, you free and equal people,

BOY:

>   Come and get your beer and your benzedrine.

PREACHER:

>   Sez here:
>   There's gonna be a world shakin', bread-breakin' day.

WOMAN:

>   Does that mean I can get a washing machine?

PREACHER:

>   Glory to ya!

ANOTHER WOMAN:

>   Can I get a waffle iron?

WOODY:

>   With your initials!

BOY:

>   Can I get a juke box?

PREACHER:

>   Sez here!

YOUNG MAN:

>   How about a helicopter?

PREACHER:

>   Helicopter?

GROUP:

>   Hallelujah!

>   On that great come-and-get-it day,
>   Won't it be fun
>   When worry is done
>   And money is hay?
>   That's the time things'll come your way,
>   On that great, great come-and-get-it day.

SHARON:

>   My gown will be a calico gown
>   My feet will dance all over the town,

WOODY:

>   'Cause word has come from Gabriel's horn,
>   The earth beneath your plow
>   Is a-buddin' and now it's yourn.

GROUP:

> Glory time's comin' for to stay
> On that great, great come-and-get-it—
> And keep it—
> And share it—
> Great, great come-and-get-it day!

(In the upstretched arms of the SHARECROPPERS *is a note of spiritual glory and a promise of material blessings to come, as*

THE CURTAIN FALLS*)*

ACT TWO

In the meetin' place, this sunny morning, some two weeks later, a few
SHARECROPPERS *and kids are watching* SUSAN *as she skips about*
the stage. Her hands are holding a package and her dancing feet are
announcing some glad tidings.

HENRY (*interpreting* SUSAN's *foot-talk*): She says it's from Shears
and Robust.

DIANA: Those are the angels who live in fairyland.

FINIAN (*entering*): It's here, it's here—that great come-and-get-
it day! Everything you ordered from Shears and Robust!
(*He motions to the people and they follow him off.*)

KIDS (*as they go*):
Last man down to Finian's hill
Is nothin' but a rotten vegetabill.
(*Now* SUSAN *brings forth from her package a bright new calico*
dress, which she waves gaily through the air. It is the fulfill-
ment of the promise which ended Act One, and the beginning
of a fashion parade which unfolds with the entrance, in turn,
of each newly bedizened sharecropper. Possession of gold [or its
equivalent: belief that they possess it] has brought them the final
cockeyed luxury. They can now afford to stop wanting things
they can buy and to start buying things they don't want. So it
is understandable that they appear in mink shorts, leopard-skin
pajamas, and gold-brocaded hunting habits. SHARON, *appear-*
ing last, is now quite the best-dressed colleen from county Glocca
Morra.)

"When the Idle Poor Become the Idle Rich"
SHARON (*singing*):
When the idle poor become the idle rich,
You'll never know just who is who—
Or who is which.

Won't it be rich
When everyone's poor relative

409

Becomes a Rockefellertive
And palms no longer itch?
What a switch!

GIRLS:

When we all have ermine and plastic teeth,
How will we determine who's who underneath?
And when all your neighbors are upper class
You won't know your Joneses from your *As*tors.

SHARON:

Let's toast the day,
The day we drink our drinkie up,
But with the little pinky up,
The day on which
The idle poor become the idle rich.

(*Interlude*)

When a rich man doesn't want to work,
He's a bon vivant,
Yes, he's a bon vivant.
But when a poor man doesn't want to work,
He's a loafer, he's a lounger, he's a lazy good for
    nothin'—

BOYS:

He's a jerk.

SHARON:

When a rich man loses on a horse,
Isn't he the sport, oh, isn't he the sport?
But when a poor man loses on a horse,
He's a gambler, he's a spender, he's a low-life,
He's a reason for divorce.

When a rich man chases after dames
He's a man about town,
A man about town.
But when a poor man chases after dames,
He's a bounder, he's a rounder, he's a rotter
And a lot o' dirty names.

SHARON and GROUP:

When the idle poor become the idle rich,
You'll never know just who is who
Or who is which.
No one will see

The Irish or the Slav in you,
For when you're on Park Avenue,
Cornelius and Mike
Look alike.

When poor Tweedledum is rich Tweedledee
This discrimination will no longer be.
When we're in the dough and off of the nut,
You won't know your banker from your *but*ler.

Let's make the switch,
With just a few annuities
We'll hide these incongruities
With cloaks from Abercrombie Fitch—
When the idle poor become the idle rich.
(*As they finish, a cacophony of automobile horns off-scene breaks the fashionable air.*)

FINIAN (*looking off*): Here they are, the sons of Gabriel, blowin' their horns of plenty—the angels of our new prosperity—Mr. Shears and Mr. Robust!
(*A new parade marches on, headed by two* SHARECROPPERS *carrying a banner inscribed*:

WELCOME TO SHEARS & ROBUST

—*Another pair and a second banner:*

SHEARS & ROBUST
FOR PRESIDENT!

—*And finally the angels of distribution themselves. Matching their monikers, one is tall and lean; the other, short and squat. They wear frock coats, striped morning trousers, and top-hats. A third banner, held by the kids, unfolds with a*—

WELCOME TO THIS EARTH!)

FINIAN: Greetings, gentlemen. It's a pleasure to welcome you to Rainbow Valley.
SHEARS (*sharply*): We're not here on pleasure. We're here on business.

ROBUST: We received your letter, McLonergan. What do you mean you can't pay us for all those tractors and clothes we sent you?

FINIAN: I explained that to you—because I can't dig up me gold.

SHEARS: Why not?

FINIAN: I'm surprised at you, gentlemen. (*With pixie belligerency.*) Do you want to ruin free enterprise?

SHEARS: God forbid!

FINIAN: Well, what stimulates free enterprise? Incentive! Right?

SHEARS: Right.

FINIAN: And what stimulates incentive? Gold! Right?

SHEARS: Right.

FINIAN: Well, if you remove gold from the ground, you remove incentive, and if you remove incentive, you wreck free enterprise. (*In a roar.*) Right?

SHEARS (*caught up in the rhythm*): Right.

FINIAN: I rest me case.

(SHEARS *and* ROBUST *go into a huddle.*)

ROBUST (*coming out of it*): There's just one thing that's not clear, McLonergan. How are you going to pay for all this merchandise?

FINIAN: We can't discuss this in public. Step into me private office, gentlemen. (*To* SHARON *as he opens imaginary door.*) Secretary, we'd like to be alone.

SHARON (*to group*): Would you mind waiting in the ante-room? (*The* GROUP *skips through the imaginary door to the imaginary ante-room.*)

FINIAN: Follow me, gentlemen. (*They enter the private office behind* FINIAN, SHEARS *bumping his head on the imaginary doorway. To* SHARON.) Shut the door. (*She obliges.* FINIAN *turns to* SHEARS *and* ROBUST, *who are sitting side by side on rim of well, with patronizing patience.*) Now, suppose I do dig up me gold and give it to you. What will you do with it?

ROBUST (*jumping up*): Send it to our bank in Chicago. (*Sits.*)

FINIAN: And what will *they* do with it?

SHEARS(*jumping up*): Transfer it to a bank in Wall Street. (*He sits.*)

FINIAN: And what will *they* do with it?

ROBUST (*jumping up*): Ship it to the Federal Reserve in Washington! (*Sits.*)

FINIAN: Now, gentlemen, what will the Federal Reserve do with it?

SHEARS and ROBUST (*jumping up and in unison*): Bury it in Fort Knox!

FINIAN: That's me whole point! Me gold is *already* buried—and *near* Fort Knox—now!

SHARON: Think of all the transportation Father is savin' ye!

(SHEARS *and* ROBUST *sink down defeated, and huddle again.*)

ROBUST (*rising out of huddle*): We don't like it.

FINIAN: Why not?

(WOODY *enters carrying suitcase.*)

ROBUST: It's un-American.

SHEARS: We don't even think you've *got* any gold!

WOODY: What's the good of gold? It can't make music—

GROUP (*a negative assent*): Mm-mm.

WOODY: Can't give milk.

GROUP: Mm—mm.

SHARON: And it doesn't taste good with mustard.

ROBUST: We're not in the *mustard* business!

SHEARS: My God, we're dealing with crackpots!

ROBUST: We'll have you blacklisted in every Chamber of Commerce in this country—and we're pulling out our equipment in the morning—all of it!

(*They start out.*)

WOODY (*stopping them—casually*): Don't be irritated—have a Lucky Gold!

(*Flustered,* ROBUST *takes it, then angrily throws it down.*)

That's no way to treat the Lucky Gold Company. They just gave me an order for forty thousand bales of tobacco—Rainbow Valley Tobacco!

(*The people cheer.* ROBUST'*s curiosity is piqued despite himself.*)

ROBUST: Why should Lucky Gold order tobacco from a piddling outfit like you?

WOODY: You've heard about the golden crispiness, the golden mellowness, the golden goldenness of Lucky Gold, haven't you?

ROBUST: They've always *claimed* that.

WOODY: When they found out about the gold in our land, feedin' our tobacco leaves, they realized it was *true*. Now they're shoutin' it out in *Life, Look, Click, Slick, Pic* and the *Nicotine Digest.*

(*The excited* SHARECROPPERS *and the* TWO INDUSTRIAL-ISTS *gather around* WOODY *to see the order, which he brings forth.*)

SHEARS (*beaming—to* WOODY): Well—this order is all the gold mine anybody needs!

ROBUST: Good sound economics!

WOODY (*imitates the tobacco auctioneer's chant, winding up with*): Sold!

WOODY, SHEARS and ROBUST (*together*): Rainbow Valley!

FINIAN: Me friends, this calls for a toast. (*He pulls the well-rope which is still slung over the limb of tree and the jug emerges into view.*)

SHARON (*pointing to jug*): Whiskey for men of distinction.

FINIAN: Won't you step up to the bar? (*Embracing* WOODY *and* SHARON *paternally.*) Woody, me boy, and, Sharon, me darlin', me mission is accomplished now. Your rainbow is just around the corner. I'll be leavin' soon. 'Twould be me lifelong dream come true if I could see you happily married before I go—but, of course, that's a decision no man should make for you. (*He makes it.*) How would next Tuesday suit everybody for the weddin'?

SHARON (*flabbergasted*): Father!

(*The* CROWD *answers with a cheer.*)

FINIAN: Then Tuesday it is, and you're all invited! Formal dress required.

(*They parade off to a reprise of "When the Idle Poor Become the Idle Rich."* BUZZ *enters with the* SHERIFF *and calls.*)

BUZZ: Hey there, Mahoney.

(WOODY *and* SHARON *stop as the others exit.*)

Where is he—where's Rawkins?

WOODY: You got me, Buzz.

BUZZ: I can't go on tellin' everybody he's restin' at White Sulphur Springs.

WOODY: We haven't seen him since the day he was struck by lightning.

SHERIFF: The D. A. is raisin' a big stink, threatenin' indictments all over the place.

SHARON: He just took to the hills and never came back.

BUZZ (*to* SHARON, *awesomely*): Well, you had something to do with it, you know.

WOODY: That's poppycock talk, Buzz. Nobody did nothin' to Rawkins.

SHERIFF: Why, there's fifty witnesses saw it happen. I suppose you're gonna deny he turned black?

WOODY: No, but that isn't good Negro black. It's just bad liver black. Psychosomatic.

BUZZ: What the psycho hell is that?

WOODY: Latest medical theory. Strawberries bring on hives, prejudice brings on jaundice. Anybody hates people like Rawkins does—it's triple jaundice.

SHERIFF: I don't know what you're talkin' about. All I know, she wished it and it happened. Give you till Tuesday to produce the corpus, or you *may* have a *murder* rap on your hands. Come on, Buzz.

BUZZ: Put that in your guitar and plunk it!

> (*They exit.*)

SHARON (*looking after them, worried*): Woody, do you think I really wished it on the Senator?

WOODY (*matter-of-factly*): Let's face it, Sharon. Ever since you came to Rainbow Valley, strange things have been happening. You've got to admit that.

SHARON: I've been worried about it myself.

WOODY: Why, this whole place is lousy with flyin' broomsticks. I felt it the first time I looked at you.

SHARON: Felt what, Woody?

WOODY: That sorta charm glitter in your eye . . . that kinda . . . conjure music in your voice. I've been bedeviled and bewitched ever since.

> (SHARON *catches on to* WOODY's *elaborate double-talk and decides to play along.*)

SHARON: Then that settles everything. I couldn't possibly marry you.

WOODY (*suddenly worried*): Why not?

SHARON: I wouldn't be a natural wife. Our children might have cloven hoofs—or two heads. You know, Father always said there was something about the McLonergans.

WOODY: And he was right. Isn't it true you voodooed me right out of that organizin' trip?

SHARON: Did I do that?

WOODY: And isn't it true you're standing there this minute,

gloating over my helplessness— (*He kisses her.*) Makin' me
putty in your hands— (*He kisses her again.*) Sweepin' me off
my feet? (*He sweeps her off her feet into a close embrace.*)

SHARON: Oh, Woody, Woody! This really *is* love, isn't it?

WOODY: Shucks, no, it's just the moon in your eyes, radiatin'
incentive.

(*They reprise "Old Devil Moon" and stroll off, arm in arm.
The lights dim. The eerie music of* SUNNY's *harmonica pierces
the night.* SUSAN *appears in a high limb of the cypress tree,
from where she has been watching* SHARON *and* WOODY. *As
if under the spell of some strange enchantment, she glides down
the gnarled trunk of the tree and into a dance. The flying feet
become more and more agitated until they are drawn as though
magnetized to the spot where the crock of gold is buried. It dif-
fuses a warm glow through the earth. In a frenzy of excitement
she digs out the crock and fondles it lovingly, like a child with
a new toy. She darts this way and that, looking for some place
to hide her treasure, then runs up the terraced rock ledges and
into the night.*)

THE CURTAINS CLOSE

SCENE 2

A wooded section of the hills which rim the valley. OG *is lying on
a fallen stump with roots and branches which form a sort of crude
couch, munching an apple and singing a phrase or two from "Glocca
Morra." A large, up-ended hollow stump stands near by.* RAWKINS
enters furtively, gives a start when he sees OG. *He is coatless, disheveled, and very unhappy-looking. Quietly he steals up behind* OG.

RAWKINS: Give me that! (*He snatches the apple and eats it
hungrily.*)

OG (*jumping up*): Oh, you needn't grab, mister. There's plenty
of apples around.

RAWKINS: Well, I don't see 'em.

OG: Naturally, you don't. Mortals never can see *all* the apples
they could have.

(*Singing to tune of "Little Brown Jug," he produces apples out
of the air.*)

An apple here,
An apple there,
Little red apples everywhere.
(*As* RAWKINS *reaches for them.*)
My, you must be hungry. Would you care for a sandwich?
(*He produces this from wherever leprechauns produce sandwiches.*)

RAWKINS (*seizing and eating it*): Wouldn't you be hungry if you'd been hiding out in this forest for two weeks, like a hunted possum? (*Sits on edge of couch.*)

OG: What were you hiding from?

RAWKINS: My wife, my people, my friends. You think I want 'em to see me this way?

OG: I see nothing wrong with you.

RAWKINS: You don't? You must be blind. Can't you see I'm black?

OG: Yes, and I think it's very becoming.

RAWKINS: But I'm a white man, dammit, a white man! At least, I was a few weeks ago.

OG: Well, *that's* a coincidence. I was *green* a few weeks ago. Don't you find an occasional change of color interesting?

RAWKINS: No, I don't! (*Darkly.*) But they won't get away with it, I tell you! They won't get away with it!

OG: You needn't get so excited, mister. I think it's just ridiculous making such a fuss about a person's color.

RAWKINS: You moron! Don't you realize what it means to be black?

OG: But you're still a human being. You can still smell bee honey and listen to bird music. A rose is still a rose, despite the color of your nose.

RAWKINS: But you can't get into a restaurant. You can't get on a street car. You can't buy yourself a cold beer on a hot day. (*With disgust.*) You can't even go into a church and pray.

OG: Who says you can't?

RAWKINS: The law says you can't.

OG: The law? Mmm . . . that's a silly law. Is it a legal law?

RAWKINS: Of course it's legal. I wrote it myself.

OG: That's too bad. I know—why don't you change your color again?

RAWKINS: How the hell am I going to do that?

OG: You said you had it changed two weeks ago.

RAWKINS: I said nothing of the kind. Some bitch wished it on me.

OG: Oh, a witch! Well, in that case, I can help you. What kind of a witch was she?

RAWKINS: How do I know? I didn't look her up in *Who's Who*.

OG: But I'm sure we can find her in *Which Is Witch*. This little book has a list of all the witches—their curses and cures— (*He brings forth a little book by magic and consults it.*) Let's see—

RAWKINS (*gruffly*): Go away, will you?

OG (*after a thoughtful pause*): I think I understand your trouble now—you're *too* unfriendly.

RAWKINS: I'm in no condition for friendship.

OG: And it's *all* that witch's fault. She gave you a new *out*side, when she should have given you a new *in*side. Very incompetent. This will give witchcraft a bad name. (*He paces worriedly.*) It may set our entire profession back a hundred years. (*Coming to a decision.*) I'm afraid we'll have to alter your personality. My whole reputation is at stake. Stand up, sir. (*He pulls* RAWKINS *up with a wave of his hand.*)

RAWKINS (*wearily*): Why don't you leave me alone?

OG (*surveying* RAWKINS, *like a couturier*): Oh, this won't be a bit hard. All we have to do is broaden out that narrow mind a little—reduce some of that bigotry—and your pomposity won't show at all. Wait till they see you in your new spring psyche. People will say you're in love! Now for the magic cure.

(*The lights dim.* RAWKINS *sinks involuntarily into a recumbent position on the couch. From inside his cape* OG *brings forth a series of vials, from which he tosses powders into the hollow tree stump. With each toss, a huge puff of smoke billows upward. Simultaneously, he circles around the stump, chanting:*)

OG:

> Fiddle, foddle, foil and fiddle,
> Cure this fuddled individdle.
> Rise, ye vapors, and unwind
> This tangled medieval mind.
> Breath of bee and bluebird wing,
> Make this scowling spirit sing.
> Balm of briar and sandalwood,

Season him with brotherhood.
Magic vapors, make this person
A better person—not a worse 'un.
(RAWKINS *has fallen into a trance-like sleep.*)
Ah, he sleeps! The cure is beginning to work!
(*Singing.*)
How are things in Glocca Morra this fine day. . . .
(*Pleased with himself,* OG *goes off. The smoke curls up and covers
the figure of* RAWKINS. *After a few moments it clears away.
The lights come up.* RAWKINS *rises and stretches, a smile on his
face, like a man emerging from a long sleep. Then he starts to
sing a joyous song.*)

RAWKINS:

Oh, dem golden slippers,
Oh, dem golden slippers,
Golden slippers I laid away,
Don't expect to wear them
Till my wedding day!
(*Three Negroes, in shabby white tails, enter and stop to listen.*)

FIRST GOSPELEER (*as* RAWKINS *finishes*): Brother, you're the
voice in the wilderness. Allow me the honor of shakin' your
hand.

RAWKINS: Thank you, friend. Sure is nice to talk to somebody
again.

SECOND GOSPELEER: Just whom, may I ask, have we the acci-
dental good fortune to meet up with in this predestined way?

RAWKINS: Well, you can just call me Bill. You fellas from
around here?

THIRD GOSPELEER: Mister, we're from around everywhere.
We travel and we sing. Haven't you ever heard of the Passion
Pilgrim Gospel Gospeleers?

RAWKINS: Well, to tell you the truth, I've been a little out of
touch with the Gospel lately.

SECOND GOSPELEER: Why, we're the prize-winninest, gospel-
singinest quartet east of the Rockies.

RAWKINS: Quartet, eh? I see only three of you.

FIRST GOSPELEER (*chanting like a revival-meetin' preacher*):
Well, you see, brother, we suffered a casualty last night, after
our triumphant performance at the First Baptist Church.

There was our Number Four man, Russ, suddenly taken with temptation. And in his desperation he cried out, "Get thee behind me, Satan"—and Satan got—and Satan pushed—and he pushed him right into the arms of a bouncin' Babylonian Jezebel from Biloxi, Mississippi. Oh, the soul was strong, but the flesh was weak. (*Matter-of-factly.*) One of our baritones is now missin'.

RAWKINS: That's too bad, losing a valuable man like that.

THIRD GOSPELEER: Brother, we only lost his body. And that's why Divine Providence led us to you. You may be Bill, but the voice inside you is Russ.

RAWKINS: I wouldn't be a bit surprised. I've been getting an awful shufflin' around lately.

THIRD GOSPELEER: Well, your shufflin' days are over. With your voice, we can go right on bein' a prize-winnin' quartet.

RAWKINS: You mean I can make a livin' singin' with you?

SECOND GOSPELEER: There's only a handful of ways. You either tote that barge, lift that bale, shine that shoe—or sing. We sing.

THIRD GOSPELEER: But before we do, either somebody got to get buried or somebody got to get married.

SECOND GOSPELEER: Over in Rainbow Valley tomorrow there's a couple achin' to be spliced and a twenty-dollar bill achin' to be split. Will you join us?

RAWKINS: Brothers, you are now a quartet!

GOSPELEERS (*ad lib*):
Well, good!
That's fine!

FIRST GOSPELEER: In preparation for this ceremony, we take our text from Genesis, wherein it says Adam and Eve begat Cain and Abel. From thence on the history of this world is just the history of who begat who.

RAWKINS: Now what do I sing in this?

THIRD GOSPELEER: You carry the big theme of this song. All you do is stress the word *Begat* and keep stressing it. Can you remember that?

RAWKINS: I've got it—I've got it!

(*Each, in turn, sounds off a note, rounding out a harmony chord.*)

"The Begat"

THE GOSPELEERS (*singing*):

The Lord made Adam, the Lord made Eve,
He made them both a little bit naive.
They lived as free as the summer breeze,
Without pajamas and without chemise—
Until they stumbled upon the apple trees.

Then she looked at him,
And he looked at her,
And they knew immejitly
What the world was fer!

He said, "Give me my cane!"
He said, "Give me my hat!
"The time has come
"To begin the Begat!"

RAWKINS:

The Begat! The Begat!

GOSPELEERS:

So they Begat Cain, and they Begat Abel,
Who Begat the rabble at the Tower of Babel.
They Begat the Cohens, and they Begat O'Rourkes,
And they Begat the people who believed in storks.

When the Begat got to gettin' under par,
They Begat the Daughters of the D.A.R.
They Begat the Babbitts of the bourgeoisie,
Who Begat the mis-begotten G.O.P.

It was pleasin' to Jezebel, pleasin' to Ruth,
It pleased the League of Women Shoppers in Duluth.
Though the movie censors tried the facts to hide,
The movie goers up and multiplied.

Soon it swept the world,
Every land and lingo,
It became the rage,

RAWKINS:

It was bigger than bingo!

GOSPELEERS:

The white Begat, the red Begat,
The folks who shoulda stood in bed Begat.
The Greeks Begat, the Swedes Begat,
Why, even Britishers in tweeds Begat.
And Lordy, Lordy, what their seeds Begat!

The Lapps and Lithuanians Begat,
Scranton, Pennsylvanians Begat,
Strict vegetarians Begat,
Honorary Aryans Begat,
Starting from Genesis, they Begat,
Fat filibusterers Begat,
Heroes and menaces Begat.
Income-tax adjusterers Begat,
'Twas natchaler and natchaler to Begat
And sometimes a bachelor, he Begat.
It didn't matter which-a-ways they Begat,
Sons of habitués Begat.

So bless them all
Who go to bat
And heed the call
Of the Begat!
(*With newly found quartet camaraderie, they exit.*)

THE CURTAINS CLOSE

SCENE 3

The meetin' place, next day, is church and reception hall for the marriage of WOODY *and* SHARON. *To a reprise of "Look to the Rainbow," sung in a hymnal mood, the bridal party marches on. The girls in bright organdies, the boys in natty Spring suits, the* MOP-PETS *festooning the procession like so many posies, create a rainbow effect of their own.* SHARON *follows the parade, in classic white, her wedding gown hooked to a train which is seemingly made of all the*

daisies in the world. It comes on majestically, endlessly, following her
around the tree in a white parabola whose end is out of sight.

JOHN, *the Negro preacher, performs the ceremony. Little* HONEY
LOU *offers the ring on traditional velvet cushion. The* GOSPELEERS,
now four with RAWKINS, *reprise a bit of "The Begat." The* BRIDES-
MAIDS *unhook the bridal train, kisses are exchanged,* SHARON *tosses*
her bouquet to FINIAN, *the newlyweds start off on a honeymoon—*
and then Southern justice bursts in, in the form of the SHERIFF,
BUZZ, *and three* DEPUTIES, *carrying shotguns.*

SHERIFF: Stand back, everybody. Don't want any trouble here.

WOODY: Well, what *do* you want?

BUZZ: Miss Sharon McLonergan.

SHARON: Mrs. Woody Mahoney.

BUZZ: Well, anyway, we got a warrant for your arrest.

FINIAN: What's the charge, gentlemen?

SHERIFF (*reading from a complaint*): People of the State of Missitucky versus Sharon McLonergan—

BUZZ (*grabbing complaint*): Demotin'! That's the charge.
Demotin' a member of the white race, namely Senator
Rawkins, to a member of the Negro race—by means of
witchcraft.

WOODY: Witchcraft? Still hunting witches, I see.

BUZZ: There's a law against witchcraft in this state.

WOODY: Yeah—passed in 1680. (*Sparring for time.*) Don't you
think it's a little obsolete by now?

SHERIFF (*defensively*): Well, she's gonna get a fair trial, Woody.

WOODY: I can just picture it—a sycamore tree for a courtroom.

FIRST DEPUTY: What do *you* suggest, lettin' her run around
loose, turnin' the whole state black?

BUZZ: Why, you couldn't tell your wife from your cook. You're
wastin' time, Sheriff. Arrest that witch.

SHERIFF (*with bravado but passing the buck*): All right, Alec—
arrest her.

SECOND DEPUTY (*afraid to tangle with any witch*): But I'm only
a deputy. You're the sheriff.

BUZZ (*to* SHERIFF): Quit stallin', Chick. Remember, there's an
election comin' up.

SHERIFF (*advancing reluctantly toward* SHARON *with the* DEPU-
TIES *behind him*): You're under arrest.

(*He backs away as* SHARON *takes a defiant step in his direction—then meekly.*)

I'm only doin' my duty, ma'am.

HENRY: Let's turn 'em into pumpkins and put candles in 'em, Sharon!

SECOND DEPUTY (*as the* DEPUTIES *quickly get together and crouch down*): D-d-don't try any hocus-pocus. (*He dusts some powder over himself and the others from a bottle.*) You can't goofer us now. That's lizard dust.

SHARON: Lizard dust . . . Witchcraft. Can you honestly accuse me of being a witch?

FINIAN (*in a sudden McLonergan flanking movement*): Don't let her bedevil you, gentlemen. A witch she is and a witch she's always been.

SHARON: Father!

DEPUTIES (*ad lib*):

    What are we waitin' for?

    He confesses.

    Her own father!

SHERIFF: Let's go!

(*They make a move to take* SHARON *off.*)

WOODY (*intercepting them*): He's tetched in the head. He doesn't know what he's sayin'!

FINIAN (*spellbinding them*): Don't I, though? Who would know better than me, her unhappy father, who found her on me doorstep, left by a fairy in the moonlight. At the age of two, she could talk with the skylarks, and decode the chirpin' of the crickets. At the age of four, she could blow a rainbow out of a bubble pipe, and then wear her panties out slidin' down it. Then, durin' her adolescence, she took a tragic turn. She began to change whiskey into milk. It was a crisis, a crisis. From then on, one change led to another, and now you are all witnesses to the unhappy climax—she's changed a white man into a black.

(*The valley people are aghast at* FINIAN's *apparent betrayal.*)

WOODY: For God's sake, Pop!

FINIAN: Quiet, Woody—I'm doin' the right thing.

(WOODY *nods his understanding.*)

SHERIFF: All right, men, take her away.

FINIAN (*with sly strategy*): Just a minute, gentlemen. Sharon can also change a black man into a white.

SHERIFF: You mean she can make Rawkins white again?

DEPUTIES:

It's a stall.

Let's get it over with.

WOODY (*carrying forward* FINIAN's *strategy to stall for time*): She'd *better* make Rawkins white again—or you guys are out of jobs. You don't think Billboard's going to be re-elected in that condition, do you? And if he ain't re-elected—you ain't re-appointed.

SHERIFF (*this is an acute political crisis*): Jeepers, that's true!

BUZZ: I never thought of that!

SHERIFF: What'll we do?

> (*The* SHERIFF, BUZZ *and the* DEPUTIES *go into a huddle as* WOODY *and* FINIAN *exchange a quick congratulatory handshake.*)
>
> (*Coming out of huddle.*)

How much time do you figure you'll need to turn him white, ma'am?

RAWKINS (*stepping forward*): I'll have somethin' to say about that!

BUZZ: My God, it's Billboard Rawkins!

RAWKINS: I ain't turnin' white or any other color to keep a pack of crooks like you in office!

SHERIFF: Calm yourself, Billboard. You're in no position to have opinions right now.

RAWKINS: Oh, no? Who the hell's in a *better* position? Boy, can I see both sides of *this* question!

SHERIFF: But you've got to see *our* side—our whole livelihood's at stake.

BUZZ (*a threat, but with respect*): Besides, Mr. Rawkins, as a Negro you've got no rights in this state—

SHERIFF: Definitely not.

BUZZ: Not even the right to stay black. So you've *gotta* turn white!

RAWKINS: I can stay black if I want to! I got congressional immunity! Furthermore, I refuse to be brought forth at any witchcraft trial as Exhibit A. It ain't progressive!

SHERIFF: We can't afford to let go of him. Tie 'im up, boys.

RAWKINS: Why, you bunch of medieval—

(FIRST DEPUTY *gags him and takes him off.*)

WOODY: Great speech, Senator, but the wrong kind of logic.

(*He slugs the* SECOND DEPUTY. *They scuffle and the* SHERIFF *knocks* WOODY *out with his gun butt.*)

SECOND DEPUTY (*to the groggy* WOODY): You're under arrest for aidin' and abettin' witchcraft!

(*He and* THIRD DEPUTY *lift* WOODY *to his feet.*)

SHERIFF: Now, how much time do you figure you'll need, ma'am?

FINIAN (*airily*): Ah, for Sharon it's child's play. Just give her till the crack of dawn.

SHERIFF: All right, the crack of dawn. Take them away, men. If she makes good, I'll withdraw all charges against both of 'em.

SECOND DEPUTY: And if she don't, there'll be three on that sycamore tree.

(*They bundle* SHARON *and* WOODY *off.*)

BUZZ: Remember, McLonergan—it's the crack of dawn or the crack of doom. (*He exits.*)

FINIAN (*jauntily, to the worried crowd*): My friends, be of good cheer. The crock's in the ground, all's right with the world. Just see that no one comes up the hill, especially a little green fella with horns in his head. He's the nemesis on me premises. Now scatter yourselves.

(*The minute they are out of sight,* FINIAN *lightheartedly dances up stage, singing as he goes, to the spot where he buried the crock. He reaches in for it—and panic sets in.*)

It's gone! It's not there! Og! Leprechaun! Nemesis! (*He runs off wildly into the lowering dusk, calling.*) Og! Og!

THE CURTAINS CLOSE

SCENE 4

The meetin' place, early next morning. SUSAN *appears and steps down the rocks, carrying her newly found treasure, a golden glow against the gray of dawn. Its thrill of enchantment still seems to tingle through her. She places it delicately inside a hollow log, covers the opening with twigs, then, satisfied it is safe, skips over and sits on the rim of the stone well. She fixes her hair, to her reflected image in the water, and, of course, does not hear the plaintive voice of* OG *calling—*

OG'S VOICE: Sharon! (*He leaps in and calls again.*)

OG: Sharon! (*And still getting no answer, he kneels at* SUSAN'S *back.*) Look at me, Sharon! I'm ninety percent mortal now— and a hundred percent miserable. It's a frenzy, a frenzy—and there's no cure for it but you. I'm feeling better already, just being near you. The scent of your hair, the touch of your hand— (*He gingerly touches her hand, which she smilingly takes. He continues with head down, not seeing her.*) Oh, the miracle of it! The sweet, sweet miracle of it!
(*Not conditioned by amatory clichés, he invents his own tribute: he bites her in the leg. She sends him sprawling on his back with a resounding slap and runs a few steps away.*)
She loves me! Her hand fits my cheek! (*He gets up, and goes over to her.*) Oh, Sharon, you are the only one, the only one! (*He stops short when he sees it is* SUSAN.) But you're not Sharon at all. You're Susan the Silent. And yet I feel the same frenzy— for you! Is this what it's like to be mortal? Is every girl the only girl? I'm beginning to like it.

"When I'm Not Near the Girl I Love"

OG (*singing*):

> Oh, my heart is beating wildly,
> And it's all because you're here,
> When I'm not near the girl I love
> I love the girl I'm near.
>
> Ev'ry femme that flutters by me
> Is a flame that must be fanned;
> When I can't fondle the hand I'm fond of
> I fondle the hand at hand.
>
> My heart's in a pickle,
> It's constantly fickle
> And not too partickle, I fear.
> When I'm not near the girl I love,
> I love the girl I'm near.

What if they're tall or tender?
What if they're small or slender?
Long as they've got that gender—
I s'rrender.
Always I can't refuse 'em,
Always my feet pursues 'em,
Long as they've got a bosom—
I woos 'em.
(*They do a little dance together.*)
I'm confessing a confession,
And I hope I'm not verbose:
When I'm not close to the kiss that I cling to
I cling to the kiss that's close.

As I'm more and more a mortal
I am more and more a case.
When I'm not facing the fact that I fancy
I fancy the face I face.

For Sharon I'm carin',
But Susan I'm choosin'—
I'm faithful to whos'n is here.
When I'm not near the girl I love,
I love the girl I'm near!
(OG*'s romantic performance, which* SUSAN *at least has heard with her eyes, melts her into his arms as he finishes singing.*)

(*A desperate and beaten-looking* FINIAN *enters, carrying a shovel.*)

FINIAN: So there you are! The wrath of Ozymandias on you! From dusk to sun-up I've searched forest and hill for you— and here you are, philanderin' in the arms of a woman.

OG (*innocently*): Is there anything wrong with that?

FINIAN: Wrong! At a moment like this? Have ye forgotten me daughter, Sharon?

OG: Of course not. (*Puts* SUSAN *down.*) She's the woman I love— present company excepted.

FINIAN: Have ye forgotten the shamrock of her eyes, and her voice like the bells of St. Mary's?

OG: Has anything happened?

FINIAN: Aye, it has. This is her last sunrise. In twenty minutes, at the crack of dawn, the glory that was Sharon and the lad that was her beloved will perish in smoke and flame.

OG: Oh, I told you that gold could only bring you doom and gloom, gloom and doom.

FINIAN: Don't blame the gold. You're the culprit!

OG: I?

FINIAN: Yes, you. If you weren't a leprechaun, you'd have had no pot of gold. If you'd had no pot of gold, I wouldn't have been forced to borrow it, I'd never have come to this primitive country, and me daughter wouldn't have burned at the stake for witchcraft.

OG: It's my fault, all my fault. The merciful saints forgive me.

FINIAN: And her poor broken father will forgive you, too, if you'll spare a little magic for her.

OG: I'll do anything! Anything, Mr. McLonergan!

FINIAN: Then turn the Senator white again, in God's name, and save Sharon's life.

OG: Why, of course. I can do it in a minute—and we'll have nineteen minutes left.

FINIAN: Thank Heaven! I knew you wouldn't fail me.

OG: But wait. Why not delay things nineteen minutes, and then we can save her at the last minute? It's more dramatic.

FINIAN: Now, Og, now, in Heaven's name! It's life and death!

OG: Very well. All I need is one little thing from you.

FINIAN: Speak, man, what is it, what is it you need?

OG: The crock of gold.

FINIAN (*livid*): Oh, give me strength. Give me strength to resist me own strength, to keep from chokin' him to death. How can you stand there that brazen and pretend you haven't got it?

OG: But I haven't got it.

FINIAN: Well, if you haven't got it, why can't I find it? I've dug more holes this weary night than all the gophers in Christendom.

OG: Think back to the night you buried it, Mr. McLonergan. Exactly what were you doing?

FINIAN (*crossing to the burial place of the crock*): Well, I was standing here with the jug of whiskey in one hand and the crock of gold in the other—

OG: —and for all you know, you might have buried the jug and swallowed the crock.

FINIAN (*furiously as he chases* OG): Why you Machiavellian half-pint pirate, stealin' me property. Where is it?

OG (*retreating to the log*): I wish I had it.

FINIAN: I'll throttle it out o' ye! (*He starts choking* OG.) Where is it, you rascally little rogue?

OG (*forced to sit on the log, over the crock*): I wish I—

FINIAN (*still choking him*): Where is it, you perfidious, scurvy, snivelin' little wretch?

OG: I wish I—

FINIAN: Tell me!

GIRL (*entering*): Sharon's calling for you, Mr. McLonergan. They're tying her and Woody to a tree!

FINIAN (*relinquishing his hold on* OG): They can't do it! They can't do it! (*Brandishing his shovel.*) It'll be one of me or a hundred of them! (*To* OG—*pleading—now a pathetic old man who would trade all the gold in Eldorado for* SHARON's *safety.*) Og, if you have a mite of merciful magic left in you, help me save Sharon.

GIRL: Hurry, Mr. McLonergan.

(FINIAN *exits with* GIRL.)

OG: Oh, Susan, it's a crisis, a crisis. They're going to kill Sharon for a witch. But she's not a witch! (*Suddenly staggered by a thought.*) She must have made a wish over the crock! (*Terribly excited.*) Susan, you must have seen her do it! Where was she standing? Oh, dear, you can't hear. I'll have to ask someone else. (*He starts off, then stops short.*) But there's no time. We've only got two minutes left! I'll dance you the question—you dance me the answer!

(*He goes into a frantic and futile little dance which* SUSAN *mistakes for more lovemaking.* OG *sits on log, defeated.*)

Oh, Susan, I love you, but I wish to God you could talk.

SUSAN (*slowly, trying out her lips for the first time*): I . . . love . . . you.

OG (*taken unaware by the double miracle*): Oh, what beautiful new words. Say them again, Susan.

SUSAN (*moving closer to* OG): I . . . love . . . you.

OG (*in a vibrato wail*): Ah, she loves me, she loves me— (*He lets out a piercing scream of realization.*) Susan, you're talking, you're talking! Tell me, where was Sharon standing?

SUSAN (*with a third inflection, still testing the new phenomenon of speech*): I . . . love . . . *you.*

OG: Oh, I know that, but— (*Bombshell.*) You're talking! That means I wished you into it! That means I was sitting over the crock! (*He scratches wildly at the twigs which block the opening— then suddenly stops in terror.*) Oh, but there's only one wish left. It's the last wish. If I use it to wish the Senator white, I can never be a leprechaun again. (*A red glow lights the sky and a doleful cry goes up from the crowd off scene.*) Oh, dear, what shall I do? I don't want to be a mortal, I want to go back to Fairyland!

(*Now* SUSAN *is very close indeed—close enough to give* OG *the first kiss of his life. His voice instantly drops to a virile bass.*)

Fairyland was never like this!

(*He grabs her and kisses her—and from now on not only does* OG's *voice change, but his character undergoes a glandular upheaval and takes on a rough, cavalier manner.*)

Gad, woman, we've only got half a minute! (*Shouting off scene in the direction of the stake ceremonies.*) Rawkins, you blackguard—I wish you white!

(*There is a crash of noise which shatters the heavens.*)

SUSAN: What's that?

OG: The crack of dawn.

(*And the dawn indeed comes up like thunder. Rose-tinged sunlight floods the scene.* SUSAN *looks on in wonder at the metamorphosis as she moves off with* OG. *The crowd surges on with* SHARON, WOODY *and* FINIAN, *singing a lusty reprise of "If This Isn't Love." At its finish,* SUSAN *dances in.*)

WOODY: What's she saying, Henry?

HENRY (*watching her feet*): She says she can talk!

(*She stops.*)

WOODY: Gee, Sis, is it true?

(*She replies with a few more brisk steps.*)

HENRY: She says cross her heart, it's true.

WOODY: Say something, Susie. I've been waiting twenty years for this moment.

(*They quiet down and listen.*)

SUSAN: I love him. I love him. I love him.

WOODY: Who's the lucky guy?

(OG *debonairly saunters in, twirling a cane and sporting a blue derby hat. He is followed by* BUZZ *and the* SHERIFF.)

OG: The name is Og. (*He hands out calling cards.*) My card. (*Greeting* SUSAN *with a kiss.*) Hi'ya, sugar. (*Turns to* FINIAN.) McLonergan, now that I'm a hundred percent mortalish, I've got a deal lined up for you. (*Indicating* BUZZ.) My client here is offering you a hundred grand to dig the gold out of your property. You keep the land. Usual ten percent for me, of course.

WOODY: Rawkins behind this too?

BUZZ: Uh—uh. Company dropped Bill from the Board.

SHERIFF: Poor fellow got his color back, but never recovered his senses.

(RAWKINS *enters with a gift box under his arm. He is now restored to his pristine whiteness, and though regenerated, is the same dynamo.*)

RAWKINS: Greetings, neighbors, greetings! (*To* HENRY *as he hands him the box.*) Mr. Henry, you're lookin' fine today!

SHERIFF: See what I mean?

OG: McLonergan, I'm a busy man. How about that gold concession deal?

BUZZ: Hundred thousand, you know, a hundred thousand.

RAWKINS: What do you mean, a hundred thousand? It's worth a quarter of a million if it's worth a quarter! (*As though making the offer himself.*) What do you say, McLonergan?

FINIAN (*coyly*): Well, I don't like this petty bickerin'. I accept.

RAWKINS: All right, Buzz, write out a check.

(BUZZ *does so.*)

WOODY: But you're not with the company any more—

RAWKINS: No, son, I'm with the people. All part of my new platform—anti–poll tax, a dam in every valley, and a rainbow in every pot. And incidentally, I'm runnin' for re-election next November.

BUZZ: Here you are, McLonergan, a quarter of a million dollars.

(BUZZ *starts to hand the check to* FINIAN, *but* SHARON *takes it.*)

SHARON (*sternly, to* FINIAN): Endorse it to the Relief Fund for Unemployed Leprechauns, Glocca Morra County, Ireland.

FINIAN: But, Sharon— (*Then gaily as he writes.*) Well, why not? There's plenty more where *it* came from—the crock's in the ground, all's right with the world.

SUSAN (*linking her arm with* OG's): Isn't he grandish, Woody? He wished me into talking.

FINIAN (*staggered*): You mean you used the crock to wish back Susan's tongue?

OG: It wasn't a cyclotron, Bub.

FINIAN: Then you've used up the third and last wish?

OG: Well, natch—can't you see I'm all mortal now?

FINIAN: Then the little gold crock has turned to worthless dross!

OG: That's right. I'll show it to you. (*He disappears behind the crowd.*)

FINIAN: This is the final crisis. Everything is collapsin' about us.

SHARON: Father, how can you say that? We have calico gowns, tobacco leaves, prosperity—

FINIAN: It's all temporary. This little boom is founded on an illusion.

OG (*comes forward with his derby covering the crock*): Dross, McLonergan, like I told you. (*He brings forth the crock of gold. But it has, alas! lost its glow, its poetry, and its shape. It is now a drab and battered kitchen utensil unworthy of even a pawnshop.*)

FINIAN (*holding it up*): Behold the little pot of gold that man has sat on so smugly for centuries.

RAWKINS: Pretty little antique. Make a nice lamp.

FINIAN (*giving* RAWKINS *the crock*): May it throw some light on you. Keep it as a souvenir of a dyin' age. Ah, things are indeed hopeless, hopeless— (*Reverting to type, with a roar.*) But they're not serious! I'm ready for reconversion! (*He picks up the little carpetbag he arrived with.*) Do you know what's in this bag? A pair of socks—and the fate of Wall Street. A toothbrush—and the wealth of empires. (*Opening the bag.*) The world of tomorrow in the palm of me hands. (*He shows them a small jagged rock.*)

RAWKINS: Why, that's just an ordinary piece of moonstone.

WOODY: He's right, Pop.

FINIAN: Ah, you're blind. You can only see what you're lookin' at. Inside this piece of stone is a whole multitude of gnomes, elves and fairy folk, like Neutron the Latent and Proton the Potent, ready to go to work for you and bring you all happiness.

HENRY: Gee, where'd you get it, Mr. McLonergan?

FINIAN: From a friend of mine, named Nicholas the Nucleus.
(*He replaces it in the bag and starts off.*)

SHARON: Father, are you leaving us?

FINIAN (*stopping*): Aye, lass. I've outlived Fort Knox.

WOODY: But where are you going?

FINIAN: To Oak Ridge, Tennessee!
(*A lovely rainbow arches over the scene.*)

HENRY: Snagdrab—a rainbow!

FINIAN: Aye, Finian's rainbow. It never fails to come up when the McLonergans are down. (*To* WOODY *and* SHARON.) I turn it over to you as Ford the First turned over his factory to Ford the Third. Sure, there's no longer a pot o' gold at the end of it—but a beautiful new world under it. Make it shine for Sharon. (*He kisses* SHARON *a tender good-bye.*) Farewell, me friends. I'll see you all some day in Glocca Morra. (*He starts away along the curving arc of the rainbow.*)

WOODY: Sharon, where *is* Glocca Morra?

SHARON (*mysteriously*): There's no such place, Woody. It's only in Father's head.
(*Singing.*)
   So to every weepin' willow,
   To each brook along the way,
   To each lad that comes a-whistlin'
   Too-ra-lay—
(*The others join their voices with hers.*)
   May we meet in Glocca Morra
   Some fine day!

THE CURTAIN FALLS

KISS ME, KATE

A MUSICAL PLAY

Music and lyrics by COLE PORTER

Book by SAMUEL *and* BELLA SPEWACK

To
W. S.
from
B. S. *and* S. S.

KISS ME, KATE

THIS is a story of show business.

It is a musical love story of the eternal serio-comic battle of male and female played against the events of an opening night of the tryout of a musical version of Shakespeare's *Taming of the Shrew* at Ford's Theatre in Baltimore.

The entire action of this musical takes place in and around the theatre, starting about five o'clock of a hot afternoon at the finish of a run-through of *The Shrew* on bare stage and winding up at midnight in full panoply.

You will meet your actors as mere mortals with toothaches and heartaches and go with them through the metamorphosis of make-up and costuming to their nightly immortality behind the footlights.

Your leading contenders in the battle of egos are Frederick Graham—actor, producer, director—and Lilli Vanessi, Hollywood star, who were once married to each other and terribly in love. They still are, on this, the first anniversary of their divorce. But neither will admit it.

The musical is a play within a play, the personal story paralleling Shakespeare's *Shrew,* and at certain points the action of one flows right into the action of the other.

Fred and Lilli are both short-tempered, selfish, lovable, and vulnerable. Both are hams. The drudgery of four weeks' rehearsal hasn't been conducive to any meeting of the minds, much less the hearts; especially as Lilli notes that Fred seems to have more than a producer's interest in Lois Lane, whom he found singing in a cheap night club. (Lois plays Bianca, younger sister to Lilli's Katharine, in *The Shrew.*)

Fred on his part can't help noting the growing interest of Harrison Howell, the "angel" of the show, in Lilli. Harrison Howell is a kind of younger statesman, whose extreme wealth allows him to play adviser to the Administration. He is a gentleman, a scholar, and a bore.

Lois Lane is strictly on the make. There's only one man for her, Bill Calhoun, a bit actor and hoofer in the show. She's

got Bill the job and kept a wary eye on him during rehearsals, knowing his weakness for gambling. But between the time
the company is dismissed after the run-through and the time it
returns to go through the opening night, Bill gets into a friendly
poker game—and loses. Lois learns that he impersonated Fred
Graham at the game, and thereby hangs our plot.

SYNOPSIS OF SCENES

MUSICAL NUMBERS

ACT ONE

Scene 1
Another O'p'nin', Another Show .... Hattie and Ensemble

Scene 2
Why Can't You Behave? .... Lois Lane

Scene 3
Wunderbar............................ Lilli and Fred
So in Love Lilli

Scene 4
Padua Street Song......Petruchio, Katharine, Bianca, Lucentio

Scene 5
Tom, Dick, or Harry ... Bianca, Lucentio, and the Two Suitors
Specialty Dance............................Lucentio
I've Come to Wive It Wealthily in Padua. ....Petruchio and
Ensemble
I Hate Men .... Katharine
Were Thine That Special Face .... Petruchio

Scene 8
I Sing of Love .... Bianca, Lucentio, and Ensemble
Finale: *Kiss Me, Kate* ....Katharine, Petruchio,
and Ensemble

ACT TWO

Scene 1
Too Darn Hot..................... Paul, Fred, and Sledge

Scene 3
Where is the Life That Late I Led?............... Petruchio

ACT ONE

SCENE I

SCENE: *The bare stage of Ford's Theatre in Baltimore, the land of Mencken and nod. It's hot. It's sticky. It's late afternoon. It's June. Numbered flats of the painted sets lean against the rear brick wall. Stagehands move leisurely in and out of the wings. The bright glare of a single bulb known in the theatre as a pilot light sharpens the faces of the actors and dancers within its orbit. They have just finished a run-through rehearsal of the musical version of* The Taming of the Shrew, *and are standing around in their street clothes in groups of two and three, presumably all ears for last-minute directorial criticism. What they're really thinking about is food and if they'll have time to eat before the show starts. Actors have to eat even if it's the opening night of a tryout.*

FREDERICK GRAHAM, *writer, director, actor, and superman, is out in the empty theatre listening to the overture as he wants it played.* LILLI VANESSI, *motion-picture star and once married to* GRAHAM, *is seated on a chair on stage right, obviously seething.* LOIS LANE *is standing, talking to* RALPH, *the stage manager, on stage left.*

CONDUCTOR (*at the end of the overture*): Is that all right, Mr. Graham?

FRED (*enters from theatre*): Yes, the cut's good, leave it in. (*Reading through notes on clipboard.*) Baptista.

    (HARRY TREVOR, *an elderly actor, steps forward.* HATTIE, LILLI's *Negro maid, enters, crosses to* LILLI *with glass of water, then exits.*)

Harry, be sure and shake off Gremio and Hortensio in that entrance in the street scene.

HARRY: *Si, signor.* Mr. Graham is it all right if—

FRED: In a minute, Harry—Bianca—

    (LOIS LANE *turns to* FRED.)

LOIS (*coyly*): Yes, Fred. I mean, Mr. Graham.

FRED: I realize, Lois, that in night-club work you don't have to cheat—

LOIS (*interrupting*): Oh, don't you though?

443

FRED: You don't have to cheat front, Miss Lane, but on stage when you're playing scenes with other people, you do. This is your first show and I know it's hard for you.

(LILLI *says nothing, but glares.*)

LOIS (*almost baby-wise*): Do you mean thus—(*of course she turns wrong*) or thus?

FRED: We'll thus it later.

(LOIS *retreats.* FRED *crosses to* RALPH *left.*)

HARRY (*crosses down left to* FRED): Mr. Graham, is it all right if I leave now? I can just make the dentist. Upper plate wobble.

FRED: In a minute, Harry. All right, let's set the curtain calls. First call all principals.

(*Principals step forward.*)

Miss Vanessi, care to join us? (LILLI *does so.*) Thank you! Leave room for me. Baptista, change places with Gremio.

(*They change places.*)

That's right. Looks like somebody's missing—Lucentio— where the hell's Lucentio?

RALPH (*looking off stage left and right, yelling*): Bill Calhoun! Bill Calhoun!

VOICE OFF STAGE: Bill Calhoun!

RALPH: He *was* here.

FRED: Give a Broadway hoofer a chance to play Shakespeare and what happens? He isn't even here.

LOIS (*who has been trying to attract their attention*): I think he went to the chiropodist.

FRED: Second call—Harry, run along to your dentist.

HARRY: Much obliged old man. . . . (*Exits left.*)

FRED: Second call, Bianca and Suitors—thank you, that looks all right. (*Hands* RALPH *clipboard and moves toward center.*) Third call—myself and Miss Vanessi.

(LILLI VANESSI *steps forward.*)

Excuse me— (*Turns from her.*) Lois!

LOIS (*stops when* FRED *calls*): Did thou call me, honey?

(*She moves toward him.* LILLI *glares.*)

FRED (*puts his arm on her shoulder*): I'd rather you didn't leave the theatre between now and opening.

LOIS (*very much gal with man*): Whatever thou say, Fred.

FRED: I want you to rest and relax, and let your mind go blank. Blank!

LOIS: How blank can it get? Honest—those *thee*'s and *thou*'s—I hope I don't louse you up. (*She exits.*)

(*Stagehands exit with ladders.* FRED *turns toward* LILLI, *who's been waiting with suppressed anger.*)

FRED: Now. Sorry to have kept you waiting, Miss Vanessi. (*To* RALPH.) Now watch it, Ralph—call it!

RALPH: Third call!

(FRED *and* LILLI *bow to each other and the audience.*)

FRED: No, I think it would look better if we came down together—and then bowed to each other.

(*They walk upstage.* FRED *takes* LILLI's *hand, walks downstage with her. They bow to audience, then to each other.* FRED *pauses in middle of bow.*)

(*To* LILLI.) Now, how about a smile, Miss Vanessi? Ready? (*She smiles, curtsies.*)

LILLI (*still curtsying and smiling, looking straight at* FRED, *as he bows*): You bastard!

(LILLI *stalks off stage right.* FRED, *startled, looks after her.*)
(*Music starts.*)

FRED (*turning back angrily*): Call them on, Ralph.

RALPH: On stage everybody!

(SINGERS, DANCERS, *and* HATTIE *enter.*)

FRED: I want to thank each and every one of you for the fine spirit you've shown all through rehearsals. There'll be a gang down from New York, don't let that worry you. This is a tryout and I know we're going to make a helluva show out of *The Shrew.* After all, we owe it to Shakespeare, not to mention the six other fellows who've been sitting up nights rewriting him. That's all. Thank you.

(*Exits angrily right. Stagehand strikes* LILLI's *chair, right, during speech.*)

(TWO SINGING GIRLS *bring* HATTIE *down center,* HATTIE *begins:*)

"Another Op'nin', Another Show"

HATTIE:

Another op'nin', another show
In Philly, Boston, or Baltimo'e,
A chance for stage-folks to say "Hello,"
Another op'nin' of another show,

Another job that you hope, at last,
Will make your future forget your past,
Another pain where the ulcers grow,
Another op'nin' of another show.
Four weeks, you rehearse and rehearse,
Three weeks, and it couldn't be worse,
One week, will it ever be right?
Then out o' the hat, it's that big first night!
The overture is about to start,
You cross your fingers and hold your heart,
It's curtain time and away we go,
Another op'nin',
Of another show.

HATTIE and ENSEMBLE:

Another op'nin', another show
In Philly, Boston, or Baltimo'e,
A chance for stage-folks to say "Hello,"
Another op'nin' of another show,
Another job that you hope, at last,
Will make your future forget your past,
Another pain where the ulcers grow,
Another op'nin' of another show.
Four weeks, you rehearse and rehearse,
Three weeks, and it couldn't be worse,
One week, will it ever be right?
Then out o' the hat, it's that big first night!
The overture is about to start,
You cross your fingers and hold your heart,
It's curtain time and away we go,
Another op'nin' of another show.

(*As* HATTIE *and* SINGERS *exit,* DANCERS *in practice costumes enter in twos and threes and go through routines of ballet exercises, waltz and jazz movements. Electricians checking on lights bathe the dancers in alternate floods of pink, blue, and amber. As the dance finishes,* HATTIE *and* SINGERS *come back on stage to join* DANCERS *in the final chorus of "Another Op'nin', Another Show."*)

HATTIE:

Four weeks, you rehearse and rehearse,

Three weeks, and it couldn't be worse.
One week, will it ever be right?
Then out o' the hat, it's that big first night!

ALL:

The overture is about to start,
You cross your fingers and hold your heart,
It's curtain time and away we go,
Another op'nin',
Just another op'nin', of another show.

BLACKOUT

SCENE 2

SCENE: *Corridor backstage. Spiral staircase stage right.* DOOR-
MAN'*s booth stage left. Coin-box telephone attached to upstage corner
of booth. Backdrop depicts corridor of theatre.*

BOYS *and* GIRLS *separate, some exit left. Others move briskly to
iron staircase and exit,* LOIS *is at telephone.* DOORMAN *in his booth.*

LOIS (*on phone*): Hello! Hello! Is Bill Calhoun there? I said Bill
    Calhoun! Well, you don't have to be so fresh about it! (*Hangs
    up.*) Pop, let me know the minute Mr. Calhoun comes in. (*She
    moves toward staircase.*)
PAUL (*bearing* FRED'*s first-act costume,* PAUL *is* FRED'*s Negro
    dresser*): Miss Lane, you got two dollars?
LOIS: What do you want two dollars for?
PAUL: It ain't for me. It's for Mr. Calhoun.
LOIS: Where is he?
    (DOORMAN *leaves booth, stands by phone.*)
PAUL: He's a prisoner of the Yellow Cab Company.
    (BILL *enters from door with* CAB DRIVER, *smoking cigarette.
    He whistles first three notes of "Bianca."*)
LOIS: Bill!
BILL: Hiya, Sarah Bernhardt!
CAB DRIVER: I want my fare.
    (HARRY *enters stage right.*)
BILL (*shaking dice*): Shoot you for it—double or nothing!
    (CAB DRIVER *shakes his head.*)
PAUL (*calling* LOIS'*s attention to* HARRY): Psst! Psst!
LOIS: Harry, you got two dollars?

HARRY: Child, if I had two dollars, I'd retire and never do a lick of work again! (*Exits.*)

LOIS: Paul, do you suppose Mr. Graham's got two dollars?

PAUL: Mr. Graham? Not him! He's a producer! (PAUL *exits.*)

LOIS (*to* CAB DRIVER): Can you wait until Saturday night? (DRIVER *shakes head, "No."*)

DOORMAN (*steps forward*): All right, Miss Lane. I'll lay it out! That'll make sixteen dollars.

> (CAB DRIVER *exits, followed by* DOORMAN. DOORMAN *returns to his stool in booth and reads racing form.*)

LOIS: Bill, you've been gambling again. And I told Mr. Graham you went to the chiropodist's.

BILL: I went to the cleaner's. (*Turning out empty trouser pockets.*)

LOIS: How much did you lose this time?

BILL: Ten G's. Ten thousand fast little bucks!

LOIS: Ten G's? Did you sign an IOU again?

BILL: Uhuh!

LOIS: Whose name did you sign this time?

BILL: Frederick Graham! (*Writes the name in the air.*)

LOIS: Mr. Graham! Oh, Bill! This is our big chance. Do you want to play night clubs all your life?

BILL: We were doing all right, weren't we?

LOIS: Yeah, it's as Mr. Graham said: "Give a Broadway hoofer a chance to play Shakespeare and . . ."

BILL: Mr. Graham—your hero!

LOIS: Mr. Graham is a great actor, a scholar, and a gentleman. He's just culturing me—but there's nothing wrong between him and I—I mean he and I.

BILL (*crosses to staircase*): I know. . . . Art!

LOIS: I'll never forgive you, Bill, if anything happens to Mr. Graham before I'm a star on Broadway. (*Crosses onto stairs.*)

BILL (*at foot of stairs*): Gee, honey, I'm sorry.

LOIS: If you only meant it! (*And* LOIS *sings.*)

"Why Can't You Behave?"
Why can't you behave?
(BILL *sits on platform.*)
Oh, why can't you behave?
After all the things you told me
And the promises that you gave,
Oh, why can't you behave?

Why can't you be good?
And do just as you should?
Won't you turn that new leaf over
So your baby can be your slave?
Oh, why can't you behave?

There's a farm I know near my old home town
Where two can go and try settlin' down,
There I'll care for you forever,
Well at least till you dig my grave,
(BILL *rises.*)
Oh, why can't you behave?
(*Takes off hat.*)

BILL:

Gee. I need yuh, kid.

LOIS:

I always knew you did
But why can't you behave?

LIGHTS FADE OUT

SCENE 3

SCENE: *Dressing-rooms, with* FRED's *room right and* LILLI's *room left. A connecting door between the rooms is open.* LILLI's *room is elaborate, with a chaise lounge, poufs, dressing-table with mirror and chair, rug on floor, and phone on table left. Elaborate screen. Dressing-table holds make-up mirror and make-up of all kinds. Also a jewel case and a small photo of a nude baby. Suitcase handy.*

FRED's *room is drab, with steam pipes showing on ceiling. Sink in upper right corner; dressing-table with make-up mirror and make-up box downstage, waste basket, old towel. An old wardrobe trunk open revealing a couple of garments. Screen and a suitcase and hatbox on a shelf, plain chair in front of table.*

FRED (*shouting angrily toward* LILLI's *room*): Calling me a bastard and on stage.
LILLI (*from her room*): I didn't say it—I just indicated it.
(RALPH *knocks at* LILLI's *door.*)
RALPH: Half hour.
LILLI: Thank you, Ralph. Oh, this heat.

RALPH (*moving to* FRED's *room*): You know Baltimore!

FRED: How's the house?

RALPH: You know Baltimore!

FRED: I know. There'll be deer running around the balcony. Next time I open a show here, I'll bring my shotgun and eat.

    (RALPH *exits, calling.*)

RALPH (*off stage*): Half hour.

FRED (*entering* LILLI's *room*): Hah! So much for a Hollywood name. Your fans must have heard you were appearing in person. (*Phone rings.*) Go on, pick it up—it's probably Harrison.

LILLI (*picks up phone*): Hello, hello, Harrison darling. I thought you'd be here by now. (*Puts part down on dressing-table.*) Oh, you're still at the White House? He is? He's taking your advice? He's getting a player piano? What? The President wants to talk to me? To unimportant little me? . . . But what'll I say? Good evening, Mr. President.

FRED (*grabbing phone and speaking into it*): Is it true, Mr. President, you're serving borscht at the White House?

LILLI (*pulls phone away from* FRED): How dare you! Mr. President, I apologize. I beg your pardon? . . . With sour cream.

FRED: What did I tell you?

LILLI: Thank you, Mr. President. . . . Hello, Harrison. . . . I wish you'd come tonight, angel, after all, it's your show. . . . Yes, angel . . . I understand . . . yes, darling . . . yes, love. I'm blowing you two kisses. (*Two kisses into phone.*)

    (FRED *blows two kisses at same time* LILLI *does.* HATTIE *enters with vase of roses.*)

FRED (*sneezing*): Roses! Get those damn roses out of here—you know I'm allergic to roses. I'll break out in a rash again and you know where.

LILLI: Hattie! Take these roses to Miss Lane's dressing-room with my compliments!

    (HATTIE *exits with roses.* LILLI *displays resplendent ring for* FRED's *benefit.*)

FRED: I see it! I see it! What is it? The Hope Diamond or Aly Khan's emerald?

LILLI: Did I show you the star sapphire Harrison sent me? It was his mother's engagement ring.

FRED: His mother must have worn it on her big toe.

LILLI (*beaming pridefully*): And now it's mine! (*Sits on couch.*)

FRED: Congratulations!

LILLI: Do you know what day this is, Fred? Our anniversary, and you forgot.

FRED: What anniversary?

LILLI (*sweetly*): The first anniversary of our divorce.

FRED: If you must know, I was thinking of sending you a cactus. But, no money. I know you're rolling in it.

LILLI: Every night before I go to bed, that's exactly what I do. Roll in my money. Wonderful for the hips. (*She pats one and moves to sit at dressing-table.*)

FRED (*bitterly*): Hollywood—swimming-pool—avocado ranches. While I—I put every penny I could scrape, borrow, or steal into my *Cyrano* in Paris. My magnum opus! But I was a huge success.

LILLI (*looking into mirror*): And you closed on Saturday? Four glorious performances!

FRED: I'll have you know, there was a general strike!

LILLI (*with mock sympathy and looking right at* FRED): Oh, you couldn't have been that bad!

FRED: Same old Lilli! (*Picks up photo on dresser.*) Who's this little monster? Harrison Howell?

LILLI: That's you at the age of two—bottoms up!

FRED: Cute little fellow. Mind if I keep it?

LILLI: No. And you can have this, too. (*Holding up cork and rising.*)

FRED: What's this? A cork?

LILLI: Our first bottle of champagne.

FRED: Our wedding breakfast?

LILLI: Yes, in my apartment.

FRED: You mean that one room of yours over the Armenian bakery?

LILLI: You're a fine one to complain. You didn't even have a room.

FRED: Why do you think I married you? (*Sits on couch.*)

LILLI (*thinking back*): That was the season we played the Barter Theatre in Virginia and they gave you a ham.

FRED (*stung*): Well, we lived on that all winter, you forget!

LILLI: *You* forget I got a job reading tea leaves in a Gypsy tea room opposite Macy's. (*Sits on couch beside him.*)

FRED: And *you* forget *I* demonstrated shaving-soap in Woolworth's.

LILLI (*suddenly remembering*): That's right. That's how I spent my honeymoon—at Woolworth's. Watching you shave.

FRED: We weren't married then?

LILLI (*nodding*): Oh yes, dear, we were. Mother was coming to stay with us. It was right after we closed on the road in a little British makeshift of a Viennese operetta that for some reason was laid in Switzerland. But the costumes were Dutch.

FRED: And so were those salaries. I could have sworn it was right after that flop revival of the *Prince of Potsdam*. Yes, I was understudying the lead. I was the youngest understudy in the business.

LILLI: No, dear. We were both in the chorus.

(*Music starts.*)

There was a waltz in it. Remember? Something about a bar. (*She starts to hum.*)

FRED (*rises*): *Ja!* Madame, you are ravishing tonight. . . . You have made me the happiest of men.

LILLI (*rising, goes to* FRED): Your Highness.

(*Both suddenly remember and speak.*)

FRED: *Wunderbar!*

LILLI: *Wunderbar!*

"Wunderbar"

FRED and LILLI:

SHE:

> *Wunderbar.*

HE:

> *Wunderbar!*

SHE:

> There's our fav'rite star above.

HE:

> What a bright-shining star!

BOTH:

> Like our love, it's *wunderbar!*
> (FRED, *back of lounge.* LILLI *sits on lounge.*)
> (*Verse*)

HE:

> Gazing down on the Jungfrau

SHE:

> From our secret chalet for two,

HE:

     Let us drink, *Liebchen mein,*

SHE:

     In the moonlight benign,

BOTH:

     To the join of our dream come true.
     (*Refrain*)

BOTH:

     Wunderbar, wunderbar!
     (*He takes her hand.*)

HE:

     What a perfect night for love,

SHE:

     Here am I, here you are,
     (*Rises.*)

HE:

     Why, it's truly *wunderbar!*

BOTH:

     Wunderbar, wunderbar!

HE:

     We're alone and hand in glove,

SHE:

     Not a cloud near or far,

HE:

     Why, it's more than *wunderbar!*

SHE:

     Say you care, dear,

HE:

     For you madly.

SHE:

     Say you long, dear,

HE:

     For your kiss.

SHE:

     Do you swear, dear?
     (*Turns and takes his hand.*)

HE:

     Darling, gladly,

SHE:

     Life's divine, dear,

HE:

> And you're mine, dear!
> (*Embrace.*)

BOTH:

> *Wunderbar, wunderbar!*

HE:

> There's our fav'rite star above,

SHE:

> What a bright-shining star!

BOTH:

> Like our love, it's *wunderbar!*
> (*They waltz a bit.*)

HE:

> And you're mine, dear!
> (*Embrace.*)

BOTH:

> *Wunderbar, wunderbar!*
> (*Sway.*)

HE:

> There's our fav'rite star above,

BOTH:

> What a bright-shining star!
> Like our love, it's *wunderbar!*
> (*They kiss at end of song.*)

> (RALPH *knocks, opens door, speaks from doorway, closes door as he leaves.*)

RALPH: Fifteen minutes.

LILLI: Whose fault was it?

FRED: It could have been your temper.

LILLI: Could have been your ego.

FRED: Let's get dressed. (*Goes into his room. Closes door.*)

> (*Lights fade out in* LILLI's *room but remain on in* FRED's *room.* FRED *sits at dressing-table.*)

> (TWO MEN *enter. They are well dressed. Too much so—from their expensive pearl-gray felt hats, and neat, hand-sewn blue suits to their over-polished shoes. They look like gunmen. They are. The soft-spoken kind. They're obviously embarrassed at being backstage and in the presence of the great* FREDERICK GRAHAM.)

FIRST MAN: Hello.

FRED (*staring*): Who are you? What are you doing backstage?

FIRST MAN: Fine-looking fella.

SECOND MAN: Clean cut.

FIRST MAN: What a figger!

SECOND MAN: What a profile!

FRED (*crosses to gunmen*): Gentlemen, I'm deeply touched by your admiration and devotion.

FIRST MAN: What diction!

SECOND MAN: Very elocutionary.

FIRST MAN: And he does not spit when he talks.

SECOND MAN (*looks*): High-type fella.

FRED: As I was saying, this is all very flattering, but I receive the public *after* the performance, not before. (*Crosses to dressing-table.*)

FIRST MAN: Oh, what grace!

SECOND MAN: If I hadda do something to him, I'd cry like a baby.

FRED: Gentlemen, come back *after* the show. I'll be very happy to present you with my autograph.

FIRST MAN (*crosses to* FRED): We got your autograph. That's why we're here.

FRED: What?

FIRST MAN: A little matter of an IOU. Here it is— (*Shows it.*) Ten G's. Mr. Hogan—that's our employer—regards this as a debt of honor. How's about it, Mr. Graham?

FRED: You're mad. Paul! Paul!

   (SECOND MAN *makes certain door is securely shut and both cross to* FRED.)

   Let's see that.

   (*Grabs for IOU.* FIRST MAN *stops him. He looks.*)

   Why, that's not even my signature!

FIRST MAN: They all say that. I'm surprised at you, Mr. Graham. You signed it only this afternoon after quite a little game down to the hotel. We wasn't there, of course. Mr. Hogan says he plied you plenty with good liquor, too.

FRED: You're really mad! I've been in this theatre since eight this morning. (*Sits and begins to apply make-up.*)

FIRST MAN: He forgot.

SECOND MAN: Yeah. That's human nature for you.

(FRED *continues making up.*)

FIRST MAN: The minute a man signs an IOU everything goes dark.

SECOND MAN: The doctors call it magnesia.

FIRST MAN: We cure it.

SECOND MAN: I'd cry like a baby, if I hadda do something to such a high-type fella. Last week—remember that high-type fella—I used up three handkerchiefs.

FIRST MAN (*looking in mirror*): I don't like my face. Do you?

SECOND MAN: No!

FRED: Gentlemen, would you mind leaving?

FIRST MAN: Ain't he virile? We now wish to express all best wishes for a magnificent opening and the success your brilliant talents deserve! I copied that out of Western Union.

SECOND MAN (*hat in hand*): Heartiest felicitations! I made that up myself!

FIRST MAN: Mr. Graham, try and jostle your memory. (*Only, he pronounces it* jostill.)

SECOND MAN: We'll be back.

(*They exit,* FRED *looks after them in amazement, shrugs, and goes on with his dressing. Lights dim in* FRED'*s room. Lights up in* LILLI'*s room.* PAUL *knocks on* LILLI'*s door, opens it, and waits there.*)

HATTIE (*turns to door*): Hello, Paul.

PAUL: Hiya, beautiful. (PAUL *gives* HATTIE *a box of flowers, and exits.*)

HATTIE: Here's some flowers. Paul gave them to me. They must be from Mr. Fred.

(LILLI *lifts lid of box—sees bouquet.*)

LILLI: Snowdrops and pansies and rosemary. My wedding bouquet! Oh, Hattie, he didn't forget.

HATTIE (*cooing*): Of course not, honey. Now, I'll get you some coffee. (*Exits.*)

(*Lights dim as* LILLI *regards the bouquet in her lap and begins to sing.*)

"So in Love"

LILLI:

> Strange, dear, but true, dear,
> When I'm close to you, dear,

The stars fill the sky,
So in love with you am I.
(*Puts box down.*)
Even without you
My arms fold about you,
You know, darling, why,
So in love with you am I.
In love with the night mysterious,
The night when you first were there,
In love with my joy delirious
When I knew that you could care.
So taunt me and hurt me,
Deceive me, desert me,
I'm yours till I die,
So in love,
So in love,
So in love with you, my love, am I.
(*Music continues as she takes flower box to dressing-table and returns to couch with bouquet. A rather sad* LILLI, *a defenseless* LILLI, *finishes with:*)
So taunt me and hurt me,
Deceive me, desert me,
I'm yours till I die,
So in love,
So in love,
So in love with you, my love, am I.

(*Lights go up in* FRED's *dressing-room.* PAUL *enters, starts helping* FRED *into his costume.*)
FRED: Paul, what the devil do you mean letting a couple of raving maniacs in here, five minutes before curtain?
PAUL: There was no one in here when I left.
FRED: Tell Ralph next time no one's to be admitted into my dressing-room with a psychoanalyst's certificate! Of course, they may have been just overwhelmed at meeting me!
PAUL: I'm sure that's it, sir! Everybody feels the magnetism of your personality, sir, off stage and on.
FRED: You know, Paul, you're not only the finest dresser I've ever had but a true connoisseur of the theatre.
PAUL: Thank you, Mr. Graham.

FRED (*sits at dressing-room table*): Did you—uh—deliver my flowers?

PAUL: Yes, sir.

FRED: Did you put the note in?

PAUL: Yes, sir.

FRED: Good. You gave them to Miss Lane personally, of course?

PAUL: Miss Lane? I thought they were for Miss Vanessi, sir.

FRED: Miss Vanessi. Don't tell me you . . . you driveling idiot!

PAUL: I'm sorry, sir. I haven't been myself since Blue Blood was scratched in the third race! (*Exits hastily.*)

FRED: Moron! (FRED *enters* LILLI's *dressing-room.*)

LILLI (*tremulous and loving*): Fred, you darling . . . You didn't forget. . . . (*Holding up bouquet.*)

FRED (*quick to pick up a cue*): You didn't think I would?
   (RALPH *opens door, sticks his head in. Overture music can be heard.*)

RALPH (*bawling*): On stage! Good luck! (*Leaves door open.*)

FRED (*snapping his fingers nervously*): Come on, let's go.

LILLI: I can't. My hands are freezing. (*Sits on lounge.*)

FRED (*begins rubbing her hands*): Now, Lilli, you're not going to whoops?

LILLI (*nervously*): Do you think they'll like me? After all, I've been away from the theatre almost . . .

FRED (*shouting*): They'll love you!
   (*As* FRED *grabs* LILLI *by the hand,* HATTIE *holds up envelope containing card.*)

HATTIE: I found it, Miss Lilli. Here's the card that came with the flowers!

LILLI: Quick, Hattie, give it to me!
   (HATTIE *does so, beaming, and exits, closing the door.* LILLI *is about to read the card.*)

FRED (*taking both her hands—aghast*): You're not going to read that now! . . . Look, I'll tell you what I wrote: "To Lilli, the only woman I've ever loved, the only artist I've ever worshipped!" Now give me the card and you can read it after the show!

LILLI: Oh, Fred, did you really mean that? (*Rises, throws arms around* FRED.)

FRED (*plenty nervous, tries to get card*): With all my heart!

LILLI: Then—that's where it's going. (*She slips card into her bosom.*) Right next to mine. I'm not nervous—I'm not going to whoops and I'll never call you a bastard—Fred dear, never!

FRED (*in grim resignation*): You will, my sweet, you will!

BLACKOUT

(*And now we go into the musical version of* The Taming of the Shrew.)

SCENE 4

SCENE: *Before the curtain, a lovely confection of yellow and pink purporting to be a map of Italy with its principal towns.*

TWO BOYS *carrying* Taming of the Shrew *banner start parade of* DANCERS *and* SINGERS, *followed by* KATHARINE, PETRUCHIO, BIANCA, LUCENTIO. *They sing.*

"Padua Street Song"

(*Verse*)

ALL:

A troupe of strolling players are we,

LILLI:

Not stars like L. B. Mayer's are we

ALL:

But just a simple band
Who roams about the land
Dispensing fol-de-rol frivolitee.
Mere folk who give distraction are we,

FRED:

No Theatre Guild attraction are we

ALL:

But just a crazy group
That never ceases to troupe
Around the map of little Italee.

(*1st Refrain*)

ALL:

We open in Venice,
We next play Verona,
Then on to Cremona,

LILLI:

Lotsa laughs in Cremona.

ALL:

> Our next jump is Parma,
> That dopey, mopey menace,
> Then Mantua, then Padua,
> Then we open again, where?
> (*2nd Refrain*)

ALL:

> We open in Venice,
> We next play Verona,
> Then on to Cremona,

BILL:

> Lotsa bars in Cremona.

ALL:

> The next jump is Parma,
> That beerless cheerless menace,
> Then Mantua, then Padua,
> Then we open again, where?
> (*3rd Refrain*)

ALL:

> We open in Venice,
> We next play Verona,
> Then on to Cremona,

LOIS:

> Lotsa dough in Cremona.

ALL:

> Our next jump is Parma,
> That stingy, dingy menace,
> Then Mantua, then Padua,
> Then we open again, where?
> (*4th Refrain*)

ALL:

> We open in Venice,
> We next play Verona,
> Then on to Cremona,

FRED:

> Lotsa quail in Cremona.

ALL:

> Our next jump is Parma,
> That heartless, tartless menace,
> Then Mantua, then Padua,

Then we open again, where?
In Venice.
(*All exit right.*)

SCENE 5

SCENE: *Piazza in Padua. To one side is the entrance and façade
of* BAPTISTA's *house with a balcony over the door. On the other side
the entrance to the inn with a shallow striped awning over it. Back of
that is a platform with drawn curtains where the mummers perform.*

*Market Day. Peddlers hawk their wares from trays. As lights come
up, dance is in progress. During dance,* BIANCA *sidles forth, carrying
a red rose, followed by* GREMIO *and* HORTENSIO *carrying nothing.*
LUCENTIO *tags along carrying books.* BIANCA, *the little flirt, exits
into house, leaving three disconsolate suitors at the door. After the
mummers finish their dance and go off stage,* BIANCA *re-enters with*
BAPTISTA, *her father.*

BIANCA (*eyes cast down, rose in hand*): Father, to your pleasure,
    humbly I subscribe, my books and my instruments shall be
    my company on them to look and practice by myself. (*She eyes*
    LUCENTIO.)
BAPTISTA: Poor child.
GREMIO and HORTENSIO (*taking* BAPTISTA *by each arm*):
    Signor Baptista.
GREMIO: Why will you let Bianca bear the penance of Katha-
    rine's tongue?
BAPTISTA (*shaking off suitors*):
    Gentlemen, importune me no farther.
    For how firmly I am resolved, you know,
    That is, not to bestow my youngest daughter
        (*Indicating* BIANCA.)
    Before I have a husband for the elder;
    Now, if either of you love Katharine
        (KATHARINE *appears on balcony with watering-can. She has
        been watering the potted plants. She listens.*)
    Leave shall you have to court her at your pleasure.
GREMIO:
    To cart her rather: she's too rough for me.
BAPTISTA (*very confidentially*):

If you Hortensio, or Signor Gremio,
If either of you can find a husband,
I would be most liberal.

HORTENSIO:

A husband? A devil.

KATHARINE (*from balcony*):

Indeed!

   (*Throws three geranium pots at* HORTENSIO. *One-two-three!*
   One is a dead hit.)

HORTENSIO (*holding head*):

Thinkst thou, sir, though you be very rich,
And many be so very a fool to be married to hell?

KATHARINE (*from balcony*):

Comb thy noddle with a three-legged stool.

   (*She hurls a stool. . . . All duck.*)

GREMIO:

I'd be as lief to take her dowry with this condition,
As to be whipped at high-cross every morning.

   (KATHARINE *throws watering-can from balcony. Suitors back*
   away. All look up.)

KATHARINE:

So, father, is it your will to make a stale of me amongst those
   males?

   (*She disappears.*)

BAPTISTA (*picking up the wreckage*):

Oh! If I could only find a man that would thoroughly woo
Her, wed her, and bed her and rid my house of her.

   (*Totters into house.*)

BIANCA (*sighing*): Ah, me!

   (GREMIO, HORTENSIO, *and* LUCENTIO *seek to assuage her*
   grief with song:)

"Tom, Dick, or Harry"

(*Verse*)

GREMIO:

   I've made a haul in all the leading rackets
   From which rip-roarin' rich I happen to be
   And if thou wouldst attain the upper brackets,
   Marry me, marry me, marry me.

LUCENTIO:

    My purse has yet to know a silver lining,
    Still lifeless is my wifeless family tree
(*Kneels.*)
    But if for love unending thou are pining,
    Marry me, marry me, marry me.

HORTENSIO:

    I come to thee, a thoroughbred patrician
    Still spraying my decaying family tree,
    To give a social goose to thy position,
    Marry me, marry me, marry.
    Marry me.

GREMIO and LUCENTIO:

    Marry me!

HORTENSIO:

    Marry me!

GREMIO and HORTENSIO:

    Marry me!

LUCENTIO:

    Marry me!

GREMIO:

    Marry me!

THREE SUITORS:

    Marry me!
    (*1st Refrain*)

BIANCA:

    I'm a maid who would marry
    And will take with no qualm
    Any Tom, Dick, or Harry,
    Any Harry, Dick, or Tom.
    I'm a maid mad to marry
    And will take double-quick
    Any Tom, Dick, or Harry,
    Any Tom, Harry, or Dick.
    (*2nd Refrain*)

GREMIO:

    I'm the man thou shouldst marry.

BIANCA:

    Howdy, Pop!

GREMIO:

    Howdy, Mom.

LUCENTIO:

    I'm the man thou shouldst marry.

BIANCA:

    Art thou Harry, Dick, or Tom?

HORTENSIO:

    I'm the man thou shouldst marry.

BIANCA:

    Howdy, pal!

HORTENSIO:

    Howdy, chick!

BIANCA:

    Art thou Tom, Dick, or Harry?

HORTENSIO:

    Call me Tom, Harry, or Dick.

    (*3rd Refrain*)

    (LUCENTIO *and* HORTENSIO *kneel on one knee to form a seat for* BIANCA. *She sits.*)

BIANCA and SUITORS:

    { I'm a maid who would marry

    { She's a maid who would marry

    And would no longer tarry,

    { I'm a maid who would marry,

    { She's a maid who would marry,

    May my hopes not miscarry!

    { I'm a maid mad to marry

    { She's a maid mad to marry

    And will take double-quick

    Any Tom, Dick, or Harry,

    Any Tom, Harry, or Dick,

BIANCA:

    A-dicka dick,

    A-dicka dick,

    A-dicka dick,

    A-dicka dick,

    A-dicka dick,

    A-dicka dick!

    (*Encore 3rd Refrain in swing time*)

BIANCA and SUITORS:

    { I'm a maid who would marry
    { She's a maid who would marry
    And would no longer tarry,
    { I'm a maid who would marry,
    { She's a maid who would marry,
    May my hopes not miscarry!
    { I'm a maid mad to marry
    { She's a maid mad to marry
    And will take double-quick
    Any Tom, Dick, or Harry,
    Any Tom, Harry, or Dick,
    A-dicka dick,
    A-dicka dick,
    A-dicka dick,
    A-dicka dick,
    A-dicka dick,
    A-dicka dick!

    (GREMIO *and* HORTENSIO *exit.* LUCENTIO *follows* BIANCA *to door of house, where she exits. She re-enters, throws him a rose, and exits.*)

LUCENTIO (*looking at rose*): Sweet Bianca, she sings as sweetly as a nightingale. She looks as clean as morning roses newly washed with dew. Sweet Bianca. (*He dances divinely with the rose, representing the fair Bianca.*)

    (*Innkeeper and waiter tactfully wait until he finishes his balletic rhapsody before they place a table in position with pewter mug and trays. To* LUCENTIO's *surprise,* GREMIO *and* HORTENSIO *enter menacingly, followed by some of their "friends."*)

GREMIO (*threateningly*):
    Are you a suitor to the maid you talk of?

    (PETRUCHIO *enters through arch, unseen by others.*)

LUCENTIO:
    And if I be, sir, is it of any offense?

GREMIO (*angrily*):
    No, if without more words, you will get you hence.

    (*During this altercation, local Paduans gather round hopefully for a fight.* LUCENTIO *sees he's vastly outnumbered, when* PETRUCHIO *advances, and pushes* GREMIO *aside.*)

PETRUCHIO:

Why, sir, I pray are not the streets as free for him as for you?

LUCENTIO:

Petruchio!

PETRUCHIO:

Lucentio!

(*They all but embrace.*)

LUCENTIO:

What happy wind blows you to Padua from old Verona?

PETRUCHIO:

Such wind as scatters young men through the world

To seek their fortunes farther than at home. And you?

LUCENTIO:

I came to study.

PETRUCHIO (*puts arm around* LUCENTIO):

I am glad that you thus

Combine your resolve

To suck the sweets of

Sweet philosophy,

The mathematics and the

Botany.

(*Indicates rose.* LUCENTIO, *embarrassed, ostentatiously tosses rose on table; that finishes the rose.*)

Fall to them as your

Stomach serves.

No profit grows where

Is no pleasure taken.

(*Removes hat and cape, along with riding-crop, places them on table.*)

In brief, sir—study—

As for me:

"I've Come to Wive It Wealthily in Padua"

(*1st Refrain*)

PETRUCHIO:

I've come to wive it wealthily in Padua,

If wealthily then happily in Padua.

If my wife has a bag of gold

Do I care if the bag is old?

I've come to wive it wealthily in Padua.

(*2nd Refrain*)

MEN OF PADUA:

    He's come to wive it wealthily in Padua.

PETRUCHIO:

    I heard you mutter: "Zounds, a loathsome lad you
        are."

    I shall not be disturbed a bit

    If she be but a quarter-wit,

    If she only can talk of clo'es

    While she powders her God-damned nose,

    I've come to wive it wealthily in Padua.

    (*3rd Refrain*)

MEN OF PADUA:

    He's come to wive it wealthily in Padua.

PETRUCHIO:

    I heard you say: "Gadzooks, completely mad you are!"

    'Twouldn't give me the slightest shock

    If her knees, now and then, should knock,

    If her eyes were a wee bit crossed,

    Were she wearing the hair she'd lost,

    Still the damsel I'll make my dame,

    In the dark they are all the same,

    I've come to wive it wealthily in Padua.

    (*4th Refrain*)

MEN OF PADUA:

    He's come to wive it wealthily in Padua.

PETRUCHIO:

    I heard you say: "Good gad but what a cad you are!"

    Do I mind if she fret and fuss,

    If she fume like Vesuvius,

    If she roar like a winter breeze

    On the rough Adriatic seas,

    If she scream like a teething brat,

    If she scratch like a tiger cat,

    If she fight like a raging boar,

    I have oft stuck a pig before,

    I've come to wive it wealthily in Padua.

    (*Coda*)

MEN OF PADUA:

    With a hunny, nunny, nunny,

    (*All move forward.*)

    And a hey, hey, hey,

PETRUCHIO:

    Not to mention money, money
    (*Stops them with a gesture.*)
    For a rainy day,

PETRUCHIO and MEN OF PADUA:

    { I've come to wive it wealthily in Padua.
    { He's come to wive it wealthily in Padua.

GREMIO (*digging* HORTENSIO *with elbow*):

    This gentleman is happily arrived!

LUCENTIO:

    Petruchio, thou'rt too much my friend. . . .
      (*To the others.*)
    I cannot wish him to a shrewd, ill-tempered wife.

HORTENSIO:

    But she is rich!

GREMIO:

    And young and beauteous.

LUCENTIO:

    But shrewd and forward so beyond all measure
    That were my state far poorer than it is
    I would not wed her for a mine of gold.

PETRUCHIO (*the cynic*):

    Peace! Lucentio, thou know'st not gold's effects. And
    Therefore, if thou know one rich enough to be Petruchio's
    Wife, tell me her father's name and 'tis enough.

GREMIO:

    Her father is Baptista Minola. Her name Katharine—
    Elder sister of the fair Bianca.
      (*Shrieks are heard from the house.*)

LUCENTIO:

    That is she! An irksome, brawling scold.

PETRUCHIO:

    Think you a little din can daunt mine ears?
    Have I not in my time heard lions roar?
    Have I not heard great ordnance in the field
    And Heaven's artillery thunder in the skies?
    And do you tell me of a woman's tongue
    That give not half so great a blow to hear
    As will a chestnut in a farmer's fire?

HORTENSIO:
Then you will woo this wildcat?
PETRUCHIO:
Will I live?
GREMIO:
I promise we will be contributors
And bear your charge of wooing, whatsoe'er.
PETRUCHIO:
Done!
GREMIO:
Let's quaff carouses to this gentleman!
(*As they exit to inn, waiter picks up hat, cloak, riding-crop, and rose from table, and exits. One can't take chances even in a university town. Incidentally, this really finishes the rose.*)
PETRUCHIO:
For all this, much thanks—
GREMIO:
Provided that you win her.
PETRUCHIO:
Go you to old Baptista and say:
"I have a husband for Katharine."
(*All exit into inn.*)
LUCENTIO (*stops* PETRUCHIO): Katharine, the curst!
PETRUCHIO: Katharine the curst! A title for a maid of all titles the worst!
(*Exits into inn. Door flies open and* BIANCA, *pursued by* KATHARINE *and* BAPTISTA, *runs past* LUCENTIO *standing near door.*)
BIANCA (*weeping*): Sister—sister—sister, content you in my discontent. (*Exits left.*)
BAPTISTA (*crosses between* BIANCA *and* KATHARINE): Katharine, Katharine—for shame, thou hilding of a devilish spirit. . . . Poor child, she weeps!
KATHARINE: She is your treasure; she must have a husband; I must dance barefoot on her wedding day—and for your love to her lead apes in hell.
BAPTISTA: Oh, oh! Was ever father thus grieved as I?
LUCENTIO (*timidly*): A word with you, kind sir.
BAPTISTA (*going into his old spiel*): Importune me no farther, good sir. . . . For how firmly am I resolved, you know. . . .

(LUCENTIO *whispers to* BAPTISTA.)

BAPTISTA: Eh? Whisper louder. . . .

(LUCENTIO *whispers some more into other ear.* BAPTISTA *brightens.*)

That is indeed news, good news! Come in, Lucentio.

(*They exit left.*)

KATHARINE (*as they exit*): Lucentio, thou meacock wretch. (*She strides to table, sits on the stool. Alone, surly and unhappy, she sings.*)

"I Hate Men"

KATHARINE:

(*1st Refrain*)

I hate men.

(*Bangs pewter mug on table.*)

I can't abide 'em even now and then,

Than ever marry one of them, I'd rest a virgin rather,

For husbands are a boring lot and only give you bother.

Of course, I'm awf'lly glad that Mother had to marry Father

But, I hate men.

Of all the types I've ever met within our democracy,

I hate the most, the athlete with his manner bold and brassy,

He may have hair upon his chest but, sister, so has Lassie,

Oh, I hate men!

(*Picks up cup and bangs upon table.*)

(*2nd Refrain*)

I hate men.

(*Bangs cup.*)

Their worth upon this earth I dinna ken.

Avoid the trav'ling salesman though a tempting Tom he may be,

From China he will bring you jade and perfume from Araby

But don't forget 'tis he who'll have the fun and thee the baby,

Oh, I hate men.

If thou shouldst wed a bus'nessman, be wary, oh be
wary.

(*Crosses to table.*)

He'll tell you he's detained in town on bus'ness
necessary,

His bus'ness is the bus'ness which he gives his
secretary,

Oh, I hate men!

(*Bangs pewter mug.*)

(BAPTISTA *enters and beats a hasty retreat as* KATHARINE
goes into:)

(*3rd Refrain*)

I hate men.

(*Bangs cup.*)

Though roosters they, I will not play the hen.

(*Crosses to center.*)

If you espouse an older man through girlish optimism,

He'll always stay at home at night and make no
criticism,

Though you may call it "love," the doctors call it
"rheumatism."

Oh, I hate men.

From all I've read, alone in bed, from A to Zed, about
'em,

Since love is blind, then from the mind, all womankind
should rout 'em.

But ladies, you must answer too, what would we do
without 'em?

Oh still, I hate men!

(*Bangs cup, crosses to center, bows.*)

(*Enter* BAPTISTA *and crosses to* KATHARINE.)

BAPTISTA: Katharine! Wonder of wonders!

KATHARINE (*belligerently*): What?

BAPTISTA (*panting*): A gentleman from Verona—desires you—
in marriage.

KATHARINE (*picks up the mug and throws it, but misses her father*):
Then he best go back there. (*She exits.*)

BAPTISTA: Heavens!

(PETRUCHIO *emerges from inn and approaches* BAPTISTA. *The ever-watchful waiter now removes mugs and trays from table and floor. Also takes stool. Unless it's nailed down, he'll take anything. He also sings tenor.*)

PETRUCHIO: Greetings, good sir. I hear sir, you have a daughter call'd Katharine, fair and virtuous.

BAPTISTA: I have a daughter, sir, called Katharine.

PETRUCHIO: I am a gentleman from Verona, sir, that hearing of her beauty and her wit, her affability and bashful modesty; her wondrous qualities and mild behavior—(*shriek is heard off stage.* PETRUCHIO *pauses for a second with a glance toward balcony, but plows on*) uh—mild behavior, am bold to make myself a forward guest within your house to make mine eye the witness of that report. Signor Baptista, my business asketh haste, and every day, I cannot come to woo.

BAPTISTA: I am afraid my daughter Katharine is not for your turn, the more my grief.

PETRUCHIO: I see you do not mean to part with her.

BAPTISTA (*follows* PETRUCHIO): Mistake me not, sir—

PETRUCHIO: Or else you like not of my company—

BAPTISTA: You are more than welcome—

PETRUCHIO (*sits on table*): Well, then—what dowry shall I have with her to wife?

BAPTISTA: After my death, the one half of my lands.

PETRUCHIO: The fertile part?

BAPTISTA: So be it!

PETRUCHIO: And in possession?

BAPTISTA: Twenty thousand crowns!

PETRUCHIO: Thirty!

(BAPTISTA *turns away,* PETRUCHIO *rises as if to go.*)

BAPTISTA (*turns back hastily*): Thirty!

PETRUCHIO: Father!

(*They embrace.*)

And for that dowry I'll assure her of her widowhood—be it that she survive me. Let specialties be therefore drawn between us, that covenants may be kept on either hand. Go, get thee to a notary.

(BAPTISTA *exits through arch. Waiter takes table off.*)

KATHARINE (*on balcony*):

Aye, when that special thing is well obtained.

That is, my love—or is that all in all?

PETRUCHIO (*looking up to balcony*): Could I but see thy face?

KATHARINE: Why, sir! 'Tis but a face like any other. . . .

PETRUCHIO: Aye—there's the rub.

(*And he sings.*)

"Were Thine That Special Face"

(KATHARINE *watches from balcony.*)

PETRUCHIO:

(*Refrain*)

Were thine that special face,
The face which fills my dreaming,
Were thine the rhythm'd grace,
Were thine the form so lithe and slender,
Were thine the arms so warm, so tender,
Were thine the kiss divine,

(*Looks at balcony.*)

Were thine the love for me,
The love which fills my dreaming,
When all these charms are thine
Then you'll be mine, all mine.

(KATHARINE *exits angrily as* DANCERS *in black rustling gowns carrying fans swish on.*)

(*Verse*)

I wrote a poem
In classic style,
I wrote it with my tongue
In my cheek
And my lips in a smile
But of late my poem

(*Crosses right center.*)

Has a meaning so new
For to my surprise
It suddenly applies to my darling, to you.

(*Looks to balcony.* KATHARINE *is gone.* PETRUCHIO *shrugs and sings to* DANCERS.)

(*Refrain repeats*)

Were thine that special face,
The face which fills my dreaming,
Were thine the rhythm'd grace,

Were thine the form so lithe and slender,
Were thine the arms so warm, so tender,
Were thine the kiss divine,
Were thine the love for me,
The love which fills my dreaming,
When all these charms are thine
Then you'll be mine, all mine.

When all these charms are thine
Then you'll be mine, all mine.
(*Lights up at end of number. Waiter moves table on stage on applause.*)

BAPTISTA (*enters*): 'Twas not to her liking.

PETRUCHIO: But that is nothing. For I tell you, father, I am as peremptory as she proud-minded. And where two raging fires meet together, they do consume the thing that feeds their fury.

I will attend her here and woo her with some spirit when she comes. If she do bid me pack—I'll give her thanks—

KATHARINE (*enters angrily from house. She holds bouquet in hand, as if it were a stiletto*): I bid thee pack.
(*This is obviously not her cue for entrance and* FRED, *as* PETRUCHIO, *is a little off guard. The others obviously sense something wrong.*)

Were thine that special face! Hah!
(LILLI *tosses bouquet at* FRED. *He barely catches it. Reaction.*)

FRED (*ad-libbing*): Grazia, signorina. (*He bows.*)

BAPTISTA (*a little nonplused, but plowing on*): And now, Petruchio, speak! (*He exits into house.*)

KATHARINE (*extracting card from bosom*): Speak, Petruchio. . . .
Though thy message is not meant for me. (*She tears up card, throws it in* PETRUCHIO'*s face.*) You bas—

PETRUCHIO (*hastily breaking in*): Good morrow, Kate.
(*In aside. Grabs her hand.*) We're on stage, now, Lilli. . . .
Good morrow, Kate, for that's your name, I hear.

KATHARINE:
Well have you heard, but somewhat hard of hearing;
They call me Katharine that do speak of me.
(*Crosses down center.*)

PETRUCHIO:

You lie, in faith; for you are called plain Kate,

And bonny Kate, and sometimes Kate the curst;

(*Throws flowers away.*)

But Kate, the prettiest Kate in Christendom;

And therefore, Kate, take this of me, Kate of my consolation;

Hearing thy mildness prais'd in every town,

Thy virtues spoke of, and thy beauty sounded,

Yet not so deeply as to thee belongs—

(*She hits him in stomach.*)

Myself am moved to woo thee for my wife.

KATHARINE:

Hah! Mov'd in good time: let him that mov'd you hither

Remove you hence; I knew you at the first you were a movable.

PETRUCHIO:

Why, what's a movable?

KATHARINE:

A joint stool.

PETRUCHIO:

Thou hast hit it. Come, sit on me.

(*Slaps knee.*)

KATHARINE:

Asses are made to bear, and so are you.

PETRUCHIO:

Women are made to bear, and so are you.

KATHARINE:

No such jade as bear you, if me you mean.

(*She bites his hand.*)

PETRUCHIO (*nursing his hand*):

Come, come, you wasp; i' faith, you are too angry.

KATHARINE:

If I be too waspish, best beware my sting.

(*Slaps* PETRUCHIO.)

PETRUCHIO:

My remedy is then to pluck it out.

KATHARINE:

Aye, if the fool could find it where it lies.

PETRUCHIO:

Who knows not where a wasp does wear his sting? In his tail.

(KATHARINE *slaps him again.* PETRUCHIO *grabs her, bends her back over his knee.*)

I swear I'll cuff you, if you strike again!

(*Aside.*) You keep on acting just the way you've been doing, Miss Vanessi, and I will give you the paddling of your life and right on stage.

KATHARINE (*breaking away*): You wouldn't dare.

PETRUCHIO (*laughs—a forced stage-laugh*): No?

KATHARINE: If you strike me you are no gentleman. What is your crest—a coxcomb? (*Holds up her hand.*)

PETRUCHIO:

A combless cock, so Kate will be my hen.

(*Grabs* KATE's *raised hand.*)

Come, give me thy hands.

KATHARINE: No! No!

(PETRUCHIO *slaps her behind, propelling her to table. From other side of table he grabs her hands and holds them down.*)

PETRUCHIO:

Come.

Setting all this chat aside,

Thus in plain terms; your father has consented

That you shall be my wife;

And will you, nill you, I will marry you.

Now, Kate, I am a husband for your turn

For by this light, whereby I see thy beauty—

Thy beauty that doth make me like thee well—

Thou must be married to no man but me.

(*Brings* KATE *around in front of table.*)

For I am he, am born to tame you, Kate;

And bring you from a wild Kate to a Kate

Conformable as other household Kates.

KATHARINE:

You devil. Father! (*Struggles to remove her hands.*)

(BAPTISTA *enters quickly and* SUITORS *enter from upstage right.*)

BAPTISTA:

And now, Signor Petruchio, how speed you with my daughter?

PETRUCHIO:

How but well! How, but well. It were impossible I should Speed amiss. We have 'greed so well together that upon

Sunday is the wedding day.

BAPTISTA (*puts his hands over theirs*):

God give you joy, son! 'Tis a match! (*Withdraws hands quickly.*)

SUITORS:

Amen, say we!

PETRUCHIO:

Father and wife and gentlemen, adieu:

(*Swings her away from him; enter crowd.*)

I will unto Venice

(*She kicks him.*)

—I'm warning you!—

to buy apparel, against the wedding day.

Sunday comes apace

And we will have rings and things and fine array and

Kiss me, Kate.

(*She slaps him.*)

All right, Miss Vanessi—you asked for this and you're going to get it! (*He takes her across his knee. He begins paddling her.*)

KATHARINE: *Oh!*

(*He paddles her harder.*)

Fred, what are you doing? *Oh!* . . . *Oh!* . . . *Oh!* . . .

(*She screams. He paddles her harder. Screams from crowd.*)

BLACKOUT

SCENE 6

SCENE: *Backstage—on stage performance of* The Shrew *is still going on, but unseen and unheard. The stagehands move about with ladders and pieces of scenery as* LILLI *enters.*

LILLI (*really angry*): Hattie! Hattie! Darn that girl!

(FRED *enters, grinning.* LILLI *turns on him.*)

That's the last time you'll ever lay your hands on me, Mr. Graham!

FRED (*laconically*): You asked for it. May I remind you, Miss Vanessi, the name of this piece is *The Taming of the Shrew,* not *He Who Gets Slapped.*

LILLI: I am a realistic actress.

FRED: Huh! Your latest picture is still in the can where it belongs.

LILLI: Cuddling up to that Copa canary!

FRED (*crosses in front of* LILLI *to center*): You're jealous—that's what's the matter with you.

LILLI: Sending my wedding bouquet to that little tramp.

FRED: That's no excuse for ad-libbing! None!

LILLI: "Let my lovely Lois shine through Bianca tonight, and there'll be a new star in the heavens." Thou jerk.

FRED: All right, all right! I sent the child some flowers—I sent her a card with the flowers. May I point out that I'm free, male, and thirty-one!

LILLI (*derisively*): Thirty-one—hah!

FRED: All right, thirty-two. What the hell has my age got to do with this? They were full, rich years and I'm proud of them. Every minute of them. Show me an actor who's done all I've done—my Peer Gynt in London—

LILLI: You never got to London.

FRED: My Hamlet in Dublin—

LILLI: You got paid in potatoes. Mashed!

FRED: That's all you ever think of—money—money—money. Miss Vanessi, you have no soul! And what the hell do you mean by poking me in the ribs?

LILLI: It's in the script!

FRED: The hell it is! I couldn't teach you manners as a wife, but by God I'll teach you manners as an actress!

LILLI: Not in this production, my pet.

FRED: What did you say?

LILLI: You heard me! And here's something to remember me by. (*Slaps him.*)

FRED: What are you trying to do? Kill me? Ralph! Ralph! Paul! (FRED *limps across, holding his cheek. Touches his cheek.*) Good God, I'm bleeding!

RALPH: Yes, Mr. Graham?

FRED: Get me some alcohol.

RALPH: Yes, sir.

FRED (*shouting*): There's a law against attempted murder—even in Baltimore. (*He feels his side.*) God, my rib—I think she broke a rib. Ralph, how can you tell if you have a broken rib?

RALPH: X-ray.

FRED: Where am I going to get an X-ray?

RALPH: All I've got is alcohol.

FRED: That monstrous female. Literally a vampire. Am I bleeding heavily, Ralph?

RALPH: I don't see any blood.

FRED: Here—what do you call that? (*Looks at his hand.*) Max Factor Number Two? Oh, I thought it was blood. Skin's bruised though, isn't it?

RALPH: I don't see anything.

FRED: Discolored?

RALPH: I don't see anything.

FRED: That's all I need. A blind stage manager!

BLACKOUT

SCENE 7

SCENE: FRED'*s and* LILLI'*s dressing-rooms. Both rooms lit.* LILLI *is on phone in* Shrew *costume.*

LILLI (*holding phone in one hand and rubbing her posterior with the other*): Harrison, I'll marry you tonight. You don't know what that villain's done to me. I can't sit down! I said: "I can't sit down!" I'm through with the theatre. Send a car for me. Better still, send an ambulance! I want to go where no one will ever find me. I'll go to Washington! I adore you, Harrison. Yes, dear . . . yes, love.

  (HATTIE *enters.*)

  Hattie, pack my things! I'll wear that blue suit. Yes, Harrison. . . . He beat me! I'm black and blue!

FRED (*enters his room, overhears her plaint and crosses into hers*): I'm a realistic actor!

LILLI: I'm quitting right now. (*Hangs up phone.*)

FRED: You don't think you can walk out of a show in the middle of a performance?

LILLI: Oh, no?

FRED: I'll have you up on charges at Equity!

LILLI: Hah! I'll be glad—glad to appear before Equity! I shall bring photographs (*indicates backside*) of what you have done to me. In Technicolor!

FRED: And I'll bring my X-rays! (*Goes to his room.*)

LILLI: Nothing you can say or do will stop me. Harrison's coming for me.

FRED (*coming back into* LILLI'*s room*): Do you think he'd let you quit? That imbecile's got two hundred thousand dollars in this show.

LILLI: He'll take it off his tax!

FRED: You don't really mean you would . . .

> (*She turns to him quickly, facing him squarely, belligerently. What* FRED *reads in her eyes frightens him. He remembers that look from the old connubial days.*)

Yes, I guess you do.

LILLI: You bet I do.

> (*The* TWO GUNMEN *quietly enter* FRED'*s room. They've been out front and are pleased.*)

FRED: You'll never play the theatre again!

LILLI: Who wants to?

FRED: You're out of your mind.

LILLI (*picking up an object*): Get out! Get out!

> (*He opens door to his room. She follows him, threatening, and* FRED *shuts door between them.*)

Get out!

> (*We leave* LILLI *for the moment and stay with* FRED.)

> (FRED, *now in his room, sees the two men.*)

FRED (*aghast*): Oh, for heaven's sake!

FIRST MAN: What a performance.

SECOND MAN: What unction!

FIRST MAN: You think the audience is getting it? It's way over their heads.

SECOND MAN: Bunch of lowbrows.

FRED: Look here—

FIRST MAN: We just want to check with you to see if you jostled your memory.

FRED: I told you I never signed anything. . . . (*Suddenly inspired.*) Well, as a matter of fact, I did sign that IOU.

FIRST MAN: He remembers.

SECOND MAN: What a relief.

FIRST MAN: When are you gonna pay this debt of honor to one of America's most respectable floating crap games?

FRED: That's just it. I haven't got it. I would have, at the end of the week, if the show could run.

FIRST MAN: It'll run. It's entertaining, vivacious, and calculated to please the discriminating theatre-goer. You can quote me.

FRED: Unfortunately, Miss Vanessi, my co-star, is quitting.

FIRST MAN: Quitting?

FRED: As of right now. Temperament. Didn't like the way I played a little scene. She's dressing to leave the theatre. I'll have to return whatever money there is in the box office.

FIRST MAN: She can't do that!

FRED: Perhaps if you talked to her, heart to heart.

FIRST MAN: That's our specialty.

    (FRED *opens the door to* LILLI'S *dressing-room.*)

FRED (*small-voiced and affable, entering* LILLI'S *room*): Lilli! Oh, Lilli!

LILLI (*without turning to look at him*): There's no use trying to persuade me to stay.

FRED: Some very ardent admirers of yours. Come in, gentlemen.

    (*The two men enter.* LILLI *turns around to meet them.*)

LILLI (*graciously*): How do you do? (*Indicates couch.*)

    (GUNMEN *sit rather gingerly, remove hats.* LILLI *sits on pouf.*)

FIRST MAN: Miss Vanessi, you been my ideal for years. I married my wife because in a certain light, when it's kinda dark, she might pass for your sister.

LILLI: How sweet.

FIRST MAN: Your glorious voice has been a inspiration to me in my work.

SECOND MAN: What a trouper!

FIRST MAN: What a personality!

SECOND MAN: Is it true, Miss Vanessi, that you're contemplating quitting this high-type entertainment?

LILLI: I am.

FIRST MAN: Now, you know, Miss Vanessi, the show must go on. (*Takes gun from shoulder holster, puts it in coat pocket.*) I'm just transferring the weight offa one side and onto the other. We've got a financial interest in the success of this show, as well as personal. And Miss Vanessi, you gotta play this show out tonight, and at least to the end of the week, when Mr. Graham pays his debt of honor.

LILLI (*rising, incensed—she's a brave girl*): Are you threatening me?

    (*Both men rise.*)

FIRST MAN: Now, Miss Vanessi, let's talk it over. (*He moves toward her, hand in gun pocket.*)

LILLI (*backing away, frightened*): Fred!

FRED (*leaning unconcernedly against the door and looking off into space*): This is an outrage!

BLACKOUT

SCENE 8

SCENE: *Front of* Shrew *curtain, a thing of colorful diamond-shaped pattern.* LOIS, LUCENTIO, *and* SINGERS.

SINGERS *enter in couples.* LOIS *and* LUCENTIO *dance on from left and right. This number gives us time to change to the next scene.*

"I Sing of Love"

ALL:
>   We sing of love,
>   We sing only of love,
>   Ye gods above,
>   May we never sing of anything but love
>   For love is the joy
>   Of ev'ry girl and boy
>   As love, later on,
>   Keeps 'em going till they're gone,
>   Yes, love is the theme
>   Of all people who dream
>   So love, let's confess,
>   (GIRLS *sit on* BOYS' *knees.*)
>   Is ev'rybody's business.
>   Oh ye gods above,
>   May we never sing of anything but love,
>   Sweet love.
>   (*1st Patter.*)

BOY:
>   I won't sing a song about battle,

GIRL:
>   I won't sing of babies who prattle,

BOY:
>   I got no glee

From songs about the sea
Or cowboys songs about cattle.

GIRL:

I won't waste a note of my patters
On socially significant matters,

ALL:

We sing of one thing and we adore it
Thank Heaven for it!

ALL:

We sing of love,
We sing of love,
Ye gods above,
May we never sing of anything but love

BIANCA:

For love is the joy
Of ev'ry girl and boy
As love, later on,
Keeps 'em going till they're gone,

LUCENTIO:

Yes, love is the theme
Of all people who dream
So love, let's confess,

ALL:

Is ev'rybody's business.
Oh ye gods above,
May we never sing of anything but love,
Sweet love.

SCENE 9

SCENE: *Exterior church, seven arches covered with greenery, with oranges and white flowers showing through.*

DANCING ENSEMBLE *begins tarantella, joined by* BIANCA *and* LUCENTIO. *At end of dance church bells ring. The ceremony within is over. Wedding guests enter, some laughing, others puzzled and disapproving.*

BAPTISTA *comes out of church, dismayed, followed by* BIANCA, LUCENTIO.

BAPTISTA:

Such a marriage never was before! The man is mad.

LUCENTIO:

And so madly mated.

BIANCA:

And in such garb! An old jerkin! And a pair of breeches thrice turned!

LUCENTIO:

A pair of boots that have candle cases and not even mates! One buckled! Another laced!

(PETRUCHIO *emerges from church carrying whip.*)

PETRUCHIO:

Come, my bonny Kate—

(*After pause, roars.*)

I said, come!

(*Cracks whip.*)

(KATHARINE *emerges in real, sullen anger, flanked by both* GUNMEN *in* Shrew *costumes.*)

Oh Kate, content thee, I prithee be not angry.

(*As* GUNMEN *enter with* KATHARINE, LUCENTIO *whispers to* BIANCA *his fear and rushes for exit.* BIANCA *catches him and drags him back.*)

KATHARINE (*moving to* PETRUCHIO. GUNMEN *move after her. Sullenly*):

I will be angry. What has thou to do?

(*Waves toward the house.*)

Forward to the bridal dinner. I see a woman may be made a fool of, if she has not spirit to resist!

PETRUCHIO:

Obey the bride, you that attend on her. Go to the feast and revel and domineer.

(PETRUCHIO *whirls first gangster downstage left, returns to center.*)

Carouse full measure to her maidenhead. Be mad, be merry, or go hang yourselves!

(*Shoves second gangster downstage right. They assume positions of guards and case the house. Snaps whip at* SECOND GUNMAN *to bring both* GUNMEN's *attention to stage.* SECOND GUNMAN *pulls gun from belt, then reassured, puts it back.*)

But for my bonny Kate, she must with me! . . . Nay, look not big, nor stamp, nor stare, nor fret—I will be master of what is mine own. She is my goods, my chattels, my horse, my ox, my ass, my anything—touch her whoever dare! I'll bring mine action on the proudest he that dares to stop my way in Padua.

(*As* KATE *attempts to run upstage, he catches her with whip.*)
(*Begins.*)

"Kiss Me, Kate"

PETRUCHIO:
> So kiss me, Kate,
> Thou lovely loon,
> Ere we start
> On our honeymoon,
> Oh, kiss me, Kate
> Darling devil divine
> For now thou shall ever be mine.

KATE:
> I'll never be thine.

PETRUCHIO, ALL OTHER PRINCIPALS, and SINGERS
> So kiss $\begin{cases} \text{me,} \\ \text{him,} \end{cases}$ Kate,

KATE:
> No!

PETRUCHIO and OTHERS:
> Thou lovely loon,

KATE:
> Go!

PETRUCHIO and OTHERS:
> Ere $\begin{cases} \text{we} \\ \text{you} \end{cases}$ start

KATE:
> Nay!

PETRUCHIO and OTHERS:
> On $\begin{cases} \text{our} \\ \text{your} \end{cases}$ honeymoon

KATE:
> Away!

PETRUCHIO and OTHERS:
> Oh, kiss $\begin{cases} \text{me,} \\ \text{him,} \end{cases}$ Kate,

KATE:
> Fred!

PETRUCHIO and OTHERS:
>Darling devil divine,

KATE:
>Kindly drop dead!

PETRUCHIO (*solo*):
>For now thou shall ever be

KATE:
>Now I shall never be

PETRUCHIO and MEN:
>Now thou shall ever be

KATE and GIRLS:
>{ Now I shall never be thine
>{ Now thou shall never be

PETRUCHIO:
>Yes, mine.

KATE:
>Not thine.

PETRUCHIO:
>Yes, mine.

KATE:
>You swine.

PETRUCHIO:
>Yes, mine.

KATE:
>You swine.

PETRUCHIO and SINGERS:
>She called.

PETRUCHIO:
>Yes, mine.

PETRUCHIO and SINGERS:
>Him a swine.

PETRUCHIO:
>So kiss me, Kate

KATE:
>I'll crack your pate.

PETRUCHIO:
>Oh, please don't pout.

KATE:
>I'll knock you out.

PETRUCHIO:

My priceless prize!

KATE:

I'll black your eyes.

PETRUCHIO:

Oh kiss me quick!

KATE:

Your rump I'll kick.

PETRUCHIO and OTHERS:

Oh, kiss $\begin{cases} \text{me!} \\ \text{him!} \end{cases}$

KATE:

Bounder!

OTHERS:

He's not her dish, he's not her dish.

PETRUCHIO and OTHERS:

Oh, kiss $\begin{cases} \text{me!} \\ \text{him!} \end{cases}$

KATE:

Flounder!

OTHERS:

A type of fish she would not wish,

PETRUCHIO and OTHERS:

Oh, kiss $\begin{cases} \text{me!} \\ \text{him!} \end{cases}$

KATE:

Dastard!

OTHERS:

What's that we heard, what's that we heard?

PETRUCHIO and OTHERS:

Oh, kiss $\begin{cases} \text{me!} \\ \text{him!} \end{cases}$

KATE:

Bastard!

OTHERS:

Oh! Katie! That's a naughty word.

PETRUCHIO and GIRLS:

Oh, kiss $\begin{cases} \text{me.} \\ \text{him.} \end{cases}$

MEN and GIRLS:
> Kiss him.

PETRUCHIO and GIRLS:
> Kiss {me. / him.}

MEN and GIRLS:
> Kiss him.

PETRUCHIO and GIRLS and BASSES:
> Kiss {me. / him.}

MEN and GIRLS:
> Kiss him.

KATE (*in a paroxysm of coloratura*):
> Never! Never—never—never . . .

(*As* KATHARINE *starts coloratura, a girl enters carrying a bird. At end of coloratura bird goes up in air.* FIRST GUNMAN *shoots at bird. Bird drops to stage, generally on* BAPTISTA'S *hat.*)

PETRUCHIO and OTHERS:
> Kiss {me, / him,} Kiss {me, / him,} {Kate, Kiss {me / him}
>
> Kiss {me, / him,} Kate, Kiss {me / him}
>
> Kiss {me, / him,} Kate, Kiss {me / him}
>
> Kiss {me, / him,} Kate, Kiss {me / him}
>
> Kiss {me, / him,} Kate, Kiss {me / him}
>
> Kiss {me, / him,} Kate
>
> Kiss {me, / him,} Kate
>
> Kiss {me, / him,} Kate
>
> Kiss {me, / him,} Kate
>
> Kiss {me, / him,} Kate.

(*Two girls unwind silken ropes to hold the wedding guests back. The* DANCERS, *now perched on top of arches, throw streamers and confetti.*)

PETRUCHIO and OTHERS:

Kiss $\begin{cases} \text{me,} \\ \text{him,} \end{cases}$ Kate

Kiss $\begin{cases} \text{me,} \\ \text{him,} \end{cases}$ Kate

Kiss (*Streamer falls from cradle above.*)

PETRUCHIO and OTHERS:

$\begin{cases} \text{me} \\ \text{him} \end{cases}$

GANGSTERS (*spoken*):

Aw—kiss him.

PETRUCHIO and OTHERS:

Kate!

(PETRUCHIO *picks up* KATHARINE *and throws her over his shoulder, carries her, kicking and pummeling him in wild, useless protest as*
Curtain falls.)

END OF ACT ONE

ACT TWO

SCENE I

SCENE: *The dimly lit alley fronting the smudgy, red-brick rear of the theatre. A single bulb over the stage door barely illuminates the black lettering on it. Through the small open windows that break the monotony of the wall, you can make out the faces of the performers in their cubicles as they give in to the heat of the night. In back, an electric-light sign indicates a distant street corner. On stage, two Negro friends of* PAUL, FRED's *dresser, are seated on an empty packing-case playing cards in desultory fashion. They're waiting to make a "touch." A working* PAUL *is legitimate prey.*

PAUL *enters, leaving stage door open. Sees his friends and we go into the number: "Too Darn Hot."*

During this number, the DANCERS *and* SINGERS *saunter out in twos and threes, drinking pop and Cokes out of bottles and lighting an occasional cigarette. They are all in* Shrew *costumes, but the men have opened up their jackets, and the women have tucked their purple-and-cerise chiffon skirts into their waistbands as high as they'll go. They fan themselves with Woolworth fans and pieces of newspaper.*

At a certain point of the number, BILL *comes out for a quiet smoke, tosses cigarette away, and joins* PAUL *and his two friends in a spirited jazz session into which the* DANCERS *throw themselves with Bacchanalian zest. We must assume that it's never too hot to dance.*

And so PAUL *and his two pals sing:*

"Too Darn Hot"

(*1st Verse*)

PAUL:

> It's too darn hot,
> It's too darn hot.
> I'd like to sup with my baby tonight
> And play the pup with my baby tonight,
> I'd like to sup with my baby tonight
> And play the pup with my baby tonight
> But I ain't up to my baby tonight
> 'Cause it's too darn hot.

BOYS:

It's too darn hot,
It's too darn hot.

PAUL:

I'd like to stop for my baby tonight
And blow my top with my baby tonight,
I'd like to stop for my baby tonight
Blow my top with my baby tonight
But I'd be a flop with my baby tonight
'Cause it's too darn hot.

BOYS:

It's too darn hot,
It's too darn hot.

PAUL:

I'd like to fool with my baby tonight,
Break ev'ry rule with my baby tonight,

TRIO:

I'd like to fool with my baby tonight,
Break ev'ry rule with my baby tonight
But pillow, you'll be my baby tonight
'Cause it's too darn hot.

(*1st Refrain*)

TRIO:

According to the Kinsey report
Ev'ry average man you know
Much prefers to play his favorite sport
When the temperature is low
But when the thermometer goes 'way up
And the weather is sizzling hot

PAUL:

Mister Adam
For his madam,
Is not.

TRIO:

'Cause it's too, too,
Too darn hot,
It's too darn hot.
It's too darn hot.

(*2nd Verse*)

BOYS:

    It's too darn hot,
    It's too darn hot.

PAUL:

    I'd like to call on my baby tonight
    And give my all to my baby tonight,

TRIO:

    I'd like to call on my baby tonight
    And give my all to my baby tonight

PAUL:

    But I can't play ball with my baby tonight
    'Cause it's too darn hot.

TRIO:

    It's too, too darn hot,
    It's too, too darn hot.

PAUL:

    I'd like to meet with my baby tonight,
    Get off my feet with my baby tonight,
    I'd like to meet with my baby tonight,
    Get off my feet with my baby tonight
    But no repeat with my baby tonight
    'Cause it's too darn hot.

BOYS:

    It's too darn hot,
    It's too darn hot.

PAUL:

    I'd like to coo to my baby tonight
    And pitch some woo with my baby tonight,
    I'd like to coo to my baby tonight
    And pitch some woo with my baby tonight
    But, brother, you bite my baby tonight
    'Cause it's too darn hot.

    (*2nd Refrain*)

TRIO:

    According to the Kinsey report
    Ev'ry average man you know
    Much prefers to play his favorite sport
    When the temperature is low
    But when the thermometer goes 'way up

And the weather is sizzling hot
Mister Gob
For his squab,
A marine
For his queen,
A G.I.
For his cutie-pie
Is not
'Cause it's too, too,
Too darn hot.
It's too darn hot,
It's too, too, too, too darn hot.

(*End of dance, blackout leaving on lights in stage door.* RALPH *enters through door.*)

RALPH: On stage everybody!
(BILL *and* DANCERS *exit through stage door.*)

BLACKOUT

SCENE 2

SCENE: *On stage again. Intermission is over. The diamond-patterned* Shrew *curtain is in place, but the stage is empty. After a second or two,* FRED GRAHAM, *in his Petruchio costume, comes quickly through the break in the curtain. Conductor in pit senses something amiss and taps baton on stand for musicians to stop playing.*

FRED: Ladies and Gentlemen, due to unavoidable circum-stances, the scene which was to have opened the second part of *The Shrew* will have to be omitted this evening. It's the scene on the mule where I, Petruchio, take Katharine, my wife, to Verona. We have a slight accident where my wife rolls off the mule into the mud and then proceeds to revile me. Miss Vanessi is unable to ride the mule this evening. We are, therefore, continuing with the next scene, which takes place in Petruchio's house. Thank you. (*Indicates to orchestra conductor to carry on, and retreats.*)

SCENE 3

SCENE: *Curtain parts to disclose main room in* PETRUCHIO'S *house. It is barely furnished. A door leads to* PETRUCHIO'S *bedroom. Long table with bowl of fruit and large vase and a low chair on either side of table comprise the furnishings.*

PETRUCHIO (*off stage*):
What—no man at the door to hold my stirrup nor to take my horse?
(*He enters before servants can get there.*)
Where be these knaves?
(*We now see* KATHARINE *grimly following* PETRUCHIO *in. She is disheveled, her wedding gown torn, her hair streaming down her back in sweet disorder.*)
Where is Nathaniel?
NATHANIEL (*entering*): Here, sir.
PETRUCHIO: Gregory.
GREGORY (*entering*): Here, sir.
PETRUCHIO: Phillip.
PHILLIP (*entering*): Here, sir.
PETRUCHIO:
You logger-headed and unpolish'd grooms! (*Pushes* NATHAN-IEL *over to other two servants.*)
(GUNMEN *enter. They're still in their ill-fitting* Shrew *costumes and street shoes.*)
What? No attendance? No regard? No duty? (*Removes cape and hat and throws them to servants.*) Go, rascals, go, and fetch my supper in.
(*Servants exit.*)
(*To* GUNMEN.) Kind strangers, thou angels in disguise who did help me in my hour of need, 'twere well you rested from your travels in yon chamber.
(*Indicates door right.* GUNMEN, *puzzled, look in direction indicated, but don't budge.*)
Get ye hence. Go to, go to— (*Indicates for them to scram.*)
FIRST MAN (*getting it, nudges his colleague*): Come to, come to— (*They exit.*)

PETRUCHIO: Food! Food! Food! Where are those . . . (*Glances at* KATHARINE *carelessly.*) Sit down, Kate. . . .

KATHARINE (*glumly*): Thou knowest full well that I cannot.

PETRUCHIO:

Well, then, stand and be merry!

(*Sits at table.*)

Some water, here; what, ho!

Where's my spaniel Troilus? Shall I have some water?

(*A servant enters with jug and cup.* PETRUCHIO *trips him.*)

Come, Kate, and wash, and welcome heartily.

You whoreson villain, will you let it fall?

(*Picks up servant and as he runs off, kicks at him. Other servants enter with food and a chair cushion.*)

KATHARINE

Patience, I pray you, 'twas a fault unwilling.

PETRUCHIO:

A whoreson beetle-headed, flap-ear'd knave!

Come, Kate, sit down; I know you have a stomach.

(*Places cushion on chair. As* KATE *goes to sit down he snatches cushion, as she almost sits on it, and gives it to servant.*)

Will you give thanks, sweet Kate, or else shall I?

What's this? Mutton?

NATHANIEL:

Aye.

PETRUCHIO (*taking it from her*): Who brought it?

PHILLIP (*stepping forward*): I.

(KATHARINE *tries to take some.*)

PETRUCHIO:

'Tis burnt, and so is all the meat,

What dogs are these? Where is the rascal cook?

How durst you, villains, bring it from the dresser,

And serve it thus to me that love it not?

Here, take it 'way, trenchers, cups, and all.

(PETRUCHIO *throws cups and plates off stage and servants scatter.* KATHARINE, *her back to* PETRUCHIO, *stuffs string of sausages down front of dress.*)

KATHARINE:

I pray you, husband, be not so disquiet,

The meat was well, if you were so contented.

PETRUCHIO:

I tell thee, Kate, 'twas burnt and dried away

And I expressly am forbid to touch it,
For it engenders choler, planteth anger, and
    (*Takes sausages out of* KATE'*s dress.*)
Better 'twere that both of us did fast
Since of ourselves, ourselves are choleric
Than feed it with such over-roasted flesh.

KATHARINE:
Did you marry me to famish me?

PETRUCHIO:
Tomorrow shall you eat, my honey love,
When we return unto thy father's house
And revel it as bravely as the best with silken coats
And caps and golden rings,
With ruffs and cuffs and fardingales and things. . . .
    (*Enter* HABERDASHER *with cap and mirror upstage left.*)
Come, let us see these ornaments.
    (*To* HABERDASHER.)
And what news with you, sir?

HABERDASHER:
The cap your worship did bespeak.

PETRUCHIO:
Aha! 'Tis for thee, Kate.
    (HABERDASHER *holds up cap.*)
Why this was molded on a porringer,
A velvet dish—
    (*Puts on cap and looks in mirror.*)
                —fie!—'tis lewd and filthy,
'Tis a cockle or a walnut shell.
Come! Let me have a bigger.

KATHARINE (*rising, takes hat*):
I'll have no bigger, this doth fit the time,
And gentlewomen wear such caps as these.

PETRUCHIO:
When you are gentle, you shall have one, too
And not till then.
    (*Takes hat from* KATE.)

KATHARINE (*in anger*):
I am no child, no babe;
Your betters have endur'd me say my mind,
And if you cannot, best you stop your ears.

My tongue will tell the anger of my heart.
Or else my heart concealing it, will break.
>   (*Grabs hat from* PETRUCHIO *and puts it on.*)

PETRUCHIO:
Why, thou say'st true, it is a paltry cap,
I love thee well in that thou lik'st it not.
>   (*Takes hat from* KATE.)

Begone! Take it hence!
>   (*Throws hat to* HABERDASHER. HABERDASHER *exits.*
>   *Assuming gentleness.*)

Well, my Kate; tomorrow we will unto your father's,
>   (*Slaps her on shoulder.*)

Even in these honest mean habiliments:
Our purses shall be proud, our garments poor;
For 'tis the mind that makes the body rich:
What, (*slap*) is the jay more precious than the lark,
Because his feathers are more beautiful?
Or is the adder better than the eel,
Because his painted skin contents the eye?
>   (*Slaps her again.*)

Oh, no, good Kate; neither art thou the worse
For this poor furniture and mean array.
Come, come, I will bring thee to thy bridal chamber.
>   (*Takes her to bedroom door.*)

KATHARINE (*in tears*):
I'm hungry.

PETRUCHIO:
How canst thou think of food at such a time?
>   (*Helps* KATHARINE *through door. Slams it shut, triumphantly.*
>   *To audience.*)

Thus have I politically begun my reign,
And 'tis my hope to end it successfully.
My falcon now is sharp, and passing empty,
And, till she stoop, she must not be full-gorged,
She ate no meat today, nor none shall eat;
Last night she slept not, nor tonight she shall not;
As with the meat, some undeserved fault
I'll find about the making of the bed,
And here I'll fling the pillow, there the bolster,
This way the coverlet, another way the sheets;

Aye, and amid this hurly I intend
That all is done in reverent care of her,
And, in conclusion, she shall watch the night,
And if she chance to nod, I'll rail and brawl,
And with the clamor keep her still awake;
This is a way to kill a wife with kindness,
And thus I'll curb her mad and headstrong humor.
    (*Turns upstage to door.*)
He that knows better how to tame a shrew,
Now let him speak, 'tis charity to show.
    (*He goes to bedroom door. Softly.*)
Kate—
    (*No answer. Louder.*)
My bonny Kate—
    (*No answer. Bawling.*)
My winsome Kate—
    (*No answer. He tries door in anger. It is locked.*)
I' faith, the woman's shot her bolt!
She has performed
While I did act the dolt!

       "Where is the Life That Late I Led?"
  (*Verse*)
    Since I reached the charming age of puberty
    And began to finger feminine curls,
    Like a show that's typically Shuberty
  (*Kicks leg.*)
    I have always had a multitude of girls,
    But now that a married man, at last, am I,
    How aware of my dear, departed past am I.
  (*1st Refrain*)
    Where is the life that late I led?
    Where is it now? Totally dead.
    Where is the fun I used to find?
    Where has it gone? Gone with the wind.
    A married life may all be well,
    But raising an heir
    Could never compare
    With raising a bit of hell.
    So I repeat what first I said,

Where is the life that late I—
(*Takes address book from waistband, consults it. 1st Patter.*)
In dear Milano, where are you, Momo,
Still selling those pictures of the scriptures in the
    Duomo?
And Carolina, where are you, Lina,
Still peddling your pizza in the streets o' Taormina?
And in Firenze, where are you, Alice,
Still there in your pretty, itty-bitty Pitti palace?
And sweet Lucretia, so young and gay-ee?
What scandalous doin's in the ruins of Pompeii!
(*2nd Refrain*)
Where is the life that late I led?
Where is it now? Totally dead.
Where is the fun I used to find?
Where has it gone? Gone with the wind.
The marriage game is quite all right,
Yes, during the day
It's easy to play,
But oh what a bore at night.
So I repeat what first I said,
Where is the life that late I—
(*Looks in book again. 2nd Patter.*)
Where is Rebecca, my Becki-weckio,
Could still she be cruising that amusing Ponte
    Vecchio?
Where is Fedora, the wild virago?
It's lucky I missed her gangster sister from Chicago.
Where is Venetia who loved to chat so,
Could still she be drinkin' in her stinkin', pink
    palazzo?
And lovely Lisa where are you, Lisa?
You gave a new meaning to the leaning tow'r of Pisa.
(*3rd Refrain*)
Where is the life that late I led?
Where is it now? Totally dead.
Where is the fun I used to find?
Where has it gone? Gone with the wind.
I've oft been told of nuptial bliss
But what do you do,

A quarter to two,
With only a shrew to kiss?
So I repeat what first I said,
Where is the life that late I led?

(*At the end of song,* PETRUCHIO *bows and backs into door. It opens. He winks, throws black address book away, and exits through door.*)

SCENE 4

SCENE: *Corridor backstage. Same setting as Act I, Scene 2. An ambulance siren, first heard faintly, then real loud and stopping as if ambulance has drawn up outside.*

DOORMAN *comes through stage door as* RALPH *enters from opposite direction.*

RALPH: Who's making all that noise? What's that siren?

DOORMAN: There's an ambulance out there for Miss Vanessi, and a gentleman by the name of Harrison Howell—

RALPH: What?

DOORMAN: He's raising a helluva rumpus.

(HOWELL *enters, followed by a doctor and two nurses. He's a dignified gentleman—not bad-looking, but a little stuffy.*)

HOWELL: I demand . . . Where is Miss Vanessi?

RALPH: Are you Mr. Harrison Howell?

HOWELL: Of course I'm Harrison Howell. Where's Miss Vanessi? How is she?

RALPH: She's doing fine.

HOWELL: Where is she?

RALPH: On stage.

HOWELL: On stage? How can she be on stage? She's ill.

RALPH: Not that I know of.

HOWELL: Of course she's ill! She told me so herself. She's been assaulted by that brute, dammit.

(FRED *enters right, followed by* TWO GUNMEN.)

FRED: Quiet, dammit!

HOWELL: Look here, Graham!

FIRST GUNMAN: He said quiet, dammit.

SECOND GUNMAN: Shhh . . .

FIRST GUNMAN (*softly*): Ain't you got no appreciation of the finer things of life?

SECOND GUNMAN (*as softly*): Man cannot live by bread alone.

HOWELL: What?

FRED (*to* GUNMEN, *very quietly*): Be tolerant, gentlemen. Remember Mr. Howell didn't have your advantages—eight years in the prison library in Atlanta!

HOWELL: What?

FRED: However, Mr. Howell is a very distinguished man. He's the only Republican who didn't run for the nomination.

HOWELL: How dare you assault my fiancée?

FRED: She hit me first!

HOWELL: I don't understand this. She asked me to bring an ambulance.

FRED: My dear Howell. You fail to take into consideration the caprices of women of talent and beauty. She may even say to you tonight: "Harrison, I am playing this show under duress. Call the F.B.I."

FIRST GUNMAN: A very efficient organization.

SECOND GUNMAN: Admirable co-ordination.

HOWELL: But why should she want the F.B.I.?

FRED: Why should she want an ambulance? My dear Howell, your fiancée may ask for chewing-gum, a miniature of the Empire State in pale ivory, or a fifth of Chanel Number Five.

RALPH: On stage, Mr. Graham.

> (LOIS *starts down stairs.*)

FRED: Why how now, Kate? I hope thou art not mad. This is a man—old—wrinkled—faded and withered. (*Clears his throat noisily and exits reciting same line.*)

LOIS (*at bottom of staircase*): Harold! . . . Why, Harold Murgatroyd!

HOWELL: All right, Doctor, nurses—I shan't need you.

> (*They exit.*)

LOIS (*crossing to* HOWELL *center*): Harold! Harold!

HOWELL: My name is not Harold! I am Harrison Howell!

LOIS: Harold, don't you remember? In front of the Harvard Club.

> (*He looks about guiltily.*)

I had something in my eye, and you took me to Atlantic City to take it out?

HOWELL: Look here, my child—

LOIS: Harold, I've still got that diamond bracelet with the rubies. I think of you all the time when I go down to my safe deposit box.

(BILL *enters, unseen by* LOIS.)

HOWELL: Very touching . . . Very touching . . . (*Looks about.*) But you must understand—

LOIS: I understand—

HOWELL: I rely on your discretion. I'm marrying Miss Vanessi, you know—

LOIS: Oh, I understand—

HOWELL: After all, I was just sowing my wild oats. Let me see—I was quite a young man at the time—barely forty-five.

LOIS: And now you're a big man in Washington!

HOWELL: Well, I have achieved a certain distinction. I'm the minority elder statesman. I have my own park bench.

RALPH: This way, Mr. Howell.

HOWELL: Thank you. (*To* LOIS.) Excuse me. (*Starts to go.*)

LOIS: One thing I've always wanted to know—what do you do about the pigeons?

HOWELL: Duck, my dear. Just duck. (*Exits.*)

BILL (*whistling first three notes of "Bianca"*): When did you initiate him?

LOIS: (*caught, therefore indignant*): What a thing to say! And about a man I haven't seen in years! I assure you there was nothing between he and I. Just because a girl is good-hearted and normal—and wants to get along—with her fellow man! (*She goes into:*)

> "Always True to You in My Fashion"
> (*Verse*)
>   Oh, Bill,
>   Why can't you behave?
>   Why can't you behave?
>   How in hell can you be jealous
>   When you know, baby, I'm your slave?
> (BILL *shrugs and exits.*)
>   I'm just mad for you,
>   And I'll always be
>   But naturally.

(*1st Refrain*)

If a custom-tailored vet
Asks me out for something wet,
When the vet begins to pet, I cry "Hooray!"
But I'm always true to you, darlin', in my fashion,
Yes, I'm always true to you, darlin', in my way.
I enjoy a tender pass
By the boss of Boston, Mass.
Though his pass is middle-class and notta Backa Bay,
But I'm always true to you, darlin', in my fashion,
Yes, I'm always true to you, darlin', in my way.
There's a madman known as "Mack"
Who is planning to attack,
If his mad attack means a Cadillac, okay!
But I'm always true to you, darlin', in my fashion,
Yes, I'm always true to you, darlin', in my way.

(*2nd Refrain*)

I've been asked to have a meal
By a big tycoon in steel,
If the meal includes a deal, accept I may,
But I'm always true to you, darlin', in my fashion,
Yes, I'm always true to you, darlin', in my way.
I could never curl my lip
To a dazzlin' diamond clip
Though the clip meant "let 'er rip," I'd not say "Nay!"
But I'm always true to you, darlin', in my fashion,
Yes, I'm always true to you, darlin', in my way.
There's an oil man known as "Tex"
Who is keen to give me checks
And his checks, I fear, mean that sex is here to stay!
But I'm always true to you, darlin', in my fashion,
Yes, I'm always true to you, darlin', in my way.

(*3rd Refrain*)

There's a wealthy Hindu priest
Who's a wolf, to say the least,
When the priest goes too far east, I also stray,
But I'm always true to you, darlin', in my fashion,
Yes, I'm always true to you, darlin', in my way.
There's a lush from Portland, Ore.
Who is rich but sich a bore

When the bore falls on the floor, I let him lay,
But I'm always true to you, darlin', in my fashion,
Yes, I'm always true to you, darlin', in my way.
Mr. Harris, plutocrat,
Wants to give my cheek a pat,
If the Harris pat
Means a Paris hat
Bé-bé
Oo-la-la
Mais je suis toujours fidèle,
Darlin' in my fashion,
Oui, je suis toujours fidèle,
Darlin' in my way.
(*4th Refrain*)
From Ohio Mister Thorne
Calls me up from night till morn,
Mister Thorne once cornered corn and that ain't hay,
  ha, ha, ha,
But I'm always true to you, darlin', in my fashion,
Yes, I'm always true to you, darlin', in my way.
From Milwaukee, Mister Fritz
Often moves me to the Ritz,
Mister Fritz is full of Schlitz and full of play,
But I'm always true to you, darlin', in my fashion,
Yes, I'm always true to you, darlin', in my way.
Mister Gable, I mean Clark,
Wants me on his boat to park,
If the Gable boat
Means a sable coat,
Anchors aweigh!
But I'm always true to you, darlin', in my fashion,
Yes, I'm always true to you, darlin', in my way.

BLACKOUT

SCENE 5

SCENE: LILLI's *dressing-room.*
   HARRISON HOWELL *is on the telephone at dressing-table.*

HOWELL: This is Harrison Howell. Give me my secretary—

Timothy? I'm waiting here for Miss Vanessi, and I thought I'd jot down my wedding itinerary. . . . Ready? We'll be married in St. Thomas's, 2:30. Got that? (*Consults notes.*) Wedding reception at the Waldorf, 4:15. Got that? Press conference, 5:38. Arrive La Guardia, 6:25. Depart, 6:30. Got that?

(FRED *enters, in dressing-gown over costume, and sits on couch.*) Arrive Washington, 9:35. Arrive White House, 9:55. Got that? Conference with President and honeymoon with wife.

FRED: It's a good trick if you can do it.

(LILLI *enters in* Shrew *outfit, followed by the* TWO GUNMEN, *also in* Shrew *costumes, who post themselves back of lounge.*)

LILLI: Harrison! They told me you were here!

HOWELL: That's all, Timothy.

LILLI: Don't hang up, Harrison. I'm playing this show under duress. Call the F.B.I.

(HARRISON *looks at* FRED. *That's what he said she'd say.*)

FRED: What did I tell you?

HOWELL (*hanging up phone*): Now, my dear—I don't mind bringing an ambulance and a doctor and two nurses. They're on my payroll. But the F.B.I. is not. I'm perfectly willing—in fact I enjoy humoring the caprices of a beautiful woman whom I happen to adore—

LILLI: Caprices? These thugs threatened me!

HOWELL: What?

LILLI: They're making me play at the point of a gun. They won't let me leave the theatre.

(HOWELL *looks at* FRED. FRED *shrugs.*)

HOWELL: Now, my dear—

LILLI: Can't you see they're gangsters?

FIRST GUNMAN: I guess it shows.

FRED (*rising and going toward* TWO GUNMEN): Are you referring to two of the most promising graduates of the Group? Not to mention the Guild Theatre, Inc., the Civic Repertory, and Miss Pennyfeather's School of Charm, whose faculty they grace!

LILLI: And you're in cahoots with them!

HOWELL: What?

FRED: What can one say to libel?

FIRST GUNMAN: Should I say something?

FRED: No.

SECOND GUNMAN: Discretion is the better part of valor.

FIRST GUNMAN: "Famous Sayings" . . . Top shelf, under Non-Fiction, right-hand corner, Atlanta . . . No talking . . . No smoking.

HOWELL (*a little dazed*): Obviously, my dear, judging by their costumes, and their speech, these men are not what you say they are.

LILLI: Harrison, darling, I tell you—

FRED (*interrupting*): Do you realize what it means to blast a reputation? Of course not. You think nothing of dragging Harrison down here—and an entire Medical Corps—for a whim!

HOWELL: Now, my dear, I'd like to go over my wedding itinerary—I just dictated it to Timothy. Now, I thought we'd be married a week from Monday. At 2:30, St. Thomas's. That'll give you just enough time to assemble a trousseau.

LILLI: Harrison darling, listen to me. I can't get out of this theatre!

HOWELL: Why not?

LILLI: These thugs won't let me.

FRED: Why don't you try it?

LILLI: What?

FRED: Go! . . . Of course you can leave the theatre. That's what you want, and I can't say I blame you. After all, what is there in the theatre to hold you? It's so tawdry—the dreary business of creating a part—the dull routine of watching a character come to life. The meaningless excitement of opening night. The boring thundering applause of the crowd—the pictures in the papers—the parties—the idiotic men and women who stare and whisper: "There goes Lilli Vanessi!" Dreadful! I don't blame you for leaving all that—when you've a chance for happiness—real happiness—with Harrison.

HOWELL: Thank you, Graham. I think I can make the little woman happy.

LILLI: I never want to see the theatre again! (*To* FRED.) Or you again!

FRED: I envy you, Harrison. Never has a man acquired a woman with more sweetness of disposition, who's more even-tempered, has more poise, more gentleness, more sheer unadulterated goodness. Yum, yum, yum . . . Yes, Lilli Vanessi is the wife for you. Get Lilli Vanessi today! This is N.B.C.!

LILLI: I hope you're enjoying yourself.

FRED: Enormously . . . And envying *you.*

LILLI: Me?

FRED: The life you're going to lead with Harrison. So different than the one you had with me.

LILLI: I'll see to that.

FRED: No quarrels—no bickering . . .

LILLI: I want peace!

FRED: And you shall have it—peace—quiet—stability.

HOWELL: I've got a place down in Georgia—thirty thousand acres. Ride for days, and not see a soul, except my tenant farmers!

FRED: You won't have to talk to a soul.

LILLI: I shall adore it!

FRED: Of course you will.

HOWELL: Wonderful life.

FRED: What do you call the place: *Solitude?*

HOWELL: No. *Contentment.*

FRED: Ah! *Contentment.* Just think. No cocktail parties. No malicious gossip. No backbiting friends. In fact, no friends at all, except an occasional mongoose who'll drop in for dinner.

LILLI: Go on! Go on!

HOWELL: We'll see all the people we want to see in Washington.

FRED: Certainly. Just think of those intimate little dinner parties for the sparkling Supreme Court. Just think of the privilege of sitting next to one of the Great Judicial Brains while he tells you the inside story of his sciatica.

HOWELL (*indicating his back*): It always hits me here. . . .

FRED: Oh, it'll be a mad whirl—

LILLI: I'll still love it.

HOWELL: I always rest up in my place in Aiken. Got a dining-room there can seat a hundred.

FRED: Marvelous!

FIRST GUNMAN: Eight years I et in a dining-room that could seat twelve hundred.

LILLI: Where did you say this was?

FRED (*quickly, crossing to left end of lounge*): The commissary at M.G.M.

HOWELL: Got my own projection room in Aiken. Got the finest collection of Mickey Mouses in the country.

FIRST GUNMAN: Where's your grammar? Mickey Mice.

SECOND GUNMAN: Don't be a purist.

HOWELL: Mickey Mice?

(*The* GUNMEN *exit, satisfied. They've corrected a millionaire.*)

FRED: Yes, I can just see life at Aiken. Morning. Harrison rises—with the aid of a valet—

HOWELL: Been with me thirty years—

FRED: Into his riding-clothes. You into yours. A brisk canter.

LILLI: I'm mad about horses.

FRED: And eventually you'll stop falling off. . . . It's yoicks and away. . . . Back to the castle. A brisk shower. A massage. An injection of Vitamin B1.

HOWELL: Making a new man out of me.

FRED: And then—Harrison takes a nap.

HOWELL: Oh, no. Breakfast first.

FRED: Ah, yes, breakfast. You sit at one end of the long, long table. Harrison at the other. You pick up your telescope and watch fondly as Harrison slops his Wheaties.

HOWELL: Wheaties are good eatin'! There's nothing finer.

FRED: And then the nap!

HOWELL: Twenty minutes. Rests the brain.

FRED: Then up. You dress. You contemplate the luxurious swamps. You toy with your toilette. Harrison wakes. You discuss this and that, topics of the day. Will Big Frost escape Dick Tracy?

HOWELL: I very much doubt it!

FRED: Time for another nap.

HOWELL: Lunch first.

FRED: Correction accepted. Lunch first.

HOWELL: Got the finest chef in the country. But I've got to watch my diet. Stick to the yolk of an egg, shredded raw carrot, and a glass of milk. Done wonders for me.

FRED: As you'll be able to see through your telescope. And then—a nice, soothing, refreshing nap!

HOWELL (*lying back*): Thirty minutes. Rests the brain.

FRED: You, too, will nap, Miss Vanessi. Thirty minutes. Rests the brain. Then up. Dress. Walk in the formal gardens. Time for tea. High tea.

HOWELL: Always refreshes me.

FRED: Time for a nap—before dinner.

HOWELL: Fifteen minutes.

FRED: A quickie . . . Rested, you rise.

> (HOWELL *starts to sit up.* FRED *pushes him back.*)

You dress for dinner. You dine in that cozy little hundred-seater. Then a brisk game of dominoes.

HOWELL: Wonderful game.

FRED (*by* HOWELL'*s head*): The mocking-bird sings. . . . The air is still. . . . You feel drowsy. . . . You yawn deliciously. . . .

> (*And* HARRISON *yawns.*)

Time for the final nap of the day—the long one. . . . You stretch out. . . .

> (HARRISON *does so.*)

Your eyes close. . . .

> (HARRISON'*s do so.*)

LILLI (*whispering fiercely*): Get out!

FRED: Sh! . . . And so the little Momma bear said to the Poppa bear: "*You bore me.* . . ."

> (HARRISON *lets out a deafening snore.*)

BLACKOUT

SCENE 6

SCENE: *Corridor, same as Act II, Scene 4.*

At opening of scene, FOUR DANCING GIRLS *are grouped on stage.* DOORMAN *is standing left center stage.* BILL CALHOUN *stage right.* FOUR SINGING GIRLS *are on staircase.*

MESSENGER *enters from* DOORMAN'*s booth carrying an exaggerated hatbox. He walks to* DOORMAN.

"Bianca"

MESSENGER: Package for Miss Lois Lane.

> (DOORMAN *indicates right.* MESSENGER *exits with box.*)

SINGING GIRLS (*from stairs*):

> For your Bianca!
> Ha, ha, ha, ha, ha.

MESSENGER (*same business. He carries box from furrier's*): Package for Miss Lois Lane.

(DOORMAN *directs. He exits.*)

SINGING GIRLS:
>*For your Bianca!*
>*Ha, ha, ha, ha, ha.*

CHAUFFEUR: (*same business. He carries bottle of champagne*):
Package for Miss Lois Lane.
>(DOORMAN *directs. He exits right.*)

BANKER (*same business. He carries two bags of money*): Package
for Miss Lois Lane.
>(DOORMAN *directs. He exits.*)

TRUCKMAN (*same business. Enters from back of booth with a barrel
of Schlitz*): Package for Miss Lois Lane.
>(DOORMAN *directs him and follows him off.*)

SINGING GIRLS:
>*Ha, ha, ha, ha, ha, ha, ha.*
>*Ha, ha, ha, ha, ha, ha, ha.*
>*Your Bianca.*
>*Ha!*

BILL (*stops them, goes to center, and sings*):
>Sweet Bianca,
>While rehearsing with Bianca
>She's the darling I adore
>Off stage I found,
>She's been around,
>But I still love her more and more.
>So I've written her a love song
>Though I'm just an amateur,
>I'll sing it through
>For all of you
>To see if it's worthy of her.
>Are you list'nin'?
>(*Refrain*)
>(BILL *sings chorus.* SINGING GIRLS *whistle.* DANCERS *dance.
>What else can they do?*)
>(*1st Chorus*)
>Bianca, Bianca,
>Oh, baby, will you be mine?

Bianca, Bianca,
You better answer yes
Or Poppa spanka.
To win you, Bianca,
There's nothing I would not do.
I would gladly give up
Coffee for Sanka,
Even Sanka, Bianca,
For you.

(*2nd Chorus*)

(BILL *sings while he and* DANCERS *go into tap routine.* SINGING GIRLS *sing from stairs.*)

(*3rd Chorus*)

(BILL *and* DANCERS *doing routine,* SINGING GIRLS *on stairs. Exit at finish. One girl ascending stairs, other three exit right.*)

(BILL *and* FOUR DANCING GIRLS *exit, with the traditional high kick of the bygone musical show.*)

(*The* TWO GUNMEN *enter, in* Shrew *outfits, and go to coin phone box.*)

FIRST GUNMAN: (*puts in dime and dials number*): Hello. Hello, Gumpy. I want to talk to Mr. Hogan. Well, I want to report in, Gumpy. Mr. Hogan likes me to report in, Gumpy. Why should I call you *Mister* Gumpy? Where's Mr. Hogan? Oh, I see. . . . Yeah. . . . I see. . . . Well, certainly, we'll pay you a visit, Mr. Gumpy.

(FRED *enters, still in dressing-gown.*)

All right, Mr. Gumpy. (*Hangs up. Points up.*) Gumpy! (*Then down.*) Hogan.

SECOND GUNMAN: You mean it?

FRED: Who's Mr. Gumpy?

FIRST GUNMAN: Mr. Graham— (*Takes out IOU.*) I guess this is the end of our very pleasant association.

SECOND GUNMAN: I guess so.

FRED: What's this?

FIRST GUNMAN: I guess we got to declare a moratorium. You see, Mr. Gumpy declared a moratorium on Mr. Hogan. His unidentified remains will be found floating in the bay tomorrow morning.

SECOND GUNMAN: Rest his soul.

    (GUNMEN *remove hats and bow heads.*)

FIRST GUNMAN: So that lets you out. . . . And we must part.

FRED: Do you think Mr. Gumpy has the executive ability, the enterprise, the initiative, and the imagination for the post?

FIRST GUNMAN (*astutely*): No, but he's got the post.

    (LILLI *enters with* HATTIE, *carrying suitcase and jewel box. Both in street attire.*)

SECOND GUNMAN (*bows in grand manner*): We want to say au revoir, Miss Vanessi.

LILLI: What?

FIRST GUNMAN (*same bow*): It's been a delightful experience.

SECOND GUNMAN: Very educational.

FIRST GUNMAN: We'll always think of you.

SECOND GUNMAN: Should old acquaintance be forgot?

FRED: What they're trying to tell you is—you're free to go. You don't have to finish the show.

SECOND GUNMAN: Au revoir. (*Bows.*)

FIRST GUNMAN: Au revoir. (*Bows.*)

    (*They exit.* FIRST GUNMAN *takes dime from phone slot on way out.*)

LILLI: Run along, Hattie.

    (HATTIE *exits to street.*)

FRED: Aren't you taking Sleeping Beauty with you?

LILLI: Let him sleep.

FRED: Don't tell me the bloom is off—the rose?

LILLI (*on the verge of tears*): You are not Louella Parsons and I don't care to discuss my personal life with you.

FRED: Same old Lilli . . . And I thought I detected a note—a new note of softness—a new humility—even a spark of affection—a glimmer of love. . . . (*Closes to her.*)

LILLI (*hesitates—then pulls away*): You're not going to hypnotize me, Svengali.

FRED: Lilli, you can't walk out on me now.

LILLI: You walked out on me once.

FRED: But I came back.

    (LILLI *hesitates.*)

DOORMAN (*from his cubbyhole*): Your cab's waiting, Miss Vanessi!

    (LILLI *leaves.* FRED, *alone, reprises:*)

"So in Love"

FRED:

Strange, dear, but true, dear,
When I'm close to you, dear,
The stars fill the sky,
So in love with you am I.
Even without you
My arms fold about you,
You know darling why,
So in love with you am I.
In love with the night mysterious
The night when you first were there,
In love with my joy delirious
When I knew that you could care,
So taunt me and hurt me,
Deceive me, desert me,
I'm yours till I die,
So in love,
So in love,
So in love with you, my love, am I.
(*Goes off as lights dim.*)

BLACKOUT

SCENE 7

SCENE: *Safety asbestos curtain with two rather Rabelaisian cherubs painted on either side. Underneath, softly, music of "Brush up Your Shakespeare." The* TWO GUNMEN, *in their hand-sewn blue suits, make their way clumsily through opening in curtain. They carry straw hats.*

FIRST GUNMAN (*as he comes through curtain*): Hey! How do we get out of here?
SECOND GUNMAN (*following him*): How'd we get in here?
FIRST GUNMAN: I don't know—on that side—no . . . (*Sees backdrop.*) Hey, look! . . .
SECOND GUNMAN (*regarding cherub*): It's a boy!
(*And off they go into:*)

"Brush Up Your Shakespeare"
(*with an intermittent soft-shoe dance*)

(*Verse*)

The girls today in society
Go for classical poetry,
So to win their hearts, one must quote with ease
Aeschylus and Euripedes,
One must know Homer, and, b'lieve me, bo,
Sophocle—also Sappo-Ho,
Unless you know Shelley and Keats and Pope,
Dainty debbies will call you a dope.
But the poet of them all
Who will start 'em simply ravin'
Is the poet people call
(*Take hats off to Shakespeare.*)
"The Bard of Stratford-on-Avon."

(*1st Refrain*)

BOTH:

Brush up your Shakespeare,
Start quoting him now,
Brush up your Shakespeare
And the women you will wow.

SECOND GUNMAN:

Just declaim a few lines from *Othella*
And they'll think you're a helluva fella,

FIRST GUNMAN:

If your blonde won't respond when you flatter 'er
Tell her what Tony told Cleopaterer.

SECOND GUNMAN:

If she fights when her clothes you are mussing,

BOTH:

What are clothes? *Much Ado About Nussing.*
Brush up your Shakespeare
And they'll all kowtow.

(*2nd Refrain*)

BOTH:

Brush up your Shakespeare.
Start quoting him now,
Brush up your Shakespeare
And the women you will wow.

FIRST GUNMAN:

With the wife of the British Embessida
Try a crack out of *Troilus and Cressida*

SECOND GUNMAN:

If she says she won't buy it or tike it
Make her tike it, what's more, *As You Like It*.

BOTH:

If she says your behavior is heinous
Kick her right in the *Coriolanus*.
Brush up your Shakespeare
And they'll all kowtow.

(*3rd Refrain*)

BOTH:

Brush up your Shakespeare,
Start quoting him now,
Brush up your Shakespeare
And the women you will wow.

SECOND GUNMAN:

If you can't be a ham and do *Hamlet*
They will not give a damn or a damn-let,

FIRST GUNMAN:

Just recite an occasional sonnet
And your lap'll have Honey upon it.

SECOND GUNMAN:

When your baby is pleading for pleasure

BOTH:

Let her sample your *Measure for Measure*.
Brush up your Shakespeare
And they'll all kowtow
Forsooth,
I' Faith.

(*4th Refrain*)

BOTH:

Brush up your Shakespeare
Start quoting him now,
Brush up your Shakespeare
And the women you will wow.

FIRST GUNMAN:

Better mention *The Merchant of Venice*
When her sweet pound o' flesh you would menace.

SECOND GUNMAN:
>   If her virtue, at first, she defends—well,
>   Just remind her that *All's Well that Ends Well*,

FIRST GUNMAN:
>   And if still she won't give you a bonus,

BOTH:
>   You know what Venus got from Adonis!
>   Brush up your Shakespeare
>   And they'll all kowtow.
>   Thinks thou
>   Odds—bodkins.

(*5th Refrain*)

BOTH:
>   Brush up your Shakespeare,
>   Start quoting him now,
>   Brush up your Shakespeare

SECOND GUNMAN:
>   And the women you will wow.
>   If your goil is a Washington Heights dream
>   Treat the kid to *A Midsummer Night's Dream*.

FIRST GUNMAN:
>   If she then wants an all-by-herself night
>   Let her rest ev'ry 'leventh or *Twelf'-Night*,

BOTH:
>   If because of your heat she gets huffy,
>   Simply play on and "Lay on, Macduffy!"
>   Brush up your Shakespeare
>   And they'll all kowtow.
>   We trow,
>   We vow.

BLACKOUT

SCENE 8

SCENE: *A splendid room in* BAPTISTA's *house, beautifully painted in black and white with touches of yellow. There's a large arch at rear on platform with three steps leading down to stage level. Full stage of wedding guests watching the dancers in a pavane based on the thematic melody of "Why Can't You Behave?"* BIANCA *and* LUCENTIO, *in dazzling white of bride and groom, come down steps, as guests applaud softly. End of pavane.* PETRUCHIO *enters, down steps.*

BAPTISTA:
   My dear Bianca, and her new-found spouse—
      (*Sees* PETRUCHIO.)
   Brother Petruchio—daughter Katharine—
   Feast with the best and welcome to my house.
      (*Then stalling.*)
   . . . But where is Katharine?
      (*To* PETRUCHIO.)
   Where is she?
      (*To one of the dancers.*)
   Sirrah, go you to Mistress Katharine.
   Say I command her to come to me.
      (NATHANIEL *exits.*)
PETRUCHIO:
   I know she will not come.
   The fouler fortune mine and there an end.
      (*Enter* KATHARINE. *Startled sighs from guests, also relief.*)
KATHARINE (*going right into part as if she'd never quit the show*):
   What is your will, sir?
PETRUCHIO (*really moved, forgetting Shakespeare*): Darling—
      (*Then, as actor, picking up play again.*)
   Katharine, that cap of yours becomes you not;
   Off with that bauble, throw it underfoot.
      (*She does so.*)
BIANCA:
   Fie! What foolish duty call you this?
PETRUCHIO:
   Kate, I charge thee, tell these headstrong women what duty
      they do owe their lords and husbands.
      (KATHARINE *does so, with Shakespeare's lyrics and Porter's
      music.*)

   "I Am Ashamed that Women Are So Simple"
KATHARINE (*moves downstage, gestures to crowd. Six girl singers
   cross to stage left*):
         I am ashamed that women are so simple
         To offer war where they should kneel for peace,
         Or seek for rule, supremacy, and sway,

When they are bound to serve, love, and obey.
Why are our bodies soft and weak and smooth
Unapt to toil and trouble in the world
But that our soft conditions and our hearts
Should well agree with our external parts?
So wife, hold your temper and meekly put
Your hand 'neath the sole of your husband's foot.
In token of which duty, if he please
(*Extends hand.*)
My hand is ready; may it do him ease.
PETRUCHIO (*taking hand and drawing her to him*):
Why! There's a wench! Come on and kiss me, Kate.
(*They kiss as* FRED *and* LILLI.)

"Shrew Finale: Full Company"

PETRUCHIO:
So kiss me, Kate,
KATE:
Caro!
PETRUCHIO:
And twice and thrice,
KATE:
Carissimo!
PETRUCHIO:
Ere we start
KATE:
Bello!
PETRUCHIO:
Living in Paradise.
KATE:
Bellissimo!
PETRUCHIO and OTHERS:
Oh, Kiss $\begin{cases} \text{me,} \\ \text{him,} \end{cases}$ Kate
KATE:
Presto!
PETRUCHIO and OTHERS:
Darling angel, divine!
KATE:
Prestissimo!

PETRUCHIO:

    For now thou shall ever be

KATE:

    Now thou shall ever be

PETRUCHIO and MEN:

    Now thou shall ever be

KATE and GIRLS:

    Now thou shall ever be

PETRUCHIO:

    Mine,

KATE:

    Mine,

PETRUCHIO and KATE:

    Darling mine,

KATE:

    And I am thine, and I am thine

PETRUCHIO and OTHERS:

    And $\left\{ \begin{array}{l} \text{I am} \\ \text{she is} \end{array} \right.$ thine, and $\left\{ \begin{array}{l} \text{I am} \\ \text{she is} \end{array} \right.$ thine,

ALL:

    All
    Thine!

(The DANCERS *start a criss-cross routine that reveals the principals in the center, in the bows rehearsed in opening scene of the play.)*

(As the curtain falls to rise again on the first note of "Brush up Your Shakespeare," the entire company is doing a waltz clog while singing:)

ALL:

    Brush up your Shakespeare.
    Start quoting him now,
    Brush up your Shakespeare
    And the women you will wow.

PETRUCHIO and KATE:

    So tonight just recite to your matey
    Kiss me, Kate, Kiss me, Kate, Kiss me, Katey.

ALL:

    Brush up your Shakespeare
    And they'll all kowtow.

CURTAIN

SOUTH PACIFIC

A MUSICAL PLAY

Music by RICHARD RODGERS

Lyrics by OSCAR HAMMERSTEIN II

Book by OSCAR HAMMERSTEIN II *and* JOSHUA LOGAN

Adapted from the Pulitzer Prize–winning novel
Tales of the South Pacific by James A. Michener

To our patient Dorothy and Nedda, who liked it even when all the parts were sung and acted by us.

The action of the play takes place on two islands in the South Pacific during the recent war. There is a week's lapse of time between the two acts.

MUSICAL NUMBERS

Act One

Dites-Moi Pourquoi	Ngana and Jerome
A Cockeyed Optimist	Nellie
Some Enchanted Evening	Emile
Bloody Mary Is the Girl I Love	Sailors, Seabees, Marines
There Is Nothing Like a Dame	Billis, Sailors, Seabees, Marines
Bali Ha'i	Bloody Mary
I'm Gonna Wash That Man Right Outa My Hair	Nellie and Nurses
I'm in Love with a Wonderful Guy	Nellie and Nurses
Younger Than Springtime	Cable
Finale	Nellie and Emile

Act Two

Soft Shoe Dance	Nurses and Seabees
Happy Talk	Bloody Mary, Liat and Cable
Honey Bun	Nellie and Billis
You've Got to Be Taught	Cable
This Nearly Was Mine	Emile
Reprise: *Some Enchanted Evening*	Nellie
Finale	

ACT ONE

SCENE I

SCENE: EMILE DE BECQUE'S *plantation home on an island in the South Pacific.*

On your right as you look at the stage is a one-storied residence. On your left is a teakwood pagoda at the edge of the cacao grove. House and pagoda are bordered and decked in the bright tropical colors of the flaming hibiscus, the purple bougainvillaea, and the more pale and delicate frangipani. Between the house and the pagoda you can see the bay below and an island on the open sea beyond the bay. Twin volcanoes rise from the island.

AT RISE: *As the curtain rises, two Eurasian children,* NGANA, *a girl about eleven, and* JEROME, *a boy about eight, are, with humorous dignity, dancing an impromptu minuet. A bird call is heard in the tree above.* JEROME *looks up and imitates the sound. The eyes of both children follow the flight of the bird.* NGANA *runs over to the pagoda and climbs up on a table and poses on it as if it were a stage.* JEROME *lifts his hands and solemnly conducts her as she sings.*

NGANA:

        Dites-moi
        Pourquoi
        La vie est belle,
        Dites-moi
        Pourquoi
        La vie est gai!
        Dites-moi
        Pourquoi,
        Chère mad'moiselle,
        Est-ce que
        Parce que
        Vous m'aimez?

(HENRY, *a servant, enters and scolds them.*)
HENRY: Allez-vous! Vite! Dans la maison!
NGANA: Non, Henri!
JEROME (*mischievously delivering an ultimatum*): Moi, je reste ici!

HENRY: Oh, oui? Nous verrons bien . . . (*He chases* JEROME *around the giggling* NGANA.) Viens, petit moustique!

> (HENRY *catches* JEROME. *He is not as angry as he pretends to be, but he grabs* JEROME *by the ear and leads him off squealing, followed by* NGANA, *who protests violently.*)

NGANA: Non, Henri . . . non . . . non!

> (*As she runs off,* NELLIE *and* EMILE *are heard offstage from around the corner of the house.*)

NELLIE'S VOICE: What's this one?

EMILE'S VOICE: That is frangipani.

NELLIE'S VOICE: But what a color!

EMILE'S VOICE: You will find many more flowers out here.

> (NELLIE *enters, looking around her, entranced by the beauty of the scene. She turns upstage to gaze out over the bay.* HENRY *comes on from downstage with a tray which he takes over to the coffee table.* EMILE, *entering a few paces behind* NELLIE, *comes down briskly and addresses* HENRY.)

EMILE: Je servirai le café.

HENRY: Oui, Monsieur.

EMILE: C'est tout.

HENRY: Oui, Monsieur de Becque.

> (HENRY *exits.* NELLIE *comes down, still under the spell of the surrounding wonder.*)

NELLIE: Well, I'm just speechless! . . . And that lunch! Wild chicken—I didn't know it was ever wild. Gosh! I had no idea people lived like this right out in the middle of the Pacific Ocean.

EMILE (*pouring coffee*): Sugar?

NELLIE: Thanks.

EMILE: One?

NELLIE: Three.

> (EMILE *smiles.*)

I know it's a big load for a demitasse to carry. All right, I'm a hick. You know so many American words, do you know what a hick is?

EMILE: A hick is one who lives in a stick.

NELLIE: Sticks. Plural. The sticks.

EMILE: Pardon. The sticks. I remember now.

NELLIE: How long did it take you to build up a plantation like this?

EMILE: I came to the Pacific when I was a young man.

(NELLIE *studies him for a moment.*)

NELLIE: Emile, is it true that all the planters on these islands—are they all running away from something?

EMILE (*pausing cautiously before he answers*): Who is not running away from something? There are fugitives everywhere—Paris, New York, even in Small Rock— (NELLIE *looks puzzled.*) Where you come from . . .

(NELLIE *suddenly understands what he means and bursts out laughing.*)

NELLIE: Oh, Little Rock!

EMILE (EMILE, *laughing with her and shouting the correction*): Little Rock! . . . You know fugitives there?

(NELLIE *runs over to where she has left her bag.*)

NELLIE: I'll show you a picture of a Little Rock fugitive. (*Taking a clipping from an envelope in the bag.*) I got this clipping from my mother today.

(*She hands it to* EMILE *who reads:*)

EMILE: "Ensign Nellie Forbush, Arkansas' own Florence Nightingale . . ."

NELLIE (*apologetically*): That was written by Mrs. Leeming, the Social Editor. She went to school with my mother. To read her, you would think that I'm practically the most important nurse in the entire Navy and that I run the fleet hospital all by myself, and it's only a matter of time before I'll be a Lady Admiral.

EMILE: In this picture you do not look much like an Admiral.

NELLIE: Oh, that was taken before I knew what rain and heat and mud could do to your disposition. But it isn't rainy today. Gosh, it's beautiful here. Just look at that yellow sun! You know, I don't think it's the end of the world like everyone else thinks. I can't work myself up to getting that low.

(*He smiles.*)

Do you think I'm crazy too? They all do over at the fleet hospital. You know what they call me? Knucklehead Nellie. I suppose I am, but I can't help it.

(*She sings:*)

> When the sky is a bright canary yellow
> I forget every cloud I've ever seen—
> So they call me a cockeyed optimist,
> Immature and incurably green!

I have heard people rant and rave and bellow
That we're done and we might as well be dead—
But I'm only a cockeyed optimist
And I can't get it into my head.

I hear the human race
Is falling on its face
And hasn't very far to go,
But every whippoorwill
Is selling me a bill
And telling me it just ain't so!

I could say life is just a bowl of jello
And appear more intelligent and smart
But I'm stuck
(Like a dope!)
With a thing called hope,
And I can't get it out of my heart . . . Not this heart!
(*She walks over to him, speaking the next line.*)
Want to know anything else about me?

EMILE: Yes. You say you are a fugitive. When you joined the
Navy, what were you running away from? (*He returns the
clipping to her.*)
NELLIE: Gosh, I don't know. It was more like running *to* some-
thing. I wanted to see what the world was like—outside Little
Rock, I mean. And I wanted to meet different kinds of people
and find out if I like them better. And I'm finding out. (*She
suddenly becomes self-conscious.*)
EMILE (*tactful*): Would you like some cognac?
NELLIE (*relieved*): I'd love some.

(EMILE *goes to the table and pours the brandy. In the following
verses,* EMILE *and* NELLIE *are not singing to each other. Each
is soliloquizing:*)

NELLIE (*thoughtfully watching* EMILE):
Wonder how I'd feel,
Living on a hillside,
Looking on an ocean,
Beautiful and still.

EMILE (*pouring the cognac*):
>   This is what I need,
>   This is what I've longed for,
>   Someone young and smiling
>   Climbing up my hill!

NELLIE:
>   We are not alike;
>   Probably I'd bore him.
>   He's a cultured Frenchman—
>   I'm a little hick.

EMILE (*pausing as he starts to pour the second glass*):
>   Younger men than I,
>   Officers and doctors,
>   Probably pursue her—
>   She could have her pick.

NELLIE (*she catches his eye. Each averts his eyes from the other*):
>   Wonder why I feel
>   Jittery and jumpy!
>   I am like a schoolgirl,
>   Waiting for a dance.

EMILE (*carrying the two filled brandy glasses, he approaches* NELLIE):
>   Can I ask her now?
>   I am like a schoolboy!
>   What will be her answer?
>   Do I have a chance?

> (*He passes* NELLIE *her brandy glass. It is a large snifter type of glass. She has apparently never drunk from one before. She watches him carefully as he lifts his to his lips, and does the same. As they drink, the music rises to great ecstatic heights. One is made aware that in this simple act of two people who are falling in love, each drinking brandy, there are turbulent thoughts and feelings going on in their hearts and brains. They lower their glasses. The music dies down.* EMILE *struggles to say something. He plunges into the middle of his subject as if continuing a thought which he assumes she has sensed.*)

EMILE: In peacetime, the boat from America comes once a month. The ladies—the wives of the planters—often go to Australia during the hot months. It can get very hot here.

NELLIE: It can get hot in Arkansas, too. (*She takes another quick swallow after this one.*)

EMILE: Ah, yes?

NELLIE (*nodding her head*): Uh-huh.

EMILE (*he puts his glass down on the table*): I have many books here . . . Marcel Proust? (*She looks blank.*) Anatole France? (*This evokes a faint smile of half-recognition from her.*) Did you study French in school?

NELLIE: Oh, yes.

EMILE: Ah, then you can read French?

NELLIE (*as though saying, "Of course not"*): No! (*Fearful of having disappointed him, she makes a feeble attempt to add a note of hope.*) I can conjugate a few verbs. (*Realizing how silly this must sound to him, she changes the subject.*) I bet you read a lot.

EMILE: Out here, one becomes hungry to learn everything. (*He rises and paces nervously.*) Not to miss anything, not to let anything good pass by.

(*He pauses and looks down at her, unable to go on. She, feeling he is coming closer to his point, looks up with a sudden encouraging smile.*)

NELLIE: Yes?

EMILE: One waits so long for what is good . . . and when at last it comes, one cannot risk to lose. (*He turns away, searching for more words.*) So . . . so one must speak and act quickly even— even if it seems almost foolish to be so quick. (*He looks at her, worried . . . has he gone too far . . . how will she accept any advance at all he may make to her? She can only smile helplessly back at him. He goes on, speaking quickly.*) I know it is only two weeks. A dinner given at your Officers' Club. Do you remember?

NELLIE: Yes.

EMILE: That is the way things happen sometimes. . . . Isn't it, Nellie?

NELLIE (*swallowing hard*): Yes, it is . . . Emile.

EMILE (*singing*):

> Some enchanted evening
> You may see a stranger,
> You may see a stranger
> Across a crowded room—
> And somehow you know

(You know even then)
That somewhere you'll see her again and again.

Some enchanted evening
Someone may be laughing,
You may hear her laughing
Across a crowded room—
And night after night
(As strange as it seems)
The sound of her laughter will sing in your dreams.

Who can explain it?
Who can tell you why?
Fools give you reasons—
Wise men never try.

Some enchanted evening
When you find your true love,
When you feel her call you
Across a crowded room—
Then fly to her side,
And make her your own,
Or all through your life you may dream all alone. . . .

Once you have found her
Never let her go,
Once you have found her
Never let her go!

(*There follow several seconds of silence. Neither moves.* EMILE *speaks.*)
I am older than you. If we have children, when I die they will be growing up. You could afford to take them back to America—if you like. Think about it.
(HENRY *enters.*)
HENRY: Monsieur de Becque, la jeep de Mademoiselle est ici.
(NELLIE *and* EMILE *turn as if awakened from a dream.*)
La jeep de Mademoiselle. (HENRY *smiles, a wide toothy smile, at* NELLIE.) Votre jeep!

NELLIE: Oh, my jeep! (*She looks at her watch.*) Gosh! Thank you, Henry. I'm on duty in ten minutes!

    (HENRY *exits.* NELLIE *holds out her hand to* EMILE.)

EMILE: Before you leave, Nellie, I want to tell you something. A while ago, you asked me a question—why did I leave France?

NELLIE: Oh, Emile, that was none of my business.

EMILE But I want to tell you. I had to leave France. I killed a man.

    (*Pause.*)

NELLIE: Why did you kill him?

EMILE: He was a wicked man, a bully. Everyone in our village was glad to see him die, and it was not to my discredit. Do you believe me, Nellie?

    (*Another pause—unbearable to him.*)

NELLIE: You have just told me that you killed a man and that it's all right. I hardly know you, and yet I know it's all right.

EMILE (*deeply moved*): Thank you, Nellie. (*His voice suddenly gay and exultant.*) And you like my place?

NELLIE: Yes.

EMILE: You will think?

NELLIE (*smiling up at him*): I will think.

    (*They are silent and motionless for a moment. Then she turns suddenly and walks off very quickly. He looks after her and starts to hum softly. He picks up the coffee cup she has left on the fountain and smiles down at it. He holds the cup up so he can examine its rim.*)

EMILE: Lipstick! . . . Three lumps of sugar in this little cup! (*He laughs aloud, then resumes his humming and walks, almost dances, across the stage in time to his own music.* NGANA *and* JEROME *enter and walk behind him across the stage, imitating his happy stride. As* EMILE *puts down the cup, the children join him, humming the same melody. He turns quickly and frowns down on them with mock sternness. They giggle.*) Eh bien!

JEROME: Bravo, Papa!

    (*The children both applaud.*)

EMILE: Merci, Monsieur!

NGANA: Nous chantons bien, aussi.

EMILE: Ah, oui?

NGANA: Attends, Papa!

JEROME (*parroting* NGANA): Attends, Papa!

(*He looks at* NGANA *for the signal to start the song. They sing . . .* EMILE *conducting them.*)

NGANA and JEROME:
> Dites moi
> Pourquoi
> La vie est belle—
> (EMILE *joins them.*)
> Dites moi
> Pourquoi
> La vie est gai!
> Dites moi
> Pourquoi,
> (EMILE *and* JEROME *make a deep bow to* NGANA.)
> Chère Mad'moiselle,
> (EMILE *picks them up, one under each arm, and starts to carry them off as they finish singing the refrain together.*)
> Est-ce que
> Parce que
> Vous m'aimez?

(*The lights fade out and a transparent curtain closes in on them. Before they are out of sight, the characters of the next scene have entered downstage in front of the curtain. All transitions from one scene to another in the play are achieved in this manner so that the effect is of one picture dissolving into the next.*)

SCENE 2

The curtain depicts no specific place but represents the abstract pattern of a large tapa-cloth. In front of this, lounge a group of Seabees, sailors and Marines. As the lights come up on them and go out on the previous scene, they are singing.

MEN:
> Bloody Mary is the girl I love,
> Bloody Mary is the girl I love,
> Bloody Mary is the girl I love—
> Now ain't that too damn bad!
> Her skin is tender as DiMaggio's glove,
> Her skin is tender as DiMaggio's glove,

Her skin is tender as DiMaggio's glove.
Now ain't that too damn bad!
(*The object of this serenade who has been hidden during the song, by two sailors, is now revealed as they move away. This is* BLOODY MARY. *She is small, yellow, with Oriental eyes. She wears black sateen trousers, and a white blouse over which is an old Marine's tunic. On her head is a peach-basket hat. Around her neck is a G.I. identification chain from which hangs a silver Marine emblem. At the end of the singing, she gives out a shrill cackle of laughter with which we shall soon learn to identify her.*)

MARY (*looking straight out at the audience*): Hallo, G.I.! (*She holds up a grass skirt.*) Grass skirt? Very saxy! Fo' dolla'? Saxy grass skirt. Fo' dolla'! Send home Chicago. You like? You buy? (*Her eyes scan the audience as if following a passer-by. Her crafty smile fades to a quick scowl as he apparently passes without buying. She calls after him.*) Where you go? Come back! Chipskate! Crummy G.I.! Sadsack. Droopy-drawers!

MARINE: Tell 'em good, Mary!

MARY: What is good?

MARINE: Tell him he's a stingy bastard!

MARY (*delighted at the sound of these new words*): Stingy bastard! (*She turns back toward the* MARINE *for approval.*) That good?

MARINE: That's great, Mary! You're learning fast.

MARY (*calling off again*): Stingy bastard! (*She cackles gaily and turns back to the* MARINE.) I learn fast . . . . Pretty soon I talk English good as any crummy Marine. (*Calling off once more.*) Stingy bastard!

(*She laughs very loud but the Marines, Seabees and sailors laugh louder and cheer her. They then resume their serenade.*)

MEN:
Bloody Mary's chewing betel nuts,
She is always chewing betel nuts,
Bloody Mary's chewing betel nuts—
And she don't use Pepsodent.
(*She grins and shows her betel-stained teeth.*)
Now ain't that too damn bad!
(*While this is being sung, the lights come up behind the tapa-cloth transparent curtain revealing:*)

SCENE: *The edge of a palm grove near the beach. Beyond the beach in the bay can be seen the same twin-peaked island that was evident from* EMILE's *hillside. On your left, as you look at the stage, is* BLOODY MARY's *kiosk. This is made of bamboo and canvas. Her merchandise, laid out in front, comprises shells, native hats, local dress material, outrigger canoes and hookahs. Several grass skirts are hanging up around the kiosk. On the right, at first making a puzzling silhouette, then as the lights come up, resolving itself into a contraption of weird detail, is a G.I. homemade washing machine. It looks partly like a giant ice-cream freezer, partly like a windmill. In front of it there is a sign which reads:*

> TWISTED AIR HAND LAUNDRY
> LUTHER BILLIS ENTERPRISES
> SPECIAL RATES FOR SEABEES

As the lights come up, the washing machine is being operated by Carpenter's Mate, Second Class, George Watts, better known as "STEWPOT." *Seabees, sailors, Marines and some Army men lounge around the scene waiting for whatever diversion* BLOODY MARY *may provide. During the singing which covers this change,* BLOODY MARY *takes a strange-looking object out of her pocket and dangles it in front of a* MARINE.

MARINE: What is that thing?
MARY (*holding the small object in her hand*): Is head. Fifty dolla'.
MARINE (*revolted*): What's it *made* of?
MARY: Made outa head! Is real human.
MARINE (*fascinated*): What makes it so small?
MARY: Shlunk! Only way to keep human head is shlink 'em.
MARINE: No, thanks. (*He leaves quickly.*)
MARY (*to a new customer as she holds a grass skirt up to her waist and starts to dance*): Fo' dolla'. Send home Chicago to saxy sweetheart! She make wave like this.
> (*She starts to dance. One of the sailors grabs her and goes into an impromptu jitterbug dance with her. Others join, and soon the beach is alive with gyrating gentlemen of the United States*

Armed Services. As this spontaneous festivity is at its height, LUTHER BILLIS *enters, followed by the* PROFESSOR, *both loaded with grass skirts. They come down in front of* BLOODY MARY *and throw the grass skirts at her feet.*)

BILLIS: Here you are, Sweaty Pie! Put them down, Professor. These beautiful skirts were made by myself, the Professor here, and three other Seabees in half the time it takes your native workers to make 'em. (*He picks up a skirt and demonstrates.*) See? No stretch! (*Throwing the skirt back on the ground.*) Look 'em over, Sweaty Pie, and give me your price.

(*At this point, an altercation starts upstage near the washing machine.*)

SAILOR: Look at that shirt!

STEWPOT: Take it up with the manager. (*He points down to* BILLIS.)

SAILOR (*coming down to him*): Hey, Big Dealer! Hey, Luther Billis!

BILLIS (*smoothly*): What can I do for you, my boy? What's the trouble?

SAILOR (*holding up his shirt which has been laundered and is in tatters*): Look at that shirt!

BILLIS: The Billis Laundry is not responsible for minor burns and tears. (*He turns back laconically to* MARY.) What do you say, Sweatso? What am I offered?

(*The* SAILOR *storms off. The* PROFESSOR, *meanwhile, is showing the beautiful work they do to some other sailors and Seabees.*)

PROFESSOR (*holding up a skirt*): All hand sewn!

SAILOR: Gee, that's mighty nice work!

BILLIS (*to* BLOODY MARY): Do you hear that, Sweaty Pie? You can probably sell these to the chumps for five or six dollars apiece. Now, I'll let you have the whole bunch for . . . say . . . eighty bucks.

MARY: Give you ten dolla'.

BILLIS: What?

MARY: Not enough?

BILLIS: You're damn well right, not enough!

MARY (*dropping the skirt at his feet*): Den you damn well keep. (*She goes down to another sailor and takes from her pocket a boar's tooth bracelet which she holds up to tempt him.*)

BILLIS (*following* BLOODY MARY): Now look here, Dragon Lady— (*Whatever he was about to say is knocked out of his head by the sight of the bracelet.* BILLIS *is an inveterate and passionate souvenir hunter.*) What's that you got there, a boar's tooth bracelet? Where'd you get that? (*He points to the twin-peaked island.*) Over there on Bali Ha'i?

MARY (*smiling craftily*): You like?

BILLIS (*taking bracelet and showing to G.I.'s who have huddled around him*): You know what that is? A bracelet made out of a single boar's tooth. They cut the tooth from the boar's mouth in a big ceremonial over there on Bali Ha'i. There ain't a souvenir you can pick up in the South Pacific as valuable as this . . . What do you want for it, Mary?

MARY: Hundred dolla'!

BILLIS: Hundred dollars! (*Shocked, but realizing he will pay it, turns to the boys and justifies himself in advance.*) That's cheap. I thought it would be more. (*He takes the money from his pocket.*)

PROFESSOR: I don't see how she can do it.

MARY: Make you special offer Big Deala'. I trade you boar's tooth bracelet for all grass skirts.

BILLIS: It's a deal.

MARY: Wait a minute. Is no deal till you throw in something for good luck.

BILLIS: Okay. What do you want me to throw in?

MARY (*taking money from his hand*): Hundred dolla'.

BILLIS: Well, for the love of . . .

MARY (*shaking his hand, grinning a big Oriental grin*): Good luck.

(*She exits with grass skirts. The men all crowd around* BILLIS, *shaking his hand in ironic "congratulation."*)

BILLIS: You don't run into these things every day. They're scarce as hens' teeth.

PROFESSOR: They're bigger, too.

BILLIS: That damned Bali Ha'i! (*Turning and looking toward the twin-peaked island.*) Why does it have to be off limits? You can get everything over there. Shrunken heads, bracelets, old ivory—

SAILOR: Young French women!

BILLIS: Knock off! I'm talking about souvenirs.

PROFESSOR: So's he.

BILLIS (*pacing restlessly*): We got to get a boat and get over there. I'm feeling held down again. I need to take a trip.

STEWPOT: Only officers can sign out boats.

BILLIS: I'll get a boat all right. I'll latch onto some officer who's got some imagination . . . that would like to see that Boar's Tooth ceremonial as much as I would . . . It's a hell of a ceremonial! Dancin', drinkin' . . . everything!

SAILOR: Why, you big phony. We all know why you want to go to Bali Ha'i.

BILLIS: Why?

SAILOR: Because the French planters put all their young women over there when they heard the G.I.'s were coming. That's why! It ain't boar's teeth . . . it's women!

BILLIS: It is boar's teeth . . . *and* women!

(*A long pause. All the men are still and thoughtful, each dreaming a similar dream—but his own. Music starts. A* SEABEE *breaks the silence.*)

SEABEE (*singing*):
> We got sunlight on the sand,
> We got moonlight on the sea.

SAILOR:
> We got mangoes and bananas
> You can pick right off a tree.

MARINE:
> We got volley ball and ping pong
> And a lot of dandy games—

BILLIS:
> What ain't we got?

ALL:
> We ain't got dames!

MARINE:
> We get packages from home,

SAILOR:
> We get movies, we get shows,

STEWPOT:
> We get speeches from our skipper

SOLDIER:
> And advice from Tokyo Rose

SEABEE:
> We get letters doused wit' poifume,

SAILOR:
> We get dizzy from the smell—

BILLIS:
> What don't we get?

ALL:
> You know damn well!

BILLIS:
> We have nothin' to put on a clean, white suit for.
> What we need is what there ain't no substitute for!

ALL:
> There is nothin' like a dame
> Nothin' in the world.
> There is nothin' you can name
> That is anythin' like a dame.

MARINE:
> We feel restless,
> We feel blue.

SEABEE:
> We feel lonely and, in brief,
> We feel every kind of feelin'

PROFESSOR:
> But the feelin' of relief.

SAILOR:
> We feel hungry as the wolf felt
> When he met Red Riding Hood—

ALL:
> What don't we feel?

STEWPOT:
> We don't feel good!

SAILOR:
> Lots of things in life are beautiful, but brother—
> There is one particular thing that is nothin' whatsoever
>   in any way shape or form like any other!

ALL:
> There is nothin' like a dame—
> Nothin' in the world.
> There is nothin' you can name
> That is anythin' like a dame.

> Nothin' else is built the same,
> Nothin' in the world
> Has a soft and wavy frame
> Like the silhouette of a dame.

MARINE (*with a deep bass voice*):

> There is absolutely nothin' like the frame of a dame!
> (*The music continues throughout the following dialogue and action.*)

GIRL'S VOICE: Hut, two, three, four! Get—your—exercise!

> (*A husky* NURSE *enters, leading several other* NURSES, *all dressed in bathing suits, playsuits, or fatigues.* NELLIE *is among them. They jog across the stage, their* LEADER *continuing the military count. The men's eyes follow them.*)

A TIRED NURSE: Can't we rest a while?

HUSKY LEADER: Come on you nurses, pick it up!

> (NELLIE *drops out of line as the others run off.*)

NELLIE (*beckoning to* BILLIS): Hey, Luther!

STEWPOT (*nudging* BILLIS): Luther!

> (BILLIS *turns and goes shyly to* NELLIE, *terribly embarrassed that the men are watching him. He is a different* BILLIS *in front of* NELLIE. *He is unassured and has lost all of his brashness. For him,* NELLIE FORBUSH *has "class."*)

BILLIS: Yes, Miss Forbush.

> (*All eyes follow him.*)

NELLIE: Have you done what you promised?

BILLIS: Yes, Miss Forbush. (*He pulls out a newspaper package from a hiding place in the roots of a tree and hands it to her.*) I did it all last night. (*With an alarmed look at his comrades, as she starts to unwrap it.*) You don't have to open it now!

> (*But* NELLIE *opens the package, much to* BILLIS' *embarrassment. It is her laundry, neatly folded.*)

NELLIE: Oh. You do beautiful work, Luther!

> (*Two men painfully cling to each other and turn their heads away.* BILLIS *tries to outglare the others in defensive defiance.*)

You've even done the pleats in my shorts!

BILLIS: Aw, pleats aren't hard. You better run along now and catch up to your gang.

NELLIE: Pleats are *very* hard. How do you do such delicate work at night, in the dark?

BILLIS: There was a moon!

STEWPOT (*in a syrupy voice*): There was a moon!

BILLIS (*he turns to the men, realizing that they have heard this, and shouts defiantly*): A full moon!

NELLIE (*she is wrapping up the package*): How much, Luther!

BILLIS (*earnestly*): Oh, no, not from you.

NELLIE: Gosh, I guess I'm just about the luckiest nurse on this island to have found you. You're a treasure. (*She turns and runs off.*) Well, good-bye, Luther. Hut, two, three, four!

(*She has gone! BILLIS turns and faces the men, trying to bluff it out. He walks belligerently over to STEWPOT who with the PROFESSOR whistles "There's Nothin' Like a Dame." Then he walks over to another group and they join STEWPOT and PROFESSOR in whistling. Soon all are whistling. BILLIS whistles too. After the refrain is finished, STEWPOT looks off reflectively at the departing NELLIE.*)

STEWPOT: *She's* a nice little girl, but some of them nurses—the officers can have them.

PROFESSOR: They got them!

STEWPOT: Well, they can have them!

MARINE (*singing*):
    So suppose a dame ain't bright,
    Or completely free from flaws,
SAILOR:
    Or as faithful as a bird dog,
SEABEE:
    Or as kind as Santa Claus,
SOLDIER:
    It's a waste of time to worry
    Over things that they have not
SAILOR:
    Be thankful for
ALL:
    The things they got!

HUSKY LEADER (*entering*): Hut, two, three, four. Hut, two, three, four!

(*The exercising nurses enter upstage, jogging in the opposite direction to their previous course. NELLIE is again with them. She turns and waves to BILLIS and points to the laundry under her arm. The boys all rise and turn upstage, their heads*

*following the girls until they're off. Then the boys continue to
turn until they're facing front again.*)

ALL:

> There is nothin' you can name
> That is anythin' like a dame!
> There are no books like a dame,
> And nothin' looks like a dame,
> There are no drinks like a dame,
> And nothin' thinks like a dame,
> Nothin' acts like a dame
> Or attracts like a dame.
> There ain't a thing that's wrong with any man here
> That can't be cured by puttin' him near
> A girly, womanly, female, feminine dame!

(BLOODY MARY *enters and starts humming the song, as she
proceeds to rearrange her new stock of grass skirts.* LT. JOSEPH
CABLE *enters. He wears suntans, overseas cap, and carries a
musette bag in his hand.* BLOODY MARY *sees him and stops
singing. They stand for a moment, looking at each other—she,
suspicious and frightened, and he, puzzled and curious.*)

MARY: Hallo.

CABLE: Hello.

(*Music of "Bali Ha'i" is played softly.*)

MARY: You mak' trouble for me?

CABLE: Hunh?

MARY: Are you crummy major?

CABLE: No, I'm even crummier than that. I'm a lieutenant.

MARY: Lootellan?

CABLE (*laughing*): Lootellan. (*He strolls away from her, toward
the men.*)

BILLIS: Hiya, Lootellan. New on the rock?

CABLE: Just came in on that PBY.

BILLIS: Yeah? Where from?

CABLE: A little island south of Marie Louise.

STEWPOT: Then you been up where they use real bullets!

CABLE: Unh-huh.

MARY (*who has been looking adoringly at* CABLE): Hey, Lootellan.
You damn saxy man!

CABLE (*rocked off his balance for a moment*): Thanks. You're looking pretty—er—fit yourself.

(*She grins happily at him, showing her betel-stained teeth and crosses, beaming, to her assistant.*)

MARY (*to assistant*): Damn saxy!

CABLE (*to* BILLIS): Who is she?

BILLIS: She's Tonkinese—used to work for a French planter.

MARY: French planters stingy bastards! (*She laughs.*)

CABLE: Say, I wonder if any of you know a French planter named de Becque?

BILLIS: Emile de Becque? I think he's the guy lives on top of that hill . . . Do you know him?

CABLE (*looking off toward the hill, thoughtfully*): No, but I'm going to.

(MARY *follows* CABLE, *taking the shrunken head from her pocket.*)

MARY: Hey, Lootellan! Real human head! . . . You got sweetheart? Send home Chicago to saxy sweetheart!

CABLE: No—er—she's a Philadelphia girl.

MARY: Whazzat, Philadelia girl? Whazzat mean? No saxy? (*With a sudden impulse.*) You like I give you free?

BILLIS: Free! You never give *me* anything free.

MARY: You not saxy like Lootellan. (*To* CABLE, *proffering the shrunken head.*) Take!

CABLE: No, thanks. Where'd you get that anyway?

MARY: Bali Ha'i.

STEWPOT (*nudging* BILLIS, *pointing to* CABLE, *as he whispers*): There's your officer! There's your officer!

BILLIS: That's that island over there with the two volcanoes. (*Significantly.*) Officers can get launches and go over there.

CABLE: (*looking out at island*): Bali Ha'i . . . What does that mean?

MARY: Bali Ha'i mean "I am your special Island" . . . mean . . . "Here I am." Bali Ha'i is *your* special Island, Lootellan. I know! You listen! You hear island call to you. Listen! You no hear something? Listen!

CABLE (*after listening for a moment*): I hear the sound of the wind and the waves, that's all.

MARY: You no hear something calling? Listen!

(*Silence.* ALL *listen.*)

STEWPOT (*trying to be helpful*): I think *I* hear something.

BILLIS (*in a harsh, threatening whisper*): Shut your big fat mouth!

MARY: Hear voice? (*She sings to* CABLE, *as he gazes out at the mysterious island.*)

> Mos' people live on a lonely island,
> Lost in de middle of a foggy sea.
> Mos' people long fo' anudder island
> One where dey know dey would lak to be . . .

> Bali Ha'i
> May call you,
> Any night, any day.
> In your heart
> You'll hear it call you
> "Come away, come away."

> Bali Ha'i
> Will whisper
> On de wind of de sea,
> "Here am I,
> Your special island!
> Come to me, come to me!"

> Your own special hopes,
> Your own special dreams
> Bloom on de hillside
> And shine in de streams.

> If you try,
> You'll find me
> Where de sky meets de sea,
> "Here am I,
> Your special island!
> Come to me, come to me!"

> Bali Ha'i!
>   Bali Ha'i!
>   Bali Ha'i!

> Some day, you'll see me,
> Floatin' in de sunshine,

My head stickin' out
F'um a low-flyin' cloud.
You'll hear me call you,
Singin' through de sunshine,
Sweet and clear as can be,
"Come to me,
Here am I,
Come to me!"

If you try,
You'll find me
Where de sky meets de sea,
"Here am I,
Your special island!
Come to me, come to me!"

Bali Ha'i!
    Bali Ha'i!
        Bali Ha'i!

(BLOODY MARY *exits.* CABLE *seems spellbound by her words.*
BILLIS *follows up with a more earthy form of salesmanship.*)
BILLIS: Of course, Lieutenant, right now that island is off limits
due to the fact that the French planters have all their young
women running around over there. (*He pauses to observe the
effect of these significant words.*) Of course, you being an officer,
you could get a launch. I'd even be willing to requisition a
boat for you. What do you say, Lieutenant?
    (*Singing throatily.*)
        Bali Ha'i may call you
        Any night any day.
        In your heart you'll
        Hear it call you—
        Bali Ha'i—Bali Ha'i . . .
Hunh, Lieutenant?
    (*Pause.*)
CABLE: No.
BILLIS (*making a quick shift*): I see what you mean, being off
limits and all. It would take a lot of persuading to get *me* to
go over there . . . But, another thing goes on over there—the

ceremonial of the boar's tooth. After they kill the boar they pass around some of that coconut liquor and women dance with just skirts on . . . (*his voice becoming evil*) and everybody gets to know everybody pretty well . . .

(*He sings.*)
   Bali Ha'i will whisper—
   (BILLIS *starts dance as he hums the melody seductively. Then he stops and talks.*)
It's just a little tribal ceremonial and I thought you being up in the shooting war for such a long time without getting any—recreation—I thought you might be interested.

CABLE: I am. But right now I've got to report to the Island Commander.

BILLIS: Oh. (*Shouting officiously.*) Professor! Take the Lieutenant up in the truck.

CABLE: Professor?

BILLIS: That's because he went to college. You go to college?

CABLE: Er—yes.

BILLIS: Where?

CABLE: A place in New Jersey.

BILLIS: Where? Rutgers?

CABLE: No . . . Princeton.

BILLIS: Oh. Folks got money, eh, Lieutenant? (*He leers wisely.*) Don't be ashamed of it. We understand. Say! Maybe you'd like to hear the Professor talk some language. What would you like to hear? Latin? Grecian? (*Grabbing the unwilling* PROFESSOR *by the arm and leading him over to* CABLE.) Aw, give him some Latin!

PROFESSOR (*the professor feels pretty silly, but proceeds*): "Rectius vives Licini—"

BILLIS: Ain't that beautiful!

PROFESSOR: ". . . neque altum
   Semper urgendo dum procellas . . ."
   (*A crowd gathers around the* PROFESSOR. BILLIS *beams at* CABLE.)

BILLIS: Now, Lieutenant, what did he say?

CABLE: I'm afraid I haven't the slightest idea.

BILLIS: What's the matter, didn't you graduate? (*Disgusted, to the* PROFESSOR.) Take the Lieutenant to the buildings.
   (CABLE *and the* PROFESSOR *start to go.*)

PROFESSOR: Aye, aye!

BILLIS (*to* STEWPOT): He'll never make Captain.

(*The* PROFESSOR, *suddenly alarmed by something he sees off-stage, turns back and starts to make strange signal-noises of warning.*)

PROFESSOR: Whoop-whoop-whoop! (*In a hoarse whisper.*) Iron Belly!

(*The men assume casual and innocent attitudes. Some make bird sounds.* MARY *looks off and walks back to her kiosk to stand defiantly in front of it.* CABLE, *puzzled, stands by to await developments. What develops is that "Iron Belly,"* CAPTAIN BRACKETT, *enters, followed by his executive officer,* COMMANDER HARBISON.)

HARBISON (*a brusque man*): Here she is, sir.

(*He points to* BLOODY MARY, *who is standing her ground doggedly in front of her kiosk.* BRACKETT *walks slowly over to her.* HARBISON *takes a few steps toward the men and they move away.* BRACKETT *glares at* MARY. *Undaunted, she glares right back.*)

BRACKETT: You are causing an economic revolution on this island. These French planters can't find a native to pick a coconut or milk a cow because you're paying them ten times as much to make these ridiculous grass skirts.

MARY: French planters stingy bastards!

(STEWPOT *drops a tin bucket. The men control themselves by great efforts, their faces contorted queerly.* BRACKETT *scowls and for the moment can think of no answer.* BILLIS *approaches him, with a snappy salute.*)

BILLIS: Sir! May I make a suggestion, sir?

BRACKETT (*returning salute*): Who are you?

BILLIS: Billis, sir, Luther Billis. (*Making an impressive announcement.*) The natives can now go back to work on the farms. The demand for grass skirts can now be met by us Seabees!

BRACKETT: Dressmakers! (*Starting to blow up.*) Do you mean to tell me the Seabees of the United States Navy are now a lot of—

BILLIS: If you don't like the idea, sir, we can drop it right here, sir. Just say the word. Just pretend I never brought it up.

HARBISON (*reflectively*): Luther Billis.

BILLIS: Yes, sir?

HARBISON: Nothing. Just making a mental note. I want to be sure not to forget your name.

(*Pause, during which* BILLIS *slowly and dejectedly retires.* BRACKETT *turns to* MARY.)

BRACKETT: I want to see you pick up every scrap of this paraphernalia now! And, for the last time, carry it way down there beyond that fence off Navy property.

(MARY *stands firmly planted and immovable.* . . . CABLE *walks to the kiosk and collapses it.*)

CABLE (*with decisive authority*): Come on, everybody. Take all this stuff and throw it over that fence.

(*The men quickly obey,* BILLIS *ostentatiously taking charge in front of the two officers.*)

BILLIS (*to men*): All right—take it way down there. Off Navy property!

CABLE (*strides over to* MARY *and points off*): You go too!

MARY (CABLE *can do no wrong in her eyes*): All right, Lootellan. Thank you.

(*She exits. By this time, all the men have gone, taking her kiosk with them.* BRACKETT, CABLE *and* HARBISON *are left.* BRACKETT *looks at* HARBISON *as if to ask who* CABLE *is.* HARBISON *shrugs his shoulders.* CABLE *turns and exchanges salutes with* BRACKETT.)

BRACKETT: Lieutenant, who are you, anyway?

CABLE: I'm Lieutenant Joseph Cable, sir. I just flew in on that PBY.

BRACKETT: A joy ride?

CABLE: No, sir. Orders.

BRACKETT: A Marine under orders to me?

CABLE: Yes, sir.

BRACKETT: I'm Captain Brackett.

CABLE: How do you do, sir?

BRACKETT: This is Commander Harbison, my Executive Officer.

(CABLE *and* HARBISON *exchange hellos, salutes and handshakes.*)

Well, what's it all about?

CABLE: My Colonel feels that all these islands are in danger because none of us has been getting first-hand intelligence, and what we need is a coast watch.

HARBISON: A coast watch?

CABLE: A man with a radio hiding out on one of those Jap-held islands, where he could watch for Jap ships when they start down the bottleneck . . . down this way.

BRACKETT (*turning to* HARBISON): What do you think, Bill?

HARBISON: Well, sir, our pilots could do a hell of a lot to Jap convoys with information like that.

BRACKETT: You'd have to sneak this man ashore at night from a submarine.

CABLE: Yes, sir.

HARBISON: Who's going to do it?

CABLE: Well, sir . . . *I've* been elected. (*Pause.*)

BRACKETT (*after exchanging a look with* HARBISON): You've got quite an assignment, son.

HARBISON: How long do you think you could last there, sending out messages, before the Japs found you?

CABLE: I think I'd be okay if I could take a man with me who really knew the country. Headquarters has found out there's a French civilian here who used to have a plantation on Marie Louise Island.

HARBISON: Marie Louise! That's a good spot. Right on the bottleneck.

BRACKETT: What's this Frenchman's name?

CABLE: Emile de Becque.

BRACKETT (*suddenly excited*): Meet me in my office in about half an hour, Cable. (*He starts off, followed by* HARBISON.)

CABLE: Yes, sir.

BRACKETT: Come on, Bill! Maybe we'll get in this war yet!
(*They exit.* CABLE *watches them off, then picks up his musette bag and starts off himself. The music of "Bali Ha'i" is played.* CABLE *stops in his tracks and listens. Then he turns and looks across at the island. . . . Softly, he starts to sing*):

CABLE:
> Bali Ha'i may call you
> Any night,
> Any day,
> In your heart you'll hear it call you,
> Come away, come away.
> Bali Ha'i, Bali Ha'i, Bali Ha'i.

SCENE 4

As CABLE *sings, the lights fade slowly. A transparent curtain closes across him.*

Downstage, several G.I.'s enter carrying bales and various articles of equipment. The lights dim out on CABLE *behind the curtain and now, illuminating the forestage, reveal the curtain as depicting a company street.*

SAILOR (*crossing stage*): When are you guys going to get that lumber down in our area?

SEABEE (*passing him*): Aw, knock it off!

SAILOR: We'll never get it finished by Thanksgiving.

(*By this time, the lights are higher on the company street. Natives and G.I.'s are constantly crossing, carrying equipment. Natives are seen sometimes wearing G.I. uniforms and sometimes just native cloths. Two nurses in white uniforms cross. Then* BILLIS *enters, in earnest conversation with* STEWPOT *and the* PROFESSOR.)

BILLIS: Did you tell those guys at the shop to stop making those grass skirts?

STEWPOT: Sure, they just turned out one of these. (*He hands him a small, dark object.*) What do you think of it?

BILLIS (*studying it a moment*): That don't look like a dried-up human head. It looks like an old orange painted with shoe polish.

STEWPOT: That's what it is.

BILLIS: Go back to the shop and tell them to try again. If I order a dried-up human head, I want a human head . . . dried up! (*He puts the orange in his pocket.*)

STEWPOT: But—

BILLIS: Fade. Here he comes.

(STEWPOT *and the* PROFESSOR *move away as* CABLE *enters.* BILLIS *crosses to him and speaks to him in a low voice, right in* CABLE'*s ear, as he walks alongside him.*)

Don't change your expression, Lieutenant. Just act like we're talking casual. I got the boat.

CABLE (*stops*): What boat?

BILLIS: Keep walking down the company street. Keep your voice down.

(CABLE *walks slowly and uncertainly.*)
I signed out a boat in your name. We're shoving off for Bali
Ha'i in forty-five minutes.

CABLE (*stopping*): No, we're not. I've got to see Captain Brackett.

BILLIS (*an injured man*): Lieutenant! What are you doing to me?
I signed this boat out in your name.

CABLE: Then you're just the man to go back and cancel it. (*Very
firmly.*) Forget the whole thing. Okay?

(CABLE *walks off.* BILLIS *looks after him with narrowing eyes
and jaw thrust forward.*)

BILLIS: Lieutenant, you and me are going on a boat trip whether
you like it or not. (*He pulls the orange, covered with shoe polish,
out of his pocket, and wishing to vent his rage somehow, he turns
and hurls it off in the direction opposite that taken by* CABLE.)

A FURIOUS VOICE (*offstage*): Hey! Who the hell threw that?

BILLIS (*spoiling for a fight with anyone at all*): I threw it! What
are you gonna do about it? (*He strides off pugnaciously in the
direction of the voice. Before he is off, the curtains have parted on
the succeeding scene.*)

SCENE 5

Inside the Island Commander's office. BRACKETT *is sitting at his
desk, reading some papers.* HARBISON *stands above him.* CABLE *sits
on a chair facing the desk.*

BRACKETT (*as curtains part*): Cable . . . we've got some dope on
your Frenchman. (*He reads a paper before him.*) Marie Louise
Island . . . moved down here sixteen years ago . . . lived with
a Polynesian woman for about five years . . . two children
by her. She died . . . Here's one thing we've got to clear up.
Seems he left France in a hurry. Killed a guy. What do you
think of that?

CABLE: Might be a handy man to have around.

(*The phone rings.*)

HARBISON (*beckoning to* CABLE): Cable.

(CABLE *joins him and they inspect a map on the wall.*)

BRACKETT (*into phone*): Good . . . send her in. No, we haven't
got time for her to change into her uniform. Tell her to come
in.

(*The men exchange looks and face the doorway where presently* NELLIE *appears.*)

Come in, Miss Forbush.

NELLIE: Captain Brackett, please excuse the way . . .

BRACKETT: You look fine. May I present Commander Harbison?

HARBISON: I have the pleasure of meeting Miss Forbush twice a week.

(BRACKETT *looks at him, surprised and curious.*)

We serve together on the G.I. Entertainment Committee.

BRACKETT: Oh. May I also present Lt. Joseph Cable . . . Miss Forbush. Sit down, Miss Forbush.

(*The three men rush to help her sit.* CABLE *gets there first.* NELLIE *sits.* BRACKETT *sits on his desk facing her.* CABLE *drops upstage.* BRACKETT *starts off with light conversation.*)

How's the Thanksgiving Entertainment coming along?

NELLIE: Very well, thank you, sir. We practice whenever we get a chance. (*She wonders why she has been sent for.*)

BRACKETT: About a week ago, you had lunch with a French planter . . . Emile de Becque.

NELLIE: Yes, sir.

BRACKETT: What do you know about him?

NELLIE (*thrown off balance*): Well, I er . . . what do I know about him?

BRACKETT: That's right.

NELLIE: I . . . we . . . met at the Officers' Club dance. He was there and I . . . met him. (*She stops, hoping they will help her along, but they say nothing, so she has to continue.*) Then I had lunch with him that day . . .

BRACKETT (*quickly*): Yes! Now, what kind of a man is he?

NELLIE: He's very nice . . . He's kind . . . He's attractive. I—er—I just don't know what you want to know, sir.

HARBISON: Miss Forbush, Captain Brackett wants to know, did you discuss politics?

NELLIE: No, sir.

BRACKETT (*after a long, pitying look at* HARBISON): Would you have discussed politics, Commander? (*Turning back to* NELLIE.) Now, what we are specifically interested in is—er—when these fellows come out from France, it's generally because they've had some trouble. (NELLIE *looks worried.*) Now . . . has he ever told you anything about that?

(NELLIE *hesitates a moment, deliberating just how far to go in her answer.* BRACKETT *tries to help her out, sensing her embarrassment.*)

What do you know about his family?

NELLIE (*glad to be able to answer a simple specific question without incriminating* EMILE): He has no family—no wife, nobody.

HARBISON: He hasn't any children?

(CABLE *and* HARBISON *exchange looks.*)

NELLIE: No, sir!

BRACKETT: And you say he's never told you why he left France? (*Pause. Then* NELLIE *answers as a Navy Ensign should.*)

NELLIE: Yes, sir. He left France because he killed a man.

(*A sigh of relief from* BRACKETT.)

HARBISON: Did he tell you why?

NELLIE: No. But he will if I ask him.

HARBISON: Well, Miss Forbush, that's exactly what we'd like to have you do. Find out as much as you can about him, his background, his opinions, and why he killed this man in France.

NELLIE: In other words, you want me to spy on him.

BRACKETT: Well, I'm afraid it *is* something like that.

NELLIE: Why? (*Alarmed, she rises and faces* BRACKETT *across his desk.*) Do you suspect him of anything?

BRACKETT (*lies do not come easy to him*): No, it's just that we don't know very much about him and he's—er . . . Will you help us, Miss Forbush?

(*Pause.*)

NELLIE: I'll try.

BRACKETT: Thank you. You may go now if you wish.

(*She starts toward the door, then turns, thoughtfully, as if asking the question of herself.*)

NELLIE: I don't know very much about him really—do I?

(*Slowly, she goes out. For a moment, the men are silent.*)

CABLE: He's kept a few secrets from her, hasn't he?

BRACKETT: Well, you don't spring a couple of Polynesian kids on a woman right off the bat!

HARBISON: I'm afraid we aren't going to get much out of her. She's obviously in love with him.

CABLE (*to* HARBISON): That's hard to believe, sir. They tell me he's a middle-aged man.

BRACKETT (*rising from his desk chair. Smoldering*): Cable! It is a common mistake for boys of your age and athletic ability to underestimate men who have reached their maturity.

CABLE: I didn't mean, sir . . .

BRACKETT: Young women frequently find a grown man attractive, strange as it may seem to you. I myself am over fifty. I am a bachelor and, Cable, I do not, by any means, consider myself—through. (*To* HARBISON *who is suppressing laughter.*) What's the matter, Bill?

HARBISON: Nothing, evidently!

BRACKETT: O.K., Cable. See you at chow. Do you play bridge?

CABLE: Yes, sir.

BRACKETT: Got any money?

CABLE: Yes, sir.

BRACKETT: I'll take it away from you.

CABLE: Yes, sir.

> (*He goes out.* BRACKETT *darts a penetrating look at* HARBISON.)

BRACKETT: What makes you so *damn sure* this mission won't work out?

HARBISON (*looking at the map*): Marie Louise Island is twenty-four miles long and three miles wide. Let's say that every time they send out a message they move to another hill. It seems to me, looking at this thing—

BRACKETT: Realistically.

HARBISON: . . . realistically, (*measuring his words*) they could last about a week.

> (*Pause.* BRACKETT *considers this.*)

BRACKETT: Of course, it would be worth it, if it were the right week. With decent information, our side might get moving. Operation Alligator might get off its can.

YEOMAN (*entering with large cardboard box*): Here it is, sir, I got it.

BRACKETT (*to* HARBISON): Okay, Bill. See you at chow.

> (HARBISON *looks at the package curiously.*)
>
> *See you at chow, Bill.*

HARBISON (*snapping out of it*): Oh, see you at chow. (*He goes out.*)

BRACKETT: Got the address right?

YEOMAN: I think so, sir. (*Reading the box lid.*) Mrs. Amelia

Fortuna. Three twenty-five Euclid Avenue, Shaker Heights, Cleveland, Ohio.

BRACKETT: That's right. I want to pack it myself.

YEOMAN: Yes, sir.

(YEOMAN *exits.* BRACKETT *starts to whistle. He opens the package and takes out a bright yellow grass skirt and shakes it out.* HARBISON *re-enters, stands in doorway, unseen by* BRACKETT, *nods as if his suspicions were confirmed and exits as the lights fade.*)

SCENE 6

As the lights are fading on the Captain's hut, the company-street curtain closes in and the activity seen here before is resumed.

G.I.'s and natives cross, carrying various items of equipment.

NELLIE *enters, walking slowly as she reads a letter. Another* NURSE *in working uniform has some letters in her hand and is moving off.*

NURSE: Going back to the beach, Nellie?

(NELLIE *nods.* NURSE *exits.* CABLE *enters and watches* NELLIE *for a moment.* NELLIE *is now standing still, reading a part of her letter that evokes an occasional groan of irritation from her.* CABLE *grins at her.*)

CABLE: Letter from home?

(NELLIE *looks up, startled by his voice, then grins back at him.*)

NELLIE: Yes. Do you get letters from your mother, telling you that everything you do is wrong?

CABLE: No. My mother thinks everything I do is right. . . . Of course, I don't tell her everything I do.

NELLIE: My mother's so prejudiced.

CABLE: Against Frenchmen?

(*She smiles to acknowledge that she gets the allusion then pursues her anti-maternal tirade.*)

NELLIE: Against anyone outside of Little Rock. She makes a big thing out of two people having different backgrounds.

CABLE (*rather hopefully*): Ages?

NELLIE: Oh, no. Mother says older men are better for girls than younger men.

CABLE (*remembering his recent lecture from* BRACKETT *on this subject*): This has been a discouraging day for me.

NELLIE: Do you agree with Mother about people having things in common? For instance, if the man likes symphony music and the girl likes Dinah Shore—and he reads Marcel Proust and she doesn't read anything . . . Well, what do *you* think? Do you think Mother's right?

CABLE: Well, she might be.

NELLIE: Well, I don't think she is.

CABLE: Well, maybe she's not.

NELLIE: Well, good-bye, Lieutenant. You've helped a lot.

CABLE: Listen, you don't know so much about that guy. You better read that letter over two or three times . . .

NELLIE: I'll show you what I think of that idea. (*She crumples the letter and throws it on the ground.*)

CABLE: Well, don't say I didn't warn you.

(*He exits.* NELLIE *comes back and picks up the letter and starts reading as she walks off.*)

SCENE 7

Before NELLIE *is off the lights come up on:*
    The beach. Several nurses are lounging about before taking their swim. More enter. One of them, DINAH, *is washing an evening dress in a tin tub. Upstage is a home-made shower bath, bearing a sign:*

BILLIS BATH CLUB
SHOWER 15¢
USE OF SOAP 5¢
NO TOWELS SUPPLIED

Two or three SEABEES *stand in attendance, part of* BILLIS' *business empire, no doubt.*

BILLIS (*entering*): Oh, I thought Miss Forbush was here. I brought some hot water for her. (*He goes to shower, climbs a ladder and pours a bucket of water into the tank on top.*) She likes to take a shampoo Fridays.

NELLIE (*entering*): Hello, Luther.

BILLIS: Hello, Miss Forbush. I brought some hot water for you.

NELLIE: Thanks. It'll do me a lot of good to get some of this sand out of my hair.

BILLIS: If you need some extra water for rinsing your hair, my bath-club concession boys will take care of you. When you're ready for the shower, just pull this chain, just like you was . . . Like you was pulling down a window shade. Take care of her, boys.

(*He exits.* NELLIE *enters the shower.*)

NURSE: What'd he want?

NELLIE: Huh?

NURSE: What'd he want?

NELLIE: Who?

NURSE: Iron Belly.

NELLIE: Captain Brackett? Oh, nothing—nothing important. Something about the Thanksgiving show.

SECOND NURSE: Then what's the trouble, Knucklehead?

NELLIE: Huh? (*She is now soaking her hair and it is difficult for her to hear.*)

SECOND NURSE: I said, what's the trouble?

NELLIE: Oh, nothing.

(*The girls look at one another.* NELLIE *comes out of the shower enclosure.*)

There's not going to be any more trouble any more because I've made up my mind about one thing. (*She takes a deep breath and looks at them dramatically.*) It's all off. (*She goes back into the shower enclosure.*)

THIRD NURSE: With him?

NELLIE (*coming right out again through the swinging doors*): Unh-hunh. (*She starts back, then stops and turns.*) I'm going to break it off clean before it's too late.

FOURTH NURSE: Knucklehead, what's happened? What'd he do?

NELLIE: *He* didn't do anything. It's just that . . . Well, I guess I don't know anything about him really and before I go any further with this thing—I just better not get started! Don't you think so, too? Diney?

DINAH: Yes, I do.

NELLIE (*unprepared for such prompt and unequivocal agreement*): You do? Well, I guess I do, too. (*She turns to the other girls.*)

Well, don't look so dramatic about it. Things like this happen every day.

(*She sings:*)
  I'm gonna wash that man right outa my hair,
  I'm gonna wash that man right outa my hair,
  I'm gonna wash that man right outa my hair,
  And send him on his way!
(*She struts around splashing soap out of her hair.*)
  Get the picture?

  I'm gonna wave that man right outa my arms,
  I'm gonna wave that man right outa my arms,
  I'm gonna wave that man right outa my arms,
  And send him on his way!

  Don't try to patch it up—
NURSES:
  Tear it up, tear it up!
NELLIE:
  Wash him out, dry him out—
NURSES:
  Push him out, fly him out!
NELLIE:
  Cancel him and let him go—
NURSES:
  Yea, sister!

  I'm gonna wash that man right outa my hair,
  I'm gonna wash that man right outa my hair,
  I'm gonna wash that man right outa my hair,
  And send him on his way!
NELLIE:
  If the man don't understand you,
  If you fly on separate beams,
  Waste no time!
  Make a change,
  Ride that man right off your range,

Rub him outa the roll call
And drum him outa your dreams!

NURSES:

Oh-ho!

DINAH:

If you laugh at different comics,

ANOTHER NURSE:

If you root for different teams,

NELLIE, DINAH, SECOND NURSE:

Waste no time,
Weep no more,
Show him what the door is for!

NURSES:

Rub him outa the roll call
And drum him outa your dreams!

NELLIE:

You can't light a fire when the wood's all wet,

GIRLS:

No!

NELLIE:

You can't make a butterfly strong,

GIRLS:

Uh-uh!

NELLIE:

You can't fix an egg when it ain't quite good,

NURSES:

And you can't fix a man when he's wrong!

NELLIE:

You can't put back a petal when it falls from a flower,
Or sweeten up a feller when he starts turning sour—
(NELLIE *goes back into the shower, turns on the water and rinses the soap out of her hair.*)

NURSES:

Oh no, Oh no!
If his eyes get dull and fishy
When you look for glints and gleams,
Waste no time,
Make a switch,
Drop him in the nearest ditch!

> Rub him outa the roll call
> And drum him outa your dreams!
> Oh-ho! Oh-ho!

NELLIE (*poking her head out from the shower, then dancing down to the nurses, as she sings*):

> I went and washed that man right outa my hair,
> I went and washed that man right outa my hair,
> I went and washed that man right outa my hair,
> And sent him on his way!

NURSES:

> She went and washed that man right outa her hair,
> She went and washed that man right outa her hair,
> She went and washed that man right outa her hair,
> (NELLIE *joining them in a triumphant finish.*)
> *And sent him on his way!*

(NELLIE *starts to dry her hair with a towel.* EMILE *enters. She cannot see him because the towel covers her eyes. The other girls quickly slip away to leave them alone, all except* DINAH, *who goes to her tin tub and takes out her evening dress.* NELLIE *is humming and dancing as she dries her hair. Suddenly, she stops. She has seen something on the ground—*EMILE's *shoe tops! She moves closer to them, holding the towel forward, as a photographer holds his cloth. She patters over to* DINAH *for confirmation, still holding the towel in this manner.* DINAH *nods, as if to say: "That's him, all right."* NELLIE *makes a dash for the shower. While* NELLIE *is putting a top-piece on over her bathing bra,* DINAH *stands in front of the shower enclosure, blocking the way, and trying to make conversation with* EMILE. *She looks and feels very silly.*)

DINAH: You'd never think this was an evening dress, would you? We're only allowed to bring two of them—evening dresses . . . only two . . . I brought . . . Yeah, sister!

(*She retreats offstage, with no grace whatever.* NELLIE *comes out of the shower and makes a naive attempt to appear surprised.*)

NELLIE: Hello!

EMILE: Hello. . . . That song . . . is it a new American song?

NELLIE: It's an American type song. We were kind of putting in our own words. (*Looking around.*) Where *is* everybody?

EMILE: It is strange with your American songs. In all of them one is either desirous to get rid of one's lover, or one weeps for a man one cannot have.

NELLIE: That's right.

EMILE: I like a song that says: "I love you and you love me . . . And isn't that fine?"

NELLIE (*not very bright at the moment*): Yes . . . that's fine.

EMILE: I left a note for you at the hospital. It was to ask you to my home for dinner next Friday.

NELLIE: Well, I don't think I'll be able to come, Emile, I—

EMILE: I have asked all my friends. The planters' colony.

NELLIE (*determined to wash him out of her hair*): A big party. Well then, if I can't come, you won't miss me.

EMILE: But it is *for* you. It is for my friends to meet you and— more important—for you to meet them; to give you an idea of what your life would be like here. I want you to know more about me . . . how I live and think—

NELLIE (*suddenly remembering her promise to "spy on him"*): More about you?

EMILE: Yes. You know very little about me.

NELLIE: That's right! (*Getting down to business.*) Would you sit down? (EMILE *sits.* NELLIE *paces like a cross-examiner.*) Do you think about politics much . . . And if so what do you think about politics?

EMILE: Do you mean my political philosophy?

NELLIE: I think that's what I mean.

EMILE: Well, to begin with, I believe in the free life—in free-dom for everyone.

NELLIE (*eagerly*): Like in the Declaration of Independence?

EMILE: C'est ça. All men are created equal, isn't it?

NELLIE: Emile! You really believe that?

EMILE: Yes.

NELLIE (*with great relief*): Well, thank goodness!

EMILE: It is why I am here. . . . Why I killed a man.

NELLIE (*brought back to her mission*): Oh, yes. I meant to ask you about that too . . . I don't want you to think I'm prying into your private life, asking a lot of questions. But . . . I always think it's interesting why a person . . . kills another person.
   (EMILE *smiles understandingly.*)

EMILE: Of course, Nellie. That has worried you. (*He turns away to compose his story. Then he begins by stating what he considers the explanation and excuse for the whole thing.*) When I was a boy, I carried my heart in my hand. . . . So . . . when this man came to our town—though my father said he was good—I thought he was bad. (*With a shrug and a smile.*) I was young . . . He attracted all the mean and cruel people to him. Soon he was running our town! He could do anything—take anything . . . I did not like that. I was young. (NELLIE *nods, understanding.*) I stood up in the public square and made a speech. I called upon everyone to stand with me against this man.

NELLIE: What did they do?

EMILE (*letting his hands fall helplessly to his side*): They walked away!

NELLIE: Why?

EMILE: Because they saw him standing behind me. I turned, and he said to me, "I am going to kill you now." We fought. I was never so strong. I knocked him to the ground. And when he fell, his head struck a stone and . . . (*He turns away and lets* NELLIE *imagine the rest.*) I ran to the waterfront and joined a cargo boat. I didn't even know where it was going. I stepped off that boat into another world . . . (*he looks around him, loving all he sees*) where I am now . . . and where I want to stay. (*He turns to* NELLIE *and impulsively steps toward her, deep sincerity and anxiety in his voice.*) Nellie, will you marry me? . . . There are so few days in our life, Nellie. The time I have with you now is precious to me . . . Have you been thinking?

NELLIE: I have been thinking.

> (*Singing, thoughtful, considering.*)
> Born on the opposite sides of the sea,
> We are as different as people can be,

EMILE:
> It's true.

NELLIE:
> And yet you want to marry me. . . .

EMILE:
> I do.

NELLIE:
> I've known you a few short weeks and yet
> Somehow you've made my heart forget

All other men I have ever met
But you . . . but you . . .

EMILE:

Some enchanted evening
You may see a stranger,
You may see a stranger
Across a crowded room,
And somehow you know,
You know even then
That somewhere you'll see her
Again and again. . . .

NELLIE:

Who can explain it?
Who can tell you why?

EMILE:

Fools give you reasons,
Wise men never try . . .
Some enchanted evening,
When you find your true love,
When you feel her call you
Across a crowded room,
Then fly to her side
And make her your own,
Or all through your life you may dream all alone!

NELLIE (*clinging to him*):

Once you have found him
Never let him go.

EMILE:

Once you have found her
Never let her go.

(*They kiss.*)

Will you come next Friday?

NELLIE (*somewhere, from out of the ether, she hears her voice murmur
an inarticulate but automatic assent*): Uh-huh.

(EMILE *kisses her again and leaves. There is the sound of a girl's
laughter offstage and a voice is heard.*)

GIRL'S VOICE (*offstage*): Well, she sure washed him out of her
hair!

(*More laughter.* NELLIE *looks defiantly off in the direction of her mocking friends.*)

NELLIE (*singing*):
> I expect every one
> Of my crowd to make fun
> Of my proud protestations of faith in romance,
> And they'll say I'm naive
> As a babe to believe
> Any fable I hear from a person in pants! . . .
>
> Fearlessly I'll face them and argue their doubts away,
> Loudly I'll sing about flowers and spring!
> Flatly I'll stand on my little flat feet and say,
> "Love is a grand and a beautiful thing!"
> I'm not ashamed to reveal the world-famous feeling I
>   feel.
>
> I'm as corny as Kansas in August,
> I'm as normal as blueberry pie.
> No more a smart
> Little girl with no heart,
> I have found me a wonderful guy.
>
> I am in a conventional dither
> With a conventional star in my eye
> And, you will note,
> There's a lump in my throat
> When I speak of that wonderful guy.
>
> I'm as trite and as gay
> As a daisy in May
> (A cliché coming true!)
> I'm bromidic and bright
> As a moon-happy night
> Pouring light on the dew.
>
> I'm as corny as Kansas in August,
> High as a flag on the Fourth of July!
> If you'll excuse

An expression I use,
I'm in love
I'm in love
I'm in love
I'm in love
I'm in love with a wonderful guy!

(*The other nurses enter and join in her song; each obviously thinking of her own wonderful guy. The "company street" curtain closes as they sing, and before the light on the girls fades out, the men are seen pursuing the activities which have characterized previous company street scenes. The music of "I'm in Love with a Wonderful Guy" has continued and now the nurses enter and resume singing it.* NELLIE *running on last and finishing in a triumphant coda to the amusement of the G.I.'s. The lights fade on them all as they exit and the next scene is revealed.*)

SCENE 8

This is BRACKETT's *office again.*

BRACKETT, HARBISON *and* CABLE *are all looking intently at* EMILE . . .

BRACKETT: Now, before you give us your answer, I want to impress you with three things. First, you are a civilian and you don't have to go. There's no way of our making you go. Second, this is a very dangerous mission and there's no guarantee that you'll survive—or that it will do any good. Third, that it might do a great good. It might be the means of turning the tide of war in this area.

EMILE: I understand all these things.

BRACKETT: Are you ready to give us your answer?

EMILE: Yes, I am. (*Pause.*) My answer must be no.

(CABLE's *foot comes down from the top of the waste-basket, on which it was resting.* HARBISON *uncrosses his arms.* BRACKETT *and* HARBISON *exchange looks.*)

When a man faces death, he must weigh values very carefully. He must weigh the sweetness of his life against the thing he is asked to die for. The probability of death is very great—for both of us. I know that island well, Lieutenant Cable. I am not certain that I believe that—what you ask me to do is . . . is—

BRACKETT: We're asking you to help us lick the Japs. It's as simple as that. We're against the Japs.

EMILE: I know what you're against. What are you for? (*He waits for an answer. They have none.*) When I was twenty-two, I thought the world hated bullies as much as I did. I was foolish—I killed one. And I was forced to flee to an island. Since then, I have asked no help from anyone or any country. I have seen these bullies multiply and grow strong. The world sat by and watched.

CABLE: Aw, to hell with this, de Becque, let's be honest! Aren't you just a guy in love with a girl and you're putting her above everything else in the world?

(EMILE *looks at* CABLE *for a moment before answering.*)

EMILE: Yes, I do care about my life with her more than anything else in the world. It is the only thing that is important to me. This I believe in. This I am sure of. This I have. I cannot risk to lose it. Good day, gentlemen.

(*He goes out. There is a pause. All three men have been rocked off their balance.*)

HARBISON (*thoughtfully*): He's an honest man, but he's wrong. Of course, we can't guarantee him a better world if we win. Point is, we can be damned sure it'll be worse if we lose. Can't we? . . . (*Hotly.*) Well, can't we?

BRACKETT (*rising*): Of course. Cable, there's a bottle of Scotch in my bottom drawer. See you tomorrow.

(*He exits quickly.* HARBISON *goes to the desk and takes a bottle from a drawer.*)

HARBISON: This is the one he means.

(*He takes two glasses and starts to pour the Scotch. A* YEOMAN *enters holding a sheaf of papers to be signed.*)

YEOMAN (*querulously*): Commander Harbison! The Old Man walked right out on me with all these orders to be signed! And there's another delegation of French planters here, complaining about that stolen pig—the one the Seabees took and barbecued. And Commander Hutton's here—

HARBISON (*grabbing papers from him, irritably*): Okay, okay! . . . I'll take care of it!

YEOMAN: Well, all right, sir!

CABLE (*as he takes his glass of Scotch*): What should I do, Commander Harbison? Go back to my outfit tonight?

HARBISON (*with his drink in his hand*): No, take a couple days off and unwind.

CABLE: Unwind?

HARBISON: Sure. Take a boat. Go fishing.

CABLE (*a light dawning on him, a memory of* BILLIS' *offer and* BLOODY MARY's *song about Bali Ha'i*): Boat!

(*He puts his glass down and exits suddenly—as if pulled out of the room.* HARBISON *takes a swallow of Scotch, puts down his glass, looks around for* CABLE, *but* CABLE *has disappeared.* HARBISON *rubs his face with the gesture of a weary man, and starts to go to work on the papers as the lights fade.*)

SCENE 9

As BRACKETT's *office recedes upstage, the tapa-cloth curtain closes and groups of French girls and native girls enter. They sing softly:*

GIRLS:

      Bali ha'i t'appele
      Dans le jour,
      Dans la nuit.
      Dans ton coeur,
      Toujours resonne,
      Par ici,
      Me voici.
      Si tu veux,
      Tu me trouvera
      Où le ciel
      Trouve la mer.
      Me voici,
      Laisse moi te prendre
      Par ici,
      Me voici,
      Bali ha'i,
        Bali ha'i,
          Bali ha'i!

(*There is a bell ringing offstage. A native* KID *shouts excitedly,* "Boat! Boat! Boat!" *He runs off left. The girls back away a few steps as* BILLIS, CABLE *and* BLOODY MARY *walk on.*)

CABLE (*as he enters*): Look, Billis, I didn't come over here to Bali Ha'i to see anybody cut any boar's teeth out.

BILLIS: It ain't the cutting of the boar's tooth exactly. It's what comes afterwards.

(*During these lines,* MARY *has whispered into a small boy's ear and sent him running off.* CABLE *has crossed the girls and looks back over his shoulder at them.*)

MARY (*smiling, understanding perfectly*): I take you with me. Come, Lootellan. You have good time. (*Calling to a native.*) Marcel! Come here! Billis, Marcel take you to boar ceremony. Lootellan come later.

(*Two French girls have caught* CABLE'S *eye, and he has about made up his mind to approach them. He takes a couple of steps toward them, but now two* NUNS *enter and engage them in conversation. Thwarted by this unhappy development,* CABLE *becomes more receptive to* MARY, *who now says:*)

Lootellan, come with me. You have good time. Come! (*She leads him off as the lights fade.*)

SCENE 10

The music swells. A concentration of light in the center of the stage reveals:

The interior of a native hut.

BLOODY MARY *comes in. Even she has to bend low to get through the doorway.* CABLE, *following her, finds himself in the darkness, blinking.*

CABLE: What's this?

MARY: You wait.

CABLE: There's nobody around here.

MARY: You wait, Lootellan.

CABLE: What's going on, Mary? What—

(*He doesn't finish because a small figure has appeared in the doorway. A girl, perhaps seventeen. Her black hair is drawn smooth over her head. Like* BLOODY MARY, *she wears a white blouse and black trousers. Barefooted, she stands, silent, shy and motionless against the wattled wall, looking at* CABLE *with the honest curiosity and admiration of a child.*)

MARY (*to* CABLE, *with a sly smile*): You like?

CABLE (*never taking his eyes from the girl*): Who is she?

MARY: Liat.

LIAT (*nodding her head and repeating it in a small voice*): Liat.

MARY: Is French name.

CABLE (*still stunned, still gazing at the girl*): Liat.

MARY: But she no French girl. She Tonkinese like me. We are ver' pretty people—No? . . .

(*She goes closer to* CABLE *and looks at him. She turns to* LIAT *and then back to* CABLE. *The two young people continue to regard each other with silent, longing interest.*)

CABLE (*over* MARY'*s head, to* LIAT): Do you speak English?

MARY: Only a few word. She talk French. (*To* LIAT.) Français!

LIAT (*smiling shyly*): Je parle Français—un peu. (*She holds her forefinger and thumb close together to show how very little French she speaks.*)

CABLE (*grinning, nearly as shy as she*): Moi, aussi—un peu.

(*He holds up his forefinger and thumb, just as she did. They both laugh, and in some strange way,* BLOODY MARY *seems to have been forgotten by both of them. She looks from one to the other. Then, with the air of one who has accomplished a purpose, she waddles to the doorway. As she goes out, she lets the bamboo curtain roll down across the opening, reducing the light inside the hut. There is a long moment of silence.*)

Are you afraid of me?

(LIAT *looks puzzled. He remembers she knows only a few words of English.*)

Oh . . . er . . . avez-vous peur?

LIAT (*her young face serious*): Non.

(*He takes a step toward her. She backs closer to the wall.*)

Oui!

(*He stops and looks at her, worried and hurt. This sign of gentleness wins her. She smiles.*)

. . . Non.

(*Now it is she who walks slowly toward him. The music builds in a rapturous upsurge.* CABLE *gathers* LIAT *in his arms. She reaches her small arms up to his neck. He lifts her off her feet. The lights fade slowly as his hand slides her blouse up her back toward her shoulders. The lights dim to complete darkness. Light projections of large and lovely Oriental blossoms are thrown against the drop. Native couples stroll across the stage, only dimly seen. The music mounts ecstatically, then diminishes. The stage is clear. The light comes up on the hut again and moonlight now comes through the opened doorway where* CABLE *stands. He has no shirt on.* LIAT *is seated on the floor, gazing up at him silently; her hair hangs loose down her back.* CABLE *smiles down at her.*)

CABLE (*trying to puzzle something out in his mind*): But you're just a kid . . . How did that Bloody Mary get a kid like you to come here and . . . I don't get it! (*Suddenly realizing that she has not understood.*) Cette vielle femme . . . votre amie?

LIAT: Ma mère.

CABLE (*horrified*): Your mother! Bloody Mary is your mother! But she didn't tell me.

   (LIAT, *to divert him from unpleasant thoughts, suddenly throws herself in his lap; they kiss. The sound of a ship's bell is heard in the distance. They sit up.* LIAT *looks panic-stricken.*)

LIAT: Non, Non! (*She covers his ears with her hands.*)

CABLE (*looking off*): It's the boat all right. (*He turns back to her, sees her little face below his, her eyes pleading with him to stay.*) Aw, let them wait.

   (*He sings.*)
      I touch your hand
      And my arms grow strong,
      Like a pair of birds
      That burst with song.
      My eyes look down
      At your lovely face
      And I hold the world
      In my embrace.

      Younger than springtime are you,
      Softer than starlight are you,
      Warmer than winds of June are the gentle lips you gave
         me.
      Gayer than laughter are you,
      Sweeter than music are you,
      Angel and lover, heaven and earth are you to me,

And when your youth and joy invade my arms

And fill my heart as now they do,

Then,

Younger than springtime am I,

Gayer than laughter am I,

Angel and lover, heaven and earth am I with you . . .

(*He releases her, goes to the door, looks off, then comes back to her. He stoops to pick up his shirt. She tries to get it first. Each has hold of one end of it. He looks down at her and repeats, softly:*)

And when your youth and joy invade my arms

And fill my heart as now they do,

Then, younger than springtime am I,

Gayer than laughter am I

Angel and lover, heaven and earth am I with you.

(*He starts. She clings to her end of his shirt for a moment, then lets it slide through her sad little fingers, and watches him go through the door—out of her life, perhaps. She sinks to her knees. The lights fade. Now, again in front of the tapa-cloth curtain, native girls bearing trays of tropical flowers and French girls are gathered in several groups.*)

SCENE 11

The girls sing and hum "Bali Ha'i" softly under the scene, as Hawaiians sing "Aloha" to all departing craft. BLOODY MARY *and* BILLIS *are looking off, anxiously awaiting* CABLE.

BILLIS (*shouting off*): Ring the bell again! Ring the bell again! (*Taking a lei from a* FLOWER-SELLER.) I'll have another one of those. (*He drapes the lei around his neck where he already has three others.*)

MARY: He come. He come. He be here soon. Don't worry, Billis.

BILLIS: Hey, Mary—Please ask those Boar Tooth ceremonial fellows not to be sore at me. I didn't think those girls would do a religious dance with only skirts on. If somebody had told me it was a religious dance, I wouldn't have gotten up and danced with them. (*Looking off.*) Oh! Here he comes! Here he comes.

(BILLIS *exits toward the boat.* CABLE *enters and crosses the stage in a kind of dream.* MARY *smiles, ecstatic, as she sees his face. Several of the French girls try to flirt with* CABLE, *but he doesn't know they're alive. He goes right by them.* MARY *then walks past them, her chin in the air, very proudly and triumphantly. The girls' voices rise, singing the final measures of "Bali Ha'i." They throw flowers offstage where* BILLIS *and* CABLE *made their exit. Cries of "Au revoir" and laughter are heard over the singing.*)

MARY (*throwing flower garland she has taken from a native girl and shouting to the others*): Is gonna be my son-in-law. (*Calling off.*) Goo' bye! Come back soon, Lootellan! Bali Ha'i! Come back soon!

THE LIGHTS FADE

SCENE 12

And other lights come up slowly on EMILE'*s terrace.*

The good-byes continue through the darkness and other good-byes from other voices blend in with these . . . all in French.

HENRY *enters with another* SERVANT. *They start to clear glasses, champagne bottles and other left-overs of a gay party which clutter the scene.*

FRENCHMAN (*offstage*): Bali Ha'i . . . Bon soir!

FRENCHWOMAN (*offstage*): Merci, Emile. Merci, mille fois!
    (EMILE *enters and addresses* HENRY.)

EMILE: Pas maintenant . . . demain!

FRENCHMAN (*offstage*): A bientôt! Bali Ha'i.
    (HENRY *and the other servant exit.*)

FRENCHWOMAN (*offstage*): Quelle charmante soirée.

NELLIE (*offstage*): Good night . . . everybody . . . Good night.

FRENCHMAN (*offstage*): Non, Non . . . Nellie . . . en Français . . . en Français.

NELLIE (*offstage, laboring with her French*): Je . . . suis . . . enchantée . . . de faire . . . votre . . . connaissance!
    (EMILE, *looking off, smiles with amusement and pride. Voices offstage shout "Bravo!" "Formidable!"* EMILE *exits.*)

FRENCHMAN (*offstage*): Bon soir, de Becque.

FRENCHWOMAN (*offstage*): Merci mille fois!!!

(*There is the sound of a motor starting loud, then growing fainter.* EMILE *and* NELLIE *enter and turn back to wave goodbye to the last guests. Then* NELLIE *turns to* EMILE, *who has been gently urging her farther into the garden. There is high excitement in her voice and she speaks very rapidly.*)

NELLIE: Emile, you know I can't stay. And I've got to get that jeep back. I stole it. Or rather, I borrowed it. Or rather a fellow stole it for me. A wonderful man named Billis. I'll have to sneak around behind the hospital as it is.

EMILE: In that case, I forbid you to go! If you have to sneak back without anyone seeing you, you might just as well sneak back later.

(NELLIE *thinks for an instant, then comes to a quick decision.*)

NELLIE (*taking off her coat*): You're absolutely right! (*She looks guiltily at* EMILE *and screams with laughter. So does he. She puts her coat on the back of a chair.*) I never had such a wonderful time in my whole life. All these lovely people and that cute old man who spoke French with me and made believe he understood me. And that exciting native couple who danced for us. Oh, it's so different from *Little Rock!*

(*She screams the last line passionately, as if she hopes Little Rock would hear.* EMILE *laughs uproariously. She suddenly becomes quiet.*)

What on earth are you laughing at? Am I drunk?

EMILE (*still laughing*): Oh, no.

NELLIE: Yes, I am. But it isn't the champagne—it's because I'm in love with a wonderful guy!

(*She sings this last line. They waltz to the music of "I'm in Love with a Wonderful Guy!"* NELLIE *resumes singing.*)

If you'll excuse an expression I use,

I'm in love, I'm in love, I'm in love—

EMILE (*also singing*):

I'm in love, I'm in love and the girl that I love—She thinks

I'm a wonderful guy!

(*They stop, exhausted and laughing. She turns and notices a half-filled glass of champagne which has been left by one of the guests. She takes it up and drinks it.*)

NELLIE: Imagine leaving all this wonderful champagne! (*She

drinks out of this one, then takes another one. She hands it to EMILE.) Here, Emile. You have some, too. It's such a waste!

EMILE: Here—here's another bottle.

(*He goes over to a long table which is under the windows on the porch. There are several buckets of champagne there. He takes one and fills two clean glasses and brings them to* NELLIE. *Meanwhile, she leans back, stretching her arms behind her head. Dreamily, she sings*):

NELLIE:

This is how it feels,

Living on a hillside . . .

(*She speaks as the melody in the orchestra continues.*)

Here we are just like two old married people. Our guests have gone home and we're alone.

EMILE (*handing her the glass of champagne, singing*):

This is what I need,

This is what I've longed for—

Someone young and smiling,

Here upon my hill—

(*The orchestra starts the music of "A Cockeyed Optimist."* NELLIE *has been thinking.*)

NELLIE: Emile, you know, my mother says we have nothing in common. But she's wrong. We have something very important in common—very much in common.

EMILE: Yes, we're both in love.

NELLIE: Yes, but more than that. We're—we're the same kind of people fundamentally—you and me. We appreciate things! We get enthusiastic about things. It's really quite exciting when two people are like that. We're not blasé. You know what I mean?

EMILE: We're both knuckleheads, cockeyed optimists.

(*They both laugh and start to sing*):

NELLIE:

I hear the human race

Is falling on its face . . .

EMILE:

And hasn't very far to go!

NELLIE:

> But every whippoorwill
> Is selling me a bill
> And telling me it just ain't so.

BOTH (*harmonizing—"Sweet Adeline" fashion*):

> I could say life is just a bowl of jello
> And appear more intelligent and smart,
> But I'm stuck,
> Like a dope,
> With a thing called hope,
> And I can't get it out of my heart . . .
> (*Dwelling on the fancy ending:*)
> Not this heart!
> (*They smile in each other's eyes.* EMILE *suddenly gets an idea and rises.*)

EMILE: Nellie, I have a surprise for you. You sit over there—something that I have been preparing for two days. Close your eyes. No peeking.

> (EMILE *looks around first for a prop, sees her coat, then makes her go over and sit by the fountain.* NELLIE *is mystified, but excited, like a child waiting for a surprise.* EMILE *takes her coat and throwing it over his head, using it to simulate a towel, he imitates her as he found her on the beach the other day.*)

> I'm going to wash that man right out of my hair,
> I'm going to wash that man right out of my hair,

NELLIE: Oh, no! No!

> (*She writhes with embarrassment and laughter as he continues.*)

EMILE:

> I'm going to wash that man right out of my hair
> And send him on his way! . . .
> (*She covers her eyes.*)
> Don't try to patch it up,
> Tear it up, tear it up,
> Wash him out, dry him out,
> Push him out, fly him out,
> Cancel him, and let him go—
> Yea, Sister!
> (*He finishes, waving his arms wildly.*)

NELLIE (*applauding*): That's wonderful, Emile.

(EMILE *lifts the coat and, looking off, sees* NGANA *and* JEROME *as they enter in their nightgowns, followed by* HENRY.)

EMILE: Bon soir!

(NELLIE *turns, looks at the children and is immediately enchanted. She kneels before the two of them, holding them at arm's length.*)

NELLIE: You're the cutest things I ever saw in my whole life! What are your names? You probably can't understand a word I'm saying, but, oh, my goodness, you're cute.

EMILE: Nellie, I want you to meet Ngana and Jerome. Ngana and Jerome, Nellie.

NGANA *and* JEROME: Nellie . . .

EMILE (*to the children*): Maintenant au lit . . . vite!

HENRY: Venez, Petits!

NGANA: Bon soir, Nellie.

JEROME: Bon soir, Nellie.

(*They wave to* NELLIE, *as* HENRY *leads them out.*)

NELLIE: Bon soir! (*Turning to* EMILE.) Oh, aren't they adorable! Those big black eyes staring at you out of those sweet little faces! Are they Henry's?

EMILE: They're mine.

NELLIE (*carrying out what she thinks is a joke*): Oh, of course, they look exactly like you, don't they? Where did you hide their mother?

EMILE: She's dead, Nellie.

NELLIE: She's—(*She turns.*) Emile, they *are* yours!

EMILE: Yes, Nellie. I'm their father.

NELLIE: And—their mother . . . was a . . . was . . . a . . .

EMILE: Polynesian.

(NELLIE *is stunned. She turns away, trying to collect herself.*)
And she was beautiful, Nellie, and charming, too.

NELLIE: But you and she . . .

EMILE: I want you to know I have no apologies. I came here as a young man. I lived as I could.

NELLIE: Of course.

EMILE: But I have not been selfish. No woman ever hated me or tried to hurt me.

NELLIE: No woman could ever want to hurt you, Emile. (*Suddenly, feeling she must get away as quickly as she can.*) Oh, what time is it? I promised to get that jeep back! (*She looks at her wrist watch.*) Oh, this is awful. Look at the time!

(*She grabs her coat.* EMILE *tries to stop her.*)

EMILE: Nellie, wait, please. I'll drive you home.

NELLIE: You will do no such thing. Anyway, I couldn't leave the jeep here. I've got to get it back by—

EMILE: Don't go now, Nellie. Don't go yet, please.

NELLIE (*rattling on very fast*): Yes, I must go now. This is terrible! I won't be able to face the girls at the hospital. You can't imagine the way they look at you when you come in late . . . I'll call you, Emile. I'll come by tomorrow. (*Suddenly remembering.*) Oh, no! Oh, dear! There are those awful rehearsals for Thanksgiving Day—I'm teaching them a dance and they want to rehearse night and day—but after that— (*Shifting quickly.*) Oh, thank you for tonight, Emile. I had a wonderful time. It was the nicest party and you're a perfect host. Goodbye. Please stay here, Emile. Don't go out to the jeep, please.

EMILE (*grabbing her arms, feeling her slipping away from him*): Nellie, I love you. Do you hear me, Nellie? I love you!

NELLIE: And I love you, too. Honestly I do— Please let me go! Please let me go!

(NELLIE *goes off. She runs as fast as she can.* EMILE *watches for a second. The motor of the jeep starts and fades away quickly, as though the jeep were driven away very, very fast. The music of "Some Enchanted Evening" swells as* EMILE *looks down and picks up a coffee cup that has been left on the fountain.*)

EMILE (*singing, as he looks down at the cup*):

Once you have found her,
Never let her go.
Once you have found her,
Never let her go!

CURTAIN

ACT TWO

SCENE I

The stage during a performance of "The Thanksgiving Follies."

A dance is in progress, four girls and four boys. NELLIE *is one of the girls. They meticulously perform the steps and evolutions of a dance routine no more distinguished or original than any that might be produced by a Navy nurse who had been the moving spirit in the amateur theatre of Little Rock. Not one of the dancers makes a single mistake. Nobody smiles. Tense concentration is evident in this laboriously perfect performance. During the course of the dance, there are solo "step-outs" after which each soloist soberly steps back into place. The most complicated unison step is saved for the exit, which they execute with vigorous precision.*

On either side, in the downstage corners of the stage, G.I.'s are sitting as if there had not been enough seats and the audience overflowed up onto the stage. There are no chairs. They are seated and sprawled on the floor of the stage.

NELLIE *returns to the stage, a sheaf of notes in her hand and talks into the microphone.*

NELLIE: It has been called to our attention that owing to some trouble with the mimeograph, the last part of the program is kind of blurry, so I will read off who did the last number. (*Reading.*) The hand-stand was by Marine Sergeant Johnson. (*Applause.*) The Barrel Roll was done by Lieutenant J. G. Bessie May Sue Ellie Jaeger. (*Applause.*) The solo featuring the hitch-kick and scissors . . . those are the names of the steps . . . was by Ensign Cora McRae. (*Applause.*) The Pin Wheel . . . you know—(*she demonstrates by waving her leg in imitation of* STEWPOT) was by Stewpot . . . I mean George Watts, Carpenter's Mate, Third Class.

(*Applause.* STEWPOT'S *head protrudes from the wings.*)
STEWPOT: Second class.

(*Applause.*)
NELLIE: The multiple revolutions and—(NELLIE *becomes self-consciously modest*) incidentally the dance steps were by Ensign Nellie Forbush. (*She bows. Applause.*) Now the next is a most

unusual treat. An exhibition of weight lifting by Marine Staff Sergeant Thomas Hassinger.

(HASSINGER *enters from right. He flexes muscles. Applause and shouts from "audience" on the corner of the stage.*)

SAILOR: Atta boy, Muscles!

(*The lights start fading.*)

NELLIE: . . . and Sergeant Johnson . . . (JOHNSON *enters.*) Marine Corporal . . .

(*The lights are out.*)

VOICE IN DARK: Hey, lights . . . the lights are out . . . Billis!

NELLIE: Bill-is . . . what the heck happened to the lights?

OTHER VOICES: "It's the generator." "Generator ran out of gas." "Switch over to the other one." "Mike . . . turn on the truck lights."

NELLIE: Keep your seats, everybody! There's nothing wrong except that the lights went out.

VOICES: "Look where you're going." "How the hell can I look when I can't see?"

(*The lights come up. The set has been changed in the darkness. We are now in:*)

SCENE 2

In back of the stage.

SEABEE: We'll have that other generator on in a minute.

BILLIS: They got the truck lights on. That's something.

(*Applause offstage, right.*)

STEWPOT (*looking off toward "stage"*): The weight-lifting act got started.

BILLIS: Good . . . (*He notices two Seabees who are pushing a large roll of cable.*) What I can't understand is how some guys ain't got the artistic imagination to put gas in a generator so a show can be a success . . . especially when they're on the committee.

FIRST SEABEE: You're on the committee, too. Why didn't you tell us it wasn't gassed up?

BILLIS: I'm acting in the show and I'm stage manager and producer. I can't figure out everything, can I?

SECOND SEABEE: Sure you can. Just put your two heads together. (*He and his companion exit, pushing the roll of cable before them.*)

BILLIS (*calling off*): Look, jerk! I got a production on my hands. (*Turning to* STEWPOT.) How's the weight-lifting act going?

STEWPOT: I can't tell. Nobody's clapping.

BILLIS: If nobody's clapping, they ain't going good. You ought to be able to figure that out. Put your two heads together.

STEWPOT: You was the one with two heads.

(EMILE *enters. He carries a bunch of flowers in his hand. He has a serious "set" expression in his eyes.*)

EMILE: Pardon, can you tell me where I can find Miss Forbush?

BILLIS (*shrewdly sensing trouble and determined to protect* NELLIE): She's on stage now. She's the Emcee. She can't talk to nobody right now. Do you want me to take the flowers in to her?

EMILE: No. I would prefer to give them to her myself.

BILLIS: Are you Mister de Becque?

EMILE: Yes.

BILLIS: Look, Mister de Becque. Do me a favor, will you? Don't try and see her tonight.

EMILE: Why?

BILLIS: We got her in a great mood tonight and I don't want anything to upset her again.

EMILE: She has been upset?

BILLIS: Upset! She's asked for a transfer to another island. And day before yesterday, she busted out crying right in the middle of rehearsal. Said she couldn't go on with the show. And she wouldn't have either unless Captain Brackett talked to her and told her how important it was to the Base. So do us all a favor—don't try to see her now.

EMILE: She's asked for a transfer?

BILLIS: Don't tell her I told you. Nobody's supposed to know.

EMILE: I must see her. Tonight!

BILLIS: Then stay out of sight till after the show. I'll take the flowers to her.

(EMILE *gives him the flowers.* BILLIS *and* STEWPOT *exit.* CABLE *enters. He doesn't see* EMILE *at first.*)

CABLE: Hey, Billis—Billis!

EMILE (*peering through the semi-darkness*): Lieutenant Cable?

CABLE (*putting his fingers to his lips in a mocking gesture*): Ssh!

Lieutenant Cable is supposed to be in his little bed over at the hospital.

EMILE: You have not been well?

CABLE: I'm okay now. Fever gone. They can't hold me in that damned place any longer. I'm looking for a guy named Billis, a great guy for getting boats. (*His voice rising, tense and shrill.*) And I need a boat right now. I've got to get to my island.

EMILE (*worried by* CABLE's *strangeness*): What?

CABLE: That damned island with the two volcanoes on it. You ever been over there?

EMILE: Why, yes, I—

CABLE: I went over there every day till this damned malaria stopped me. Have you sailed over early in the morning? With warm rain playing across your face?

(LIAT *enters. He sees her, but doesn't believe his eyes.*)

Beginning to see her again like last night.

LIAT (*calling offstage*): Ma mère! C'est lui!

(*She turns and, like a young deer, glides over to the amazed* CABLE *and embraces him before the equally amazed* EMILE. MARY *waddles on.*)

CABLE (*holding* LIAT *tight*): I thought I was dreaming.

LIAT (*laughing*): Non. (*She holds him tighter.*)

CABLE (*he holds her away from him and looks at her*): What are you doing over here?

MARY (*grimly*): She come in big white boat—bigger than your boat. Belong Jacques Barrere. He want to marry Liat. (*To* EMILE.) You know him.

(EMILE *nods. She turns back to* CABLE.)

Is white man, too. And very rich!

CABLE (*to* LIAT): Is that the old planter you told me about? The one who drinks?

(*His eye catches* EMILE's. EMILE *nods.* CABLE *cries out as if hurt.*)

Oh, my God! (*He turns angrily to* MARY.) You can't let her marry a man like that.

MARY: Hokay! Then *you* marry her.

EMILE (*angrily, to* MARY): Tais-toi! Il est malade! . . . Tu comprends?

(MARY *is temporarily silenced.* EMILE *turns to* CABLE *and his voice becomes gentle and sympathetic.*)

Lieutenant, I am worried about you. You are ill. Will you allow me to see you back to the hospital?

CABLE: You're worried about me! That's funny. The fellow who says he lives on an island all by himself and doesn't worry about anybody—Japs, Americans, Germans—anybody. Why pick out *me* to worry about?

EMILE (*stiffly*): Forgive me. I'm sorry, Lieutenant.

(*He leaves.* MARY *goes to* CABLE *to make one last plea for her daughter's dream.*)

MARY: Lootellan, you like Liat. . . . Marry Liat! You have good life here. Look, Lootellan, I am rich. I save six hundred dolla' before war. Since war I make two thousand dolla' . . . war go on I make maybe more. Sell grass skirts, boar's teeth, real human heads. Give all de money to you an' Liat. You no have to work. I work for you. . . . (*Soft music is played.*) All day long, you and Liat be together! Walk through woods, swim in sea, sing, dance, talk happy. No think about Philadelia. Is no good. Talk about beautiful things and make love all day long. You like? You buy?

(*She sings. Throughout the song,* LIAT *performs what seem to be traditional gestures.*)

> Happy Talk,
> Keep talkin' Happy Talk!
> Talk about tings you'd like to do.
> You got to have a dream—
> If you don' have a dream
> How you gonna have a dream come true?

> Talk about a moon
> Floatin' in de sky,
> Lookin' like a lily on a lake:
> Talk about a bird
> Learnin' how to fly,
> Makin' all de music he can make.

> Happy Talk,
> Keep talkin' Happy Talk!
> Talk about tings you'd like to do.

You got to have a dream—
If you don' have a dream
How you gonna have a dream come true?

Talk about a star
Lookin' like a toy,
Peekin' through de branches of a tree.
Talk about a girl,
Talk about a boy
Countin' all de ripples on de sea.

Happy Talk,
Keep talkin' Happy Talk!
Talk about tings you'd like to do.
You got to have a dream—
If you don' have a dream
How you gonna have a dream come true?
(LIAT *now performs a gentle, childish dance. At the end of it, she returns to* CABLE's *side and* MARY *resumes her song:*)
Talk about a boy
Sayin' to de girl,
"Golly, baby, I'm a lucky cuss!"
Talk about a girl
Saying to de boy,
"You an' me is lucky to be us."
(LIAT *and* CABLE *kiss.* MARY's *voice becomes triumphant.*)
Happy Talk,
Keep talkin' Happy Talk!
Talk about tings you'd like to do.
You got to have a dream—
If you don' have a dream
How you gonna have a dream come true?

If you don' talk happy
An' you never have a dream
Den you'll never have a dream come true.

(*Speaking eagerly.*)
Is good idea . . . you like?

(*She laughs gaily and looks in* CABLE'*s eyes, anxious to see the answer.* CABLE *is deeply disturbed. He takes a gold watch from his pocket and puts it in* LIAT'*s hand.*)

CABLE: Liat, I want you to have this. It's a man's watch but it's a good one—belonged to my grandfather. It's kind of a lucky piece, too. My dad carried it all through the last war. Beautiful, isn't it?

(LIAT *has taken the watch, her eyes gleaming with pride.*)

MARY: When I see you firs' time. I know you good man for Liat. And she good girl for you. You have special good babies.

(*Pause.* CABLE *looks tortured.*)

CABLE (*forcing the words out*): Mary, I can't . . . marry . . . Liat.

MARY (*letting out her rage and disappointment in a shout, as she grabs* LIAT'*s arm*): Was your las' chance! Now she marry Jacques Barrere. Come, Liat!

(LIAT *runs to* CABLE, MARY *pulls her away.*)

Give me watch.

(LIAT *clasps it tight in her hands.* MARY *wrests it from her and yells at* CABLE.)

Stingy bastard!

(*She throws it on the ground and it smashes.* CABLE *looks on, dazed, stunned.* MARY *pulls* LIAT *off.* CABLE *kneels down, gathers up the pieces and puts them in his pocket. Meanwhile, several of the men come on, dressed for the finale of the show. They are looking back over their shoulders at* LIAT *and* MARY *whom they must have just passed.*)

PROFESSOR: Hey! Did you get a load of that little Tonkinese girl?

(*They continue up to the stage door as they speak.*)

MARINE: Yeah.

(*Applause off.* NELLIE'*s voice is heard through the loudspeaker.*)

NELLIE (*offstage*): Now, boys, before we come to the last act of our show, it is my great pleasure to bring you our skipper, Captain George Brackett.

(*Applause.* CABLE *looks off at* LIAT *as she passes out of his life.*)

CABLE (*singing*):

> Younger than springtime were you,
> Softer than starlight were you,
> Angel and lover, heaven and earth
> Were you to me. . . .

SCENE 3

The lights fade to complete darkness. BRACKETT's *voice is heard in the loudspeaker. During his speech, the lights come up, revealing: The G.I. Stage, as before.* BRACKETT *is speaking into a microphone.*

BRACKETT: Up to now, our side has been having the hell beat out of it in two hemispheres and we're not going to get to go home until that situation is reversed. It may take a long time before we can get any big operation under way, so it's things like this, like this show tonight, that keep us going. Now I understand that I am not generally considered a sentimental type.
    (*Laughter and cries of "Oh, boy!" "Check," "You can say that again," etc., from the boys on the corners of the stage.*)
Once or twice I understand I have been referred to as "Old Iron Belly."
VOICES: "Once or twice." "Just about a million times." (*Loud laughter.*)
BRACKETT: I resent that very much because I had already chosen that as my private name for our Executive Officer, Commander Harbison. (*Big laugh. Applause.* BRACKETT *calls into the wings.*) Take a bow, Commander.
    (*Two of the girls pull* COMMANDER HARBISON *out.*)
SAILOR: I wish I was a commander!
    (HARBISON, *flanked by the two girls, stands beside* BRACKETT *as he continues:*)
BRACKETT: I want you to know that both "Old Iron Bellies" sat here tonight and had a hell of a good time. And we want to thank that hard working committee of Nurses and Sea-bees who made the costumes out of rope and mosquito nets, comic books and newspapers . . . (*He fingers the comic-paper skirt of one of the girls.*)
SAILOR: Ah, ah—captain!
    (BRACKETT *frowns, but pulls himself together.*)
BRACKETT: . . . and thought up these jokes and these grand songs. And I just want to say on this Thanksgiving Day, to all of them from all of us, thank you. (*Applause from the boys, but it is comically feeble. Obviously, they'd like to get on with the show.*) And now I'm going to ask Commander Harbison to

announce the next act which is the Finale of our Thanksgiving entertainment.

(*He hands* HARBISON *a paper.* HARBISON *reads from a small card.*)

HARBISON: The next and last will be a song sung by Bosun Butch Forbush . . . (*he looks kind of puzzled*) . . . and that Siren of the Coral Sea . . . gorgeous, voluptuous and petite Mademoiselle Lutheria . . . (*ending in a high, surprised voice, as he reads the name of his pet abomination*) . . . Billis!

BRACKETT (*laughing*): Come on, Bill.

(*He leads off* HARBISON, *who is looking at the paper, puzzled. The music of "Honey-Bun" starts and* NELLIE *enters, dressed as a sailor, in a borrowed white sailor suit, three times too big for her.*)

NELLIE (*singing*):

> My doll is as dainty as a sparrow,
> Her figure is something to applaud.
> Where she's narrow, she's as narrow as an arrow
> And she's broad where a broad should be broad!

> A hundred and one
> Pounds of fun—
> That's my little Honey-Bun!
> Get a load of Honey-Bun tonight!

> I'm speakin' of my
> Sweetie Pie,
> Only sixty inches high—
> Ev'ry inch is packed with dynamite!

> Her hair is blonde and curly,
> Her curls are hurly-burly.
> Her lips are pips!
> I call her hips:
> "Twirly"
> And "Whirly."
> She's my baby,
> I'm her Pap!
> I'm her booby,

She's my trap!
I am caught and I don't wanta run
'Cause I'm havin' so much fun with Honey-Bun!
(NELLIE *starts a second refrain, meanwhile having considerable difficulty with her sagging trousers. Now* BILLIS *enters, dressed as a South Sea siren in a straw-colored wig, long lashes fantastically painted on his eyelids, lips painted in bright carmine, two coconut shells on his chest to simulate "femininity" and a battle-ship tatooed on his bare midriff. He and* NELLIE *dance. For an exit, she leads him off, singing a special ending.*)

NELLIE:
She's my baby,
I'm her Pap!
I'm her booby,
She's my trap!
I am caught and I don't wanta run
'Cause I'm havin' so much fun with Honey-Bun!
(Believe me, sonny)
She's a cookie who can cook you till you're done,
(Ain't bein' funny)
Sonny,
Put your money
On my Honey-Bun!
(*After they exit,* NELLIE *returns for a bow. Then* BILLIS *enters with* EMILE's *flowers and presents them to her. Thinking they are from* BILLIS, *she kisses him. He exits in a delirious daze. She exits as the girls enter, singing.*)

GIRLS:
A hundred and one
Pounds of fun—
That's my little Honey-Bun
Get a load of Honey-Bun tonight.

I'm speakin' of my
Sweetie Pie,
Only sixty inches high—
Every inch is packed with dynamite.
(*The girls are dressed in home-made costumes representing island natives. The materials are fish-net, parachute cloth, large tropical leaves and flowers—anything they could find and*

sew together. At the end of their line is BILLIS *still dressed as a girl. As the song proceeds, he is the butt of many a slur from his comrades. While passing one of them, he is shocked and infuriated to feel a hand thrust up his skirt. He turns to swing on him, but he can't get out of line and spoil the number; "On with the show!" He is grim and stoic—even when another boy lifts one of the coconuts in his "brassiere" and steals a package of cigarettes therefrom. The girls and* BILLIS *continue singing through these impromptu shenanigans.*)

GIRLS:

> Her hair is blonde and curly,
> Her curls are hurly-burly.
> Her lips are pips!
> I call her hips:
> "Twirly" and "Whirly."
>
> She's my baby,
> I'm her Pap!
> I'm her booby,
> She's my trap!
> I am caught and I don't wanta run
> 'Cause I'm havin' so much fun with Honey-Bun!
> (*All lining up for finale.*)
> And that's the finish,
> And it's time to go for now the show is done.
> (*Balance of* "COMPANY" *comes on.*)
> We hope you liked us,
> And we hope that when you leave your seat and run
> Down to the Mess Hall
> You'll enjoy your dinner each and every one.

(NELLIE *makes a special entrance, now wearing a new costume.*)

NELLIE (*very brightly*):

> Enjoy your turkey.

ALL (*pointing to* BILLIS):

> And put some chestnut dressing on our Honey-Bun!
> (*The curtain is slow.* NELLIE *signals for it and jumps up to help pull it down. The lights are off. Boys on the stage wave their flashlights out at the audience, addressing them as if they were all G.I.'s. "See you down at the mess hall," etc. When the clamor dies down, two lines are distinguishable.*)

SAILOR: How d'ye like the show?
MARINE: It stunk!

SCENE 4

Now the lights come up on the scene behind the stage.

The girls come off the stage and file into their dressing shack. BILLIS *follows them in. After a few moments, he comes hurtling out, minus his wig. A few seconds later, the wig is thrown out by one of the girls in the dressing room.*

BILLIS: Oh, I beg your pardon. (*At this moment, he turns and faces* NELLIE, *who has just come down the steps from the stage with another girl.*)

NELLIE (*seeing* BILLIS): Oh, Luther, you really are a honey-bun! These beautiful flowers! I needed someone to think of me tonight. I appreciate it, Luther—you don't know how much.

BILLIS (*very emotionally*): Miss Forbush, I would like you to know I consider you the most wonderful woman in the entire world—officer and all. And I just can't go on being such a heel as to let you think I thought of giving you those flowers.

NELLIE: But you did give them to me and I—

BILLIS (*shoving a card at* NELLIE): Here's the card that came with them. (*She reads the card, then turns away—deeply affected.*) Are you all right, Miss Forbush? (*She nods her head.*) I'll be waiting around the area here in case you need me. Just—just sing out.

(*He exits.* NELLIE *is on the point of tears.* CABLE, *who has been sitting on a bench below the ladies' dressing shack, now rises and approaches* NELLIE.)

CABLE (*sympathetically, but taking a light tone*): What's the matter, Nellie the nurse? Having diplomatic difficulties with France?

(NELLIE *turns, startled.*)

NELLIE (*immediately becoming the professional nurse*): Joe Cable! Who let you out of the hospital?

CABLE: Me. I'm okay.

(*She leads him to the bench and feels his forehead and pulse.*)

NELLIE (*accusingly*): Joe! You're trying to get over to Bali Ha'i. That little girl you told me about!

CABLE (*nodding thoughtfully*): Liat. I've just seen her for the last time, I guess. I love her and yet I just heard myself saying I can't marry her. What's the matter with me, Nellie? What kind of a guy am I, anyway?

NELLIE: You're all right. You're just far away from home. We're both so far away from home.

(*She looks at the card. He takes her hand.* EMILE *enters. He is earnest and importunate.*)

EMILE: Nellie! I must see you.

NELLIE: Emile! I—

EMILE: Will you excuse us, Lieutenant Cable?

(CABLE *starts to leave.*)

NELLIE: No, wait a minute, Joe. Stay. Please! (*To* EMILE.) I've been meaning to call you but—

EMILE: You have asked for a transfer, why? What does it mean?

NELLIE: I'll explain it to you tomorrow, Emile. I'm—

EMILE: No. Now. What does it mean, Nellie?

NELLIE: It means that I can't marry you. Do you understand? I can't marry you.

EMILE: Nellie—Because of my children?

NELLIE: Not because of your children. They're sweet.

EMILE: It is their Polynesian mother then—their mother and I.

NELLIE: . . . Yes. I can't help it. It isn't as if I could give you a good reason. There is no reason. This is emotional. This is something that is born in me.

EMILE (*shouting the words in bitter protest*): It is not. I do not believe this is born in you.

NELLIE: Then why do I feel the way I do? All I know is that I can't help it. I can't help it! Explain how we feel, Joe—

(JOE *gives her no help. She runs up to the door of the dressing shack.*)

EMILE: Nellie!

NELLIE (*calling in*): Dinah, are you ready?

NURSE: Yes, Nellie.

NELLIE: I'll go with you.

(*The other nurse comes out and they exit quickly.* EMILE *turns angrily to* CABLE.)

EMILE: What makes her talk like that? Why do you have this feeling, you and she? I do not believe it is born in you. I do not believe it.

CABLE: It's not born in you! It happens *after* you're born . . .
(CABLE *sings the following words, as if figuring this whole question out for the first time.*)

You've got to be taught to hate and fear,
You've got to be taught from year to year,
It's got to be drummed in your dear little ear—
You've got to be carefully taught!

You've got to be taught to be afraid
Of people whose eyes are oddly made,
And people whose skin is a different shade—
You've got to be carefully taught.

You've got to be taught before it's too late,
Before you are six or seven or eight,
To hate all the people your relatives hate—
You've got to be carefully taught!
You've got to be carefully taught!

(*Speaking, going close to* EMILE, *his voice filled with the emotion of discovery and firm in a new determination.*)
You've got the right idea, de Becque—live on an island. Yes, sir, if I get out of this thing alive, I'm not going back there! I'm coming here. All I care about is right here. To hell with the rest.

EMILE (*thoughtfully*): When all you care about is here . . . this is a good place to be. When all you care about is taken away from you, there is no place . . . (*Walking away from* CABLE, *now talking to himself.*) I came so close to it . . . so close.
(*Singing:*)
One dream in my heart,
One love to be living for,
One love to be living for—
This nearly was mine.

One girl for my dreams,
One partner in Paradise,
This promise of Paradise—
This nearly was mine.

Close to my heart she came,
Only to fly away,
Only to fly as day
Flies from moonlight!

Now, now I'm alone,
Still dreaming of Paradise.
Still saying that Paradise
Once nearly was mine.

So clear and deep are my fancies
Of things I wish were true,
I'll keep remembering evenings
I wish I'd spent with you.
I'll keep remembering kisses
From lips I'll never own
And all the lovely adventures
That we have never known.

One dream in my heart
One love to be living for
One love to be living for—
This nearly was mine.

One girl for my dreams,
One partner in Paradise.
This promise of Paradise—
This nearly was mine.

Close to my heart she came,
Only to fly away,
Only to fly as day
Flies from moonlight!

Now . . . now I'm alone,
Still dreaming of Paradise,
Still saying that Paradise
Once nearly was mine.
(*He drops to the bench, a lonely and disconsolate figure.*)

CABLE (*going to him*): De Becque, would you reconsider going up there with me to Marie Louise Island? I mean, now that you haven't got so much to lose? We could do a good job, I think—you and I. (EMILE *doesn't answer.*) You know, back home when *I* used to get in a jam, I used to go hunting. That's what I think I'll do now. Good hunting up there around Marie Louise. Jap carriers . . . cargo boats . . . troopships . . . big game. (*He looks at* EMILE, *craftily considering how much headway he has made.* EMILE *smiles a little.*) When I go up, what side of the island should I land on?

EMILE: The south side.

CABLE: Why?

EMILE: There's a cove there . . . and rocks. I have sailed in behind these rocks many times.

CABLE: Could a submarine get in between those rocks without being observed?

EMILE: Yes. If you know the channel.

CABLE: And after I land, what will I do?

EMILE: You will get in touch with my friends, Basile and Inato—two black men—wonderful hunters. They will hide us in the hills.

CABLE (*his eyes lighting up*): Us? Are you going with me?

EMILE (*a new strength in his voice*): Of course. You are too young to be out alone. Let's go and find Captain Brackett.

CABLE (*delirious*): Wait till that old bastard Brackett hears this. He'll jump out of his skin!

EMILE: I would like to see this kind of a jump. Come on!

(*They go off quickly together.* BILLIS *rushes on and looks after them. Obviously, he's been listening. He thinks it over for a moment, "dopes it out." Then, with sudden decision, he takes one last puff on a cigarette butt, flings it away, and follows after them.*)

SCENE 5

The lights go out and almost immediately the sound of an airplane motor is heard, revving up, ready for the take-off. The lights come up between the tapa-cloth and the dark-green drop.

Several Naval Aircraft mechanics are standing with their backs to the audience— They look off, watching tensely. As the plane is heard taking off, they raise their hands and shout in an exultant, defiant manner.

The music reaches a climax and the lights fade out on them, as they exit.

Lights in center come on simultaneously, revealing:

SCENE 6

This is the communications office or radio room. The back wall is covered with communications equipment of all sorts: boards, lights, switches. There is a speaker, a small table with a receiving set, various telephones and sending equipment. A COMMUNICATIONS ENLISTED MAN *is sitting at the table with earphones. He is working the dials in front of him.* CAPTAIN BRACKETT *is seated on an upturned waste basket. On the floor, are several empty Coca-Cola bottles and several full ones. He is eating a sandwich and alternately guzzling from a bottle of Coca-Cola. There are a couple of empty Coca-Cola bottles on the* ENLISTED MAN's *desk, too.* BRACKETT *is listening avidly for any possible sound that might come from the loudspeaker. After a moment, there is a crackle.*

BRACKETT (*excitedly*): What's that? What's that?

> (*The* ENLISTED MAN *cannot hear him, because he has earphones.* BRACKETT *suddenly becomes conscious of this. He pokes the* ENLISTED MAN *in the back. The* ENLISTED MAN, *controlling himself, turns and looks at* BRACKETT, *as a nurse would at an anxious, complaining patient. He pulls the earphones away from his ear.*)

What was that?

ENLISTED MAN (*quietly*): That was . . . nothing, sir.

> (*He readjusts his earphones and turns to his dials again.* BRACKETT, *unsatisfied by this, pokes the* ENLISTED MAN *again. The* ENLISTED MAN *winces, then patiently takes the earphones from his ears.*)

BRACKETT: Sounded to me like someone trying to send a message . . . sounded like code.

ENLISTED MAN: That was not code, sir. That sound you just

heard was the contraction of the tin roof. It's the metal, cooling off at night.

BRACKETT: Oh.

ENLISTED MAN: Sir, if you'd like to go back to your office, I'll let you know as soon as . . .

BRACKETT: No, no, I'll stay right here. I don't want to add to your problems.

ENLISTED MAN (*he turns back to his dials*): Yes, sir.

> (BRACKETT *impatiently looks at his watch and compares it with the watch on the* ENLISTED MAN's *desk. He talks to the* ENLISTED MAN *who cannot hear him.*)

BRACKETT: We ought to be getting a message now. We ought to be getting a message, that's all. They'd have time to land and establish some sort of an observation post by now, don't you think so? (*He realizes that the* ENLISTED MAN *cannot hear.*) Oh.

> (*He sits back in a position of listening.* HARBISON *enters. He is very stern, more upset than we have ever seen him.*)

HARBISON: Captain Brackett?

BRACKETT: Yeah, what is it? What is it? Don't interrupt me now, Bill. I'm very busy.

HARBISON: It's about this Seabee out here, sir, Billis! Commander Perkins over at Operations estimates that Billis' act this morning cost the Navy over six hundred thousand dollars!

BRACKETT: Six hundred— By God, I'm going to chew that guy's—send him in here!

HARBISON: Yes, sir.

> (*He exits.* BRACKETT *goes over and taps the* ENLISTED MAN *on the shoulder. The* ENLISTED MAN *removes earphones.*)

BRACKETT: Let me know the moment you get any word. No matter what I'm doing, you just break right in.

ENLISTED MAN: Yes, sir.

> (*He goes back to his work.* BRACKETT *paces another second and then* BILLIS *enters, wary, on guard; his face is flaming red, his nose is a white triangle, covered with zinc-oxide. He wears an undershirt. His arms are red, except for two patches of zinc-oxide on his shoulders. He is followed by* LIEUTENANT BUS ADAMS *and* COMMANDER HARBISON, *who closes the door.*)

HARBISON (*pushing* BILLIS *in*): Get in there! Captain Brackett, this is Lieutenant Bus Adams, who flew the mission.

BRACKETT: H'y'a, Adams.

ADAMS: Captain.

    (BRACKETT *beckons* BILLIS *to him.* BILLIS *walks over to him slowly, not knowing what may hit him.*)

BRACKETT: One man like you in an outfit is like a rotten apple in a barrel. Just what did you feel like—sitting down there all day long in that rubber boat in the middle of Empress Augusta Bay with the whole damn Navy Air Force trying to rescue you? And how the hell can you fall out of a PBY anyway?

BILLIS: Well, sir, the Jap anti-aircraft busted a hole in the side of the plane and—I fell through . . . the wind just sucked me out.

BRACKETT: So I'm to understand that you deliberately hid in the baggage compartment of a plane that you knew was taking off on a very dangerous mission. You had sand enough to do that all right. And then the moment an anti-aircraft gun hit the plane you fell out. The wind just sucked you out . . . you and your little parachute! I don't think you fell out, Billis, I think you jumped out. Which did you do?

BILLIS: Well, sir . . . er . . . it was sort of half and half . . . if you get the picture.

BRACKETT: This is one of the most humiliating things that ever happened to me. Adams, when did you discover he was on the plane?

ADAMS: Well, sir, we'd been out about an hour—it was still dark, I know. Well, we were flying across Marie Louise. The Jap anti-aircraft spotted us and made that hit. That's when Luther . . . er . . . this fellow here . . . that's when he . . . left the ship. I just circled once . . . time enough to drop him a rubber boat. Some New Zealanders in P-40s spotted him though and kept circling around him while I flew across the island and landed alongside the sub, let Joe and the Frenchman off. By the time I got back to the other side of the island, our Navy planes were flying around in the air above this guy like a thick swarm of bees. (*He turns to grin at* HARBISON, *who gives him no returning grin. He clears his throat and turns back to* BRACKETT.) They kept the Jap guns occupied while I slipped down and scooped him off the rubber boat. You'd have thought this guy was a ninety-million-dollar cruiser they were out to protect. There must have been fifty-five or sixty planes.

BILLIS: Sixty-two.

BRACKETT: You're not far off, Adams. Harbison tells me this thing cost the Navy about six hundred thousand dollars.

BILLIS (*his face lighting up*): Six hundred thous . . . !

BRACKETT: What the hell are you so happy about?

BILLIS: I was just thinking about my uncle. (*To* ADAMS.) Remember my uncle I was telling you about? He used to tell my old man I'd never be worth a dime! Him and his lousy slot machines. . . . Can you imagine a guy . . . (*He catches sight of* HARBISON'*s scowl and shuts up quickly.*)

BRACKETT: Why the hell did you do this anyway, Billis? What would make a man do a thing like this?

BILLIS: Well, sir, a fellow has to keep moving. You know . . . you get kind of held down. If you're itching to take a trip to pick up a few souvenirs, you got to kind of horn in . . . if you get the picture.

BRACKETT: How did you know about it?

BILLIS: I didn't know about it, exactly. It's just when I heard Lieutenant Cable talking to that fellow de Becque, right away I know something's in the air. A project. That's what I like, Captain. Projects. Don't you?

HARBISON: Billis, you've broken every regulation in the book. And, by God, Captain Brackett and I are going to throw it at you.

ADAMS: Sir. May I barge in? My co-pilot watched this whole thing, you know, and he thinks that this fellow Billis down there in the rubber boat with all those planes over him caused a kind of diversionary action. While all those Japs were busy shooting at the planes and at Billis on the other side of the island, that sub was sliding into that little cove and depositing the Frenchman and Joe Cable in behind those rocks.

BRACKETT: What the hell do you want me to do? Give this guy a Bronze Star?

BILLIS: I don't want any Bronze Star, Captain. But I could use a little freedom. A little room to swing around in . . . if you know what I mean. If you get the picture.

BRACKETT: Get out of here. Get the hell out of here!

(*Moving up after* BILLIS. BILLIS *flees through the door.*)

HARBISON: I'd have thrown him in the brig. And I will too, if I get the ghost of a chance.

(*Suddenly, the* RADIO OPERATOR *becomes very excited and waves his arm at* CAPTAIN BRACKETT. *We begin to hear squeaks and static from the loudspeaker and through it we hear* EMILE DE BECQUE's *voice. Everyone on the stage turns. All eyes and ears are focused on the loudspeaker.*)

EMILE'S VOICE: —And so we are here. This is our first chance to send news to you. We have made contact with former friends of mine. We have set up quarters in a mango tree—no room but a lovely view. . . . First the weather: rain clouds over Bougainville, The Treasuries, Choiseul and New Georgia. We expect rain in this region from nine o'clock to two o'clock. Pardon? Oh—my friend Joe corrects me. Oh—nine hundred to fourteen hundred. And now, our military expert, Joe.

CABLE'S VOICE: All you Navy, Marine and Army Pilots write this down.

(ADAMS *whips out his notebook and writes it as* CABLE *speaks.*)

Surface craft—nineteen troop barges headed down the bottle neck; speed about eleven knots. Ought to pass Banika at about twenty hundred tonight, escorted by heavy warships.

(BRACKETT *and* HARBISON *smile triumphantly.*)

There ought to be some way to knock off a few of these.

(CABLE's *voice continues under the following speeches.*)

ADAMS: Oh, boy! (*He goes to door.*)

HARBISON: Where you going?

ADAMS: Don't want to miss that take-off. We'll be going out in waves tonight—waves—

(*He exits quickly.* BRACKETT *sits down on waste basket and opens another Coke.*)

BRACKETT: Sit down, Bill.

(HARBISON *sits, listening intently.* BRACKETT *hands him a Coca-Cola.* HARBISON *takes it.*)

Here.

HARBISON: Thanks.

BRACKETT: You know what I like, Bill? Projects—don't you?

(*Lights start to fade.*)

CABLE'S VOICE (*which has been continuing over above dialogue*): As for aircraft, there is little indication of activity at the moment. But twenty-two bombers—Bettys—went by at 0600, headed

southwest. There was fighter escort, not heavy . . . They should
reach—

> (*The lights are now off the scene, but another part of the stage
> is lighted, revealing a group of pilots around a radio set, being
> briefed by an* OPERATIONS OFFICER.)

SCENE 7

OPERATIONS OFFICER: Listen carefully.

EMILE'S VOICE: Ceiling today unlimited. Thirty-three fighters—
Zeros—have moved in from Bougainville. Their course is
approximately 23 degrees— Undoubtedly, heavy bombers will
follow.

OFFICER (*to pilots who are writing*): Got that?

> (*Lights out. Light hits another group.*)

NAVY PILOT (*to a group of officers*): Well, gentlemen, here's the
hot tip for today. Joe and the Frenchman have sighted twenty
surface craft heading southeast from Vella Lavella. Christmas is just two weeks away. Let's give those two characters a
present—a beautiful view of no ships coming back.

AN OFFICER: Okay, that's all right with me.

> (*They exit. Lights fade off and return to center of stage,
> revealing:*)

SCENE 8

The Radio Shack again.

> BRACKETT *is pacing up and down.* HARBISON *is standing near
> the door, a pleading expression on his face.*

HARBISON: Sir, you just have to tell her something some time.
She hasn't seen him for two weeks. She might as well know
it now.

BRACKETT: Okay. Send her in. Send her in. I always have to do
the tough jobs.

> (HARBISON *exits. A second later,* NELLIE *enters, followed by*
> HARBISON. *She goes to* BRACKETT *and immediately plunges
> into the subject closest to her heart. Her speech is unplanned. She
> knows she has no right to ask her question, but she must have
> an answer.*)

NELLIE: Captain Brackett, I know this isn't regular. . . . It's about Emile de Becque. I went to his house a week ago to . . . You know how people have arguments and then days later you think of a good answer. . . . Well, I went to his house, and he wasn't there. I even asked the children . . . he has two little children . . . and they didn't seem to know where he'd gone. At least, I think that's what they said—they only speak French. And then tonight while I was on duty in the ward—we have a lot of fighter pilots over there, the boys who knocked out that convoy yesterday—you know how fighter pilots talk—about "Immelmanns" and "wingovers" and things. I never listen usually but they kept talking about a Frenchman—the Frenchman said this, and the Frenchman said that . . . and I was wondering if this Frenchman they were talking about could be—*my* Frenchman.

(*Pause.*)

BRACKETT: Yes, Miss Forbush, it is. I couldn't tell you before but . . . As a matter of fact, if you wait here a few minutes, you can hear his voice.

NELLIE: His voice? Where is he?

BRACKETT: With Lieutenant Cable behind enemy lines.

NELLIE: Behind . . . ?

(*The* RADIO OPERATOR *snaps his fingers. All heads turn up toward the loudspeaker. They listen to* EMILE's *voice on the radio.*)

EMILE'S VOICE: Hello. Hello, my friends and allies. My message today must be brief . . . and sad. Lieutenant Cable, my friend, Joe, died last night. He died from wounds he received three days ago. I will never know a finer man. I wish he could have told you the good news. The Japanese are pulling out and there is great confusion. Our guess is that the Japs will try to evacuate troops from Cape Esperance tonight. You may not hear from us for several days. We must move again. Two planes are overhead. They are looking for us, we think. We believe that . . . (*His speech is interrupted. There is the sound of a plane motor.* EMILE's *voice is heard shouting excitedly "off mike."*) What? . . . What? ("*In mike.*") Good-bye!

(*There is a moment's silence. The* RADIO OPERATOR *works the dials.*)

BRACKETT: Is that all? Is that all? Can't you get them back?

RADIO OPERATOR: No, sir. They're cut off.

NELLIE (*tears in her eyes*): Poor Joe. Poor little Joe Cable. (*She grabs* BRACKETT *and holds tightly to his arms.*) Captain Brackett . . . Do you think there's a chance I'll ever see Emile de Becque again? If you don't think so, will you tell me?

BRACKETT: There's a chance . . . of course there's a chance.

NELLIE (*turning to* HARBISON): I didn't know he was going.

BRACKETT: Of course not. How could he tell you he was going? Now don't blame Emile de Becque. He's okay . . . he's a wonderful guy!

    (NELLIE *tries to answer, swallows hard, and can make only an inarticulate sound of assent.*)

NELLIE: Uh-huh! (*She exits quickly.*)

BRACKETT: He has got a chance, hasn't he, Bill?

HARBISON (*hoarsely*): Of course. There's always a chance!

BRACKETT: Come on! Let's get out of here!

    (*Both exit, as the shack recedes upstage and a group of officers and nurses enter downstage to walk across the company street.*)

SCENE 9

The officers and nurses are singing the refrain of "I'm in Love with a Wonderful Guy."

    NELLIE *walks on from the opposite side, looking straight ahead of her, a set expression on her face.*

NURSE (*as they pass her*): Coming to the dance, Nellie?

    (NELLIE *just shakes her head and passes them.*)

A LIEUTENANT: What's the matter with her?

    (*Three girls in a trio and in a spirit of kidding* NELLIE, *sing back over their shoulders at her,* "She's in love, she's in love, she's in love, she's in love with a wonderful guy." *Even before they have reached the end of this, the lights have started to dim. Now the lights come up in back, revealing:*)

SCENE 10

The Beach.

    NELLIE *walks on. The strain of "I'm in love, I'm in love, I'm in love" ringing in her ears and cutting deeply into her heart.* NELLIE *walks up and looks over the sea.*

Pause. Then she speaks softly.

NELLIE: Come back so I can tell you something. I know what counts now. You. All those other things—the woman you had before—her color . . . (*She laughs bitterly.*) What piffle! What a pinhead I was! Come back so I can tell you. Oh, my God, don't die until I can tell you! All that matters is you and I being together. That's all! Just together— The way we wanted it to be the first night we met! Remember? . . . Remember?

    (*She sings:*)
        Some enchanted evening
        When you find your true love,
        When you feel him call you
        Across a crowded room—
        Then fly to his side,
        And make him your own,
        Or all through your life you may dream all alone . . .
    (*Music continues. She speaks.*)
Don't die, Emile.
    (*As the last line of the refrain is played,* BLOODY MARY *walks on and addresses* NELLIE, *timidly.*)
MARY: Miss Nurse!
    (NELLIE, *shocked by the sudden sound of an intruding voice, turns and emits a startled scream.*)
Please, please, Miss Nurse?
NELLIE: Who are you? What do you want?
MARY: Where is Lootellan Cable?
NELLIE: Who *are* you?
MARY: I am mother of Liat.
NELLIE: Who?
MARY: Liat. She won't marry no one but Lootellan Cable.
    (LIAT *walks on slowly.* MARY *moves her forward and shows her to* NELLIE. NELLIE *looks at this girl and realizes who she is.*)
NELLIE: Oh. (NELLIE *rushes to her impulsively and embraces her.*) Oh, my darling!
    (*As she clasps* LIAT *in her arms, the noises of the company street burst harshly as the curtains close and we are plunged abruptly into:*)

SCENE II

The company street is crowded with members of all Forces, ready to embark. There are sounds of truck convoys passing. Over the loud-speaker the following is heard:

VOICE ON LOUDSPEAKER: All right, hear this. All those outfits that are waiting for loading, please keep in position. We'll get to you as soon as your boat is ready for you.

    (BILLIS, STEWPOT *and the* PROFESSOR *enter.*)

STEWPOT: Hey, Billis, let's head back, huh? Our gang's about a mile back down the beach. Suppose they call our names?

PROFESSOR: Yeah! They may be ready for us to go aboard.

BILLIS: They won't be ready for hours yet . . . this is the Navy. (*He turns and regards the scene offstage.*) Eager Beavers! Look at that beach . . . swarmin' with 10,000 guys—all jerks! (*Picking out a likely "jerk."*) Hey, are you a Marine?

MARINE (*turning*): Yeah!

BILLIS: Are you booked on one of those LCT's?

MARINE: I guess so, why?

BILLIS: They'll shake the belly off you, you know. (*He takes out a small package.*) Five bucks and you can have it.

MARINE: What is it?

BILLIS: Seasick remedy. You'll be needing it.

MARINE: Aw, knock off! (*Pulls out a handful of packages from his pocket.*) That stuff's issued. We all got it. Who are you tryin' to fool?

BILLIS (*turning to* STEWPOT): These Marines are getting smarter every day.

OFFICER (*passing through*): All right, all right. Stay with your own unit. (*To a nurse in combat uniform.*) Ensign, you too. For Heaven's sake, don't get spread out over here. We're trying to get this thing organized as quickly as possible, so for God's sake, stay with your outfit! (*To* BILLIS.) Say, Seabee . . . you belong down the beach.

BILLIS (*saluting officer*): Excuse me, sir, could you tell me where we could find Captain Brackett?

OFFICER: He's up at the head of the company street. He'll be along any minute now.

BILLIS (*saluting*): Thank you, sir. That's all, sir.

(*The* OFFICER, *having started off, stops in his tracks, stunned and rocked off his balance by being thus "dismissed" by* BILLIS. *Oh, well—too many important things to be done right now! He goes on his way, shouting:*)

OFFICER: All right! Stay in line! How many times have I told you . . .

(*He is off. A* NURSE *comes by.*)

BILLIS: Hello, Miss McGregor. You nurses going too?

NURSE: Only a few of us. We're going to fly back some wounded.

BILLIS: Is Miss Forbush going with you?

NURSE: I don't know. She may be staying here with the hospital. (*She starts to leave.*)

BILLIS: Oh, Miss McGregor . . . you don't get airsick, do you? I was thinking maybe if you got three bucks handy, you might be able to use this little package I got here.

NURSE (*looking down at it*): Oh, that stuff's no good . . . we gave that up last month.

BILLIS (*turning to* STEWPOT): That's a female jerk!

(BRACKETT *and* HARBISON *enter.*)

I beg pardon, sir . . . could I speak to you a minute?

BRACKETT (*peering through the semi-darkness*): Who's that?

BILLIS: Billis, sir . . . Luther Billis.

BRACKETT: Oh. What do you want, Billis? We're moving out pretty soon.

BILLIS: Yes, sir, I know. I'd like to do something for Miss Forbush, sir. Stewpot and the Professor and me was wondering if anything is being done about rescuing the Frenchman off that island. We hereby volunteer for such a project . . . a triple diversionary activity, like I done to get 'em on there. You could drop us in three rubber boats on three different sides of the island . . . confuse the hell out of the Japs. . . . Get the picture?

BRACKETT: It's very fine of you, Billis . . . but you're too late for diversionary activity. That started this morning before the sun came up. Operation Alligator got under way. Landings were made on fourteen Japanese-held islands.

BILLIS: I think that's very unfair, sir. The first thing they should have done was try to rescue that Frenchman.

HARBISON: The Admiral agrees with you, Billis. Marie Louise was the first island they hit.

BILLIS: Did they get him? Is he alive?

BRACKETT: We don't know. Lieutenant Bus Adams flew up there to find out. He hasn't come back. But if the Frenchman's dead, it *is* unfair. It's too damned bad if a part of this huge operation couldn't have saved one of the two guys who made it all possible.

HARBISON (*gazing off*): Look at the beach . . . far as you can see . . . men waiting to board ships. The whole picture of the South Pacific has changed. We're going the other way.

OFFICER: Captain Brackett, sir . . . the launch is ready to take you to your ship.

BILLIS: You got a ship, sir?

BRACKETT: Yes, Harbison and I've got a ship. I'm no longer a lousy Island Commander. Come on, Bill.

BILLIS: Good-bye, Commander Harbison.

HARBISON: Good-bye, Billis. Oh, by the way, I never did get you in the brig . . . did I?

BILLIS (*laughing almost too heartily at his triumph*): No! Ha-ha.

HARBISON: Oh, I forgot!

BILLIS (*still laughing*): Forgot what, sir?

HARBISON: Your unit'll be on our ship. I'll be seeing all of you.
(*Dismay from* BILLIS, STEWPOT *and the* PROFESSOR.)

BRACKETT: Come on, Bill.
(BRACKETT *and* HARBISON *exit.*)

OFFICER (*entering*): All right . . . let's start those trucks moving out—all units on the company street. We're ready to load you. All Nurses will board assigned planes—Seabees to embark on Carrier 6. All Marines to board LCT's. Any questions? MOVE OUT!
(*The sound trucks roar. The music which has been playing under the scene mounts in volume. The men march off. Nurses in hospital uniform stand waving to the men and the nurses in combat uniform who leave with them. Soon the groups are all dispersed and lights come up in back, revealing:*)

SCENE 12

EMILE'*s terrace.*

It is late afternoon. Sunset—reddish light. The drone of planes can be heard. JEROME *stands on a table.* NELLIE *holds him.* NGANA *is beside her. All look off.*

NELLIE (*pointing off*): The big ones are battleships and the little ones are destroyers—or cruisers—I never can tell the difference. (*She looks up in the air.*) And what on earth are those?

JEROME: P-40s.

NELLIE: Oh, that's right. They're all moving out, you see, because, well . . . there's been a big change. They won't be around here much any more, just off and on, a few of us. Did you understand anything I said? Vous ne comprenez pas?

NGANA: Oui, oui, nous comprenons.

(JEROME *nods his head.*)

JEROME: Oui.

NELLIE: Now, while I'm down at the hospital, you've got to promise me to mangez everything—everything that's put before you on the table—sur le tobler. Sur la tobler?

NGANA (*smiling patiently*): Sur la table.

NELLIE (*she smiles, congratulating herself*): Now come back here, Jerome, and sit down. (*She starts to place the children at the table, on which a bowl of soup and some plates have been set. At this point,* BUS ADAMS *appears upstage—a weary figure. Behind him comes* EMILE *in dirt-stained uniform, helmet, paratroop boots and musette bag.* BUS *calls his attention to the planes droning above. Neither sees* NELLIE *or the children.* NELLIE *pushes the kids down, on the bench, as they playfully balk at being seated.*) Ass—say—yay—voo. (*They sit.* EMILE *turns sharply at the sound of her voice.*) Now you have to learn to mind me when I talk to you and be nice to me too. Because I love you very much. Now, *mangez.*

(EMILE's *face lights up with grateful happiness.* BUS *knows it's time for him to shove off, and he does.* NELLIE *proceeds to ladle soup from the large bowl into three small bowls.*)

JEROME (*his eyes twinkling mischievously*): Chantez, Nellie.

NELLIE: I will not sing that song. You just want to laugh at my French accent. (*The kids put their spoons down—on strike.*) All right, but you've got to help me.

NELLIE, NGANA and JEROME:

    Dites moi

    Pourquoi

    (NELLIE *is stuck. The children sing the next line without her.*)

    La vie est belle.

NELLIE (*repeating, quickly, to catch up to them*):
>La vie est belle.
>
>(*Meanwhile* EMILE *has crossed behind them.* NELLIE *is looking out front, not seeing him, trying to remember the lyrics, continues to sing with the children.*)
>
>Dites moi
>Pourquoi . . .
>
>(*She turns to the children.*)

Pourquoi what?

>(*She sees* EMILE.)

EMILE (*answering her, singing*):
>La vie est gai!
>
>(NELLIE *gazes at him, hypnotized—her voice gone. The children rush to embrace him.*)

EMILE, NGANA and JEROME:
>Dites moi
>Pourquoi,
>Chère mad'moiselle—
>
>(EMILE *leans forward and sings straight at* NELLIE.)

EMILE:
>Est-ce que
>Parce que
>Vous m'aimez—
>
>(*The music continues. The children drink their soup.* NELLIE *comes back to consciousness enough to realize that* EMILE *must be hungry. She leans over and hands him the large bowl of soup with an air of "nothing's-too-good-for-the-boss!" Then she passes him the soup ladle! But he doesn't use it. Instead, he thrusts his hand forward.* NELLIE *clasps it. Looking into each other's eyes, they hold this position as the curtain falls.*)

Additional Lyrics

MIS'RY'S COMIN' AROUN'
from *Show Boat*

Sung by Queenie and the Cotton Blossom's *black workers,
"Mis'ry's Comin' Aroun'" was cut after the first pre-Broadway
tryout performance in Washington, D.C., on November 15, 1927.
Jerome Kern kept musical passages from it in the show's overture,
however, and included it in its entirety in the 1928 complete vocal
score.*

*The song was recorded for the first time in 1988, as part of an
EMI archival studio recording, conducted by John McGlinn.
The 1994 Broadway revival of* Show Boat *restored the song to
its original place in the show, a choice adopted by several subsequent productions in various opera houses, both in America and
abroad.*

QUEENIE:
> Mis'ry's comin' aroun',
> De mis'ry's comin' aroun'.
> I knows it's comin' aroun',
> Don't know to who.

QUEENIE and COLORED WOMEN:
> Mis'ry's comin' aroun',
> De mis'ry's comin' aroun'.
> We knows it's comin' aroun',
> Don't know to who.
> (ENSEMBLE *hums under dialogue.*)

A WOMAN:
> Heaven keep dat devil away.

TWO WOMEN:
> Keep dat misery far away.

TWO OTHER WOMEN:
> An' if he is a-comin' today—

WOMEN and MEN:
> Heaven, don'cha let him stay!
> (ENSEMBLE *hums under dialogue.*)

QUEENIE:
> Mis'ry's comin' aroun',
> So if you done any wrong,

> Den lif' yo' feet off de groun'
> An' fly away.

MEN:

> If you done any wrong,
> Jes' lif' yo' feet off de groun'
> An' fly away,
> An' fly away.
> (ENSEMBLE *hums under dialogue.*)

QUEENIE:

> I know misery's near.
> I don't know why it is here.

MEN:

> I only knows it's near.

QUEENIE:

> Don't know for who.

MEN:

> Don't know for who.

QUEENIE:

> Don't know for why.

MEN:

> I don't know for—

QUEENIE and MEN:

> Why dat misery's near.

A MAN:

> I knows misery done come here.

JULIE:

> When I dies, let me rest
> With a dish on my breast.
> Some give nickel, some give dime,
> All dem folks is fren's o' mine.

QUEENIE, JULIE, and WOMEN:

> On my back in a hack,
> In a fo'ty-dollar hack.
> No mo' gin, no mo' rum,
> Oh, de misery's done come!

MEN:

> Upon my poor ol' back
> Within a liv'ry hack.
> With no mo' rum
> Oh, de misery's done come!

I HAVE THE ROOM ABOVE HER
from *Show Boat*

Written for the 1936 film of Show Boat, *in which it was sung by Allan Jones (as Ravenal) and Irene Dunne (as Magnolia). "I Have the Room Above Her" was subsequently added to the 1994 revival.*

(*Refrain 1*)

RAVENAL:

> I have the room above her.
> She doesn't know I love her.
> How could she know I love her,
> Sitting in her room below?
> Sitting in her room below,
> How could she dream how far a dream could go?
> Sometimes we meet.
> She smiles, and, oh, her smile's divine.
> It's such a treat to hear her say,
> "Hasn't the weather been fine?"
> I blush and stammer badly;
> My heart is beating madly.
> Then she goes into her room,
> And I go sadly up to mine.

(*Interlude*)

RAVENAL:

> A lover more impetuous than I
> Would say his say or know the reason why;
> But when I get my chance,
> I let my chance go by.

(*Refrain 2*)

RAVENAL:

> I have the room above her.
> She doesn't know I love her.
> How could she know I love her,
> Sitting in her room below?
> Sitting in her room below,
> How could she dream how far a dream could go?

MAGNOLIA:

> Sometimes we meet.
> He smiles, and, oh, his smile's divine.
> It's such a treat to hear him say,
> "Hasn't the weather been fine?"
> I blush and stammer badly;
> My heart is beating madly.
> Then he goes up to his room,
> And I go sadly into mine.

NOBODY ELSE BUT ME
from *Show Boat*

The last collaboration by Kern and Oscar Hammerstein II, "Nobody Else But Me" was written for the 1946 Broadway revival. It was sung by Jan Clayton (as Kim), in the second act, as a replacement for the specialty number performed by Norma Terris in the original production. Clayton recorded the song on the cast album of the 1946 production for Columbia Records; it went on to become a jazz and popular standard. (See also Note 95.5–17.)

(*Verse 1*)

GIRL:

> I was a shy, demure type,
> Inhibited, insecure type of girl.
> A pearl of no great price was I
> Till a certain cutie called me "sweetie pie."
> Now I'm smug and snooty
> And my nose is high!

(*Refrain 1*)

GIRL:

> I want to be no one but me—
> I am in love with a lover
> Who likes me the way I am!
> I have my faults;
> He likes my faults.
> I'm not very bright;
> He's not very bright.

He thinks I'm grand—
That's grand for me!
He may be wrong,
But if we get along,
What do we care, say we.
When he holds me close,
Close as we can be,
I tell the lad
That I'm grateful and I'm glad
That I'm nobody else but me!

(*Verse 2*)

BOY:

Once I was meek and fearful,
Unconfident and uncheerful, afraid.
I stayed within my little shell
Till a certain party told me I was swell.
Now I'm hail and hearty—
I have rung the bell!

(*Refrain 2*)

BOY:

I want to be no one but me—
I am in love with a lady
Who likes me the way I am!
I have my faults;
She likes my faults.
I'm not very bright;
She's not very bright.
She thinks I'm grand—
That's grand for me!
She may be wrong,
But if we get along,
What do we care, say we!
Walking on the shore,
Swimming in the sea,
When I am with her,
I'm glad the boy who's with her
Is nobody else but me!

I'M TALKING TO MY PAL
from *Pal Joey*

"I'm Talking To My Pal," sung by Joey Evans toward the end of the first act, was cut in the Philadelphia tryouts in 1940. It was reinstated for the 1995 Encores! presentation of Pal Joey *at New York City Center, where it was moved to the conclusion of the second act. Peter Gallagher performed Joey in that presentation and recorded the song for DRG Records; the 2008 Broadway revival added the song to a similar spot in the second act.*

OZZIE:

(*Verse*)

I'm independent.
I'm a descendant
Of quite a family of heels.
I'm never lonely,
I and I only
Know how my pal Joey feels.
Who else would pay for my meals?

(*Refrain*)

I'm talking to my pal,
Myself, my closest friend.
And that's the only pal
On whom I can depend.
When I come home at night,
A bit too tight to see,
My wallet is all right—
I'd never steal from me.
My friend stands pat
When I am flat.
He only cheats when I do.
I can't be sure of girls,
I'm not at home with men—
I'm ending up with me again.

GABEY'S COMIN'
from *On the Town*

"Gabey's Comin'," which followed the "Presentation of Miss Turnstiles" in the first act, was dropped after the show's Boston

tryout. It was recorded for the first time in 1993 in a studio recording for Deutsche Grammophon, conducted by Michael Tilson Thomas, and was subsequently included in the 1998 Broadway revival.

OZZIE and CHIP:

        Gabey's comin',
        Gabey's comin' to town!
        He's on the town.
        With a day to burn,
        You're gonna turn
        New York City upside down!

GABEY, CHIP, and OZZIE:

        Gaby's comin' to town!

    (*A number of* GIRLS *enter and pose.*)

OZZIE: Here's the way you do it!

    (*To the* GIRLS, *for* GABEY's *instructions:*)

        Hello, baby, gosh you're pretty;
        I'm so tall and strong and witty;
        God's great gift to New York City.
        How's about a date tonight?

CHIP:

        When a guy is feeling tender
        He don't want no solo bender,
        What he craves is sweet surrender.
        How's about a date tonight?

GIRLS (*excited*):

        Date tonight? Date tonight? Love it!

        Gabey's comin',
        Gabey's comin' to town!
        He's on the town!
        Gonna brush my teeth
        Down underneath,
        Slip into my sheerest gown
        Gabey's comin' to town!

OZZIE:

        Hello, babe, you look delicious
        You're the answer to my wishes.
        Let's start by buying breakfast dishes.

> How's about a date tonight?

CHIP:

> Aren't we having lovely weather?
> We're two birdies of a feather;
> We could make such tunes together.
> How's about a date tonight?

GIRLS:

> Date tonight? Date tonight? Love it!
>
> Gabey's comin',
> Gabey's comin' to town!
> He's on the town!
>
> Gonna take a dive
> In Chanel Five,
> For that lover,

GIRLS and GABEY:

> For that lover,

GIRLS, GABEY, CHIP, and OZZIE:

> For that lover of renown!
> Gabey's comin' to town!

MY GIRL BACK HOME
from *South Pacific*

Originally sung after the Thanksgiving show in Act Two, "My Girl Back Home" was cut from South Pacific *after the Boston tryout. It was reinstated for the 1958 film, sung by Bill Lee (as the dubbed voice of Cable) and Mitzi Gaynor. It was subsequently interpolated into the 2001 television version (but ultimately cut) and the 2008 Broadway revival, sung by Matthew Morrison and Kelli O'Hara and placed in Act One.*

CABLE:

> My girl back home—
> I'd almost forgot!
> A blue-eyed kid—
> I liked her a lot.
> We got engaged—

Both families were glad;
And I was told
By my uncle and Dad
That if I were clever and able
They'd make me a part of a partnership
Cable, Cable—and Cable!

How far away!
Philadelphia, PA—
Princeton, NJ—
How far are they
From coconut palms
And banyan trees
And coral sands
And Tonkinese!

NELLIE:

How far away!
Little Rock, Ark.—

CABLE:

Princeton, NJ—
How far are they—

NELLIE:

How far are they—

BOTH:

From coconut palms
And banyan trees
And coral sands
And—
(*They are interrupted.*)

BIOGRAPHICAL NOTES

BROADWAY PRODUCTION NOTES

NOTE ON THE TEXTS

NOTES

SOURCES AND ACKNOWLEDGMENTS

Biographical Notes

Irving Berlin (May 11, 1888–September 22, 1989) was born Israel Beilin, the youngest of eight children of Moishe Beilin, a butcher and cantor, and Liah (Lipkin) Beilin, probably near Mogilev in present-day Belarus; he emigrated to the U.S. with his parents in 1893. As a young man, he sang on street corners, worked as a singing waiter, and performed in vaudeville. He published his first song, "Marie (From Sunny Italy)," in 1907, under the name Irving Berlin (his family had changed their last name to "Baline" after emigrating to America). From 1909 to 1911 he worked as a lyricist for the Ted Snyder Music Company, contributing lyrics for dozens of vaudeville songs. After several hit songs beginning with "Alexander's Ragtime Band" in 1911, he wrote two successful Broadway shows, *Watch Your Step* (1914) and *Stop! Look! Listen!* (1915). He married Dorothy Goetz in 1912, but she died of typhoid fever six months later, inspiring Berlin to compose "When I Lost You." Drafted during World War I, he created and performed in the patriotic revue *Yip Yip Yaphank* (1918). After the war he started his own music publishing company and became a cofounder of ASCAP, of which he later served as president. He wrote songs and scores for many Broadway musicals, including four *Music Box Revues* (1921–24), *The Cocoanuts* (1925; film 1929), *Face the Music* (1932), *As Thousands Cheer* (1933), *Louisiana Purchase* (1940), *This Is the Army* (1942; film 1943), *Annie Get Your Gun* (1946; film 1950), *Miss Liberty* (1949), and *Call Me Madam* (1950; film 1953); his film credits include *Puttin' on the Ritz* (1930), *Top Hat* (1935), *Follow the Fleet* (1936), *On the Avenue* (1937), *Alexander's Ragtime Band* (1938), *Second Fiddle* (1939), *Holiday Inn* (1942), *Easter Parade* (1948), and *There's No Business Like Show Business* (1954). Hit songs not written for stage or screen include "Always," "Blue Skies," "Marie," and "God Bless America." He retired in New York City after the Broadway debut of the musical *Mr. President* (1962). His wife of sixty-three years, Ellin Mackay, died in 1988.

Leonard Bernstein (August 25, 1918–October 14, 1990), the first child of Ukrainian immigrants Jennie (Resnick) Bernstein and Samuel Bernstein, was born in Lawrence, Massachusetts; his father ran a business supplying barber and beauty shops. He studied music at Harvard, where he wrote a thesis on "The Absorption of Race Elements into American Music" and met Aaron Copland, a major influence on his later compositions. He subsequently did graduate training at the Curtis Institute and studied with conductor Serge Koussevitzky at Tanglewood. Named assistant conductor of the New York Philharmonic in 1943, he began a long and celebrated international career as a conductor, principally associated with the Philharmonic; during his tenure as its music director (1958–69), he led the orchestra on many world tours and dramatically increased its American audience. He made his first contribution to the Broadway stage in 1944 with *On the Town*—loosely suggested by his 1944 ballet piece *Fancy Free* and written in collaboration with Betty Comden and Adolph Green—and went on to write scores for *Wonderful Town* (1953, with Comden and Green); *Candide* (1956, with Richard Wilbur, John Latouche, and Dorothy Parker); *West Side Story* (1957, with Stephen Sondheim); and *1600 Pennsylvania Avenue* (1976, with Alan Jay Lerner). He also wrote music in a variety of forms, including three symphonies (*Jeremiah*, 1942; *The Age of Anxiety*, 1949; *Kaddish*, 1963) and other orchestral works; two operas (*Trouble in Tahiti*, 1952; *A Quiet Place*, 1983); piano and choral works; ballet pieces (*Facsimile—Choreographic Essay for Orchestra*, 1946; *Dybbuk*, 1974); and the score for the film *On the Waterfront* (1954). He died in New York City, days after announcing his retirement from conducting.

Betty Comden and **Adolph Green** met in 1938 and began performing (with Judy Holliday) as The Revuers, at the Village Vanguard. Their professional partnership continued for the rest of their lives: together, they wrote the books, lyrics, and screenplays for dozens of Broadway and Hollywood musicals. Comden (May 3, 1917–November 23, 2006) was born Basya Cohen in Brooklyn; her mother Rebecca (Sadvoransky) Cohen worked as a schoolteacher and her father Leo Cohen as a lawyer; she graduated from New York University and married Stephen Kyle in 1942. Green (December 2, 1914–October 23, 2002) was the son of Helen (Weiss) and Daniel Green, Hungarian immigrants from the Bronx; he aspired, like Comden, to be an actor. In 1944, at the suggestion of Leonard Bernstein—who had occasionally accompanied them on the piano at the Village Vanguard—they wrote the book and lyrics for *On the Town*, while also performing as Claire and Ozzie in the production. Their next two musicals, *Billion Dollar Baby* (1945) and *Bonanza Bound* (1947), were not successful, and the duo moved to Hollywood to work for MGM producer Arthur Freed. They collaborated on screenplays for a succession of MGM films: *Good News* (1947), *The Barkleys of Broadway* (1949), *On the Town* (1949, using only two songs from the stage version), *Singin' in the Rain* (1952), *The Band Wagon*

(1953), *It's Always Fair Weather* (1955), *Auntie Mame* (1958), and *Bells Are Ringing* (1960). Their final film, in 1964, was the 20th Century-Fox comedy *What a Way to Go!* They continued to write for Broadway as well, contributing to revues and musicals, including *Two on the Aisle* (composer, Jule Styne, 1951), *Wonderful Town* (Bernstein, 1953), *Peter Pan* (Styne and others, 1954), *Bells Are Ringing* (Styne, 1956), *Say, Darling* (Styne, 1958), *Do Re Mi* (Styne, 1960), *Subways Are for Sleeping* (Styne, 1961), *Fade Out-Fade In* (Styne, 1964), *Hallelujah, Baby!* (Styne, 1967), *Applause* (book only, 1970), *Lorelei* (Styne, 1974), *On the Twentieth Century* (Cy Coleman, 1978), *A Doll's Life* (Larry Grossman, 1982), and *The Will Rogers Follies* (Coleman, 1991). They both wrote and performed in the 1958 revue *A Party with Betty Comden and Adolph Green*, revived in 1977. In 1995 Comden published a memoir, *Off Stage*. Both died in New York City.

Oscar Hammerstein II (July 12, 1895–August 23, 1960) was born into a family prominent in New York theater: his grandfather, the first Oscar Hammerstein, was an opera impresario; his father, William, managed the family's vaudeville interests; and his uncle, Arthur, worked as a producer, usually of operettas for Broadway. While his father attempted to dissuade him from a career in show business, his mother, Alice (née Nimmo), encouraged him. After two years as a law student at Columbia—and newly married, to Myra Finn—he took a job as stage manager for his uncle's out-of-town productions. He soon attempted his first play, *The Light* (1919), which closed out-of-town. Under his uncle's wing, he learned the craft of writing libretti for operettas and musical comedies on shows including *Always You* (1920), *Tickle Me* (1920), *Jimmie* (1920), *Wildflower* (1923), *Rose-Marie* (Rudolf Friml, 1924), *Sunny* (Jerome Kern, 1925), *Song of the Flame* (1925), and *The Desert Song* (Sigmund Romberg, 1926). Following the success of the groundbreaking musical *Show Boat* (1927), Hammerstein worked with Jerome Kern on several other projects—*Sweet Adeline* (1929), *Music in the Air* (1932), and *Very Warm for May* (1939) among them—but none of these shows, or the other musicals to which he contributed in the 1930s, met with anything like the same kind of success. During an unhappy time in Hollywood in the late 1930s, he wrote the lyrics to "The Folks Who Live on the Hill" and "The Last Time I Saw Paris," both with Kern. Shortly before World War II, Hammerstein moved to a farm in Bucks County, Pennsylvania, and worked on an adaptation of Bizet's *Carmen* for the Broadway stage. In 1942 he was asked by composer Richard Rodgers to collaborate on *Oklahoma!* (1943), which ran for 2,212 performances in its opening run; *Carmen Jones*, with its all-black cast, came to Broadway the following season and was also a substantial hit. For the Broadway stage, Rodgers and Hammerstein would go on to write *Carousel* (1945), *Allegro* (1947), *South Pacific* (1949), *The King and I* (1951), *Me and Juliet* (1953), *Pipe Dream* (1955), *Flower Drum Song* (1958), and *The Sound of Music* (1959), many of which were adapted into successful films, often with Rodgers and Hammerstein serving as executive producers. They also worked together on the original movie musical *State Fair* (1945, which included "It Might as Well be Spring," an Academy Award winner) and on *Cinderella* (1957) for CBS. Hammerstein was diagnosed with cancer in 1959, shortly before *The Sound of Music* opened on Broadway. He died in Doylestown, Pennsylvania.

E. Y. "Yip" Harburg (April 8, 1896–March 5, 1981) was the son of Mary (Ricing) Hochburg and Louis Hochberg, both garment workers who had emigrated from Russia to the Lower East Side of New York in 1889. Born Isidore Hochberg, he acquired the nickname "Yip" as a child, and later changed his name to Edgar Yipsel Harburg. He attended the College of the City of New York (with high-school friend Ira Gershwin) and then began a commercial career, managing the Uruguayan office of a meatpacking firm and starting an electrical appliance business in Brooklyn. He married Alice G. Richmond in 1923. Forced into bankruptcy in 1929, he turned to writing lyrics for Broadway revues and plays, with songs such as "Brother, Can You Spare a Dime?" (1932, with Jay Gorney), "It's Only a Paper Moon" (1933, with Harold Arlen and Billy Rose), and "April in Paris" (1932, with Vernon Duke). In 1934 he collaborated with Ira Gershwin and Arlen on the revue *Life Begins at 8:40*, and worked with Arlen again on the revue *The Show Is On* (1936) and the musical *Hooray for What!* (1937). He worked in Hollywood through the 1930s and early 1940s, most notably writing the lyrics for *The Wizard of Oz* (1939); its central song, "Over the Rainbow," won an Academy Award for Arlen and Harburg. His lyrics also appeared in the films *At the Circus* (1939), *Cabin in the Sky* (1943), and later the animated feature *Gay Purr-ee* (1962). *Bloomer Girl* (1944) brought Harburg back to Broadway, and *Finian's Rainbow* (1947, with Burton Lane and Fred Saidy) won three Tony Awards. Because of his progressive political convictions, Harburg was blacklisted from further work in Hollywood after 1950, interrupting a planned musical adaptation of *Huckleberry Finn*. Harburg continued to work on the Broadway stage, conceiving and writing lyrics for the unsuccessful anti-McCarthy satire *Flahooey* (Sammy Fain, 1951). In 1957 he collaborated once again with Arlen and Saidy on *Jamaica*, a successful vehicle starring Lena Horne and Ricardo Montalbán, but the experience was, creatively, an unhappy one for Harburg. He went on to write lyrics for *The Happiest*

Girl in the World (1961)—an adaptation of Aristophanes' *Lysistrata*, to the music of Jacques Offenbach—and *Darling of the Day* (Jule Styne, 1968), starring Vincent Price. He died in Hollywood of a heart attack.

Lorenz Hart (May 2, 1895–November 22, 1943) was born in New York City, the first of two sons of Max and Frieda (Isenberg) Hart, both German-Jewish immigrants. His father worked as an entrepreneur and real estate agent. At Columbia, he wrote and performed in undergraduate theatricals, sometimes in collaboration with Oscar Hammerstein II. In 1919, Hart was introduced to the much younger Richard Rodgers; they immediately collaborated on songs for various variety shows and charities. During the early 1920s Hart and Rodgers worked on many amateur productions and saw some of their songs performed on Broadway (*Poor Little Ritz Girl* in 1920 featured several), but a Broadway career eluded them. In 1925, they contributed the hit song "Manhattan" to the revue *The Garrick Gaieties*, which put them firmly on the path to success. Among their well-received musicals of the decade were *Dearest Enemy* (1925), *Peggy-Ann* (1926), *A Connecticut Yankee* (1927), *Present Arms* (1928), *Spring Is Here* (1929), *Simple Simon* (1930), and *Ever Green* (West End, 1930). Moving to Hollywood after the stock market crash, they wrote songs for the movie musicals *Love Me Tonight* (1932), *The Phantom President* (1932), and *Hallelujah, I'm a Bum* (1933), as well as their one tune released solely for commercial purposes, "Blue Moon." They returned to Broadway to work on *Jumbo* (1935), launching an unprecedented run of groundbreaking musicals with collaborators who included George Abbott, George Kaufman and Moss Hart: *On Your Toes* (1936), *Babes in Arms* (1937), *I'd Rather Be Right* (1937), *The Boys from Syracuse* (1937), and *Pal Joey* (1940, with a book by John O'Hara). Hart's health disintegrated, due to alcoholism, and in the early 1940s his working relationship with Rodgers began to fray; *By Jupiter* in 1942 was their last completely new work. Hart's independent collaboration with Emmerich Kalman and Paul Gallico, *Miss Underground*, was left unfinished. In 1943 Hart was able to contribute several new songs with Rodgers to a revival of *A Connecticut Yankee*, but died of pneumonia in New York, during a wartime blackout, five days after its premiere.

Moss Hart (October 24, 1904–December 20, 1961) was born into a working-class Jewish family and raised in the Bronx and Brooklyn. As a teenager, he worked as an office boy for the theatrical road producer Augustus Pitou, who later produced *The Hold-Up Man* (1925, also titled *The Beloved Bandit*), which Hart had written under a pseudonym. In 1929, he wrote *Once in a Lifetime*, a satire about Hollywood, and brought it to the revered playwright George S. Kaufman in search of a collaborator. After the 1930 success of the comedy, he worked with Irving Berlin on the musical comedy *Face the Music* (1932) and the revue *As Thousands Cheer* (1933), and he provided the book adaptation for *The Great Waltz* (1934). Again collaborating with Kaufman, Hart wrote *Merrily We Roll Along* in 1934. In 1935, he wrote *Jubilee*, a musical satire of British royalty, with Cole Porter. He resumed his partnership with Kaufman on *You Can't Take It with You* (1936) and *I'd Rather Be Right* (1937, with a score by Richard Rodgers and Lorenz Hart), *The Fabulous Invalid* (1938), *The American Way* (1939), *The Man Who Came to Dinner* (1939), and *George Washington Slept Here* (1940). In 1941 he wrote and directed the musical *Lady in the Dark*, with a score by Kurt Weill and Ira Gershwin. Another solo effort was *Winged Victory* (1943), a tribute to the Air Force, which Hart also directed. He had successes as a director with the comedies *Junior Miss* (1941) and *Anniversary Waltz* (1954); as a Hollywood screenwriter with *Gentleman's Agreement* (1947, Academy Award for Best Picture, with a nomination for Hart), *Hans Christian Andersen* (1952), the Judy Garland vehicle *A Star Is Born* (1954), among others; and as a playwright and director with *Christopher Blake* (1946), *Light Up the Sky* (1948), and *The Climate of Eden* (1952). He married the actress and singer Kitty Carlisle in 1946. In 1956, he directed Lerner and Loewe's *My Fair Lady* and won the Tony Award for Best Direction; a blockbuster success in New York, the musical was also a hit in London in 1958. In 1959 he published a memoir, *Act One*, which became a best seller. Hart worked with Lerner and Loewe again on *Camelot* (1960), but during its tryout in Toronto, Hart suffered a heart attack, although he was able to continue working on the show after its Broadway opening. Hart and his wife moved to Palm Springs, California; he had begun what he called a "comedy of manners" when he died of heart failure.

Jerome Kern (January 27, 1885–November 11, 1945) was born in New York City. His father, Henry Kern, earned his living as a merchant; his mother, Fannie (Kakeles) Kern, taught him the piano. While studying at the New York College of Music he worked for music publisher Edward B. Marks and saw his first songs published. By 1904, he began writing songs to be interpolated into imported European musicals and visited England, where he collaborated with P. G. Wodehouse on songs for *The Beauty of Bath* (1906). In 1910 he married Eva Leale. Returning to America, Kern started his fruitful collaboration with librettist Guy Bolton and lyricist Wodehouse on various shows for the petite Princess Theatre on Broadway, including *Nobody Home* (1915), *Very Good Eddie* (1915), *Oh Boy!* (1917), *Leave It to Jane* (1917), and *Oh*

Lady! Lady! (1918). Kern worked with lyricist Oscar Hammerstein II on *Sunny* (1925), *Show Boat* (1927), *Sweet Adeline* (1929), and *Music in the Air* (1932). He also worked as a Hollywood composer, writing songs for the films *Roberta* (1935, with Otto Harbach, Dorothy Fields, and Jimmy McHugh, an adaptation of his Broadway success of 1933), *Swing Time* (1936, with Fields), for which he won his first Academy Award for Best Song, "The Way You Look Tonight," and *Joy of Living* (1939). By the time of his final Broadway show, *Very Warm for May* (1939, with Hammerstein), he had settled in Hollywood, contributing songs to movies such as *You Were Never Lovelier* (1942, with Johnny Mercer) and *Cover Girl* (1944, with Ira Gershwin), including "I'm Old Fashioned" and "Long Ago (and Far Away)." In the fall of 1945, Kern returned to New York in order to work with Hammerstein on a revival of *Show Boat* and to write an original score for a musical based on Annie Oakley; weeks later, he collapsed on the street due to a cerebral hemorrhage. He died in New York City.

Burton Lane (February 2, 1912–January 5, 1997) was born Burton Levy in New York City, the younger of two children of real estate agent Lazarus Levy and amateur pianist Frances Fink. Interested in musical composition from an early age, he was introduced to George Gershwin at eleven and published his first song, "Broken Butterfly," at fifteen. In the early 1930s, he contributed music to songs in several revues, including *Three's a Crowd*, *The Third Little Show*, and *Earl Carroll's Vanities*. He moved to Hollywood to work for MGM in 1933, writing several musicals with Harold Adamson. He is credited with bringing the young Frances Gumm to the attention of MGM executives, who signed her and changed her name to Judy Garland. In 1935 he married Marion Seaman. He collaborated with Frank Loesser on the films *Spawn of the North* (1938), *Cocoanut Grove* (1938), *Some Like It Hot* (1939), and *Dancing on a Dime* (1940), after which he wrote the Broadway score for *Hold on to Your Hats* (1940), an Al Jolson vehicle with lyrics by E. Y. Harburg. He went on to partner with Harburg on the film *Ship Ahoy* (1942) and the musical *Finian's Rainbow* (1947); *Laffing Room Only*, a musical for which he contributed both music and lyrics, began a successful Broadway run at the end of 1944. Other Hollywood scores include *Royal Wedding* (1951, with Alan Jay Lerner), *Give a Girl a Break* (1953, with Ira Gershwin), and *Jupiter's Darling* (1955, with Harold Adamson); Lane also led the newly formed Songwriters' Protective Association in its advocacy efforts in Washington, D.C. He divorced in 1961 and was remarried to Lynn Daroff Kaye. His two last scores for Broadway were written in collaboration with Alan Jay Lerner: *On a Clear Day You Can See Forever* (1965) and *Carmelina*

(1979). In 1990 Lane accompanied pianist/singer Michael Feinstein for *The Burton Lane Songbook*, a retrospective double-CD anthology. He died in New York.

Joshua Logan (October 5, 1908–July 12, 1988), born in Texarkana, Texas, was the son of Joshua Lockwood and Susan (Nabors) Logan; his father committed suicide when he was three, and he later took the surname of his stepfather, an Army officer. After four years at Princeton, where he acted with the Triangle Club, he studied with Constantin Stanislavski at the Moscow Art Theatre and began an acting career. He soon turned his talents to directing, working as dialogue director on the films *Garden of Allah* (1936) and *I Met My Love Again* (1937), several Broadway plays, and the Rodgers and Hart musicals *I Married an Angel* (1938) and *By Jupiter* (1942). After World War II, in which he served as an Air Force combat intelligence officer, he returned to Broadway as director of *Annie Get Your Gun* (1946) and *John Loves Mary* (1946). In 1948, his adaptation of Thomas Heggen's novel *Mister Roberts* (which he also directed) won the Tony Award for Best Play. He followed this success as director and coauthor, with Rodgers and Hammerstein, of *South Pacific* (1949), for which he won a Tony Award and shared the Pulitzer Prize. His subsequent credits as Broadway director included *The Wisteria Trees* (1950), *Wish You Were Here* (1952), *Picnic* (1953), *Kind Sir* (1953), *Fanny* (1954), *Middle of the Night* (1956), *Blue Denim* (1958), *The World of Suzy Wong* (1959), *There Was a Little Girl* (1960), *All American* (1961), *Mr. President* (1962), *Tiger, Tiger, Burning Bright* (1962), *Ready When You Are, C. B.* (1964), *Look to the Lilies* (1970), and *Miss Moffat* (1974). In Hollywood, he directed *Picnic* (1955), *Bus Stop* (1956), *Sayonara* (1957), *South Pacific* (1957), *Tall Story* (1959), *Fanny* (1960), *Ensign Pulver* (1963), *Camelot* (1967), and *Paint Your Wagon* (1968). Later in life he published two books of memoirs, *Josh: My Up and Down, In and Out Life* (1976) and *Movie Stars, Real People, and Me* (1978). He died in New York City.

John O'Hara (January 31, 1905–April 11, 1970), born in Pottsville, Pennsylvania, was the oldest of eight children of surgeon Patrick O'Hara and Katherine Delaney. Expelled from several high schools, he took a job at the *Pottsville Journal*, and in 1928 became a reporter for the *New York Herald Tribune*. While writing for the *Tribune* and other papers, he also began publishing short stories. His first novel, *Appointment in Samarra* (1934), proved a critical and commercial success; he followed it with *BUtterfield 8* (1935) and *Hope of Heaven* (1938) and the story collections *The Doctor's Son* (1935) and *Files on Parade* (1939). In 1940 he collaborated with Rodgers and Hart on the musical *Pal Joey*, based on his short stories collected in 1940 under the same title; it ran for over 350 performances on Broadway, was revived in 1952, and was radically adapted in Hollywood in 1957. His subsequent books included the novels *A Rage to Live* (1949), *Ten North Frederick* (1955, winner of the National Book Award), *From the Terrace* (1958), and *Ourselves to Know* (1960), and many collections of stories. He was married three times, to Helen Ritchie Petit in 1931, Belle Mulford Wylie in 1937, and Katharine Barnes Bryan in 1955. He died in Princeton, New Jersey.

Cole Porter (June 9, 1891–October 15, 1964), the only child of Kate (Cole) and Samuel Porter, was born in Peru, Indiana; his maternal grandfather was one of the state's wealthiest men. He toured Europe before enrolling at Yale, where he wrote musical scores and songs and was active in the Glee Club and the Whiffenpoofs. He entered Harvard Law School in 1913 but instead studied music, and by 1915 saw his first song in a Broadway show: "Esmeralda" in the revue *Hands Up*. In 1916, he wrote the music and lyrics for *See America First*, a comic opera that closed after only fifteen performances. Porter moved to Paris after America's entry into World War I and worked for a volunteer relief organization. Remaining abroad throughout most of the 1920s, he married Kentucky socialite Linda Lee Thomas; they travelled extensively throughout Europe and entertained lavishly. From his home base in Paris, Porter contributed songs to revues in London and New York, collaborated on the ballet *Within the Quota* (1923, with Gerald Murphy), and became a kind of legend among songwriters in New York. He returned to Broadway with his first hit musical, *Paris*—which included the song "Let's Do It (Let's Fall in Love)"—in 1928. Finally established on the American scene, Porter followed the show in quick succession with *Wake Up and Dream* (1929) in London, *Fifty Million Frenchmen* (1929) on Broadway, and *The Battle of Paris* (1929) for Hollywood. During the 1930s his Broadway shows included *The New Yorkers* (1930), the Fred Astaire vehicle *Gay Divorcee* (1932, which became the 1934 film *The Gay Divorcee*), and *Anything Goes* (1934), starring Ethel Merman; he also wrote *Nymph Errant* (1933) for the West End. In 1935 he sailed around the world with Moss Hart, collaborating on *Jubilee* (1935), which disappointed at the box office. He signed a contract with MGM the same year and moved to Hollywood, where he contributed scores for *Born to Dance* (1936) and *Rosalie* (1937). Late in 1937 he suffered a crippling equestrian accident that left him in near-constant pain for the rest of his life. He nevertheless continued to work on scores for Broadway, including *Leave It to Me* (1938), *Panama Hattie* (1940), *Let's Face It!* (1941), *Something for the Boys* (1943), *Mexican Hayride* (1944), *Seven Lively Arts* (1944), and *Around the World* (1946). In between musicals he wrote for Hollywood. In 1946 the biopic *Night and Day*, starring Cary Grant, featured his songs along with a fictionalized version of his life. *Kiss Me, Kate* (1948), on which he collaborated with Sam and Bella Spewack, won a Tony Award for Best Musical and ran for 1,077 performances, the longest run of his career; he followed it with *Out of This World* (1950), *Can-Can* (1952), and *Silk Stockings* (1955). His song "True Love," from the film *High Society* (1956), won an Academy Award. After 1958, his health declined and he no longer wrote for the stage. He died of kidney failure in Santa Monica.

Jerome Robbins (October 11, 1918–July 29, 1998) was born Jerome Rabinowitz in New York City to Harry Rabinowitz, the owner of a corset company, and Lena Rips. He showed an early aptitude for dancing and theatrics, and graduated from Woodrow Wilson High School in 1935. The Depression curtailed his higher educational ambitions and instead he studied dance at Senya Gluck-Sandor's Dance Center and appeared in the Yiddish Art Theatre. In the summer of 1937, he began dancing and choreographing at Tamiment, a progressive-movement summer resort; some of those dances were part of *The Straw Hat Revue*, which opened on Broadway in 1939. In the summer of 1940, he was accepted into the recently formed Ballet Theatre as a dancer and, eventually, a choreographer. In 1944, his short piece, *Fancy Free*, with a score by Leonard Bernstein, was a sensation and was further developed as *On the Town* (also 1944, with a new score by Bernstein and Betty Comden and Adolph Green). That led to other Broadway musicals, choreographing *Billion Dollar Baby* (1946); *High Button Shoes* (1948); *Look, Ma, I'm Dancin'* (which he co-directed with George Abbott, 1948). In 1949 he left Ballet Theater to join George Balanchine's New York City Ballet, as Associate Artistic Director. He choreographed groundbreaking ballets such as *The Guests* (1949, score by Marc Blitzstein), *The Age of Anxiety* (1950, Bernstein), and *The Cage* (1951, Stravinsky). He continued to work on Broadway, as the choreographer of *Miss Liberty* (1949), *Call Me Madam* (1950), and *The King and I* (1951). He returned to co-directing on *The Pajama Game* (with George Abbott, 1954) on Broadway; conceived, directed, and choreographed *Peter Pan* (1954); directed and co-choreographed *Bells Are Ringing* (1956); and choreographed the film version of *The King and I* (1956). Meanwhile at New York City Ballet he created *Afternoon of a Faun* (1953) and *The Concert* (1956), among other works. In 1957 he teamed up once again with Leonard Bernstein (along with Stephen Sondheim and Arthur Laurents) on *West Side Story* (film version 1961, for which he also choreographed and co-directed). He formed his own company, Ballet: USA, and directed and choreographed *Gypsy* (1959) with Ethel Merman. In 1964, he directed and choreographed his last original musical, *Fiddler on the Roof*, the most successful musical of its day. Retired from Broadway (with the exception of his 1989 anthology show, *Jerome Robbins' Broadway*), he devoted himself to new works for American Ballet Theatre (*Les Noces*, 1965) and New York City Ballet, where his career culminated with ballets such as *Dances at a Gathering* (1969), *Watermill* (1972), and *The Dybbuk Variations* (score by Bernstein, 1974), revised as *A Suite of Dances* (1980). He continued with ballets to music by Philip Glass (*Glass Pieces*, 1983) and Steve Reich (*Octet*, 1985), as well as music by Bach for *A Suite of Dances* (1994) for Mikhail Baryshnikov. By the mid-1990s, he was in fragile health. He died at his home in New York.

Richard Rodgers (June 28, 1902–December 30, 1979), the son of Mamie (Levy) Rodgers and William Rodgers, a physician, was born in Arverne, New York. He attended Columbia and the Institute of Musical Art in New York City; writing songs for the Columbia Varsity Show, he first encountered lyricist Lorenz Hart. He and Hart placed their first song on Broadway in 1919, but had to wait until 1925 to achieve real success. Beginning with *The Garrick Gaieties* (1925), they wrote the scores to more than a dozen shows, including *The Girl Friend* (1926) and *A Connecticut Yankee* (1927), before moving to Hollywood in 1930. Under contract to Paramount, they wrote several screen musicals, including *Love Me Tonight* (1932, "Isn't It Romantic?"). Returning to Broadway in 1934, Rodgers and Hart contributed music and lyrics (and occasionally the book) for *Jumbo* (1935), *On Your Toes* (1936), *Babes in Arms* (1937), *I'd Rather Be Right* (1937), *The Boys from Syracuse* (1938), *I Married an Angel* (1938), *Too Many Girls* (1939), *Higher and Higher* (1940), *Pal Joey* (1940), and *By Jupiter* (1942). Separately, Rodgers also composed the ballets *Nursery Ballet* (1938) and *Ghost Town* (1939). Shortly before Hart's death in 1943, he found a new collaborator in Oscar Hammerstein II: their first musical together, *Oklahoma!* (1943), ran for an unprecedented 2,212 performances. They went on to work together on *Carousel* (1945), *Allegro* (1947), *South Pacific* (1949, Pulitzer Prize), *The King and I* (1951), *Me and Juliet* (1953), *Pipe Dream* (1955), *Flower Drum Song* (1958), and *The Sound of Music* (1960). After Hammerstein's death in 1960, he contributed both music and lyrics for the show *No Strings* (1962), and collaborated on *Do I Hear a Waltz?* (1965, with Stephen Sondheim), *Two by Two* (1970, with Martin Charnin), *Rex* (1976, with Sheldon Harnick), and *I Remember Mama* (1979, with Charnin). Rodgers was also active as a producer or coproducer on many of his musicals and was president of the Music Theater of Lincoln Center, which in the 1960s presented several revivals of his shows.

He died in New York City, survived by his wife of forty-nine years, Dorothy Feiner, and two daughters.

Fred Saidy (February 11, 1907–May 14, 1982) was born Fareed Milhem Saidy in Los Angeles, the son of Lebanese immigrants Mejiba (Abilan) and Milhem Saidy. He was raised in Manitou Springs, Colorado, where his father and uncles ran a curio store for tourists visiting Pikes Peak; at age eleven, he contributed sports columns to the *Manitou Springs Journal*. As an undergraduate he served as drama critic and editorial director for the *New York University Daily News*. While searching for a career in journalism, he continued to earn his living as a salesman in his family's retail stores in Brooklyn and Los Angeles until at least 1940. He married Marie Dolores Mallouk; they had three children. In 1942, with Arthur Ross, he cowrote the musical revue *Rally 'Round the Girls*, which was performed in Los Angeles; sketches from the revue were included in the film *Star Spangled Rhythm* the same year. He cowrote screenplays for the films *I Dood It* (1943) and *Meet the People* (1944), both with Sig Herzig. He met E. Y. Harburg during the filming of *Meet the People*, on which Harburg served as producer, beginning a long collaborative relationship. In 1944, with Sig Herzig, he cowrote the book for the Broadway musical *Bloomer Girl*, with music by Harold Arlen and lyrics by Harburg. With Harburg, he wrote the book for *Finian's Rainbow* (1947), *Flahooley* (1951), and *Jamaica* (1957), and collaborated on *The Happiest Girl in the World* (1961, book with Henry Myers). During the 1950s he worked to bring a number of musicals to live television with producer Max Liebman, including *Babes in Toyland* (1954), *Best Foot Forward* (1954), *Satins and Spurs* (1954), *Promenade* (1955), and an adaptation of *Bloomer Girl* (1956). He died in Los Angeles.

Samuel and **Bella Spewack** met at nineteen, while reporting on the same story for different newspapers, he for the New York *World* and she for the *New York Call*. They married in 1922 and collaborated throughout their lives on plays, musicals, and movies. Samuel (September 16, 1899–October 14, 1971) was born in the Ukraine and raised on Staten Island by his parents Noel and Sema (Zelavetski) Spewack; his father ran a laundry. Bella (March 25, 1899–April 2, 1990) was the daughter of Fanny Cohen and Adolphe Loebel, natives of Transylvania. She emigrated to the Lower East Side of New York with her mother, who was a factory worker and seamstress, when she was three. Sam left Columbia after three and a half years to take a job as a police reporter. Bella earned a living as a reporter and publicity agent and published short stories in magazines such as *Argosy*, *Live Stories*, and *The Touchstone*.

1. Sheet music cover for *Show Boat* (1927).

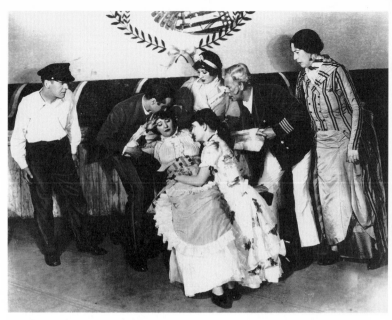

2. Julie (Helen Morgan) faints, in a prelude to the discovery of her racial background, from Act One, Scene 4 of *Show Boat* (l. to r.: Francis X. Mahoney, Charles Ellis, Morgan, Norma Terris, Eva Puck, Charles Winninger, Edna May Oliver).

3. Joe (Jules Bledsoe) contemplates life and time along the Mississippi in Act Two, Scene 7.

4. Cap'n Andy (Charles Winninger) comes to the rescue, following a disastrous performance of *The Parson's Bride*; in *Show Boat*, Act One, Scene 6.

5. Sheet music cover for *As Thousands Cheer* (1933).

6. The cast performs the Prologue, Scene 3: "Man Bites Dog." The newspaper headline motif defined the production.

7. Herbert Hoover (Leslie Adams) and his First Lady, Lou (Helen Broderick), select some souvenirs in "Franklin D. Roosevelt Inaugurated Tomorrow" in Act One.

8. Ethel Waters starts a "Heat Wave" in Act One of *As Thousands Cheer*.

9. Handbill for *Pal Joey* (1940).

10. Joey Evans (Gene Kelly) works his way through the chorus line in Act One of *Pal Joey*.

11. On the dance floor of the new Chez Joey in Act Two, Scene 1, Victor (Van Johnson) leads Gladys Bumps (June Havoc) in a new routine.

12. In Act Two, Scene 4, Vera Simpson (Vivienne Segal) gives the heave-ho to Joey (Gene Kelly) in front of his "mouse," Linda (Leila Ernst).

13. Cover of the souvenir book for *Oklahoma!* (1943).

14. Jud Fry (Howard Da Silva) is serenaded by Curly (Alfred Drake) in "Pore Jud," about his own demise, in Act One, Scene 2.

15. The joyous box social that opens Act Two of *Oklahoma!*

16. The conclusion of *Oklahoma!*: Curly (Alfred Drake, center) and Laurey (Joan Roberts) will soon be married and living in a brand-new state. Joining them are (l. to.r.) Will Parker (Lee Dixon), Ado Annie (Celeste Holm), Ali Hakim (Joseph Buloff), and Aunt Eller (Betty Garde).

17. Show poster for *On the Town* (1944).

18. Hildy (Nancy Walker, right) entreats Chip (Cris Alexander) to come up to her place in Act One, Scene 5 of *On The Town*.

19. Times Square is alive with sailors and their gals in the ballet that closes Act One.

20. Enjoying the late evening hours in a nightclub at the top of Act Two, Claire and Ozzie (Betty Comden and Adolph Green, center; also the musical's librettists) are joined by Lucy Schmeeler (Alice Pearce), a reluctant Gabey (John Battles), Chip (Cris Alexander), and Hildy (Nancy Walker).

21. Show poster for *Finian's Rainbow* (1947).

22. Sharon (Ella Logan) and her father Finian (Albert Sharpe) arrive from Ireland with some essential belongings in Act One, Scene 1.

23. Delores Martin teaches the Missitucky sharecroppers about the values of "Necessity" in Act One, Scene 5 of *Finian's Rainbow*.

24. In Act Two, Scene 2, the Passion Pilgrim Gospeleers (Jerry Laws, Lorenzo Fuller, Louis Sharp) are joined by an unlikely "fourth" in their rendition of "The Begat": a transformed Senator Billboard Rawkins (Robert Pitkin).

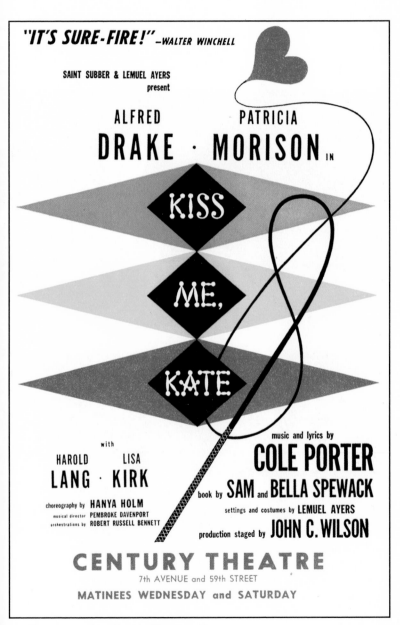

25. Show poster for *Kiss Me, Kate* (1948).

26. Fred Graham (Alfred Drake), in the guise of Petruchio, teaches his ex-wife, Lilli Vanessi (Patricia Morison), some manners in the Act One finale of *Kiss Me, Kate*.

27. In a front-cloth number from Act Two, Scene 6, First Gunman (Harry Clark) and Second Gunman (Jack Diamond) brush up their Shakespeare.

28. Show poster for *South Pacific* (1949).

29. In Act One, Scene 1, Emile de Becque (Ezio Pinza) and Nellie Forbush (Mary Martin) contemplate the frangipani on his plantation, as well as their romantic future.

30. Luther Billis (Myron McCormick, center), surrounded by his fellow Seabees, shows uncharacteristic respect for Navy nurse—and dame—Nellie Forbush (Mary Martin) in Act One, Scene 3.

31. Lieutenant Cable (William Tabbert) discovers in the arms of Liat (Betta St. John) ardent charms that are "Younger Than Springtime" in Act One, Scene 10 of *South Pacific*.

After several years as journalists in Europe and New York, they wrote their first play together, *The Solitaire Man* (1927); it was adapted for film in 1933. They followed this with *The War Song* (1928), *Poppa* (1928), *Clear All Wires!* (1932; filmed 1933), *Spring Song* (1934), and *Boy Meets Girl* (1935; filmed 1938). In 1938 they wrote their first musical, *Leave It to Me!*, an adaptation of *Clear All Wires!* with music and lyrics by Cole Porter; it ran for 291 performances. The movie *My Favorite Wife* (1940), for which they contributed both the original story and screenplay, won them an Academy Award nomination. During World War II, Sam made films for the Office of War Information in London and worked as a press attaché in Moscow; Bella remained home in New Hope, Pennsylvania, but after the war toured Eastern Europe for the United Nations Relief and Rehabilitation Agency. They returned to the theater with the farce *Woman Bites Dog* (1946). In 1948, collaborating again with Cole Porter, they wrote *Kiss Me, Kate*, which won the first Tony Award given to a musical; it was filmed in 1953. Sam afterward wrote several plays on his own: *Two Blind Mice* (1949), *The Golden State* (1950), and *Under the Sycamore Tree* (1952), which opened in London with Alec Guinness. Their last joint effort to succeed at the box office was the play *My Three Angels* in 1953; *Festival* (1955) and *Once There Was a Russian* (1961) closed after brief runs. They devoted much time in their later years to philanthropy.

Broadway Production Notes

SHOW BOAT

Show Boat was first presented by Florenz Ziegfeld, Jr. at the Ziegfeld Theatre on December 27, 1927, and closed on May 4, 1929, after 572 performances. It was revived on Broadway in 1932, 1946, 1983, and 1994. The original cast and production staff are listed below.

WINDY . . . . Alan Campbell
STEVE . . . . Charles Ellis
PETE . . . . Bert Chapman
QUEENIE . . . . Tess ("Aunt Jemima") Gardella
PARTHY ANN HAWKS . . . . Edna May Oliver
CAP'N ANDY. . . . . .Charles Winninger
ELLIE . . . . .Eva Puck
FRANK . . . . Sammy White
RUBBER-FACE . . . . .Francis X. Mahoney
JULIE . . . . Helen Morgan
GAYLORD RAVENAL . . . . .Howard Marsh
VALLON . . . . Thomas Gunn
MAGNOLIA. . . . . Norma Terris
JOE . . . . Jules Bledsoe
FARO DEALER . . . . Jack Wynn
GAMBLER. . . . . Phil Sheridan
BACKWOODSMAN . . . . .Jack Daley
JEB . . . . Jack Wynn
LA BELLE FATIMA . . . . .Dorothy Denese
OLD SPORT. . . . . Bert Chapman
ETHEL . . . . .Estelle Floyd
LANDLADY. . . . . .Annie Hart
SISTER . . . . Annette Harding
MOTHER SUPERIOR. . . . . Mildred Schwenke
KIM (*child*) . . . . Eleanor Shaw
JAKE . . . . Robert Farley

JIM . . . . Jack Daley

MAN WITH GUITAR. . . . . Ted Daniels

CHARLIE . . . . J. Lewis Johnson

LOTTIE. . . . . .Tana Kamp

DOLLY. . . . . Dagmar Oakland

HAZEL . . . . Maurine Holmes

KIM (*young woman*) . . . . Norma Terris

OLD LADY ON LEVEE. . . . . .Laura Clairon

Directed by Zeke Colvan and Oscar Hammerstein II
Choreographed by Sammy Lee
Scene design by Joseph Urban
Costume design by John Harkrider
Musical direction by Victor Baravalle
Choral direction by Will Vodery
Orchestrations by Robert Russell Bennett

AS THOUSANDS CHEER

As Thousands Cheer was first presented by Sam H. Harris at the Music Box Theatre on September 30, 1933, and closed on September 8, 1934, after 400 performances. The original cast and production staff are listed below.

LANGLEY . . . . .Hal Forde

MR. GEORGE ANDREWS . . . . Leslie Adams

MRS. EMILY ANDREWS . . . . .Helen Broderick

REPORTER . . . . .Harry Stockwell

EDITOR. . . . . Jerome Cowan

MR. HOOVER . . . . Leslie Adams

MRS. HOOVER . . . . .Helen Broderick

FRANK . . . . .Hamtree Harrington

BARBARA HUTTON . . . . Marilyn Miller

PRINCE DONATELLI . . . . Jay Hunter

PRINCE AUSTERLIEBE. . . . . Paul Pierce

PRINCE HOHENSTEIN. . . . . Chester O'Brien

PRINCE DELUNEVILLE . . . . .Harold Murray

PRINCE ALEXIS MDIVANI . . . . Clifton Webb

"HEAT WAVE" (PERFORMER). Ethel Waters
DANCERS . . . . Letitia Ide, José Limón

JOAN CRAWFORD. . . . . Marilyn Miller
WILL HAYS. . . . . Leslie Adams
DOUGLAS FAIRBANKS JR. . . . . Clifton Webb
FIRST REPORTER. . . . . Harold Murray
SECOND REPORTER. . . . . Jerome Cowan
TWO CAMERAMEN . . . . Ward Tallmon, John Perkins

ENGLAND, ITALY, GERMANY,
    AND FRANCE. . . . . Leslie Adams, Jerome Cowan,
                                    Hal Forde, Harry Stockwell
STATUE OF LIBERTY . . . . Helen Broderick

"LONELY HEART" (PERFORMER) . . . . Harry Stockwell
DANCERS . . . . Letitia Ide, José Limón

MRS. JOHN D. ROCKEFELLER JR. . . . . Helen Broderick
JOHN D. ROCKEFELLER JR. . . . . Leslie Adams
CHILDREN . . . . Peggy Cornell, Jerome Cowan,
                                    Thomas Hamilton, Harold Murray
REPORTER . . . . Hal Forde
CAMERAMEN . . . . Jay Hunter, Harold Murray, Ward Tallmon
JOHN D. ROCKEFELLER SR. . . . . Clifton Webb

"THE FUNNIES" (PERFORMER) . . . . Marilyn Miller

MAN . . . . Hamtree Harrington
WOMAN . . . . Ethel Waters
"TO BE OR NOT TO BE" (PERFORMER) . . . . Ethel Waters

"HER EASTER BONNET" (PERFORMERS) . . . . .Marilyn Miller,
                                                Clifton Webb

"METROPOLITAN OPENING" (PERFORMERS). . . . . Company
ANNOUNCER . . . . Jerome Cowan
MONSIEUR PEPPITON . . . . Clifton Webb
MOTHER WILLIAMS . . . . Helen Broderick

RUTHIE WILLIAMS . . . . Marilyn Miller

FATHER WILLIAMS . . . . Leslie Adams

"SUPPER TIME" (PERFORMER) . . . . Ethel Waters

NICK. . . . . Hal Forde

CAMERAMAN. . . . . (not credited)

MAHATMA GANDHI. . . . . Clifton Webb

NATIVE. . . . . Ward Tallmon

AIMEE SEMPLE MCPHERSON . . . . Helen Broderick

REVOLT IN CUBA: RUMBA NUMBER
    (DANCERS) . . . . Letitia Ide, José Limón

FIRST BELL BOY. . . . . Ward Tallmon

SECOND BELL BOY. . . . . Harold Murray

MRS. FISCHER . . . . Helen Broderick

ELLA. . . . . Ethel Waters

AGGIE REILLY . . . . Marilyn Miller

HENRY PERLMUTTER . . . . Clifton Webb

WINDOW CLEANER . . . . Leslie Adams

MAN. . . . . Clifton Webb

WOMAN. . . . . Marilyn Miller

"OUR WEDDING DAY"

BRIDESMAIDS . . . Jeannette Bradley, Elsie Duffy, Dorothy Dodd,
        Helen Ericson, Irene McBride, Jeannette Mundell,
        Toni Sorel, Lucille Taylor, Elsa Walbridge, Teddy West

USHERS . . . . Jack Barnes, Robert Castaire, Arthur Craig,
            JAY HUNTER, FRED MAYON, CHESTER
            O'BRIEN, MORTIMER O'BRIEN, JOHN
                        PERKINS,
                WARD TALLMON, JACK VOETH

KING GEORGE . . . . Leslie Adams

QUEEN MARY. . . . . Helen Broderick

THE PRINCE OF WALES . . . . Thomas Hamilton

LACKEY . . . . Harold Voeth

RAMSAY MACDONALD. . . . . Hal Forde

CHAUFFEUR . . . . (not credited)

PERSONAL MAID . . . . (not credited)

JOSEPHINE BAKER .... Ethel Waters

SECRETARY .... Jerome Cowan

"HARLEM ON MY MIND" (PERFORMER) .... Ethel Waters

"THROUGH A KEYHOLE" (PERFORMER) .... Clifton Webb

"NOT FOR ALL THE RICE IN CHINA"
    (LEADING PERFORMERS) .... Marilyn Miller, Clifton Webb

    GIRLS .... Jeanette Bradley, Dorothy Dodd, Elise Duffy,
        Helen Ericson, Katherine Litz, Irene McBride,
        Katherine Mulowney, Jeanette Mundell,
        Margaret Sande Toni Sorel, Lucille Taylor,
        Ella Walbridge, Teddy West

    BOYS .... Jack Barnes, Robert Castaine, Arthur Craig,
        Jay Hunter, Fred Mayon, Chester O'Brien,
        Mortimer O'Brien, John Perkins, Paul Pierce,
        Ward Tallmon, Harold Voeth, Jack Voeth

    CHARLES WEIDMAN DANCERS... Helen Backe, Debby Coleman,
        Robert Gorham, Letitia Ide (*leading dancer*),
        Harry Joyce, José Limón (*leading dancer*),
        William Matons, Paula Yasgour

Directed by Hassard Short
Choreographed by Charles Weidman
Scenic design by Albert R. Johnson
Lighting design by Hassard Short
Costume design by Varady, Irene Sharaff
Musical direction by Frank Tours
Orchestrations by Adolph Deutsch, Frank Tours, Ed Powell, Russell
Wooding, Helmy Kresa

PAL JOEY

Pal Joey was first presented by George Abbott at the Ethel Barrymore
Theatre on December 25, 1940, and closed on November 29, 1941, after
374 performances. It was revived on Broadway in 1952, 1976, and 2008.
The original cast and production staff are listed below.

JOEY EVANS .... Gene Kelly

MIKE SPEARS........................... Robert J. Mulligan

THE KID.................................... Sondra Barrett

GLADYS .... June Havoc
AGNES .... Diane Sinclair
LINDA ENGLISH............................... Leila Ernst
VALERIE................................... Amarilla Morris
ALBERT DOANE .... Stanley Donen
VERA SIMPSON .... Vivienne Segal
ESCORT..................................... Edison Rice
TERRY...................................... Jane Fraser
VICTOR..................................... Van Johnson
ERNEST .... John Clarke
STAGEHAND................................. Jerry Whyte
MAX .... Averell Harris
THE TENOR .... Nelson Rae
MELBA SNYDER .... Jean Castro
WAITER .... Dummy Spevlin
LUDLOW LOWELL .... Jack Durant
COMMISSIONER O'BRIEN .... James Lane
ASSISTANT HOTEL MANAGER .... Clifford Dunstan

SPECIALTY DANCER........................... Shirley Paige
DANCING GIRLS ..... Claire Anderson, Sondra Barrett, Alice Craig,
      Louise de Forest, Enez Early, Tilda Getze, Charlene Harkins,
      Frances Krell, Janet Lavis, June Leroy, Amarilla Morris, Olive
      Nicolson, Mildred Patterson, Dorothy Poplar, Diane Sinclair,
      Mildred Solly, Jeanne Trybom, Marie Vanneman

DANCING BOYS ... Adrian Anthony, John Benton, Milton Chisolm,
            Stanley Donen, Henning Irgens, Van Johnson,
            Howard Ledig, Michael Moore, Albert Ruiz

Directed by George Abbott
Choreographed by Robert Alton
Scene and lighting design by Jo Mielziner
Costume design by John Koenig
Orchestrations by Hans Spialek

OKLAHOMA!

Oklahoma! was first presented by the Theatre Guild (Theresa Helburn and Lawrence Langner, administrative directors) at the St. James Theatre on March 31, 1943, and closed on May 29, 1948, after 374 performances. It was revived on Broadway in 1979 and 2002. The original cast and production staff are listed below.

AUNT ELLER. . . . . Betty Garde
CURLY . . . . Alfred Drake
LAUREY . . . . Joan Roberts
IKE SKIDMORE . . . . Barry Kelley
FRED . . . . .Edwin Clay
SLIM . . . . Herbert Rissman
WILL PARKER . . . . .Lee Dixon
JUD FRY . . . . Howard Da Silva
ADO ANNIE CARNES . . . . Celeste Holm
ALI HAKIM. . . . . Joseph Buloff
GERTIE CUMMINGS. . . . . Jane Lawrence
ELLEN. . . . . Katharine Sergava
KATE. . . . . Ellen Love
SYLVIE . . . . .Joan McCracken
ARMINA . . . . .Kate Friedlich
AGGIE. . . . . Bambi Linn
ANDREW CARNES . . . . Ralph Riggs
CORD ELAM . . . . .Owen Martin
JESS . . . . .George Church
CHALMERS. . . . . .Marc Platt
MIKE . . . . Paul Shiers
JOE . . . . George Irving
SAM . . . . Hayes Gordon

Directed by Rouben Mamoulian
Dances by Agnes de Mille
Settings by Lemuel Ayers
Costumes by Miles White
Orchestra directed by Joseph Schwartzdorf
Orchestrations by Robert Russell Bennett

ON THE TOWN

On the Town was first presented by Oliver Smith and Paul Feigay at the Adelphi Theatre on December 28, 1944, and closed on February 2, 1946, after 462 performances. It was revived on Broadway in 1971 and 1998. The original cast and production staff are listed below.

WORKMAN	Marten Sameth
2ND WORKMAN	Frank Milton
3RD WORKMAN	Herbert Greene
OZZIE	Adolph Green
CHIP	Cris Alexander
SAILOR	Lyle Clark
GABEY	John Battles
ANDY	Frank Westbrook
TOM	Richard D'Arcy
FLOSSIE	Florence McMichael
FLOSSIE'S FRIEND	Marion Kohler
BILL POSTER	Larry Bolton
LITTLE OLD LADY	Maxine Arnold
POLICEMAN	Lonny Jackson
S. UPERMAN	Milton Taubman
HILDY	Nancy Walker
POLICEMAN	Roger Treat
FIGMENT	Remo Bufano
CLAIRE	Betty Comden
HIGH SCHOOL GIRL	Nellie Fisher
SAILOR IN BLUE	Richard D'Arcy
MAUDE P. DILLY	Susan Steell
IVY	Sono Osato
LUCY SCHMEELER	Alice Pearce
PITKIN	Robert Chisholm
MASTER OF CEREMONIES	Frank Milton
SINGER	Frances Cassard
WAITER	Herbert Greene
SPANISH SINGER	Jeanne Gordon
THE GREAT LOVER	Ray Harrison
CONDUCTOR	Herbert Greene

BIMMY . . . . Robert Lorenz

DANCERS . . . . Barbara Gaye, Lavina Nielsen, Atty Vandenberg,
Dorothy McNichols, Cyprienne Gabelman, Jean Handy,
Virginia Miller, Nelle Fisher, Royce Wallace, Allyn Ann McLerie,
Malka Farber, Aza Bard, Ray Harrison, Frank Neal, Carle Ebrele,
James Flashe Riley, Ben Piazza, Douglas Matheson, Duncan Noble,
Frank Westbrook, John Butler, Richard D'Arcy, Lyle Clark

SINGERS . . . . Frances Cassard, Jeanne Gordon,
Lila King, Frances Lager, Marion Kohler,
Dorothy Johnson, Regina Owens, Shirley
Ann Burton, Frank Milton, Roger Treat,
Marten Sameth, Benjamin Trotman,
Milton Taubman, Herbert Greene,
Lonny Jackson, Melvin Howard,
Sam Adams, Robert Lorenz

Directed by George Abbott
Musical numbers and choreography staged by Jerome Robbins
Production designed by Oliver Smith
Costumes designed by Alvin Colt
Musical direction by Max Goberman

FINIAN'S RAINBOW

Finian's Rainbow was first presented by Lee Sabinson and William R. Katzell at the 46th Street Theatre on January 10, 1947, and closed on October 2, 1948, after 725 performances. It was revived on Broadway in 1960 (transferred from City Center) and 2009. The original cast and production staff are listed below.

SUNNY (*harmonica player*) . . . . Sonny Terry
BUZZ COLLINS . . . . Eddie Bruce
SHERIFF . . . . Tom McElhany
FIRST SHARECROPPER . . . . Alan Gilbert
SECOND SHARECROPPER . . . . Robert Eric Carlson
SUSAN MAHONEY . . . . Anita Alvarez
HENRY . . . . Augustus Smith, Jr.
THIRD SHARECROPPER . . . . Maude Simmons
FINIAN MCLONERGAN . . . . Albert Sharpe
SHARON MCLONERGAN . . . . Ella Logan
WOODY MAHONEY . . . . Donald Richards

FOURTH SHARECROPPER . . . . William Scully

OG (*a leprechaun*) . . . . David Wayne

HOWARD . . . . .William Greaves

SENATOR BILLBOARD RAWKINS. . . . . Robert Pitkin

FIRST GEOLOGIST . . . . Nathaniel Dickerson

SECOND GEOLOGIST . . . . .Lucas Aço

DIANE . . . . Diane Woods

JANE. . . . . Jane Earle

JOHN (*the preacher*) . . . . Roland Skinner

MR. ROBUST. . . . . .Arthur Tell

MR. SHEARS. . . . . Royal Dano

FIRST PASSION PILGRIM GOSPELEER. . . . . Jerry Laws

SECOND PASSION PILGRIM GOSPELEER . . . . Lorenzo Fuller

THIRD PASSION PILGRIM GOSPELEER. . . . . Louis Sharp

FIRST DEPUTY . . . . .Michael Ellis

SECOND DEPUTY . . . . .Robert Eric Carlson

THIRD DEPUTY . . . . Harry Day

OTHER CHILDREN . . . . .Norma Jane Marlowe, Elayne Richards

DANCERS

GIRLS . . . . .Freda Flier, Annabelle Gold, Eleanore Gregory,
Ann Hutchinson, Erona Harris, Anna Mitten,
Kathleen Stanford, Lavinia Williams

BOYS . . . . Lucas Aco, Harry Day, Daniel Floyd, J. C. McCord,
Frank Neal, Arthur Partington, James Flash Riley,
Don Weissmuller

SINGERS

GIRLS . . . . Arlene Anderson, Connie Baxter, Carroll Brooks,
Lyn Joi, Mimi Kelly, Delores Martin,
Marijane Maricle, Maude Simmons

BOYS . . . . Robert Eric Carlson, Ralph Waldo Cummings,
Nathaniel Dickerson, Alan Gilbert, Theodore Hines,
Morty Rappe, William Scully, Roland Skinner

Directed by Bretaigne Windust
Scenery and lighting by Jo Mielziner
Choreography by Michael Kidd
Costumes by Eleanore Goldsmith
Orchestrations by Robert Russell Bennett and Don Walker
Vocal arrangements by Lyn Murray
Musical direction by Milton Rosenstock

KISS ME, KATE

Kiss Me, Kate was first presented by Saint Subber and Lemuel Ayers at the New Century Theatre on December 30, 1948, and closed on July 28, 1951, after 1,077 performances. It was revived on Broadway in 1999. The original cast and production staff are listed below.

FRED GRAHAM . . . . Alfred Drake

HARRY TREVOR . . . . Thomas Hoier

LOIS LANE . . . . .Lisa Kirk

RALPH (*stage manager*) . . . . Don Mayo

LILLI VANESSI . . . . .Patricia Morison

HATTIE . . . . Annabelle Hill

PAUL . . . . .Lorenzo Fuller

BILL CALHOUN . . . . .Harold Lang

FIRST MAN . . . . Harry Clark

SECOND MAN . . . . .Jack Diamond

STAGE DOORMAN . . . . Dan Brennan

HARRISON HOWELL . . . . Denis Green

SPECIALTY DANCERS . . . . Fred Davis, Eddie Sledge

"TAMING OF THE SHREW" PLAYERS

    BIANCA (LOIS LANE) . . . . .Lisa Kirk

    BAPTISTA (HARRY TREVOR) . . . . Thomas Hoier

    GREMIO (FIRST SUITOR) . . . . Noel Gordon

    HORTENSIO (SECOND SUITOR) . . . . .Charles Wood

    LUCENTIO (BILL CALHOUN) .Harold Lang

    KATHARINE (LILLI VANESSI) . . . . .Patricia Morison

    PETRUCHIO (FRED GRAHAM) . . . . Alfred Drake

HABERDASHER . . . . John Castello

SINGING ENSEMBLE . . . . Peggy Ferris, Christine Matsios, Joan Kibrig, Gay Laurence, Ethel Madsen, Helen Rice, Matilda Strazza, Tom Bole, George Cassidy, Herb Fields, Edwin Clay, Allan Lowell, Stan Rose, Charles Wood

DANCERS . . . . .Janet Gaylord, Jean Houloose, Doreen Oswald, Cynthia Risely, Ingrid Secretan, Gissela Svetlik, Jean Haas, Harry Asmus, Marc Breaux, John Castello, Victor Duntiere, Tom Hansen, Glen Tetley, Rudy Tone

Directed by John C. Wilson
Choreography by Hanya Holm

Settings and costumes by Lemuel Ayers
Musical direction by Pembroke Davenport
Orchestrations by Robert Russell Bennett
Instrumental ballet music by Genevieve Pitot

SOUTH PACIFIC

South Pacific was first presented by Richard Rodgers and Oscar Hammerstein II in association with Leland Hayward and Joshua Logan at the Majestic Theatre on April 7, 1949, and closed on January 16, 1954, after 1,925 performances. It was revived on Broadway in 2008. The original cast and production staff are listed below.

NGANA . . . . Barbara Luna

JEROME . . . . Michael De Leon, Noel De Leon

HENRY . . . . Richard Silvera

ENSIGN NELLIE FORBUSH . . . . Mary Martin

EMILE DE BECQUE. . . . . Ezio Pinza

BLOODY MARY . . . . Juanita Hall

BLOODY MARY'S ASSISTANT . . . . Musa Williams

ABNER . . . . Archie Savage

STEWPOT . . . . Henry Slate

LUTHER BILLIS . . . . Myron McCormick

PROFESSOR . . . . Fred Sadoff

LT. JOSEPH CABLE, U.S.M.C. William Tabbert

CAPT. GEORGE BRACKETT, U.S.N. . . . . Martin Wolfson

CMDR. WILLIAM HARBISON, U.S.N. . . . . Harvey Stephens

YEOMAN HERBERT QUALE . . . . Alan Gilbert

SGT. KENNETH JOHNSON . . . . Thomas Gleason

SEABEE RICHARD WEST . . . . Dickinson Eastham

SEABEE MORTON WISE . . . . Henry Michel

SEAMAN TOM O'BRIEN . . . . Bill Dwyer

RADIO OPERATOR BOB MCCAFFREY . . . . Biff McGuire

MARINE CPL. HAMILTON STEEVES . . . . Jim Hawthorne

STAFF SGT. THOMAS HASSINGER . . . . Jack Fontan

SEAMAN JAMES HAYES . . . . Beau Tilden

LT. GENEVIEVE MARSHALL . . . . Jacqueline Fisher

ENSIGN DINAH MURPHY .... Roslyn Lowe

ENSIGN JANET MACGREGOR...................... Sandra Deel

ENSIGN CORA MACRAE...................... Bernice Saunders

ENSIGN SUE YAEGER........................ Pat Northrop

ENSIGN LISA MINELLI........................... Gloria Meli

ENSIGN CONNIE WALEWSKA .... Mardi Bayne

ENSIGN PAMELA WHITMORE .... Evelyn Colby

ENSIGN BESSIE NOONAN .... Helena Schurgot

LIAT .... Betta St. John

MARCEL, HENRY'S ASSISTANT .... Richard Loo

LT. BUZZ ADAMS .... Don Fellows

ISLANDERS, SAILORS, MARINES, OFFICERS ..... Mary Ann Reeve,
Chin Yu, Alex Nicol, Eugene Smith,
Richard Loo, William Ferguson

Book and musical numbers staged by Joshua Logan
Scenery and lighting by Jo Mielziner
Costumes by Motley
Orchestra directed by Salvatore Dell'Isola
Orchestrations by Robert Russell Bennett

Note on the Texts

This volume gathers texts of eight musicals first performed on Broadway from 1927 to 1949: *Show Boat* (1927), *As Thousands Cheer* (1933), *Pal Joey* (1940), *Oklahoma!* (1943), *On the Town* (1944), *Finian's Rainbow* (1947), *Kiss Me, Kate* (1948), and *South Pacific* (1949). A companion volume in the Library of America series, *American Musicals, 1950–1969*, presents eight later musicals: *Guys and Dolls* (1950), *The Pajama Game* (1954), *My Fair Lady* (1956), *Gypsy* (1959), *A Funny Thing Happened on the Way to the Forum* (1962), *Fiddler on the Roof* (1964), *Cabaret* (1966), and *1776* (1969). Most of these works have been revived and revised since they premiered, some of them many times, and most exist in multiple textual forms, including those found in original production scripts, book editions published for general readers, and scripts subsequently issued for licensed performances. The texts in the present volume have been chosen and prepared in order to represent each musical, to the greatest extent possible, as it originally opened on Broadway. A selection of lyrics not performed on opening night but that have come to be associated with these shows over the course of their production histories is included as an appendix, and some alternate versions of book scenes are included in the notes.

Texts of four of the eight musicals included here—*Oklahoma!*, *Finian's Rainbow*, *Kiss Me, Kate*, and *South Pacific*—have been taken from the first book editions. These editions, all but one published within a year of opening night, reflect what is known about each musical's opening night state from the evidence of playbills, reviews, and subsequent scholarship. (*Kiss Me, Kate* was not published until 1953, five years after that show's Broadway debut, but it too follows the form of the original production without later alteration.) Texts of the remaining four musicals—*Show Boat*, *As Thousands Cheer*, *Pal Joey*, and *On the Town*—have been taken from typescripts associated with the first Broadway production of each show. *Show Boat*, *Pal Joey*, and *On the Town* have been published elsewhere in versions that contain substantial subsequent revision; *As Thousands Cheer*, it is believed, is published here in its entirety for the first time.

The production typescripts chosen as copy-texts for *Show Boat*, *As Thousands Cheer*, *Pal Joey*, and *On the Town* were not intended for wider publication in the form in which they were originally circulated. As working documents, they include technical cues for actors and musicians not usually present in editions of Broadway musicals prepared for a general reading audience. They occasionally indicate musical numbers by title alone, omitting the lyrics, which were provided to the performers separately; or they include lyrics in a form less complete or less carefully rendered than in contemporary sheet music or subsequent collected editions of the lyricists' work. They sometimes lack attribution of parts in musical numbers, or assign speaking parts using the names of the actors in the original cast rather than the characters they ultimately represented, or include song titles or act and scene divisions inconsistently. Several features of these typescripts have been silently emended in the present volume. Titles of works, names of vessels, and taxonomic binomials have been printed in italics. Quotation marks have been added around quoted material. The length of dashes and ellipses, punctuation associated with quotation marks, and the capitalization of character names have been regularized. Directions made unnecessary by the typographical design of the present volume, such as "(*Dialogue*)" where dialogue is clearly indicated by the typesetting, have been omitted. Abbreviations in stage directions have been expanded. Musical and lighting directions typed in the margins, such as "CLIMAX FOR CURTAIN" and "MUSIC CUE," have been excised. Blocking instructions for actors have been simplified or excised (for instance, "THE SISTER and KIM exit R. 1." becomes "THE SISTER and KIM exit."). Parts indicated with the name of an actor rather than that of the character represented have been changed to reflect the latter. Where lyrics are presented without complete attribution of singing parts, these parts have been supplied. Where act and scene divisions are absent or incompletely indicated, these have been added. Where song or scene titles have been included inconsistently, missing titles have been inserted.

A variety of sources—including opening night programs, music scores, sheet music, separate book editions of lyrics, cast recordings, other versions both published and unpublished, and secondary studies—have been consulted as evidence in establishing complete and accurate opening night reading texts for each work. In the case of two of the eight musicals included here—*As Thousands Cheer* and *Pal Joey*—no existing text fully reflects the state in which the work was first presented in New York. As described in more detail below, the best available texts of these two musicals have been further emended, and material from other sources has been interpolated, to bring them into conformity with the work as it is known to have been originally performed.

Show Boat. Unlike most major musicals in subsequent decades (as Miles Kreuger explains in his 1977 book *Show Boat: The Story of a Classic American Musical*), the original Broadway *Show Boat* "never had an official script or score." A text published by Chappell & Co. in London in 1928 was "vastly altered," following changes made on the London stage. A text published in 1962 by the Rodgers & Hammerstein Theatre Library in New York, and another, without date, by T. B. Harms, incorporate numerous substantial alterations made over the years by Oscar Hammerstein II, his son William, and others, some "for length," some "to trim some of the comedy scenes originally intended simply to cover long scene changes," some "to reflect the nation's changing racial attitudes."

The text of *Show Boat* in the present volume has been taken from a copy generously provided by the Rodgers and Hammerstein Organization of a typescript once the property of Hammerstein and bearing his extensive holograph emendations. Two identical typescripts, without these emendations, are present in the Billy Rose Theatre Collection at the New York Public Library. Hammerstein's emendations evidently postdate the show's Broadway opening and have not been adopted here, but the underlying typescript follows the form in which the musical opened on Broadway, and appears to have been used as a final production script.

The text of the Hammerstein typescript has been emended at several points in the present volume. A stage direction in Act 1, Scene 4—"(ELLIE *stands at side, waiting for something to happen.*)"—has been moved so that it precedes rather than interrupts the subsequent line of dialogue. The names of attractions at the Chicago World's Fair— "DALEY," "PRINCESS FATIMA," "SHERIDAN," "WYNN," "DAHOMEY VILLAGE," "CONGRESS OF BEAUTY"—typed in the margin of the scene description at the beginning of Act 2, have been omitted. The lyrics sung at the beginning of Act 2, Scene 4, tipped into the typescript on a separate sheet before the scene description, have been printed in the present volume as part of the scene description. At the end of Act 2, Scene 8, the typescript abbreviates a reprise of "You Are Love"; the present volume supplies the lyrics. Punctuation and spelling in the lyrics of "Ol' Man River," "Make Believe," "Can't Help Lovin' Dat Man," "You Are Love," and "Why Do I Love You?" have been emended following the text of these lyrics in Hammerstein's *Lyrics* (New York: Simon & Schuster, 1949).

As Thousands Cheer. The text of *As Thousands Cheer* in the present volume has been taken from a typescript, now in the Sam Harris Collection (Box 3) at the Princeton University Library (Manuscripts Division, Department of Rare Books and Special Collections), associated with the show's original 1933–34 Broadway run. Two of Moss Hart's sketches, "Franklin D. Roosevelt To Be Inaugurated Tomorrow" and "World's Wealthiest Man Celebrates Ninety-Fourth Birthday," are included in *The Greatest Revue Sketches*, an anthology edited by Donald Oliver and published by Avon Books in 1982, and Irving Berlin's songs have been published as sheet music and in separate editions of lyrics, but *As Thousands Cheer* is not otherwise known to have appeared in print. An undated manuscript in the Moss Hart and Kitty Carlisle Papers at the Wisconsin Historical Society (Box 4, Folder 1) contains the text of an early draft of the show.

The Harris typescript evidently postdates the show's Broadway opening, albeit narrowly: it lacks the song "Through a Keyhole," which was cut during the show's run. In other respects, however, the typescript follows the order of sketches and musical numbers described in the opening night program, and probably contains little or no further revision. A number of aspects of the typescript text have been emended in the present volume. The lyrics of "Through a Keyhole"—from *The Complete Lyrics of Irving Berlin*, edited by Robert Kimball and Linda Emmet (New York: Alfred A. Knopf, 2001)—have been added. Irving Berlin's byline, included after some songs, has been omitted. "Headline" titles for each sketch, not consistently included in the typescript, have been supplied from the opening night program and other contemporary sources. The scene descriptions at the beginning of the sketches "Franklin D. Roosevelt Inaugurated Tomorrow," "World's Wealthiest Man Celebrates Ninety-Fourth Birthday," and "Green Pastures Starts Third Road Season"—not present in the typescript—have been interpolated from Hart's manuscript draft. A stage direction, "*Curtains part to reveal* BRIDEGROOM *and* BRIDE *in bed together*," has been added in the sketch "Society Wedding of the Season Outside St. Thomases," which otherwise lacks such directions. Aside from these emendations, the text in the present volume follows the Harris typescript.

Pal Joey. *Pal Joey* first appeared in print in 1952 in an edition published by Random House in New York; the text of the Random House edition contains numerous changes introduced for the show's 1952 Broadway revival. The text of *Pal Joey* in the present volume is based on an undated typescript provided by the Rodgers and Hammerstein Organization, a copy of which is also available in the Goodman Theatre Archives at the Chicago Public Library. This typescript reflects the form in which *Pal Joey* opened on Broadway in 1940 more closely than any other known to be extant, though in a number of particulars it may postdate the Broadway opening. The opening night program lists an appearance by Stanley Donen as Albert Doane, a character not included in the typescript. No mention is made in the program of the character Mickey, played by Phyllis Dorne in 1952 and included in the typescript. Fragmentary indications of a character named Max are evident in the typescript—Max was played by Averill Harris on opening night, and no longer appears in the 1952 Random House text—but Max's lines have been cancelled by hand in the typescript and reassigned to a character Mike; it is not possible to restore the character to its original state simply by reversing the cancellations. The song "What is a Man?," which concludes Act 1, Scene 4, in the typescript, is not listed in programs until May 12, 1941, more than four months after the show had opened; the opening night program calls instead for a song titled "Love Is My Friend." Metrically identical, the variant titles probably both referred to the same song; no distinct version of "Love Is My Friend" is known to be extant.

Several aspects of the typescript text have been emended in the present volume. The names of a few minor characters, indicated in the typescript by the names of the actors playing them and not given in the opening night program, have been supplied from context or from the 1952 Random House text. For example, the typescript's [Edison] "Rice"—an "Escort" in the opening night program—is rendered in the present volume as "Escort" in Act 1, Scene 5 (where he is Vera Simpson's escort), but as "Scholtz" in Act 2, Scene 1 (where he speaks from offstage as a lighting technician named Scholtz), and then as "Delivery Boy" in the same scene (when he comes onstage carrying a crate of eggs). In three places, stage directions have been added to note entrances and exits indicated by internal or other evidence. The opening verse of the song "Take Him" appears to have been inadvertently omitted in the typescript text; lyrics have been supplied from *The Complete Lyrics of Lorenz Hart*, edited by Dorothy Hart and Robert Kimball and published by Alfred A. Knopf in 1986. In the same way, the lyrics of "Bewitched, Bothered and Bewildered" have been taken from *The Complete Lyrics* rather than the typescript, which includes them in abbreviated, placeholding form. In all other particulars the text in the present volume follows the Rodgers and Hammerstein typescript.

Oklahoma! Oklahoma! was first published by Random House in New York in 1943, in an edition that follows the form in which the musical opened on Broadway. The text of *Oklahoma!* in the present volume has been taken from the Random House first edition.

On the Town. On the Town was not published in an edition intended for general readers until 1997, when it was included in *The New York Musicals of Comden & Green* (New York: Applause Books); an undated script used for licensed performances (New York: Tams-Witmark) was probably prepared around 1970, before the show's 1971 revival. These later texts appear to derive from the show's final 1944 production script, a copy of which is now in the Jerome Robbins Papers (Box 63, Folder 9) at the New York Public Library. Both expand and correct the 1944 text at points where it abbreviates lyrics or contains typographical errors; both also introduce a number of transcription errors and omit a minor character (the "Delicate Type" hailing a taxi in Act 1, Scene 5) along with short sections of original dialogue and scene description. In *The New York Musicals of Comden & Green*, the song "Gabey's Comin'"—not performed on opening night, but added in revival performances—appears. ("Gabey's Comin'" is printed in the present volume among the "Additional Lyrics" included as an appendix.) The text of *On the Town* in the present volume has been taken from the 1944 Jerome Robbins Papers typescript.

Finian's Rainbow. In the present volume, the text of *Finian's Rainbow* has been taken from the first book edition, which follows the musical's opening night form; it was published by Random House in 1947.

Kiss Me, Kate. *Kiss Me, Kate* remained unpublished until late 1953, when Alfred A. Knopf produced an edition timed to coincide with the release of an MGM film version of the musical. In spite of the delay, the text of the Knopf edition follows the musical's original Broadway form, without evidence of subsequent alteration. The text of *Kiss Me, Kate* in the present volume is that of the 1953 Knopf first printing.

South Pacific. The text of *South Pacific* in the present volume has been taken from the first book edition, published by Random House in 1949; this edition follows the form in which *South Pacific* opened on Broadway.

A section of "Additional Lyrics" has been included as an appendix to the present volume; it contains the lyrics of several songs that were not performed on opening night, but that have subsequently been associated with *Show Boat*, *On the Town*, and *South Pacific*. Texts have been taken from the following sources:

"Mis'ry's Comin' Aroun'"; "I Have the Room Above Her"; "Nobody Else But Me" (from *Show Boat*): *The Complete Lyrics of Oscar Hammerstein II*. New York: Alfred A. Knopf, 2008, 114–16.

"I'm Talking to My Pal" (from *Pal Joey*): *The Complete Lyrics of Lorenz Hart*. New York: Alfred A. Knopf, 1986, 275.

"Gabey's Comin'" (from *On the Town*): *The New York Musicals of Comden & Green*. New York: Applause Books, 1997, 14–16.

"My Girl Back Home" (from *South Pacific*): *The Complete Lyrics of Oscar Hammerstein II*. New York: Alfred A. Knopf, 2008, 342.

This volume presents the texts of the original printings and typescripts chosen for inclusion here, but it does not attempt to reproduce features of their typographic design. The texts are presented here without change, except for the emendations specifically described above and for the correction of typographical errors. Spelling, punctuation, and capitalization are often expressive features, and they are not altered, even when inconsistent or irregular. The following is a list of typographical errors, cited by page and line number: 6.24, *exits Show*; 6.36, *beruffles,*; 7.1, Laverne; 8.5, papa!; 9.21, Andy, Captain Candy; 9.25, Andy, Captain Andy.; 9.26, dandy,; 10.17, *exits in*; 10.23, Hey-Rubberface; 10.40, Julia; 11.10, *prop smile*; 12.1, *with much*; 12.13, *stage*, PETE; 13.5, skylarking always playing; 15.37, Of; 18.11, conventions; 19.12, *knife picks*; 21.31, Ah, declare ef; 22.19, *impossible,*; 22.36, no account; 23.27, F'sho' Ah; 24.30, *picks apple*; 26.23, Cute; 26.40, RIDE WITH THEM; 31.34, *it the*; 32.2, *Stage*; 32.9–10, —now [missing speaker]; 32.13, (SHE; 32.26, *count—slurred*; 32.38, "Y'; 33.29, —Guess; 34.26, *him, she looks at* STEVE, *horrified*, ELLIE; 36.3, much darling; 36.17, Miscegenation; 37.21, keel boatin'; 38.22, *"Misery" First*; 38.22–24, *hummed.*) / On [missing speaker]; 39.10, mother!; 41.3, No—responsibility; 41.28 (and *passim*), mother; 42.28, ANDY (*Leads*; 45.2, *astride*; 46.3, *exit in*; 46.40, *Exit on*; 49.15, of' breath; 50.16, Twilight; 51.1, ELLIE (*Rises*; 50.30, Twilight; 51.1, MAGNOLIA (MAGNOLIA *paces*; 51.8, *Parson played*; 52.13, *repulsive grisly*; 53.5, *open mouth*; 53.7, FRANK (*Pushing*; 53.8, *making exit*; 53.11, Shultz; 53.12, here [no punctuation]; 53.29, comewhen; 53.36, ain'tgoin'; 54.25, Thewages; 55.23, Nola!; 56.30, And; 58.4, *flare*; 59.24, There's; 61.5, that man; 62.17, BETTER; 62.17, CHILLSON . . . *well known*; 62.20, *their*; 66.20–21, *the streets of Cairo*; 66.36, *Couchie-couchie*; 67.2, Dohomey; 67.6, Wives; 68.22, two.; 68.26, wherefor; 69.14, DOHEMEYS; 69.24, check uncha; 71.1, *Dahomey*; 71.7, *(1904)* [no punctuation]; 74.21 *bills Her*; 74.29, *played in*; 76.8, *well executed*; 76.13, *too anxious*; 79.13, *impressarios*; 79.18, Never see; 79.23, *guitar, across*; 79.25, *That Man*; 83.34, *Eve* [no punctuation]; 83.36, *enter* [no punctuation]; 85.28, *they start*; 87.38, river [no punctuation]; 88.9, who'; 88.37, now—; 90.31, Mah.; 92.9, *radio,*; 92.13, *That Man*; 93.5, jus-t; 95.11, you; 96.24, Andy,; 96.30, *gave*; 109.35, Wise cracking; 110.4, Engineers; 110.28, Boys; 110.37, Medicine Ball; 111.29, Oboe yes; 114.23, she dances; 115.29, Hays gentlemen I; 117.6, anybodys; 117.8, Love; 117.14, Her; 117.30, afinal; 117.36, You; 118.11, MR. HAYS; 120.23, U.S.A.; 120.24, STATUTE; 121.12, *Spangle*; 121.24, lovely as; 122.13, shout?; 122.17, Yes Father; 122.29, That gentlemen,; 128.34, shakespere; 130.1, 'cause; 131.5 Parade [no punctuation]; 133.32 (and *passim*), Muellers; 134.4, Chef; 134.9–10, Housewives; 134.35 (and *passim*), Moma!; 136.16, Curtains; 139.17, works.—; 140.20, white rock; 141.6, For; 141.37, that,; 141.40, mam!; 142.1–2, Rielly; 142.30, waiter.; 143.24, Giaconda!; 144.8, sloughedoff; 144.18, Lunts; 145.17, Bangkoh; 147.37, (*Chorus*); 149.1, Exactly David; 149.5, THE PRINCE; 150.32, Yorke; 150.33, McDonald.; 151.14, Ed.; 151.30, America.; 153.20, unenthusiastically [no punctuation]; 153.23, Folies Bergere; 154.20, am I [no punctuation]; 154.25, know / Why [no punctuation]; 154.37, cherie; 163.7, Fay?; 164.37, bubly; 165.29, life. (GLADYS *enters*.) My love.; 168.2, wire haired; 168.4, Hy,; 168.25, Airdale; 171.35, Lille,; 171.36, *Byfield's*; 173.25, Joey; 173.27, Chicagoen; 173.26, Club. Name; 173.31, back.; 173.34, minute I'm; 175.15, your're; 179.30, Why the; 185.25, wheter; 186.4, aan-yteem; 186.7–8, "Maysure a dam."; 186.35, Bros.; 189.23, bother,; 191.9–10, time. / If [missing speaker]; 191.23, trilum; 192.12, colum; 193.33–34, Darda nella, Who; 194.4 (and *passim*), Frere; 195.3, Minski.; 195.12, Lippman; 195.25, passe; 195.30, Alah; 196.6, sickyl; 196.24, guy. (JOEY *enters*.) You; 196.28, OOh; 198.5, Don't round; 199.5, *pats his face*; 209.7, hasno; 213.20, Ten; 217.34, *red lined*; 242.5, *Exit*.); 250.21, peeked-lookin'; 300.13, city; 300.23, office. [no closing quote] (and *passim*); 301.34–35, her. / Obviously [missing speaker]; 303.6, Part; 305.35, *awakes*; 307.1, felles; 312.6, apre; 312.36, *status*; 313.15, *take*; 315.26, they you; 317.16, fefence; 318.10, an a; 319.9, hist; 320.17, they she'd; 321.2, GIRSL *enter*; 321.6, ambarrassment; 322.1, *lefts*; 323.36, vocalize—; 328.8, dolico-clphalic; 331.7, *inhalor*; 331.34, *reeth*; 341.9, Rodny; 341.26, Babe; 342.12, *cowing*; 344.16, *Congo*; 348.25, *mods*; 350.23, Dawn; 355.25, (*Introducing*; 357.25, *the the*; 358.8, the romance and dager; 358.16, battery's; 366.6, collaterel; 381.8, *organizer* [no punctuation]; 449.22, *longue*; 512.3, let's; 512.20, GUNMEN; 548.8, *immovable!*; 567.11, *room!*; 571.34, oh!; 580.11–12, *eyes*.) // Pardon [missing speaker].

Notes

In the notes below, the reference numbers denote page and line of the present volume (the line count includes titles and headings but not spaces). No note is made for material included in standard desk-reference works. Quotations from Shakespeare are keyed to *The Riverside Shakespeare*, ed. G. Blakemore Evans (Boston: Houghton Mifflin, 1974). For further information on the musicals included in the present volume and their creators, and references to other studies, see: Steven Bach, *Dazzler: The Life and Times of Moss Hart* (New York: Alfred A. Knopf, 2001); Laurence Bergreen, *As Thousands Cheer: The Life of Irving Berlin* (New York: Viking, 1990); Todd Decker, *Show Boat: Performing Race in an American Musical* (New York: Oxford University Press, 2012); Miles Kreuger, *Show Boat: The Story of a Classic American Musical* (New York: Oxford University Press, 1977); William McBrien, *Cole Porter: A Biography* (New York: Alfred A. Knopf, 1998); Jeffrey Magee, *Irving Berlin's American Musical Theater* (New York: Oxford University Press, 2012); Laurence Maslon, *The South Pacific Companion* (New York: Simon & Schuster, 2008); Harold Meyerson and Ernie Harburg, *Who Put the Rainbow in "The Wizard of Oz"?* (Ann Arbor: University of Michigan Press, 1993); Amanda Vaill, *Somewhere: The Life of Jerome Robbins* (New York: Broadway, 2006); Max Wilk, *OK! The Story of Oklahoma!* (New York: Grove Press, 1993).

The editor would like to thank Ted Chapin, Bruce Pomahac, Bert Fink and Victoria Traube of the Rodgers & Hammerstein Organization; Mark Eden Horowitz of the Music Division of the Library of Congress; Robert Kimball; Ernie Harburg; Nick Markovich, archivist of the Yip Harburg Foundation; Steve Nelson; Susan Ivory; Sheldon Harnick; Charles Kopelman and Sarah Douglas of Abrams Artists; Keith Edwards; Tom Lehrer; Jack Viertel; Tom Lisanti and the staff of the New York Public Library for the Performing Arts for their advice and assistance in selecting and preparing *American Musicals (1927–1969)*.

SHOW BOAT

Show Boat was the most advanced and adventurous musical of its day. As Stephen Sondheim put it, in the documentary *Broadway: The American Musical*, "What Oscar [Hammerstein] did was to marry European operetta and American musical comedy tradition. One of the reasons *Show Boat* turned out as well as it did is that [Jerome] Kern knew what Oscar was trying to do, and he was just as interested in doing it—attempting to tell some kind of story about character."

The novelist and playwright Edna Ferber first became interested in the performance tradition of the floating show boats in 1925, and spent months researching the few still-existing show boats along the North Carolina tidewaters. Her novel *Show Boat* was serialized in *Woman's Home Companion* beginning in April 1926, and appeared in book form from Doubleday in August of that year.

Jerome Kern read the novel in October, and immediately saw it as the kind of material he was looking for, more textured, serious, and inherently musical than the star-oriented vehicles of the 1920s. On October 12, during the intermission of the new musical *Criss Cross* (for which Kern had written the music), the composer was introduced to Ferber by critic Alexander Woollcott and broached the idea of adapting her book into a musical. Although Ferber initially expressed reservations about the appropriateness of her large-scale novel for the musical stage, she came to an agreement with Kern and his collaborator, Oscar Hammerstein II. (Kern had written to Hammerstein: "Would you like to do a show for Ziegfeld? It's got a million dollar title: *Show Boat*." Hammerstein immediately said yes.)

Kern and Hammerstein worked quickly and by November 29 auditioned a first act for producer Florenz Ziegfeld, who wrote a telegram the next day to a tenor he was hoping to interest in the role of Gaylord Ravenal: "This is the best musical comedy I have ever been fortunate to get hold of; it looks wonderful, and there are two of the greatest parts that have ever been written." Kern and Hammerstein signed contracts with Ziegfeld on December 11, promising a working script by January 1, 1927, for a proposed mid-April premiere. Ziegfeld's experience with getting shows up and onstage quickly did not prepare him for the care and time that Kern and Hammerstein would need to adapt a sprawling narrative to the stage, so the creators and the producer argued frequently about the timetable.

Hammerstein's task of bringing Ferber's nineteen-chapter novel to the musical stage was without precedent in the American theater. No serious work of fiction with such narrative scope had previously been adapted into a musical. Ferber's novel was elaborate in structure, beginning in 1889, moving back and forth in chronology, and featuring lengthy digressions that Hammerstein was obliged to elide. He retained the novel's major through-lines, while softening some of its more tragic elements, such as the death of Cap'n Andy and other important characters. Ferber's Ellie Chipley is far less sympathetic to Julie's plight as the victim of antimiscegenation laws, and in the novel Julie herself ends up not as a ruined singer in Chicago, but as a haggard secretary to Chicago's most notorious madam.

The novel's last three chapters, bringing the story into the 1920s and with action occurring in several different cities, provided the most trouble for Hammerstein. Most of the rewriting in early drafts of *Show Boat* involved various attempts to condense the action. For example, in the earliest extant draft (dated to 1927), the penultimate scene in Act Two (set in 1926) has Cap'n Andy and Ravenal bringing each other up to date, with Andy recounting that Joe and Queenie's grandson has grown up to become the famous singer Paul Robeson. (The intention was to have Robeson himself come onstage at this point to give a brief recital.) Robeson had been actively sought by Kern and Hammerstein to

play Joe, and his professional commitments contributed to a delay in the production schedule; as it turned out, Joe was played by Jules Bledsoe, although
Robeson appeared in several subsequent versions, beginning with the London
production of 1928.

Show Boat made its out-of-town debut at the National Theatre in Washington, D.C., on November 15, with a running time of over four hours. The
collaborators continued to revise the musical as it proceeded to Pittsburgh and
Cleveland, shortening it considerably, and its form was largely set by the time it
opened in Philadelphia on December 5. *Show Boat* finally arrived in New York
on December 27 at the new Ziegfeld Theatre, designed by Joseph Urban, who
was also responsible for the show's stage design. (Ziegfeld cut short the run
of the theater's opening attraction, *Rio Rita*, to make way for *Show Boat*.) The
musical ran for 577 performances and was so successful that Ziegfeld revived it
on Broadway as early as 1932.

Show Boat was filmed in 1929, 1936, and 1951. There were Broadway revivals
in 1946, 1983, and 1994, and it was also performed at New York City Center
in 1948 and 1954. In 1988, a three-CD recording of the score released on EMI
Records (supervised, conducted, and directed by John McGlinn in consulta-
tion with Miles Kreuger) contained every variation in the score written or
authorized by Kern and Hammerstein.

5.3 *Natchez*] In the 1946 production of *Show Boat*, Natchez was replaced by
Greenville.

5.11 Niggers all work] Beginning with Paul Robeson's performance as Joe in
the 1928 London production of *Show Boat* (and continuing through his subsequent performances in the 1930 Broadway revival and the 1936 film), there was
strong resistance among black cast members to singing these lyrics as written.
Thus the creators (and other hands) variously changed this reference to "Darkies all work," "Colored folk work," or "Here we all work" in stage and film
productions up to the present day.

10.20 Rubber-Face Smith] The character of Rubber-Face was played by
Francis X. Mahoney in the original 1927 production of *Show Boat*. Mahoney
(1884–1948) was a former carnival performer with elastic features; when he
was not available to play the part in subsequent productions the character was
frequently cut.

14.14–15 *The Heart of an Ethiopian*] An invented melodrama.

17.15 *The Village Drunkard*] An invented melodrama.

24.34 *coon shuffle*] In the 1936 film of *Show Boat*, Irene Dunne as Magnolia
performs the step in this number.

25.20 SCENE 3] This scene was cut in its entirety for the 1946 production.
Background exposition about Ravenal's past and the miscegenation laws was
placed variously in Act One, Scene 1 and Scene 4 (subsequently Scene 3) and
the song "Life Upon the Wicked Stage" was placed into the subsequent Scene

3 with a minor change in context. "Till Good Luck Comes My Way" was cut entirely.

31.31 SCENE 4] During *Show Boat*'s first out-of-town tryout—in Washington, D.C., in November 1927—this scene began with Queenie, Julie, and the black chorus (the Jubilee Singers) singing "Mis'ry's Comin' Aroun'." The number was subsequently cut, though the music, reportedly among Kern's favorites, was retained in the original overture and four lines of the text are sung later in the scene. For the complete text of the lyrics, see pages 611–612 in this volume.

36.17 miscegenation case] An 1880 Mississippi statute made the marriage of "a white person and a negro or mulatto or person who shall have one-fourth or more of negro blood" a crime punishable by up to ten years in state prison. The 1890 state constitution extended the prohibition to persons having "one-eighth or more of negro blood," and antimiscegenation laws remained in effect in Mississippi until the 1967 U.S. Supreme Court decision in *Loving v. Virginia*.

36.28 Julie—Dozier] Elsewhere in *Show Boat* the character is introduced as Miss Julia La Verne, presumably a stage name.

42.35 East Lynne] A stage adaptation of the 1861 sensation novel of the same title, by English writer Mrs. Henry Wood (Ellen Wood, 1814–1857).

46.8 "I Might Fall Back on You"] This song was cut in the 1946 production. A bit of whimsical dialogue between Frank and Ellie and the addition of some admiring young girls allowed for "Life Upon the Wicked Stage" (cut from Act One, Scene 3) to be interpolated in its place.

48.25 dicky] Probably a variant of "dicty"—African American slang for "fashionable."

49.27–28 The Parson's Bride] An invented melodrama.

54.37 Camilleys] Camille—the title character of many English-language adaptations of *La Dame aux camélias*, a widely popular 1848 novel by Alexandre Dumas *fils* (1824–1895)—was an epitome of the fallen woman.

55.6 olio] This was part of a vaudeville (or showboat) performance, where a curtain was dropped between sections of a longer melodrama or narrative show. The curtain usually was adorned with advertisements and singers or dancers performed various musical numbers while the scenery was changed.

55.12 SCENE 7] In the 1936 film *Show Boat*, Kern and Hammerstein added the original song "I Have the Room Above Her."

57.32 SCENE 8] In the 1946 production of *Show Boat*, the wedding ensemble's choruses were significantly cut.

58.32 Know we're . . . congratulate you!] A technical note follows this line in Hammerstein's production script of *Show Boat*: "(At this point the lyric is split into parts for sopranos, altos, tenors, and basses which can not be indicated clearly here.)"

61.6–8   ANDY *arranges . . .* FALLS.)] The concluding stage direction was emended in 1946 to read: "Girls pull carriage and flowers are tossed from upper deck—Everyone following carriage and waving as—THE CURTAIN FALLS."

62.3   *The Midway Plaisance . . . Fair—1893*] The World's Columbian Exposition, celebrating the four hundredth anniversary of Columbus's discovery of America, ran from May until the end of October; it was attended by more than twenty-five million people. This scene takes place along the Midway Plaisance, a mile-long promenade at the fair featuring foreign and private exhibitions and sideshow attractions.

62.7–8   *"World's Congress of Beauty"*] An exhibit of women's fashion from around the world, featuring "40 Ladies from 40 Nations."

62.10   *Dahomey Village*] An exhibition simulating a village of the Fon tribe of Dahomey (now Benin), occupied by about one hundred Dahomeans who performed songs and dances, reenacted battles, and sold souvenirs; Frederick Douglass complained they were "African savages brought here to act the monkey."

62.12–13   "couchie-couchie" . . . *Streets of Cairo*"] "The Streets of Cairo," an exhibition simulating the atmosphere of a Middle Eastern city, featured replicas of mosques and other Arab-Islamic buildings as well as camel rides, musicians, and street performers. The most famous of these performers was "Little Egypt," a belly dancer who performed the "Hootchy-Kootchy" dance. "Little Egypt" was actually three different performers during the course of the fair, including Fatima Djamile, whose "Coochee Coochee Dance" was filmed by Edison in 1896.

62.17–18   HETTY CHILSON . . . *in tow*] In Edna Ferber's novel *Show Boat* (1926) and in an early draft of the musical, Chilson is the madam of an elegant Chicago brothel; Ravenal frequents and Julie ultimately resides in her establishment. The character and her scenes were cut before *Show Boat* arrived onstage, but she makes a brief appearance here.

63.7   Sandow] Eugen Sandow (1867–1925), a German bodybuilder and strongman, made his American debut at the Columbian Exposition in 1893; he was managed there by Florenz Ziegfeld Jr., the eventual producer of *Show Boat*.

67.25   the Palmer House] One of Chicago's major hotels, built in 1875.

67.27   Rector's] Rector's Oyster House, a famous Chicago restaurant.

71.13   *"Good Morning Carrie!"*] A 1901 song in "Negro" dialect composed by Chris Smith (1879–1949) and Elmer Bowman (c. 1879–1916), with lyrics by Richard C. McPherson (1883–1944).

74.4   the Trocadero] A "music garden" and vaudeville stage owned by Florenz Ziegfeld Sr. (1841–1923), the father of *Show Boat*'s producer.

76.35   "Bill"] "Bill" was written originally for *Oh Lady! Lady!!*, a 1919 musical comedy by Jerome Kern and P. G. Wodehouse. It was dropped out of town at the last minute. The song resurfaced a year later in a flop called *Zip Goes a Million* but was also cut. The song was resurrected a second time for *Show Boat* as a second-act torch song for Helen Morgan. With some further doctoring by both Kern and Hammerstein (and a contractual credit to Wodehouse), the song found a permanent place in the show.

79.11   Coon songs] A subgenre of ragtime music, extremely popular from 1880 until its precipitous decline around 1910. It played on African American stereotypes, often with a black narrator or a situation in which there was some calamity that needed to be solved.

83.28   *She starts to march off*] In the 1946 revival of *Show Boat*, a final line was added for Kim: "Yes, Daddy—I'll tell her."

83.33   SCENE 5] This "front cloth" scene was cut in 1946 and has rarely been restored.

85.32–33   *Ballet dance in progress*] In 1927, the entertainment at the Trocadero began with a dance by the Sidell Sisters, Violet ("Billie," 1904–1989) and Piera (b. 1908–?). In the 1946 revival they were replaced by the team of "Schultz and Schultz."

86.1–2   a Parisian novelty, the Apache Dance] A dramatic, violent dance inspired by Les Apaches, a fin-de-siècle Parisian street gang.

86.5   "Goodbye, My Lady Love"] Popular song (1904) by Joseph E. Howard (1878–1961).

88.14   "After the Ball"] Popular song (1891) by Charles K. Harris (1867–1930). It was unusual for a composer of Kern's eminence to interpolate other song-writers' work into an original score.

89.20   SCENE 7] This "front cloth" scene was cut from the 1946 production of *Show Boat*; Joe's reprise of "Ol' Man River" was moved into what had been Scene 8.

89.22   *"Lindbergh Arrives in Mexico City"*] Charles Lindbergh (1902–1974) arrived in Mexico on December 14, 1927, after a nonstop flight from Washington, D.C.; *Show Boat* opened on Broadway on December 27.

89.26   "Ol' Man River"] In the 1936 film version of *Show Boat*, Kern and Hammerstein wrote a new song for Paul Robeson (Joe), "Ah Still Suits Me."

90.7–9   Folks git mad . . . what for] In the 1946 revival of *Show Boat* these lines were altered as follows:

> Wars go on an' some folks die.
> De res' ferget
> De reason why.

92.1   SCENE 8] In early drafts of *Show Boat*, Hammerstein experimented with scenes in which Kim took New York City café society by storm. In one, she sings at a cocktail party accompanied by a talented young jazz pianist named George.

95.5–17   imitation of your mother . . . *imitation.*] The imitations given by Kim are of contemporary entertainers: actress Ethel Barrymore (1879–1959), bandleader Ted Lewis (1890–1971), and, apparently, revue star Beatrice Lillie (1894–1989). "That's all there is" was Ethel Barrymore's catchphrase, supposedly first said when an applauding audience wouldn't leave the theater at the end of one of her shows. Norma Terris, the actress who played both Kim and Magnolia in *Show Boat* in 1927, counted imitations among her specialties; in subsequent productions without Terris, these imitations were replaced with new songs, including "Dance Away the Night" (London, 1928) and "Nobody Else But Me" (New York revival, 1946; see also pages 614–615).

95.39   mid-Victrola!] Changed to "illegitimate!" for the 1946 revival of *Show Boat*.

AS THOUSANDS CHEER

As Thousands Cheer represents the best, and one of the last, examples of the revue form. In addition, as a time capsule of America's social and cultural preoccupations in the early 1930s—created by Irving Berlin and Moss Hart at the peak of their powers—the show is without peer.

The revue form—which alternated sketches, songs, and dance numbers—had been a staple of the Broadway musical scene since the early twentieth century. Annual revues produced by the likes of Florenz Ziegfeld and (after World War I) George White, Earl Carroll, and Irving Berlin constituted the most elaborate and popular offerings of any given theatrical season. The revue was a fertile ground for originating the popular songs that would make up the American Songbook. Such Irving Berlin classics as "Say It With Music," "All Alone," and "What'll I Do?," for example, were first heard in several revues that Berlin produced in the 1920s at his Music Box Theatre on West 45th Street.

As Thousands Cheer appeared at the tail end of the revue era and was the second collaboration between Berlin and Moss Hart, who had written the book for the musical comedy *Face the Music* in 1932. As Hart told *The New York Times* in October 1933, "the idea for *As Thousands Cheer* was broached to me by Mr. Berlin more than a year ago, before I had journeyed westward to the city of dreadful night known as Hollywood. We both agreed that we had no desire to do a conventional sort of revue with the usual blackout sketches, songs and dances. So we hit upon the idea of writing a topical revue right off the front pages of the newspapers." Berlin and Hart signed a contract with producer Sam H. Harris in December 1932, and in late April 1933 the pair travelled to Bermuda to work on the show. After a few weeks—looking through recent newspapers for material to work with—they had finished a first act and laid out a second. "Whatever satire there may be in the piece," Berlin told an interviewer, was "really implicit in the news items." In the production, each song or sketch was introduced by a projected newspaper headline, one that either contextualized the material to follow or provided an ironic contrast.

Berlin's clout and the ambitiousness of the piece allowed them to cast many leading revue performers of the period, including Marilyn Miller, Clifton Webb, Ethel Waters, and Helen Broderick. Berlin and Hart made a number of important changes to the initial script during late summer rehearsals in New York and a two-week tryout at Philadelphia's Forrest Theatre beginning September 9. Typically for the revue format, the tryout necessitated a good deal of reordering and refocusing of the musical numbers. The intended finale, "Park Avenue Takes Up Skating Craze," was to feature the entire cast on roller skates, but the technical challenges of having the cast perform the number proved insurmountable and the scene (including the song "Skate With Me") was cut. "Revolt in Cuba," a dance number reflecting recent news stories, was added during Philadelphia tryouts. Another such late addition was the head-line sketch "Josephine Baker Still the Rage of Paris," which concluded with Waters's song "Harlem on My Mind." Waters's performance was so strong that Clifton Webb, who followed her with "Through a Keyhole" in the sketch "Broadway Gossip Columnist," threatened to quit unless Waters's number was dropped or moved, or a new one written for him. After some contentious discussion *As Thousands Cheer* opened with "Through a Keyhole" following "Harlem on My Mind," although within months Webb's number was dropped from the show entirely.

As Thousands Cheer opened at the Music Box on September 30, 1933, and ran for four hundred performances. It was the second biggest hit of Berlin's prewar career, running only forty performances fewer than *The Music Box Revue of 1921*. There was a subsequent national tour. It was never filmed or revived on Broadway; the 1943 MGM film *Thousands Cheer* bears no relation to the Berlin/ Hart musical, although songs from the show appear in such films as *Easter Parade*, *Blue Skies*, and *Alexander's Ragtime Band*.

106.33   the Drys] Supporters of Prohibition, which would be repealed on December 5, 1933.

107.5   Arthur Brisbane] Brisbane (1864–1936) was an editor, columnist, and essayist, most notably for the Hearst syndicates' *New York Journal*. His daily column, "Today," was read by millions.

107.15–18   Heywood Broun . . . June] Broun (1888–1939) often used his column "It Seems to Me," in the New York *World-Telegram*, to focus attention on social injustices.

107.20   Walter Lippmann] Lippmann (1889–1974) was one of the most influential political journalists and columnists of his time; he wrote for the *New York World*, and from 1931 on, the *New York Herald Tribune*.

107.30–33   Winchell's . . . "mom"] Winchell (1897–1972), a radio personality and author of the gossip column "On Broadway" for the *New York Daily*

Mirror, frequently made announcements of pregnancies ("infanticipation"), births ("blessed event"), and divorces ("Reno-vation").

108.3–4 FRANKLIN D. ROOSEVELT INAUGURATED TOMORROW] In the 1932 presidential election, Democratic nominee Franklin D. Roosevelt defeated the Republican incumbent Herbert Hoover by 57.4 to 39.6 percent of the popular vote. Hoover and his wife read the returns at their Palo Alto home.

109.20–21 (*It is Washington.*)] The stage direction has been added to the present volume; it does not appear in the original production typescript of *As Thousands Cheer.*

110.18 Ogden Mills] Mills (1884–1937) succeeded Andrew Mellon as Hoover's secretary of the Treasury on February 12, 1932.

110.37 A medicine ball] Hoover often played an arduous version of volleyball (using a medicine ball) with his staff on the South Lawn of the White House; they became known as the Medicine Ball Cabinet.

111.4 Charlie Curtis] Charles Curtis (1860–1936) served as Hoover's vice president. He was of Kaw tribe extraction.

111.7 Dolly Gann] Dorothy Curtis Gann (1863–1953) was Vice President Curtis's half sister; when Curtis's wife died, she assumed the role of his social ambassador. When she "pulled rank" over other congressional wives at state dinners and functions, she created a scandal that embarrassed Curtis.

111.13–14 Andrew Mellon and Henry Stimson] Mellon (1855–1937), a wealthy industrialist, served as Hoover's secretary of the Treasury until February 12, 1932; he resigned his position after impeachment proceedings were begun against him in Congress and accepted an appointment as ambassador to the Court of St. James. Stimson (1867–1950) was secretary of state.

112.22–23 Tony's wife . . . wife] From "Tony's Wife," a popular song (1933) by Harold Adamson (1906–1980) and Burton Lane (1912–1977).

112.25 Fit as a fiddle . . . love] From "Fit as a Fiddle (And Ready for Love)," a popular song (1932) by Arthur Freed (1894–1973), Al Hoffman (1902–1960), and Al Goodhart (1905–1955).

112.31–32 BARBARA HUTTON TO WED PRINCE MDIVANI] Hutton (1912–1979), sheltered heiress to the Woolworth fortune, met the recently divorced Georgian aristocrat and fortune-hunter Alexis Mdivani (1905–1935) during a springtime tour of the Far East in 1933; they were married in June in a lavish Paris ceremony.

114.18–19 "Heat Wave" . . . Waters] Waters was accompanied, as she sang this number, by the dancers Letitia Ide and José Limón, who were choreographed by Charles Weidman.

115.18–19 JOAN CRAWFORD . . . FAIRBANKS, JR.] Joan Crawford (1904–1977), Hollywood actress and former Broadway chorus girl, married

Douglas Fairbanks Jr. (1909–2000)—the son of movie stars Douglas Fairbanks and Mary Pickford—in June of 1929. They were a glamorous couple and made one film together, *Our Modern Maidens* (1929). By 1932, Crawford had begun an affair with costar Clark Gable and despite attempts at reconciliation (abetted by, among others, Crawford's boss at MGM, studio chief Louis B. Mayer), the couple divorced on May 12, 1933.

115.22   WILL HAYS] Beginning in 1922, former postmaster general Hays (1879–1954) became president of the Motion Pictures Producers and Distributors of America, a self-regulating group that attempted to enforce morality in Hollywood; in 1930, Hays would oversee what was called the Production Code, a specific list of rules and regulations often called "the Hays Code."

116.18–19   the Brown Derby or the Cocoanut Grove] Los Angeles restaurants popular with film industry celebrities.

117.17–18   Constance Bennett's] Bennett (1904–1965), a two-time divorcee when *As Thousands Cheer* opened on Broadway, had recently starred in films, including *The Easiest Way* (1931) and *What Price Hollywood?* (1932).

117.19–21   Ruth Chatterton's . . . Forbes] Chatterton (1892–1961), an Academy Award nominee for *Madame X* (1932), divorced Forbes (1904–1951), a serviceable but less prominent actor in action films and melodramas, in 1932; the day after the divorce was finalized she married her frequent costar George Brent.

118.38   Mary Pickford–Douglas Fairbanks separation] Mary Pickford (1892–1979) and Douglas Fairbanks (1883–1939), both leading stars of the silent era, separated in 1933; neither had supported Fairbanks Jr.'s marriage to Crawford.

119.14   Louie B. Mayer] Mayer (1884–1957) headed Metro-Goldwyn-Mayer beginning in 1924.

120.2–8   to discuss the debts . . . lovely conference] The United States, which had loaned Allied nations approximately eleven billion dollars during World War I, had consistently rejected European calls for debt forgiveness and proposed several repayment schemes during the 1920s. In December 1932, Congress rejected a solution agreed upon by England, France, and Germany at the Lausanne Conference earlier in the year, to link forgiveness of German reparation payments to forgiveness of other war debt. Debt forgiveness was again on the agenda at the London Economic Conference of June–July 1933, but the issue was never formally resolved, and every Allied debtor but Finland defaulted.

120.29   Off the Gold Standard] President Roosevelt took the United States off the gold standard by executive order on April 5, 1933.

122.1–3   WORLD'S WEALTHIEST . . . BIRTHDAY] John D. Rockefeller (1839–1937) celebrated his ninety-fourth birthday on July 8, 1933; he had earned his extraordinary fortune as a cofounder and president of Standard Oil. He had a propensity for handing out dimes to little children and frequently to adults as well.

122.26   to build that thing] In 1928, John D. Rockefeller Jr. (1874–1960), heir to the Rockefeller fortune, leased a parcel of land between Fifth and Sixth avenues in Manhattan, from 48th to 51st streets. He intended a grand complex of buildings that would include the Metropolitan Opera as its centerpiece, but the Met later withdrew from the project. Rockefeller continued with what would become one of the largest real estate developments in the city's history: fourteen Art Deco office buildings taking up three city blocks. Construction began in 1930 and would eventually cost Rockefeller, who financed the project personally, a quarter of a billion dollars. Rockefeller Center's folly was initially compounded by the vast decrease in the need for office space during the Depression.

125.29   Muscle Shoals] A small Alabama city that experienced a boom in real estate speculation after Henry Ford, in 1921, proposed to buy the nearby Wilson Dam and to develop the city into a major metropolis.

126.7   Roxy] Samuel Lionel Rothafel (1882–1936), nicknamed "Roxy," a prominent theatrical impresario with whom Rockefeller Jr. collaborated on the construction of Radio City Music Hall, a mammoth 6,201-seat theater that opened on December 27, 1932.

127.14   THE FUNNIES] In this number, a little girl (played by Marilyn Miller) reads the Sunday papers and various comic strip characters leap off the pages.

128.1   Katzenjammers] From *The Katzenjammer Kids*, a comic strip created by Rudolph Dirks (1887–1968) and drawn by Harold H. Knerr (1882–1949) from 1912 to 1949.

128.3   "Bringing Father Up,"] *Bringing Up Father*, comic strip (1913–2000) created and originally drawn by George McManus (1884–1954).

128.4   "Skippy"] Comic strip (1923–45) by Percy Crosby (1891–1964).

128.11   The Dempseys or the Tunneys] Professional boxers like Jack Dempsey (1893–1983) or Gene Tunney (1897–1978).

128.19–20   GREEN PASTURES STARTS THIRD ROAD SEASON] *The Green Pastures* by Marc Connelly (1890–1980) opened in May of 1930 and subsequently ran for 640 performances, making it one of the most successful plays of the 1930s. It also toured in nearly every city in America until 1935. The conceit of Connelly's play was to cast a series of stories from the Old Testament as they would have been imagined by a group of black children in the rural South. One critic called it a "celestial fish fry" and the play had easily the largest African American cast of its time, playing various characters from the Bible. "De Lawd" was played by Richard B. Harrison (1864–1935), whose prior career had included the recitation of dramatic monologues and Shakespeare's soliloquies; the aspiring actor in this skit is apparently a spoof of Harrison.

An early draft of *As Thousands Cheer* now at the Wisconsin Historical Society contains the following variant opening:

ETHEL: I'm getting mighty fed up with all this Shakespeare stuff and I ain't just talking. What d'ya think you're doing, boy? You ain't gonna play "Hamlet"—you ain't even going back to "Green Pastures" if I have anything to say in this flat. Boy, that show sure ruined you. Coming around here and talking about Marc Connelly and F.P.A. I don't care that you saw George Kaufman getting out of a taxi—he don't mean anything up in Harlem.

MAN: How do you expect me to capture the essence of this if you keep interrupting with me all the time? What's the matter with you?

130.8–10 ROTOGRAVURE SECTION . . . 1883] Newspapers of the 1930s often included pictorial inserts printed by the sepia-toned rotogravure process; the process was first adopted by *The New York Times* in 1912. This musical number dramatized a New York Easter parade of 1883, with scenery and costumes in various shades of brown and gray. "Easter Parade" borrowed its melody from a song Irving Berlin had written in 1917, "Smile and Show Your Dimple."

132.2–3 METROPOLITAN OPERA . . . SPLENDOR] The Metropolitan Opera Radio broadcasts began in 1931, with the first transmission of a full opera (*Tristan und Isolde*) in March 1933 on the NBC radio network. Initial sponsors included the American Tobacco Company and Listerine, but the Depression made sponsorship sporadic until Texaco underwrote the series in 1940.

132.22 Mr. Belmont] August Belmont Jr. (1853–1924), a prominent financier and sportsman.

132.24–28 Mr. Rubin . . . famous] Arnold Reuben (1883–1970), the German-born proprietor of Reuben's Delicatessen, has been credited with the invention of the reuben sandwich, made of corned beef and melted Swiss cheese.

132.29–31 Mr. Klein . . . Union Square] S. Klein on the Square was one of New York's most popular bargain-priced department stores.

133.1 William Fox] Fox (1879–1952), who began his career as an entrepreneur in the garment industry, founded Fox Film Corporation in 1915 but lost control of the company in the wake of the market crash of 1929, and filed for bankruptcy in 1932.

133.2–3 Nat Lewis . . . socks] Lewis (c. 1882–1956) owned a famous haberdashery to the stars in the Theatre District.

135.20–21 UNKNOWN NEGRO . . . MOB] In 1932, the NAACP recorded eleven lynchings in the South; other sources list as many as twenty-eight in the year 1933.

136.13–14 GANDHI GOES ON NEW HUNGER STRIKE] In May 1933, Mahatma Gandhi (1869–1948) started a twenty-one-day hunger strike against British authorities while in prison to protest their treatment of the Untouchables in India. He had also participated in highly publicized hunger strikes in

1926 and 1932. In an earlier draft of this sketch, Gandhi is seated in a restaurant, photographed by the press while abstaining from dinner; an obnoxious British couple sits next to him and orders a four-course meal.

137.20 Aimee Semple McPherson] McPherson (1890–1944) was a travelling evangelist and preacher who settled in Los Angeles in 1923 and built the Angelus Temple as a cornerstone for her work. The church held 5,300 people and when she preached, it was filled to capacity three times each day, seven days a week. She founded the International Gospel of the Foursquare Church and owned her own radio station. A masterly manipulator of the media, she became a national celebrity with her highly dramatic sermons and tent meetings. In 1926, she was the purported victim of a kidnapping, the circumstances of which are still unknown.

138.18 *She Done Him Wrong*] A 1933 box office hit starring Mae West (1893–1980), based on her play *Diamond Lil* (1928).

139.11 a safety pin] Ostensibly holding up Gandhi's dhoti.

139.32 "Pale hands I loved"] The beginning of "Kashmiri Song" by British composer Amy Woodforde-Finden (1860–1919), from her 1902 collection *Four Indian Love Lyrics*; the text was taken from a 1901 poem by Ada Florence Nicolson (1865–1904), published under the pseudonym Laurence Hope.

139.35 *42nd Street*] A 1933 Warner Brothers musical starring Warner Baxter and Ruby Keeler and featuring the choreography of Busby Berkeley (1895–1976).

140.14–15 REVOLT IN CUBA . . . Dance] José Limón dancers dramatized a recent populist uprising against Cuban dictator Gerardo Machado (1871–1939).

140.16–18 NOEL COWARD . . . ENGLAND] Coward (1899–1973), British playwright, actor, and composer, had eleven separate productions of plays and revues on Broadway from 1925 to 1933; he acted in four of them.

141.10–15 *Design for Living* . . . each other] Coward's 1933 play *Design for Living*, in which he starred with Alfred Lunt and Lynn Fontanne, chronicles what one character refers to as a "three-sided erotic hodge-podge" involving a designer, a playwright, and a painter; it was considered mildly scandalous at the time.

141.33 that Mr. Lonsdale] Frederick Lonsdale (1881–1954), British playwright who wrote several comedies of manners in the 1920s, including *Aren't We All?* (1923), *The Last of Mrs. Cheyney* (1925), and *On Approval* (1927).

143.12 medieval megaphone] See Coward's *Design for Living* (1933), Act One: "OTTO: What is a wimple? / LEO: A sort of medieval megaphone, made of linen. Guinevere had one."

143.33 "Destiny's Tot."] A sobriquet given to Coward by the American theater critic, essayist, and raconteur Alexander Woollcott.

144.21   Max Gordon] Gordon (1892–1978) was a highly successful Broadway producer from the 1920s on.

144.29   Elsa Maxwell] Maxwell (1883–1963) was a prominent society hostess and gossip columnist.

144.36   *Cavalcade*] Coward's 1931 play—a major hit and subsequently an Academy Award–winning film (1933)—followed the lives of the members of a British household over three decades. It was not produced in the United States.

145.3–4   The Duke . . . always is.] See Coward's *Private Lives* (1930), Act One: "AMANDA: Whose yacht is that? / ELYOT: The Duke of Westminster's, I expect. It always is."

146.28   Cholly Knickerbocker] The *New York Journal-American*'s pseudonymous syndicated gossip columnist. Maury Paul (1890–1942) wrote the column from 1917 until his death in 1942, after which it was continued by others.

147.14–15   (*Curtains part . . . bed together.*)] The stage direction, not present in the original typescript of *As Thousands Cheer*, has been added for the present volume.

148.6–7   PRINCE OF WALES RUMORED ENGAGED] King George V of England and Queen Mary waited in vain for their firstborn son, Edward, the Prince of Wales, to get married and begin to consider his dynastic responsibilities more seriously. In 1933, the Prince of Wales ("David" to his immediate family) was thirty-eight years old, one of the most well-known men in the world, and an incorrigible bachelor and playboy, who had two known affairs with married women. When *As Thousands Cheer* opened, he was just embarking on another affair, unknown to the public, with an American divorcée named Mrs. Wallis Simpson, for whom he would later renounce the throne.

148.19   those stamps] George V was an accomplished philatelist, with one of the world's great collections.

150.1   *Goona-Goona*] A melodrama (1932) shot in Bali, in Technicolor, by André Roosevelt (1879–1962) and Armand Denis (1896–1971); the film featured a scantily clad native cast.

150.22–23   the N.R.A. and Samuel Insull] The National Recovery Administration, a New Deal agency established under the National Industrial Recovery Act of 1933, was charged with reregulating industrial practices and setting prices. Insull (1859–1938), a wealthy businessman whose utility and railroad holding companies collapsed during the Great Depression, was indicted for mail and wire fraud in 1932 and 1933.

150.25   Charley Dawes] Charles G. Dawes (1865–1951) served as Herbert Hoover's ambassador to Great Britain from 1929 to 1932; he caused a minor scandal by refusing to wear the knee breeches traditionally required by diplomats to the Court of St. James.

150.28–29   Woodin . . . violin] William H. Woodin (1868–1934), who served as Franklin Delano Roosevelt's secretary of the Treasury in 1933, was an accomplished violinist and composer.

151.1   the Duke of York] Prince Albert (1895–1952), who would later assume the throne as George VI after his older brother's abdication in 1936.

151.16   Mrs. Roosevelt] Following the 1932 presidential election, Eleanor Roosevelt was contracted to deliver twelve radio news commentaries for the Pond's cold cream company. She continued to broadcast into 1933 as First Lady.

151.22–23   Eddie Cantor . . . Marx Brothers] Cantor (1892–1982), Pearl (1894–1982), and Wynn (1886–1966) were all popular radio comedians of the day; Groucho (1890–1977) and Chico Marx (1887–1961) had a short-lived radio series entitled *Flywheel, Shyster, and Flywheel* in 1932 and 1933.

153.4–5   Havelock Ellis] British physician and psychologist (1859–1939) who wrote pioneering studies on homosexuality and sexual fetishes; his *Studies in the Psychology of Sex* was published in seven volumes from 1897 to 1928.

153.9–10   JOSEPHINE BAKER . . . PARIS] Josephine Baker (1906–1975) was a St. Louis–born singer and dancer who had some success in various Harlem-based revues and musicals. In 1925, she toured in Paris with a show called *La Revue Nègre* and became an immediate sensation. Her exotic dances and sensual songs made her a legendary headliner, called variously Black Venus and *La Bakhair*. She parlayed her stay in Paris into a career of major celebrity, returning briefly to the United States in 1936.

153.31   Folies Bergères] The Folies Bergère, a Paris music hall; Baker first appeared there in *La Folie du jour* in 1926.

155.10   hi-de-ho] The call-and-response refrain from Cotton Club legend Cab Calloway's 1931 song "Minnie the Moocher."

155.14   Lady Mendel] Elsie de Wolfe (c. 1865–1950), known as Lady Mendl after her marriage in 1926, a flamboyant interior designer and socialite.

PAL JOEY

Composer Richard Rodgers said that *Pal Joey* was "the first musical to deal with the facts of life." Rodgers and Lorenz Hart provided a bifurcated score that alternated brilliantly between the cheesy world of a seedy Chicago nightclub and the more sophisticated and deluded mating dances of its leading characters. If John O'Hara's book graciously stepped out of the way on occasion to allow for a few unmotivated specialty numbers in the score, *Pal Joey* still appealed to a mature audience, as *The New Yorker*'s Wolcott Gibbs noted at the time: "The idea of equipping a song-and-dance production with a few living characters behaving like human beings may no longer strike the boys in the business as merely fantastic."

It was in the October 22, 1938, issue of *The New Yorker* that John O'Hara began publishing a series of thirteen short stories centered on a Chicago-based nightclub dancer and host named Joey Evans. Written in epistolary form to his "pal Ted," Joey's letters—filled with malapropisms, misspellings, and poor grammar—detail his ups and downs trying to make it big in the Chicago nightclub world while relentlessly pursuing an unending stream of women—or "mouses," as he calls them. O'Hara claimed that he was inspired by a particularly debilitating alcoholic bender to create a character even more debauched than himself.

It was O'Hara who contacted Rodgers and Hart with the idea of creating a musical around the "Pal Joey" stories sometime between October 1939 and early 1940. By the end of the 1930s, Rodgers and Hart had emerged as the most successful and ambitious musical theater songwriting team on Broadway. Intrigued by the challenges of the Joey character and nightclub milieu, they accepted the offer and brought on board producer/director George Abbott, who had already directed and collaborated on four previous Rodgers and Hart musicals, including *The Boys from Syracuse* (1938).

The plot of O'Hara's libretto is mostly original, although it borrows the character of Linda English from "Bow Wow," the character of Melba from "A Bit of a Shock," and elaborates on an incident in "Joey and Mavis" to establish the romantic relationship between Joey and Vera Simpson. In his memoir *"Mister Abbott"* (1963), Abbott remembered O'Hara's early script as "a disorganized set of scenes without a good story line"; it required revision before rehearsals could begin. Although Hart had a fabled reputation for missed deadlines and unreliability in rehearsal, O'Hara apparently did him one better. Abbott often was forced to rewrite material in rehearsal in O'Hara's absence, and would need to wait until O'Hara's eventual reappearance for his approval. (All the stories were collected in the collection *Pal Joey*, published in September 1940, but O'Hara never returned to the Joey Evans character in print once the show opened.)

By mid-September 1940, Rodgers and Hart were half finished with their score; rehearsals began in November, with Gene Kelly, fresh from his acting success in William Saroyan's *The Time of Your Life*, as Joey, and Vivienne Segal, who had starred in Rodgers and Hart's *I Married an Angel* (1938), as Vera Simpson. The show had its out-of-town tryout in Philadelphia, December 16–22, and opened in New York at the Ethel Barrymore Theatre on December 25. Critical reaction was mixed, with *The New York Times*' Brooks Atkinson citing the milieu and characters as inappropriate for a musical comedy: "How can you draw sweet water from so foul a well?" Nevertheless *Pal Joey* ran for eleven months.

More problematic for Rodgers and Hart was a radio boycott of ASCAP-licensed songs that began January 1, 1941, and lasted ten months, as a result of which none of their new songs from *Pal Joey* received significant airplay. In the late 1940s, the song "Bewitched, Bothered and Bewildered" was rediscovered by popular bands and singers, including Doris Day, who had a big hit with the song in 1949. The success of the songs on radio and recordings led to a 1950

Columbia Records studio recording of the score—the first ever—with Vivienne Segal re-creating her role opposite Harold Lang. The Columbia recording stirred new interest in the score, which led to a 1952 stage revival starring Segal and Lang and produced by composer Jule Styne. O'Hara returned to revise several scenes in the second act and Rodgers revised several lyrics; Hart had died in 1943. (Some of these changes are noted below.) The revival received rave reviews, with Atkinson revising his original opinion, and ran for fifteen months.

Pal Joey has been revived on Broadway twice since the 1952 production, in 1977 and 2008. A 1957 film version starring Frank Sinatra significantly revised the setting and characters (Joey was turned into a singer to accommodate Sinatra), and interpolated several Rodgers and Hart tunes while deleting many others.

163.6 *finished singing*] What Joey sings as the curtain goes up is not specified in texts or the score of the 1940 *Pal Joey*, but in the 1952 revival he was given the song "Chicago" (included in the present volume on page 171).

163.7 Alice Faye?] A notably attractive film actress, Faye (1915–1998) had recently starred in *In Old Chicago* (1937), about the Chicago fire.

164.20–21 Richman . . . Crosby] Harry Richman (1895–1972), Morton Downey (1901–1985), and Bing Crosby (1903–1977) were famous tenor crooners of the 1930s.

164.31–32 Tony de Marco . . . Yolanda] Tony De Marco (1898–1965), Frank Veloz (1902–1981), and Yolanda Casazza (1908–1995) were among the leading American ballroom dancers of the 1930s and 1940s, De Marco with a succession of partners and "Veloz and Yolanda" as a husband-and-wife team.

166.10 tab show] A shortened and downsized version of a musical show, usually on tour, or used as a transitional act in a vaudeville show.

166.32 "You Mustn't Kick It Around"] The 1952 revival of *Pal Joey* included additional dialogue after this song before Gladys repeats its refrain, as follows:

MIKE: Hey, Joey, come here.
JOEY: Yeah, Mike. (*To* GIRLS.) Go ahead, keep on rehearsing.
    (MIKE *and* JOEY *exit.*)
GLADYS: Keep on rehearsing, that's what he thinks.
SANDRA: My feet hurt.
WAGNER: What does he think this is, the Follies?
KYLE: This is a hell of a way to make a living.
FRANCINE: Rehearse all day and work all night.
ADELE: You're lucky you got a job.
FRANCINE: Oh yeah.
DOTTIE: Hey, look at her—Miss Ambitious 1935.
DOLORES: My mother told me.

AD LIB: My mother told me.

SANDRA: I used to get by just showing my shape. Now I have to dance my fanny off for fifty bucks a week.

GLADYS: You said it.

WAGNER: Wish I was tall enough to be a show girl, then I wouldn't have to dance.

GLADYS: You ain't kidding.

DOTTIE: Who did you ever think I saw yesterday?

SANDRA: Who ever?

DOTTIE: Muriel, ever. She's working at Marshall Field's.

SANDRA: What as?

DOTTIE: Floorwalker.

SANDRA: Don't talk dirty.

MIKE (*enters. To* GIRLS): Come on—get up—you heard Joey. Keep on rehearsing.

GLADYS (*an aside*): This crumb is but *really* taking over.

MICKEY: Me, I think he's cute.

GLADYS: Who *don't* you think is cute?

MIKE: Come on—come on—keep on rehearsing.

171.34–36   Beatrice Lillie . . . Byfield's] Lillie (1894–1989), Coward (1899–1973), and Lawrence (1898–1952) were all prominent performers unlikely to appear at Joey's nightclub, as were many of the celebrities who frequented The Pump Room, a restaurant and bar owned by Chicago personality Ernie Byfield (1890–1950).

173.13–14   Miss Armour and Mr. Swift] Armour and Swift were leading meat-packing companies in Chicago.

176.11   *The Man Who Came to Dinner*] Kaufman and Hart's *The Man Who Came to Dinner* opened on Broadway in October 1939.

177.18–24   What is a man . . . this thing called man.] The concluding lyrics of "What is a Man" were altered when *Pal Joey* was revived in 1952, as follows:

> What is a man:
> Is he an ornament,
> Useless by day,
> Handy by night,
> Nature's mistake
> Since the world began?
>
> They're all alike,
> They're all I like,
> What is this thing called Man?

181.32   SCENE 6] During *Pal Joey*'s out-of-town tryouts, Joey performed the song "I'm Talking to My Pal" in this scene; it was cut before the show opened on Broadway. The lyrics are included in the present volume on page 616.

182.30 "Bewitched, Bothered and Bewildered"] The lyrics of this song in the present volume have been taken from *The Complete Lyrics of Lorenz Hart* (1986), which presents them in a form that probably reflects what was sung on *Pal Joey*'s opening night. In the only available typescript associated with *Pal Joey*'s original Broadway run, produced after opening night, the lyrics vary in a number of particulars. The typescript's opening verse reads as follows:

> He's a fool, and don't I know it—
> But a fool can have his charms;
> I'm in love and don't I show it,
> Like a babe in arms.
> Men are not a new sensation,
> I've done pretty well, I think;
> But this half-pint imitation
> Puts me on the blink.

The typescript's third chorus also varies:

> Sweet again
> Petite again
> And on my proverbial seat again.
> Bewitched, bothered and bewildered am I.
> What am I?
> To think that he loves me
> So hot am I.
> Bewitched, bothered and bewildered am I.
> We can fight—we start shrieking
> Always end in a row,
> Horizontally speaking is not the whole thing now.
> When your dream boat is leaking
> And your pal ain't your pal
> Geometrically speaking just keep it vertical.
> I'm dumb again
> And numb again
> Like Fanny Brice singing "Mon Homme" again.
> Bewitched, bothered and bewildered am I.

184.10 Than Roebuck is to Sears] Alvah C. Roebuck (1864–1948) and Richard Warren Sears (1863–1914) founded the mail-order retail firm Sears, Roebuck & Co. in 1893; they sold a wide range of general merchandise from compendious illustrated catalogs.

185.12–13 Albert Payson Terhune] A dog breeder and author (1872–1942) whose novel about a faithful collie, *Lad: A Dog*, was a best seller in 1919.

186.9 "Valentina"] Probably "Valentine," a song by Maurice Chevalier (1888–1972).

188.29 ("*Chez Joey Ballet.*")] The scenario for the Act One finale dance number, choreographed by Robert Alton, was not described by the authors. Costume and prop notes from the production script suggest that the finale began in the old nightclub, with Joey surrounded by waiters, scrubwomen, and dancers in rehearsal clothes. This was followed by a transition into "Chez Joey," where the clientele now included couples in evening finery, as well as "a roué," "an ambassador," and "a countess." There were also reporters and photographers. The production script also lists future film star Van Johnson and future film director Stanley Donen as appearing in the finale, along with Gene Kelly (as Joey). In his memoir "*Mister Abbott*," George Abbott credits set designer Jo Mielziner with "suggesting that the curtain of Act One be a scene in which Joey envisions his future in the magnificent club which his girl friend is going to buy him. It cost ten thousand dollars to build the set, a good deal of money in those days when a musical had a budget of one hundred thousand dollars, but I accepted the suggestion unhesitatingly."

193.13–14 colleges where Betty Grable's always going] Grable (1916–1973) was typecast in a number of college films in the late 1930s, including *Pigskin Parade* (1936), *This Way Please* (1937), *College Swing* (1938), and *Man About Town* (1939).

193.31–32 "Dardanella," "Who?"] "Dardanella" was a popular dance band song of 1919, written by Felix Bernard (1897–1944) and Johnny S. Black (1891–1936) with lyrics by Fred Fisher (1875–1942); "Who?," from the 1925 musical *Sunny*, was written by Jerome Kern (1885–1945) with lyrics by Otto Harbach (1873–1963) and Oscar Hammerstein II (1895–1960).

194.12 Pops Whiteman] Paul "Pops" Whiteman (1890–1967), a popular bandleader.

194.36–37 I've interviewed . . . Coward] Howard (1893–1943) was a leading English stage and film actor; for Coward, see note 140.14–16. In 1952, the lyric was altered to "I've interviewed Pablo Picasso / And a countess named di Frasso."

195.1 Minsky] Minsky's Burlesque, originally based in Brooklyn, moved to Times Square for the first half of the 1930s.

195.4 Miss Lee] Gypsy Rose Lee (1911–1970), the most famous striptease artist of her time, adding wit, humor, and intelligence to her act; she performed for four years at Minsky's Burlesque in Times Square during the 1930s.

195.10 Walter Lippmann] See note 107.20.

195.11 Saroyan] William Saroyan (1908–1981), playwright awarded the Pulitzer Prize for his 1939 play, *The Time of Your Life*.

195.14 Zorina] Vera Zorina (1917–2003), classically trained ballerina, later musical stage and film star. She appeared as the lead character in Rodgers and Hart's 1938 musical, *I Married an Angel*, choreographed by her husband, George Balanchine.

195.15 Cobina] Probably Cobina Wright Jr. (1921–2011), a socialite named the "most attractive girl of the 1939 season" and awarded the title of Miss Manhattan; her mother, Cobina Wright Sr. (1887–1970), was also a socialite.

195.21 Margie Hart] Hart (1913–2000), a red-haired, statuesque stripper, also performed at Minsky's.

195.25–26 Hearing Rhumba bands . . . Mrs. Perkins] Frances Perkins (1880–1965), socially progressive U.S. secretary of labor (1933–45). In 1952, the lyric was altered to "Zip! English people don't say clerk, they say clark. / Zip! Anybody who says clark is a jark."

195.30–31 Whistler's Mother, Charley's Aunt, or Shubert's brother] An iconic American painting (1871) by James McNeill Whistler (1834–1903); a British farce (1892) by Brandon Thomas (1848–1914), revived on Broadway in October 1940, shortly before the opening of *Pal Joey*; Lee Shubert (1873?–1963), Samuel S. Shubert (1875?–1905), or Jacob J. Shubert (1879?–1963), prominent theatrical managers and producers.

195.34 Sally Rand] Rand (1904–1979), burlesque stripper known for her bubble dances and fan dances.

195.36 That Stokowski] Leopold Stokowski (1882–1977), principal conductor of the Philadelphia Orchestra from 1936 to 1940, and conductor of Disney's 1939 film *Fantasia*. In 1952, "that Stokowski" was changed to "Toscanini."

195.39 Tyrone Power] Hollywood matinee idol (1914–1958).

196.1 luscious Lucius] Lucius Beebe (1902–1966), society columnist for the *New York Herald Tribune*.

195.3–4 either Mickey . . . Rooney] Mickey Mouse had recently appeared in *Fantasia* (1939), and Mickey Rooney (1920–2014) in *Love Finds Andy Hardy* (1938) and *Babes in Arms* (1939).

196.6–7 classic and choice . . . Rosita Royce] Royce (1918–1954), a dark-haired burlesque stripper, was known for her act using live doves. In 1952, the lyric was altered to "Zip! My artistic taste is classic and dear. / Zip! Who the hell's Lili St. Cyr?"

199.35 "Plant You Now, Dig You Later"] In the 1952 revival of *Pal Joey*, "Plant You Now, Dig You Later!" is reassigned to Gladys and the ladies of the chorus as a nightclub number.

203.6 Tchaikowski's "1812" sounds great] When *Pal Joey* was revived in 1952, this lyric was altered to read: "Ravel's *Bolero* works just great."

206.27 "Do It the Hard Way"] In the 1952 version of *Pal Joey*, this song was performed by Joey at the beginning of Act Two, Scene 7, and instead of Lowell's song, "Chicago" was reprised, with the word "Morocco" replacing "Chicago" in the lyrics.

216.33 *Dinner at Eight-Thirty*] A 1932 play by George S. Kaufman (1889–1961) and Edna Ferber (1885–1968), filmed in 1933, was titled *Dinner at Eight. Tonight at 8:30*, a series of short plays by Noël Coward, had appeared on Broadway in 1936.

218.22 And thanks—thanks a million.] The 1952 revival of *Pal Joey* included a final stage direction:

> He turns back to the pet shop. A Girl enters from the left, passes JOEY, stops and looks at the pets, then exits right. After she leaves, JOEY turns again toward stage left, where LINDA exited, moves left, turns slowly and exits right as the
>
> Curtain Falls

OKLAHOMA!

Rodgers and Hammerstein were already pioneers in their respective fields of music and words when they joined together in 1942 to write about pioneers in the Oklahoma territory. The result of their collaboration was to reveal new possibilities for the narrative musical. The trajectories of their characters' lives were conveyed without concession to show biz: no specialty dances, no clever-for-the-sake-of-cleverness songs, no extended gags for the supporting comedian. There was just a story, with dialogue, song, and dance complementing one another.

Oklahoma!'s source was Lynn Riggs's *Green Grow the Lilacs*, a play with American folk songs set in the Oklahoma territory at the turn of the twentieth century, which opened on Broadway at the Theatre Guild on January 26, 1931. Starring Franchot Tone as the cowboy Curly, the show ran for sixty-four performances. In July 1940, one of the Guild's coproducers, Theresa Helburn, attended a summer stock production of the play at the Westport Country Playhouse. (The folk dances for the one-week run were choreographed by Gene Kelly.) Helburn felt the play was felicitous material for a musical adaptation, and was able to interest Richard Rodgers—who, with Lorenz Hart, had written songs for the Guild's *Garrick Gaieties* in 1925—in writing the score.

Hart was not interested when Rodgers suggested adapting the Riggs play, and the two turned instead, as a follow-up to *Pal Joey*, to writing *By Jupiter* as a vehicle for Ray Bolger. Prodded by the Guild's continued investment in a musical adaptation of *Green Grow the Lilacs*, Rodgers sounded out Oscar Hammerstein to see if he would be interested in supplying the book for the project. Hammerstein himself had independently considered the play as musical material, but his songwriting partner at the time, Jerome Kern, was not compelled by the play either. After *By Jupiter*'s successful debut in June 1942, Rodgers turned one last time to Hart, who again refused to work on the new show, and so Rodgers officially became the writing partner of Oscar Hammerstein. The new team went to work in the late summer of 1942.

Hammerstein made several major changes in the source material. In the play, Curly is arrested for the murder of Jud Fry on his wedding night (in which the "shivaree" is much more violent than in the musical version), and escapes from jail in order to be with Laurey. In addition to expanding the size of the cast, Hammerstein invented the character of Will Parker and renamed Curly's nemesis, farmhand Jeeter Fry, as Jud Fry (perhaps to avoid confusion with Jeeter Lester, the leading character in the long-running play *Tobacco Road*).

The Theatre Guild spent the rest of that year arduously raising money for the production—now called *Away We Go!*—as well as hiring a director, Rouben Mamoulian, and a choreographer, Agnes de Mille. The show went into rehearsals on February 8, 1943, with a relatively unknown cast, including Alfred Drake and Joan Roberts. The show moved to New Haven for a split week of performances, March 11–13, in the process shedding one song ("Boys and Girls Like You and Me") and some dance numbers. The show moved to Boston for two weeks, March 15–27, during which time a reprise of the song "Oklahoma" was added and the title of the musical was changed. *Oklahoma!* opened at the St. James Theatre in New York on March 31, 1943.

Oklahoma! achieved a run of 2,212 performances (by far the longest in Broadway history of its time), and received an unprecedented citation from the Pulitzer Prize committee in 1944 (there was no award for drama that year). Its impact as a cultural phenomenon was broadened by the popularity of its original cast album, released by Decca Records on six 78 rpm disks. The show was presented at New York City Center in 1951 and 1953, and was revived on Broadway in 1979 and 2002. A film version, of which Rodgers and Hammerstein were the executive producers, appeared in 1955.

221.11 *Indian Territory (Now Oklahoma)*] An area in the southwestern United States that was used before the Civil War to resettle numbers of the Cherokee, Chickasaw, Choctaw, Creek, and Seminole tribes as they were forcibly removed from their lands east of the Mississippi. In 1890 Congress divided the existing territory into Oklahoma Territory in the west and Indian Territory in the east. Parcels of land not settled by the Indian tribes were opened up by Congress to white settlers in exchange for a committment to cultivate the land and make it usable for farming and livestock. Within a year, 50,000 settlers migrated into the area, nearly 3,000 square miles. Non-Indian settlers in both territories sought statehood, and in 1907 the two territories were combined to form the new state of Oklahoma.

223.4–9 *"It is a radiant . . . pass away."*] A direct quotation from the play on which *Oklahoma!* was based, Lynn Riggs's play *Green Grow the Lilacs* (1930).

225.9 Box Social] A communal charity tradition where women auction off a packed meal and the promise of their company for its consumption. In *Oklahoma!*, the men will compete to pay for the privilege of eating a box lunch with one of the young ladies in the community; the money will go to improving the local school.

228.2 Claremore] *Oklahoma!* is set in the Verdigris Valley within a few miles of Claremore, a town established in the heart of Indian Territory in the mid-1870s. By 1900, Claremore had a population of 855, a rail station, a post office, and several hotels. It became the county seat of Rogers County in 1907, when Oklahoma achieved statehood.

229.26   Bushyhead] Named for a former chief of the Cherokee Nation, Bushy-head is approximately thirteen miles northeast of Claremore.

238.5   Persian] Although the character of Ali Hakim refers to himself as "Persian," it has been the stage performance tradition that the character be played by a recognizably Jewish actor, with Jewish (or Yiddish) diction and inflections. In *Green Grow the Lilacs*' original production, the character (known only as "The Peddler" in the credits) was played by Lee Strasberg; in the original *Oklahoma!*, the character was played by Joseph Buloff, who had started his American career playing over two hundred roles (in Yiddish) at Maurice Schwartz's Yiddish Art Theatre.

238.16   Catoosie] Catoosa, a small cattle town at the basin of the Verdigris Valley.

257.10   Quapaw] The largest town in northeastern Oklahoma, across the border from Kansas; seventy miles from Claremore.

259.11   Dutch rub] Grabbing someone around the neck, and pulling him under your arm with one hand while you drag your knuckles across his scalp with the other hand.

263.36   Police Gazette] The *National Police Gazette* (1845–1977) reported sensationally on prostitution, vice squads, outlaws, and murder cases; its covers often featured engravings or photographs of scantily clad women.

284.20   Darby and Jones] Darby and Joan are a proverbial married couple whose devotion runs into their twilight years. The phrase made its first appearance in a 1735 poem entitled "The Joys of Love never forgot" by Henry Sampson Woodfall. It became a Victorian commonplace and was used in Oscar Hammerstein's 1937 ballad (music by Jerome Kern) "The Folks Who Live on the Hill."

288.13   shivoree] Also spelled *shivaree* or *charivari*: a mock serenade to newly-wed couples, usually in a boisterous and intentionally disrespectful manner.

ON THE TOWN

The Second World War opened the door for a new generation of Broadway songwriters: Lerner and Loewe, Frank Loesser, Jule Styne, and others. At about the time the tide was turning to the Allies' favor overseas, *On the Town* introduced an impossibly young team to the Theatre District: Leonard Bernstein, Betty Comden, and Adolph Green, inspired and overseen by Jerome Robbins. Their twenty-four-hour snapshot of a nation at war buoyed the weary spirits of New York and beyond. As Adolph Green put it, *On the Town* was "about the feeling of what a brief moment life and joy can be."

Choreographer Jerome Robbins had made his American Ballet Theatre debut on April 18, 1944, at the Metropolitan Opera House with a dance piece entitled *Fancy Free*, performed as part of a bill of short works, and featuring music by Bernstein and set design by Oliver Smith. The contemporary vignette of three sailors on shore leave trying to impress various girls at a local bar was an immediate sensation, and the Ballet Theatre extended the bill's run in its repertory.

Almost immediately after the run concluded, Smith and a relatively untried producer named Paul Feigay persuaded Robbins and Bernstein to turn their dance scenario into a full-length musical comedy. After several false starts with different book writers and lyricists (including Arthur Laurents), the duo turned to Comden and Green, two young writers and friends of Bernstein who had performed with him as The Revuers, a Greenwich Village nightclub act. The team expanded the story of *Fancy Free* and changed its focus to three sailors on leave in New York City, each following a different girl. Not one note of Bernstein's music for the ballet appears in *On the Town*.

In the summer of 1944, Robbins and his collaborators began writing the new show. As he told an interviewer in 1999: "I think what was so new about it is that it was all very contemporary. The war was still on, the sailors were around. Life was right there on the streets for us to see. And then we thought, the idea of picking at New York as if it were a new place for some people to try to find their way around was also very good." As Smith and Feigay struggled to raise capital during the fall of 1944, the team acquired veteran director George Abbott to guide the material. Comden and Green also cast themselves in the show, in the comic parts of Clare and Ozzie. During its December tryout in New Haven and an additional two weeks in Boston, *On the Town* lost an opening scene set in a night court (which framed a flashback), as well as "Gabey's Comin'." In addition, Abbott had Robbins divide the lengthy "Coney Island Ballet" into two parts. At Abbott's insistence all specific references to the war were deleted.

The show opened on December 28, 1944, at the Adelphi Theatre and transferred to two other theaters—the 44th Street Theatre and the Martin Beck—during the course of its 462-performance run. *On the Town* was revived on Broadway in 1971 and 1998. The 1950 film version features only two full songs composed by Bernstein (the other songs were composed by Roger Edens, with lyrics by Comden and Green) and moves the action forward to 1949, beyond the time frame of World War II.

300.20–21 Betty Hutton] Comedienne and singer (1921–2007) who made nine Hollywood films from 1942 to 1944.

301.29–30 "Miss Turnstiles for the Month"] "Miss Turnstiles" was based on "Miss Subways" (1941–76), a monthly contest run by a company called New York Subways Advertising.

303.32 Nedick's] A New York fast-food restaurant chain known for their orange drink and donuts.

304.2 "Gabey's coming."] A song titled "Gabey's Comin'" was cut from *On the Town* prior to its Broadway opening. Subsequent productions (such as the 1998 Broadway revival) have included it. See pages 616–618 of the present volume.

308.13 Hippodrome] Built in 1905, the Hippodrome arena filled an entire city block along Sixth Avenue, between 43rd and 44th streets. It was torn down in 1939.

309.1 *Tobacco Road*] Jack Kirkland's 1933 drama about an impoverished family in the hills of Georgia was the longest-running Broadway show of its time, achieving a record 3,182 performances (most of them at Forrest Theatre) before it closed in 1941.

309.14 *Angel Street*] A 1938 British thriller by Patrick Hamilton; it ran for more than one thousand performances from 1941 to 1944, at the John Golden Theatre.

309.22 Aquarium] The New York Aquarium opened at Castle Clinton in Battery Park in 1896. It was relocated to the Bronx in 1941 and relocated again to Brooklyn in 1957.

310.4–5 highest spot . . . Woolworth Tower] The Woolworth Building was the tallest building in the world from 1913 to 1929, when it was surpassed first by the Chrysler Building and then by the Empire State Building.

314.5 Quasimodo] The title character of Victor Hugo's 1831 novel *Notre-Dame de Paris* (*The Hunchback of Notre Dame*).

321.15 Lakmé] Opera (1883) by Léo Delibes (1836–1891).

321.17–20 "Down, down . . . Down King!"] See Shakespeare's *Richard II*, III.iii.178–82.

323.35 vocalise] A singer's warm-up exercises, using nonverbal sounds corresponding to the musical scale; pronounced *voc-a-leez*.

324.5 Jack Ballantine—Jack Robinson.] Madame Dilly may be thinking of Ballantine's scotch whisky. (When *On the Town* was collected in *The New York Musicals of Comden & Green* in 1997, the line was altered to "Jack Daniels—Jack Robinson.")

329.32 I.R.T.] Interborough Rapid Transit, the first private subway line in New York City, in operation since 1904. By 1940, the IRT had become part of the city's public transit system.

332.10 Goodbye, Mr. Chips] Title of a 1934 British novel by James Hilton (1900–1954); it was filmed in 1939.

334.2 a big Navy "E"] The Army-Navy "E" (Production) Award, given jointly by the War Department and the Navy Department beginning in 1942, for "individual plants which have achieved outstanding performance on war production." Winning plants were given a pennant and their employees a badge or ribbon with an "E" insignia.

348.16   Out—of my lodge at Eventi-i-i-d-d-e!!] The opening line of "Pale Moon," a popular song of 1920 composed by Frederick Knight Logan (1871–1928) with lyrics by Jesse G. M. Glick (1874–1938).

353.24–25   HILDY *embraces* . . . "Some Other Time"] In the original typescript from which the text of *On the Town* has been taken in the present volume, the stage direction reads "*They embrace*," and the song title "Oh Well." The former has been emended to clarify the meaning, and the latter to correspond to the form in which the title appears in the opening night program and subsequent texts.

FINIAN'S RAINBOW

Lyricist and librettist E. Y. "Yip" Harburg had spent much of his two-decade career trying to raise the level of discourse in the American musical in such shows as the political satire *Hooray for What!* (1937), while subsidizing this quixotic task by writing standards for Hollywood such as "Over the Rainbow" and "Happiness Is a Thing Called Joe." The postwar Broadway scene was more open to his brand of social satire and anarchic spirit. If *Finian's Rainbow* had contributed nothing more than "How Are Things in Glocca Morra?," "Old Devil Moon," and "Look to the Rainbow," it would rate as a classic, but Harburg's attempts to wrestle with commercialism, hypocrisy, greed, nuclear warfare, and, above all, racism in a popular art form put this show in another, higher category. A rare original musical in what was increasingly an age of adaptations, *Finian's Rainbow* captures the preoccupations of a postwar America attempting to define its priorities.

Harburg conceived of *Finian's Rainbow* apparently as early as October 1944, immediately following the Broadway debut of *Bloomer Girl*. He proposed his idea to that show's co-librettist, Fred Saidy, and eventually to its composer, Harold Arlen, who turned down the idea. Harburg's original concept allowed him to fuse three distinct "streams of thought" (as he remembered in a 1978 lecture at the Northwood Institute in Midland, Michigan): his sense of the "idiocy" of the transfer of gold bullion to Fort Knox and the wider failures of America's economic system; his love of Irish literature, especially James Stephens's novel *The Crock of Gold* (1912); and his "outrage" at the racist pronouncements of Senator Theodore Bilbo and Congressman John Rankin. (Bilbo was a governor, then senator, in Mississippi during the 1930s and 1940s who virulently advocated against African Americans having access to the polls in 1946; Rankin was a sixteen-term Mississippi congressman who was anti-Semitic and segregationist, questioning the bravery of black soldiers in World War II.) Harburg spoke about the musical's genesis in 1978:

> It was written in Roosevelt's time. For the first time, the black man was being given some recognition. So it occurred to me to do a show about Bilbo and Rankin. The only way I could assuage my outrage against

their bigotry was to have one of them turn black and live under his own
[Jim Crow] laws and see how he felt about it. I was making a point to
every white person: "Look—we use the word reincarnation. You might
come back as a black, and here's how you'll be treated if you do. How do
you like it?" I said to myself, "Gee, this is a great idea; how can I make
it into a musical?" Well, it was a little grim. So I put it in my notebook
for future reference and forgot about it.

By late 1944, Harburg had been collaborating with composer Earl Robinson, a folksinger with a progressive social agenda who had written the melodies
to "Joe Hill" (1936) and "Ballad for Americans" (1939). Robinson's political
interests coincided with Harburg's and Harburg enlisted him on the project
as composer. Harburg and Saidy wrote an outline for the script in Los Angeles
in 1945 and by March of 1946, *Finnian's* [sic] *Rainbow* was announced by *The
New York Times* as a project with both Robinson and composer Burton Lane,
with whom Harburg had been collaborating on various stage and film musicals
since 1932. By the summer of 1946, Robinson had left the project, profess-
ing himself unequal to the task of writing a full Broadway score, and Lane
remained as *Finian's Rainbow*'s sole composer.

The project had a difficult summer and fall. Harburg, writing the script
with Saidy in Hollywood, pushed back the schedule, according to the *Times*,
"on account I am learning to golf and Broadway in August is no place for a
nineteenth hole." The show's relatively inexperienced producers, Lee Sabinson
and William R. Katzell, had difficulty assembling a cast and postponed the
opening to the end of the year; even during its late December tryout in Philadelphia in 1946, the team had not yet secured a New York theater.

Finian's Rainbow eventually opened at the 46th Street Theatre on January 10, 1947, where it ran for 724 performances. The song "How Are Things
in Glocca Morra?" had preceded the show itself on the airwaves—as was the
custom for potential hit songs at the time—and had become popular in a
rendition by Buddy Clark, released in October 1946. On April 6, 1947, for
their contributions to the show, actor David Wayne (Og) and choreographer
Michael Kidd would win the very first Tony Awards ever given. The show was
revived at New York City Center in 1955 and 1960 and on Broadway in 2009.
A 1968 film, updated to the 1960s, was directed by Francis Ford Coppola and
featured Fred Astaire and Petula Clark.

372.7   Mr. Serutan] Serutan was a widely advertised brand of laxative.

372.34   *"Talking Union Blues"*] A 1941 "talking blues" song written for the
Congress of Industrial Organizations (CIO) by members of the Almanac Sing-
ers, including Millard Lampell (1919–1997), Lee Hays (1914–1981), and Pete
Seeger (1919–2014).

373.21–22   poll tax] Begun during the Reconstruction era, a poll tax was a fee
levied on individuals seeking to vote in local elections; used in the South for

decades as a way of excluding blacks and poorer whites, it was outlawed by the 24th Amendment in 1964.

394.26   Carmen Miranda] Flamboyant Brazilian singer and movie star (1909–1955).

395.27–396.2   such a hungry yearning . . . under me skin] In the course of this exchange Og and Finian quote several popular songs: "Night and Day" (1932) by Cole Porter (1891–1964); "All the Things You Are" (1939), composed by Jerome Kern (1885–1945) with lyrics by Oscar Hammerstein II (1895–1960); "Smoke Gets in Your Eyes" (1933) by Kern and lyricist Otto Harbach (1873–1963); "That Old Black Magic" (1942), composed by Harold Arlen (1905–1986) with lyrics by Johnny Mercer (1909–1976); and Porter's "I've Got You Under My Skin" (1936).

397.12   John Henry] A legendary African American railroad worker, the subject of hundreds of ballads and tales, said to have died defeating a steam drill in a tunnel-digging contest.

397.25   *Sears-Roebuck catalogue*] See note 184.10.

399.24–25   Bogart . . . Baby Bacall's] Lauren Bacall (b. 1924) had first appeared on screen in *To Have and Have Not* in 1944 opposite Humphrey Bogart (1899–1957); they were married in 1945 and starred in *The Big Sleep* in 1946.

401.20   Teresa] Pronounced "Te-*ress*-a."

411.3   Cornelius] The first name of one of the richest men in American history, Cornelius Vanderbilt (1794–1877), whose grandson was Cornelius Vanderbilt II (1843–1899) and great-grandson Cornelius Vanderbilt III (1873–1942).

414.32–33   White Sulphur Springs] An exclusive West Virginia resort community.

416.35   *"Little Brown Jug,"*] A popular song, originally written by Joseph Eastburn Winner (1837–1918) in 1869.

419.14–18   Oh, dem golden slippers . . . wedding day!] The opening lines of "Oh, Dem Golden Slippers," an 1879 minstrel song by James A. Bland (1854–1911).

420.18   tote that barge, lift that bale] From "Ol' Man River," a song in the 1927 musical *Show Boat*; see page 19 in this volume.

421.24   the D.A.R.] The Daughters of the American Revolution, a women's group whose members could demonstrate descent from a Revolutionary War soldier or supporter. The group was involved in several controversies in the 1930s and 1940s, in which its "white performers only" policy kept African Americans, including Marion Anderson, from singing at their headquarters at Constitution Hall.

421.25   the Babbitts of the bourgeoisie] Conformist, materialistic, middle-class men, like the character George F. Babbitt in the novel *Babbitt* (1922) by Sinclair Lewis (1885–1951).

432.3–434.32   OG *debonairly saunters . . .* CURTAIN FALLS] E. Y. Harburg and Fred Saidy revised the text of *Finian's Rainbow* in 1980 and their changes were incorporated in a revival of the musical at the St. James Theatre in 2009. Their most substantial alterations were to the show's final scene. The text of the ending of 2009, including a final curtain call, is as follows:

> (OG *enters, now a man of the world, derby-hatted and sporting a cane.*)
>
> OG: The name is Og. My card. (*He tries to magically produce his calling card, then pulls one out of his pocket and gives it to* WOODY. *He greets* SUSAN *with a kiss.*) Hi'ya, sugar.
>
> > (OG *sweeps* SUSAN *off her feet, twirling her to one side. A commotion is heard offstage as* RAWKINS, *now white, enters berating the* SHERIFF *and* BUZZ *who are trying to hide in the crowd.*)
>
> RAWKINS: Where are they? . . . Just let me get my hands on 'em. (*To the crowd.*) Where are they?
>
> > (*Everyone points to the* SHERIFF *and* BUZZ. RAWKINS *chases them to down center.*)
>
> You! You're done. Demoted. (*Ripping his badge off.*) Term-in-ated.
>
> SHERIFF: But boss, we was only . . .
>
> BUZZ: Now calm yourself, Senator. Remember, your blood pressure.
>
> RAWKINS: And you, you squirmy little snake. You're lucky 'cause I'm gonna let you slither away from here and keep your slimy hide. I don't want to see either of you within forty miles of Rainbow Valley for as long as I live.
>
> SHERIFF & BUZZ (*ad libs*): Now, Boss. But, Senator, we
>
> RAWKINS: Git!!
>
> SHERIFF & BUZZ: Yes, Boss. (*And they trip and fall over each other trying to be the first to get the farthest from* RAWKINS'S *grip as they start to exit.*)
>
> SHERIFF: Poor fella got his color back but never recovered his senses.
>
> > (RAWKINS *slowly crosses in amongst the* SHARECROPPERS.)
>
> WOODY: Well, Senator, looks like they'll be some changes in the valley.
>
> RAWKINS: Yes Woody my boy, and about time. (*Stepping down to the middle of the crowd and getting to know them.*) Greetings neighbors friends. I just want to let you know that I'm running for re-election next November and it would be a privilege to represent you
>
> > (*Crosses to* HOWARD *and shakes his hand.*)
>
> All of you. (RAWKINS *pulls out his now rainbow colored handkerchief, and mops his brow.*)
>
> SUSAN (*crossing to* WOODY): Isn't it grandish, Woody? He wished me into talking.
>
> FINIAN (*buttonholing* OG): You wished? You used up the third and last wish?
>
> OG: Well, natch. Can't you see I'm all mortal now?

FINIAN: Then the gold crock has turned to

OG: worthless dross. (*He pulls it out and shows it to* FINIAN.)

FINIAN: This is the final crisis! Everything is collapsin' about us.

SHARON: Father, how can you say that?

FINIAN: Sharon, I failed. I swore you'd have everything that you'd be rich.

SHARON: Father, I am rich.

FINIAN: What have I ever given you but a rootless, wanderin' life? (*Sinks to sit on stump, hands covering face, bent over.*) Ahhh, things are hopeless hopeless (*Springs up, with eyes shining.*) But they're not serious! (*With renewed purpose.*) It's time to move on

SHARON: But Father, we have a new home, friends to fill it with and a good man who loves me.

WOODY: You gave us hope, Mr. McLonergan.

FINIAN (*skeptical—then a lightbulb*): I did that?

SHARON: Father, we're home. This is home. It's journey's end.

FINIAN: No, Sharon, not for me. This is just the beginning

SHARON: Father, what are you saying?

FINIAN (*picking up the little carpetbag he first arrived with*): My dear one, I love you, and that will always be. But you don't need me any longer. You've got a life to build and I've got work to do. I'm needed needed to keep those dreams out there, the wee ones as well as the grand ones, bubblin' up 'til they spill over and flood a life.

(*A rainbow appears.*)

HENRY: Snagdrab—a rainbow!

FINIAN: Aye, Finian's rainbow. Sure there's no pot of gold at the end of it, but a beautiful new world under it. It led us to this blessed valley, so I'll trust it to set my feet on the right path. Goodbye, darlin', we'll meet again. (*He kisses* SHARON *goodbye.*) Farewell, my friends. I'll see you someday in Glocca Morra.

(*Music. He picks up his carpetbag and starts off following the rainbow. He pauses a moment to look back at them.*)

WOODY: Sharon, where is Glocca Morra?

SHARON: You won't find it on any map, Woody. It's that far away place in everyone's heart—a little beyond your reach, but never beyond your hope.

(SHARON *starts to sing "May We Meet in Glocca-Morra Some Fine Day." The* OTHERS *join in.*)

(*As they sing,* FINIAN *opens his carpetbag, pulls out his telescope and scans the horizon. Briskly, he closes up the telescope, picks up his bag and marches off to a new adventure.*)

SHARON:

> So to every weepin' willow,
> To each brook along the way,
> To each lad that
> Comes a whistling too-ra-lay

FULL COMPANY:

> May we meet in Glocca-Morra
> One fine day.

SLOW CURTAIN

CURTAIN RISES

ALL:

> Won't it be fun when worry is done
> And money is hay?
> That's the time things'll come your way.
> On that great, great come and get it day.
> I'll get my gal, that calico gown,
> I'll get my mule, that acre of groun'
> 'Cause word has come from Gabriel's horn
> The Earth beneath your plough
> Is a buddin' and now it's your'n
> Glory time's comin' for to stay
> On that great, great come and get it,
> And keep it,
> And share it,
> Come and get it day.

CURTAIN

434.10   Oak Ridge, Tennessee] A town built by the U.S. Army Corps of Engineers beginning in 1942 as part of the Manhattan Project, to house workers and production facilities for the development of the atomic bomb.

KISS ME, KATE

The success of the narrative-driven Rodgers and Hammerstein musicals (which by 1948 would include the masterful *Carousel* and the experimental *Allegro*) forced even the most accomplished Broadway hands to confront the challenges of the evolved form; Irving Berlin confessed himself baffled by the demands of what he called "a situation show." Cole Porter hesitantly brought his unique talents to the narrative form, but by confining himself to the sweeping emotions of the main characters rather than a sweepingly complicated plot, Porter wrote his deepest score for *Kiss Me, Kate*—one of the handful of perfect scores in the Broadway canon—and his biggest hit, the crown jewel of a gilded career.

Porter had five musicals running on Broadway at various points during World War II, but though several succeeded commercially, none was as lucrative or highly acclaimed as the works that had made his reputation in the 1930s. After his version of *Around the World in 80 Days*, directed by Orson Welles, proved a flop in 1946, Porter decamped to Hollywood, where he could write songs on an easier schedule and be close to the doctor attending his severe spinal injuries, the result of a horseback-riding accident in 1937.

Porter's road back to Broadway came in a roundabout way through the Theatre Guild, Broadway's most prestigious organization since the mid-1920s. When the Guild was at its height in the mid-1930s, its reputation was upheld by one of Broadway's preeminent couples, husband and wife Alfred Lunt and Lynn Fontanne. From 1928 to 1960, the American-born Lunt and the British-born Fontanne would only appear onstage opposite each other in dozens of plays, including the world premieres of *Design for Living* (with its author, Noël Coward), *Idiot's Delight*, and *There Shall Be No Night*, along with such classic plays as *The Seagull* and *The Taming of the Shrew*—these last two, among others, produced by the Theatre Guild.

During their 1935 Broadway engagement in *The Taming of the Shrew*, a young starstruck hanger-on named Arnold Saint Subber noticed that Lunt and Fontanne carried their onstage feuds offstage into the dressing room, where their egos clashed nightly. Over the course of the following decade, Saint Subber worked his way up as a production assistant on Broadway and kept nurturing an idea that the star turns of the Lunts might form the basis of a musical. Along with *Oklahoma!*'s set designer, Lemuel Ayers, he approached comic playwright Bella Spewack about creating a book that folded together Shakespeare's play with the backstage antics of a similar pair. Spewack's initial instinct was to go straight to Cole Porter, with whom she and her estranged husband, Sam, had written *Leave It to Me* in 1938.

The producing partners, however, were uninterested in employing Porter, whom they considered passé. Compounding the difficulty, Porter was, at best, skeptical about the project. Adapting Shakespeare seemed like a commercially unappealing prospect, and he preferred to stay in Hollywood. Spewack pleaded with him and Porter maintained a passing interest in the project only by having Spewack synopsize the subplots for him—he claimed he simply couldn't get through the original *Shrew*. By spring 1948, Spewack had worn down his resistance and Porter pronounced himself enchanted by the drafts of her libretto. The leading character of Fred Graham evolved into a figure less like Alfred Lunt and more like Orson Welles, or José Ferrer, who had set up shop at the New York City Center at the beginning of 1948, producing, directing, and starring in a variety of classical and modern roles in repertoire.

To complement the musical's romantic moments, Saint Subber and Ayers felt that *Kiss Me, Kate* needed more accessible humor and prevailed upon Bella Spewack to allow her ex-husband Sam to join the team; he added the two misplaced gangsters to the proceedings.

The show had a relatively seamless out-of-town tryout in Philadelphia beginning on December 2, 1948, without losing a single musical number. It moved practically intact to the New Century Theatre on Broadway, debuting only two days before the beginning of 1949. It ran for 1,077 performances, and won five (of the recently created) Tony Awards, including for Best Musical. A Hollywood version was made by MGM in 1954 (featuring a character called "Cole Porter") and it was revived on Broadway for the first time in 1999.

Samuel and Bella Spewack wrote an introduction for the first edition of *Kiss Me, Kate*, published in New York by Alfred A. Knopf in 1953. It is reprinted below:

HOW TO WRITE A MUSICAL COMEDY

An Esoteric Analysis of a New Art Form

Books are being written about it, symposiums held, and letters exchanged between savants of Akron and Ankara. It is therefore fitting that we, the undersigned, having written two (2) examples of the New Art Form, enter the discussion forthwith.

Ordinarily we write plays—just plays. But about every ten years we tiptoe with typewriters into musical meadows. Thus, in 1938 we emerged with *Leave It to Me*, a study of a Kansan who is made Ambassador to Soviet Russia against his will, and who devotes himself to the business of getting recalled. This was before the era of the New Art Form. So we ran a year in New York and a year on the road.

In 1948 we wrote *Kiss Me, Kate*. Definitely New Art Form.

For both, Cole Porter provided wonderful music and lyrics.

Ergo, if we all live long enough, 1958 should see a third collaboration.

But while we're still fresh and in our right senses we want to contribute our mite to the study of the New Art Form.

You may remember that the old musical comedy consisted of a story (book), songs, dances, scenery, girls, and boys. On the other hand, the New Art Form consists of a story (book), songs, dances, scenery, girls, and boys.

But there is an indefinable "something else" in the New Art Form. Is it the product of a mysterious blending of kinetics, plastics, social significance, abstractionism, atonal atavism, a fluid capitalist structure, and plenty of money in the hands of the wrong people?

We realized when we embarked on *Kiss Me, Kate* that just having fun with Victor Moore as an Ambassador to Russia would not be enough. That was all right in 1938. But 1948 was made of sterner stuff. The New Art Form required a message.

For instance, *Call Me Madam*: money ain't everything. *Pal Joey*: don't be a heel. These crusades, articulated for the first time in the New Art Form, have had a profound effect upon our society. We have a message, too. It's Shakespeare's: slap your wife around; she'll thank you for it.

Sociologists have not yet measured the influence of *Kiss Me, Kate* upon domestic relations, but when they do get around to it they will discover that a preponderant number of wedding anniversaries (ranging from the first to the fiftieth) were celebrated by happy or resigned couples scattered nightly throughout the audience during its run. Our mail orders generally began with an explanation that tickets were wanted for the anniversary date.

The cultural impact of the comedy has been profound. At its British debut, in Oxford, two natives of that damp ancient seat of learning met during the intermission for this bit of dialogue:

"Difficult to follow, what?"

"It's a skit on Shakespeare, you know."

"Really?"

Fortunately this was not a typical reaction. From New York to California, in Australia and New Zealand, in the Scandinavian countries and wherever else Western culture still reigns, men and women quenched their thirst for the New Art Form and were pathetically grateful—for they had only the music and literature of the ages to draw upon, and thus were in a pitiable condition until we rescued them with *Kiss Me, Kate*.

Now, how did our contribution to this miracle of the New Art Form come about?

Devious and intricate and thorny was the path. But after all the legal beagles got their licks in and the Dramatists Guild contract was duly signed and sealed and mislaid, we embarked on the business of writing a play with a play cum musica. The newest parlay in town became the triple play, Shakespeare to Spewack to Porter.

How to Collaborate with W. Shakespeare

If you want to collaborate with Shakespeare, get two inexpensive copies of any one of his plays. Tear them out of their bindings and spread the pages on a large table or bed or floor, so that you can spot at a glance what you will retain and what you will discard. Take well-sharpened pencil, or pen that works, and so indicate.

Then with shears cut out the parts you intend using, and if you're handy with the paste-pot, paste up in sequence on ordinary copy paper. If allergic to paste or glue, use stapler. If you have no stapler, your lawyer is sure to have one.

Do not throw away discarded pages. Some wonderful ideas for songs may be among them. Or you can run up your own lampshade.

Total outlay: many, many sleepless nights and haggard days; cash $2.50.

How to Collaborate with C. Porter

With Porter it is a little bit different. You can't attack him with shears and paste, and you can't spread him out on the bed or the floor. If it's your own play, it's comparatively easy to get Porter to accept the idea. But if it's Shakespeare's play it takes a deal of persuasion. When we approached him with the notion of making a musical version of *The Taming of the Shrew* he whispered: "What?" At the second discussion of the same theme, he told us that he had tried reading the play and had then had it read to him.

"I don't understand a word of it," he sighed.

At the third meeting we had jotted down likely song titles from Shakespeare's own lines: "I've Come to Wive It Wealthily," "Where Is the Life that Late I Led?" and "Were Thine That Special Face." Mr. Porter brightened.

"Well, let's try."

In our not at all humble opinion, Mr. Porter then wrote his finest score. The song, "Were Thine That Special Face," by itself may very well live as more than a minor classic.

The process of welding book, music, and lyrics into one organic whole was not easy. Mr. Porter not only probed each characterization and motivation, but in turn asked us to do the same with his lyrics.

For example:

> PORTER: *Tell me about Lois Lane. She's not a bad girl, is she?*
>
> SPEWACKS: *Oh, no. She's unmoral rather than immoral.*
>
> PORTER: *Just what do you mean by that?*
>
> SPEWACKS: *Well, Lois Lane at the age of fourteen started a career that should have landed her in the reformatory by this time.*
>
> PORTER: *All the time she's really in love with Bill Calhoun the hoofer, isn't she?*
>
> SPEWACKS: *Not in love, Cole. She loves him the way a mother loves a child. Mostly for his weakness—like his gambling and his lack of ambition—and of course she thinks he's a wonderful dancer.*
>
> PORTER: *She really cares for him?*
>
> SPEWACKS: *In her way, yes.*

New scenes about Lois and Bill were sent to Porter the next day. And the next 2 a.m. the phone rang.

"Are you asleep?" asked Porter.

We were.

"Stay right where you are and listen."

Porter played and sang "Why Can't You Behave?" over the telephone, and the next day the Lois–Bill scenes were cut again and again. They became smaller and smaller in rehearsal—and never did authors care less.

One night, as we were about to leave, Porter asked if we knew who had written a poem with the line, "I have been faithful to thee."

"Cynara! in my fashion," we finished for him.

We guessed Ernest Dowson or Alan Seeger, and of course it was Ernest Dowson. That poem was required quoting in the twenties.

About a week later Porter played and sang for us "Always True to You in My Fashion." It's five years since we heard it first, but we knew then that we were destined to hear it over and over again.

There is evidently something in the chemical blending of our collaboration that moves Porter to his bawdiest. Both "Fashion" and "My Heart Belongs to Daddy" (from *Leave It to Me*) are piquant narrations of the confession school. While insisting on the essential purity of the heroine, they are case histories with a lusty twist.

Lyrically the song "Why Can't You Behave?" has tragic implications, but the scene that led to it was meant to be funny. By the time of the Philadelphia tryout the parts of Lois and Bill contained only the essentials for plot and song cues. We could afford to be ruthless in cutting our own lines, but we hated to cut Shakespeare, and we hated to cut Porter. Three songs dropped out during rehearsal, and we fought to retain at least one of them. But in the face of seventeen numbers, it was well we lost that battle. We were a long show.

Porter was in California when we airmailed him the finished draft of the book, and he wired: "The best musical comedy book I have ever read arrived this morning. Congratulations."

In addition, Porter sent Katharine's song of capitulation, "I Am Ashamed that Women Are So Simple," using the only lyrics by Shakespeare in the comedy; then, later, the lengthy, punning "Brush up Your Shakespeare." Accompanying these lyrics Porter wrote: "Belle will probably cut her throat when she gets this." As it had been agreed at the outset that Porter would write no songs for our gunmen, we were rather surprised, but we realized that according to the classic standards of Broadway it was a "boff" number—a show-stopper, if you please. Perhaps not a New Art Form, but definitely a must for the male patron. So instead of any throat-cutting, we dropped the final scene (all Shakespeare) and a beautiful dance for which the stairs had been built. We had exactly three minutes left in which to finish our show.

Our collaborative correspondence swelled and waned as the weeks grew into months. And Cole's letters, which had once started with "Bellissima Carissima," veered to the accusation that the Spewack obstinacy was the defect of "charming Roumanian-Hungarian nature." In a later letter to the fledgling producers he said: "Whenever I try to talk sense to Bella it is like trying to talk sense to Russia."

Bella, hurt, wrote: "Russia will now reply and retreat into Mongolian silence."

The loves and hates that go with the production of a play are laid to rest as soon as the play is on, whether it's a hit or a failure. Where all has been peaches and cream you generally have a flop. Mutual admiration at a tryout is deadly. The biggest fight in regard to this production was the spotting of "Were Thine That Special Face." The producers did not like the song and wanted to place it in the second half where it could be dropped easily. It stayed in the first act.

During rehearsal Porter himself wanted to drop "Tom, Dick, or Harry," the quartet number with Bianca and her suitors. We fought against that—insisted on its being restaged. The performers concocted a jazz finish for it, and when it was all done Porter clapped his hands delightedly, applause that was multiplied a thousandfold when we opened in Philadelphia four weeks later.

We have always tried to let a song tell part of the story where it could do so, and we have always been willing to cut large passages of book, as certainly we did in *Kiss Me, Kate*. The spoken word in a musical comedy must compete with music, dance, color, and movement. When a spoken scene does compete successfully with these powerfully appealing elements, the writers can take pride in their craftsmanship. But anyone writing the book for a musical must be prepared to cut—and cut—and cut. There is no room for the writer's love of his own words. "Love" lingers longest in lyrics.

Summing Up

The writing of musical comedy is a craft in itself, just as writing a play or a screenplay is. But they all have three things in common: situation, dialogue, and hard work.

In the realm of the musical show there are: first, the play with music; second, the operetta; third, the musical comedy; and fourth, the spectacle or extravaganza with music. In the first and last categories the songs do not carry forward the plot—or shall we say the story? In the operetta (and in the opera, for that matter) the songs do. In the musical comedy the songs should serve a similar function, but occasionally they serve a mood function instead; someone feels happy or sad and you get "Oh, What a Beautiful Morning!" or "Why Was I Born?"

Musicals can be based on anything. *The King and I* had for its predecessor *Anna and the King of Siam*, the experiences of an Englishwoman assigned to teach the children of the King of Siam during the last century. It was a best-seller as a book and an equally successful film before it was equipped with songs and a ballet. *My Darlin' Aida* emanated from the opera without My and Darlin'. The adaptation kept the original music, but showed the events as occurring in the South during the Civil War, A.D. instead of in Egypt, B.C. *Pal Joey* is based on a fiction series of letters from a heel of a hoofer to a friend, which first appeared in The New Yorker.

And yet the musical comedy cannot revolve around just anything. It must not only be about something; it must also be entertaining. Unlike the straight play, this form is elastic—provided it can be made to serve the ear and the eye.

For example, *Leave It to Me* can be called a play with music, for none of the songs that Cole Porter wrote for that comedy of ours advanced the story one iota. "My Heart Belongs to Daddy" merely repeated what Dolly had already told Buck Thomas: that she had to leave him because she listened to her heart and not her head. When it was sung by Mary Martin, who cared if she had already told her reasons? Of the musical fact that her heart belonged to Daddy the public could not get enough. Incidentally, that was Mary Martin's first appearance on Broadway and the first time a strip-tease took place in snowbound Siberia.

But in *Kiss Me, Kate* Cole Porter's songs served the story, especially in Shakespeare's *Shrew*, the play within the play. When Petruchio sings "I've Come to Wive It Wealthily," or when Lucentio, Gremio, and Hortensio join with Bianca to sing "Tom, Dick, or Harry," Shakespeare's deathless words of plottage go into limbo. Where Porter's melodious substitution takes about five minutes with encores, Shakespeare takes twenty.

For in order to keep the actors in his stock company loyal and contented, Shakespeare frequently padded the parts of his lesser characters, and the audience did not object because in those days nobody had to make the 11:20 to the suburbs.

In adapting *The Shrew* for the play within the play, it was necessary to drop the entire opening. From the body of the piece it was necessary to drop the servants of Lucentio's and Petruchio's ménage, as well as the scene with the Pedant. Here and there among the omitted passages were lines that we wanted to keep, and these we blithely distributed to the characters that remained. They came in handy when, during rehearsal, an actor would say "I feel I need another line," or "I'd like a handle for this speech."

There was plenty of misgiving when *Kiss Me, Kate* was about to open in England, Shakespeare's own land. Would the English be offended or would they appreciate that we had been faithful to the Bard in our fashion? The tryout was in Oxford, and if the New Theatre had been triple its size it would still not have been adequate accommodation for the crowds who wanted to see it. In London there were one million paying customers at the Coliseum despite the handicap of a stage where the Old and New Testaments could be played simultaneously. And on tour in England, Scotland, and Wales, *Kiss Me, Kate* has to date played for fourteen months—with an all-British cast. A second touring company starts next month.

Scandinavia also knows and loves its Shakespeare, but there too *Kiss Me, Kate* has been given a hospitable welcome. As of this writing it is the most successful musical in Scandinavian theatrical history. A touring company is still making the trek, perhaps, by this time, in Lapland.

Whatever was used of Shakespeare was used à la mot. Only two lines were borrowed from other Shakespeare sources—one from *Hamlet* and one from *Macbeth*. You find them.

Vital Statistics

The Taming of the Shrew was played in New York as far back as 1768, and again in 1785. About one hundred years later it was revived by Augustin Daly with John Drew and Ada Rehan, who took it on the road in 1902 with Otis Skinner as Petruchio. Several years later Charles Richman took part. Sothern and Marlowe used it in their repertory, and in 1927 Basil Sidney and Mary Ellis played it in modern costumes. Alfred Lunt and Lynn Fontanne revived it in 1935. On December 30, 1948, *Kiss Me, Kate* opened, to establish the longest run *The Shrew* ever had anywhere, any time, including Shakespeare's own.

Statistically, the performances in New York numbered 1077, and across the United States it played 1064 times. More than four million Americans have seen and heard it.

Since its closing *Kiss Me, Kate* lives on in summer and winter stock, indoor and outdoor presentations in tent, stadium, and arena productions. This summer, performances are scheduled with municipal light opera companies in Kansas City, St. Louis, Dallas, Los Angeles, and San Francisco.

The race horse, *Kiss Me, Kate*, paid $17.94 at Belmont on May 23, 1951.

437.6   Ford's Theatre] A major touring house in Baltimore, opened in 1871 and demolished in 1964.

443.35   cheat] When *Kiss Me, Kate* was published by Alfred A. Knopf in 1953, a footnote was provided: "Theatrical expression to cover actor's appearing to play scene with another actor but actually aiming his lines out to the audience."

449.35   Half hour] The stage manager's warning that actors have thirty minutes before "places"—their call to the stage.

450.15   He's getting a player piano?] Truman took piano lessons as a young man and briefly considered a career as a professional pianist. Once he entered the White House, he continued the play the piano, often at the least provocation, and frequently to accompany his daughter, Margaret.

450.19   borscht at the White House] Truman was a particularly strong advocate for a Jewish homeland in Israel and, under his direct order, the United States was the first nation to recognize the State of Israel on May 14, 1948.

451.13   my *Cyrano*] *Cyrano de Bergerac* (1897), a play by Edmond Rostand (1868–1918).

451.35–36   the Barter Theatre] Founded in 1933 in Abingdon, Virginia, the Barter Theatre got its name by accepting the barter of food or other goods in lieu of paid admission to its plays.

452.9   the *Prince of Potsdam*] An apparently invented operetta.

452.37   the Jungfrau] The third highest peak in the Bernese Alps.

459.18   L. B. Mayer's] See note 119.14.

466.35–36   I've come to wive . . . happily in Padua] See *The Taming of the Shrew*, I.ii.75–76.

477.7–15   Father and wife . . . Kiss me, Kate] See *The Taming of the Shrew*, II.i.321–24.

477.34 *He Who Gets Slapped*] A 1914 play by Russian author Leonid Andreyev (1871–1919), filmed in 1924.

478.17 Peer Gynt] The hero of Henrik Ibsen's 1866 play.

479.33 Equity] Actors Equity, the major trade union for actors appearing in the theater.

491.24 the Kinsey report] The first of Alfred Kinsey's two pioneering studies of human sexuality, *Sexual Behavior in the American Male*, was published in 1948.

498.25 typically Shuberty] The Shubert Brothers' annual revues of 1912–24, entitled *The Passing Show*, were particularly known for their leggy chorines.

499.6–7 Carolina . . . pizza] When *Kiss Me, Kate* was published by Alfred A. Knopf in 1953, footnotes were provided: "Pronounced *Caroleena*," "Pronounced *Leena*," and "Pronounced *peetsa*."

499.32 Lisa] When *Kiss Me, Kate* was published by Alfred A. Knopf in 1953, a footnote was provided: "Pronounced *Leeza*."

501.10 the only Republican . . . nomination] In the months prior to the 1948 presidential election, fifteen different candidates vied for the Republican nomination, which was ultimately given to Thomas A. Dewey.

505.33–34 the Group . . . Guild Theatre . . . Civic Repertory] Some of New York's most famous theater companies between the wars: the Group Theatre (1931–1941), known for the works of Clifford Odets and its intense ensemble preparation; the Theatre Guild (see page 696); and the Civic Repertory Theatre, managed by and featuring Eva Le Gallienne.

508.26–27 Will Big Frost escape Dick Tracy?] Mobster Big Frost was one of the many eccentric villains who ran through the panels of Chester Gould's detective strip, *Dick Tracy*; he appeared in 1948.

512.27 Louella Parsons] Hollywood gossip columnist (1881–1972) for the Hearst newspapers.

512.33 Svengali] The villainous and manipulative Hungarian hypnotist in George du Maurier's 1894 novel, *Trilby*.

517.34 "I Am Ashamed that Women Are So Simple"] In the first published book edition of *Kiss Me, Kate*, the title appears here as "Women Are So Simple"; it has been emended in the present volume to follow the form in which the title appears in the list of musical numbers at the front of the same edition, and in the opening night program.

SOUTH PACIFIC

The decades since 1949 may not have dulled *South Pacific*'s emotional power, but the show's piercing topicality has, understandably, dimmed somewhat with time. Yet the masterfully constructed and superbly scored *South Pacific* can rank comfortably among other postwar books, plays, and films that sought to memorialize the American experience in World War II: *The Naked and the Dead, All My Sons, The Best Years of Our Lives*. It's hard to imagine that there was anyone in the audience of the Majestic Theatre in 1949 untouched by the Theater of War in the South Pacific, and this show puts that overwhelming experience into accessible context.

In October 1942, a thirty-five-year-old book editor at Macmillan named James Michener enlisted in the Navy; by April 1944, Michener, now a lieutenant senior grade, was posted to the Solomon Islands, where he served for the next twenty months as a communications officer, naval historian, and informal troubleshooter. During his time there, he wrote a series of nineteen short stories about the American occupation of the South Pacific, roughly from the spring of 1942 to the assault on Tarawa in late November 1943. They would ultimately be organized into a manuscript called *Tales of the South Pacific*.

The stories are related by a single narrator who holds the same sort of military appointment as Michener's, but the details of his duties are unclear and the point of view shifts frequently. Characters appear in one story, then disappear in the next, only to reemerge in later stories and in different places. Though Michener fictionalizes the names of most of the locations in his short stories, the tales are set in the New Hebrides, which the Allies held throughout the war, and the Solomon Islands, which they began to fight for in the summer of 1942. During this stage of the war, the Allies attempted to capture the Solomons one by one, in their quest to drive the Japanese from the South Pacific. All of the plotlines in *Tales*, however vaguely related, culminate in the story "The Landing on Kuralei," which describes the massive invasion of a Japanese-held island. The invasion of Kuralei in Michener in many respects resembles the military assault on Tarawa Atoll in the Gilbert Islands, which was staged in part from the New Hebrides.

Upon Michener's return to civilian life in early 1946, he submitted his manuscript to Macmillan, which—following the serialization of several stories in the *Saturday Evening Post* in December 1946—published the full version, *Tales of the South Pacific*, at the beginning of 1947. The stories made the rounds of various Hollywood script departments, but were largely ignored until Kenneth MacKenna, the head of MGM's literary department, mentioned them to director and playwright Joshua Logan. Logan had been working on a stage adaptation of Thomas Heggen's *Mister Roberts*, also set in the South Pacific. In the winter of 1947, Logan and producer Leland Hayward optioned the rights to Michener's "Fo' Dolla," and Logan mentioned the project to Richard Rodgers, who had been looking for a new musical project with his collaborator Oscar Hammerstein.

By mid-February of 1948, Rodgers and Hammerstein had been signed to write the score (and Hammerstein the book) for an adaptation of Michener's material. Rodgers and Hammerstein insisted on optioning rights to all nineteen Michener stories and by the spring, Logan had joined Hammerstein as co-librettist (a rarity in Hammerstein's career) and director. In April, Michener's short stories won the Pulitzer Prize for fiction, and with the engagement of Metropolitan Opera star Ezio Pinza as Emile de Becque and Broadway star Mary Martin as Nellie Forbush, plans were under way for a late 1948 opening on Broadway for the new musical, now titled *South Pacific*.

In crafting their libretto, Hammerstein and Logan use the same names and locations as Michener. The action of *South Pacific* takes place on the (unnamed) island of Espiritu Santo in the New Hebrides (now Vanuatu), before and after the battle of Guadalcanal (August 1942–February 1943), mostly in the weeks leading up to Thanksgiving 1943.

Of the nineteen tales that comprise Michener's collection, *South Pacific* borrows most heavily from two, "Our Heroine" and "Fo' Dolla." "Our Heroine" is the tale of Ensign Nellie Forbush and her romance with the French planter Emile De Becque (capital "D" in Michener), while "Fo' Dolla" recounts a sexual affair between Lieutenant Cable and Liat on the island of Bali Ha'i. The character of Luther Billis appears in several stories, including "Dry Rot" and "A Boar's Tooth." Hammerstein and Logan borrow considerably from "The Cave" for their second act. In "The Cave," a local expatriate planter from England agrees to help the Allies by hiding out on a nearby island in order to broadcast Japanese troop movements back to the Americans. He and his compatriots are eventually discovered and killed by the Japanese. Hammerstein, Logan, and Rodgers borrowed numerous other names, characters, incidents, and insights from nearly all of the remaining Michener stories.

Rehearsals began in New York on February 3, 1949, with tryout performances in New Haven (March 7–12, 1949) and Boston (March 15–April 2, 1949): among many other changes, the songs "Will My Love Come Home To Me" (also known as "Loneliness of Evening"), "My Girl Back Home," and "Now Is the Time" were dropped out of town. Several critics (as well as friends of Michener's) strongly suggested that "You've Got to Be Carefully Taught" was too controversial and should be cut; Rodgers and Hammerstein resisted, defending the song as integral to the theme of the show (Michener concurred).

South Pacific opened at the Majestic Theatre on April 7, 1949, and ran for 1,925 performances. It was awarded an unprecedented nine Tony Awards (including awards for performers in each of the four acting categories) and in 1950, the musical was also awarded the Pulitzer Prize, making it the only musical to have won a Pulitzer for both its source material and its musical adaptation. The song "Some Enchanted Evening" reached the Number One spot in the pop charts in 1949, in a version covered by Perry Como; the song also entered the charts in 1949 with versions covered by Frank Sinatra, Bing Crosby, Al Jolson, and Ezio Pinza from the original cast album. *South Pacific* was not revived in a Broadway theater until 2008, under the auspices of the Lincoln Center Theater.

Rodgers and Hammerstein both contributed short accounts of the making of *South Pacific* for a souvenir program distributed during its original Broadway run. Hammerstein's "How 'South Pacific' Was Written" and Rodgers's "Adapting 'Tales of the South Pacific' to the Stage" are reprinted below:

How "South Pacific" Was Written

Who creates a play?

As my temples become more tinged with grey—only tinged, you understand—I become more and more convinced that no writer creates anything, and no good writer tries. He knows he is an agent of the world he lives in, the world of his time and centuries before his time.

What and who created this one musical play? The libretto derives from a book, "Tales of the South Pacific," a group of stories which last year won the Pulitzer Prize for fiction. How did James Michener "create" these? Out of his head? Out of a typewriter? No. It seems he had a job in the Navy, a roving job that flew him back and forth among the islands of the New Hebrides and New Guinea groups. In these journeys he met people and found them in situations partly created by a world war. I say partly created because their reactions to these situations were determined by their characters, and their characters were moulded by their immediate environments and heredities and the history of religion and science and poetry up to the time they were born. Michener took actualities and realities and fictionized them into a group of stories, some amusing, some deeply romantic.

Next step in "creation": Leland Hayward thought these stories would make a good musical play. Next step: So did Rodgers and Hammerstein. Amusing sidelight: When negotiations were opened to acquire the rights from Michener, it was found that he lived a five-minute walk from me in Bucks County, Pennsylvania, and up to that time we had never met.

For three months, Dick Rodgers, Josh Logan and I wrote nothing. We struggled with the problem of selection. There were so many stories we liked. We couldn't use them all. We settled finally on two: "Our Heroine"—about a Navy nurse who falls in love with a French planter—and "Fo' Dolla"—about a Marine Lieutenant to whom a strange old Tonkinese woman presents her seventeen-year-old daughter. We borrowed a few of our favorite characters from some of the other stories, and our next job was to combine all these into one coherent narrative. It took us a year to make this adaptation. Neither Dick nor Josh nor I wrote or produced anything else in that time. We cannot, however, say that our work was the end of "South Pacific's" creation, for the theatre is a place of complex mass collaboration, and anyone who seeks to claim sole credit for any play is a blind egomaniac.

This play emerged as the combined work of the composer, the authors, the director, Mary Martin, Ezio Pinza and their supporting cast, Jo Mielziner, designer of the scenery, Elizabeth Montgomery, designer of the costumes, Russell Bennett, the orchestrator, Salvatore Dell'Isola, the conductor, and many more who must be included as sources of creation.

After all these had contributed their talents and energies, the final factor in creation was the audience. An audience must apply its composite heart and mind to a play, create it as something it believes should exist or destroy it as something it believes should not exist. So when the curtain rose on the opening night, the circle was complete.

This tale of the South Pacific, taken out of the living world and crystallized in theatrical form, was offered back to the living world for approval.

ADAPTING "TALES OF THE SOUTH PACIFIC" TO THE STAGE

I had one deep reservation about doing a musical version of "Tales of the South Pacific." An island in the South Pacific could mean only one thing musically, and that was the sound of a steel guitar and a xylophone, or perhaps a marimba, struck with what is known as a "soft stick." This is a particularly mushy, decayed sound and one which is entirely abhorrent to me. The prospect of having to deal with it for a full evening was far from enticing.

The moment eventually arrived when we met James Michener for the first time. This, of course, was at lunch because in the theatre you are not allowed to meet anybody for the first time anywhere else. I could hardly get my martini down because I was so anxious to find out just what kind of steel guitar they used on Mr. Michener's particular island.

To my amazement and joy I found out that in this particular area of the Pacific there was no instrumental music of any kind and the nearest approach to it was simple percussion, such as drums made of hollow logs which could be beaten in the conventional way. There was also the long tubular type of drum which could be struck against the ground to produce sound, but there was no music in the accepted occidental sense of tonality.

This caused a complete shift in my approach to the problem of doing a score for the piece. I realized I could use what is known as a legitimate orchestra, that is, the same instrumental combination that one finds in symphony; smaller of course, but basically the same and with no trick instruments of any kind for atmosphere. I would also be allowed to do what I had always wanted to do by way of construction—give each character the sort of music that went with the particular character, rather than with the locale in which we found him.

Emile de Becque, for example, is an expatriated Frenchman, and I tried to invest his songs with his personality—romantic, rather powerful and not too uninvolved. (This also happens to fit a man named

Pinza.) Nellie Forbush is a Navy nurse from a small town in Arkansas. Her musical and cultural background would have been confined to radio, a certain number of movies, and perhaps that one trip to Chicago where she saw a touring musical comedy.

This immediately did a fine thing for me as the composer. It gave me a change of musical pace, for I wrote light, contemporary, rhythmic music for her. Boys in the Navy are boys in the Navy, and there's not much that you can write for them except songs that are fun for them to sing. With a little luck this makes fun for the audience, too, and provides another change of pace.

In the whole score there are two songs that could even remotely be considered "native." These are sung by a Tonkinese woman, and here I made no attempt whatever to be authentic or realistic. This music is simply my impression of the woman and her surroundings in the same sense that a painter might give you the impression of a bowl of flowers rather than try to provide a photographic resemblance.

From the point of view of the composer there was another problem and perhaps an even more difficult one. In the construction of musical plays we have always been able to resort to "groups" for the development of the songs. There has always been a choral group to back up the soloist or it has been possible to follow the soloist with a dance group of one sort or another.

"South Pacific," however, is quite a serious story, and when we thought of backing up our principals with a ballet or a singing ensemble, we feared that sincerity would go out the nearest exit, and we would be back in artificial and unemotional form. It was easy enough to say no groups, but it wasn't easy to find a substitute for them in developing the songs.

It happens that the simple direct answer is often the easiest one. We decided that the only thing to do was to try to make the songs good enough and have them sung so well that they would stand on their own and need no further development. I might say it's a very interesting experience to hear Mr. Pinza sing one simple refrain and stop the show cold with it. Of course, it takes Pinza to do it. It is also equally clear now that Mary Martin needs no more help than thirty-two bars' worth of words and music to hit the audience with the impact of a Diesel locomotive.

I hope this won't be construed as a rejection on my part of choral and dancing groups in the theatre. I think they are indispensable in any musical play approaching fantasy. Certainly the fantasy in "Carousel" and in "Oklahoma!" could not have existed without the help of concerted singing and dancing. But "South Pacific" is never fantastic, and it would have been hurt badly by any attempt to mix the medium of realism with that of fantasy.

There are boys and girls, and enough of them, in the play, but we have tried desperately—and I think successfully—to make them individuals rather than members of an ensemble. Thus, they are called upon to make a direct contribution to the total feeling of the play and are not interpolated figures.

The final resolution of our problem came from Joshua Logan in the extraordinary way in which he has managed to stage the songs, as though they were book and dialogue and not pleasant little interruptions in the scheme of the play. His extraordinary sense of balance has made it possible for the small values in the songs to create a large effect. He has been able to follow a rare, subdued technique, but never has he neglected showmanship or refused to allow the audience what I consider its greatest joy—that of being able to applaud.

525.20–31 Dites-moi . . . m'aimez?] French: Tell me why life is beautiful, / Tell me why life is happy, / Tell me why, dear miss, / Is it because you love me?

525.33–526.2 Allez-vous! . . . petit moustique!] French: HENRY: Go! Quickly! In the house! / NGANA: No, Henry! / JEROME: I'm staying here! / HENRY: Oh, yes? We'll see . . . Come, little mosquito!

533.27 Seabees] Men serving in the Naval Construction Battalions. Formed in 1942, the battalions built airfields, roads, and port facilities on islands throughout the Pacific.

537.1–2 Dragon Lady] The Dragon Lady was a sinister, seductive villainess from Milton Caniff's adventure comic strip *Terry and the Pirates* about derring-do in the Far East. She made her first appearance in 1935.

538.39 Tokyo Rose] Generic name given to the nearly dozen separate female radio announcers who broadcast Japanese propaganda during World War II.

542.32 PBY] A twin-engine long-range flying boat used by the U.S. Navy for reconnaissance and bombing missions.

542.34 Marie Louise] A fictional island probably based on Santa Isabel or Vella Lavella in the Solomon Islands.

543.5 Tonkinese] A native of the French protectorate of Tonkin, now part of Vietnam. The Tonkinese frequently served as indentured laborers in the Solomon Islands.

546.29–33 "Rectius vives . . . procellas"] See Horace, *Ode* 2.10: "You will live more prudently, Licinius, by neither always keeping out at sea. . . ."

549.4 the bottleneck] The New Georgia Sound, running from the northwest to the southeast through the Solomon Islands, was often referred to by the Allies during World War II as "the Slot"; it was the scene of several naval battles in 1942–43.

567.19–36 Bali ha'i t'appele . . . Bali ha'i!] French: Bali ha'i calls you / During the day, / During the night. / In your heart, / Still resonates, / Here, / Here I am. / If you want, / You will find me / Where the sky / Meets the sea. / Here I am, / Let me take you / Here I am / Bali h'ai.

569.30   avez-vous peur?] French: are you afraid?

570.12–13   Cette vieille femme . . . mère.] French: That old lady—is she your friend? LIAT: My mother.

575.5   *"Sweet Adeline"*] A 1903 ballad that has become a standard of the barbershop repertoire; it was composed by Harry Armstrong (1879–1951) with lyrics by Richard H. Gerard (1876–1948).

576.13–14   Maintenant . . . Petits!] French: Now to bed quickly! HENRY: Come, Little Ones!

576.29   Polynesian] In the original Michener tale "Our Heroine," Nellie refers to the mother of De Becque's children as a "nigger." During the out-of-town tryouts of *South Pacific*, Nellie referred to her, with revulsion, as "colored."

581.26   Jacques Barrere] The character as found in Michener is known as Jacques Benoit; Hammerstein substituted the name of *South Pacific*'s stage manager.

581.37–38   Tais-toi! Il est malade! . . . Tu comprends?] French: Hush! He is sick! . . . You understand?

596.9–10   Empress Augusta Bay] A bay on the western side of Bougainville Island, in the northern Solomon Islands.

596.32   P-40s] Single-engine land-based U.S. fighter aircraft flown in the South Pacific by the U.S. Army Air Forces and the Australian and New Zealand air forces.

598.21   Banika] An island southwest of New Georgia, in the Solomons.

598.41   Bettys] Twin-engine land-based Japanese bombers.

599.9   Zeros] Single-engine Japanese fighter aircraft.

600.11   "Immelmans" and "wingovers"] Maneuvers used by fighter pilots.

603.17   LCT's] Landing Craft Tank, used for amphibious assaults.

Sources and Acknowledgments

ADDITIONAL LYRICS

NOTES

Kiss Me, Kate   "Introduction: How To Write a Musical Comedy: An Esoteric Analysis of a New Art Form," by Samuel and Bella Spewack, from *Kiss Me, Kate: A Musical Play* (New York: Alfred A. Knopf, 1953). Reprinted by permission of Tams-Witmark Music Library, Inc.

South Pacific   "How *South Pacific* Was Written," by Oscar Hammerstein II, from *The Boston Post*. Reprinted by permission of Rodgers and Hammerstein: an Imagem Company. "Adapting 'Tales of the South Pacific' to the Stage," by Richard Rodgers, from *The N.Y. Herald-Tribune*. Reprinted by permission of Rodgers and Hammerstein: An Imagem Company.

ILLUSTRATIONS
(See photo insert following page 634.)

Courtesy of Photofest: 1, 4, 5, 9, 13, 15, 17, 21, 25, 26, 28
Courtesy of Rodgers & Hammerstein: An Imagem Company, www.rnh.com: 2, 12, 14, 16, 29, 30
Courtesy of Culver Pictures, Inc.: 3, 6
Courtesy of Vandamm Studio/© Billy Rose Theatre Division, The New York Public Library for the Performing Arts: 7, 11, 18, 20
Courtesy of Vanity Fair/The Condé Nast Collection, copyright © Anton Bruehl: 8
Courtesy of Time & Life Pictures/Getty Images: 10, 27
Courtesy of Eileen Darby Images, Inc.: 19
Photograph by Fred Fehl, courtesy of Gabriel Pinski/Billy Rose Theatre Division, The New York Public Library for the Performing Arts: 22, 23, 24
Courtesy of Philippe Halsman and Magnum Photos/© Billy Rose Theatre Division, The New York Public Library of the Performing Arts: 31

This book is set in 10 point ITC Galliard, a
face designed for digital composition by Matthew Carter
and based on the sixteenth-century face Granjon. The paper
is acid-free lightweight opaque and meets the requirements for
permanence of the American National Standards Institute.
The binding material is Brillianta, a woven rayon cloth
made by Van Heek–Scholco Textielfabrieken, Holland.
Composition by Publishers' Design and Production Services, Inc.
Printing and binding by Edwards Brothers Malloy, Ann Arbor.
Designed by Bruce Campbell.

THE LIBRARY OF AMERICA SERIES

The Library of America fosters appreciation and pride in America's literary heritage by publishing, and keeping permanently in print, authoritative editions of America's best and most significant writing. An independent nonprofit organization, it was founded in 1979 with seed funding from the National Endowment for the Humanities and the Ford Foundation.

To subscribe to the series or to order individual copies, please visit www.loa.org or call (800) 964-5778.

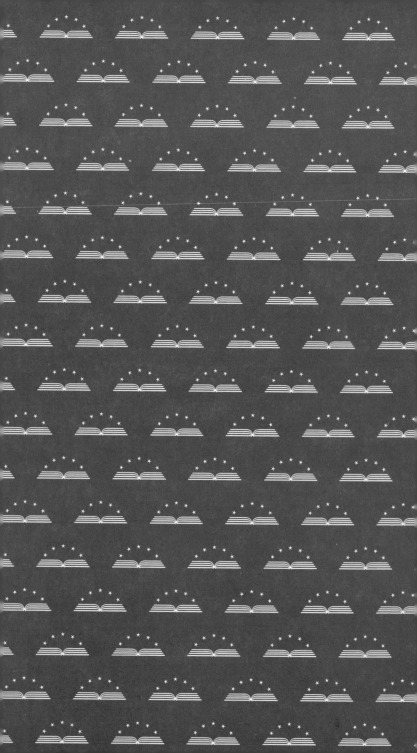